MW01012778

Adapted Physical Activity Across the Life Span

Carol Leitschuh, PhD
Research Associate, Retired
School of Kinesiology
University of Minnesota

Marquell Johnson, PhD
Professor, Director of Rehabilitation Science Program
Department of Kinesiology
University of Wisconsin—Eau Claire

HUMAN KINETICS

Library of Congress Cataloging-in-Publication Data

Names: Leitschuh, Carol, 1948- author. | Johnson, Marquell, 1978- author.
Title: Adapted physical activity across the life span / Carol Leitschuh,
  Marquell Johnson.
Description: Champaign, IL : Human Kinetics, [2024] | Includes
  bibliographical references and index.
Identifiers: LCCN 2023007517 (print) | LCCN 2023007518 (ebook) | ISBN
  9781718213364 (paperback) | ISBN 9781718213371 (epub) | ISBN
  9781718213388 (pdf)
Subjects: LCSH: Physical education and training--Textbooks. | Physical
  fitness--Textbooks. | People with
  disabilities--Rehabilitation--Textbooks. | BISAC: EDUCATION / Teaching /
  Subjects / Physical Education | SPORTS & RECREATION / Disability Sports
Classification: LCC GV341 .L36 2024 (print) | LCC GV341 (ebook) | DDC
  796.071--dc23/eng/20230523
LC record available at https://lccn.loc.gov/2023007517
LC ebook record available at https://lccn.loc.gov/2023007518

ISBN: 978-1-7182-1336-4 (print)

The web addresses cited in this text were current as of March 2023, unless otherwise noted.

Acquisitions Editor: Scott Wikgren
Developmental Editor: Judy Park
Managing Editor: Derek Campbell
Copyeditor: Janet Kiefer
Indexer: Dan Connolly
Permissions Manager: Laurel Mitchell
Senior Graphic Designer: Nancy Rasmus
Graphic Designer: Denise Lowry
Cover Designer: Keri Evans
Cover Design Specialist: Susan Rothermel Allen
Photographs (cover): Halfpoint Images/Moment RF/Getty Images (running, basketball); Trevor Williams/DigitalVision/Getty Images (yoga); 10'000 Hours/DigitalVision/Getty Images (pickleball)
Photographs (interior): © Human Kinetics, unless otherwise noted
Photo Asset Manager: Laura Fitch
Photo Production Manager: Jason Allen
Senior Art Manager: Kelly Hendren
Illustrations: © Human Kinetics, unless otherwise noted
Printer: Sheridan Books

Printed in the United States of America   10 9 8 7 6 5 4 3 2 1

The paper in this book is certified under a sustainable forestry program.

Human Kinetics
1607 N. Market Street
Champaign, IL 61820
USA

United States and International
Website: **US.HumanKinetics.com**
Email: info@hkusa.com
Phone: 1-800-747-4457

Canada
Website: **Canada.HumanKinetics.com**
Email: info@hkcanada.com

E8627

We respond with heartfelt gratitude toward the ones gone before us, and those with us today, who have dedicated their lives to serving individuals with disabilities to ensure engagement in and enjoyment of physical activity experiences. Their collective contribution of scholarship and practice has defined the literature, expanded the knowledge, and advanced the skills for teaching, coaching, training, managing, consulting, and speaking and thinking. We acknowledge this contribution and seek to grow in that fertile ground a new future of broad collaborations in an interdisciplinary language that accelerate the reach and refine the service where health and well-being are intrinsically linked to adapted physical activity participation for everyone, from our infants to our oldest of old.

CONTENTS

Adapted Physical Activity Across the Life Span artic-ulates the interdisciplinary nature of educating undergraduate students to work together as edu-cators and clinicians in facilitating physical activity engagement that is adapted for and with infants through to the oldest of the old. Current definitions of health and disability are applied in detail. Health is now understood as distinct from function because good health can exist in the presence of limitations. Disabilities are now defined due to a health condi-tion that occurs in the context of one's environment and are influenced by personal factions.

The beginnings of this textbook are traced in direct authorship on special physical education for over 70 years and the privilege of our authorship association with the influence of Dr. Hollis Fait. He wrote the first textbook in adapted physical activity in the 1960s referencing *activity*, not *edu-cation*, because special education had not been established. Today, Dr. Fait would be the first to recognize there is a shift in higher education train-ing to meet the needs of adapted physical activity engagement across the life span, not just the chil-dren and youth he addressed. Data now identify increasing numbers of undergraduate students from other disciplines rushing into classes on adapted physical activity, outstripping numbers of physical education majors by as much as 300 percent. These other disciplines represent students headed toward the allied health professions of kinesiology, such

as occupational therapy, physical therapy, speech and language pathology, nursing, and medicine, as well as subdisciplines within kinesiology, such as sport psychology, exercise physiology, therapeutic recreation, coaching, and athletic training. Also, the physical educator and adapted physical educator have an honored and stated place in the execution of special education for children and youth with disabilities. They set an early positive basis for a life in physical activity with adaptation.

Adapted physical education remains a solid area of academic study and as such is presented in com-prehensive form with emphasis on the collaboration required with education and allied health roles applied for today's infants, toddlers, preschoolers, kindergarteners, early and late grade schoolers, and high school youth.

Reflecting the current model in aging, the named disciplines are understood to interact with adults as they age *into* disability and *with* disability. These two groups have history in physical activity that can influence how professionals approach the person in adulthood to facilitate participation in adapted physical activity. Health-related fitness, leisure activity, and adapted sports are offered with contemporary guidelines for assessment and engagement in physical activity for those who are sedentary, fragile, and have chronic diseases.

In the end, every individual across the life span can be physically active.

ACKNOWLEDGMENTS

We acknowledge the following individuals for their contributions to our lives and to the physically active lives of people with disabilities:

Paul H. Leitschuh, MD—Orthopedic surgeon and specialist in sports medicine. His life from 1949 to 2018.

Winston Kennedy, DPT, MPH, PhD—Scholar who is exciting the future models of the ecology of adapted physical activity engagement clinically and educationally.

Gloria Krahn, PhD, MPH—Scholar of disability-related health disparities. Formerly of the Centers for Disease Control and Prevention. Consultant to projects reaching around the globe.

Paula Scraba, OSF, PhD, CAPE—Professor and ultimate educator never wavering in commitment to her students and adapted physical education's clientele.

Heidi Stanish, PhD—Professor with sustained enthusiasm for scholarship promoting health and physical activity for those with intellectual and developmental disabilities.

Joonkoo (JK) Yun, PhD—Professor, Chair of Kinesiology, College of Health and Human Performance. Scholar of measurement in adapted physical education, published in exercise physiology and disability, contextual understanding of adapted physical activity, professional practice in physical education, and adapted physical activity. A textbook on adapted physical activity across the life span was his idea.

PART I

Overview and Scope

Physical Activity and Disability

FatCamera/E+/Getty Images

CHAPTER OBJECTIVES

After completing this chapter, you will be able to do the following:

- Gain an appreciation for the historical context of the disability movement.
- Understand the life course perspective of disabilities.
- Identify and describe the four disability models utilized by educational and rehabilitation professionals.
- Identify and describe characteristics of children with disabilities that make them susceptible to physical inactivity.
- Identify and describe characteristics of adults with disabilities that make them susceptible to physical inactivity.
- Identify and describe the barriers and facilitators to physical activity for populations with disabilities across the life span.

What are some of the first words, expressions, or visual illustrations that come to your mind when you hear the word *disability*? If you have no previous experiences interacting with people with disabilities, your response will typically render an unfavorable expression or one that focuses on what this population is unable to do or that describes what this population needs assistance doing. If you have some experiences interacting with people with disabilities, your response will typically be more favorable or one that highlights specific attributes of this population that you enjoyed. As you embark on a career that will require authentic interactions with populations with a disability, you should ask yourself the following questions:

- What were my childhood interactions with populations with a disability?
- What were my interactions with populations with a disability attending school for grades K to 12?
- What have my adulthood interactions with populations with a disability been like?
- What am I doing as a preprofessional student to increase my interaction with this population?

History of Professional Disability Service

To begin an exploration of disability and physical activity, we must first take into consideration the historical treatment of this marginalized population. This historical context is not meant to be exhaustive but will attempt to demonstrate that the physical activity needs and concerns for healthy living have not always been prioritized for this population. Throughout time, the inferior economic and social status of people with disabilities has been viewed as the inevitable consequence of the physical and mental differences imposed by a disability (Ward, 2009). An inability to contribute to society's workforce and revenue streams determined one's contributory status in the community as nonexistent. For many years, disability was viewed as a punishment from God or as indicating the presence of demonic possession (Ward, 2009). People with disabilities were not treated well overall and were unfavorably thought of by most society members. These most fervent belief systems about disability led to the justification of institutionalization of this population to protect society from its members. Long-term institutionalization and dehumanization

of individuals with disabilities was the norm. The basic needs for becoming a contributing member of society were viewed as different than those for populations without a disability.

As awareness of institutionalized mistreatment of populations with a disability grew, the belief systems of some professionals providing services to them began to change. A facility-based approach to providing services to this population included contributions from "social rehabilitators" and "medical rehabilitators" (Ward, 2009; Reid, 2003). The social rehabilitator's role was to educate the person with a disability and attempt to change the cultural perspective of the greater society regarding the treatment of this population. The medical rehabilitator's role was to attempt to fix the person with a disability through surgery and therapy. The return of many veterans with disabilities during postwar eras contributed to the changing attitudes and beliefs about populations with a disability. Societal views regarding this subpopulation were that they were deserving and worthy of public support for their contributions to defending their country. The service-based approach to providing services to populations with a disability led to the deinstitutionalization movement and was in part mandated by legislation passed to ensure the livelihoods of wounded veterans and curb the mistreatment of other disability groups. Educational preparedness for children with a disability and vocational training opportunities for adults with a disability highlighted this period (Reid, 2003; Ward, 2009). During this time, specific educational and rehabilitation service professions such as adapted physical education specialists, physical therapists, occupational therapists, and vocational rehabilitation specialists came to the forefront.

Using the support-based approach to providing services, populations with a disability would be best served in environments alongside populations without disability to ensure successful learning, working experiences, and community integration (Reid, 2003; Ward, 2009). Types of supports that assisted individuals with a disability to function in inclusive settings were technical, natural, or human. Professional terminology and philosophy that appeared during this time included adapted physical activity, inclusion, and disability sport organizations. A common thread amongst facility-based, service-based, and support-based approaches was the dependency on a professional expert to deliver what was needed to populations with a disability. Along with the passage of legislation that addressed both access to public education and protection of civil rights, advocacy groups along with continued litigation have emphasized that individuals with disabilities should have freedom to make personal decisions about their lives, rather than being dependent upon others. This service approach has been identified as the empowerment or self-determination approach (Reid, 2003).

Understanding Disability

People with disabilities are a diverse group who share the experience of living with significant limitations in functioning and, as a result, often experience exclusions from full participation in their communities (Krahn et al., 2015). Multiple definitions of disability exist to allow populations with disabilities to receive services and protection of civil rights at the local, state, national, and international levels (see table 1.1). These definitions have also been used for multiple research and public health purposes and will be covered in more detail in chapter 3. Definition differences also reflect an evolution in our understanding of disability and its relationship to health, the relative value society has placed on people with disabilities, and how program eligibility has been addressed (Krahn et al., 2015).

Education and rehabilitation science professionals have utilized various disability models to provide necessary services and supports for people with disabilities. Conceptual models assist understanding by allowing one to examine and think about something that is based on partial knowledge of that concept. Drum (2009) broadly defined four major categories of disability models: medical, functional, social, and integrated. The *medical model* views disability as a problem inherent in the person requiring a medical cure and classifies disabilities categorically based on medical diagnoses (e.g., multiple sclerosis or cerebral palsy). The *functional model* emphasizes functional limitations arising from impairments and focuses on improving functioning with rehabilitation. *Social models* view disability not as an attribute of the person, but as an experience caused by architectural, social, and political barriers that should be eliminated through social change. Finally, *integrated models* view disability as a multidimensional experience that arises from both personal and environmental factors (Agiovlasitis et al., 2018; Drum, 2009). Professionals who subscribe to the medical model are believed to engage in activities that marginalize and oppress people with disabilities. The medical model considers only the medical aspect of the disability and does not consider the important role physical, cultural, environmental, and political factors play in determining disability status. The most favorable utilization of this model is to determine eligibility for governmental services. The functional model categorizes people into those with functional limitations (disability) and those without functional limitations (nondisability). It typically overlooks

TABLE 1.1   Definitions of Disability

Definition source	Disability definition
Individuals With Disabilities Education Act (IDEA)	*Child with a disability* means a child evaluated in accordance with §§300.304 through 300.311 as having an intellectual disability, a hearing impairment (including deafness), a speech or language impairment, a visual impairment (including blindness), a serious emotional disturbance (referred to in this part as emotional disturbance), an orthopedic impairment, autism, traumatic brain injury, other health impairment, a specific learning disability, deafblindness, or multiple disabilities, and who, by reason thereof, needs special education and related services.
Americans With Disabilities Act (ADA)	A *person with a disability* is a person who has a physical or mental impairment that substantially limits one or more major life activities.
Social Security Disability Insurance (SSDI)	The term *disability* means inability to engage in any substantial gainful activity by reason of any medically determinable physical or mental impairment that can be expected to result in death or which has lasted or can be expected to last for a continuous period of not less than 12 months.
World Health Organization (WHO)	*Disability* is the umbrella term for impairments, activity limitations, and participation restrictions that refers to the negative aspects of the interaction between an individual with a health condition and that individual's contextual environmental and personal factors.

or neglects the role of external factors (e.g., socioeconomic status and accessibility concerns). In the social model, the ability to undertake activities is dependent upon accessible environments. Four environmental dimensions to consider include the social, physical, economic, and political. The need for integrated models becomes apparent as several disability models are concurrently operating and require professionals to communicate effectively and work collaboratively in attempting to eliminate the health disparities that persons living with disabilities experience (Agiovlasitis et al., 2018).

Life Course Perspective

When examining the relationship between disability and physical activity, there is a need to use a life course perspective. This perspective is based on the life course theory, which is a conceptual framework that helps explain health and disease patterns, particularly health disparities across populations and over time. Instead of focusing on differences in health patterns one disease or condition at a time, life course theory points to broad social, economic, and environmental factors as underlying causes of persistent inequalities in health for a wide range of diseases and conditions across population groups (USDHHS, 2010b). The life course perspective on disability recognizes that health trajectories are particularly affected at certain times in life:

- During infancy and the early stages of disability diagnosis, families are provided early intervention and access to community supports that will allow for proper foundational development.
- During the school-age years, the individual is provided with direct and related services that will allow for opportunities to develop appropriate functional behaviors that will maximize participation in their communities.
- During adulthood, appropriate services in recreational and physical activity, vocations, health care, and wellness allow for successful aging with a disability.

A life course perspective advocates for (1) improved training of educational and rehabilitation science professionals to support earlier identification and intervention in children, (2) improved services for children with disabilities transitioning out of school programs into adulthood, (3) the efficiency of the many systems that adults with disabilities rely on, and (4) improved health care and health promotion for adults with disabilities. The first two components will be covered in more detail in part II of the textbook. The last two components will be covered in more detail in part III of the textbook.

Health for populations without disabilities is defined as the absence of disease that shifts back and forth on a continuum from poor to excellent. The World Health Organization (2003) defines health as "a state of complete physical, mental, and social well-being and not merely the absence of disease" (p. 1). This definition acknowledges that health involves all aspects of people's lived experiences and that it is inherently multifactorial (Agiovlasitis et al., 2018). People with disabilities often start at the lower end of the health continuum due to secondary conditions that overlap with their primary disability (Rimmer et al., 2009). Secondary conditions are those physical, medical, cognitive, emotional, or psychosocial consequences to which persons with disabilities are more susceptible by virtue of an underlying impairment, including adverse outcomes in health, wellness, participation, and quality of life (Rimmer, 1999).

Populations with disabilities are at risk of experiencing secondary conditions no matter their age. Health for populations with disabilities involves the management of the primary disability and reducing the effects of secondary conditions. Some have suggested that the high costs of direct health care for a disability are a result of earlier insufficient attention to secondary and other health needs of individuals with disabilities (Rimmer et al., 2009; USDHHS, 2005). For populations with disabilities, experiencing health also means that they can access appropriate, integrated, culturally sensitive, and respectful health care that meets the needs of a whole person, not just a disability (USDHHS, 2005). According to Krahn and colleagues (2015), a life course perspective is needed to

- map a trajectory for successful adult living,
- establish that successful adult living is the result of interaction between impairment, personal factors, and environment over time (a child's life), and
- change current clinical approaches to developmental progress that focus on activities (e.g., performance on most standardized tests) to measurement of participation (e.g., test performance versus how one fares in the real world).

Health care professionals are not necessarily well informed about the primary health care needs of populations with disabilities, the prevention and management of secondary health conditions, the challenges that adults face in aging with disabilities, and the transition of young people with disabilities from pediatric to adult services (Krahn et al., 2015; USDHHS, 2005). The absence of professional training on disability competency issues for educational and rehabilitation science professionals is one of the most significant barriers preventing people with disabilities from receiving appropriate and effective health care (Krahn et al., 2015; Rimmer et al., 2004; USDHHS, 2005). A life course perspective, beginning in childhood, would promote coordination and continuity of health care between pediatric and adult systems, as well as education, social, and community services and supports (Palisano et al., 2018). According to the U.S. surgeon general's report (USDHHS, 2005), one of the challenges is to identify ways in which the health and wellness of populations with disabilities can be brought to the consciousness of the American public as an issue warranting effective action and ongoing attention.

Sixty-one million adults of all ages, races, ethnicities, socioeconomic statuses, and levels of educational attainment in the United States live with at least one disability. This number amounts to one in four U.S. adults having some type of functional disability (see figure 1.1). The National Survey of Children's Health identified nearly one in five children ages 12 to 17 as having special health care needs (USDHHS, 2022). In 2018 to 19, the number of students ages 3 to 21 who received special education services under the Individuals With Disabilities Education Act (IDEA) was 7.1 million, or 14 percent of all public school students. As the U.S. population ages, the percentage of people with disabilities increases. In the United States in 2016, fewer than 1 percent of those under 5 years old had a disability. The rates for other ages were 5.6 percent for those ages 5 to 17, 10.6 percent for ages 18 to 64, and 35.2 percent for people ages 65 and older (Kraus et al., 2018). This data demonstrates that fewer people are aging *with* a disability than are aging *into* a disability. The increase in the prevalence of disability also is a product of advances in preventing infant and child mortality from both the birth process and trauma-related impairments (USDHHS, 2005). As children and youth with disabilities of all kinds live longer, they will contribute to growing rates of disability in each age group to which they advance over the years (Kraus et al., 2018; USDHHS, 2005). Health expenditures associated with disabilities, including medical care and long-term services, have been estimated at $868 billion annually, with 70 percent of these costs covered through public (government) programs (Anderson et al., 2010; Khavjou et al., 2020; Krahn et al., 2015). Healthy People 2020 included a disability and health topic,

Erik McGregor/LightRocket via Getty Images

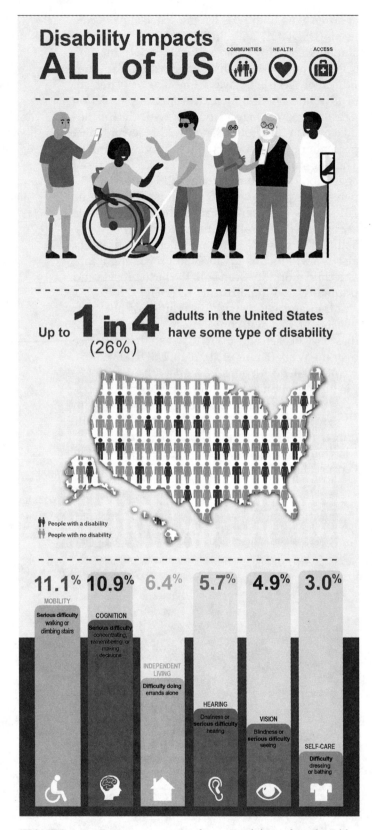

FIGURE 1.1   The percentage of people living with disabilities.

Reprinted from National Center on Birth Defects and Developmental Disabilities, Centers for Disease Control and Prevention, last modified January 5, 2023, www.cdc.gov/ncbddd/disabilityandhealth/infographic-disability-impacts-all.html.

and subsequently, Healthy People 2030 prioritized the goal to improve health and well-being in people with disabilities.

Healthy People 2020 recognized that what defines individuals with disabilities, their abilities, and their health outcomes more often depends on their community, including social and environmental circumstances. To be healthy, all individuals with or without disabilities must have opportunities to take part in meaningful daily activities that add to their growth, development, fulfillment, and community contribution (USDHHS, 2010a). Highlighted measurable objectives under the disability and health topic included the following:

- Increase the proportion of youth with special health care needs whose health care provider has discussed transition planning from pediatric to adult health care

- Reduce the proportion of adults with disabilities aged 18 and older who experience physical or program barriers that limit or prevent them from using available local health and wellness programs

- Increase the proportion of children with disabilities, birth through age two years, who receive early intervention services in home or community-based settings

- Increase the proportion of children and youth with disabilities who spend at least 80 percent of their time in general education programs

- Increase the proportion of adults with disabilities aged 18 years and older who participate in leisure, social, religious, or community activities

There is a critical need to address disparities experienced by children with disabilities and develop health transition plans to minimize the effect of disparities that may occur in adulthood. Children with disabilities experience disparities in important functional outcomes like school, community engagement, employment, and independent living arrangements compared to peers without disabilities. Participation in activities that provide a sense of accomplishment and enjoyment during childhood and youth helps to foster positive development into adulthood. Swanson and Bolen (2011) identified eight functional areas affected by childhood disability:

1. Overall health status
2. Self-management of health
3. Physical activity, obesity, or nutritional status

4. Emotional well-being

5. Employment

6. Personal relationships

7. Participation in recreation, spiritual, and civic activities in the community

8. Independent living arrangements

These aforementioned areas and subsequent opportunities for growth were shown to be necessary for adequate preparation for children with disabilities to go from childhood to adulthood (Palisano et al., 2018). Children with disabilities are susceptible to poorer housing and neighborhood quality (Atkinson et al., 2015; Mattson et al., 2019); food insecurity (Mattson et al., 2019; Rose-Jacobs et al., 2016); adverse childhood experiences (e.g., abuse and domestic violence) (Mattson et al., 2019); and additional family stressors (e.g., caregiver burden, financial problems, lack of coping skills) (Halfon et al., 2012; Mattson et al., 2019).

It appears that the biological, physical, emotional, and social environments strongly affect the capacity for children to be healthy over the life span (Berry et al., 2010; Mattson et al., 2019; USDHHS, 2010b), and if all of these environments are not addressed through intervention, children with disabilities may not reach their full potential. For youth with and without disability, obesity is a primary concern. Children with disabilities have been shown to reach higher rates of obesity compared to children without disabilities (Bedell et al., 2013; Rimmer et al., 2007). Obesity rates are exacerbated in youth with disabilities because they are typically less active than their counterparts without disabilities (USDHHS, 2018). Students with disabilities participate at a lower rate in athletics and other organized programs compared to their peers without disabilities (U.S. GAO, 2010). Youth with disabilities should work with a health care professional (e.g., physician, therapist) or physical activity specialist (e.g., adapted physical education teacher, certified therapeutic recreational specialist) to understand the types and amounts of physical activity appropriate for them. It has been shown that as children age, their physical activity behaviors decrease dramatically (Belcher et al., 2010; Kann et al., 2018). Bassett and colleagues (2015) identified the following five explanations to physical activity behavior change in youth without disabilities:

1. Children living in highly technological societies

2. Active commuting to school

3. School physical education

4. High school sports

5. Outdoor play

What applicability do these explanatory factors have on the physical activity behavior of youth with disabilities? When given options, children with a disability will select a sedentary-oriented activity rather than a more physically active option (Rimmer & Rowland, 2008). Like youth without a disability, problems with neighborhood safety and conducive routes to school have a negative impact on active commuting to school. Also consider that most public schools provide transportation for students with disabilities receiving services under IDEA, greatly reducing the chance that these children will walk or bike to school. A reduction in instructional physical education has been happening for some time for all students, and it has been shown that students with disabilities receive instructional physical education less often than their peers without disability (U.S. GAO, 2010). The United States Government Accountability Office (2010) found that students with disabilities participated in lower rates of organized athletics, club sports, and intramurals. Active participation of children with disabilities in organized activities is influenced by functional ability, program cost, and program availability (Rimmer & Rowland, 2008). Given the inherent inaccessibility of the outdoor environment, especially for students with physical and sensory disability, reduced participation in outdoor play is expected. Children and adolescents with disabilities have disproportionately lower levels of physical activity and fitness compared to their peers without disabilities (McDonald, 2002; Rimmer & Rowland, 2008).

Categories of Barriers to Physical Activity in Children With Disabilities

1. *Physical barriers:* These barriers include playgrounds and ball fields that are inaccessible to youth who use wheelchairs.

2. *Programmatic barriers:* These barriers include not having the necessary staffing or support to accommodate the child during the activity.

3. *Attitudinal barriers:* These barriers include overprotection from parents.

Adapted from Rimmer and Rowland (2008).

If health disparities of children with disabilities are not addressed, then this population becomes adults with compromised opportunities at experiencing good health. Health trajectories in populations without disabilities are typically affected by lifestyle behaviors and genetics, yet there is a third, less understood, dimension in populations with disabilities: the onset and course of secondary health conditions and their weighted or additive effect on changes in health and function (Kinne, 2008; Rimmer & Lai, 2017). Secondary conditions in adults with a disability can be broken down into two categories (physical and psychosocial). Some of the most frequently reported physical secondary conditions include pain, fatigue, and deconditioning (Rimmer et al., 2011; Rimmer & Lai, 2017). The most frequently reported psychosocial secondary conditions include anxiety, isolation, and depression (Kinne et al., 2004; Rimmer & Lai, 2017). The functional disability type with the largest percentage of adults is the mobility category, operationally defined as serious difficulty walking or climbing stairs, and the functional disability type with the smallest percentage of adults is the self-care category, operationally defined as having difficulty dressing or bathing.

In the United States, people with disabilities are 4 to 10 times more likely to be victimized than people without disabilities (BJS, 2021;). Victimization includes abuse, violence, and harm caused on purpose and typically takes place either at home or in a hospital setting. Disability-associated health care expenditures per person with a disability are $11,637 per year; collectively they are $7.8 billion per year (Anderson et al., 2010). In the United States in 2016, 35.9 percent of people with disabilities ages 18 to 64 living in the community were employed. The employment percentage was more than double for people without disabilities at 76.6 percent (Kraus et al., 2018). This trend has been consistent over the years, demonstrating limited income earning power and continued reliance on governmental support well into adulthood. Working-age adults with disabilities who get no aerobic physical activity are 50 percent more likely than their active peers to have a chronic disease such as cancer, diabetes, stroke, or heart disease (Carroll et al., 2014). Only about 44 percent of adults with disabilities who saw a doctor in the past year got a recommendation for physical activity. Adults with disabilities were 82 percent more likely to be physically active if their doctor recommended it (Carroll et al., 2014). This underscores the importance of having health care providers who are trained and knowledgeable about the needs of populations with disabilities.

The obesity rate among populations with disabilities is alarming, because this group may require additional monitoring or medical care and may have higher expenditures (Anderson et al., 2013; Kraus et al., 2018). Anderson and colleagues (2013) demonstrated additional obesity expenditures are much higher for people with disabilities than for those without disabilities, emphasizing the need to focus on prevention, reduction, or better control of secondary conditions for this segment of the population.

SDI Productions/E+/Getty Images

What Do We Know About Adults With Disabilities and Their Physical Activity Participation?

- About 12 percent of adults with disabilities had heart disease compared to 4 percent of adults without disabilities.
- About 16 percent of adults with disabilities had diabetes compared to 7 percent of adults without disabilities.
- About 39 percent of adults with disabilities were categorized as obese, compared to 28 percent of adults without disabilities.
- Roughly 42 percent of adults with disabilities reported experiencing depression, compared to 12 percent of adults without disabilities.
- About 26 percent of adults with disabilities reported smoking, compared to 13 percent of adults without disabilities.
- Approximately 39 percent of adults with disabilities reported participating in sufficient aerobic physical activity, compared to 54 percent of adults without disabilities.
- Only 15 percent of adults with disabilities reported meeting the physical activity guidelines for aerobic and muscle-strengthening activity, compared to 23 percent of adults without disabilities.
- About 42 percent of adults with disabilities reported being inactive (no participation in physical activity), compared to 24 percent of adults without disabilities.

Data from Centers for Disease Control and Prevention, National Center on Birth Defects and Developmental Disabilities, Division of Human Development and Disability. Disability and Health Data System, last modified May 19, 2022, https://dhds.cdc.gov.

© Steve Nagy/age fotostock

The Physical Activity Guidelines for Americans provide detailed prescriptions for children and adolescents, adults, and older adults. Additional physical activity guidance for adults with disabilities is also included and highlights the health benefits for this underserved population. The benefits of physical activity for those with disabilities have been studied in diverse groups with disabilities related to traumatic events or to chronic health conditions. These groups include stroke survivors and people with spinal cord injury, multiple sclerosis, Parkinson's disease, muscular dystrophy, cerebral palsy, traumatic brain injury, limb amputations, mental illness, intellectual disability, and Alzheimer's disease and other dementias (USDHHS, 2018). Benefits of engaging in regular physical activity include improved cardiovascular and muscle fitness, improved brain health, and better ability to do tasks of daily life. In consultation with a health care professional or physical activity specialist, people with chronic conditions or disabilities should understand how their disease or disability affects their ability to do physical activity. This underscores the importance of having health care providers that are trained and knowledgeable about the needs of populations with disabilities.

The Physical Activity and Sedentary Behavior Guidelines for Adults With Disabilities sidebar includes key physical activity and sedentary behavior guidelines for adults with disabilities that health care providers should adhere to when prescribing physical activity and advocating for reduced sedentary behavior.

Populations with disabilities encounter substantial obstacles to participating in physical activities due to physical and social environments that limit fitness and recreation opportunities. Fitness facilities and other locations such as community parks, play-

Physical Activity and Sedentary Behavior Guidelines for Adults With Disabilities

Physical Activity Guidelines

- Adults with chronic conditions or disabilities, who are able, should do 150 minutes (2 hours and 30 minutes) to 300 minutes (5 hours) a week of moderate-intensity aerobic physical activity or 75 minutes (1 hour and 15 minutes) to 150 minutes (2 hours and 30 minutes) a week of vigorous-intensity aerobic physical activity, or an equivalent combination of moderate- and vigorous-intensity aerobic activity. Preferably, aerobic activity should be spread throughout the week.

- Adults with chronic conditions or disabilities, who are able, should also do muscle-strengthening activities of moderate or greater intensity and that involve all major muscle groups on two or more days a week, as these activities provide additional health benefits.

- When adults with chronic conditions or disabilities are not able to meet the previous key guidelines, they should engage in regular physical activity according to their abilities and should avoid inactivity.

- Adults with chronic conditions or disabilities should be under the care of a health care provider. People with chronic conditions can consult a health care professional or physical activity specialist about the types and amounts of activity appropriate for their abilities and chronic conditions.

Sedentary Behavior Guidelines

- Adults living with a disability should limit the amount of time spent being sedentary. Replacing sedentary time with physical activity of any intensity (including light intensity) provides health benefits.

- To help reduce the detrimental effects of high levels of sedentary behavior on health, adults living with a disability should aim to do more than the recommended levels of moderate- to vigorous-intensity physical activity.

Data from the Physical Activity Guidelines for Americans, 2nd edition and World Health Organization Guidelines on Physical Activity and Sedentary Behavior.

grounds, and ball fields used for competitive games and sports often lack accessibility (i.e., they have uneven terrain, grass, or gravel surfaces), thereby limiting opportunities for participation by individuals with disabilities (Johnson et al., 2012; Rimmer et al., 2017). Barriers to physical activity are obstacles individuals face when participating in physical activity (Booth et al., 2002). Facilitators to physical activity are supports individuals receive when participating in physical activity (Rimmer et al., 2004). Rimmer and colleagues (2004) identified 10 categories of barriers and facilitators to physical activity participation among populations with disabilities. Table 1.2 includes examples of barriers and facilitators for each category of physical activity participation.

Summary

The lived experiences of populations with disabilities have been fraught with cruelties and inadequate inclusion throughout history into present-day society. Educational and health care professionals can improve the overall health of these populations through an understanding of the life course perspective and the realization that health results from the cumulative impact of experiences in the past and the present. Barriers and facilitators to physical activity opportunities persist across the life span, and professionals would benefit from increased knowledge, more favorable attitudes when interacting with disabled individuals, and increased advocacy efforts.

TABLE 1.2 Barriers and Facilitators to the 10 Categories of Physical Activity Participation

Categories	Barriers	Facilitators
Built and natural environments	Lack of curb cuts, lack of elevators, narrow entrances, inability to access all amenities	Providing adequate number of accessible parking spaces, nonslip mats in locker rooms, push-button operated doors
Cost/economics	Full compliance with ADA requirements, maintaining facilities, and cost of accessible equipment	Designing and building accessible facilities from the outset, sliding fees, free trial membership
Equipment	Not enough space between exercise equipment for assistive devices	Seek input from people with disabilities regarding exercise, sport, and recreational equipment
Guidelines, codes, regulations, and laws	View of ADA accessibility guidelines as recommendations rather than as strict regulations	Create legislation that will enforce ADA guidelines
Information related	Lack of information regarding available and accessible facilities and programs in the community	Continued education and training of professional staff
Emotional and psychological	Perception that fitness and recreational facilities are unfriendly environments for individuals with disabilities	Presentation by professionals as being more friendly and motivated when interacting with persons with disabilities
Policies and procedures	Lack of policies at fitness and recreation facilities that are relevant to persons with disabilities	Prorating membership fees based on facility accessibility
Lack of resources	Lack of transportation and accessible facilities and problems regarding facility staffing	Communities pooling their resources to provide accessible facilities and programs
Perceptions and attitudes related to accessibility and disability	Professionals' negative attitudes toward persons with disabilities	Professional awareness of and empathy toward the needs of persons with disabilities
Knowledge, education, and training	Inability of staff to perform a proper wheelchair transfer	Utilization of person-first language when interacting with populations with disabilities

CHAPTER 2

Professional Roles in Adapted Physical Activity

Wavebreakmedia/iStockphoto/Getty Images

CHAPTER OBJECTIVES

After completing this chapter, you will be able to do the following:

- Identify professions that serve and support individuals with disabilities in adapted physical activity.
- Describe the roles of the professionals who serve and support individuals with disabilities in adapted physical activity.
- Explain the interdisciplinary approach to adapted physical education (APE) of the preK to 12th grade educational professionals in community schools.
- Explain the roles of the preK to 12th grade allied health professionals in serving children and youth with disabilities in APE or general physical education (GPE) in community schools.
- Describe the various programs that serve individuals with disabilities and their sponsorship in the community.
- Describe the roles of select health care professionals in the community serving individuals with disabilities as engaged directly or indirectly in adapted physical activity (APA).

Knowledgeable and skilled professionals in education and health care are the key to developing, sustaining, and advancing the human right to engagement in healthy physical activity with ensuing happiness. In serving children and youth with disabilities in physical activity, the professionals reach across adapted physical education, general physical education, and the allied health fields such as occupational therapy, physical therapy, speech and language pathology, nursing, and medicine, as well as other fields of kinesiology, such as coaching, athletic training, sports psychology, and exercise physiology. Professionals serving adults with disabilities cross disciplines to adapt physical activity while working in disease processes and with injuries of their clientele. Today, the interdisciplinary nature of service in adapted physical activity begins in the earliest ages and continues with professionals who instruct and nurture the physical activity of the oldest of our communities. This is a life span of approaching health and happiness through adapted physical environments and experiences.

Physical activity support for those with a disability requires professionals with an understanding of adapted physical activity, a mastery of instructional techniques, the capability to identify abilities and interests, and the ability to adapt the principles of physical activity engagement as the person meets them at any age.

Professionals engaged in this dynamic service to individuals with disabilities stride into interdisciplinary territory and commit to understanding the contribution each profession makes toward the well-being of those they serve in an integrated approach. A delineation of the professions will contribute to understanding one another's expertise, including when and how they address adapted physical activity with their clientele.

A clear example of the interdisciplinary nature of adapted physical activity (APA) professionals is found in the underpinning of the education of children with disabilities. Federal education law mandates that all children are entitled to attend public school, and this depends on many professions coming together to design services for children with specific disability categories. These professions share responsibility for the adapted physical education program of a student by discussing assessments, designing educational plans, teaching the student, and then reassembling to review the progress of the student. The professions represented are varied depending on the student's needs and can include adapted physical education, general physical education, physical and occupational therapy, speech

and language pathology, and general and special education.

In health care, a classic collaborative example is an inpatient rehabilitation program. The individuals may have head or back injuries, or they might be in difficult stages of a disease process. The individual's team comes together to share their assessments, design interventions, implement therapies, and reassess. They repeatedly listen, discuss, and try to move health care goals forward. The team includes a rehabilitation doctor, nurses, occupational and physical therapists, speech and language pathologists, psychological services (counseling, social work, psychiatry, clinical psychologist), and prosthetics and mobility specialists.

Some professions involved in adapted physical activity are better understood than others. Physical education is well known throughout the world. The same is now true for adapted physical education (APE). APE began formally in the 1970s in the United States with the passage of federal educational law now reauthorized and renamed the Individuals with Disabilities Education Improvement Act of 2004 (known as IDEA, 2004), discussed in more detail in chapter 3. In the United States, research has grown to show that general physical education (GPE) and APE professionals are colleagues who collaborate regularly (e.g., Wilson et. al., 2020). They understand each other's expertise better than they did decades ago. Together, adapted physical education and activity experiences are established on the practice of individualized goals created out of valid assessments by working together with the parents and other caregivers and members of the team forming the student's individualized education program. Organizations like the International Federation of Adapted Physical Activity and its European section support the provision of adapted physical activity.

Professional Disciplines

Kinesiology is the study of human movement, and it is a course of study leading to a degree. In higher education, kinesiology departments house subdiscipline specializations that result in professional occupational pursuits addressing, in part or totally, adapted physical activity for individuals with disabilities (table 2.1). In addition, students seeking graduate training in the allied health occupations of kinesiology often acquire a clinical emphasis in kinesiology and identify, for example, as pre-OT (occupational therapy) and pre-PT (physical therapy) to pursue graduate training in those fields. The many classic subdisciplines of kinesiology take up

TABLE 2.1   Kinesiology Subdisciplines and Settings for APA

Kinesiology subdisciplines*	Settings for adapted physical activity			
	Schools: education	Schools: allied health	Community	Health care
APE	X			
GPE	X			
Coaching	X		X	
Therapeutic recreation	X	X	X	X
Sports management	X		X	
Athletic training	X	X	X	
Sport psychology			X	X
Exercise physiology			X	X
Biomechanics			X	X

*Many colleges and universities offer training in these identified subdisciplines using departmental titles other than kinesiology, such as exercise and sport science, health and kinesiology, human movement sciences, kinesiology and leisure studies, and health, exercise science, and recreation.

Subdiscipline terms from Hoffman & Knudson (2018).

research or direct service in adapted physical activity for people with disabilities. For example, exercise physiologists have made invaluable contributions through research to the assessment of people with disabilities for exercise (see chapters 14 and 15).

Tables 2.2 through 2.5 in the following sections are designed to elaborate on the occupations and indicate their direct and indirect roles in facilitating adapted physical activity. The professions are established in the schools, the community, and the health care system. For each setting, those identified professionals listed in the tables participated in conversations and reviewed the content to be sure it reflected their field. The results are outlines that offer a framework to commence understanding and discussions across a multitude of occupations.

Professionals in the Schools

School settings discussed in this text are to be understood as preschool and kindergarten through the 12th grade (preK-12). Table 2.2 lists the professions present in a school district. Note the distinctions between GPE, APE and APA:

- *GPE* denotes the education program established in that school district for a grade level.
- *APE* is the physical education curriculum adapted for students with disabilities when they meet criteria for services in their state.

- *APA* includes adapted physical education and other activities such as sports where qualified athletes with disabilities participate.

When considering service delivery within the educational setting, the terms *direct* and *indirect* used in the tables designate roles with the population served in APE and APA (table 2.2).

- *Direct:* The professional is meeting with the student face to face in the activity, such as in teaching, observing, and assessing.
- *Indirect:* The professional's work is in the facilitation of APE for a student, such as individualized education program (IEP) meeting collaborations and writing evaluations, or in collaboration on APA.

The types of services that students with disabilities receive in the educational setting are determined by the IEP. This is the written goals created for the student's education and is based on extensive interdisciplinary assessments in consultation with the student's parents or caregivers.

Education administrators are experts on the management of the whole school. As such they are very important to the academic program in physical education. They or their representative are required by law to attend the IEP meetings. General physical educators and adapted physical educators need their support in running programs

TABLE 2.2   Education-Based Occupations and APA Roles in Schools

Professional occupation	Roles in APA
Education administrator	*Indirect:* Supervises staff and program development addressing students with a disability in GPE, APE, or the physical activity of the after-school programs. Attends IEP meetings when necessary.
School psychologist	*Direct:* Assists with the behavioral plans of the IEP for APA. *Indirect:* Provides assessments and intervention plans with the IEP team.
Adapted physical education teacher	*Direct:* Teaches adapted physical education for students who qualify. Provides assessments and evaluations. *Indirect:* Consults in GPE for mainstreamed students with disabilities. Is an IEP team member and collaborator. Advocates for students.
General physical education teacher	*Direct:* Teaches students with identified disabilities participating in the GPE. Provides assessments and evaluations. Referred to as GPE teacher. *Indirect:* Collaborates with the IEP team.
Special education teacher	*Direct:* In some states, may also teach APE classes with consultation from APE, particularly at the younger ages. *Indirect:* Often advise on current behavioral and learning strategies of the student's IEP to assist in student participation for GPE and APE.
General education teacher	*Direct:* Teaches in an inclusive classroom. *Indirect:* Share behavioral and instructional strategies being employed in their classroom for application in a student's APE and GPE program.
Paraprofessional	*Direct:* Actively assists with students with a disability in their GPE and APE classes. Works under supervision of the GPE or APE teacher when in those classes.
Recreation therapist	*Direct:* Addresses the APE content regarding transition from high school to community life. Teaches, consults, assesses, and evaluates toward graduation goals. *Indirect:* Collaborates with the IEP team.
Intramural sports director	*Direct:* May have the role as coach for a specific team composed of students with disability. *Indirect:* Supervises the staff responsible for the sports programs where participants are students with disability.
Coach	*Direct:* Coaches individuals with disability participating in sports teams of the school if the student is qualified. Also coaches those individual athletes in disability sport-specific teams such as Special Olympics as a part of such activity as the after-school programs.
Athletic trainer	*Direct:* Cares for athletes with disabilities injured during sport participation in provision of immediate first aid; later with implementation of rehabilitation exercises and injury prevention recommendations.
After-school program director	*Indirect:* Supervises staff and facilitates program development for participation of students with a disability in APA in the after-school program.
After-school staff	*Direct:* Assists students with disabilities in recreation, play, and sport activity in the programs in which they participate.

and having essentials like equipment, well-trained paraprofessionals or volunteers, and cooperative colleagues. Parents often seek administrators to uphold their concerns about their child's education. If that includes the physical education program participation, then the administrator needs all the facts from the content expert like the GPE and APE with an open line of communication to solve problems.

School psychologists are invaluable to ascertaining a clear picture of the students' cognitive, social, and emotional abilities and how to support educational success. In many cases they can observe a child struggling in a physical activity class to provide input for interventions. Their work is data driven in that the selection of an intervention is based on what behavior is getting in the way of student learning and what will lead to success in the classroom. It takes time to try interventions, check for positive trends in the resolution of inappropriate behavior, and potentially readjust goals. School psychologists are also adept at conferring with parents.

Recreation therapists are employed in the schools, in the community, and in health care (table 2.1). In schools, they are essential in the assessment of students that leads to IEP goals in high school for the development of postgraduation leisure skills in physical activity. Here, the recreation therapist considers the desires of the student and their family and the resources for recreation in the community. Students no longer spend time working on balance per se in their PE or APE classes but on activities that are age appropriate for leisure time. When the IEP plan is developed in high school, the training goes out in the community as the naturally occurring environment for the activity. If a student wants to learn to bowl in their community that has bowling and an accessible bowling alley, training takes place in that setting and includes entering the building, obtaining shoes for the game, and learning the rules of the game, as well as skills for ball control and social skills for the setting and any team play.

Adapted physical education teachers in some districts work strictly in a consultation capacity whereby they assess and, in their evaluation, make recommendations for the student's IEP in physical education whether in GPE or APE. They then train staff, including in some cases the special education teacher, to carry out the IEP plan for APE or GPE. In other districts, they work directly with students in their APE program. In some cases, they both consult and work directly with the students.

GPE teachers have often had some courses in working with students with disabilities, while others have had none. They are experts in the curriculum of the more typically developing child from grade school through high school depending on their license and their state's requirements for teaching. Many students with disabilities are in inclusive (mainstreamed) classes because of the placement decisions of the IEP team. This team includes the parent, who must give permission for this placement. The child may be in the GPE with consultation from the APE for either the whole program or just certain activities. The GPE teacher is also used to working with occupational therapists (OTs) and physical therapists (PTs) in their classrooms. The GPE teacher has a lot of children to work with in class, and consulting APE personnel make every effort to increase participation of the identified children and increase the teacher's clarity for inclusion. Referencing the student's IEP is important for both GPE and APE teachers, but the day-to-day activity isn't to teach to the IEP. The student needs to be involved in the age-appropriate activity of their grade as specified in the IEP. More information on instructional strategies is found in chapter 5.

Special education teachers and *general education teachers* are invaluable resources for an APE and GPE teacher regarding the behavioral IEP of a student with a disability and its implementation in their classroom—be it the gymnasium or on a community outing—or in specific units such as swimming or bowling. The special education teachers often have specific areas of teaching expertise such in autism spectrum disorder, learning disabilities, and sensory impairments.

Paraprofessionals are assigned to a student with a disability to assist in the educational day. See table 2.2 and the relationship to APE. According to Paula Scraba, OFS, PhD, CAPE, the work of a paraprofessional in the schools is usually one to one with students with disabilities with any background and at least an associate of arts degree.

> But I know a number of professionals in our field that did not get a job teaching right away and came into APE as a paraprofessional. . . . That is how I started a Missouri School for the Blind in St. Louis, and by Christmas I was the classroom teacher, and by the end of the school year, Assistant Principal for the Deaf/Blind Program.
>
> Scraba, personal communication, July 7, 2021.

Coaches and intramural sports directors can engage the athlete with a disability who qualifies to play on an integrated team without adaptations, participates in a segregated program such as Special Olympics, or participates in a mainstreamed program with adaptations. A popular video circulating among physical educators is an example of coaching that stunned a high school, the athlete, and his classmates. A graduating senior who was on the autism spectrum had spent his high school years managing the basketball

Interview With a Professional

Lauren Allard, MS, CAPE
Adapted Physical Education Specialist

Question 1: *What did you learn in your master's program that is particularly helpful in your work as an itinerant adapted physical educator?*

Classroom management is one of the most integral skills I learned from my program. My students have a very broad variety of behaviors, and it is important to be able to have strong management skills. This enables me to have successful lessons where students are physically active and on task. Management includes selecting, designing, and creating the visuals for students, which I studied and implemented in my training. Now, I make lots of token boards, visual schedules, and reward systems for students. For instance, my middle school class has difficulty staying on task and being safe. If they follow the class rules of safe, kind, and respectful, they earn a stamp on their hand that they show to their classroom teacher after APE, and they earn five minutes of choice time. If students break the rules once, they have a warning. If they break them twice, they lose their stamp and the choice time. The third time, they fill out a behavior sheet with their classroom teacher and have it signed by parents.

It has been hugely helpful for me to have had experience writing lesson plans and preparing to order equipment. I don't have time to write out extensive lesson plans anymore as I am at 14 sites and barely have a prep period. At OSU, we wrote out lesson plans with modifications to support all students in the general physical education setting and for Friday evening's IMPACT. IMPACT was a federally funded training program where we had time with the students in the pool and then time in the gym. We practiced teaching them, including practicing transitions. This helped me understand itinerant teaching. At OSU, writing out the modifications for specific students gave me a breadth of modifications to use with all students. We planned a whole year's curriculum and filled out the order sheets for all the equipment in our curriculum. The right equipment goes hand in hand with a successful yearlong curriculum of lessons.

Question 2: *What physical activities do you particularly like teaching?*

I particularly like teaching cardio drumming, basketball, yoga, dance, swimming, and the lifetime physical activity unit I created for my adult students [high school]. I also enjoy teaching our Paralympics unit! In this unit, I typically have all students seated for three of the four sports: one week of seated bocce ball, volleyball, badminton, and goalball. These are sports they might see at the Paralympics on TV.

Question 3: *Describe a good day as an adapted physical educator in the public schools.*

A great day for me starts with me getting to my first middle school on time and getting set up in the best location for success for my students. I text the general education PE teachers to learn what space they are in, and then decide based on our unit what space makes sense for us. We either use the blacktop, a small indoor portable space, or the gym. My middle school students arrive on time, we complete fitness activities and the lesson focus. Recently for my middle and high schoolers it has been volleyball. (My upper elementary students have been working on teamwork activities, and my younger elementary students are working on throwing and catching.) The students persevere when they get tired, encourage one another, are safe, are kind, and ask for breaks when they need them. The students help me pack up, I check in with staff, and I depart on time to my next site, a nonpublic site. These are students with self-injurious behaviors who perform similar activities for their age. On a good day, they are successful, and no challenging behaviors (refusal, throwing things, etc.) are present. I drive to my office, and I set up for my virtual elementary student. I teach that student, their parent is supportive, and the student is able to attempt all tasks. I eat lunch and get my full 40 minutes! To finish the day, I have two classes on-site (two high school students and a group of five middle school students). Once again, the students do their best, work together, and are kind and supportive.

All day long, I use management systems the students and I created together such as a reward system of five minutes free time after APE, a dance party at the end of the lesson, raffle tickets, positive behavior intervention supports, and music choice. I return to my office at the end of the day, unpack, clean up, and head home on time feeling there were many moments of joy throughout the day!

team and participated in every practice with the team over the years. On the last game of his high school career with the team ahead, the coach sent him into the game for the last few minutes. He entered the game, got the ball, and missed the basket. Then he got the ball again and hit a three-pointer! The crowd went wild! He then shot two more three-pointers. Although his team won by a comfortable margin, his buzzer beater felt like a game winner, and the crowd and all the players were sent into a frenzy.

Athletic trainers treat the athlete with disabilities when injured in a sport endeavor. In universities, select students majoring in athletic training have gone on to do their master's thesis with coursework in disability sport.

After-school program directors and staff are vital in modeling and promoting the acceptance of children with disabilities with their nondisabled age peers, and in creating the fun in being physically active

after a long academic school day. These professionals know the students, their interests, their families, and their rhythm of a day. Over time, they are in a good position to know when it is a good day and when it is tough for the student, adjusting activity accordingly.

Table 2.3 represents the allied health professions brought into the preK-12 educational system with the IDEA (2004) federal education mandate. These clinicians are trained specifically for the needs of student learning in the school, not hospital inpatient care or outpatient care. Those in the professions of OT, PT, and speech and language pathology (SLP) function as school therapists. There is a lot to understand about the difference between these services in the school settings versus these services in clinical settings. Nurses are also typically in schools and include the students with disabilities in their care.

The allied health professionals in the schools work specifically on skills needed for learning in

TABLE 2.3   Allied Health Occupations and APA Roles in Schools

Allied health–specific occupation	Roles in APA
Occupational therapist (OT)	*Direct:* Conducts assessments and evaluations that include strategies specific to physical activity engagement in APE and GPE classes. May teach in APE for transition skill development for community engagement. *Indirect:* Consults on skill performance, such as catch and release of projectiles and grasping equipment for games and sports. Positioning for APA. Conducts training on specific disability and adapted physical activity, such as cerebral palsy and adapted equipment for play and games, transfers from assistive equipment, and personal hygiene and APA. Consults on high school APA transition plans from high school to community life.
Physical therapist (PT)	*Direct:* Conducts assessments and evaluations for student participation in APE or GPE class, including locomotion when using a wheelchair or other assistive devices and adaptive equipment. Evaluates positioning for APA, particularly transfers from wheelchairs for physical activity. *Indirect:* Consults on transition plans for APA community engagement. Training on specific disabilities and APA.
Speech and language pathologist (SLP)	*Indirect:* Consults with the APE and GPE teachers on use of communication skills for a student's participation in activities of the class. May offer specific expertise in disabilities such as autism spectrum disorder.
Registered nurse (RN)	*Direct:* Administers medications. *Indirect:* Consults on and monitors medical needs for participation in APE or GPE. Communicates with the family on medication and dosage regulation during the APE and GPE classes.

the classroom. As such, the service differs from the work these professions perform in hospitals and clinics. In the schools, the therapists

- offer interventions in the naturally occurring environment of the students' school day;
- facilitate the students' engagement across the curriculum (e.g., reading, math, physical education) and the learning environment (e.g., eliminates physical barriers); and
- identify adaptations enabling the student to participate (e.g., assistive communication, equipment in physical activity).

The adapted physical education of children and youth with disabilities is often dependent on input from OT, PT, SLP, and the school nurse (RN). Communication is important at the very start of service and either continually or during episodes of difficulty. This is why special education is a collaborative process. The APE and GPE access knowledge about movement and disability working collaboratively with their therapy colleagues. Together with the allied health colleagues, APE and GPE teachers work within the student's IEP.

Occupational therapists work within activities that support activities of daily living in the school environment (e.g., self-care, toileting, organizational skills for homework); recommend assistive technology for classroom participation (e.g., pencil grips, computer software, seat positioning and modification); address sensory needs to enhance learning through calming, positive regard, and development of social skills; and assist with the IEP transition plans for participation in the student's home community upon graduation.

A current OT trend is a strengths-based approach, whereby the whole individual's context, motivation, and interests are considered, not just the isolated skill (Dunn, 2017). Dr. Winnie Dunn described current trends and approaches in occupational therapy (personal communication July 10, 2021):

- Finding out people's and families' interests and priorities so therapy is within their life pattern
- Meeting people in their authentic contexts and activities to discover what is supporting or interfering with participation
- Finding therapeutic opportunities in the everyday routines (rather than having therapy protocols)
- Using telehealth and coaching to serve those at a distance from professional services (or

whose circumstances make this an easier option)
- Creating ways to support *everyone*, not just those who are in health care or education and have a diagnosis (e.g., creating parent tips for children whose behavior is challenging)

Dr. Dunn emphasizes that the OT works with the knowledge that the individual has indicated they want and need the life activity. She advocates that stronger bodies are ones able to carry out their own life activities, leading directly into physical activity participation. Professionals listed in table 2.3 could benefit from adapting Dr. Dunn's modern trend observations.

Suggestions for implementing Dr. Dunn's identified trends are:

- In the school, ask, Who is this child and what are their interests in participating in their classroom writing projects (classically an OT area of expertise)? Or ask, In the activities of physical education using their wheelchair (classically a PT area of expertise), what are the student's interests?
- In the school setting, consider what is supporting the student's participation in the gymnasium for activities like appropriately handling equipment (OT or PT expertise) or understanding the directions (SLP expertise).
- With consultation in any of the therapies for a student, the teacher and therapist collaborate to embed an intervention naturally into the student's routine day (e.g., taking turns, moving across the classroom or gym, or asking for help).
- Compliment the student on their participation on one day a week (if positive feedback is an intervention area). Ask the student to name one thing they or the teacher did well that day in class. Have a brief discussion on the parent's interest in an upcoming special activity (just to get their take on it). Consult with SLP on ways to be successful with children with attention-deficit/hyperactivity disorder in the gym.

A *physical therapist* in the school ensures that the student has physical access to their educational life. Physical therapists want the student to be able to move well around the classroom, use and transfer in and out of any adaptive equipment (e.g., crutches, wheelchair) while navigating the school environment, engage in their learning tasks, and progress in learning without undue physical barriers. During the IEP transition activities in high school PE, the physical therapist works with the student in the use of the community for physical activity upon graduation. See the sidebar for examples of when PT is required or not.

Speech and language pathologists (SLPs) are adept at communication for the physical activity setting. Children with disabilities often present with atypical communication skills, and the guidance of the SLP is invaluable in knowing how to present instructions, give feedback, and understand what the child is communicating or not communicating.

The *registered nurse* cares for all the children in the school and can assist in the physical activity engagement of the student with disabilities around issues with medication administration, medical emergencies, medication changes, and the resulting monitoring of behavior. These nurses also communicate with authority to parents and caregivers, as well as with other medical personnel.

School-Based Physical Therapy Situations

Shasha is a pleasant preschool child, age four years, who moves awkwardly in her classroom. She wobbles and comes close to running into tables and chairs. She joins in classroom games but is slow to understand the rules. Shasha is functional in the motor room activities, even if a bit slower. Shasha's classroom teacher shares staff concerns with her parents, who have also noticed the awkwardness. Shasha's teacher believes that Shasha could have a global developmental delay. As the conversation proceeds, Shasha's teacher suggests that her parents can have their child assessed by the special education team. They can better address global developmental delay with the parents.

Why is school-based PT *not appropriate* at this time for Shasha? Shasha is accessing all her educational activities. She is making slow academic progress in the classroom and the motor room where she needs no adaptations for physically engaging in the physical activities. She is globally showing progress across all settings at school, albeit slowly. This may be more than just a physical therapy issue.

John, age 13, struggles in his wheelchair to perform movement activities in his general education class and participate in his adapted physical education class. He leans to the right in his wheelchair, slumps down, and isn't able to do what the other students are doing. His parents report he is going through an early growth spurt. None of his jackets or his long pants fit.

Why is school-based PT *required* at this time for John? Despite implementing the IEP team's adaptations from both PT and OT in the APE classes, John is unable to participate fully in the class. He reports not being happy with not fully participating in his PE class. There are questions to consider for his ongoing OT and PT service. Is his growth spurt affecting his posture in the wheelchair and his overall comfort in the wheelchair for learning? What else is physically affecting him in movement? Does his position in the wheelchair impede his visual line for getting the full instructions? Does he need a recommended place in the classroom for better accessing information?

Professionals in the Community

Adapted physical activity programs in the community are typically geared toward high school students through adults and older adults with disabilities (table 2.4). Specific programs such as Paralympics, Special Olympics, and Unified Sports are covered in chapter 16. In larger cities, medical center community education programs offer seniors a broad array of wellness classes including activities like yoga, tai chi for better balance, and mindfulness and stress reduction. Many classes are offered through online platforms and can reach far outside of the city and across the state to satellite hospital-based programs and into people's homes.

Therapeutic recreation specialists and staff, such as an adapted recreation coordinator and an inclusive service coordinator, work to foster inclusion for individuals with disabilities in city recreation programs.

The sidebars in this section outline the roles in the administration of programs to coach athletes with disabilities in programs such as the Special Olympics and how those roles eventually led to management of the program. Another facet is discussed with the Unified Sports program of Special Olympics, where individuals without an intellectual disability are teammates with those with intellectual disabilities.

TABLE 2.4   Community Practitioner APA Roles and Sponsorship

Community practitioner occupation	Programs sponsorship
Therapeutic recreation specialists	*Direct:* City parks and recreation and specialized programs in APA offer activities such as dances, fitness and weight training, day camps, swimming, and bowling where therapeutic recreation staff actively organize and lead the program. *Indirect:* Administration of overall programs and training of staff and seasonal staff for direct segregated programs and inclusion programs. *Sponsorship:* Municipal taxes, sometimes supplemented with participant fees.
Directors and coaches	*Indirect:* The administration of sports leagues for individuals with disabilities, such as Paralympics, Special Olympics, and Unified Sports, and an integrated program of athletes from Special Olympics matched with athletes without intellectual disabilities. *Direct:* Coaches for any of the aforementioned teams. *Sponsorship:* Fees, grants, and donations from individuals, groups, and businesses.
Directors and instructors	*Direct:* Teaching classes in APA. *Indirect:* Administration of city parks and recreation programs either segregated or integrated with assistance for individuals with disabilities under various names (e.g., inclusive recreation). Special events may be offered seasonally for clubs within the programs. *Sponsorship:* City programs are tax supported with some use of class fee. Clubs have a membership with some classes charging an additional fee. Senior clients enrolled in Silver and Fit might be covered by their Medicare supplemental insurance. Silver and Fit programs are based in city community centers, private clubs, and hospital-based community education classes.
Personal trainers	*Direct:* Instructs clients with disabilities on physical activity engagement. An instructor might direct a class for individuals with a disability. A personal trainer typically meets one on one with a client. *Sponsorship:* Fitness classes can be a part of the senior adult Silver and Fit programs and might be free whether offered in a club or community center. Otherwise, fitness classes taught by fitness instructors are fee based. Personal trainers typically charge fees.

Interview With a Professional

Philippe Neubauer, MS

Coach and Teaching Assistant

Question 1: What led you to the management of Special Olympics programs?

I was a part of the physical activity club at St. Bonaventure University, where I did my under-graduate work in sport studies with a concentration in sport management. Through the physical activity club, I was given the opportunity to work with Special Olympics programs during the New York State AHPERD [Association for Health, Physical Education, Recreation and Dance] Conference in Verona, New York, in both 2017 and 2018. We conducted a Unified Sports demonstration basketball activity to emphasize the importance of an inclusive sport (people with and without disability) in the athlete's chosen activity. I also worked with Special Olympics programs during Women in Sports Day at St. Bonaventure, emphasizing the importance of daily healthy habits for students to maintain an active lifestyle. Working with Special Olympics during my undergraduate studies was a great opportunity to develop leadership and management skills, which led me to my current career path in sport-based youth development.

Question 2: What skills have you observed in your staff that are effective in engaging the athletes of Special Olympics in their chosen activity?

The many skills I observed in staff resulted in their athletes' demonstration of self-management, self-awareness, and social-emotional learning. During the basketball demonstration activity at the AHPERD Conference, the athletes expressed self-management by being able to follow the rules properly, and they expressed self-awareness by knowing what is expected from them in the activity and by doing their best. These skills came together, enabling the athletes to participate in the activity while learning the proper motor movements. These three skills couldn't have been possible without the impact and instruction of the Special Olympics staff members.

Directors often have training that qualifies them for working directly with clients. These professionals are often certified by numerous bodies or have advanced training from their academic degrees. Certification from the American College of Sports Medicine (ACSM) is considered the most rigorous certification. There are several professional bodies offering certificates. *Instructors* in hospital-based programs are typically clinically certified by such bodies as the ACSM. Instructors in community programs (such as autism exercise specialist or inclusive fitness trainer) can also be certified by ACSM.

Employment opportunities include:

- Public centers such as city parks and recreation community centers
- Private clubs focused on fitness, health, and athletic endeavors, such as the YMCA, the YWCA, Jewish Community Centers, or LA Fitness
- Medical center community education programs offering APA fitness classes such as Parkinson's fitness, low-impact aerobics,

water aerobics, yoga, tai chi, and classes with titles that address bone health and balance (Better Bones and Balance) and muscle strength (Strong for Life)

For *fitness instructors* and *personal trainers*, two resources enhance the quality of adapted physical activity offerings. One is the surge in certifications for working with individuals with special needs. The second is hospital-based community wellness classes that include instructed-fitness classes.

Instructors in community wellness classes associated with medical centers, or classes like spinning, yoga, or Zumba at clubs, are typically certified to teach fitness to their older clientele or specialized group. Staff with ACSM certifications are more frequently found working in the community as certified personal trainers, certified exercise physiologists, certified group exercise instructors, instructors with an exercise in medicine credential, cancer exercise trainers, or certified inclusive fitness trainers. Their job title might be personal trainer, but look at the qualifications listed with marketing material on the class.

The ACSM/NCHPAD Certified Inclusive Fitness Trainer certificate is a collaborative project with the National Center on Health, Physical Activity and Disability (NCHPAD) and the ACSM. These trainers work with healthy individuals with physical, sensory, or cognitive disability in community and public health settings (e.g., the YMCA or city parks), and they have expertise in addressing physical barriers to accessing fitness venues. The goal is a healthy lifestyle and one where there is community access. Fitness instructors typically come from backgrounds in the movement sciences.

When identifying classes for people with disabilities, it is very important to note the instructor's qualifications to teach. They can have any number of different job titles, but their certifications as described here are strong indicators they are well-trained to engage the person with a disability in exercise.

Professionals in Health Care

Adapted physical activity engagement is part of many health care professionals' roles, including service to both children and adults. Table 2.5 describes many health care professions and their valuable roles in facilitating adapted physical activity in the community for individuals with disabilities and those otherwise needing access to physical activity.

Physical therapists (PT) and *occupational therapists* (OT) in the clinic are a point of referral from medical doctors for individuals of all ages. Clinical work in rehabilitation centers, as a part of hospital outpatient programs, includes any number of specialties of which OT and PT are a part. People come there for evaluation resulting in a treatment.

Physical therapy aides and *occupational therapy aides* work under the direction of either the physical therapist or occupational therapist. They can execute part of the treatment plan with the patient in the clinic. Sometimes that plan includes engagement in physical activity in the community. When the patient comes to clinic, the aide can inquire about that engagement and either answer or direct questions to the PT or OT. The aide is a part of a team to engage the patient in physical activity that regularly encourages the patient.

Interview With a Professional

Mana Shintani, BS, MS, ACSM-CEP
Fitness Specialist

Question 1: What was your professional study, and what led you to that study and eventually to your current work?

I have always loved watching sports since I was a child. In our home, baseball, soccer, rugby, golf, tennis, or any kind of sports were always on the TV when I was growing up. So, I wanted to be involved with sports. I went to the University of Georgia and studied exercise science with an emphasis in athletic training. I became a certified athletic trainer and I got to work with Division I collegiate athletes. I helped with athletes' injury prevention, treatment, and preparing them for surgery, and in their clinical rehabilitation program including after discharge into the community or to home. Then I decided to get my master's degree in clinical exercise physiology and work at a cardiac rehabilitation clinic, helping mostly elderly patients who were deconditioned. Currently, I work at a fitness center with a demographic of senior citizens. My background in athletic training, especially with the knowledge in biomechanics, anatomy, and physiology, helps a lot because most seniors have some physical ailments that require adjustments to a conventional exercise itself and a program overall.

Question 2: What do you see as the greatest benefit for the adults you serve when they participate in adapted physical activity?

The greatest benefit for the adults to participating in adapted physical activity is the ability to live life to the fullest. Being mobile, able to socialize, and able to be independent is a great way to *live*. Anyone, at any age, with any ailment, can participate in physical activity. It is my mission to find exercise that works for everyone.

TABLE 2.5   Health Care Professionals and APA Roles in the Community

Health care professional	Roles
Physical therapist (PT)	*Direct:* Works to improve functional movement involving skills such as walking; balancing; stair use; engagement in age-appropriate play, recreation, and sports; recovery of joint function following surgical procedures; and recovery of function following injury to muscles, ligaments, joints, and the like.
Physical therapy assistant	*Direct:* Works under the direction and supervision of a PT carrying out treatment plans. Often in a position of regular encouragement during treatment recovery.
Occupational therapist (OT)	*Direct:* Employs activity, practice, and adaptations to support people in the everyday life activities they need and want to do, such as eating, typing, cooking, bathing, and dressing, which support physical activity such as running errands, learning, working, and recreation. Addresses recovery from injury or surgical procedures, such as of the hand, arm, and wrist.
Occupational therapy assistant	*Direct:* Works under the direction and supervision of an OT to implement treatment plans including those that will serve the individual well in their leisure time. Often in a position of being able to provide regular encouragement during clinical care.
Speech and language pathologist (SLP)	*Direct:* Recovery or establishment of communication skills for play, leisure, recreation, sports, and other age-appropriate physical activity.
Physician	
General pediatrician*	*Direct:* Manages the health of children and adolescents for physical activity engagement. *Indirect:* Makes referrals to OT, PT, and child psychology for the child with a disability to support engagement in physical activity (APE, APA) if needed. This follows the role of the developmental pediatrician.
Developmental pediatrician	*Direct:* Physical assessments for participation in age-appropriate activity of GPE, APE, and sport programs if specialized disability knowledge is required. *Indirect:* Makes referrals to OT, PT, or recreation therapists if necessary for concentrated efforts to increase functional and age-appropriate movement skills for physically active play, games, sports, and leisure pursuits. In the case of social-emotional concerns, referrals are made to child psychology to address mood and are often accompanied by recommendations for a boost by engagement in physical activity.
Primary care physician (PCP)	*Direct:* Diagnose, treat, and manage medical care, referring and collaborating whenever necessary. Concentrated efforts are made to encourage participation in community APA offerings. *Indirect:* When injury, diseases, and disabilities affect client participation in physical activity, individuals are referred to experts in the health system such as nutrition and physical therapy. Support by clinical focus can support the individual.
Physician's assistant	*Indirect:* Physician's assistants can provide referrals for APA experts or suggest community offerings based on medical needs.
Physiatrist	*Direct:* This physician heads up teams of professionals, to whom participation in adapted physical activity is paramount in rehabilitation and treatment, particularly in the outpatient phase and upon discharge in planning and ongoing follow-up.
Child psychiatrist	*Direct:* Can address recreational activity to improve the overall physical and mental health of the child. Within residential and day treatment programs, they advocate for child involvement in physical activity adapted for the child's psychological needs, such as anger and temper control.
Adult psychiatrist	*Direct:* Often addresses engagement in physical activity for improved mental health outcomes. *Indirect:* Can refer to community programs for physical activity with ability to adapt if necessary, or to OT or PT for treatment and evaluation for participation in adapted physical activity.

> *continued*

TABLE 2.5   *> continued*

Health care	Roles
Nurse	
School	*Direct:* Often advises on APA participation and the student's prescribed medication timing and amount. Works as a team member monitoring participation of special needs students for intensity and duration of a physical activity.
Residential care	*Direct:* In the recreation program of the adult residential care facility, the nurse participates in monitoring medication and fitness for physical activity and establishing participation with the professional team to the fullest extent possible for the resident.
Assisted living	*Direct:* Assisted living, like residential care, has a strong focus on adapted physical activity in the day-to-day program and in special events.
Nursing home	*Direct:* Nurses assist with medication use and assist with advising on APA.
Community or public health	*Direct:* Administration of medicines for individuals not traditionally served in private clinics, including vaccinations for COVID-19, flu, and shingles and numerous immunizations for children and youth. This care supports their participation in physical activity by boosting health outcomes. Nurses are often in positions to discuss day-to-day life and can advise of physical activity in the community for health.
Nurse practitioner	*Direct:* Adapted physical activity can be a part of their referral responsibilities in any one of these areas: education, counseling, guiding people, health promotion, and injury prevention. *Indirect:* Consulting with other health professionals and community resources on behalf of the individuals they serve to engage them in adapted physical activity.

*Pediatric. Children's age in years: 0 to 1, infants; 1 to 2, toddlers; 3 to 5, preschoolers; 4 to 11, mid-childhood; 12 to 19, adolescence (CDC, 2021).

SLP professionals work to establish communication skills for those who have specific disabilities affecting speech or those who do not have verbal speech and instead use assistive communication, and they are invaluable in creating a way for a person to explain themselves. Specific disabilities result in atypical communication, and the SLP can work to make the person more easily understood by the family and school personnel in APE, GPE, and APA, as well as train the individual in communication. When an individual has a stroke, their communication is often impaired. SLP professionals across the country sponsor Stroke Camp, where participants use adapted physical activity, improve their communication skills, relax, and enjoy the outdoors (Stroke Camp, n.d.). It is a very popular program reporting positive outcomes.

General pediatricians are focused on the physical health of children and adolescents that supports APA and GPE or APE. When young children lag in movement skill performance, the general pediatrician can refer families to OT and PT for assessments. These assessments can be a part of special education services, or they can be offered through private service. For the very young child, services are typically conducted in the home when possible, which is the natural occurring environment for the

child. This is the beginning of the child's participation in a physically active life using modifications and adaptations if needed for involvement in play. *Developmental pediatricians* work in a subspeciality of pediatrics caring for the health of children and youth with disabilities, and they support engagement in APA, GPE, and APE.

Primary care physicians (PCPs) are medical doctors providing comprehensive care from birth to old age. *Physicians' assistants* work under the direction of a medical doctor in areas such as orthopedics and primary care, psychiatry, addiction medicine, pain management, and public health. The PCP is a relatively new evolution of medical practice, having emerged from the profession of family practice. The implementation of the Affordable Care Act increased the number of health care centers staffed by primary care physicians (Kurtzman & Barnow, 2017). Every effort is made to engage patients in a healthy lifestyle, which often calls for engagement in adapted physical activity. A review of services from hospital outpatient centers includes questions about exercise, measurements to be taken, time set to listen to patient concerns (across all ages) and referrals made to community activities or to necessary specialty clinics. PCPs also have specialties such as obstetrics and gynecology, adolescent medicine, or

Interview With a Professional

Katrina Schenck, DPT
Physical Therapist

Question 1: What area did you specialize in during your studies in physical therapy (PT)? And has that changed?

I initially chose to focus on general orthopedics, and then shortly after graduating from PT school, I took continuing education courses to be able to treat patients with vestibular disorders and pelvic floor dysfunction. I have since moved away from treating patients with pelvic floor dysfunction and am now more focused on treating patients following a concussion and working with athletes, while continuing working with those with vestibular disorders. Some examples of the adults I treat in our outpatient clinic are those who have been in car accidents, home accidents; athletes with sports injuries; and those who have balance or vestibular problems driven by inner ear dysfunctions and other complex disorders. In all these instances, life is significantly disrupted.

Question 2: What do you like about your work with adults in physical therapy?

I love helping patients learn how to heal and manage their injuries or chronic conditions using movement and lifestyle changes as opposed to just using medication. In due time, their medication used for pain decreases, and in most cases, it is discontinued. I see daily how we can empower patients to improve their health through exercise.

Question 3: What happens clinically if a person can engage in community-adapted physical activity as a part of their physical therapy program?

Being able to engage in community-adapted physical activity as a part of a physical therapy program often sets a patient up for success, especially once formal PT concludes. Initiating this activity while in treatment provides numerous benefits, such as developing a supportive community of people going through similar issues, and it fosters a routine that helps lead to long-term maintenance of an active lifestyle. While in therapy, we can talk about aspects of their adapted physical activity engagement. I can guide and problem solve with the individual. In the end, I've observed this approach build confidence for physical activity engagement once therapy goals have been reached, and it leads to an ease with committing to physical activity engagement.

geriatrics, as well as sexuality and gender identity. The PCP team includes nurse practitioners and physicians' assistants. This team provides referrals when necessary and collaborates to provide comprehensive care for their patients with and without disabilities.

Physiatrists or *physical medicine and rehabilitation doctors* are medical doctors specializing in rehabilitation medicine caring for people with disabling conditions needing a concentrated multidisciplinary clinical team approach for recovery (illness, injury, or phase of a disease process). For example, they may lead a multidisciplinary team in collaborating in the care of people with spinal cord injuries, those with disability conditions, and those with serious illnesses, all in critical need of recovery to health and being functional. The modern program includes an inpatient phase and an outpatient phase.

Child psychiatrists are medical doctors trained in the mental illnesses of children and adolescents that affect participation in APA. They are keenly aware of the isolated child, unhappy and needing play and recreation. Often this doctor works directly with the family to sort out how play and recreation can occur for the child, in conjunction with talking with the child if they are willing and capable. Art and music therapy often helps these children express themselves better; this therapy is adapted if needed for participation. *Adult psychiatrists* are medical doctors trained in diagnosis and treatment of mental illnesses in adults.

School nurses attend to the medical needs of students while in their school program. *Residential care nurses* and *assisted living nurses* assist with medication use and, if necessary, guidelines for engagement in APA. *Nursing homes nurses* use APA as a primary

Interview With a Professional

Amanda Johnson, MS, OTR/L
Occupational Therapist

Question 1: *With the adults you meet at the outpatient clinic, what are some of the common functional issues you help them with in their life?*

My focus is with patients with neurological deficits. Specifically, I work with regaining movement and coordination of their arms, hands, fingers, and eyes. I help them regain their ability to take care of themselves, complete household activities, and participate in community events. I help their caregiver understand the support the patients might need.

Question 2: *In thinking about using a home exercise program (HEP) along with visits to the clinic for an adult's rehabilitation, what elements are important to consider for setting them up for success?*

Whenever possible, I like to work with developing a home exercise program (HEP) with my patients to supplement what is done during clinic visits. One thing that I have found very important is to have a good discussion with the patient that gets at their honest assessment of their motivation and ability to complete a HEP. Many patients are able and desire a HEP. However, some know they most likely won't complete a HEP. With this knowledge, I can schedule them for more frequent office visits. Also, it is important to keep in mind whether there is special knowledge or physical or cognitive abilities required to complete the HEP, that neither the patient nor the caregiver has. Does the patient need to know more about the injury they have, or more about why we are doing a specific exercise? Can I do this gradually? What else? Lastly, for those able and desiring a HEP, I look at how the HEP is provided. In our clinic, we have software programs that can print the HEP that is individualized for our patient and based on my work with them. Many of my patients can't read small fonts or can't interpret a picture that is used with the software. Some speak a language that is not used in the software. I can help with all these obstacles, but over the years, I have found that the patient may not even be able to bring them to my attention. When these are addressed, the patient has a much easier time with the home exercise program. It complements what we are doing in the clinic and helps to progress them toward improved function and enjoyment in their day-to-day life.

Question 3: *What do you most enjoy in your work as an occupational therapist?*

What I enjoy most about being an occupational therapist is seeing hope come into patient's lives as they begin to understand their condition and how to improve their functional abilities. It is very inspiring to see patients work so hard and regain abilities that they have considered impossible to regain.

modality in engaging residents in their health and for fun, relaxation, and recreational purposes.

Public health nurses work in a vast array of health agencies, both public and private. Mental health nursing is prominent in caring for individuals who have a mental health diagnosis and, for example, are poor, homeless, experiencing food scarcity, and runaways. In caring for these individuals, along with medical interventions, consultations for inexpensive recreational outlets such as city parks and recreation programs, parks, and age-appropriate APA can be made.

Nurse practitioners have advanced training beyond their bachelor's degree in nursing, specializing in clinical care in family practice, gerontology, primary care, emergency family care, and other areas. "Nurse practitioners provide high-quality care in diverse settings, including clinics, hospitals, emergency rooms, urgent care sites, private physician or NP practices, nursing homes, schools, colleges and public health departments. . . . [They] assess, diagnose and treat acute and chronic diseases, as well as counsel, coordinate care and educate patients regarding their illnesses" (American Association of Nurse Practitioners, n.d.).

War and Rehabilitative Medicine

The neurosurgeon Sir Ludwig Guttman believed that physical activity was paramount in the return of human dignity and physical health for those injured in wars. In 1943, he became the director of the new National Spinal Injury Center at the Emergency Services Hospital at Stoke Mandeville, England. Guttman is considered the first to introduce the rehabilitation approach, promoting

- an active life versus the accepted inactive confinement to bed,
- rehabilitation units as teams of professionals, and
- referrals made to athletic competition.

He included nurses and physiotherapists in his rounds. As the patients improved, they were referred to sports participation. Athletic participation became the potent drug in rehabilitation and the patients became people participating in a full life. A colleague, Dr. John Silver, described a young man who came to them in 1956 nearly dead, having waited 18 months for his transfer to Stoke. Silver explained that Guttman "cured" the young man and sent him out to a meaningful life.

Guttman's patients' athletic endeavors eventually became the Stoke Mandeville Games. In England, these games were offered at the Stoke Mandeville Hospital in 1948, noticeably coinciding with the Olympic Games. In 1961, Guttman founded the British Sports Association for the Disabled. His games became international, and he was the first editor of *Paraplegia*. After being knighted in 1966, he lobbied heavily for association with the International Olympic Committee, resulting in the Paralympic movement. Thus, he earned the name *Father of the Paralympics*.

Interview With a Professional

David Tempest, MD

Physiatrist

Question: Please describe how adapted physical activity works in recovery programs for your patients.

The focus on the inpatient side with newly diagnosed conditions has to be on exercise to learn independence in basic self-care skills and mobility in the house and then in the community . . . some of my favorite people of all time have been the therapeutic recreation staff on our team. Every inpatient goes through a crash course in community integration, both practical experience with community outings and with resource materials.

Often for an inpatient, endurance training, strengthening, and flexibility protocols are used to lay a foundation to tolerate participation in home and community activities. The focus is on basic self-care and mobility with an introduction to longer term opportunities, but there is simply not time for in-depth education in adapted physical activity. Note that inpatient stays are so short now that exposure to adapted physical activity is woefully limited and so much is happening that clients are often overwhelmed with limited carryover. Thus, much has to be done on the outpatient side.

In the early outpatient days, the focus is on the successful transition back to managing basic home and community skills. I think many centers drop the ball here regarding introducing people with new disabilities to recreational and athletic opportunities.

Because the ball may get dropped, I think it is so important to link people up with peer support and support groups. Peer counseling in the hospital is invaluable in introducing an inpatient to someone who has been there and leads a successful, active life. Some successful examples of support groups for outpatients can be found in the stroke, amputee, and spinal cord injury populations (e.g., the Harbor View Amputee Support Group in Seattle, Washington).

I tried to direct people that I was working with to community programs that do hands-on exposure to activities. Outdoors for All is my favorite. Absolutely a remarkable group. Skiing, sailing, bicycling, bowling, rock climbing . . . they'll work with anyone no matter what and figure out a way to participate. Wounded Warriors comes to mind. Adapted swim teams, wheelchair rugby teams, and basketball. The Paralyzed Veterans of America has excellent resources.

I always told people, I provided care for formal physical and occupational therapies that are time limited, and that the patient's job was to not just go through therapy, but to learn how to do their own therapy. The point being, therapy isn't a discrete program that ends—it's a lifelong routine. I focus on how forced use can improve recovery over years, with no end point. Get into recreational activities that are often better therapy than formal sessions with the PT or OT. For instance, I worked with a young (30ish) guy about two years out from his motor vehicle accident with a T-12 paraplegia (an injury at the 12th thoracic vertebra, resulting in a paralysis of the lower body and limbs). He worked and worked with PT to improve balance and strength. Then he hooked up with Outdoors for All and began to learn to sit-ski. When I saw him a few months later, he was really excited and said (I'm paraphrasing) . . . "Skiing is *way* better than PT for learning balance, trunk control, and core strength." And he had a blast with it, and it could be a lifelong activity.

Interview With a Professional

Courtesy of the University of Northern Colorado.

Scott Douglas, PhD

Professor, Department of Kinesiology, Dietetics, and Nutrition

University of Northern Colorado

Question 1: *What drew you to competitive adapted sports?*

I love to play, and I love competition. Setting goals and trying to achieve them (and win) has always been and still is a part of me—it's in my blood. Since I can remember, from four-year-old tee ball or the neighborhood game of flashlight tag after dark up through high school and college athletics, and ultimately three U.S. Paralympic Teams, I've strived to win. Any sport, any game, any carnival booth, or even a friendly kayak race on a quiet lake sparks my fire.

As an 18-year-old freshman at the University of Utah, I took every opportunity to head to the mountains to ski. On one cold Sunday morning my life was changed forever. While skiing with a friend at Snowbird, Utah, I lost an edge and slid backward at speed into an unpadded lift tower located directly in the middle of the trail. After a helicopter ride down the canyon and a lot of poking and prodding, the surgeon at the hospital told my family I had a spinal cord injury and might never walk again. To me and my parents that meant I might not do *anything* again, including sports.

My three-month long rehabilitation program was all about making me whole again—but really, I wanted to walk again. Walking was everything. Otherwise, my life was over. I just wanted to walk down the aisle at my wedding. Walking had no other meaning or purpose in the long term to me. It was at the encouragement of my physical therapist at the rehab center that my true rehabilitation took place. While in the hospital rehabilitating, I became frustrated by the constant inactivity and boredom. On many days, I chose to provide a lame excuse to just stay in bed and watch television. Looking back, I'm sure I was depressed at some level. I was told my feelings were normal, but I felt like a prisoner of my own fear of the unknown. Would I ever walk or play sports again? Would the pain go away? What would life be like using a wheelchair? Could I still have a family? Thankfully, my physical therapist took the extra time and energy needed to get to know me and discover what motivated me—what made me tick. It was sports.

One evening, this PT signed me out of the hospital and drove me 40 miles in the hospital van to see Patrick Ewing play a basketball game for Georgetown in the NCAA tournament. I remember overhearing my physical therapist trying to convince my very conservative and conventional physiatrist that it was okay for me to leave the hospital for a few hours. He would be responsible for my well-being while we drove to Provo, Utah, to see the game. It was my first time out of the hospital since my crash. I wore a full upper-torso body brace, sat in a reclining rehab special wheelchair, and was in excruciating pain the entire time. I loved every minute of it!

A few weeks later, I was getting stronger and attended an outing on the hospital's outdoor patio. My PT grabbed a basketball out of the bushes, brushed the snow off the ball, dribbled it a couple times, and then handed it to me. There was a 10-foot regulation basketball hoop in the courtyard, and we rolled over to check it out. "Go for it," he said—and with both hands I did, barely reaching the bottom of the net. It was the first of many airballs I would shoot in my career, but more importantly, my next shot did not miss. This was one of many shots I would make in my career, only this one changed my entire outlook on life! It turned on my internal light. I could still play sports. I could be normal again—thanks to my PT.

> continued

Scott Douglas   *> continued*

> **Question 2:** *When you competed, what did your teammates share with you in mindset, experience, and benefit of competition?*
>
> My teammates were vital to my own life experiences living with a disability. Many of these people became part of my inner circle of friends, and many are still close to me today. These were the people who showed me the ropes of living life and playing sports from a wheelchair. First, they enlightened me about how to manage my day-to-day living with a spinal cord injury. In rehabilitation I made it all about just walking again—and not about learning how to jump curbs or ride an escalator in my wheelchair. My teammates showed me, through their own life experience, about all the other possibilities that life still had to offer. They taught me lessons like traveling, getting an apartment by myself, attending college again, pursuing a normal relationship with my girlfriend (now wife of 40 years), camping in the mountains, whitewater rafting, alpine skiing, water-skiing, and playing wheelchair softball. They also introduced me to the newest sport wheelchairs available to play basketball and tennis. The biggest reason that I was successful and jumped up the ranks quickly in adapted sport is because I was able to access these lightweight sport wheelchairs.
>
> As I started playing against all the best wheelchair athletes in the country, I began to seek out knowledge and information from them and prominent coaches about how to be better—the best. My goal was to learn and apply some of their training, competition strategies, and past sport experiences to my own parasport career. I wanted to be a Paralympian, and my goal was always to win a gold medal for my country. A huge piece in fueling my success was the advice from many teammates and rivals to act like an athlete. This transformed my mindset from being a former able-bodied multisport athlete to a world-class wheelchair athlete. This shift provided me with the confidence and personal tools to develop and maintain my current growth mindset that influences everything I do in my life, personally and professionally.

Orthopedists

Orthopedists are trained in the diagnosis and treatment of bone disease and injury to bones and surrounding joints and ligaments. This includes the delineation of procedures to care for an individual until surgery or after a surgical procedure. Nonsurgical interventions may be prescribed (e.g., physical therapy, injections, medicines, physical activity). They are not trained to have discussions about engaging in physical activity except to say it is a good idea. Adults with or without disability often complain that their orthopedist was not concerned about them and their life after surgery. The following information is offered to help this situation.

Orthopedists are easily able to describe limitations and give a time frame for physical activity modification. There are two phases in orthopedics for patient engagement in physical activity. One is the acute phase of recovery from surgery or accident (rehabilitative), and the second is the gradual entry into the patient's preferred physical activities, or developing new interests and finding community resources. During any of these phases the orthopedist can quickly advise, but the best route is to make clinical referrals to appropriate specialists (e.g., PT or OT, prosthetics). There is only so much time allotted now for seeing a patient, but it doesn't take long for the surgeon to share advice and refer to a specialist whose job encompasses the process of evaluation for physical activity and the individual's assimilation and application of that information. Orthopedists regularly refer to physical therapy for their patient population.

Summary

The professionals involved in promoting the involvement of people with disabilities in adapted physical activity are much expanded from the early days of the Individuals with Disabilities Education Improvement Act of 2004. Now more than ever, these professionals need training to bring their expertise to settings where, across the age spectrum, people with disabilities live and can be physically active. The settings include public schools, homes, community recreation centers, private clubs, hospital rehabilitation inpatient and outpatient programs, and medical clinics for primary care and specialized medical care. In this chapter, detailed tables delineate professional roles and describe delivery of services to those with disabilities as either mandated by law or encompassed in an agency's service provision. Each has implications for higher education training programs.

CHAPTER 3

Disability and the Law

Dennis Brack-Pool/Getty Images

CHAPTER OBJECTIVES

After completing this chapter, you will be able to do the following:

- Identify federal definitions of disability from infancy to old age.
- Understand and identify federal laws that mandate adapted physical education for individuals with disabilities from birth through age 21.
- Identify and describe the value of the individualized education program (IEP) and the individual family service plan (IFSP).
- Describe the goal of placement options within the physical education setting and describe some of those options.
- Acknowledge the role of a variety of professionals on an IEP team.
- Describe what is meant by a transition plan.

The Constitution of the United States was written in 1787; it lays down the rights of people of America whereby the government is to serve the people. Amendments are made to the Constitution as history passes, and related laws are passed as well. The Civil Rights Act of 1964 abolished institutional racial segregation and discrimination.

Civil rights for those with disabilities extends into the schools, and people with disabilities cannot be discriminated against in programs because of their disability. If physical education is a part of the curriculum of a school, physical education must be offered to those with disabilities as well. The right to sports and other club programs must also be extended to students with disabilities who qualify for the activity.

Individuals with Disabilities Education Improvement Act of 2004

The Individuals with Disabilities Education Improvement Act of 2004 (abbreviated as IDEA [2004]) is the federal law mandating education for those with disabilities from infants to seniors in high school who qualify. This law stems from one of the most important laws passed in 1975, the Education for All Handicapped Children Act (EAHCA). Prior to the enactment of EAHCA, children who had disabilities were not in the public schools, or in many cases, not in school at all. In the United States, there were specialized schools like schools for the blind that dated back to the 1800s. One of these is the famous Perkins School for the Blind, where Helen Keller attended classes. (Presently, there remain 49 residential schools and 52 day schools in the United States for deaf students.) After EAHCA passed in 1975, federal monies were directed, by way of grants, to educate teachers in special education and to create curricula for those teachers and for the children and youth themselves.

IDEA guides monies allotted to run special education and mandates the documents created within IDEA for teaching, specifically the individualized education program (IEP) and the individual family service plan (IFSP) for infants and toddlers. Teachers need to know the specifics of their legal instructional responsibilities under IDEA. Teaching includes advocacy, and the law is a tool that teachers use to both serve children and their families and advocate for their education.

IDEA (2004) mandates the following:

- That all children or youth up to 21 years old in public schools have a right to a free,

appropriate, public education. This originally applied to just 1st to 12th grades but, through amendments, now includes infants, toddlers, preschoolers, and kindergarteners.
- That children with disabilities are educated in the least restrictive environment with their age peers.

Schools must provide students who qualify for special education in their state with the following:

- An individualized education program (IEP) written by a team of professionals (e.g., adapted physical educators, occupational therapists, physical therapists, speech and language pathologists) for students ages 3 to 21 years
- An individual family service plan (IFSP) written for infants and toddlers if they are ages zero to two years (to age three in some states)

IDEA requires that physical education teachers and allied health professionals in the schools know the law to deliver services. The law purposely gave leeway to states to administer the law, which is vague in places. Historically this meant litigating to solve concerns. By litigating, parents, special interest groups, and school districts advocated for the rights of children and youth to be appropriately educated in the public schools. Understanding the law informs the physical educators in the schools and their colleagues in designing the IEP and IFSP. These plans and programs are legal documents and must follow the law.

Without the federal mandate to serve children in the schools, there would be a major inability to provide education to infants, toddlers, preschoolers, school-age children, and youth with disabilities or suspected disabilities.

This law has consequences for students with specific categories of disabilities participating in adapted physical education. Professionals involved with adapted physical education in the schools need the following legal information as a point of advocacy for a student and to perform their work. Professionals working under this mandate include adapted physical education, general physical education, plus occupational and physical therapy, and speech and language pathology, as well as coaching and school administration (see chapter 2).

Infants and toddlers with a disability have an individual family service plan (IFSP) constructed by the child's educational team with the family. The IFSP necessitates an emphasis on family involvement due to the young age of the children. Physical educators do not work with infants and toddlers leaving that area of service delivery to occupational therapy, physical therapy, speech and language pathology, and a few others. APE with specialized training work with the preschool and kindergarten child with a disability given the importance of physical development often requiring interdisciplinary expertise. IFSPs are discussed later in the chapter; see Individual Family Service Plan.

For very young children with a disability, it is imperative that intervention begin as soon as possible to stave off negative developmental trajectories and boost early brain development (Shonkoff & Phillips, 2000). Other scientists have long reported the cumulative developmental risk if delay is not detected early and intervention begun (Sameroff & Chandler, 1975). Intervening early is a positive approach to helping children and families before undetected problems multiply and grow. Knowledgeable parents can better understand how their child is developing and how to support that development. Although Shonkoff and Phillips always contend that even if a delay is detected later, beginning intervention then will also help the child.

The IEP and the IFSP teams are important professionals whose roles are to work with the family and advocate for the student by collaborating on the student's academic plans and interventions. Together, assessments by these multiple professionals are discussed. This IEP team includes the parents and the educators (e.g., physical educator, adapted physical educator, classroom teacher, and special education teacher) and associated health care professionals (e.g., occupational therapists, physical therapists, and speech and language pathologists) plus other specialists (e.g., recreation therapists and mobility trainers). (Refer to chapter 2, table 2.2 and table 2.3.) The placement of a student in a program is, to the extent possible, to be integrated with the student's age peers. The educational placement is termed *least restrictive environment* and is discussed by the team on a case-by-case basis. Some states extend their IFSP into preschool; most do not and leave it for infants and toddlers, birth through 2 years of age. The IFSP team includes pediatric occupational and physical therapists, speech and language pathologists, an adapted physical educator (in states that extend the IFSP) as appropriate, and others deemed important. Placement for infants and toddlers is often in the home with services coming to the family or in centers in the community with services coordinated there.

Defining Physical Education

Public Law 108-446, Individuals with Disabilities Education Improvement Act of 2004 (referred to as IDEA 2004), defines physical education as:

> The development of physical and motor fitness; fundamental motor skills and patterns; and skills in aquatics, dance, and individual and group games and sports (including intramural and lifetime sports); and includes special physical education, adapted physical education, movement education, and motor development.

IDEA (2004, § 300.39[b][2]).

> General. Physical education services, specially designed if necessary, must be made available to every child with a disability receiving FAPE [free, appropriate, public education].
>
> Regular physical education. Each child with a disability must be afforded the opportunity to participate in the regular physical education program available to nondisabled children unless the child is enrolled full time in a separate facility; or the child needs specially designed physical education, as prescribed in the child's IEP.
>
> Special physical education. If specially designed physical education is prescribed in a child's IEP, the public agency responsible for the education of that child shall provide the services directly or make arrangements for those services to be provided through other public or private programs.

IDEA (2004, § 300.108[a, b, c]).

Special physical education is the legal term in IDEA (2004) and since the beginning of special education under EAHCA (1975). Today we refer to it as *adapted physical education*. Under IDEA (2004), *special physical education* means that if a specially designed physical education is prescribed in a child's IEP, the public agency responsible for the education of that child shall provide the services directly or make arrangements for those services to be provided through other public or private programs.

Owing to IDEA (2004), special education services are established in public schools from preschool through 12th grade to serve students with disabilities. States vary in their qualification criteria for this special education service. Adaptations are individualized based on assessments, educational planning decisions, and resources of the district. (All of this is discussed in later chapters.) In addition, two other federal laws mandate services: the Elementary and Secondary Education Act and Section 504 of the Rehabilitation Act affect students with disabilities.

As it currently stands in IDEA (2004), physical education is not *a required academic area* under the law for qualifying special education students, particularly if students without disabilities are not receiving physical education. Yet the definition of physical education in federal education law has remained the same since the seminal Education for All Handicapped Children Act of 1975 when physical education was a recognized academic area.

The reason physical education is defined and remains in the law is that states and their school districts often choose to offer physical education and adapted physical education within special education services (e.g., Minnesota Rules—DAPE criteria 3525.1352). State rules superseded federal education law. The spirit of the federal law or the intent of the law clearly indicates that, if a child with a disability needs modification or adaptation, the school uses its resources to make reasonable accommodations for the child to succeed. The spirit of the law is often decided in the courts.

Defining and Categorizing Disability

There are specific primary categories included in IDEA under the lead definition of *child with a disability*. These federal terms and definitions guide how states define disability and who is eligible for a free, appropriate, public education under federal education law (see the sidebar, Categories of Disability Under IDEA [2004]). To fully meet the definition of child with a disability (and eligibility for special education and related services), the student's educational performance must be adversely affected due to

Categories of Disability Under IDEA (2004)

1. Autism means a developmental disability significantly affecting verbal and nonverbal communication and social interaction, generally evident before age three, that adversely affects a child's educational performance. Other characteristics often associated with autism are engagement in repetitive activities and stereotyped movements, resistance to environmental change or change in daily routines, and unusual responses to sensory experiences.

Autism does not apply if a child's educational performance is adversely affected primarily because the child has an emotional disturbance, as defined in paragraph (c)(4) of this section.

A child who manifests the characteristics of autism after age three could be identified as having autism if the criteria in paragraph (c)(1)(i) of this section are satisfied.

2. Deaf-blindness means concomitant hearing and visual impairments, the combination of which causes such severe communication and other developmental and educational needs that they cannot be accommodated in special education programs solely for children with deafness or children with blindness.

3. Deafness means a hearing impairment that is so severe that the child is impaired in processing linguistic information through hearing, with or without amplification, that adversely affects a child's educational performance.

4. Emotional disturbance means a condition exhibiting one or more of the following characteristics over a long period of time and to a marked degree that adversely affects a child's educational performance:

   ○ An inability to learn that cannot be explained by intellectual, sensory, or health factors.

   ○ An inability to build or maintain satisfactory interpersonal relationships with peers and teachers.

   ○ Inappropriate types of behavior or feelings under normal circumstances.

   ○ A general pervasive mood of unhappiness or depression.

   ○ A tendency to develop physical symptoms or fears associated with personal or school problems.

Emotional disturbance includes schizophrenia. The term does not apply to children who are socially maladjusted, unless it is determined that they have an emotional disturbance under paragraph (c)(4)(i) of this section.

5. Hearing impairment means an impairment in hearing, whether permanent or fluctuating, that adversely affects a child's educational performance but that is not included under the definition of deafness in this section.

6. Intellectual disability means significantly subaverage general intellectual functioning, existing concurrently with deficits in adaptive behavior and manifested during the developmental period, that adversely affects a child's educational performance. The term "intellectual disability" was formerly termed "mental retardation."

7. Multiple disabilities means concomitant impairments (such as intellectual disability-blindness or intellectual disability-orthopedic impairment), the combination of which causes such severe educational needs that they cannot be accommodated in special education programs solely for one of the impairments. Multiple disabilities does not include deaf-blindness.

8. Orthopedic impairment means a severe orthopedic impairment that adversely affects a child's educational performance. The term includes impairments caused by a congenital anomaly, impairments caused by disease (e.g., poliomyelitis, bone tuberculosis), and impairments from other causes (e.g., cerebral palsy, amputations, and fractures or burns that cause contractures).

9. Other health impairment means having limited strength, vitality, or alertness, including a heightened alertness to environmental stimuli, that results in limited alertness with respect to the educational environment, that—

  ○ Is due to chronic or acute health problems such as asthma, attention deficit disorder or attention deficit hyperactivity disorder, diabetes, epilepsy, a heart condition, hemophilia, lead poisoning, leukemia, nephritis, rheumatic fever, sickle cell anemia, and Tourette syndrome; and

  ○ Adversely affects a child's educational performance.

10. Specific learning disability—

  ○ General. Specific learning disability means a disorder in one or more of the basic psychological processes involved in understanding or in using language, spoken or written, that may manifest itself in the imperfect ability to listen, think, speak, read, write, spell, or to do mathematical calculations, including conditions such as perceptual disabilities, brain injury, minimal brain dysfunction, dyslexia, and developmental aphasia.

  ○ Disorders not included. Specific learning disability does not include learning problems that are primarily the result of visual, hearing, or motor disabilities, of intellectual disability, of emotional disturbance, or of environmental, cultural, or economic disadvantage.

11. Speech or language impairment means a communication disorder, such as stuttering, impaired articulation, a language impairment, or a voice impairment, that adversely affects a child's educational performance.

12. Traumatic brain injury means an acquired injury to the brain caused by an external physical force, resulting in total or partial functional disability or psychosocial impairment, or both, that adversely affects a child's educational performance. Traumatic brain injury applies to open or closed head injuries resulting in impairments in one or more areas, such as cognition; language; memory; attention; reasoning; abstract thinking; judgment; problem-solving; sensory, perceptual, and motor abilities; psychosocial behavior; physical functions; information processing; and speech. Traumatic brain injury does not apply to brain injuries that are congenital or degenerative, or to brain injuries induced by birth trauma.

13. Visual impairment including blindness means an impairment in vision that, even with correction, adversely affects a child's educational performance. The term includes both partial sight and blindness.

Reprinted from IDEA, Section 300.8, "Child with a Disability," modified July 11, 2017, https://sites.ed.gov/idea/statuteregulations/.

the disability. For example, cerebral palsy may affect cognition and locomotion, thus requiring accommodations for material presentation and ambulation from point A to point B as well as academic content adaptations.

IDEA (2004) uses a category of developmental delay that has served children experiencing delays in their development without a specific diagnosis for preschool and kindergarten children to age nine in early elementary school. In the amendments of IDEA (2004), infants and toddlers were included in the service under the criteria of developmental delay or at risk for developmental delay (see chapter 4).

Since state educational law overrides federal educational law, some states limit service under developmental delay to kindergarten, rather than to age nine years. In those states, if the child meets state criteria, beginning in first grade, the child is categorized as to the child with a disability and the categories of IDEA disability.

Professionals from both the schools and community health care contribute to the diagnosis of disability. In addition, medical expertise contributes to the discussion around the diagnosis from orthopedists, neurologists, ophthalmologists, audiologists, and other specialties. These professionals contribute assessment data and evaluation reports understanding whether a delay is present and if so,

its extent. It is not the role of many of the professionals named in table 2.2 and table 2.3 to diagnose but rather to present information to enable a diagnosis, possibly made by the school psychologist or other school specialist, or in medicine by one such as the developmental pediatrician or the orthopedist.

It is always tempting to speculate on a diagnosis for a child developing atypically. Every decade seems to have a popular diagnosis. Today, the diagnosis of autism spectrum disorder is a common consideration. More clinicians understand this disorder and more assessment tools are available than there were in the early 2010s. Yet often it takes a seasoned professional to determine the appropriate diagnosis for many of these categories of disability. The diagnosis is made to secure funding for special education in the schools, or medical reimbursement in clinical settings from health insurance and to help the child, the family, and the IEP and IFSP team. Note in some of the definitions that follow how exclusions are described. For example, the diagnosis of autism spectrum disorder does not apply if the child's educational performance is adversely affected primarily because the child has an emotional disturbance. Here is where the skilled professional can assess the degree to which the behavior is evidence of emotional disturbance or one of autism.

In adulthood, there are federal government criteria defining disability. These are different from any federal special education law's definition of disability. According to the United States Centers for Disease Control and Prevention (CDC, 2000), individuals 18 years and older have a disability if *any* of the following three conditions is true:

1. When the individual was age 5 years or older, reported a sensory, physical, mental, or self-care disability.

2. When the individual was 16 years old or older with difficulty going outside of the home.

3. The individual is 16 to 64 years old and reported an employment disability.

Disability for adults was defined by CDC (2020) in an annual survey (Behavioral Risk Factor Surveillance System) if they reported having one or more of the six disability types:

- *Mobility:* Serious difficulty walking or climbing stairs
- *Cognition:* Serious difficulty concentrating, remembering, or making decisions
- *Hearing:* Deafness or serious difficulty hearing

Realistic Reflections/Getty Images

- *Vision:* Blindness or serious difficulty seeing
- *Independent living:* Difficulty doing errands alone
- *Self-care:* Difficulty dressing or bathing

Still another source of definition of adult disability is described in the Americans with Disabilities Act (ADA). It was specifically revised in 2008 to better define *disability* beyond the initial description in the law as:

1. a physical or mental impairment that substantially limits one or more major life activities;
2. a record (or history) of such an impairment; or
3. being regarded as having a disability.

These descriptions remain in the law. In amending the law, the Department of Justice specified in great detail what is and is not disability. The ADA is about equality under the law, and an individual's disability status cannot be a basis for discrimination in such areas as employment, use of transportation, and telecommunication.

The World Health Organization (WHO) reports and cares for individuals with a disability from a worldwide perspective. Around the world, adults with disabilities are less likely to be employed. This worldwide definition of disability is included to increase communication and understanding when adapted physical educators or others providing adapted physical activity work around the world.

For WHO, disability is an umbrella term that includes "impairments, activity limitations and participant restrictions, referring to the negative aspects of the interaction of the individual (with a health condition) and that individual's contextual factors (environmental and personal factors)" (WHO 2021, pp. 3-4). The committee charged with this definition was guided by parameters begging for cross-discipline cooperation and research:

> . . . a definition of disability should be: applicable to all people, without segregation into groups such as "the visually impaired" or "wheelchair users" or those with a chronic illness, and be able to describe the experience of disability across many areas of functioning. The definition should allow comparison of severity across different types of disability, be flexible enough for different applications

> (e.g., statistical or clinical use), be able to describe all types of disability, and recognize the effects of the environment on a person's disability. Finally, the definition should not include stipulations about the causes of any disability.

> Only when disability is accurately defined can the many issues in health and social policy be tackled and appropriate studies designed to assess which interventions have the best health and health-related outcomes to improve the life and wellbeing of all people living with disability.

> Leonardi et al. (2006, pp. 1219-1221).

WHO devised the International Classification of Functioning in conjunction with persons with disabilities, practitioners, clinicians, and researchers. WHO is committed to a cross-discipline approach in increasing the health outcomes for people with disabilities. WHO combines the rights for development of services for people with disabilities with human rights, promoting inclusive development in the mainstream of society, empowering people with disabilities and family members using practical suggestions and easily accessed community-based rehabilitation services. WHO reported on the disastrous effect that COVID-19 had on people with disabilities in countries that did not protect them from infection or care for them while they were sick (2021).

IDEA and the Vocation and Rehabilitation Act of 1973, Section 504

If a student does not have a disability identified in IDEA but requires modifications and adaptations in the educational setting, services can be received through Section 504 of the Vocation and Rehabilitation Act of 1973. It is very broad civil rights law encompassing all aspects of the individual's life and has implications for students. The major concept of Section 504 is that individuals may not be discriminated against because of a disability. This law reinforces the rights of students with disabilities to participate in all educational learning experiences, including physical education.

This is a challenging area requiring professionals to determine that the student does not meet IDEA criteria. Furthermore, states have differing criteria. For example, an eight-year-old student is tested and scores above the cutoff for IDEA qualification in her state (1.5 SD below the mean) on a standardized test of motor development. The IEP team determines that she is clearly struggling across many settings in school, and it would not be prudent to have her continue to fall further and further behind without appropriate support. They recommend to the mother to use a 504 plan instead of an IEP. The 504 plan is still free for her daughter's public school education and includes adaptations for her physical education program.

For older students, the 504 plan from high school does not follow the student to college. Yet the students are still protected from discrimination at a college or university because of their disability. They is also protected under the ADA for the rest of their lives.

Americans with Disabilities Act Amendments Act of 2008

American with Disabilities Act of 1990 (ADA, 1990) was the seminal civil rights law for individuals with disabilities that stated that individuals with disabilities cannot be discriminated against. On the 20th anniversary of the establishment of the ADA, President Obama proclaimed:

Today, as we commemorate what the ADA accomplished, we celebrate who the ADA was all about. It was about the young girl in Washington State who just wanted to see a movie at her hometown theater, but was turned away because she had cerebral palsy; or the young man in Indiana who showed up at a worksite, able to do the work, excited for the opportunity, but was turned away and called a cripple because of a minor disability he had already trained himself to work with; or the student in California who was eager and able to attend the college of his dreams, and refused to let the iron grip of polio keep him from the classroom—each of whom became integral to this cause.

And it was about all of you. You understand these stories because you or someone you loved lived them. And that sparked a movement. It began when Americans no longer saw their own disabilities as a barrier to their success, and set out to tear down the physical and social barriers that were. It grew when you realized you weren't alone. It became a massive wave of bottom-up change that swept across the country as you refused to accept the world as it was. And when you were told, no, don't try, you can't [sic]—you responded with that age-old American creed: Yes, we can.

The White House (July 26, 2010).

This federal law is referred to as the ADA Amendments Act of 2008, ADAAA 2008, or ADAAA. When the ADA was first established in 1990, it was a watershed moment, the result of which was enormous change by offering legal protection for individuals with disabilities with equal status under the law and reasonable accommodation if needed for inclusion. ADAAA 2008 further clarified disability. (Typically the term *ADA* is used to reference this law instead of *ADAAA*.) Up to the early 1970s, in the United States, individuals with disabilities could not attend public schools. They were sent to live in state institutions; they were not allowed to vote; they had been involuntarily sterilized; they lived under "ugly laws" in some municipalities mandated not to be seen in public (McKeever, 2020); and they were physically denied access to public buildings, restrooms, and the walkways of cities, towns, and parks.

The ADA prohibits discrimination on the basis of disability just as other civil rights laws prohibit discrimination on the basis of race, color, sex, national origin, age, and religion. The ADA guarantees that people with disabilities have the same opportunities as everyone else to enjoy employment opportunities, purchase goods and services, and participate in state and local government programs. . . . To prevent discrimination against people with disabilities, the ADA sets out requirements that apply to many of the situations you encounter in everyday life. Employers, state and local governments, businesses that are open to the public, commercial facilities, transportation providers, and telecommunication companies all have to follow the requirements of the ADA.

ADA.gov (n.d.).

ADA touches many aspects of adapted physical activity service in the schools, in the community, and in health care. It is a civil right for individuals with disabilities to access programs, buildings, transportation systems and communication systems to participate in the adapted physical activity programs.

As of 2008, there exists enormous legal protection for individuals with disabilities enabling their equal access in education. In sum, prohibiting discrimination against students with disabilities was further fortified by the ADAAA given the prior passage of the Rehabilitation Act Amendments of 1973, Section 504; and IDEA (2004). These laws prohibit discrimination in education against students with disabilities *under two civil rights purposes*: not to be discriminated against based solely on their disabilities and the right to reasonable accommodations in education (Turnbull et al., 2009).

An example of this comes from the state of Minnesota, where the cutoff score on standardized tests of psychomotor skills is set at 7 percent to qualify for adapted physical education (referred to as developmental adapted physical education in Minnesota).

Those performing at greater than 7 percent do not qualify for adapted physical education services under IDEA (2004), unless otherwise determined by the IEP team. But some children who have a disability just over that 7 percent cutoff desperately need modifications in order to be successful in their physical education activities. Being served under a Section 504 plan can facilitate the assistance the child would need. Overall, the ADA has established the civil rights of this child. ADA has no educational IEP or 504 plan. It is a civil right, now in place for rights in education.

Every Student Succeeds Act of 2015

The federal education law for all children referenced as the No Child Left Behind Act of 2001 addressed elementary and secondary education in America. The negative side of this law was an onslaught of paperwork, and testing of student educational progress was by standardized testing only. This

Extracurricular Sports and the Vocation and Rehabilitation Act of 1973

In January 2013, the Office for Civil Rights of the U.S. Department of Education reported that there had not been adequate implementation of Section 504 of the Vocation and Rehabilitation Act of 1973 by the American educational system. The Office for Civil Rights issued the following statement:

> Extracurricular athletics—which include club, intramural, or interscholastic (e.g., freshman, junior varsity, varsity) athletics at all education levels—are an important component of an overall education program. The United States Government Accountability Office (GAO) published a report that underscored that access to, and participation in, extracurricular athletic opportunities provide important health and social benefits to all students, particularly those with disabilities. These benefits can include socialization, improved teamwork and leadership skills, and fitness. Unfortunately, the GAO found that students with disabilities are not being afforded an equal opportunity to participate in extracurricular athletics in public elementary and secondary schools.

U.S. Department of Education, Office for Civil Rights (2013).

The office issued a letter reiterating that this law requires the schools to offer participation in the extracurricular athletic opportunities if it is offered to persons without a disability. It specified that if the individual was qualified to participate, no unnecessary separate activity would be offered. For example, if an athletic track program is available for students at a high school, and a student with a disability is qualified (e.g., student is hearing impaired and running the 200 meters), then that student can participate. For example, the hearing-impaired student could start the race given a cue card versus starting to the sound of the gun.

If a student with a disability cannot participate *with reasonable accommodation*, then a different type of activity should be offered. The bottom line is that these types of activities offer social, leadership, and health benefits to students and are to be offered to all students.

approach to measurement of success was aimed at specific grades across the country, using the same test for poor children in Mississippi as the very rich in New York City. These tests were not known to reflect the curriculum in these respective school systems, and the results were disastrous. In addition, teachers and administrators' jobs were based on the results whereby "teaching to the test" was common, rather than teaching within a curriculum of cultural sensitivity and appropriate topics using exploration and multimodality teaching. Scandals erupted when it was discovered teachers changed students' incorrect answers with correct answers. President Barack Obama signed the Every Student Succeeds Act (ESSA) in 2015. ESSA amended the No Child Left Behind Act. The hope in passing this law was to systematically address the ills of the No Child Left Behind Act so that, as the law implies, every child succeeds in school. Approaches to testing student progress were drastically changed, as were teacher retention and measures of school success. In addition, monies were allocated to grants that described new ways to support underperforming students and schools, as well as to innovative educational programs.

Dr. Joe Winnick, considered an eminent scholar in adapted physical education and activity, was quick to point out that ESSA's definition of a well-rounded education included health and physical education, which enables school districts to seek funding through their state departments of education, which was not the case with the No Child Left Behind Act. He went on to say,

The potential benefit of ESSA relative to health and physical education is immeasurable. This is particularly true relative to in-school and out-of-school physical education and physical activity programs. In order to gain these benefits, professionals associated with adapted physical education and sport will need to conceptualize programs, serve as program advocates, and develop relevant needs assessment information for school districts to support projects submitted to states designed to benefit children and youth with disabilities.

Winnick & Porretta (2017, p. 16).

Individualized Education Program

One of the significant features of IDEA (2004) is the requirement that an IEP be developed for each student with disabilities. This mandate has been there since 1975 under EAHCA. There are two main parts of the IEP requirement, as described in federal law and the regulations that accompany this law:

1. The IEP meeting(s), at which parents or caregivers and school personnel (both direct and indirect service providers) jointly make decisions about a student's educational program

2. The IEP document itself, which is a written record of the decisions reached at the meetings

The IEP process is designed to accommodate several important functions. Some of these, as identified by the federal government, are indicated in the following paragraphs (U.S. Department of Education, 1981, p. 5460).

• The IEP meeting serves as a communication vehicle between parents and school personnel, thus allowing them as equal participants to jointly decide the student's educational needs and to identify the necessary special education and related services. The IEP meeting also helps resolve potential differences between parents and school officials concerning the educational programs as well as anticipated outcomes.

• A practical purpose of the IEP is to identify in writing the resources necessary to enable the student to benefit from the educational program that has been developed. Furthermore, the IEP is a management tool that is used to ensure that each student with a disability is provided special education and related services appropriate to the student's special learning needs.

The IEP also may be used as a compliance or monitoring device. Local school personnel as well as state department of education officials can review individual IEPs to determine whether a student is receiving the educational program agreed to by the parents and the school. An evaluation of the student's progress toward meeting the stated educational goals and objectives is also possible by periodically examining the IEP.

IEP Team Members

This team is also legally referred to as the multidisciplinary team. Although the exact composition of the IEP team will vary from one school system to the next, IDEA (1997) specified that certain participants must be included in all IEP discussions, and the amendments of IDEA (2004) are listed herein. School officials require that the following participants are present at the IEP meeting. The following is adapted from Lieberman & Houston-Wilson (2009):

• *Parents or guardians:* Their educational concerns and any information they provide about their child must be addressed. One of the basic premises of IDEA (1997 and 2004) is that parent input into the IEP is considered extremely important. For this reason, school systems should take whatever steps

Weekend Images Inc/E+/Getty Images

are necessary to ensure that parents are involved in the IEP deliberations. This means scheduling the meeting at a time convenient for parents as well as informing parents of their right to disagree with the recommended IEP.

Some parents also may require the assistance of an interpreter if they are deaf or their native language is one other than English. Regardless of the provisions made to solicit parent input, a small percentage of parents will elect not to become involved in the IEP process. In these cases, the IEP meeting may still be held, but school officials should be prepared to document their attempts to solicit parent input. In some cases, the state department of education will appoint surrogate parents for students living in state institutions whose parents are deceased, unknown, or express no interest in their child's welfare.

• *The student with a disability:* The inclusion of the student depends on their age, disability, and ability to communicate. The team must listen to their wants and preferences. Students with disabilities, like their nondisabled peers, frequently have helpful comments to make about the educational experiences that are to be provided for them. It is for this reason IDEA (1997) emphasized the importance of student input. The final decision as to whether the student will participate as a member of the IEP team rests with the parents, except in cases where the student is of majority age. IDEA (2004) continues this focus.

• *The child's teacher:* The person selected to fill this role is the teacher who has the most contact with the student and who coordinates the student's education. IDEA (1997) specified that the child's regular education teacher must be present. Therefore, those present can be the regular classroom teacher, a special educator, or a specialist such as a speech therapist or physical educator. Of primary importance is that the person selected to fill this role cannot also serve as the school's representative to the team.

• *Representative of the public agency:* Various individuals, including building principals, counselors, and special education administrators are normally selected to fulfill this role. The key factor is that the person selected must be thoroughly familiar with the local school's special education program, and federal and state law and ensure that the appropriate services are brought into the student's IEP.

• *School psychologist:* This person meets with the student and conducts testing and interprets evaluations in compliance with IDEA (2004) and is helpful in supporting the student psychologically in their school programs.

• *Transition service representative:* This is only necessary for older students preparing for transitioning out of high school. By law, this must begin at age 16, but some districts start at age 14.

• *Other individuals at the discretion of the parents or agency:* This last category for membership on the IEP team simply indicates that both the local school and the parents have the right to invite others to participate as members of the IEP team. For the school this means that on occasion it may be desirable to have additional school personnel involved in the IEP deliberations. Likewise, parents may feel the need to be accompanied by a relative or friend who is more knowledgeable about education and its relationship to their student. At times, parents have also felt it necessary to be accompanied by legal representation. The important point is that both the parents and the school may invite others to participate.

The basis for interdisciplinary service for children and youth in the schools is seen in the *recommended* memberships of the IEP team for physical education. These disciplines are as follows:

• Adapted physical education
• General physical education
• Paraeducator
• Physical therapist
• Occupational therapist
• Speech and language pathologist
• Nurse
• Audiologist (for students with hearing loss)
• Vision specialist (for students with visual impairments)
• Orientation and mobility specialists (for students with visual impairments)

Adapted physical educators have begun working more and more as consultants rather than delivering direct service with a large caseload. Here, they give guidance to the general physical educator and the educational aides on meeting student needs, evaluate student performance, adjust expected IEP goals, and provide in-service training, answer questions, and encourage and support direct teaching. Consultants are best selected from the professionals with a record in direct service of physical education. As one physical educator with many years of experience claimed, "To be a good adapted physical educator, you have to first be a good physical educator."

These consultants are either hired by a district or are consultants with their own business.

Because physical education is an integral part of special education, the IEP team must decide on the physical education program and a placement for the student. If a school does not offer physical education, then there is no physical education program for the student with a disability. Fortunately, this is very rare.

If the program design and the placement are not handled properly, the student may receive inappropriate physical education services. Some of the potential difficulty arises because of the absence of a person knowledgeable about the area of physical education. Some school systems have resolved this problem by inviting a representative of physical education to serve on the IEP team, particularly for the student needing greater levels of support in the educational placement. Other school systems, desiring to keep the official IEP team small, have used pre-IEP meetings to obtain the input of specialists such as adapted physical educators. The IEP team makes critical decisions that affect the student's physical education placement and curricular content using information supplied by the adapted physical educator as well as other members of the team, often those in special education, OT, PT, and SLP.

Physical education representatives (APE, GPE) should bring the following to the IEP meeting (Lieberman & Houston Wilson, 2009):

- Description of how the student learns
- Assessment results for present level of performance (PLP)
- Suggested goals (or objectives if the district requires them; IDEA 2004 does not)
- Suggestions about inclusion in general physical education
- Suggestions on modifications to the curriculum needed to support placement

IEP Content

As a legal document, the IEP specifies the special education programs and services to be provided the student. Each IEP must include the following information, which is strategically dependent on assessment data presented and discussed by the team members:

1. *Present level of educational performance:* A statement of the child's present level of educational performance

2. *Annual goals:* A statement of annual goals. IDEA (2004) only requires goal statements not objectives.

3. *Specific services:* A statement of the specific special education and related services to be provided to the student.

4. *Inclusion:* The extent to which the child will be able to participate in general education programs.

5. *Dates:* The projected dates for initiation of services and the anticipated duration of the services based on the educational time (e.g., nine months).

6. *Evaluation procedures:* Appropriate objective measures versus subjective criteria are used in the evaluation procedures. Schedules for determining, on at least an annual basis, whether the instructional goals are being achieved by the student.

7. *Transition services:* A statement of the needed transition services for students beginning *no later* than age 16 and annually thereafter (and when determined appropriate for the individual, beginning at age 14 or younger), including, when appropriate, a statement of the interagency responsibilities or linkages (or both) before the student leaves the school setting. Transition services are addressed in a transition conference under IDEA (2004) as a part of the IFSP when the child leaves early intervention and enters early childhood special education. When the child leaves early childhood special education, there is no law specifying transitioning to school at age six. It is considered best practice that the early childhood special education program work with the new school and the child and parents to make it easier for the child to move on.

Present Level of Educational Performance

Present level of educational performance simply means those physical education skills the student presently possesses, typically referred to as the present level of performance (PLP). To ascertain this information requires that a report is generated by an assessment of the student's physical and motor fitness levels. For the high school students, a functional assessment of age-appropriate physical activity is presented. Without this array of information, the IEP meeting is disadvantaged when called upon to make recommendations concerning the student's special physical education needs. Physical educators must be aware of federal mandates on assessments as well as their state's laws regarding eligibility criteria.

Annual Goals

Under IDEA (2004), the goals will become the guideposts for determining whether the student with a disability is benefiting from the educational program developed by the IEP team. Goals provide direction and serve to communicate to the student and members of the team that a particular area needs attention in physical education. States determine the way the goals are written. The goal is aimed for the duration of a school year's completion. The following are examples of physical education goals, although some states may require different content:

- Joe will improve his overhand throw from a push-out to a throw that meets all the criteria as measured by the Test of Gross Motor Development-3, by the end of the academic school year.

- James will run around the track five times in one session, by the end of the academic school year.

Many school districts have computerized goal statements to ease the burden of creating them. Although a child with a disability is unique, despite a common category of disability, sometimes the overall goal for that student can be generalized and implemented, and sometimes it cannot. The Brockport Physical Fitness Test has a computer-generated list of goals and objectives categorized by disability area. But that is the exception.

Specific Services

Physical educators and adapted physical educators may need to utilize the services of other related professionals to best determine the physical education placement. Related services include the following: speech therapy, physical therapy, occupational therapy, mobility trainers, and recreation therapists. In the law, these professionals are related services to distinguish them from the direct service of special education. The related service personnel provide invaluable assessments, consultations, training, and in-school therapy to enable the students to learn. Thus, physical educators and the students they teach benefit from the assistance of many professionals from various fields identified in IDEA (2004). The IEP team determines the student's placement for physical education.

Under IDEA (2004), physical education is mandated as a special education service when there is a

physical education program offered at the school *and* the student meets state qualifications for adapted programs. The student must first be assessed using the general physical education curriculum of the school for the student's grade. Based on the results, assessments may continue to determine what the student *can do*. If the student fails in general physical education without supports, then the process continues for adapted services. What supports does the student need to be successful in their physical education class? And which class? These days, every effort is directed toward an inclusive educational placement with the student's age peers.

By law, the service of physical education is in the least restrictive environment when at all possible. Specifically, where is the student placed? Does the student's present level of educational performance support whether placement in the general physical education program is appropriate? Another option is placement that is both in a general and a segregated physical education setting. Some individuals may simply need the assistance of an aide, peer, or volunteer to succeed in the general education class. Of course, students with severe disabilities may require help that can best be met in a segregated adapted physical education experience.

Inclusion

Lieberman and Houston-Wilson provide a model of continuum of supports and placement (2018) that recognizes many options to best serve the student.

Inclusion Options
- Inclusion without adaptations
- Inclusion with adaptations and modifications
- Inclusion with trained peer tutors
- Inclusion with paraeducators
- Inclusion with specialists
- Inclusion with a small class of peers with typical movement

Part-Time Self-Contained and Part-Time Integrated Options
- Split placement without support
- Split placement with support

Community-Based Placement Options
- Part-time community, part-time school-based
- Full-time community-based

Self-Contained Within [General] School Options
- Self-contained, no support
- Reverse integration with typically developing peers being added

- One on one with a paraprofessional

Other Options
- Day school for specific needs
- Residential school for specific needs
- Home schooling
- Institution
- Hospital

Dates

Under IDEA (1997), each IEP is normally written to cover a period of up to 12 months. IDEA (2004) assumes a similar approach to goal attainment. For each goal, a time line is established to provide a general estimate of when the student should achieve a particular goal. When the teacher sees unusual deviations from the projected time line, it is best to request that the school personnel call for an IEP meeting to identify, with parent consultation, new goals with more realistic time lines from those previously developed.

Evaluation Procedures

The IEP must include a plan that specifies the procedure to be used to evaluate the student's progress. This review must be done at least annually. Many school systems have responded to this requirement by indicating the extent to which the student has achieved the goals specified in the IEP. It should be emphasized, however, that the IEP is not a performance contract that imposes liability on a teacher or public agency if a student does not meet the IEP objectives. According to the rules and regulations for the EAHCA, a stipulation that has continued with the reauthorization of IDEA (2004) is that,

> While the agency must provide special education and related services in accordance with each handicapped [disabled] child's IEP, the act does not require that the agency, the teacher, or other persons be held accountable if the child does not achieve the growth projected in the written statement.

EAHCA (1981, p. 830).

Transition Services

Healthy People 2030 has drawn attention to transitions that occur from pediatric care to primary care for all individuals. According to many, the transition service is one area of IDEA (2004) that has grown in

importance. Transition services address the needs of students moving from early intervention programs into preschool programs, as well as those students moving out of the school program and into the community after high school. Specifically, IDEA (2004) provides a definition of transition services to students' IEPs in high school, and in the case of early intervention, to the IFSP during the second year of life. The term *transition services* means a coordinated set of activities for a student who is leaving the known educational service. The IFSP is designed for smooth transition for infants and toddlers to preschool at age three. For much older students, the transition from high school includes IEP goals for an array of options including postsecondary education, vocational training, integrated employment, continuing and adult education, adult services, independent living, and community participation in physical activities. The goal, of course, is to ensure that students and community resources are fully integrated to the extent that students with disabilities can use other environments, including those used for various recreational pursuits. Physical educators are expected to be cognizant of procedures for ensuring that skills and activities learned in the school setting can be generalized successfully into a particular student's interests in the community and home settings (e.g., community fitness centers for stationary biking, roller skating rinks for free skate, and swimming pools for lap swim). The infants and toddlers' transition plans of the IFSP are typically coordained and monitored by an assigned lead therapist from the child's IFSP team.

IDEA (2004) also made it clear that cooperating and participating agencies are responsible for providing services identified within the IEP. Specifically, the law states that where a participating agency, other than the educational agency, fails to provide agreed-upon services, the educational agency shall reconvene the IEP team to identify alternative strategies to meet the transition objectives. This, of course, places the school in a unique position to work cooperatively with participating agencies and monitor the quality of their services.

Individualized Family Service Plan

Closely related to the IEP is the individualized family service plan (IFSP) mandated by the Education of the Handicapped Act Amendments of 1986. The law has been amended to include infants, toddlers, and preschool children. One of the critical aspects of IDEA (2004) has been the IFSP for infants and toddlers. The major components of the IFSP include

- a statement of the child's present levels of development (cognitive, motor, speech, language, psychosocial, and self-help);
- a statement of the family's strengths and needs relating to enhancing the child's development;
- a statement of major outcomes expected to be achieved for the child and family;
- the criteria, procedures, and time lines for determining progress;
- the specific early intervention services necessary to meet the unique needs of the child and family including the method, frequency, and intensity of service; and
- the projected dates for the initiation of services and expected duration.

While there are many similarities between the IEP and the IFSP, there are also some differences. First, the IFSP is family centered with as much commitment and emphasis placed on the family as on the individual child. As Deal and colleagues (1989) stated,

> Major emphasis is placed on both enabling and empowering families. Enabling families means creating opportunities for family members to become more competent and self-sustaining with respect to their abilities to mobilize their social networks, to get needs met and attain desired goals. Empowering families means carrying out interventions in a manner in which family members acquire a sense of control over their own development course as a result of their effort to meet needs.

Deal et al. (1989, p. 33).

Second, the IFSP is designed to make certain that for the infant (ages zero to two) that there is a transition plan to ensure a smooth integration into preschool at age three.

Summary

Legal mandates support access to adapted physical activity. The Individuals with Disabilities Improvement Act (IDEA, 2004) is a U.S. educational law mandating that all children have *free appropriate public education*, including children with disabilities. If school-age children do not qualify under IDEA for adapted physical education but need modifications to participate, they can be served under Section 504 of the Rehabilitation Act if they meet eligibility criteria. Placement of children in schools is to be in the mainstream (inclusive) with their age peers to the extent that it is possible (the least restrictive environment). The individual family service plan (IFSP) for infants and toddlers and the individualized education program (IEP) for the children from age 3 through 21 have professional memberships and roles prescribed by the federal education law IDEA 2004. This law is also explicit about goal statements for the IEP.

The Americans with Disabilities Act Amendments Act of 2008 is the civil rights law for those with disabilities stipulating there can be no discrimination in the United States because a person has a disability. The law has implications for the physically active life for those with disabilities across school, community, and health care settings. Federal agencies define a disability for individuals across the ages. For our purposes, IDEA (2004) drives children's definitions of disability for educational services, while the federal government serves as a basis for definitions influencing medical care and other important services to support a whole and active life. Understanding the legal aspects of disability allows those professionals working with the individuals and their families to serve in an important advocacy role.

CHAPTER 4

Designing Life Span Programs

Maskot/Maskot/Getty Images

CHAPTER OBJECTIVES

After completing this chapter, you will be able to do the following:

- Apply the term *developmental delay* to the work of physical activity engagement with infants and toddlers.
- Examine the ecological theory of Bronfenbrenner and its usefulness in adapted physical activity assessment and instruction.
- Describe the term *developmentally appropriate* and its application in teaching adapted physical activity in the educational setting.
- Explain the opportunities for health care providers to foster physical activity engagement in the lives of young adults with disabilities.
- Distinguish between *aging with disabilities* and *aging into disabilities* terminologies for adults with disabilities.
- Explain how interdisciplinary collaboration is necessary for the engagement in community physical activity programs for people with disabilities.

Indisputably, engagement in physical activity, *across all ages*, promotes health.

> Abundant scientific evidence has demonstrated that physically active people of all age groups and ethnicities have higher levels of cardiorespiratory fitness, health, and wellness, and a lower risk for developing several chronic medical illnesses, . . . even small amounts of PA [physical activity] provide protective health benefits.
>
> Fletcher et al. (2018, p. 1622).

This chapter addresses engagement across a lifetime in adapted physical activity and specifies the services of support across disciplines for individuals with disabilities from earliest childhood to oldest adulthood to engage in physical activity. In this chapter, we focus on a call to a life course perspective (USDHHS, 2005) where the whole person is addressed—and not just by their disability (Krahn et al., 2015). In the community where people reside, an array of interdisciplinary professional roles supporting the engagement in adapted physical activity are identified (Agiovlasitis et al., 2018). Healthy People 2030 goals for the United States focus on physical activity involvement (USDHHS, 2018) and detail physical activity frequency, intensity, and duration across childhood, adolescence, adulthood, and older adulthood. To accomplish this, ". . . physical activity across the country will require the efforts of individuals, families, and many sectors of society . . ." (p. 95).

To physically be moving is critical to a healthy life:

- Clinically, infants who move are considered developing well when they present movement skills appropriate for age. Thus, functional movement assessments have been recommended to be performed by clinical staff and developmental progress to be communicated to families and other staff (Cioni, 1997).

- Participation in physical activity reports robust increases in the cognitive domain in children, adolescents, and older adults (Erickson et al., 2019); improvements in the student's behaviors in the classroom and in reading and math skills (Álvarez-Bueno et al., 2017; Singh et al., 2019).

- Adults who are physically active reportedly have a lower mental health burden (WHO, 2019), a lifting of depression and loneliness (Kim et al., 2017; Yen et al., 2018), and increased fitness for their day (Vader et al., 2021).

Physical Activity Program Goals

We share the belief that feelings of enjoyment bring greater participation and greater participation brings more health benefits especially for those with a disability. Enjoyment is a goal for school age students with disabilities in physical education (Jin et al., 2018). The U.S. Department of Health and Human Services holds that "It is important to provide young people opportunities and encouragement to participate in physical activities that are appropriate for their age, that are enjoyable, and that offer variety" (2018, p. 48). This is the beginning for many individuals with disabilities for participating in physical activity—they enjoy the activity.

Table 4.1 details enjoyment in physical activity and includes for each age group the skills for that age group in physical activity, instructional strategies, and the professional support needed across disciplines including sample narratives. Each aspect is a best practice and is research-based.

People with a disability need to be heard when they are lost, sad, or without resources. Individuals with disabilities have repeatedly told us how important physical activity is while participating in Paralympics, Special Olympics, programs of rehabilitation centers, adapted school sports, and community-based physical activity programs. One participating athlete in Special Olympics noted the best thing about Special Olympics was exercising (McCarty et al., 2022)!

Participants in these programs need support from many services and professionals, volunteers, friends, and family members. We find that the *interdisciplinary* nature of the work informs within identified conditions of disability, illnesses altering life courses, and the complications of aging through life's end. Infants through the oldest receiving services must always be observed and listened to and understood for their uniqueness and preferences, likes, and dislikes. These gestures inform their interaction with their family, friends, physical education teachers, recreation specialists, trainers, coaches, and health care team.

Physical activity engagement across the life span is facilitated, in part, by the *modification and adaptation* of physical activity. For some, these accommodations begin early in life and continue throughout

TABLE 4.1   Considerations for Creating Enjoyment in Life Span Adapted Physical Activity Programs

Age group	Infant to toddler	Preschooler to early elementary	Middle school to high school
Movement category*	**Early movement skills**	**Fundamental movement skills**	**Specialized movement skills**
• Engaged in activity recognizing developmental skill and activity across maturation • Individualized exposure to a broad array of activity • Success while learning with emphasis on recognition of age-appropriate activity and use of recognized teaching strategies and program development (e.g., task analysis, ecological task analysis; standards)	• Locomotor: roll over, crawl, sit, pull to stand, cruise, walk, run • Object control: reach, grasp, release • Games and play	• Locomotor: run, horizontal jump, gallop, hop, skip, slide • Ball skills: strike, bounce, catch, kick, throw • Games and play • Simple lead-up games to sports • Recreational activity with a geographical community physical activity focus	Middle school: • Lead-up games to sports; later, sports themselves and sport clubs • Broad range of recreational age-appropriate physical activity commensurate with community physical activity High school: • Exposure to a broad range of PA/APA • Training in community use in leisure time for physical activity with geographical, community, or family activity focus • Training in community use for work-related activity where physical capacity requires attention by APE/GPE
Success with continuous level of support	Roll over, sit, reach	Sit, stand, walk, grasp, release, throw	Functional age-appropriate APA of student interests for fun and fitness in community
Professional support			
Success supported by professionals	• Special education: Early childhood special education teacher • Pediatric OT • Pediatric PT • SLP • Health care: MD: pediatrician, developmental pediatrician, neonatologist, neurologist, cardiologist • Community nurse (RN)/visiting nurse (RN), pediatric RNP	• APE • GPE • School-based OT, PT, SLP • Special education teacher • General education teacher • Health care: MD: pediatrician, specialists (e.g., orthopedists, neurologists, cardiologists) • Nurses (RN, LPN, RNP); community OT, PT, SLP	• APE • GPE • School-based OT, PT, SLP • Special education teacher • General education teacher • Recreation therapist (CTRS) either in the school system or in the community • Coach • Mobility trainers • Health care: MD: Pediatrician or PCP, MD specialists; RNs; community OT, PT, SLP
• Showing interest in the child's physical activity. • Naming the activity for the child and family. • Positive regard shown to the individual for engaging in physical activity and their family for supporting that engagement.	Use of comments such as: • *"You are crawling, Peter."* • *"You are happy with the ball, Peter."* • *"Helen, you are doing the right things by having Peter on the floor playing."*	Use of comments such as: • *"You are swimming in your PE class!"* • *"It's good for Peter to stay so active at the swimming pool with his classmates, and you and your family."*	Use of comments such as: • *"I hear you are in Special Olympics this summer. That is great."* • *"I hope Paul and his team have fun."* • *"You and your dad are going hiking. That is going to be fun!"*

Abbreviations: APE = adapted physical educator; GPE = general physical educator; OT = occupational therapist; PT = physical therapist; SLP = speech and language pathologist; ADLs = activities of daily living; MD = medical doctor; CTRS = certified therapeutic recreation specialist; RN = registered nurse; LPN = licensed practical nurse; RNP = registered nurse practitioner; PCP = primary care physician.

Movement category terms from Burton and Miller (1998).

their life. For others, they are episodic, and for still others the needs arrive later in life. People sometimes use the terms *modification* and *adaptation* interchangeably. They are, in fact, different.

Most understand that to increase learning for all participants, we *modify the curriculum or the program* and then we *adapt the activities* of that curriculum or program (Winnick, 2017). To increase participation for an individual, we have changed the established curriculum or program, thus modifying it. Then we take the activities of that program, and where needed, adapt them.

There are recommended guidelines for both modification and adaptation. According to Lieberman and Huston-Wilson, we modify in four areas to increase physical activity participation: equipment, rules, environment, and instruction (2018). According to Winnick, we best adapt by considering if we should increase interaction, meeting the needs of all without jeopardizing the education (activity) of just a few; or if we should increase the physical activity of all, providing a safe environment and maintaining the self-esteem of all (2017). Again, we apply this

to physical activity for all ages, even though these recommendations focused on school-age adapted physical education activity.

Infants and Toddlers

To understand atypical development, one must understand typical development. Infancy and toddlerhood comprise the first two years of life; infancy is the first year, and toddlerhood is the typically the second year as the infant begins to walk unassisted.

Having a child with a disability is a surprise for families—often a shock (Barnett et al., 2003). As many first-time parent(s) often report, coming home from the hospital, they ask themselves, "What do we do now?" Parents of a baby born prematurely spend the first weeks or months of their baby's life visiting the intensive care unit while the baby is treated for prematurity and its myriad of medical complications. The family eventually takes their baby home with lots of information. They carry with them feelings. One is fear in caring for their baby

and another is feeling very much alone. Parents of a baby with an obvious disability need time to adjust to losing the perfect baby (Wright, 2008).

There is a specific vocabulary in working with very young children that is used in communicating within many disciplines and within the health and education systems. There are federal and state education supports for a child with a disability. These supports begin at the child's birth. Intervention activities are embedded in the day-to-day early life of the baby to support developmental skills. Interventions are started as early as possible, to be sure the child develops to their top capacity at every age (Shonkoff & Phillips, 2000).

Infants are totally dependent on others to care for them. In the best sense, the *other* understands their respectful relationship with the vulnerable baby. Magda Gerber made this her life's work, and she influenced the guidelines of the National Association for the Education of Young Children.

> To me, a mature, evolved person shows love by respecting . . . the beloved. You become a good parent not only by listening to your instinctive messages but by paying close attention to your baby . . . Sensitive observation flows from respect . . .
>
> Gerber (2002, pp. 45-46).

Typical and Atypical Development

New parents wonder what typical development is. Is their baby developing well? Experts in child development espouse an interaction of the variables of nature and nurture as the basis for understanding how a child is developing (Posner & Rothbart, 2007; Rothbart et al., 2012). Each child has a unique expression of the interaction between their inherited genes (nature) and their unique family and life experiences influencing the expression of their developmental skills (nurture). What is typical and what is atypical development in infants and toddlers? Table 4.1 identifies a few of the early movement skills. To understand further what is typical and atypical, it is important to understand there is a range of the expression of the expected skills considered normal.

Young children develop within a range of what is considered a normal or typical expression of that skill given their age. For example, the skill of independent walking is early at 8 months and late at around 18 months. This full range is considered normal. Sometimes a child can be behind on a skill but on target for many other skills. Why? Well, that is always a matter of looking more carefully at the child. If all the other skills are on target, then maybe it's just a matter of opportunity. Create more opportunity to know and practice that skill. If there is more broad delay in the onset of skills, we want interventions to bump up the expression of those skills. We can sleuth with theoretical understanding how development is taking place, within a context.

The *domains* of development are intertwined across early development: social-emotional, cognitive, communication, physical (e.g., movement) (Center on the Developing Child, 2007). For example, as much as we think that we are observing only the physical, we are really observing the skills the baby has for cognition and social-emotional skill and communication. These domains are intertwined, and we can observe many domains of development as the child plays. For example, a child of 11 months of age is sitting and playing with a few toys in front of her. She picks up a toy, extends her arm and looks at her father sitting on the floor near to her. She presents the toy to him, saying "Dada." The domains of development are observed as such:

- *Social-emotional:* The child obtained eye contact with father and wanted to talk with him. She was asking for engagement, not ignoring him but wanting his attention. She has a positive regard for her father.

- *Cognitive:* The child was sorting toys and picked one of interest to her. She wasn't randomly banging on them but rather focused and engaged.

- *Communication:* She used *Dada* appropriately when turning to her father for a request.

- *Physical:* She could reach, grasp, and extend her arm toward her father to engage him in her play.

This activity is *typical* for a young child. It is an example of how the domains of development are intertwined with multiple domains expressed within one activity. Given the same setting, *atypical* development might have the child gazing at the toys, sitting still; or banging on the toys frantically; scattering the toys, and screaming; crying and failing to regard the father. Yes, this could happen if the child was having a bad day. But, if this behavior is usual for this child, she is developing atypically.

Early Intervention

When atypical development is apparent with infants and toddlers, their development is supported by early intervention (EI) services. In the United States, each state is mandated to provide early intervention services to support families and very young children under the Individuals with Disabilities Education Improvement Act (IDEA, 2004). Each state determines its own qualification criteria for services for their infants and toddlers. The federal program Child Find is written into IDEA (2004), calling for each state to find the young children who need early intervention.

The names of these EI programs vary across the country. For instance, there is First Steps in Illinois, Birth to 3 in Wisconsin, Early On in Michigan, Early Steps in Florida, Making Connections in Hawaii, Babies Can't Wait in Georgia, BabyNet in South Carolina. To search an EI program in any state, typically search within the Department of Education in that state using the term "early intervention."

IDEA (2004), as an educational law, requires interventions to be carried out in this naturally occurring environment of the child's life, and this is best practice in EI (OSEP TA, 2008). This approach separates itself from clinical care. Clinical care is offered according to Bronfenbrenner ". . . in [the] strangest of places, with the strangest of people, asking the child to do the strangest of things" (Bronfenbrenner, 1977, p. 513). He argued for developmental assessments conducted in the naturally occurring environments of the child's life. Otherwise, Bronfenbrenner claimed that the data obtained was probably not valid. Instead, he believed that developmental assessments were better carried out in places familiar to the child and in the presence of a familiar person. All of this eventually became best practice in the field of early intervention services.

The child's natural environments are often home, a relative's home, or a childcare setting. When interventions are devised, they are placed within the routines of that child's day in the place they reside. This is referred to as *routines-based interventions* (McWilliam, 2010). These interventions are then very functional. They are what the child does every day. They are not performed in a clinician's office carried out with a specialist who is unfamiliar to the child (although these clinicians have their place in medical care). They are ongoing interventions that are embedded in the child's day and required to help the child's development. Families provide valuable information about the day, the family concerns, and hoped-for outcomes for their child. These then are translated into the individualized family service plan (IFSP) (Pletcher & Younggren, 2017). This IFSP is the bedrock for the child's early intervention services.

Developmental Delay

Children qualify for intervention services if they have a developmental delay (DD), which is a known disability category of IDEA. This DD category is used when there is a delay noted on assessments that has no obvious ideology but nonetheless, the child is delayed. And it is also used if the child is at risk for developmental delay. For example, in some states, prenatal drug exposure is an automatic entrance into early intervention services, thus qualifying a child and their family for intervention services.

Infants and toddlers who are lagging in typical developmental skills for unknown reasons receive services in EI under the category of DD if they meet criteria in their state, as each state sets their criteria for how much delay means that a child needs services. Children are difficult to accurately assess at early ages, and caution is important. This caution allows for intervention to begin without identifying a known reason for the delay. It often takes time to accurately diagnose a disability in young children. With time and access to early intervention, the child may catch up in development; or the reason for the delay might become more apparent, allowing services to be further specialized.

Disability

A very young infant can be diagnosed with a category of disability. Not all categories of disability defined in chapter 3 are relevant for an infant, which is why infants can be served under the category of DD until they enter elementary school. Down syndrome, however, can be diagnosed early. A baby who has Down syndrome has distinct facial features and can be diagnosed at birth. Down syndrome is associated with intellectual disability and as such is a category of disability under IDEA (2004). Astute specialists in pediatrics are also able to diagnose forms of prenatal alcohol exposure in infancy, as well as forms of cerebral palsy. If the disability isn't diagnosed in infancy, the diagnosis is often clearer by toddlerhood. There are specialized clinicians able to diagnose autism spectrum disorder within infancy, but typically with delay and some suspicion, it is confirmed or dismissed in toddlerhood or by age three years.

At Risk

IDEA Section 303.5 defines an at-risk infant or toddler as a child less than three years of age who would be at risk of experiencing a substantial developmental delay if early intervention services were not provided to the child. These are children experiencing developmental delays because of biological or environmental factors that can be identified by low birth weight, respiratory distress as a newborn, lack of oxygen, brain hemorrhage, infection, nutritional deprivation, a history of abuse or neglect, and being directly affected by illegal substance abuse or withdrawal symptoms resulting from prenatal drug exposure. As stated, each state determines which at-risk categories automatically mean a child can be enrolled in EI services.

In addition to those risk factors mentioned in the law, risk factors classically include poverty, drug abuse in the home, teen motherhood; and in present times, homelessness and nutritional scarcity for the family. In fact, poverty has for a long time been considered one of the most detrimental risk factors in early development (Odom & Pungello, 2012). Risk that is not ameliorated grows and accumulates more risk; thus, the term *cumulative risk*. For example, a teen mother lacks maturity to care for her baby without supports from others. In the better scenarios, schools have programs for teen mothers and provide childcare so the mother can finish school. The childcare center also is a lab where these teens learn about child development and how to play with and physically care for their baby. This supports the development of the baby and the young mother. If the teen mother comes from poverty, the risk is increased, and social services can work to engage essential nutritional support. Intervention changes the potential negative developmental trajectory for this young dyad of mother and baby. Early intervention is founded on research that reports families who engage in early intervention service can change the potential negative developmental trajectory for their child.

Protective Factors and Cumulative Risk

Child development research reports that protective factors mediate risk factors (Masten & Garmezy, 1985; Masten & Wright, 1998). An engaged, attentive, and supportive mother (biological or otherwise) is a documented protective factor. An attentive and supportive father as the primary caregiver would also be a protective factor. A child born into poverty who has a mother who is attentive, involved in an early intervention program, and follows through on the support offered does well. If a child is born prenatally exposed to drugs and lives with a supportive foster family, she has protection from the risk factors of a mother who is addicted to drugs and unable to care for her baby. In many cases, the mother may want to care for her baby, but cannot because drugs have overtaken her life at this time.

When babies are born prematurely, before the 40 weeks of gestation is complete, they are at risk for negative developmental trajectories. As time passes, the premature child will face negative developmental outcomes across early aging, as the negative trajectory in motor skill will continue unless intervention takes place to avoid cumulative risk. EI services will follow these children and work with the family to support their early growth. The Center on the Developing Child at Harvard (2010) espouses that early health "is strengthened by positive early experiences . . . [this] provides a foundation for the construction of sturdy brain architecture and the associated achievement of a broad range of abilities and learning capacities" (p. 1). With known intervention strategies in place in the home, the risks are lowered or completely ameliorated.

In some states, children referred to EI face a long waiting list, or for various reasons, children are not enrolled in EI services until they are older than an infant. When delay in development is identified, intervention needs to begin as soon as possible, no matter how late (Shonkoff & Phillips, 2000). In this area, Shonkoff and colleagues at Harvard are strong and vocal advocates for protecting the developing brain from toxic stress in early childhood (2021). Today, some of the stresses identified are racism, both cultural and institutional, and interpersonal discrimination, thus creating public health challenges requiring a multidimensional framework for addressing the challenges.

Brain Development

Early intervention services are founded on the neuroscience of early brain development and the reality that an appropriately stimulated brain is the building block for development:

> Brain architecture is built over a succession of sensitive periods, each of which is associated with the formation of specific circuits that are associated with specific abilities. The development of increasingly complex skills and their underlying circuits build on the circuits and skills that were formed earlier. Through this process, early experiences create a foundation for lifelong learning, behavior, and both physical and mental health. A strong foundation in the early years increases the probability of positive outcomes and a weak foundation increases the odds of later difficulties.

Center on the Developing Child (2007, p. 5).

From the beginning of life, the brain of a baby has neurological circuits (neuronal connections) and the potential to build more circuits. Stimulation by touch, sight, sound, and movement grows the brain. The connections that are stimulated will grow strong. Scientists have emphasized that without stimulation, the brain does not grow; there is no firm foundation for early life and the life ahead.

The ability of the brain to form new circuits is called *brain plasticity*, which allows the brain not only to build more circuits, but to reform circuits.

This is the reason that intervention, even if it is late, is so essential. The brain will still reform itself. For example, if it is discovered that an 18-month-old child is constantly placed in a stroller, is still crawling, lacks much in the way of verbalizations, and has a very depressed, unengaged mother who is his only parent, he will test as a child with *global developmental delay*. Typical developmental skills should find him walking and talking, and he should have a mother who regards him in some positive nurturing ways like holding him, smiling, and looking at him. Instead, his brain lacks the stimulation needed for growth, and he has essentially been a disregarded child. He needs intervention in the form of specific skill development and emotional engagement from his mother. How much he will catch up to typical 18-month-old markers of development is not known, but new growth in his brain will begin as his mother responds to her child, shares toys with him, and learns from the therapists how to encourage more movement toward walking. Across his early life, the back-and-forth interactions with an attentive caregiver is the foremost strategy in developing his brain. Referred to as "serve and return," the child initiates (serves), and the adult responds with support and encouragement (return) (Center on the Developing Child, 2019). In our case, if the mother is amenable, the early intervention team can coach her through these steps and refer her for help with her depression.

Movement and Early Brain Development

Moving is critical for brain development of the infant. Early assessment tools for healthy neurological status rely on the baby moving. If you stimulate the cheek of a baby, the baby should turn to that side of the body (a reflexive response). Later, after the brain has developed more, the involuntary movements of the reflexes give way to voluntary movements, and clinicians test skills such as raising the head up from a prone (on the tummy) position, eventually rolling over from the prone position, sitting up unassisted, pulling up to a standing position, and initiation of independent walking.

Language is developed by experiences with moving. Many clinicians will regard the development of language as the most important skill of early childhood. Yet, without moving, the child has no experience to attach language to persons, places, or things.

The child delayed in motor skill needs activities geared to their level of success, therefore, they need child-centered activities. They will progress. Occupational and physical therapists and some adapted physical educators work with the parents in reaching EI goals in movement skills of early childhood listed in table 4.1. Chapters 5 and 6 cover teaching movement skills for young children and the assessment of early movement skills.

Nonlinear Expression of Skills

Development in early childhood is nonlinear (Campos et al., 2000). As children learn a skill, they explore using it by repeating it many times. In this repetition, they go back to a former, less-skilled activity and use that. Time can pass and they begin using the newly learned skill again. A concrete example of this occurs when a child first tries an independent walk. Typically, it is shaky, and if they really want to get somewhere fast, they use a crawl. Parents often observe this regression and feel their child has a problem, when in fact, this is a typical path to developing their skills.

Repeated Practice, Play, and Exploration

For children to learn a skill, they need repeated practice and exploration of the skill (Adolph, 1997, Dunn & Leitschuh, 2014, MNDAPE, 2023). This repetition is often boring or misunderstood by adults. Parents report how tired they get reading *Goodnight Moon* with their child at night. They wear out of the repetition of going back to a slide or a swing in the park. But every time they read that book or return to that swing, the child is learning, and the brain connections (neuronal pathways) are getting stronger and stronger. All the domains of development are engaged (Adolph, 1997).

Young children gravitate to places that interest them; they repeatedly return to these places of play, and in doing so continue to learn more about themselves, the objects there, and the environment. They refine their physical skills, which also engages emotional-social skills and cognitive skill. All in all,

their brains are strengthened by this repeated exploration. It is not wasted time. It is essential to learning.

Preschoolers

When children turn age three years in the United States, they attend preschool if their state offers the program. Children can attend preschool programs based on the resources of the community and the decisions of the family and the IFSP team. Certain children attend preschool for a longer day than others. Others attend a few days a week, or a few half-days a week. Best practice for preschoolers receiving special education is to have their interventions embedded into the activities of their day (McWilliam, 2010).

At this time, children who have received services under the DD category can now move into a different category of disability for service if they still need service, although the DD category lasts to age nine years of age in select states. Moving out of the DD category into a more specific disability category, to better serve the needs of the child, is determined by the IEP or IFSP team members. By this time, the educational team, which includes the parents or caregivers, has had more time to observe. Is the real reason for the developmental delay autism spectrum disorder or intellectual disability? Sometimes it just takes time, observation, testing, and discussion to decide what the root causes of the delay are.

Transition Plan

The transition for toddlers (up to two years) to a preschool program (three to five years of age) is part of IDEA (2004), Section 300.124. It has its own plan within the IFSP and guides the toddler and family into the preschool setting (Pletcher & Younggren, 2017). The sidebar about Tamiya illustrates a transition plan into preschool from toddlerhood.

Home Services to School Transition

Tamiya is leaving her early intervention program of home services to a preschool program. Tamiya's team of professionals and her family has decided that Tamiya will attend an inclusive preschool program. This means that Tamiya's preschool will include her with her typically developing peers. Both the mother and present teacher know this is the best for Tamiya but they both have concerns. Her transition plan will include meeting her preschool teacher, visiting the school, and at some point, sharing information on both sides regarding their concerns. Many of these concerns can be addressed in the transition plan before Tamiya begins preschool there.

IDEA Disability Categories

Children in preschool are eligible for special education if they have a disability or developmental delay. Referred to as Part B of IDEA (2004), these preschoolers are like Tamiya and have been receiving services as infants and toddlers under Part C. In some cases, parents want their child to continue in Part B services through preschool and kindergarten to entry into grade school, which some states allow.

These preschool children have a disability and are experiencing developmental delays, as identified by their state, using appropriate diagnostic instruments and procedures and their state's criteria. The delay in one or more of the following areas of development is required: physical, cognitive, communication, social or emotional, or adaptive.

Movement Skill Development and Instruction

As with any group of children, children at age three years are not a homogeneous group. Some children are slow in developing and expressing the movement skills of infancy and toddlerhood. Some entering the early preschool years are still learning the skills of toddlerhood. When teaching children with atypical development, expect to apply the knowledge of teaching movement skills of infancy into toddlerhood, and those of toddlerhood into the preschool years.

Teaching this age group is not like teaching later elementary school age children. The environment has to be set up so that the children learn without many instructions, are engaged in the activity, and have repeated opportunities to perform the skills. There is less emphasis on form and more on engagement. Teaching movement skills and games is important (Active Learning, 2003). See table 4.1 for the selected fundamental movement skills of the preschooler.

In preschool, the physical activity program is often taught by the classroom teacher, although sometimes a school district has a physical education teacher who consults. If a child has an IFSP or an IEP in motor skills, there are occupational and physical therapists who may also be consulting on positioning and modifications and adaptations. If a child cannot participate even with modifications or adaptations, then a substitute activity can be used.

Other activities of preschooler programs include body awareness like identifying body parts, spatial awareness like moving through an obstacle course, body actions (bending, stretching, animal walks), play skills like pedaling a wheeled toy and group games with a parachute (MNDAPE, 2023). Instructions on how to modify, adapt, and teach an activity for participation are explained by disability in chapters 7 through 13.

Some key points on teaching these young children with delays are:

- *Use a child-centered approach:* Teach where the child is successful in the skill and build from there.

- *Teaching is critical:* It is a fallacy that young children just pick up their movement skills. Children don't learn to read by standing in a library. They learn to read by having material to read and a teacher trained to teach them. The same is true for learning movement skills and the games and activities of young children. They need the opportunity, the equipment, the teachers, and the time to repeat and explore the activities. It is never about perfect form at these very young ages.

- *Preschoolers have a short attention span:* The attention span of preschooler is shorter than their older age kindergartener classmates. Expect and plan for that.

Repetition

Young children need to repeat movement activity over and over, and in doing so, they learn. Leave plenty of time for discovery and repetition to enable the child to learn. All their systems—physical, cognitive, social-emotional, and communication—are working together to produce coordinated movement; and all those systems grow because of the stimulation of movement. Campos and colleagues reported significant gains in attending to this phenomenon, demonstrating locomotor acquisition that paralleled an explosion in cognitive skills (2000).

Sex Differences

Research has reported that by age three, there is a difference between the expression of movement skills in typical development by girls versus boys using the Test of Gross Motor Development (TGMD; Ulrich, 2000). In select skills, girls do better than boys and the reverse is true in other skills. When Ulrich updated to the TGMD-3 (2017), these differences were written into the tables used to calculate overall scores in motor development for children ages 3 to 10 years. Ulrich and colleagues tested the validity of the TGMD-3 (Maeng et al., 2016; Webster & Ulrich, 2017), reporting results thus continuing the separation of girl and boy calculation tables. For now, this separation is owed to the reality that there are too few numbers of young children identifying as other than male or female to statistically influence a change in the record. Select fundamental movement skills and activities of the preschool years are noted in table 4.1.

Kindergarteners

In most states, by age five, children with and without typical development attend kindergarten before entering elementary school in the fall of their sixth year. In kindergarten, many schools offer physical education, hence a trained teacher runs the program. School districts should have standards for each age group in the district, and teachers should have a district curriculum for physical education.

As a kindergartener, the child with a disability is more mature than they were in preschool, and their movement skills are more developed (see table 4.1). They have grown in all aspects of their life. In general, at these young ages, the differences between them and their typically developing peers is not necessarily as highly noted. (Disability with more pronounced physical manifestations such as some forms of cerebral palsy might be the exception.) A child with Down syndrome is walking and running—though maybe slower—and attempting to catch and throw like their classmates, many of whom are typically developing children still learning these skills themselves. What is so important to instill is the same: their success and an enjoyment of movement time with their peers.

Transition Plan

There is another transition when leaving preschool and entering kindergarten, though it is just a part of moving on to the next year of school. Procedures for creating another IFSP or an IEP are part of the advancement of the child educationally. In some states an IFSP is retained, and in others the child moves to an IEP. IDEA (2004) does not require a transition plan from preschool to kindergarten.

Placement and Inclusion

Inclusion is the term used today to address integration with typically developing peers in the classroom. Since its inception in 1975, special education has always stated that the child with a disability is to be educated *to the extent possible within the mainstream of their educational community*. In the early days of special education, *mainstreaming* was the term used. It is still in the language of the law, but today *inclusion* is the appropriate term.

Placement of the child in a setting of inclusion is based on the IEP team's goals for the child (or IFSP in some states); the team considers the needs of the child and the resources available. Smaller communities with fewer resources face different challenges for inclusion than larger communities with more resources. Nonetheless, inclusion is discussed in the IEP or IFSP meetings to determine what the children's educational placement will be. As the children move into settings for kindergarten, they learn in the least restrictive environment as stated by IDEA (2004). The least restrictive environment for some children could be a segregated class where the children have needs that are not meet in an integrated setting with their typically developing peers. This is the environment that provides the most opportunity for them, whereas the fully integrated classroom with their peers would restrict them too much. Most children in kindergarten learn in the integrated classroom setting.

Movement Skill Development and Instruction

The skills of the child in kindergarten expand developmentally from the skills they had in the preschool years (see table 4.1). When a child is three years of age and running, they don't engage the upper part of their body, but by the time they are six, they are moving their arms in opposition to their legs (e.g., when they are in a running motion, the left leg goes forward and the right arm is back; then as they take another step in the run, the right leg comes forward and the left arm goes back). This is typical development. A child with a disability may be running using a form based on what they can do and not doing it in the typical fashion for anyone but themselves! At this time, kindergarteners also begin learning more physical activity games geared to their age group.

This group of children remain a heterogenous group with some children still developing the skills of the five-year-old. Some children are slower to develop physically than others and this influences how they can perform their fundamental skills (Haywood & Getchell, 2019). Now, depending on many variables considered by Bronfenbrenner's theory (Bronfenbrenner, 1977; Bronfenbrenner & Morris, 2006), some children begin to excel in their skills given an opportunity and considering such influences as adult or parental involvement and natural inherited ability. During the Olympics, it is always interesting to note the athletes whose parents were outstanding athletes. Paralympians are also noted for having had athletic backgrounds themselves before an injury or illness or having had a parent recognized for athletic accomplishments. For that matter, early family videos of current sport stars that are posted on the Internet often show an outstanding star at age six! Despite any prowess in physical activity, kindergartners do better without competitive physical activity. Winning isn't important. Participating, moving, and having fun are much more important to their overall development.

Occupational and physical therapy can advise on modifications or adaptations for engagement of children with disabilities in the physical activity programs of the class. As in the state of New York, physical educators teach in the kindergarten classes.

In kindergarten, follow all the same previously mentioned teaching strategies used with the preschoolers. What you teach, and how you teach it, change because the children are more physically mature than they were in preschool. They have a longer attention span (but they are still just six years of age). The following are some additional instructional strategies for kindergarteners.

• *The class:* There should be a beginning, a middle, and an end to your classes. Follow a plan to teach the fundamentals over time. Introduce the children to games for their age.

• *Partner up:* If needed, for some of the activity, the children can all partner up, which helps many children besides the one or two with a disability who need a partner in a game or activity. This is the approach of universal design for learning (Lieberman et al., 2020), where instead of one child with an adaptation, all share in the adaptation.

Transition Plan

There is no transition plan for kindergarten to first grade required by IDEA (2004). Best practice does facilitate this in other ways with teachers and parents discussing concerns. This is particularly true with students placed in inclusive settings either full time or part time.

Elementary School Ages

The literature suggests that parents of a child with a disability want their child to be included with age peers in physical education, recess, and in any sport programs, where their child is qualified. They also want their child to be happy and have friends. They want their child to be safe. They desire the physical education teacher to care about their child and be competent in making modifications and adaptations for participation success.

Research shows that being successful in skills performance is linked to the enjoyment of physical education and engagement in physical activity (e.g., Jin et al., 2018). The opposite is also true: those children who experience failure or prejudice in skills and games performance in physical education have negative feelings, often over a lifetime, toward participation in physical activity (Hodge et al., 2017).

Table 4.1 lists selected fundamental movement skills of these early grade school years. These same skills span across the whole age spectrum from preschool up to around age 10 years of age. The younger child is not as proficient as the older child. The horizontal jump of a kindergartener is not as mature as that of a child who is older. Typically, the lower body of younger children is more engaged when performing the skill (e.g., certain bending of the legs and some jumping out), and with age, the upper body becomes more involved (e.g., arms decidedly bend, thrust back, swinging forward; as the legs bend deep and spring out far). Many criterion-referenced assessment tools of motor development make this clear (e.g., TGMD-3; Ulrich, 2017). A child with a disability may not be able to perform the skill or may have their own way of performance not established in standardized testing. For example, a child with cerebral palsy may not run using the TGMD-3 criteria, but they run.

Social Skills

For many children with disabilities, social skills need to be taught, especially in physical activity with other children. The role of educators is to model and intervene with knowledge to create opportunities for children with disabilities to play with their nondisabled peers. Teachers trained in systematic social skills development for their students with disabilities find opportunity on the playgrounds at school, in the classroom, in the gymnasium, and in consultation with parents to use this knowledge. If the whole school takes social skill development on, the results have broader collaborative interventions and therefore will be more effective (Anaby et al., 2019). For children who have a behavior disorder, chapter 10 has detailed interventions that shape appropriate social response in the physical education classes.

Bullying occurs in schools at higher rates for children with disabilities than without (Bills, 2020). This occurs on playgrounds, in the classrooms, and in the athletic programs and clubs of the school. Bullying is unwanted physical or verbal harassment, aggression to insult or violate another individual, and is four times higher for students with disabilities than without (Bills, 2019). Participation in school athletics by students with a disability decreased bullying but participating in nonathletic extracurricular activities does not (Bills, 2020). For students with disabilities, schoolwork, friends, and self-esteem all improved given their status as athletes.

In a 2021 review of 14 studies from the previous 20 years, 114 children who were blind reported bullying in school physical education programs initiated by the physical educators (50 percent), paraeducators (7 percent), and their peers (93 percent). The bullying occurred in class (93 percent) and in the locker room (21 percent) (Ball et al., 2021). In particular, to reduce bullying, greater training was highly recommended for physical educators and paraeducators working with blind students, including assessments, modifications, and adaptations in activities of the physical education (PE) class. Students with visual impairments wanted increased communication from the PE teacher (Haegele et al., 2020). The Olweus Bullying Prevention Program was recommended for a whole-school approach. Bullying by a teacher can influence the freedom in which their peers feel enabled to bully their classmate. The authors did not believe their research could be generalized to all children who are blind.

Movement Skill Development and Instruction

Participation in the physical education program at the early elementary ages is designed to develop basic motor skills and introduce children to a variety of age-appropriate games and sport activities referred to as lead-up games to sports. Students with disabilities participate with their peers in physical education to the extent possible. Selected substitutions in the established curriculum can be made for students with disabilities, as determined by their IEP team. Modifications are made to the curriculum. Sometimes all the students benefit from the modification, for example when there is a choice between two units.

Teachers of physical education are encouraged to develop student friendships and positive interactions, which are often referred to as creating the opportunity for students to learn social skills. This is the basis for children with disabilities being placed in their peer groups in physical education or adapted physical education. A standard teaching technique for increasing enjoyment is to reduce any wait time in a class (waiting to throw the ball or be a part of a game) as would increasing choice

in PE. Recess is seen as challenging for children with disabilities who often need more structure and more play options, with different play areas available, with diverse equipment available, and with teaching staff supervising.

PE is an academic area like no other academic area in elementary and secondary school in that it exposes the student to the view of others. Events in a physical education class that can be humiliating for a student with disabilities include moving awkwardly, losing the game, repeatedly missing the shot, being chosen last to participate, being unable to hold the bat well, being unable to hear the calls of others in a game, and not understanding the directions.

Positive Regard

Lavay and colleagues promote use of positive regard by teaching staff, in all its different forms, during engagement in physical activity for children and youth (Lavay et al., 2016). Here are some forms of positive regard:

- Modeling of positive regard by teachers by using the student's name and specific positives (for example, "Mark, that touch-and-turn at the end of the pool was done very well").
- Acceptance by the teachers and school allied health care professionals (OT and PT) of how each student strives to perform at their *personal best*.
- Decreased competition in class activities and create more opportunity for cooperation.

A tenet of learning is that the more a concept is reinforced across a child's day, the greater likelihood learning will take place. Individuals who can influence enjoyment in physical activity are identified in table 4.1. One area of great influence is the positive verbal regard by health care professionals to either the young student or their family in

- showing interest in the individual's physical activity participation;
- encouraging the student or parent to describe a physical activity at school that the student likes;
- keeping a note in the medical chart;
- naming that activity or the skill for the child;
- talking about the activity, or in the least, naming the activity;
- making positive statements such as "I'm so glad you are enjoying your swimming program, Jeanne"; and

- exhibiting positive regard geared toward the family for getting the child to the activity (maybe even participating).

For health care professionals and teachers, these comments can come while walking down the hallway at school, when greeting a family at a parent meeting, when talking with a child in the clinic, or when standing on the sidelines of the playing field (see table 4.1). Comments from medical personnel can astonish a child and family. Overall, medical personnel often have the "surprise reinforcement effect" where there is a good relationship with the health care personnel. Health care personnel are critical in keeping the individual healthy physically. Begun in early elementary school, their part extends all through the school system to high school graduation.

Developmentally Appropriate Practice

The activity presented in physical activity classes should meet the physical capability of the student; this is known as being developmentally appropriate. Children will not succeed and therefore will not enjoy the activity if it is beyond their physical capacity. Kicking to a target is a developmentally appropriate movement skill across the preschool to early elementary ages. To kick the ball to a target, young children position themselves closer to a target that is large. In time, they can be farther away and kick to a smaller target. Then certain children can kick a ball while running and kick a ball to someone who is running. This is an early soccer skill. None of this would be enjoyable if the teacher misses the developmentally expected physical capacity of that student. When the student is ready for the next step, explain that step briefly and provide lots of opportunities. Back off if the student is getting too frustrated. Return to the next step later.

Other strategies for teaching in developmentally appropriate practice include a *task analysis*, whereby there is a breaking down of the skill into smaller performance parts to achieve the whole skill. Educators also use an ecological task analysis that considers the variables of the individual, the environment, and the task to better understand how the individual will succeed in the movement performance. (Both task analyses and ecological task analyses are explained in more detail in chapter 5.) In some cases, the rules of a game are modified to include the child with or without a disability and to build up the child's skill while increasing participation.

Developmentally appropriate also encompasses the social and emotional skills for age. Physical activity in the gym, motor room, track, or swimming pool isn't just about the physical body, it is about the mind and body and the child's social and emotional life. If these skills are lacking or underdeveloped for the activity, the child will also struggle or fail. For this child, social and emotional skills need to be taught. They have a developmental delineation. A task analysis or ecological task analysis can be used to teach these skills. A delay in one domain may or may not mean a delay across all domains. A child may have appropriate social skills like taking turns with ease in the gym but lack skills in being positive with classmates when losing a game played outside.

Physical educators and adapted physical educators, coaches, and others involved with the physical activity of children and youth with disabilities know the expected state competencies for grades, as well as the SHAPE America guidelines that define a student as literate, knowledgeable, and skilled about themselves in physical activity. These identified grade-level activities can inform and guide interventions when teaching toward success.

Enjoyable Physical Activity

Enjoyable is defined as observing a student display a pleasant affect or their reporting that they like an activity or are having fun (Jin et al., 2018). Individual enjoyment boosts participation and increases health outcomes in school-based programs of physical activity. Historically, most children, and particularly children with disabilities, have not met recommended levels of physical activity participation. Yet, in a study of 241 youngsters 5 to 15 years of age with disabilities, their health was directly and positively influenced by enjoyment in their physical education class and in increased physical activity outside of school (Jin et al., 2018). Overall, physically active children are known to be healthier, and those with regular access to physical education and recess attend better and have higher cognitive aptitude in the school day (AAP, 2013; Pedro Ángel et al., 2021). Sports psychologists reported that children will remain involved in sports programs if the participation is fun (e.g., Scanlan & Simons, 1992). This finding has held true.

Young children with or without disabilities may not have a vocabulary for physical activity and may not know the names of games or skills. In a school day, comments from education staff are also effective in reinforcing the names of physical activities and ongoing engagement. Naming exercise in a positive light is a boon to physical activity participation. Examples include statements such as "You went fast on the slide"; "You did your best in the

game today, Aaron, and you looked happy"; and "You rolled down the mat!" The students benefit from knowing their teacher noticed them.

Middle to High School Ages

Developmental appropriateness continues to the end of high school. Now some of the activity has a measure. "School-age youth should participate daily in 60 minutes or more of moderate to vigorous physical activity that is developmentally appropriate, enjoyable, and involves a variety of activities" (Strong et al., 2005). This statement has been built into the Healthy People guidelines from the Centers for Disease Control and Prevention over many decades and it is part of the SHAPE America standards. The guidelines of the federal government and standards of our professional organizations are geared, in part, toward participation in a variety of activities. The goal is to enable a student to choose to participate in physical activities because they know they can and they like them. This is also a part of becoming an adult. This is facilitated by the transition plan in their IEP.

Movement Skill Development and Instruction

Learning the specialized movement skills of the middle schooler to high schooler turns from learning basic movement skills to functional physical activity involvement. What the student can do as a basic skill is relatively apparent as they enter middle school as well as when they are in high school. These skills (e.g., strike, kick) have been applied in games and sports in the early elementary physical education classes. Now the students are further advanced, participating in age-appropriate physical activity in practical, efficient ways, using adaptations if necessary. Wheelchair basketball is a functional participation in the game of basketball for those using a wheelchair for ambulation. Sit-ski is functional skiing for students with lower-limb paralysis.

By middle school and high school, chronological age—time on Earth—is confusing when people are programming in physical activity and note the discrepancy with the developmental age and the chronological age of the student with a disability. The appropriate approach in programming is carried out by recognizing the student's chronological age for selecting program content and the developmental age for how the content is taught. A student who is 15 years old with an intellectual disability should be participating in physical activities of those age 15 while being taught by considering what supports or instructions they need based on their developmental age. More of this discussion takes place in chapter 7 on intellectual disability. Table 4.1 lists the specialized movement skills for high schoolers and emphasizes chronological age-appropriate activity.

Another important aspect of high school physical education for those who have been on IEPs for increasing skills in basic motor skills is that, by now, any repetitious focus on basics doesn't help the students and is terribly boring. High school is a time to leave that training, in and of itself, and apply basic skills to the age-appropriate physical activities of teens. The focus in high school is educating for a physically fit and healthy teen life. Curricula are planned with some researchers advocating for added time in the classroom to talk about fitness for life (Corbin et al., 2020), which is reaping positive effects on activity engagement.

By experiencing a variety of physical activities in the physical education program that is both sensitive to locale and of the child's interests, the student has a chance to understand what it means for them to be physically active and enjoying activity. Enjoyment is paradoxical. Everyone knows that to report enjoyment in an activity is not to say everything was easy or fun. Getting up from a fall on a ski run on the slopes is hard and challenging but overshadowed by that great run down the trail. Hiking up a hill for longer than expected is a surprise and hard, but the view at the top is worth it. Dancing socially in the gymnasium for the first time is anxiety producing until time passes, friends are encouraging, and your favorite song is played. In each of these scenarios, many participants report that they enjoyed the activity!

A curriculum that includes leisure time pursuits like bike riding, roller skating, dancing, downhill skiing, and hiking is age appropriate for middle and high school students. If the youth in schools are enjoying their physical education classes and recess times and have a choice within these times, they are more likely to participate and achieve, sustain, or gain in health through the chosen activity.

The sum, years of physical education, and community-based physical activity participation exposes the individual to a broad array of physical activities starting from a very young age, building on positive feedback and success as the student ages through early grade school, middle school, and high school. This allows the student a broad and positive understanding of themselves as physically active. Physical skills, rules of the games, and recreational activity plus the associated social skills are funneled into these final years in high school for use after graduation.

Transition Plan

Engagement in age-appropriate physical activity during the teen years is solidified in the curriculum by the transitional IEP goals required by IDEA (2004) to prepare the student to graduate and participate in physical activity in their postgraduation community. To achieve this, the physical education assessment takes into account the student's interests, skills, family interests, and community resources. The physical education curriculum broadens the exposure of the student to a variety of

recreational activities, often based on locale. Youth with disabilities in Hawaii learn to surf. In Colorado, youth learn to downhill ski, and in Minnesota, they learn to cross-country ski.

In high school, a student with a disability and the IEP team must, by IDEA (2004), begin this transition and work toward graduation to a life in the community. Referenced unofficially or locally as the transition or transitional IEP, "it assures that planning and services are available and coordinated to assist young adults with disabilities in moving from school to community-based programs, agencies, and services" (Colarusso et al., 2017, p. 75). The student, along with their family and school personnel, begins to plan for this transition to work or continued education, as well as for recreational physical activity. The transitional IEP team can engage other educational and medical specialists. Therapeutic recreation personnel can assess and collaborate in training high school students to use their community for physical recreation. Certain school districts have specialists who are identified in IDEA (2004). The therapeutic recreation person works in an interdisciplinary fashion with other members of the student's transition team.

This IEP must begin by age 16; some school districts begin earlier. Colleagues report positive outcomes by focusing on functional goals, especially for those not going on to higher education. For physical activity planning, assessments of the student's interests in leisure activities and community resources, the family's interests in physically active recreation, and their interests for their teenager upon graduation are conducted. Other professionals in the schools have other responsibilities for areas such as vocational training or college preparatory work.

Sometimes students enjoy an activity even though they may not be that skilled in it. Parents are invaluable in an effective transition for the teen into the community. Questions to prompt discussions of recreation activities include:

- What are their interests for their teen regarding physical activity engagement?
- What does the student want to do when they graduate?
- Is the student reasonable?
- Do the parents need support at this time of transition out of school?
- Do the parents feel strapped or unable to assist their teen? For example, is there food scarcity, parental unemployment, or uncer-

tainty as to whether the student can be transported to recreation classes and activities?

- Does the student know about community activities in which they would like to participate? If not, where does school training need to begin?

- What interest does the family have for their teen's community recreation that are similar to their own interests? Dissimilar? What are some first-step goals?

- What needs to be specified in the IEP?

Adults

The definition of the student's disability was spelled out by federal education law, IDEA (2004), and used throughout their primary and secondary education. This allows the school to serve the student in special education through their 21st year of age. Those with a new 504 plan might have a more recent evaluation report for services. The definition of disability broadens after the departure from high school, because the federal government has different criteria used across many settings in adulthood.

Adults with disabilities have usually been considered as one group, but a new paradigm of aging has emerged that divides this group into two: those identified early with a disability are referred to as *aging with disability* (such as having a diagnosis of cerebral palsy or Down syndrome), and those identified later in life are said to be *aging into disability* (such as having arthritis or cardiac conditions) (Molton & Yorkston, 2017). With this, a new direction for research in aging is the model of long-term service, which supports focusing on home and community-based services (Putnam, 2014, 2017). These new models necessitate cross-disciplinary collaboration to support the lives of those with disabilities (Molton & Ordway, 2019). These distinctions are essential today in considering physical activity participation.

In looking at the physical activity engagement of adults with disabilities, we will be as clear as possible about who we are addressing and what we are recommending. Adulthood covers a broad range from young adult (mostly beginning around age 18 years of age) to old adult (over 85 years of age). Our groupings of adulthood are young adults (ages 18 to near 40 years), middle-aged adults (ages 40 to near 60 years), older aged adult (ages 60 to near 80 years), and oldest adults (age 80 and older).

Aging and Disability

In America, many adults with disabilities have participated in adapted physical activity from early childhood through their graduation from high school (owing to IDEA [2004]). Others, as young adults, qualify as having a disability by federal description—they have *acquired* a disease or incurred an injury. What are the implications for adapted physical activity engagement given this new paradigm? Our research and the practitioners' work of adapted physical activity engagement is perfectly aligned when reviewing the themes inherent in the new paradigms of aging with disability and aging into disability. The effort is to improve the lives of individuals with disabilities (Molton & Ordway, 2019, pp. 10S-11S) in specific ways. These efforts are listed with our added commentary on adapted physical activity under each:

- *Increasing effective health promotion and disease prevention programs.*

Adapted physical activity engagement has a long history of making contributions to the health of individuals with disabilities at any age. Participation in this activity has long been known to prevent disease onset and to ease progressions as with diabetes and arthritis. This focus on adults is presented in detail in part III.

- *Focus on the utilization of rehabilitation, services and other supports.*

The invaluable interdisciplinary work conducted in rehabilitation centers to facilitate the

Government Support and Research Groups

There is solace in the federal establishment of the Administration for Community Living, which includes the Administration on Aging, the National Institutes on Disability, Independent Living, and Rehabilitation Research, and the Administration on Disabilities. Here, merging of research is among aging and disability disciplines, which affects understanding supports and services. Research in adapted physical activity has been calling for greater cross-disciplinary collaboration for individuals with disabilities, enabling a physically active life (Agiovlasitis et al., 2018). Adapted physical activity takes place in the community and in the home, and this is where the new research with cross-disciplinary collaboration is finding an essential focus.

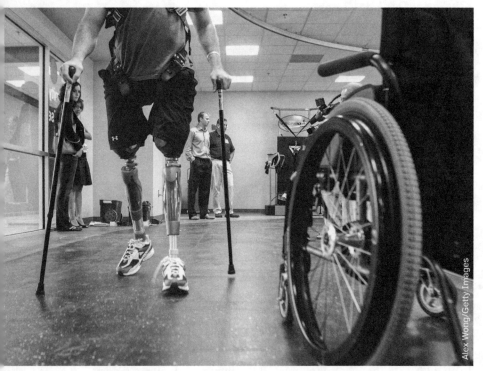

Alex Wong/Getty Images

same as with IDEA (2004). Instead, it is a general term for those diagnosed in early childhood with cognition, hearing, or vision impairments.)

Another interesting development has been to enroll younger adults with a long-term disability (those aging with disability, before middle age) into a fall-prevention program (Eagen et al., 2019). This group has a known risk for falls as its members age. The researchers didn't expect those with long-term disability to attend as well as their matched peers—those adults without long-term disability—but they were surprised when those with long-term disabilities actually surpassed their peers (90 percent versus 63 percent). Even though it was difficult at times for the those with long-term disabilities to attend, they solved the problem. Researchers noted an increase in social skill interactions with this group. Since fear of falling is a risk factor leading to activity restriction and physical decline, decreasing fear was statistically significant for those with long-term disability. The program was offered to discussion groups conducted by *trained* community members, not clinicians.

The findings of the research reinforce the benefit of having programs offered in the home community of the individuals with disability and of training their community members to offer instruction based on the use of auditory (listening) and visual presentation along with a physical component. This instructional approach is discussed in chapter 5.

• *Improving opportunities for meaningful social and community participation.*

Adapted physical activity engagement has a social commitment whether the individual is an introvert or an extrovert. Those who desire to be alone in an activity such as walking or swimming laps should be allowed to do so. Likewise, others might desire greater involvement with others, so activities such as skiing, dancing, hiking, exercise classes would be in order. More and more, the emphasis should be on this engagement taking place in the individual's community, and issues of transportation must be addressed.

• *Living life consistent with personal goals and values in the context of disability.*

The respect of individuals with disabilities has always been a tenet of the work of professionals facilitating adapted physical activity. New questions

successful engagement of individuals with disabilities in adapted physical activity in their lives and communities is identified in chapter 2 . This will be directed to a more nuanced understanding of those who have long lived with a disability as well as those with a newly acquired impairment such as a spinal cord injury, and those who have a new disease condition who are aging into a disability.

Together we may be learning new ways to approach the interventions needed given the disability status of the new paradigms. What other services and supports do we need to find, link, and utilize? For example, the established Chronic Disease Self-Management Program has reported success in increasing an individual's physical activity engagement and decreasing depression (Ferretti & McCallion, 2019). Originally developed at Stanford University for individuals living with a chronic disease such as arthritis or diabetes, researchers successfully adapted the program for older adults with developmental disabilities (mild and moderate developmental disabilities) who received their medical care for a chronic disease in the community. In one component, the individuals devised a long-term physical activity program and formed a plan on how to maintain it. The researchers emphasized that making self-management programs available to those with developmental disabilities in mainstreamed settings can support engagement for adults with developmental disabilities as they age. (In this literature, *developmental disabilities* is not the are now being asked to gain access to what the individual values, and thus, where and how they can be involved. In theory, engagement in adapted physical activity for a person with a disability centers them in their community as a common and equal member. Understanding what supports are important for this to happen are built into the models of adaptation and modification.

As individuals with disabilities advance into middle age and older age, the levels of support change based on the many variables that need to be considered using the framework of life course health development (Halfon & Forrest, 2018; Halfon & Hochstein, 2002). One variable that changes across *all adults* is their interests in physical activity. Where once in high school an individual might have enjoyed team sports, over time the interest may shift to dual sports, or single sports such as swimming. Another variable that broadly changes across all adults over time is health status. For some, it affects the frequency, intensity, and duration of a loved physical activity. Running gives way to any number of activities like hiking, biking, or walking because the knees hurt or the back doesn't support the pounding of running. For others, it leads to depression and a disengagement in physical activity. Survey data identifying the barriers to participating in physical activity for adults with disabilities, such as low motivation, income or rural residency (e.g., Trost et al., 2002), can't be ignored. The effort to engage individuals with disabilities in physical activity that supports a healthy lifestyle is many pronged involving many disciplines. We have a vast array of knowledge of adapting physical activity for those with disabilities. With what we know now, we encourage the following.

Connect the physical activity interests with engagement in adapted physical activity concomitant with a psychological state. The adult person's identity is formed by the interplay of their child development, their parental influences, the social and cultural context in which they have lived, and by political crises occurring in their life (Erikson, 1978). Understanding oneself and planning in middle age for older age creates social well-being (Erikson et al., 1994). The tenet of obtaining physical literacy throughout life complements this approach, whereby one understands oneself in physical activity including those with disabilities (Pushkarenko et al., 2021). What follows herein is a description of an adult psychosocial stage of development, a discussion of adapted physical activity opportunity, and the professional involvement. Physical activity suggestions for adults are expanded on in part III.

Young Adults

Young adults with disabilities are healthier than their predecessors a decade ago, and going forward, there is a call for the United States to ask for cooperation across health care professionals and organizations to continue physical activity engagement for health maintenance (Thompson & Eijsvogels, 2018). This new mark of health is critical at the point when young adults leave high school and enter their home community in new ways. Engagement changes with health care professionals, educators, community practitioners, and their families from the way it was when individuals with disabilities were in school. With broad interdisciplinary support, young adults with disabilities can continue regular participation in physical activity and mediate chronic disease as they age (Bauer et al., 2014).

Upon graduating from high school, young adults with disabilities pursue new paths. Options include attending college or a vocational school, beginning employment, or attending day programs. They also transition from a pediatric health care practitioner to an adult health care practitioner. They may reside in the family home, a group home, or with others in an apartment. According to the United States Bureau of Labor Statistics for 2021, 44 percent of those with a disability are in the labor force. The COVID-19 pandemic disrupted (and continues to do so) training and employment across the labor market in the United States with a reduction of at least 5 percent employment level for those with disability (Houtenville, 2021).

Younger adulthood is roughly attributed to ages 18 to 40 years, as a stage of moving toward the advancement of intimacy in one's life rather than isolation (McLeod, 2018). The word *intimacy* is an emotionally charged word describing a range of close personal relationships. Curriculum, training, and discussion in disability services address sex education and disability, providing an education in intimacy (e.g., Frawley & O'Shea, 2020; Grove, 2018; Rowe et. al., 2018). It is important and necessary. We take a broad interpretation of intimacy. Is it not intimate in the sharing of experiences in an outdoor hike—recounting life stories as one trudges along the trail or sitting on a hillside, sandwich in hand, viewing the mountain range next to your climbing friends? Is it not intimate riding on the bus with your teammates after the joyful experience of swimming in the Special Olympics regional competition? Is it not intimate at the dance at the parks and recreation building where you picked your special person for the slow dance? Is the doubles tennis match with your partner not intimate? Furthermore, it is wonderful finding a loving relationship in life.

Scientists of aging note that without meaningful social connections, the isolation and resulting loneliness and depression are detrimental to health. Interestingly, in England, Emerson and colleagues reported that disability status *was not* the highest contributor to loneliness in younger people with disabilities (2021). Instead, what contributed to a greater sense of loneliness was being poor and living alone in neighborhoods that were termed *deprived and without environmental assets*. This is helpful to know and translate. Can we use a tailored approach to engaging the individual in adapted physical activity out of the home, out of the neighborhood, at no or low cost? Or is there a safe place in the neighborhood where young adults can gather to exercise and socialize? Yes, the larger picture will take an interagency, interdisciplinary response to address the conditions contributing to the environmental loneliness these individuals feel. But a known and validated antidote to depression is physical activity engagement, and when depression is mitigated and support systems are in place in the community, we know many individuals can find motivation to help themselves—the self-management discussed earlier.

By virtue of being young adults, many individuals with disabilities desire the social engagement and the intimacy associated with being a young adult. Is this individual intrinsically motivated to be involved in physical activity with others in their home community? Or is this a challenge for the individual? Has their education in being physically active been so positive they are looking forward to this time after high school? Is their residential living, circle of friends, or family unit sufficiently informed to understand how important physical activity is and how it will happen? Are they incentivized to be physically active?

In behavioral psychology, experiencing enjoyment or pleasure is an *intrinsic motivator* for behavior and is more desirable because it comes from within the individual, not put upon them by someone else. It is within their values, likes, and dislikes. It is in line with who they are. An *extrinsic motivator* depends on someone outside the individual to motivate them by varying means. B. F. Skinner is known for his work for shaping behavior by extrinsic means (1938). By rewarding a student with something tangible and desirable, the student's behavior can be changed. Educators have used extrinsic rewards to shape behavior for decades, but current literature supports the more desirable strength of the intrinsically motivated student. These are some of the questions to be answered either by the individual themselves or the individual in conjunction with their family or care givers. The answers they provide now will help shape the quest for a physically active life postgraduation.

Transition Plan

For the recently graduated high school student, the transitional IEP goals in physical activity are now applied. It has addressed the *unique aspects* of the young adult with a disability as they enter their postgraduate life with needs and plans for a physically active young adult life. In theory, through the last two years before graduation, this has been the student's focus in their adapted physical education program. Hopefully, the responsibility for implementing the IEP goals was addressed. The level of support must have been addressed for each individual so they can enjoy being physically active. Importantly, do they receive continual support or hardly any?

Postsecondary Institution Recreation Programs   For those individuals with disabilities pursuing postsecondary education, there are physical activity resources and social outlets to be considered. Community colleges, colleges, and universities often offer recreation programs on campus and in the greater community in which the institution is located. Buildings are set aside for these activities. There are classes offered to balance the often-sedentary lifestyle of student life.

The facilities can have open equipment rooms with stationary bicycles, elliptical machines, treadmills, free weights, weight machines, and other implements. There are classes scheduled for fitness. Hiking, canoeing, basketball, dancing, fitness classes, surfing, walking, and biking are typically social and physical activities. Sometimes these programs come as a club activity. Clubs are often associated with the recreation center's offerings. For any young adult engaged in a postsecondary education, joining a club on their campus means a social opportunity for individuals who share a similar interest.

Municipal Programs   Communities often have municipal recreation programs. Their schedules often list inclusion or adapted recreation programs among their web-based classes, and they might offer either integrated or segregated activities for those with disabilities. Community recreation personnel are trained and sensitive to the initial inquiry about joining a class or outing. They can suggest the individual observe the class first or that a program volunteer partners with the individual for the first few sessions. Often it is helpful to review or preteach the participation in the class. In such a case, someone can meet with the individual and explain the outline of the class, keeping things simple. This could happen at the activity's location just before the class starts.

Fitness and Wellness Centers   Another method of getting into physical activity is to seek out fitness and wellness centers that are affordable and find which classes are suitable. Pick one class and meet with the instructor, if needed, to ease the initial participation. Explore any classes that might be set up for special needs. Make sure the class is age appropriate for the younger adult. Look for staff with certificates in aspects of disability. The stationary equipment might be on option for the individual, depending on their level of training. For example, an adult who is blind may have had training in using free weights, stationary weight machines, or stationary bicycles. Laps are also an option for those individuals who know how to swim. Aqua aerobics is an option for an instructor-led class with low-impact exercise, because the water is buoyant and supportive.

Sport   Young adults, their energy level, and social interests find themselves suited to sport. Adapted sport competitions for adults are discussed in detail in chapter 16. Programs like Special Olympics, the Paralympics, and sport programs for disability-specific groups (e.g., those who are blind or have spina bifida) are explained. Special Olympics is widely popular among young adults with intellectual disability, many of whom began participating in the programs when they were younger.

Many young adults who fought in wars and received life-changing injuries have been introduced to high-level sports competition through the Paralympics. Other Paralympic athletes have histories of sport participation when a disabling condition developed later in life. Together, these athletes are training and competing regularly, some with specialized coaches. The Paralympic program began in 2001 and offers competition in 27 summer sports such as swimming and tennis and in 21 winter sports such as alpine skiing and wheelchair curling. Team USA is the umbrella organization for both Olympic and Paralympic athletes.

Middle-Aged Adults

For our purposes, middle adulthood is somewhere around 40 to 55 years of age. It is difficult to pinpoint this age range. Subgroups of adulthood vary across disciplines and federal agencies. A common approach is to lump adulthood into ages 18 to 65 years of age. This large range does not allow an adequate description of adapted physical activity engagement and disability. We also recognize the aging into disability taking place in the population where those who did not previously have a disability are now aware of an impairment (Molton & Ordway, 2019). This a group new to adaptations for physical activities engagement.

With common diseases of aging like osteoarthritis, seniors need access to services that are integrated and include community-based rehabilitation. They might need assistance with activities of daily living, support with community participation and transportation, and community health promotion (ACSM, 2009; Molton & Yorkston, 2017; Rimmer & Lai, 2017; USDHHS, 2005). This approach has benefits for life. For example, active adults with intellectual disabilities gain in health outcomes with aging, even when they are below cutoff scores for people without disabilities as published by the American College of Sports Medicine (ACSM) (Oppewal et al., 2020).

Interestingly, researchers studying aging report successful aging if *there is little or no disability*. Most of us realize this is a biological impossibility. Aging means the acquisition of some differences in physical activity engagement because we are older. Rather, those studying disability could report that living well with a disability is a success. There is a reality that "Freedom from chronic illness or disability is necessary to age successfully . . ." this has been cited by most of the empirical studies as the gold standard of successful aging (Molton & Yorkston, 2017, p. 291). Those without any disability in older age are not superior to those with disability. In addition, the attainment of no disabilities in the aging process is *not* supported by population studies. All people age, and all will deal with some form of modification and adaptation to physical activities because of it. Therefore, there is great support for the broad reach of adapted physical activity knowledge and skill applied to disability and aging.

Middle age is the life phase of generativity (Erikson, 1978; Erikson et al., 1994) that occurs at around 40 to 60 years of age. It is a time where individuals want to be productive and engaged in making contributions that are important to them, in employment, in family commitments, and in connections to their community. They reached out from themselves to be for and with others, as opposed to solely living inwardly for themselves. They are in relationships with challenges, compromises, disappointments, and rewards. It is a time of feeling more independence in life to commit more closely to a family, a created family, and professional and health groups in ways that match the individual's personality.

Exercise Prescription

According to the Centers for Disease Control and Prevention, when a medical doctor prescribes exercise for an individual with a disability, more than 82 percent follow through (2014). (The Centers for Disease Control and Prevention uses a broader definition of disability than the IDEA [2004] categories.) The campaign Exercise Is Medicine wants doctors' attention on assessing physical activity participation during visits with a person with a disability. Advice on discussions doctors could have with patients with disabilities follows.

- Ask how much physical activity patients are engaging in each week.
  - The U.S. Department of Health and Human Services program Move Your Way recommends starting slow with physical activity engagement, doing what can be done (USDHHS, 2023). It does not dismiss even a five-minute walk, which can build up to more activity over time.
  - The eventual goal is about 25 minutes, 6 days a week or 30 minutes, 5 days a week of moderate-intensity exercise (the individual is exerting effort but can still carry on a conversation). Those who are not thoroughly verbal should watch for signs of overexertion like heavy breathing.
  - Adapt intensity or hours of physical activity to engage the individual in physical activity. Since most people do not reach the stated goal set by DHHS and numerous other federal agencies, the goal of 2 hours, 30 minutes per week seems to beg for adaptation.
- Ask what patients enjoy in physical activity.
  - Match the person's abilities to connect them to resources.
  - Suggest activities based on abilities (e.g., a brisk walk, wheeling in their wheelchair, swimming laps, water aerobics, adapted bicycling).
  - Check that the patient understands the recommendation.
  - Consider ways the person regularly receives information and communicates what they understand. Write down and verbally describe the information.
  - The National Center on Health, Physical Activity and Disability (NCHPAD) encourages physicians to pledge to talk to their patients about physical activity. Physicians can offer prescriptions for activities like water aerobics, walking, and yoga, and they can write their recommendations on a prescription pad.
- Ask about barriers to participation. Listen for physical or emotional barriers.
- Follow up on conversations from prior visits using notes in the patient's chart.
- Ask if the person has any questions about a physical activity or wants more recommendations.
- It is important for the medical doctor to take the lead, but due to limited time to see people in the office, a different member of the doctor's team may be responsible for referring the person to resources or people.

All in all, individuals with disabilities are encouraged to share information about physical activity engagement when attending medical appointments with their primary care physician. Also communicate this information to medical specialists like orthopedics and neurology. They can use pointed questions such as "How long should I walk?" This information is often entered into the follow-up notes from the appointment that are shared with the patient that day. This approach keeps the medical personnel in the loop about physical activity and encourages discussion (even if it is just social) about being physically active.

Choosing health includes connecting to a community of activity where others are similarly engaged, such as in relationship status, occupation, or activities. The opposite of engagement is isolation (Erikson et al., 1994). Isolation is not to be confused with an introversion, in which a person chooses to have connections but chooses them in ways that match their interests with fewer social engagements and commitments (King & Mason, 2020; Sahono et al., 2020).

Starting or Maintaining Physical Activity   Physical activity choices often change by age 40 and then continue changing through middle age. Some people choose more health-related physical activity, others drift away and still others are abruptly reminded that their health is at stake and requires physical activity. For those faced with a sudden need to be physically active, starting and maintaining a physical activity program in middle age has benefits for their health. Researchers have reported that physical activity engagement helps to reduce the effects of declines in health related to illnesses, and this engagement need not be extreme. Emphasized is that physical activity (PA) engagement

> . . . reduced [the] risk of cardiovascular disease (CVD), including reductions in coronary heart disease, stroke, hypertension, and heart failure. PA . . . increase[s] capacity for activities of daily living, and enhance[s] regulation of physiological systems. . . . The preponderance of evidence suggests that PA need not be high-intensity exercise to produce health benefits but that maintenance of PA is critical . . .

Emory et. al., (2022, p. 379).

These declines are often experienced in middle age and older. An older gentlemen encountered an extended hospital stay for complications of the heart and pulmonary function. "I thought I'd just come home and go back to my life. It hasn't turned out that way." On the other hand, muscle is quick to build in middle age and older, and the heart is a muscle (Oliver, 2021). Physical activity engagement is a strong deterrent for cardiovascular disease.

Lear and colleagues from around the world reported that:

> Higher recreational and non-recreational physical activity was associated with a lower risk of mortality and cardiovascular disease events in individuals from low-income, middle-income, and high-income countries. Increasing physical activity is a simple, widely applicable, low-cost global strategy that could reduce deaths and cardiovascular disease in middle age.

Lear et al. (2017, p. 2,643).

To obtain these findings, researchers enrolled 130,000 participants to determine if there was a difference in cardiovascular disease for poor people who engage in physical activity out of necessity versus people from higher income countries who engage in physical activity as recreation. Along a continuum from lower income to higher income, all benefited from engagement in physical activity, no matter the type, and prevented or significantly lowered cardiovascular disease incidents.

Chapters 14 and 15 address adapted physical activity for health-related fitness and leisure, which fit this age group well.

Physical Literacy   Promoting physical literacy with adults with disabilities, and particularly older adults with disabilities, could benefit from teaching approaches used in adult education. Adult education acknowledges the autonomy of the individual in decision making. This is stressed in the literature on successful aging and is emphasized in our discussions of successfully engaging in physical activity in older age. In physical activity promotions, while instructing classes, and in health care settings and community agencies serving adults with disabilities, attention must be paid to what we say, both in the printed word *and* in our dialogues. Our words should

- motivate adults with disabilities to participate in physical activity,
- provide positive feedback,
- inspire confidence in being physically active,
- provide positive feedback about seeing them again in classes,
- place overall value on physical activity's place in life enough to make a commitment to a lifetime of engagement, and
- emphasize to participants that exercise is for today as they build strong bodies for their life. Focus on the present time and enjoying their physically active life now!

Pushkarenko and colleagues recently argued that application of physical literacy as inclusion has been weak regarding those experiencing disabilities despite a long history of believing that it was in place (2021). Instead, individuals with disabilities are learning that their body is less than the body without disability, and through adaptations they are fitting into an able-bodied society. No doubt, the future holds exciting debates on this. Indeed, physical literacy has been described as a narrative that needs a definition in its "grand promises of physically literate citizens" (Quennerstedt et al., 2021). These academics hope for better dialogue to establish ". . . what physical literacy reasonably can be held accountable for" (p. 846), meaning that physical literacy for those with disabilities is still unfolding.

Older Adults and Disability

Older adults, age 65 years and older, both with and without disability, engage in less physical activity than young adults. This is one very important reason to group by age sets when discussing aging and physical activity. With advancing age, structural and functional deterioration occurs in most physiological systems, even in the absence of discernable disease (ACSM, 2009; Cunningham et al., 2020). Aging can also affect activities of daily living and the preservation of physical independence; changing body composition has profound effects on health and physical function among older adults with and without disabilities; and there is increased chronic disease risk (ACSM, 2009; Cunningham et al., 2020; Rimmer & Lai, 2017; USDHHS, 2005). Chronic fatigue and pain have been the most deleterious effect associated with adults aging with disabilities (Molton et al., 2014). The components of the aging process include (1) the primary aging (cellular aging) process, (2) secondary aging—resulting from chronic disease and lifestyle behaviors, and (3) genetic factors (ACSM, 2009). It appears that the secondary aging component can be modified through physical activity engagement to decrease the deleterious effects of aging and chronic disease risk. The developmental life course indicates that for individuals without disabilities in their younger years, significant disability tends to develop late in life (ages 65 and over), and for individuals with disabilities prior to the elder years, onset of disability is typically in the first four decades (Molton & Yorkston, 2016).

The Centers for Disease Control and Prevention reports that 6 in 10 adults have a chronic disease and 4 in 10 have two chronic diseases (e.g., heart disease, lung disease, diabetes), which makes adults the largest portion of the populations with disabilities (2022). The cumulative effects of living with a disability condition for many years contribute to premature declines in health that can include early onset of chronic medical comorbidities and secondary conditions (Molton & Yorkston, 2017; Rimmer, 2015; USDHHS, 2018). For those aging with a disability, the complex interaction of the medical and social factors and their timing and impact in the developmental life course create an especially challenging environment for successful aging (Molton & Yorkston, 2017; Rimmer & Lai, 2017).

Molton and Yorkston (2017) held focus groups of older adults with disabilities to talk about successful aging. The researchers were able to come up with four themes related to successful aging for adults with disabilities: (1) resilience and adaptation, (2) autonomy, (3) social connectedness, and (4) physical health. *Clearly there is overlap in successful aging for those with and without disabilities.* What differs is the access to a means for achieving the goals. People with disabilities struggle. Larger societal changes are required, as well as establishing changes at the local neighborhood, family, and individual levels.

Older Adults Aging

The American College of Sports Medicine position stand on exercise and physical activity for older adults (2009) provided elements for successful aging in populations. These elements include the following:

- *Exercising regularly:* This is espoused in the *Physical Activity Guidelines for Americans, Second Edition* (2018).

- *Maintaining a social network:* A social network positively influences our behavior and physical health. Yang and colleagues found a dose-related response whereby a higher degree of social integration was directly associated with lower physiological dysregulation later in life (2016).

- *Maintaining a positive mental attitude:* This staves off the impact of the trend toward an exercise-aging cycle where less physical activity engagement results in poor physiological health and increased psychological distress (i.e., depression).

According to later opinions in chapter 14, an understanding of aging is that everyone ages with disability.

Engagement in adapted physical activity crosses many of the elements that support successful aging for people with disabilities. This includes the following:

1. *Resilience and adaptation:* This refers to emotional mastery and the avoidance of negative chronic mood states. National efforts are needed to ensure those without disabilities understand that populations with disabilities can lead long, healthy, and productive lives (USDHHS, 2005). Educational and rehabilitation service providers can utilize person-first language when interacting with populations with disabilities and their respective families (or designated care provider when appropriate).

   ○ *Adapted physical activity:* Engaging in physical exercise does increase a positive mood state. Engaging regularly in physical activity adds significantly to better physical health outcomes. Listen to what the individual wants to participate in given the choices in the community and find it, offer it, or advocate for it. Recognize that interests change, seasons change. Be proactive by reflecting that the seasons are going to change and maybe the interests or offerings will change. New friends met through physical activity classes might influence interests, too.

   ○ *Person-first language:* Use the person's name before any disability. If there is no need to identify a disability, then do not include it. Examples include the following statements:

     - "John, you were at the Special Olympics track day."

     - "Azizah, did you know there is a hike on Saturday?"

     - "I like your red tennis shoes, Mark!"

     - "Scott, are you headed to the Paralympics this year?"

2. *Autonomy:* This is the ability to maintain a sense of personal agency, self-efficacy, and choice as one ages. For aging populations with disabilities, there are usually minimum program offerings to choose from that align with their abilities. More opportunities need to be made available so they can promote their own good health by developing and maintaining healthy lifestyles (Rimmer & Lai, 2017; USDHHS, 2005, 2018). More research and outreach are needed to identify and support effective health promotion programs for persons with disabilities (Agiovlasitis et al., 2018; Rimmer & Lai, 2017; USDHHS, 2005, 2018).

   ○ *Adapted physical activity:* When assembling the choices for exercising in a community, attempt to include as broad an array of activity as possible. If that would be confusing for an individual, at least provide a few choices. Be sensitive to times that work well for the individual and cross that with times known for class offerings. Does the Parkinson's disease exercise class meet at 10:00 a.m., and is there another offering at 1:00 p.m.?

   ○ *Positive feedback:* To increase motivation, if that is a concern, or to sustain participation or give positive feedback about participation in physical activity. Attempt to be specific. For example, you might say, "Gramma, I love hearing about your exercise class. What did you like doing today?"

3. *Social connectedness:* Availability of support or assistance from a variety of sources. Along with friends, family, and social support groups (e.g., those that are disability specific), populations with disabilities view the personal connections with educational and rehabilitation services providers as an integral value-added component to their health and wellness.

   ○ *Adapted physical activity:* In the course of providing health care, continue to ask about physical activity and share interests back and forth. While staying professional, it is appropriate to let your clients know that you, too, are physically active. If you are helping them with positions or duration of exercises, use metaphors from physical activity or the client's personal life as you know it. Examples include: "Hello, Anne. Did you watch any of the Olympics?" or "Put your foot down here like you are beginning to waltz."

   ○ *Use of personal names:* When leading adapted physical activities, build into the program the use of people's names to personalize the experience for participants and to allow others to get to know each other's names. Encourage socialization before and after class if possible. Wander over to early arrival groupings or chat with late departers. These social connections are vital to health.

4. *Physical health:* This includes maintenance of current physical health and access to appropriate healthcare. Aging adults with disabilities acknowledged that managing secondary health conditions requires access to appropriate health care resources. Educational and rehabilitation

service providers need to relate to persons with disabilities in ways that recognize their value, dignity, and capabilities, whether communicating in person, electronically, or in writing (USDHHS, 2005). Advance accountability by all educational and rehabilitation service delivery programs, including clinical and community preventive services, to ensure that persons with disabilities have full access to their services (Rimmer & Lai, 2017; USDHHS, 2005).

○ *Adapted physical activity:* As managers of physical activity programs for older adults with disabilities, greet staff with respect and ensure that they are respecting the scope of ability in a given class. Many physical activity leaders or teachers can offer on-the-spot adaptations to an exercise, making it normal to do so—for example, "If this position is too much, then . . . the arms can go to here, or to here; the leg can cross here, or here. You can hold onto the chair as you stand here if you need to." This is very common in an exercise class for older adults. The participants appreciate the adaptations and can then pace themselves and experience the gradual increase in strength, endurance, and balance.

○ *Clearly labeled programs:* Classes that are clearly labeled in the program offerings by qualification can be offered. Examples include: low-impact aerobics, gentle stretches, chair yoga. Most older adults are sensitive to pounding with the legs on the floor, as their arthritis doesn't allow for that activity without causing pain in the knees or hips. Agencies often give catchy, descriptive names to these programs, allowing the participant to match their ability to the class. Participants can ask their health care provider about a specific class to determine if they should enroll and if there are adaptations for them. The health care provider may not know all that is going on in the community, but given a description, they can usually determine if this program will be enjoyable for the individual and will match their capacities.

Older adults may have additional factors that keep them from being physically active, like transportation, fear of injury, cost of programs, lack of reasonable accommodations, and difficulty getting physically into a facility (CDC, 2020). To address this, fitness and wellness centers should list in the program bus stops near the facility, encourage participants to call and talk to the instructor with questions or concerns, and describe the background of the instructor with expertise for leading this class for seniors. Also, health care providers can reassure the participant that they can talk about their concerns for the class or activity involvement. Most agencies and programs also list sliding fees or connections to physical activity programs like Silver Sneakers or Silver and Fit, associated with Medicare supplemental health insurance, which has cooperating facilities that offer the programs for free at a particular facility for specific classes.

In closing this section on adults in adapted physical activity, there is much more information in part III on sports, fitness, and leisure for adults with disabilities. In subsequent chapters we concentrate on very young children to high school students with detailed information on how to teach these populations adapted physical activity and physical activity (chapter 5) and how to assess skills for physical activity (chapter 6). There is also specific information by category of disability (IDEA 2004) on engaging these young individuals in physical activity (chapters 7 through 13).

Summary

This chapter addresses a lifetime of engagement in adapted physical activity for individuals with disabilities and identifies the professionals that work together for successful adapted physical activity to take place. Research has identified enjoyment as critical to engaging and sustaining an individual in physical activity. Table 4.1 elaborates this reality to be applied to adapted physical activity. From the beginning of life, a cadre of professionals apply interdisciplinary interventions to increase age-appropriate physical activity. When required, the curriculum might need to be modified or the activity itself adapted. The professional language for working with very young infants and toddlers differs from school-age children and youth. For children in school, the appropriate approach in programming is carried out recognizing the individual's chronological age and using it to select program content that is taught considering the developmental age. With adults, a new approach to aging recognizes that adults living with disabilities acquired in early childhood are aging *with* disability and those who acquired disabilities around middle age or older are aging *into* disability. This distinction is important for the practitioner to understand and thus is important to enable a more successful engagement in adapted physical activity for the individual.

PART II

Adapted Physical Activity in Schools

CHAPTER 5

Instructional Strategies

CHAPTER OBJECTIVES

After completing this chapter, you will be able to do the following:

- Examine the ecological theory of Bronfenbrenner and its usefulness in adapted physical activity assessment and instruction.
- Explain developmental systems theory (DST) and life course health development theory and how, if applied to physical activity engagement, it can engage those whose lives are seemingly lost in society.
- Describe the universal design for learning in physical education (UDL in PE) and its effect on inclusion in general physical education programs.
- Explain how using goal setting can aid a student with a disability when trying to boost self-esteem and motivation.
- Describe the direct and indirect methods of teaching and their application for students with disabilities in physical education.
- Explain the necessity of culturally responsive respect when teaching.
- Recognize the value of task analysis, as well as ecological task analysis and peer tutors, in teaching physical education to students with disabilities.
- Understand the need for verbal, visual, and kinesthetic instructional strategies when teaching physical education for students with disabilities.
- Describe the hierarchy of cues used in instruction.
- Describe how behavior management is implemented in a class to effectively assist a particular student.

Teachers know that learning specific games like goalball and tennis will not take place for a student if only the space and equipment are available without guidance. More broadly, it doesn't work to stand them in a stadium, place them in a pool, lean them on the goalposts, place the baby on the floor, have the ice skates on, the boogie board drifting at the water's edge, or the racket in hand. All this is limited if the desired outcome is a game or activity participation or to progressively learn a movement skill. The teachers have to engage the student, select materials for the activity, know the student, design instruction, and evaluate progress. The professional goal in physical education is an active, healthy person who has choices and interests to pursue in physical activity (SHAPE America, n.d.).

Successfully engaging the student in adapted physical activity requires physical educators, adapted physical educators, school allied health professionals, parents, and others to work together during the school years from preschool through 12th grade. It requires the successful writing and implementation of the individualized education programs (IEPs) mandated by federal education law. It also requires the general physical educator (GPE) to apply universal design for learning (UDL) to their age-grade curriculum, modifying that curriculum so all the students can participate (Lieberman et al., 2021). It requires the ongoing evaluation of progress on IEPs and overall physical education programming. These evaluations point the way to the flexibility required today to educate for the student's present-day physically active life. This is a hope that early in life, good teaching will reap enormous benefits as that student's life in physical activity unfolds.

Heavily researched understanding in human development supports that a positive home and appropriate parenting have a positive and profound effect on the domains of development in the present and is also a hope for the future positive development as life unfolds (e.g., Baker & Mott, 1992; Guttentag, et al., 2014; Rogers et al., 1991). The hope is that powerful known variables supported in early life produce future positive life experiences. Knowing oneself in physical activity is certainly a lifesaver in adulthood. For example, there is the father who returns to competitive tennis after his teenage son dies of cancer; the medical student who continues running marathons during arduous years of study; and the woman with autism spectrum disorder describing the utter joy of ice skating alone while trying to handle adult life. In these scenarios, professionals have instructed young children and youth with the realization that the many rewards of a physically active life abound into adulthood.

This chapter addresses the best practice in instructional strategies for educating individuals with disabilities in physical activity in the school setting. These instructional strategies are then exemplified by specific disability categories of children and youth in chapters 7 through 12. As outlined in chapter 3, federal educational law IDEA (2004) lays out the legal mandate to serve these children and youth. Theory guides research, which guides what we know and what is embedded in the services provided. Theory and its resulting theoretical framework guide us into best practice. Theory has directed us to solve problems in gaining access to physically active lives. This chapter begins with theories and frameworks to guide instructional approaches and then moves to style and techniques.

Ecological Theory

We must understand the full person—all the different aspects of the individual—to understand how to engage them successfully in physical activity. In child development, Uri Bronfenbrenner's theory is well known and well employed. Most assessment tools of early childhood are based on his ecological theory. Problem-solving on lagging development in early childhood is typically based on this theoretical approach. It is not esoteric. It is practical and very helpful.

Bronfenbrenner's ecological theory of development in context (Bronfenbrenner, 1977; Bronfenbrenner & Morris, 2006) resonates in current issues of identity, inclusion, and diversity of the unique child. There are multiple reasons why a child with a disability can struggle in the home and community, in the gymnasium, on the athletic field, in the swimming pool, and on the neighborhood playground. Risk factors for positive development affect why children are not doing well in these environments. Using Bronfenbrenner's theory, we examine the child's development in context. Laid out are specific variables to explore, beginning with a child's unique primary dyad (e.g., mother–child) and widening out to her community, state, and nation, which are all known to influence development (figure 5.1). It is within these ecological contexts that we best understand how this person is growing or why they are faltering. Is their mother depressed? Is their neighborhood unsafe for play outside? Has the state cancelled physical education in the schools?

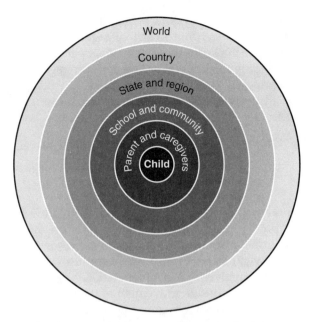

FIGURE 5.1 Bronfenbrenner's ecological theory of development with the child at the center and identified variables known to influence their physically active lives.

Adapted from Bronfenbrenner (1977); Bronfenbrenner and Morris (2006).

Developmental Systems Theory

Developmental systems theory (DST) is currently used by professionals in the human sciences to help understand how people *of all ages calibrate and do well with enormous changes* (Lerner, 2005). It is a theory about systems. DST grew out of the study of resilience in child development, begun in the 1970s, reporting on children in dire life circumstances whose lives resulted in positive developmental trajectories versus the expected negative ones (Masten, 2015). Ann Masten, a recognized scholar in resilience, explains:

> Resilience is defined as the capacity of a system to adapt successfully to challenges that threaten the function, survival, or future development of the system. This definition is scalable across system levels and across disciplines, applicable to resilience in a person, a family, a health care system, a community, an economy, or other systems.

Masten (2015, p. 18).

DST has been used across the systems of education and health science. At Harvard's Center for the Developing Child, Shonkoff and his colleagues are not satisfied reporting solely on the main effects of an intervention study on young children's development (2021). They go beyond asking questions about why intervention A was statistically more significant than intervention B. They urge and provide models for a more intricate analysis of multiple systems influencing a child's life, finding subgroups of children who did better or worse.

An example of the positive effects of DST-based research in physical activity comes from Donohue and colleagues (2020)) as they turned their attention to youth drug abuse in low-income neighborhoods in a U.S. city involving youth whose lives are difficult if not disastrous. They asked, "How can these youth be reached?" and "How can their lives be improved?" Going to where the youth were hanging out, the intervention was formed by sport participation and discussion groups offered in their community at places like the YMCA. Young men, in turn, selected any number of others (friends or relatives) and showed up. Together they discussed how to make their lives better and identified goals and attainment strategies. Using DST as a theoretical approach, with basketball and discussion, the researchers reported success in getting the young people out of a drug-abusing life.

Life Course Health Development

Life course health development is a framework (Halfon & Forrest, 2018, Halfon & Hochstein, 2002) for the study of development across a life span examining what leads to optimal health. Although stated in simplistic terms here, this framework is applied at points across the unfolding life span, *recognizing a complexity at a specific timing in biological development*. On the one hand, the framework was used to study the policy effects of paid family leave that resulted in unintended detrimental effects on some families (Halfon & Hochstein, 2002). On the other hand, Hirschfeld and colleagues (2021) used the life course health development framework in developing the PRISM health measurement model precisely because measuring health in children is complex. PRISM is the title the researchers gave to their way of viewing into "four fundamental dimensions of health measurement—Potential, Adaptability, Performance, and Experience" (p. 1).

In developing the PRISM health measurement model, the researchers communicated that

> Health is a multidimensional concept that is challenging to measure, and . . . requires a dynamic approach to accurately capture the transitions, and overall arc of a complex process of internal and external interactions . . .
>
> The process of child development is often viewed as the outcome of an orderly series of changes in structure and function. In recent years, with development of the field of neuroscience, biomedical and psychological developmental research has become much more integrated. However, these fields focus on individual level processes. Although individually focused, Bronfenbrenner's highly influential bioecological model of human development broadens our perspective to include the multiple types of contexts and levels of environmental influences by situating the child in his/her social contexts . . .
>
> Hirschfeld et al. (2021, pp. 1, 2).

In the field of kinesiology, applying DST theory and a life course health development framework to assessment and intervention recognizes that the movement performance is not only dependent on the unique person with a disability but also on the uniqueness of their family (e.g., privileged, homeless, immigrant, food scarcity) and their neighborhood (e.g., it has gangs or it is isolated or rural). In addition, this process can account for those influences from infancy through high school, to all stages of adulthood, including a physically active life in their community.

These perspectives produce findings for use in providing adapted physical activity. They reach across disciplines because they must. Adapted physical activity engagement across the life span is no longer always a question of "Did Mark catch the ball or not?" or "Did Henry attend his Parkinson's bicycle class or not?" Although these are important questions to ask and have an important place in the delivery of service, we cannot stop here. Today, the practitioner can tell you Mark cannot catch a ball because he has had little practice doing this (he is

a unique individual) and his family doesn't have the means to get him to school regularly. Today, across the life span, these theoretical perspectives are guiding the understanding of the engagement in a physically active life, from infancy to old age, for all individuals and especially for those with disability.

Universal Design for Learning

Universal design for learning (UDL) is new to adapted physical activity. It expands on modifications and adaptations for one person in a class or clinical setting. It then applies them to the entire activity environment. UDL grew out of the universal design movement at the time of the implementation of the Americans With Disabilities Act of 1990.

Universal design had its beginnings in the removal of architectural barriers so people with disabilities could enter public buildings or buildings receiving public support, such as a library on a university campus (Kennedy & Yun, 2019). In New England, the Center for Applied Special Technology (CAST) was formed to apply universal design to education, later termed universal design for learning (UDL). UDL is a theoretical framework to assist in the design and ongoing development of curriculum—that includes *all* students in the learning environments using materials in flexible ways that offer options for all learners to comprehend information, demonstrate their knowledge and skills, and be motivated to learn (Hall et al., 2012; Meyer et al., 2014; Pisha & Coyne, 2001; Rogers-Shaw et. al., 2018).

Using a simple metaphor is helpful here: if the library is accessible, then the books and the instructions need to be accessible too. If the school buildings are accessible, then the programs offered inside need to be accessible for all.

Rich instructional supports include materials, methods, and environments for all students (CAST, 2000) in UDL, and this work has been applied to both educational and clinical settings. Within the education setting, the term universal design in physical education (UDL in PE) has been used (Lieberman et al., 2021). Lieberman explains that "UDL is embedded ahead of time into the lesson throughout, AND the variations in instruction (multiple means of representation), motivation (multiple means of engagement), and assessment (multiple means of action and expression) are for every child." (Personal communication, October 25, 2021). This is a new support for all learners being applied around the world.

This framework is reaching into physical education (Lieberman et al., 2021). NCHPAD, in conjunction with the National Consortium of Physical Education for Individuals with Disabilities (NCHPAD and NCPEID, n.d.), prepared an interactive infographic containing the three main principles of the UDL framework and applications using UDL in PE:

1. *Engagement:* To stimulate interest and motivation for students to learn in a variety of ways. *Example:* Music is inviting as it plays when the students enter the gymnasium.

2. *Representation:* To present material in multiple formats so all students can engage. *Example:* Selecting across audio, visual, and kinesthetic instruction as supports to engage students in the class.

3. *Expression:* Allow for a variety of ways and means for students to express their learning. *Example:* All students are assessed according to both their abilities and skills; not just one is used in assessments.

NCHPAD/NCPEID provides a free tool kit on UDL in PE on its website.

The instructional strategies found in UDL in PE are familiar to adapted physical education, such as task analysis, systematic use of verbal instruction, and physical modeling; and within class, choice of equipment to fit student ability. It also points to being culturally sensitive. According to Lieberman and colleagues, these learning strategies in the UDL in PE framework are efficient for all students with and without disabilities (2021). This is exactly why it is so valuable to adapted physical education. With the UDL framework, the general physical education program is set up to instruct many more learners than ever before, in ways known to support students with IEPs. We predict that students with IEPs will come into these physical education programs more effectively included.

General physical educators can use UDL in PE to have curricula meet the students' needs even before they enter the program (Kennedy & Yun, 2019). Instead of changing the curriculum for a student's inclusion in a physical education class, the curriculum is already designed proactively, in many ways, for variability in student learning. The application of this framework does justice to the general physical education curriculum when those educators include students with disabilities in the planning for their programs. This means that teachers determine the goals for their program and goals for the students ahead of classes. Next, they

incorporate UDL's flexibility in every aspect of the learning (e.g., flexibility in assessment). Future research will provide practitioners in both general and adapted physical education with continued guidance.

Motivation and Disability

Various theoretical concepts exist as the basis for ways to motivate behavior. The theories do overlap, so that it is possible to utilize styles advocated by different theories in combination to produce the best results in motivating the learner. Also, certain concepts of various theoretical bases appear to be more effective in motivating some individuals than do others.

Humanism and Behaviorism

The theories of humanism and behaviorism are the two theories most utilized by educators. Basic to the humanistic approach is that a reasoning process is evoked in the learners so that they arrive at decisions that are best for themselves, as individuals and for the society in which they live. Then they act upon the decisions accordingly. Intrinsic rewards rather than extrinsic ones are used to motivate and reinforce learning.

The *behavioristic approach* emphasizes extrinsic rewards and relies primarily on manipulation of the external environment to produce the desired behavior (Schellenberg, 1978; Skinner, 1976). In theory, there is more concern for the outcome than how the outcome is achieved. B.F. Skinner conducted experiments in the application of behaviorism and is commonly associated with the popular use of behaviorism in education today. According to Delprato and Midgley (1992), Skinner believed that "Behavior is what an organism is doing" (Skinner, 1938, p. 6) and that this can be determined in observation within an environment. He claimed that "properly used behaviorism is very powerful" (Skinner Quotes, n.d.) He emphasized positive reinforcement to shape behavior, which remained a powerful teaching tool.

Researchers have found the use of extrinsic rewards to be very effective in producing desired behavior in those with intellectual disabilities and with behavioral disabilities. However, the preponderance of research indicates that although extrinsic rewards can be quite effective in altering behavior temporarily in a controlled setting, such rewards are less influential in effecting changes of a permanent nature outside the nonreinforcing

environment. This is one of the reasons to fade the reinforcement. Fading allows for a gradual removal of the reinforcer or even a change in reinforcement that is more cumulative.

Goal Setting

For decades, child psychologists at a popular interdisciplinary outpatient clinic in Portland, Oregon, has successfully trained children who are highly active and impulsive to set goals. They also train their parents to support their child in goal setting. Training in this skill increases the child's success in school, at home, and in the community. Most importantly, the child has a skill that lends itself to control in their day. Of course, this is one of many skills the children learn in the class, but it is critical to gaining self-esteem and control.

Children need help in analyzing their abilities to determine their possible level of achievement. Yet, in the Oregon clinic setting discussed in the previous paragraph, the children first select their level of achievement. Then they try the skill. Next, they are asked if they came close or not. If they didn't or if they came close . . . what is their next goal? (Trying again.) This is a gamelike approach to goal setting for those who can manage the concepts.

This can also be applied to a whole class. For example, a gym teacher might ask, "How many seconds will it take our class to put the balls back in the gym bag [or other container]? Take two guesses, one from all those who have on blue pants and the other from those who have on a different color of pants." The teacher writes the numbers where they can be seen, then says, "Ready, set, *go!*" Then the students pick up the balls and put them in the container. The gym teacher runs the stopwatch to monitor the time. When the students are done, they kneel on one knee. The teacher announces the time and determines who came the closest to the goal. The objective here isn't to be the fastest but to correctly estimate how long it will take their class to put the balls away, given their composition of students, with the way the balls are spread out, and so on. At the end of the next class, they try this again. If there is a constant group effort to set these goals, and it is fun, then individuals can be gradually introduced to their own goal setting for other class purposes.

Repeating these activities in playlike ways gets the students out of competition with themselves, or others, into a clearer understanding of what a group of students can do. Psychologically, it also transfers the notion of the teacher setting the goal to the student-to-student engagement in their class and taking responsibility.

Instructional Style

Teaching is an art. A teaching style is used by the teacher to help the student understand and apply the learning content (Goldberger et al., 2012). The best style is the one that matches the teacher's skills and preferences, the content, the learners, and the environment. In physical education, selected styles are (Collier, 2017):

Direct Teacher Involvement

- *Command:* The teacher directly makes all the decisions.
- *Practice: The teacher provides individual feedback at a given student's individual practice.*
- *Reciprocate:* Partners provide feedback to each other. The criteria are set by teacher.
- *Self-check:* The student checks task accomplishments. The criteria are set by the teacher.

Indirect Teacher Role

- *Guided discovery:* Given an experience, students answer a question proposed by the teacher.
- *Divergent discovery:* Students discover multiple answers to a single question.

In actual practice, many physical education teachers combine the traditional direct style of teaching and the indirect problem-solving style. It unites the best of each style and permits flexibility so that the teacher can choose the style best suited to a specific student or their class.

A synthesis of the two styles is likely to be more effective in helping students to achieve the objectives of the program than the exclusive use of either style. It allows students to be creative and experimental. But if, at any time, the teacher senses a lack of security among the students with the problem-solving style or confusion arising from failure to solve the motor task, the instructor can shift to a more direct approach. According to Goldberger and colleagues, Mosston

> . . . believed each style to contribute in its unique ways. He never envisioned individual styles in opposition with each other. Rather, he viewed the styles as complimentary [sic] to one another. . . . teachers rarely, if ever, use the same teaching style all day.
>
> Goldberger et al. (2012, pp. 272, 275).

In the direct style, the teacher selects the activity or skill to be learned and instructs the students by describing the skill using evidenced-based, best-practice instructional strategies.

In the indirect teaching style, the learning experiences are mediated by the student (Mosston & Ashworth, 2002). Examples of some of indirect teaching styles are as follows (Collier, 2017; Roth et al., 2016):

- In *convergent discovery*, the student mediates this line of learning given higher level demands of a physical activity. Having learned how to kick a soccer ball under a direct learning style, the student then learns skills for planning strategies for the game of soccer. For example, how to attack the goal with teammates requires higher level skills. *Converge* means to bring together. This is what this teaching approach does when it potentially allows the students to explore how the surge to the goal will occur. Some teachers, of course, will want to directly teach these team plays, and if so, they should do so. But if they are inclined to allow the team some options and exploration, then this is an indirect teaching style.

- In *guided discovery*, the teacher poses questions for the student to solve in the physical activity class. How many ways can you go through the doorway? Can you make yourself go fast like an airplane? Can you and a friend hop to the door? This is often referred to as movement exploration.

- For *reciprocal style*, the teacher sets up the activity including identifying what is considered success, and the students are partnered with a learning buddy. Here the partners give each other feedback. Learning buddies for the whole class allow everyone to participate using a buddy, including the student with a disability. Peer tutors are named as such in the professional literature.

Instructional Techniques

Techniques of teaching may be defined as ways the teacher handles instructional problems efficiently and deals effectively with the varied responses of different children. Teaching techniques used by physical education teachers are of three general types: verbalization, visualization, and kinesthesis. *Any of the techniques may be used with any style of teaching.* Before examining how they are used with a specific teaching style, the various techniques will be described to provide the background necessary for understanding the use of the terms in the later discussion.

Differentiated Instruction

One of the hallmarks of special education and adapted physical education and activity is to address the differences the children might have in their ability to learn in the general education program and instruct them in a child-centered way to enable learning. Child-centered learning is beginning instruction where the child is achieving and building new learning from there. It takes the expertise of a team of people (IEP or individualized family service plan team) to assess and determine where, to the best of their knowledge, the student is achieving. Depending on how the team understands the assessments, the modifications to a school's curriculum and the adaptations to the activities can begin. All this specialization points to differentiated instruction. It is solidly based in assessment, inclusive of understanding the total student, not just the student's physical skills (in the case of physical education) but their unique cognitive, social-emotional, and affective traits.

In the meeting on the IEP or IFSP, there are broad goals spelled out by the team. A placement is determined throughout that academic year's physical education curriculum with attention to the appropriateness of activities in a gym, swimming pool, bowling alley, track, baseball field, or other locations. It is here that ongoing observation on performance continues, and the instruction's flexibility is apparent. Comments such as these arise: "Kathleen is progressing in the swim unit"; "Linus is moving well through his soccer unit with his peer tutor in place"; "Mykara is catching up on her developmental lag when we offer her choices of age-appropriate physical activity"; and "Moses loves being outside playing and he struggles to stay on tasks inside. What do we need to consider for him?"

Culturally Responsive Teaching

Sociocultural diversity is receiving attention in vast platforms across the country. There is a call to issues of diversity as it relates to race, ethnicity, gender, sexual orientation, religious affiliation, disability status, social class, culture, and other aspects of sociocultural life (Fuentes et al., 2021). Refer to our sidebar.

There is ample reason to know that as teachers of physical education, whether adapted or general, our students come from multicultural backgrounds, speak many languages, or have life experiences that may differ from most PE teachers. In the United States, the race of PE teachers is predominantly White (71 percent), followed by Asian (10 percent) and African or Black (10 percent) (U.S. Bureau of Labor Statistics and U.S. Census Bureau, 2021).

Social justice pedagogies in physical education are advocated in physical education training to assist in preparing teachers to identify and combat inequity in schools (Hodge et al., 2017). Chubbuck and colleagues (Chubbuck, 2010; Chubbuck & Zembylas, 2016) define *socially just teaching* as action to improve learning opportunities in "curricula, pedagogies, teacher expectations and interactional styles" (p. 6) for each student. They advocate for the transformation of educational structures or policies that are unjust and thus diminish students' learning.

Selected guidelines for creating high-quality and socially just physical education programs (Hodge et al., 2017) include the following:

- Listen to your students with disabilities to understand their messages.
- Examine your own beliefs about students with disabilities. Measure how these will affect your interactions and expectations.
- Become culturally competent by understanding your students' interaction styles, norms, customs, traditions, foods, and dominant language spoken at home.
- Learn and pronounce students' names accurately.
- Have a no-tolerance policy for bullying, negative stereotypes, or racist, homophobic, or sexist comments. When any of these happens, reemphasize social responsibility and encourage cooperation and respect.
- Become culturally aware of others and understand that definitions and expectations of student behavior are culturally influenced.
- Understand that diversity is socially constructed.
  - *Ethnicity* refers to the cultural or geographical construction of family ancestries, practices, traditions, and languages (e.g., Irish Americans, Mexican Americans, Asian Americans, African Americans).
  - *Race* is a categorization based on visible biological features. That said, there is an argument in America that this categorization system is invalid. Instead, we are American. *Race logic* makes a link between color of skin and stereotyped behaviors.

Sex and Gender

The term *sex* is used to identify the biology of an individual, and *gender* is the social identity. Johns Hopkins All Children's Hospital describes *sexual orientation* as a process begun as a teenager (2021) that is ambiguous at times, and it advocates respect and support for the youth.

> It can help to talk to someone about the confusing feelings that go with growing up—whether that someone is a parent or other family member, a close friend or sibling, or a school counselor . . . most medical experts understand sexual orientation is not something that a person voluntarily chooses . . . Instead, sexual orientation is just a natural part of who a person is.
>
> Johns Hopkins (2021).

LGBTQ stands for lesbian, gay, bisexual, transgender, and questioning. (Note that there are other variations, with this being the most general.) Johns Hopkins explains that transgender is not a sexual orientation; it is gender identity—what the individual feels they are most comfortable as (Johns Hopkins, 2021). About 5 to 10 percent of the high school population is gay or lesbian, which Hodge and colleagues note matches the society at large (Hodge et al., 2017). Educators must do a self-assessment around these issues and be mindful that their professional role calls for respect in teaching all students.

- In physical education, don't assume student abilities.
- Monitor feedback to equally include boys and girls.

Task Analysis

Skills for physical activity can be taught by presenting the easier components of the activity and then moving to more difficult components. This process is referred to as task analysis, a technique in which the components of an activity are identified and then ordered according to their level of difficulty. Each component can then be further subdivided into smaller instructional units so that a student is taught at a level where they achieve initial success before moving to more advanced levels. Task analysis is an instructional strategy as well as an assessment tool for evaluating progress. Figure 5.2 shows how physical assistance can be used to support the initial learning of the skill of kicking.

Lieberman and Houston-Wilson have promoted rubrics used with task analyses of physical activity that is functional (2018). Functional means the skill relates to everyday life of a student. In assessments for physical education, having to place arms extended out from the shoulders and then alternately bring one in to place a finger to tap on one's nose is a measure of coordination, but it is not functional. There is no time in a child's daily life when they need to perform that skill. Hopping like a bunny is functionally part of young child's play and requires coordination.

Throwing a tennis ball to a target and then picking it up to use it again is part of a game for young children, and therefore it is functional and requires coordination. Task analysis for a stationary kick is presented here, adapted from Lieberman and Houston-Wilson (2009).

Skill: Student Kicks a Stationary Ball

Components: Using a three-step approach, the trunk is inclined backward during contact, there is a forward swing of the opposite arm and follow-through.

- Level 1, with any form
- Level 2, using a three-step approach, walking or running during most kicks
- Level 3, using a three-step approach, the trunk is reclined backward during contact during most kicks
- Level 4, using a three-step approach, the trunk is reclined backward during contact, and there is a forward swing of the opposite arm during most kicks
- Level 5, using a three-step approach, the trunk is reclined backward during contact, and there is a forward swing of the opposite arm during three out of five kicks
- Level 6, using a three-step approach, the trunk is reclined backward during contact, and there is a forward swing of the opposite arm and follow-through, propelling the ball 30 feet

FIGURE 5.2   Task analysis of a skill assists in teaching kicking to a student needing instructional steps.

- Level 7, using a three-step approach, the trunk is reclined backward during contact, and there is a forward swing of the opposite arm and follow-through, propelling the ball 60 feet

Here, in level 3 of the task analysis, there is flexibility if the components need to be further delineated for the student. Perhaps there is a need to substitute a larger or lighter ball than a standard soccer ball.

Alternatively, level 3 might need to be branched by "Using a three-step approach, the trunk is inclined backward during contact, and the student is *running* during most kicks." Then, as the child's speed picks up, the arm will most likely swing in opposition, moving the child to level 4.

In using the instructional strategy of task analysis modification for the game of basketball, one of the examples covers equipment, rules, environment,

and the instruction include (Lieberman & Houston-Wilson, 2009, p. 123):

- *Equipment:* Bright ball, auditory ball, low basket
- *Rules:* No double dribble rule, pass x number of times before a shot is attempted
- *Environment:* Modify court size, use stations
- *Instruction:* Peer tutor; use of verbal cues, demonstration and physical assistance

Skill: Dribbling a Basketball Around Cones and Inactive Defensive Players

Components: The student uses proper form (the student uses fingertips at waist height, with the ball contacting the floor in front of or near the foot on the same side as the dribbling hand) and control (around cones and inactive defensive players).

- Level 1, while dribbling in place, the student uses their fingertips at waist height, with the ball contacting the floor in front of or near foot on the same side as the dribbling hand most of the time.
- Level 2, while walking around eight cones placed five feet apart, with the ball contacting the floor in front of or near the foot on the same side as the dribbling hand most of the time.
- Level 3, with proper form, while walking around eight cones placed five feet apart 50 percent of the time.
- Level 4, with proper form, while jogging around eight cones placed five feet apart 50 percent of the time.
- Level 5, with proper form, while jogging around eight cones placed five feet apart 75 percent of the time.
- Level 6, with proper form, while jogging around eight cones placed five feet apart 50 percent of the time with the dominant hand and 50 percent of the time with the nondominant hand.
- Level 7, with proper form, while jogging around eight stationary defenders placed five feet apart 75 percent of the time with the dominant hand and 50 percent of the time with the nondominant hand.

Branching approaches that might be needed for students:

- Level 4
  - with proper form, while jogging around eight cones placed five feet apart 50 percent of the time.
  - with proper form, while jogging around six cones and two stationary players placed five feet apart 50 percent of the time.
  - with proper form, while jogging around four cones and four stationary players placed five feet apart 50 percent of the time.
- Level 5, with proper form, while jogging around eight cones placed five feet apart 75 percent of the time.
- Level 6
  - with proper form, while jogging around eight cones placed five feet apart 50 percent of the time with the dominant hand

and 50 percent of the time with the nondominant hand.
  - with proper form, while jogging around four cones and four stationary players placed five feet apart 50 percent of the time with the dominant hand and 50 percent of the time with the nondominant hand.
- Level 7, with proper form, while jogging around eight stationary defenders placed five feet apart 75 percent of the time with the dominant hand and 50 percent of the time with the nondominant hand.

The task-analysis approach is an essential instructional strategy to assist teachers creating positive and successful educational experiences. While task analysis continues to be a very effective instructional approach, particularly for individuals with severe disabilities (e.g., Dunn, Morehouse, & Fredericks, 1986), Davis and Burton (1991) cautioned that this approach is not without limitations. They argued that traditional approaches to task analysis focused too much on the task while forgetting about the learner and the environment in which the task is to be performed. This is where ecological task analysis can be a very helpful tool for the physical educator, particularly if more information is needed for instruction to be successful.

Ecological Task Analysis

Building on the work of others, namely Gibson (1979) and Newell (1986), Burton and Davis (1996) offered an approach to task analysis known as an ecological task analysis (ETA). This ecological approach focuses on the environment, the performer, and the task in predicting the movement performance (figure 5.3). Burton and Davis argued that the primary difference between the ETA and task analysis is that in ETA, the wholeness of the skill to be learned is not divided. Instead, the unique characteristics of the environment, the performer, and the task are all considered in a movement performance. With ETA, the correctness of the response is based on the performer's perception of the task, the environment, and his or her personal attributes. In theory, this could mean that whatever the task is, the child who comes to the gymnasium repeatedly upset could be giving her best behavior given the turmoil in the home (her personal attribute) and the loudness of the gym (environment). But the point really is in this case, how can this be a better experience for her not only motorically but also psychologically?

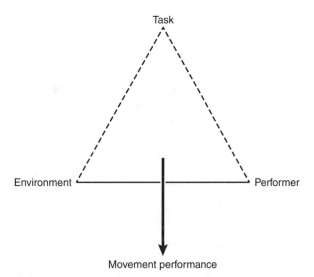

FIGURE 5.3 Ecological task analysis helps analyze the effects of the environment, task, and performer in the movement performance of the student.

Adapted by permission from W.E. Davis and A.W. Burton, "Ecological Task Analysis: Translating Movement Behavior Theory Into Practice," *Adapted Physical Activity Quarterly* 8 (1991): 154-177.

Another example of the scope of ETA application is if an eight-year-old child is playing games and is constantly getting angry and stomping away. Why are they not able to stay in the game? There are many possibilities to explore. Are the tasks in the game ones that they can't perform? Is the environment conducive to her learning? Did something just happen to the child before coming into the gymnasium? As the performer, does the child have any documented vision difficulties? Once we understand some of these questions, the teacher can better help. If observation tells the teacher that the child needs support with the skills, preteaching some skills or providing a peer-tutor might be the answer.

Addressing the variable of the individual performer (the student) is where ETA is poignant in its usefulness to an adapted and general physical educator. Gathering that information is possible initially through the IEP and the individualized family service plan process as all the members contribute. It is appropriate to use objective terms versus subjective terms about a child's participation in physical activity. For example, we could say, "Marcus is full of energy every day and all day. How do we present the directions of the activity to him in the gym?" Problem-solving here at the start of the IEP or individualized family service plan process may be the initial positive experience that sets up rapport, allowing issues to be addressed as the school year progresses.

Cues and Prompts

The instructional strategies referred to as verbalization, visualization, and kinesthesis have been incorporated into a well-recognized use of cues or prompts when working with individuals with disabilities in physical activity. Cues and prompts are used in a hierarchy to enable students to learn skills and develop knowledge in movement performance. The terms *cue* and *prompt* are often used interchangeably in special education. The hierarchy of cues and prompts is as follows from the highest to the lowest level of effective intrusion or demand on the student.

- *Physical:* Tapping a body part (leg) or moving a limb (right hand) or in other ways touching the student to indicate a move in a direction (guiding toward a forward motion)
- *Visual:* Assistive directions with pictures or signs, symbols, gestures
- *Verbal:* Speaking to the student

Through evidenced-based practice, we know that applying a physical prompt is a starting point in learning a physical skill if the student needs assistance. After time passes, the student can learn that movement with a visual prompt, and finally we can use a particular verbal prompt. For example, when we say to a group of young children, "Line up by the wall" and point to the wall, we are using both a verbal and a visual prompt. We know we don't need a physical cue (holding hands with a buddy to the wall) because the students have successfully used the buddy system many times before. Later when the children have accomplished the task with the visual and verbal, we will explore use of the verbal alone, such as "Line up by the door." It may take a while.

Individuals have a preferred method of learning. Some prefer auditory methods, some visual, and some moving or kinesthetic. Many physical educators readily admit that they learn through moving, whereas music teachers are often auditory learners as well as kinesthetic learners. (Both vocalists and instrumentalists learn to move their body for effect when singing or playing.)

Some students have auditory processing difficulties, and therefore auditory methods are not their preferred mode of learning. For them auditory instructions are confusing, and they become lost in the gym. To overcome this, the physical education teacher uses a multimodality approach: verbal, visual and physical instructions. This ensures that the students will have their mode of learning addressed. She might say, "John, Amy, Teresa, and Mark, stand here by me (and blow her whistle in a friendly way, making it a privilege). John, take Amy to the red hoops. Mark, take Teresa to the blue hoops." This has an auditory and visual component in the instructions. (This may not be your style, but you can see how the multiple modes of learning are employed.)

The prompt hierarchy is useful when teaching skills. A student with intellectual disability may learn a skill by seeing a demonstration of the skill (visual) and then listening to *key words* used (verbal) as they are being physically assisted through the movement (kinesthetic).

Verbalization

Verbalization refers to the use of the spoken word in the process of teaching. Describing a skill and explaining the strategy are examples of the use of the technique. For example, in the demonstration of a skill, verbalization is frequently employed to clarify an action or concept. In figure 5.4, the instructor is delivering verbal instructions *at eye level with the student*. She has the child's attention as the instructions are provided. Having the attention of the student is crucial to any instruction, especially for those delivered verbally. Always keep the verbal instructions and feedback simple and short. Typically and atypically developing students will lose attention otherwise.

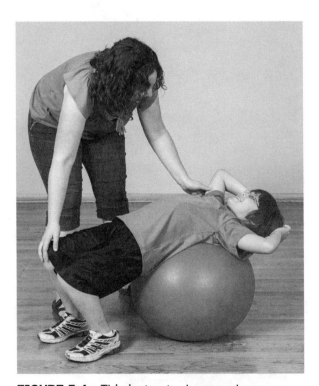

FIGURE 5.4 This instructor has good eye contact with this student as well as the student's attention. This increases the ability of the student to benefit from instructions.

The auditory input helps many students especially when using music to set the tone to start and engage in an activity (such as running with arms out as though flying like airplanes), when learning rhythms, and when using relaxation techniques to finish a particularly rowdy class. Some students have difficulty with loud noises, but that can be mediated. Rhythmic verbal beats are helpful to performance. With a swimming unit, use "One, two, three, *go*," followed by "stroke, stroke, stroke . . ." or, when teaching swinging on a swing, "Push up and back. Push up and back."

Visualization

Visualization is a technique that employs the optical attention of the students. Demonstration is a most effective tool, particularly when used with the traditional style of teaching. An appropriate demonstration in physical activity is one where the skill is modeled In correct form one or more times for the student. The student then attempts to perform the skill by duplicating the movements *observed*. In modeling the skill, the teacher needs to be mindful of where they are standing in relationship to their student. Some demonstrations are best done in front of the student facing the same direction, then moving from side to side.

Besides a demonstration, also included under this general heading of visualizations are films, videos, Internet resources such as YouTube showing skills performed by individuals with disabilities, which are sometimes effective or motivational.

Pictures, posters, and diagrams may be used effectively to illustrate correct skill techniques. Pictures of performers executing the skills are less desirable than ones in which an adapted technique is illustrated, but they are nevertheless extremely useful. Diagrams of plays on the blackboard are used to good advantage in teaching students with disabilities who may be less familiar with the strategy of games. As discussed in chapter 8, students with autism are successfully taught the skill and the schedule for physical education using visual aids, particularly in the form of pictures.

The use of *the printed word* is a technique that has been largely overlooked as an effective teaching tool in physical education but now is taking off with the use of the computer and cell phones. Depending on their reading level, students with disabilities may be assigned to read about a game before the class begins that activity in the PE class. This helps with the terminology and the general performance of the activity. Effective and well-organized teachers can manage to bring additional information to their classes. Worksheets are helpful for some students (see figure 5.5).

Technique	Common errors	My errors and corrections
Grip	Gripping too high on the handle	
Bounce the ball	Bouncing too high or too low to strike the ball	
Strike ball to target on a wall	Allowing the ball to drop too low before striking	
	Swinging racket too early to strike ball	
	Swinging too late to strike the ball	
	Ball does not travel to target area	

FIGURE 5.5   Sample worksheet used for student self-correction in striking a ball with a racket.

Kinesthesis

The use of kinesthesis refers to the involvement of muscular activity in the teaching–learning situation. There are different ways of using kinesthesis as a teaching technique, although it must be taken into consideration that this type of learning has different phases.

When students attempt to perform a skill and must make an adjustment in stance or grip because it does not feel right, they are making use of kinesthesis. Of course, beginners will not know how the correct form feels. In fact, the correct form may feel more awkward than the incorrect. It is only after students begin to associate the desired result with the correct form that they will begin to feel right about their performance.

In a sense, the adjustment that students make when their muscular movements have not achieved satisfactory results is a phase of kinesthesis. Adjusting the serve in table tennis after the ball has fallen short of the net is a learning related to kinesthesis. For some, the eyes tell the player that the serve was no good, but the adjustment in the muscular movement made to perform the skill more accurately is kinesthetic.

Attempts to correct errors to achieve a more satisfactory performance are referred to as *exploratory kinesthesis*. Such exploration is an integral phase of the learning of any new activity and is particularly to be fostered among students who are disabled. This is the reason free time and repeated practice is part of learning a movement skill. Freely making more and more attempts and correcting them can be fun.

Still another area of teaching that employs kinesthesis is that of actually leading the student's hand, arm, or part of the body involved in the activity, through the performance of the skill. This technique

is called *manual kinesthesis* (figure 5.6) and is built into the notion of a physical cue. It is extremely helpful to students who have failed to grasp the fundamentals through visualization or verbalization. With students who have sensory impairments, as in the case of blindness, the technique is invaluable. These students learn by feeling the movements involved in an execution of a task.

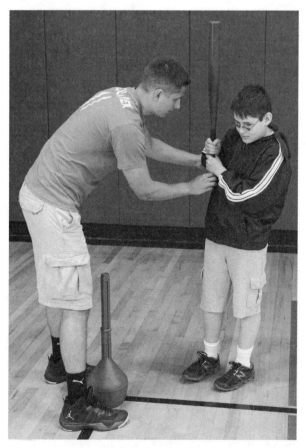

FIGURE 5.6   Manual kinesthesis is helpful as this student learns to hit a ball.

Class-Wide Peer Tutoring

Class-wide peer tutoring (CWPT) has been shown to greatly benefit students in classrooms, as the students direct, teach, and even evaluate their peers in the classroom (Greenwood et al., 2002). "Class wide peer tutoring is a class of instructional strategies wherein students are taught by their peers who have been trained and are supervised by the classroom teacher" (Greenwood, p. 611). The effective use of this approach has extended to physical education settings where Houston-Wilson, Dunn, and colleagues (1997) and Houston-Wilson, Lieberman, and colleagues (1997) found that trained peer tutors were very effective in helping students with developmental disabilities increase their opportunity to respond in physical education. The opportunity to respond is vital to achieving desired learning objectives for students with disabilities. "CWPT is a form of peer-mediated instruction that is reciprocal. CWPT allows students to instruct each other while also practicing certain skills" (Houston-Wilson, Lieberman, et al., 1997, p. 42). The peers must be trained and supervised. In looking at opportunity to respond, trained tutors took turns with their peer with a disability while using the data sheets created by the teacher describing an activity. CWPT was used in a kindergarten class with data collected on two pairs: one child with autism spectrum disorder and one without. The children with autism spectrum disorder showed more improvement in their correct and total number of catches with a peer tutor compared to their classmate without.

Effective teachers can manage CWPT so students obtain the maximum time participating in class goals. Academic learning time which offers a student engagement in the planned activity of the class (Harrison, 1987), increases. Other investigators have suggested that the frequency with which students have an opportunity to respond in physical education may be as important as the amount of on-task instructional time.

Behavior Management

Dr. Barry Lavay contends that you cannot teach if you cannot manage and motivate your students. He describes his first year of teaching adapted physical education where his students with intellectual disabilities just sat down in the gym. He couldn't teach them *anything*, much less the planned fitness lesson he had prepared. After more than 35 years in adapted physical education, he has published behavior management concepts that he has found supports student learning (Lavay, 2019). Embedded in his list are concepts for the program and the face-to-face

Response to Intervention

The allowance of special education monies to be spent on early intervening services was strengthened in IDEA (2004). This addresses students who are not formally classified under IDEA but who need "additional academic and behavioral support to succeed in a general education environment" (Turnbull et al., 2009, Section 1413[f]). This means that a student who is lagging educationally but who is not formally entered into the special education system can be identified for extra academic assistance. If that assistance is successful, in many cases, special education is not warranted. One term given to this assistance is *response to intervention* (RtI). Here educators can plan educational interventions and set a timetable for evaluating the success of the plan. If the student shows success, then referral for assessment for special education services is not needed. Teachers receive special training to use response to intervention appropriately. In fact, response to intervention holds promise for assisting children who need more assistance in the classroom but for whom special education services are not needed. The Council for Exceptional Children (2008) emphasizes that response to intervention is a schoolwide initiative that works with families to identify needs of learners early, even in preschool, and does not delay the referral of a child who is suspected of having a disability from a comprehensive evaluation. Its policy statement includes guidelines for interventions, team roles, resources, and professional knowledge and skills.

teaching with students. The concepts are directed to teachers but can easily be applied to coaches.

> . . . behavior management, when applied positively, systematically and artfully, can be a powerful way to motivate and promote student learning, especially when teaching different students. Fortunately, today's educators are moving away from a discipline-first approach and recognizing that positive behavior supports are an effective way to empower students.
>
> Positive Behavioral Interventions and Supports (2018, p. 5).

Lavay's Crucial Behavior Management Concepts for Instructors

- *Connection:* Really caring about the students earns their trust and respect, and then they will follow your directions. Learn their names, likes, and idiosyncrasies.

- *Culture:* No matter what others do, stay positive and respectful in your setting. This influences others to do the same.

- *Action:* Think before reacting. Stay calm, and students can function better.

- *Planning:* Manage behavior *not* out of desperation. Be proactive in thinking about which student behaviors will enhance the learning and which will detract. Then establish expectations (rules) and routines.

- *Expectation and routine:* Establish immediately in the first orientation! Use input from students when possible. Expect listening to instructions, doing *your* best, and getting cooperation from others. Develop routines for entering and exiting the class, grouping students, and transitioning into and out of activities.

- *Consequences:* What are the consequences for not following the established class rules? Be consistent. Do not cave in even when the class is difficult. Students learn they are accountable for their behavior. Have a strong daily commitment to being calm, clear, and consistent.

- *Attentiveness:* Be tuned in to your class. Be observant and aware of misbehavior. Be able to address issues quickly. Be in position to see the whole class while teaching. When the class is large, place your back to the wall to quickly scan the whole class.

- *Positivity:* Reinforce those who are behaving appropriately. They often are ignored! Provide specific social praise. Positively pinpoint praise at random times. Set this teaching goal: Provide four positives to one corrective (4:1).

- *Transition clarity:* With clear, concrete transitions in a fast-paced physical activity class, use verbal and visual countdowns.

- *Proximity:* Stand near students who are off task. Sometimes that is enough. You can also make eye contact or use the student's name or use a visual cue intervention.

- *Eclectic:* What contributes to the behavior that is inappropriate? Explore various theoretical perspectives:
  - *Behavioral:* What in the environment can be changed? *Action:* Reinforce with extra free throws if the student does warm-up and skill learning.
  - *Humanistic:* Why is there a problem? *Action:* Ask one student to help one of their fellow students during a game.
  - *Biophysical:* What of the individual's physiology or biological contributes? *Action:* Learn from the school nurse about medication for a student.

- *Behavior:* Understand the ABC analysis and use it artfully and systematically (see Block, Henderson & Lavay, 2016). Identify the event happening *before* (antecedent [A] to) the inappropriate behavior (B), and what was the consequence (C) of the student's behavior. The consequence is usually identified as "what reward was there for the student?" Manipulate those variables to increase or decrease the behavior. This is explained in greater detail in chapter 10.

- *Extrinsic or intrinsic reward:* These are types of motivators for a student. Reward that is outside of the student is extrinsic (e.g., a ribbon or a certificate), whereas the intrinsic reward is internal to the student (e.g., he feels performed better in a skill; she had fun). The goal is to fade the reward that is extrinsic so the reward becomes intrinsic.

- *Bag of tricks:* Use a variety of behavior rewards for management of a class that fits different students. Your toolbox can be nonverbal, verbal, or tangible (such as access to a favorite physical activity or privileges) for the student.

- *Premack principle:* Use if–then statements, whereby the student performs *their* least preferred behavior for a reward of participation in *their* favored activity. You can say, "If you can participate in the warm-ups today, then you can shoot baskets later." This strategy is not effective if immediate reinforcement is necessary (e.g., if there are cognitive limitations). Reinforcement does not need to be expensive. Free is good.

- *Responsibility:* Each student takes in the social needs of others and has personal ownership. Some strategies include asking "Who did you help today?" or "What rules should we have for this game class?" The teacher provides feedback at end of class.

- *Continuum of systematic, flexible practices:* Your program and students are unique. The continuum is composed of proactive strategies (expectations and routines) that are the beginning of a program of communication. Then move to positive methods (reinforcements) to punishment or redirect inappropriate behaviors when necessary (planned ignoring, time-out). Do not use exercise as a punishment.

- *Evaluate:* Is the intervention increasing participation?

Adapted from Lavay (2019).

Summary

Instructional strategies for teaching children and youth with disabilities in physical education and adapted physical education are based in best practice. These practices are the result of research and practitioner verification that collectively affect how children and youth with disabilities can learn their movement skills and later their games, sports, and recreational physical activities. Today, culturally responsive teaching respects all students and their race, ethnicity, religion, gender, sexual orientation, religious affiliation, disability status, social class, culture, and other aspects of sociocultural life. Specific strategies presented included the application of universal design for learning to the physical education classroom, referred to as UDL in PE. Instructional strategies described in detail are task analysis, ecological task analysis; the use of techniques of instruction through verbalization, visualization, and kinesthesis; using a hierarchy of visual, verbal, and physical cues and prompts. Behavior management is stressed as an extremely necessary knowledge base for teaching. If the class is out of control, no one learns.

CHAPTER 6

Assessment and Evaluation

CHAPTER OBJECTIVES

After completing this chapter, you will be able to do the following:

- Explain the difference between the terms *assessment* and *evaluation* in providing adapted physical education service.
- Describe the differences between the bottom-up approach to assessment and the top-down approach and which students would benefit from their use.
- Understand and explain why all students with disability do not automatically receive adapted physical education (APE) service.
- Discuss the various assessment tools used in APE services.
- Explain a norm-referenced test and a criterion-referenced test and their use in special education.
- Identify the difference between a standardized and a nonstandardized assessment tool and the reason for choosing each of these in APE services provision.
- Identify the place that functional assessment has in delivering adapted physical education services.
- Describe the impact of assessments and evaluation on the transitional individualized education program (IEP) and identify the participants and their input roles.

Assessment is an art despite the numeric of measurement. It takes skill, understanding, an ability to communicate, an interest in the individual, and commitment to representing their ability and how we will instruct them. Sound assessments in the hands of competent professionals lead to evaluation reports that markedly assist interventions in adapted physical education and physical activity experiences for infants, toddlers, preschoolers, kindergarteners, grade schoolers, middle schoolers, and high schoolers. This chapter devotes attention to these age groups while later chapters (14, 15, and 16) focus on adults.

This chapter begins with assessment categories pointing out appropriate use with children and youth in measuring movement performance. Selected tools are defined to call attention to parameters for use. It will become apparent why an older student with intellectual disability cannot be tested with a tool that has been standardized on young children or why a student who has autism spectrum disorder can be tested using adjustments to instructions with the Test of Gross Motor Development-3 (Allen et al., 2017).

The terms *assessment* and *evaluation* are often used interchangeably in special education. For our purposes, assessment is the assigning of numbers to a movement performance, and evaluation is the resulting judgment(s), made by the professional, based on the assessment data.

The interpretation of standardized, nonstandardized, observational, and functional assessment data uses any combination of the expertise of the adapted physical educator, general physical educator, educational allied health colleagues, and other members of the special education team. This chapter will illustrate the factors to be considered for making those professional judgments for adapted physical education eligibility, placement, and the ongoing assessment of the student's progress in learning.

The assessment of students with disabilities or delays is driven by the federal education law IDEA (2004). In IDEA (2004), *special physical education* is the term for adapted physical education (APE). APE is physical education with curriculum modification or adaptation to support the student with a disability. That is not special but inclusive.

Assessment Process

Children with disabilities who are now in school have most likely been served in early intervention programs (ages 0-2) and early childhood special education (ages 3-5). These categories of disability

are identified in IDEA (2004) and can be found in the chapter 3 sidebar, Categories of Disability Under IDEA (2004). They could have received interdisciplinary services from pediatric occupational therapy, physical therapy, or speech and language pathology. The adapted physical educator works closely with other members of the individualized education program (IEP) team when the children reach school age. The occupational and physical therapists and the speech and language pathologists are common contributors of assessment information that is directly applicable to the physical education plan for the child. Later in high school, the transitional IEP initiates a myriad of other disciplines to assess and plan for the student's graduation into their community. The transitional IEP and the professionals involved were identified in chapters 2 and 3 and continue in specific disability chapters going forward in this textbook.

Often, administrators, teachers, and special education teachers are not aware that physical education must be addressed in the IEP process if the school offers physical education programs (Lieberman & Houston-Wilson, 2011). Instead, many feel occupational therapy and physical therapy can substitute for physical education. These experts are a very important part of the whole educational team and the process of creating an IEP. Occupational therapy and physical therapy are support services under the federal educational law and are used to do just that: support learning in the classroom including the gymnasium and other locations of the general physical education (GPE) program and APE program. Occupational therapy and physical therapy are used *to assist* the GPE and the APE teacher in the modifications and adaptations needed for the student to learn. Occupational therapists and physical therapists do not teach fundamental movement skills, games, and sports to students. They support the learning of those activities in the GPE and APE. They are not subservient to APE; they are highly trained, equal partners, and they care about the students.

For APE consideration, IDEA (2004) requires a student with a disability to first be evaluated in the *GPE curriculum for their age*. The question is: Can the student participate in the GPE program without support? If not, then the first part of IDEA (2004) is met. The process is then initiated to determine whether the student meets eligibility requirements for APE services. Each state determines its own eligibility requirements given the federal mandate to provide a free, appropriate, public education for all students.

Next, what modifications and adaptations does the student require to be successful in the GPE or the APE? The assessment should also include information from the IEP team in other domains of development (cognitive, communication, social and emotional) as necessary, to determine what supports are necessary for the spectrum of inclusion in the GPE program or if they need a separate APE class.

Section 504 Referrals

Access to physical education for students with disabilities is only required *if the other students are also receiving physical education*. Many school districts have continued to work to meet the needs of students with disabilities in physical education, and intense lobbying by parents and professional associations press for change when IDEA (2004) comes up for reauthorization. Plans based on Section 504 can be triggered if IDEA (2004) is not available for accessing APE.

The assessment process for providing APE service begins with screening and referral and continues with establishing eligibility for service through appropriate assessment. From there, the team develops the IEP. Assessments and the resulting evaluations are the cornerstone of a student's meaningful IEP. Annual instructional goals are the foundation upon which an appropriate placement into GPE or an APE program can be built specific to the needs of the student.

Screening and Referral

Informal screening occurs when professionals or parents observe that a student is performing in movement skills or with developmentally appropriate games and sports at a level significantly below his or her peers. Sometimes this is referred to as the concern and reflection stage in the referral process (Colarusso et al., 2017). In informal ways, observations are made by parents in the home and community, physicians in their offices, special educators at recess time, and GPE teachers in the gymnasium, pools, tracks, and play areas. Sometimes observations can be systematic and repeated in a similar setting across a similar time. If there is an unofficial consensus that a problem exists, or if deep parental concern is voiced, then formal screening assessments can be initiated, which can lead to comprehensive assessments for special education eligibility.

Screening is common in the early years because of the category of developmental delay in movement skill (very young). If the child is screened and found to be at risk for delay, then more formal testing can be initiated or a response to intervention (RtI) can be initiated.

RtI is a strategy used to determine whether a formal referral to the special education team is needed. This is a prereferral process that bypasses direct referral to consideration for special education services. In APE, the prereferral has been more helpful than not. In special education in general, this prereferral and resulting level of intervention has reduced the number of inappropriate referrals for special education especially with younger children (Colarusso et al., 2017).

People and time are involved when a full referral is initiated for special education. It saves time and money to first try a few interventions. If they work, the full special education services may not be needed. RtI is required in some states before referring a student for special education (Dykeman, 2006).

Overall, the prereferral RtI has three tiers as implied by the law and used in practice. Tier I looks at the student's engagement in a high-quality classroom instruction (e.g., the student is not failing because the instruction is poor), screening, and use of group instruction (e.g., research-based interventions). If the student is not making progress in the larger group, then tier II is initiated with more targeted interventions devised in smaller groups. When tier II fails, then tier III begins using more intensive interventions, and a comprehensive evaluation is done to design a more specialized intervention (Colarusso et al., 2017).

Establish Eligibility for Service

A second purpose of an assessment program is to establish whether the student is eligible for APE services. This eligibility is determined by each state. Further testing pinpoints the student's specific strengths and weaknesses and particular educational needs. At this stage, the question of the need for APE services is answered.

The law requires that more than one assessment is conducted to qualify for services. This means that more than one discipline is involved in assessing the student. The overall assessment strategy is directed at gathering information that is functional for the student in school, is conducted with attention to developmental expectations, and is related to academic achievement (Dykeman, 2006). Functionality has become much more prominent in special education assessment and services. IDEA (2004) states that ". . . the [assessment be] sufficiently comprehensive to identify all of the child's special education and related service's needs . . ." (§ 300.304[c][6]).

Only by collecting data through a variety of approaches (e.g., observations, interviews, tests, curriculum-based assessment, and so on) and from a variety of sources (parents, teachers, specialists, child) can an adequate picture be obtained of the child's strengths and weaknesses. (Parent Training and Information Centers, 2021).

Evaluation Process

After the student has been assessed and started their APE program, the next steps are to analyze educational progress, review curricular effectiveness, and communicate between home and school.

Analyze Educational Progress

A periodic review of the annual goals, which are required by IDEA (2004), and objectives, if they are required by the state, coupled with further evaluation provides a mechanism whereby the effectiveness of the physical education can be determined. Information obtained through this process informs the teacher, parents, and students about the extent to which educational progress has occurred. Areas where significant gains were made are identified, as well as areas where the instructional gains were minimal. Teachers can adjust instructional methodology, material, or the environment in which the experi-

ences are provided. The student cannot be adjusted. The IEP is the cornerstone of communication.

Review Curricular Effectiveness

Evaluation of student progress has curricular ramifications. For instance, the lack of improvement in a student's physical fitness program may be due to the insufficient time allocated for the program. Likewise, some students will not progress because the curricular sequences are too difficult, requiring that skills be further broken down into smaller steps based on a task analysis. A review of the progress of a student who has recently been integrated into a GPE class can only be effectively conducted if sufficient evaluative data are available.

Communicate Between Home and School

Communication with students and their parents is greatly enhanced if the evaluation plans of the IEP goals for the student are monitored. Teachers naturally feel more comfortable talking about a student's achievement if some objective data are available. Parents and students more readily accept objective data than subjective remarks. (Sample objective statement: Sam is quiet and always participates fully in the activities of the class. Sample subjective statement: I don't know what Sam really likes in class.) Parents often appreciate efforts to determine progress in their child's performance as well as hearing about positive attributes such as consideration and respect for teammates or others in class.

Courtesy of Michael Beets.

Legal Assessment Requirements

There are numerous legalities in the execution of IDEA (2004). The following sections of IDEA (2004) highlight the importance of being attentive to what is required in the legal IEP document.

- Prior written notice must be given to parents before an initial evaluation to determine if the child has a disability; parents must give consent before assessment (§ 300.300, parental consent). If parents do not respond, the evaluation can take place unless otherwise indicated by the state.
- Assessments must be selected and administered so that they are not racially or culturally discriminatory (§ 1414[b][3])
- Assessments must be provided and administered in the child's native language or other mode of communication, in a form most likely to produce accurate information. (§ 1414[b][3])
- Trained professionals must administer assessments according to the test instructions (§ 1414[b][3])
- Assessments must have been validated for the specific purpose for which they are used (§ 1414[b][3])
- Assessments must be selected so that they do not discriminate against the individual on the basis of disability (unless their purpose is the identification of the disabling condition) (§ 1414[b][3])
- No one procedure may be used as the sole criterion for determination of the educational program, the IEP; assessments selected for use in evaluation must include not merely those that yield a single general IQ score (§ 1414[b][3])
- Individuals must be assessed in all areas related to the suspected disability (e.g., health, vision, hearing, social and emotional status, general intelligence, academic performance, communicative status, motor ability) (§ 1414[b][3])
- Information from a variety of sources (aptitude and achievement assessments, teacher recommendations, physical condition, social and cultural background, adaptive behavior) must be documented and carefully considered (§ 1414[b][3])

It is important that all educators, including teachers of physical education, have a clear and comprehensive understanding of federal law for students with disabilities and the provisions related to evaluation.

- *Identification:* Every state is required to develop a plan for identifying, locating, and evaluating all students with disabilities within the state. Most state departments of education work in cooperation with local education agencies to implement a plan for identifying school-age students to deliver services to individuals with disabling conditions. Teachers have a responsibility to refer those students whose motor and physical fitness levels deviate significantly.
- *Prereferral:* We have already mentioned the prereferral plan or RtI employed by most school systems. Standardized tests are used, as are other informal techniques, such as teacher checklists and systematic observation of student performance. Scholars like Dykeman added to the list: functional assessments, authentic assessment, curriculum-based measurement, and applied behavioral analysis (2006). School records may also be consulted as a source of information. If two interventions fail, then a referral for eligibility for APE is made.
- *Due process:* Federal law ensures that children with disabilities and their parents are guaranteed procedural safeguards. This protection, commonly known as due process, means that parents and their children will be informed of their rights, with the provision that they may challenge educational decisions that they feel are unfair. For this reason, most local education agencies assign this responsibility to an administrator, normally the director of special education.
- *The evaluation report:* Persons who are knowledgeable about the assessments administered must be available to respond to any questions the parents may have about the assessment process or the evaluation report. The report generated by the physical education specialist considers all the assessments conducted and reports the findings in a manner that can be understood by the parents and the team at a meeting. In this meeting, the parents must be told whether their child qualifies under IDEA (2004) for APE. The basics of an evaluation report are outlined in the sidebar.
- *Outside evaluation:* If the parent wishes, an independent evaluation of the student can be conducted to confirm or refute the findings of the local school. According to IDEA (2004), the assessment ". . . must be the same as the criteria that the public agency uses when it initiates an evaluation, to the extent those criteria are consistent with the parent's right to an independent educational evaluation" (IDEA, 2004, § 300.502[e][1]). Paying for the evaluation is complicated and is best discussed by both parties involved. For example, if all criteria are met by the outside evaluator and the results differ from

the information previously provided by the school system, the cost is borne by the school district.

• *Hearings:* If the parents and the school system cannot agree on the evaluation findings, efforts to mediate the differences should be undertaken. This process normally requires that both sides review their positions and continue to talk and negotiate to resolve the differences. When mediation fails, an impartial hearing officer is appointed to hear both parties, review the available information, and render a decision.

• *Confidentiality of records:* Only parents of the student and authorized school personnel are permitted to review the student's records. This confidentiality clause includes all available evaluation reports. Other persons who request to review the file may do so only after the parents have given written permission.

• *Standards for evaluation:* The legal requirements of the federal educational law not only help to ensure that an assessment process will be utilized but also help to establish standards in the evaluation process. This is a marked departure from some of the past practices when the student's intelligence quotient, without concern for the performance capabilities, was used for eligibility. The safeguards continue to be in place under IDEA (2004).

• *Test selection:* The instruments used to gather assessment data for APE must be valid tools designed to reflect the student's achievement level, rather than reflecting the student's impaired sensory or speaking skills. Refer to the state criteria for assessment tools per area of service. For example, in Minnesota, if using a standardized tool, then only one assessment is required; if nonstandardized tools are used, then two are required.

• *Test administration:* Many students with disabilities have communication problems. Tests must be administered in such a way that they measure the student's *physical ability* rather than their communication skills. Adaptations in assessment protocol may be necessary, and if so, this must be noted in the evaluation report. For example, students who have visual and hearing impairments may need adaptations (see chapter 11 on sensory impairments). In some cases, where the adaptations changed the assessment items or protocols, standardized scores *are not* reported because the standardized use of the test has been altered. Instead, raw scores can be used in the evaluation report, and the assessor can describe what the student *was able to do* given the test. For example, if the student with visual impairment needs extra physical assistance in the Test of Gross Motor Development-3 (Ulrich, 2020),

Evaluation Reports

Evaluation reports in most states are written using a state or district template, where the assessor fills in the necessary data. Important data are the student's name and birth date, the date of the assessment, the calculated age of the student at assessment (particularly for younger students); and a description of the student in objective terms of how they present for testing and if the assessor judges the performance to be a valid representation of the student's ability (or skills) to date. Then there is a statement of the referral request and the instruments chosen for the assessment. The instruments are fully named and their purpose stated. (For example, the Test of Gross Motor Development-3 was used and is considered a valid and reliable measure of locomotor and balls skills for children 3 years through 10 years of age.) When other measures are employed, name the checklist, curriculum assessment, and whether it is standardized or not; every tool has a name and should be able to be located and reviewed if legally necessary.

In the case of interviews, the interview is labeled, and there is an indication of who was interviewed, the date, where and how, followed by a summary of the information defined in objective terms (Mrs. Chin was crying through our interview today and reported that they have had a difficult time understanding how to engage their son in physical activity in their home and community.) In the conclusion, statements are made to the referral questions one by one, in order, as listed at the beginning of the report.

The signature of the assessor includes their full professional name, any certificate or license abbreviations from their profession or education, and their professional position for assessing the student, as well as their affiliation, such as school district or business name. Usually, the record form from a test is attached and noted in the report that it is attached. Attaching raw interview data is at the discretion of the interviewer. Summaries of interviews usually suffice and are, as stated, included in the report. Raw interview data may need to be kept in a password-protected file either with the school district or with the consulting professional (or both).

such assistance is noted, and the physical activity performance of the fundamental movement skills are reported in raw scores, but the norms are not.

• *Test examiners:* Professionals involved in the assessment process must be trained and qualified to administer and interpret test results in their area of expertise. While federal law emphasizes the importance of qualified assessment administrators, it does not specify the qualifications necessary to administer tests. These decisions are made by local school districts. Assigning the responsibility for the student's physical education program to *adapted physical educators* is logical. In addition to their own assessment(s), the APE takes in valuable data from others on the IEP team, part of assuming the overall responsibility in managing the full report for their student.

Approaches to Assessment

The approaches to testing in physical education are either bottom-up or top-down (Winnick & Porretta, 2022). A graphic display of curriculum is presented in figure 6.1. Although it is an older model, it is still widely used to guide overall curriculum in physical education and indicates the type of activity taking place in the GPE classes.

Bottom-up testing is considered the classic developmental approach. In it, a hierarchy of movement skills is identified beginning at the younger ages. The skills build and progress into high school.

Using the bottom-up approach, the student is not allowed to progress to the next level or activity until competency has been reached in the lower skill areas (Burton & Miller, 1998). It is felt that lower skill accomplishment contributes to more complicated skill accomplishment later. Therefore, the instructional strategy is to move the student along a developmental progression that is both normative and curriculum based.

The top-down approach recognizes that functional ability in a skill or game area may be reachable by the student without all the assumed prerequisite skills. This is particularly appropriate for students with disabilities who may never be able to perform all the lower-level skills in a manner that is normative. For example, a child with a brain injury may never demonstrate the criterion of throwing as described on the Test of Gross Motor Development-3 (Ulrich, 2020). Yet, this child can throw a ball. It is functional. In other standardized tests, they may not walk on a balance beam, but they can navigate a school classroom or gymnasium in a functional manner. They can participate in the games of their age peers in an inclusive GPE class. Their GPE placement will benefit from using the universal design for learning in physical education (Lieberman et al., 2021). The top-down approach is well linked into functional assessment and supported by IDEA (2004).

Some children with cerebral palsy never crawl (e.g., they have too much tone in their legs), but some will, in time, sit up, shuffle forward on their

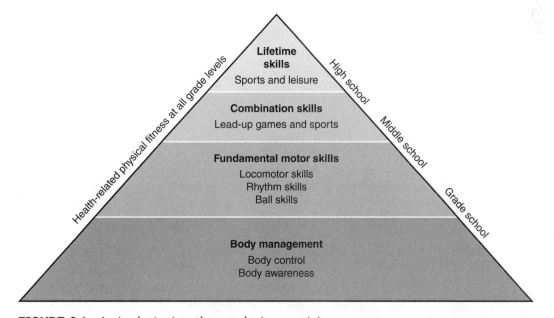

FIGURE 6.1 A physical education curriculum model.
Adapted by permission from A.E. Burton and D.E. Miller, *Movement Skill Assessment* (Champaign, IL: Human Kinetics, 1998).

bottom (scoot), or roll along with their whole body toward something or someone. Eventually some can get into a standing position and walk with or without assistive devices (chapter 12). Thus, the top-down approach is useful with younger children. Top-down approaches are very useful for teens with disabilities in assessing for sports, games, and fitness participation. Those with severe disabilities also benefit from a top-down approach for physical activity in their teens.

Assessing from a top-down approach is seen in figure 6.2. The *goal is identified*, and then the *student is given choices* in the movement skill sequence like setting out different types of balls if the skill is throwing or kicking. The student selects which balls they will throw or kick. The instructor observes the movement task and records whether the student can perform the task and with which ball. If they have difficulty, then a series of steps are taken by the instructor to ascertain whether manipulating some of the variables (e.g., equipment/ball choices; environment/distance from the ball for the movement to begin) makes any difference to the performance. In the top-down assessment approach, there is a fine line between assessment and when teaching takes over the process. When the student is finally successful in the task, then instruction takes over and the assessment process has ended.

Screening Test Selection

After the student has been identified with a disability category, they must then be tested to determine if they meet state eligibility requirements for APE services. Having a disability does not mean that the student receives services in all academic areas addressed in special education, as each state establishes its own criteria for special education services (e.g., the student must be a certain number of standard deviations [SDs] from the mean).

Some states have higher eligibility cut off scores on standardized tests (such as one and a half SD from the mean). This allows more children to receive services. Others have lower scores, such as two SD from the mean. Figure 6.3 depicts the standard normal curve, with noted areas under the curve for percentiles and SD values.

For example, in Minnesota, the criteria for eligibility have two main subsections: the first approach for eligibility is based on the use of a standardized, norm-referenced, or criterion-referenced test. To be eligible for services in APE, the student must be one and a half SD below the mean for their age (see figure 6.3). If the student cannot be tested using a standardized assessment tool, then the second approach for eligibility allows alternative methods of documenting the need for APE. As mentioned earlier in this chapter, this situation calls for two tools be used. The choices are from alternative methods like motor and skill checklists, criterion-referenced measures, curriculum-based assessment, medical history and reports, parent and staff interviews, systematic observations, and social, emotional, and behavioral assessments.

Alternative methods are also referred to as nonstandardized methods and informal assessments. In the early days of the federal education law, PL-94-142, the Education of All Handicapped Children Act (1975), the standardized, norm-referenced assessment tool was the gold standard. Fortunately, over the years, we have come to understand that this tool does not necessarily assess in valid ways the performance of a student with a disability for a physical education program. Now there are many more tools and literature to support the validity of using these nonstandardized (alternative to

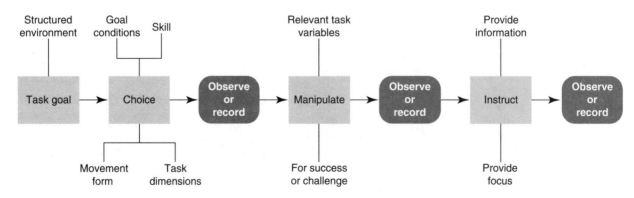

FIGURE 6.2   Top-down approach using ETA.

Reprinted by permission from W.E. Davis and A.W. Burton, "Ecological Task Analysis: Translating Movement Theory into Practice," *Adapted Physical Activity Quarterly* 8, no. 2 (1991): 154-177.

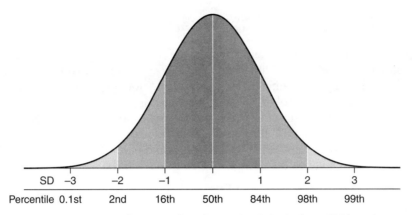

FIGURE 6.3 Standard normal curve with associated standard deviations (SD) and percentiles under the curve. Note that while SD is never a negative value it is typically expressed as such to show directionality when below the mean.

standardized, and informal) tools that meet the requirements of IDEA (2004).

These alternative forms of assessment require the application of the PE and APE teacher's professional judgment, based on the data collected, to document skill performance. With the IEP team, this then contributes to the design of appropriate IEP goals in the motor performance and placement decisions. For example, a systematic observation of a student in a GPE class can document where the student is performing compared their peers. Then this data is combined with data from a checklist of what the student can do in a curriculum-based assessment in GPE for their grade. This can be evidence that the student needs support, hence APE.

See figure 6.4 for an example of curriculum-based assessment.

One of the greatest challenges in selecting a test is that sometimes there is no standardized test that could produce a valid representation of the skills for that student with that disability. For example, the norming sample for the test never included a representation of the student's specific disability. Perhaps the test protocols cannot be used well by the student being tested. A student with autism spectrum disorder (ASD) may not be able to follow the very specific protocols of a standardized tool. Maybe the student's understanding doesn't match the test logic. For example, the verbal prompt plus a visual demonstration for "run fast to the cone,

Jump

1. Demonstrate jumping forward:
    - Knees and hips are flexed and arms swing backwards ☐
    - Swing both arms forward and upward as knees and ankles extend ☐
    - Land lightly on two feet, bending knees and ankles to cushion the shock of landing ☐
2. Jump forward rather than in place ☐

Kick

Use a toe kick to propel a ball to a partner 20 feet away ☐

Body Awareness

1. Correctly identify the right and left sides of the body ☐
2. Correctly move the body upon command: forward, backward; sideways, right, left ☐
3. Demonstrate walking forward and turning ☐

FIGURE 6.4 A curriculum-based assessment for second graders—sample skills.

Take Care

What is important is to find the student's age in the heading of the tables in the instructor's manual for standardized tests. This then identifies the correct numbers for the evaluation report. We have all observed a highly trained and skilled professional report a spurious number that catches the attention of an alert colleague in a team meeting when the professional had calculated the wrong age! This had a domino effect, leaving the child seemingly much more impaired than the team had experienced with its assessments. Calculating age is simple math, but if that isn't done correctly including using the year, month, and day for the birth date using the date of testing, then the wrong tables in the manual are employed. If the age is correct, but the wrong table is selected, the results are just as invalid.

pick up the stick, and come back here" may not mean anything to a student. When this is the case, alternate testing is very appropriate.

Finally, the goal in selecting a tool for assessment is to obtain data about *what the student can do*. In the past, an assessor could use a test that produced mostly zeros in their evaluation report. Then the student qualified for APE. But this data is not a valid selection of an assessment tool that can ascertain what the student can do. A different assessment needs to be conducted because the IEP team cannot create goals from zeros. If a student is low functioning motorically, there are tools for assessing their skills. For example, the Mobility Opportunities Via Education curriculum is a functional, top-down assessment that is used when students have fewer skills for physical activity (Bidabe & Lolar, 1990).

There are validity and reliability quotients associated with standardized assessment tools. In the simplest of terms, a tool that is *valid* means that it has been found to test what it says it is testing. A tool that is *reliable* means that assessors can obtain similar results testing the same student at the same time given the same tool. There are measurement terms associated with validity and reliability found in the instructor's manual of the test instrument. Validity and reliability are important numbers to pay attention to both when selecting a test instrument and when including it in the evaluation report.

Purpose of the Test

Fundamental question 1: What is the purpose of the test, and does your selection of it match the purpose for which the test was designed? Of the list that follows, what is your reason for using the test chosen?

- Screening for delay
- Comprehensive assessment for services
- Comprehensive assessment for re-evaluation for services

- Check on progress within a unit in the curriculum
- Assist in teaching a skill within a curriculum

Companies collaborate with authors of assessment tools in promoting the tools; they market them for the professional tasks needed. Thus, the test purposes are boldly explained in the test manual and in the advertising for the tool.

Measuring change over time in weeks or a few months is not well measured by norm-referenced tests where the time lapse between testing again is minimally six months. Criterion-referenced tests that are norm referenced follow the same guide. Checklists are valuable to mark the change over time, as are curriculum-based assessments, and both can be used more frequently. This is true for tools that assist in teaching such as task analysis, ecological task analysis, rubrics, and the like.

Fundamental question 2: For what ages is the test appropriate?

- Testing instruments with or without standardized procedures must match the students identified age, thus within the identified ages for which the test was designed. If it is not, the test results would be invalid.

- Some disabilities are associated with intellectual disability, and some students have both an identified disability and an intellectual disability. People sometimes make the erroneous assumption that they can match a motor assessment to the understood intellectual disability instead of to the student. Instead, chronological age (CA) is matched for testing. CA places the student with their age peers whenever possible (IDEA, 2004) within an age curriculum, with modifications and adaptations that support that student. Thus, assessment for participation in the APE program is by age. A student of 16 years of age with an intellectual disability cannot be assessed by the TGMD-3 because that test is not normed on 16-year-olds but rather on children ages 3 years to 10 years, 11 months.

• Comprehensive assessments of young children require the recording of the year, month, and day of the child's birth and the year, month, and day of the testing. The child's testing age is calculated from these dates, and the calculated age is used to find the right chart in the user manual. A few months of development make a huge difference in the early years of life. Some assessments, like Ages and Stages, come with an online calculator (Squires & Bricker, 2018).

Administrative Factors

Purchasing assessments or selecting them for use depend on an analysis of

- the ease with which a test may be given at the school,
- the amount of time required for administration,
- the distance required for some tasks,
- the portability of the test or storage of the items, and
- the cost.

Assessments of physical fitness vary considerably in the amount of time required to administer them. Some require only a few minutes, whereas others involve several test sessions over a two-day period. Some tests can be given in bouts. Assessors and the student can return at a later time or day to complete the test. If a test is long but provides needed information, then it should be used.

Assessments designed primarily as screening instruments to identify students who may need further evaluation must be constructed so that they are time efficient, thus increasing the probability of their widespread use to screen. Caution must be exercised when attempting to shorten the necessary testing time by evaluating a group of students together. The performance of some students is dramatically affected when peers are permitted to observe their motor skill evaluation.

Each test should be reviewed carefully to determine the level of training required for potential users of the test. Even though many of the motor performance assessments can be routinely administered and evaluated by personnel with preparation as physical educators, some do require additional expertise and training. Training is necessary to administer tests to some students with disabilities. For instance, personnel who test students with hearing impairments will need sufficient signing skills to communicate effectively so that the results will not be invalid. Likewise, examiners of individuals with intellectual disability should have sufficient training to ensure that a given test is assessing the student's motor rather than cognitive level.

The quality of information obtained through the evaluation process is closely related to the skills of the examiner. Every effort must be made to utilize personnel who have a thorough background in APE and who are knowledgeable about appropriate motor assessments and their use with special populations.

Norm-Referenced Assessments

Historically, most assessments used in physical education were norm referenced, meaning they had a standard that had to be followed to administer the test, and raw scores were transformed into standardized scores that allowed the assessor to compare what typical ages can do. In creating a norm, the test is administered to a group of individuals (the normative group), and the norm becomes the average score of performance on an item by age. This normative sample becomes the criteria against in which the student being tested is compared. The data collected when testing a student is raw score data (e.g., how fast, how much, how many, how far?). The test manual includes tables that convert raw scores into standardized scores. The raw score is listed in the manual alongside the standardized score listed by an age.

The examiner's manual that accompanies norm-referenced assessments contains information on the standard way of administering the test, scoring, and interpreting the assessment data. It is very important when selecting a norm-referenced test to know who composed the normative group. If there were no children with an intellectual disability in the sample, then the test is not valid for those children. For the most part, the newer editions do, and they explain the level of intellectual disability.

If the test is used with someone whose disability was not represented in the normative population, the assessor doesn't report using the norms. Instead, if the test is used for its items, which the assessor modified to help the student perform the test items, then the assessor indicates in the report that there was "modification to the test in the following way(s) . . ." then the assessor reports the findings in some way to compare to grade expectations.

Close Cutoff Scores

In a situation where the test score is close to a state cutoff, and thus the student technically does not qualify for APE, some options are available. A student whose scores are very close to the cutoff is obviously in need of services. The use of norms and the state's cutoff scores are typically one and a half or two SD below the mean. A student who is one and a half SD below the average (0) under the normal curve is in the seventh percentile. That means 93 percent of the test population technically are more competent. At two SD from the mean of the test population, that marks the student at the second percentile, with 98 percent of the students above them. Both of these percentiles are a very low criteria to meet.

A student who has scores calculated just a bit above these low percentages of 7 percent or 2 percent is very much needing help if, for example, 7 percent is the state cutoff. In any given test, there is error on the part of the test itself, the assessor, and the testee. Suffice it to say that another test can be administered that might do a better job of capturing the student's level of skills. A more practical approach is for the assessor to add an interview with the current physical education teacher *and* an observation of the student in physical education to support placement in the APE with a level of support. This is not to ridicule the rules of the states but only to allow for reason and the spirit of the law to enter into the equation. Those who know how can use the standard error of measurement (SEM) to calculate the student's score to determine if the lower score qualifies the student for services, which in these cases it surely would.

The examiner must pay attention to the age range of the normative group because this is the basis for indicating the ages for whom the test is intended. Sometimes people want to use a test standardized on children ages 3 to 10 years with older students with an intellectual disability. They rationalize that the individual with an intellectual disability functions at a developmental age lower than their chronological age. But that is an incorrect use of the norm-referenced test, because the student being tested is older than the population sample that composes the norms. Despite cognitive

deficits compared to age peers without intellectual disabilities, their body has grown, hormones have developed, and other developments have occurred. However, the norm-referenced test can be used as a checklist if that type of information is helpful in teaching a student, and the student is near the age of the normative sample. For students in high school, their physical education program has other goals, and thus testing motor development of fundamental skills (e.g., running, jumping, and hopping) is not appropriate.

Test of Gross Motor Development

The Test of Gross Motor Development-3 (TGMD-3) developed by Ulrich (2020) is a widely used assessment of fundamental movement skills (running, jumping, skipping, throwing, etc.). The purpose of the TGMD-3 is to identify children ages 3 years through 10 years, 11 months who lag in the execution of gross motor skills. Two subtests—locomotion and ball skills—assess different aspects of gross motor development.

For example, when using the TGMD-3, we accumulate data on what a four-year-old is performing overall to obtain a gross motor index (GMI). Tables are listed in the TGMD-3 instructor's manual that are ready-made for these purposes. The cover of the examiner record form indicates where the scores obtained from the manual are placed for use in further discussions and planning (figure 6.5).

The TGMD-3 uses an overall gross motor index to describe overall performance (locomotor + ball skills). A gross motor index of 70 or below (<70) indicates impairment or delay, followed by gross motor indices with corresponding scores identifying a student as borderline impaired or delayed, below average, average, above average, superior and gifted, or very advanced. Most assessors find it is important to be sensitive when reporting and interpreting scores to parents. It is very disheartening to report age equivalents when the scores are vastly below a child's age. The term *delayed* is sufficient to indicate that the child qualifies for APE service and the IEP lays out "this is where we will start . . . and this is where we expect to be at the end of the school year."

TGMD for Those With Visual Impairments

The Test of Gross Motor Development-3 (TGMD-3) (Ulrich, 2020) has reported validity for children with visual impairments ages 6 to 12 years (Brian et al., 2018). The TGMD-3 assesses fundamental motor skills.

TGMD for Those With Autism Spectrum Disorder

Numerous articles attested to the validity and reliability of the TGMD-3 and its use with children with ASD. These included Allen and colleagues (2017), who stated that

> . . . before motor performance can be considered as a principal characteristic of ASD, it is essential to establish a valid and reliable motor assessment for use in children with ASD that incorporates appropriate adaptations to facilitate task understanding and to ensure an accurate evaluation of motor performance can be achieved.
>
> Allen et al. (2017, p. 813).

Using the TGMD-3, these researchers used extra picture cards, short verbal prompts, and physical demonstrations with their students with ASD, as well as with their control group. Both groups were assessed using the traditional TGMD-3. The children with ASD performed better with the addition of the extra cues. Researchers recommended visual prompts to be simple and attentive to the age of the child across the age spectrum of the TGMD-3.

TGMD for Those With Cerebral Palsy and Orthopedic Impairments

The Test of Gross Motor Development-2 (Ulrich, 2000) has been broadly used in APE and was problematic for students with cerebral palsy if they use a wheelchair for locomotion; thus, the locomotor subsection is not appropriate. No score can be given in that subsection, and then an overall gross motor quotient cannot be calculated. But the TGMD is a valuable tool because it assesses the functional movement skills used in physical education classes for children ages 3 to 10 years or age. For students with cerebral palsy, it is appropriate is to use the TGMD as a checklist versus a criterion-referenced test with standardized procedures and norms. Ulrich later published the TGMD-3 (2020), and it can be used in the same manner as the TGMD-2 was—as a checklist. Leave out the locomotor norms if the skills can't be assessed. A child with cerebral palsy can run, but they don't run using the criterion of the TGMD. An assessor can note that in the report. Thus, used as a checklist, the test results as raw scores can be reported but not the norms. This approach can also be used with students older than 10 if it is appropriate to assess some of the basic skills for games and sports or establish a task analysis. But

//

Examiner Record Form

Ages 3-0 to 10-11   Dale A. Ulrich

Section 1: Identifying Information

Name _____

☐ Female   ☐ Male

School _____

Examiner's name _____

Examiner's title _____

	Year	Month	Day	
				Preferred hand ☐ Right ☐ Left ☐ Not established
Date tested	____	____	____	Preferred foot ☐ Right ☐ Left ☐ Not established
Date of birth	____	____	____	
Age	____	____	____	

*When accessing the normative tables, use years and months. Do not round up.

Section 2: Subtest Performance

Subtest	Raw score	Age equivalent	%ile rank	Scaled score	__ % Confidence interval	Descriptive term	Difference between scaled scores
Locomotor							
Ball skills							
Sum of scaled scores =							☐ Not important ☐ Statistical ☐ Clinical

Section 3: Composite Performance

	Sum of scaled scores	%ile rank	Gross motor index	__ % Confidence interval	Descriptive term
Gross motor					

Section 4: Descriptive Terms

Scaled scores	1-3	4-5	6-7	8-12	13-14	15-16	17-20
Descriptive term	Impaired or delayed	Borderline impaired or delayed	Below average	Average	Above average	Superior	Gifted or very advanced
Index score	<70	70-79	80-89	90-109	110-119	120-129	>129

//

FIGURE 6.5   Cover of the examiner record form, Test of Gross Motor Development-3.

again, it is a checklist. In the end, it might be more an observation of whether the child can throw and reporting that it is functional!

Bruininks-Oseretsky Test of Motor Proficiency II

The Bruininks-Oseretsky Test of Motor Proficiency II (Bruininks & Bruininks, 2005) measures motor ability, those underlying skills that contribute to motor performance (Burton & Miller, 1998), such as balance and coordination. This test is also referenced as the BOT-2 in practice and in research (e.g., Jírovec et al., 2019). Balance has such tasks as standing on a preferred lower extremity on the floor, on the balance beam, with eyes closed on the balance beam; walking forward on a floor line, on the balance beam, heel-to-toe on a floor-line; and stepping over a designated measuring stick from the test kit on a balance beam. The assessment yields overall scores as well as subscores for gross motor and fine motor skill. Assessment time is at least 1 hour for the long form and about 15 to 20 minutes for the short form. Presently the test kit is considered expensive, and the results are well associated with validity and reliability measures that are attractive to selected special education systems and professionals.

The challenge for many physical educators is to translate assessment data into the functional day-to-day physical education curriculum to be used in developing the student's IEP and developing the supports necessary for APE. Use of this tool with occupational therapy, physical therapy, and the APE can often yield helpful functional data. The occupational and physical therapists use the BOT-2. Their evaluation report can be translated into specific activities found in the functional activities of the physical education curriculum: how to best situate a student for catching, throwing, kicking; and determining what modifications might be necessary within the grade curriculum. This is teamwork.

The Mobility Opportunities Via Education (MOVE) (Bidabe & Lolar, 1990) is an assessment tool used *with* students with severe limits on physical skill execution and severe intellectual disability requiring high levels of support and who may also have additional impairments. The curriculum has produced a top-down motor milestone test. This test is useful in understanding the basic skills of sitting, standing, and walking as they relate to being a physically active individual engaged in functional activity. In some school districts, the physical and occupational therapists do more of the assessments for these students with recommendations for an APE program. They may use the MOVE curriculum. This can also provide a guide for students to engage in the Special Olympics Motor Activity Training Program (MATP), which develops physical activity skill and is not competitive but fun (Special Olympics, n.d.).

BOT-2 and Cerebral Palsy

It is important to choose tools for assessing students with cerebral palsy for physical education that produce data on what students *can do*. In the past, special education primarily used tools that used standardized procedures that produced normative data on the child. Despite BOT-2 renorming in 2010, the tool has fallen out of favor in physical education with special needs children for physical education assessment. For the most part, these children receive too many zeros for speed, accuracy, and coordination. Zeros tell the IEP team what the child cannot do more than what they can do. This is particularly apparent when attempting to use the BOT-2 for students with cerebral palsy. The student ends up failing many of the items because of the cerebral palsy and the lack of ability to move quickly, exhibit good balance, or to be precise with skills like throwing. Also, the test results of the BOT-2 do not easily translate into intervention strategies for use in the curriculum of physical education except as used by occupational therapists or physical therapists.

The Brockport Physical Fitness Test (Winnick & Short, 1999) is an appropriate tool for students with cerebral palsy. It was developed in part for these students. It is also used with other disability areas as specified in the user's manual.

Burton's top-down approach may be the best way to assess the student with orthopedic disabilities for physical education and activity. The underlying theme in using the top-down approach is that for a child with cerebral palsy, they can throw the ball, but it does not meet any of the TGMD-3 criteria for form. Adaptations may need to be made to the game's equipment (such as adding hook-and-loop fasteners to a catcher's mitt) or other areas where the child can be very functional and enjoy playing in the activity.

Early Movement Interdisciplinary Assessment

Infancy to Toddlerhood

Early movement milestones are identified as locomotor and object control skills performed *before* the child is upright in bipedal locomotion (Burton & Miller, 1998). Pediatric occupational and physical therapists play a large role in the assessment of infant movement, qualifying them for early intervention (ages 0-2 years) and providing direct services to facilitate movement considered adapted physical activity (APA). At this young age, the services are offered in the home or are center-based.

Toddlerhood to Preschool (APA to APE)

Fundamental movement skills are performed once the child is upright and moving and are classified as locomotor (e.g., walking and running) and object control (e.g., throwing and kicking). This begins with toddlers and develops through early school age. A two-year-old's skill of throwing develops across ages and looks different in execution to a three-, four-, or five-year-old's throwing skill. Pediatric occupational and physical therapists assess in toddlerhood for movement concerns, and the children participate in adapted physical activity when needed.

Most adapted physical educators do not work with infants and toddlers, but some do work with preschoolers, and many work with kindergarteners. Also, pediatric occupational therapists, physical therapists, and speech and language pathologists contribute to IEP development as do assessments by child psychology, community nursing, and community clinical practices.

Tests

- *Peabody Developmental Motor Scales-3 (PDMS-3; Folio & Fewell, 2023):* These scales are used to determine a Gross Motor Quotient that includes testing body transport, object control, hand manipulation, and eye–hand coordination; reflexes, stationary ability, locomotion, and object manipulation; and a supplemental assessment for fitness. The fitness assessment responds to concerns for early obesity, overweight, and fitness in preschool. PDMS-3 is used with children from infancy (e.g., APA) to 6 years of age (e.g., APE).

- *Bayley Scales of Infant and Toddler Development-4 (Bayley & Aylward, 2019):* The Bayley test has both a motor quotient and an intelligence quotient. This test and the Peabody scales are often conducted by the psychologist on the eligibility team for qualification for early intervention services and for the development of the individual family service plan (IFSP) or individualized education plan (IEP) services, or results come from an outside clinical practice to the special education team.

- *Brigance Inventory of Early Development III (IED III) (Brigance, 2020):* This tool assesses across the main domains of development in early childhood, including the motor domain for those 0 to 35 *months* of age and also children who are 3 to 5 *years* of age. Months are used when analyzing the data from assessing very young children to track development, and later the data is analyzed in years. There are now guidelines for virtual administration and use of the IED III (Brigance, 2020). This information can also be used as a criterion-referenced checkup on skills for children already in programs. (APA)

Curriculum-Based Assessments

- *The Assessment, Evaluation, and Programming System for Infants and Children, Third Edition (Bricker et al., 2021):* Ages of children assessed are from infancy to age six years old. The components of assessment are gross and fine motor, adaptive, social-emotional, social-communication, cognitive, literacy, and math. All the components of assessment are linked directly into the curriculum. (APA to APE)

- *Ages and Stages Questionnaire, Third Edition:* This is used with children from birth to five years of age. It is a screening tool. Gross motor skill is a component of the questions. This is a parent questionnaire with validity reported (Lipkin & Macias, 2020). This is a formal screening tool and one that is validated and recommended by the Centers for Disease Control and Prevention for use at regular intervals with pediatric checkups for children at ages 9 months, 18 months, and 30 months of age (CDC, 2021). (APA)

- *The Hawaii Early Learning Profile 0-3 and Hawaii Early Learning Profile 3-6:* These are criterion-referenced, curriculum-based assessment tools used with infants, toddlers, and early learners covering cognitive, language, gross motor, fine motor, social-emotional, and self-help domains (Parks, 1992/2013; Parks, 1992/2006). One is for children up to three years old, and the other is for those ages three to six. The 3-6 version is used in the Head Start program. (APA to APE)

- *The Carolina Curriculum:* There are two assessments—the Carolina Curriculum for Infants & Toddlers With Special Needs (ages 0-36 months) and the Carolina Curriculum for Preschoolers With Special Needs (ages 24-60 months). Both are criterion-referenced assessments and are curriculum based for teaching skills across five domains: cognition, communication, personal-social, fine motor, and gross motor (Johnson-Martin, 2007). The Carolina assessments link into interventions. (ADA)

Nonstandardized Assessments

Nonstandardized assessment is a valid assessment strategy for qualifying a child for special physical education, particularly for students for whom assessment tools are not normed on their disability area. The physical educator uses their professional judgment to present valid information to the IEP team for an appropriate placement of the student. This approach includes the following tools: criterion-referenced assessments, task analysis assessments, checklists and rubrics, systematic observation, interviews, and curriculum-based assessments. With the results of these assessments, a determination can made about the extent to which the student will be participating in the GPE curriculum or whether the student needs other placements. In addition, it points to what supports are needed in either or both settings.

Criterion-Referenced Assessments

Criterion-referenced assessments are well suited to assessment in physical education. Here, a criterion or level of mastery of certain skills is established for each item of the test. See figure 6.6 for an example for balls skills. The score achieved by the student describes how much of the criterion was met. (How much of the criteria does the student meet? What of that amount is age appropriate?) Some criterion-referenced assessments have a standardized procedure and norms and are therefore both criterion-referenced and norm-referenced (e.g., TGMD-3). If there are no norms reported for a criterion-referenced test, then it can be classified as a nonstandardized assessment. Criterion-referenced assessments with norms have validity and reliability quotients reported in the instructor's manual. These measures tell the user how strong the psychometrics are, and the strength can be included in the evaluation report. Most often, a general statement will suffice. For example, some tests report test–retest reliability as good at 0.75. A general statement is that reliability is good. This data is very attractive, particularly where the assessor likes the content and it relates to the curriculum specific to the child.

Task Analysis Assessment

A task analysis assessment procedure is closely related to the criterion-referenced process. With task analysis, the components of a specific skill are identified and then arranged from most complex to least. Students are evaluated on where they are in relationship to the final skill. The last step may be thought of as the criterion. If the student cannot master the final step, then branching occurs to further simplify the steps to meet the criteria. As we have discussed, a branching can be conducted at any point along the way to further instruct the student. Assessment using a task-analyzed approach provides a great deal of useful information for instruction. See figure 6.7 for an example of a task analysis for striking a ball off the batting tee in the TGMD. This example includes a task analysis of the performance objectives.

Analysis of the value of task-analytic evaluation procedures was challenged and strengthened by the close work by Davis and Burton back in 1991. They argued correctly that teachers need to be very careful about developing a sequence of a specific skill and then assuming that all learners will master the skill following precisely the order of subtasks as they have defined them. The traditional task-analytic approach, which normally uses either an anatomical or developmental perspective, if used rigidly, places too much emphasis on the sequence of the skill and

Skill	Materials	Directions	Performance criteria	Trial 1	Trial 2	Score
1. Two-hand strike of a stationary ball	A 4-inch lightweight ball, a plastic bat, and a batting tee	Place the ball on the batting tee at the child's belt level. Tell the child to hit the ball hard. Repeat a second trial.	1. Child's preferred hand grips bat above non-preferred hand			
			2. Child's non-preferred hip and shoulder face straight ahead			
			3. Hip and shoulder rotate and derotate during swing			
			4. Steps with non-preferred foot			
			5. Hits ball sending it straight ahead			
					Skill Score =	
2. One-hand forehand strike of self-bounced ball	A tennis ball, a light plastic paddle, and a wall	Hand the plastic paddle and ball to child. Tell child to hold ball up and drop it (so it bounces about waist height); off the bounce, hit the ball toward the wall. Point toward the wall. Repeat a second trial.	1. Child takes a backswing with the paddle when the ball is bounced			
			2. Steps with non-preferred foot			
			3. Strikes the ball toward the wall			
			4. Paddle follows through toward non-preferred shoulder			
					Skill Score =	

FIGURE 6.6   Criterion-referenced ball skills from TGMD-3. The TGMD-3 is both criterion-referenced and norm-referenced.

fails to adequately consider individual variation found within groups of learners (figure 6.7). Davis and Burton recommended that the traditional approach to task analysis be modified to recognize that the capability of the performer varies due to individual and environmental constraints. That is the way the top-down strategy was promoted by them in what they called task analysis applied to ecological task analysis. For example, the approach used by a student with cerebral palsy to catch a ball can be different than a student with an intellectual disability. Likewise, environmental constraints (e.g., the size of the ball and elements such as wind) should be considered in assessing the performance of any student. In using task-analytic procedures, it is important to make sure that the parts (subtasks) of the skill are similar to the whole task so that

the desired goal of catching a ball is recognizable. Some of the new thoughts and arguments regarding task-analytic assessment approaches have helped reinforce the need to always be attentive to individual differences and focus on what students *can* do. Today it is important to look more closely at the performer considerations beyond the typical hand-size and disability considerations to child development literature related to risk factors (e.g., poverty of the home environment).

Lieberman and Houston-Wilson (2009) have focused on physical education unit modifications. In figure 6.8, a circle is used to indicate if the skill has been introduced by the instructor. A check is used to identify which of the modifications would be appropriate for the given student. This form of modifying and adapting the activity is based in ecological task

//

Desired or target behavior: The child will demonstrate a mature two-hand striking pattern by hitting a foam ball with a wiffle-ball bat successfully off a batting tee 9 out of 10 times. (Other types of balls and striking implements may be substituted for the bat and ball in accordance with the individual's skill level.)

Steps (Task analysis of the desired or target behavior)

1. Demonstrates familiarity with the equipment that will be used to perform the striking pattern.
2. Both hands are held correctly on the bat, with the dominant hand on top.
3. Visually attends to the object (ball) that will be used to perform the striking pattern. (Use brightly colored balls.)
4. Is in proper position in relation to the batting tee. (If necessary, a physical cue such as footsteps taped on the floor can be used.)
5. Brings the bat 2 inches back from the batting tee and strikes the foam ball in a horizontal plane.
6. Brings the bat 1 foot back from the batting tee and strikes the foam ball in a horizontal plane.
7. Brings the bat back to shoulder height with both elbows flexed and strikes the object in a horizontal plane.
8. Develops proper contact and follow-through upon contacting the ball.

Once the process of the task is mastered the instructor can have the individual increase the striking velocity. (However, do not increase the swinging velocity at the expense of sacrificing control of the striking pattern.)

If an individual is displaying difficulty moving from one step to the next, then the task analysis may need to be altered or broken down to smaller steps. Dunn, Morehouse, and Fredericks (1986) define this procedure as branching. For example, the child accomplishes the following:

1. Brings the implement back to shoulder height with both elbows flexed and strikes the object in a horizontal plane
2. Properly grips the bat and brings it back to shoulder height with both elbows flexed
3. Stands with feet shoulder-width apart and knees comfortably flexed
4. Turns body slightly to the side
5. Turns the head and eyes toward the object on the batting tee
6. Positions weight on the back foot
7. Begins the horizontal swing with a lateral step forward on the front foot
8. Begins to extend the arms forward toward the object on the tee
9. Rotates the hips in the direction of the object
10. Shifts weight to the front foot upon contacting the object

//

FIGURE 6.7   Task analysis of a strike.

analysis. Their work is easily understood and has been applied since its inception.

Checklists and Rubrics

Checklists are typically created to teach a specific skill (e.g., free throw). Many coaches create their preferred checklist for teaching skills for games and sports. Checklists are also used to teach in authentic situations rather than in more isolated skills sets. For example, an authentic assessment of bowling is done in the bowling alley with a checklist developed for competencies.

Rubrics combine checklists, task analyses, and rating scale methods to make it clear to the student what is expected, as well as inform teachers, paraprofessionals, and parents what is being taught. Sometimes class rubrics are developed, and at other times one student has a rubric. It is motivating for students to see their improvement via this checklist.

Soccer: Potential Modifications and Adaptations

Equipment	Rules	Environment	Instruction
— Soccer balls	— Hands permitted for protection	— Cones as boundaries	— Verbal cues
— Large balls	— No heading	— Bright boundaries	— Demonstration
— Small balls	— Walk with ball	— Ropes as boundaries	— Modeling
— Bright balls	— Peer places ball on ground for kick	— Beeper or auditory boundaries	— Tactile modeling
— Textured balls	— Undefended	— Visual shooting line	— Physical assistance
— Heavy balls	— No defense for certain number of seconds	— Smooth surface	— Task cards (enlarged if needed)
— Light balls	— Free shooting (no defense)	— Modified field size	— Pictures
— Foam balls	— Everyone touches ball before shots on goal	— Stations	— Guided discovery
— Nerf balls	— Pass certain number of times before shots on goal		— Problem-solving
— Beach balls	— Vary playing times		— Task analysis
— Deflated balls	— Limit boundaries		— Proximity
— Auditory balls	— Lane soccer		— Individualized
— Bell balls	— Small-sided games		— Sign language
— Balls on strings			— Feedback
— Front bumper on chair			— Peer tutor
— Bells on net			— Paraeducator
— Buzzer on net			— Interpreter
— Wide goal			
— Small goal			
— Bright goal			
— Flags			
— Cones			
— Shin guards			

Reprinted by permission from L.J. Lieberman and C. Houston-Wilson, *Strategies for Inclusion: Physical Education for Everyone*, 3rd ed. (Champaign, IL: Human Kinetics, 2017), 146.

FIGURE 6.8   Unit modifications and adaptations for soccer. In filling out the form, a *check* indicates the modification works well; a *circle* indicates instructor has tried the variable; a circle with a line through it indicates instructor tried the variable but it did not work; the date is added to the right after every line.

Rubrics are similar to a task-analytic approach to teaching, as are as checklists and teacher rating scales. Rubrics are believed to be easily translated into curriculum content for the student and can be discussed in the IEP meeting (table 6.1).

Specialized Movement Skills for Games and Sports

Specialized movement skills are those fundamental movement skills used in combinations to accomplish specific tasks such as shooting a free throw or spiking a volleyball (Burton & Miller, 1998). They are the skills most physical educators understand as part of the curriculum as students get older. Examples of these assessments are the self-made checklists constructed by a GPE or APE teacher and are based on their observation and experience. The Aquatics Checklist (Houston-Wilson in Lieberman & Houston-Wilson, 2018) is an excellent example of specialized skill assessment in its application to teaching swimming. It is flexible, and branching is easily applied.

Brockport Physical Fitness: A Health-Related Test for Youth With Physical Disabilities and Mental Disabilities (Winnick & Short, 1999) was designed

TABLE 6.1   Rubric for Soccer

Dribbling	
Task	Student dribbles using inside and outside of foot against a defender.
Scale components	(a) Form, (b) velocity of performance, (c) radius of direction change, (d) number of defenders

Rubric level and color	Rubric descriptors
1. White	Student dribbles with dominant foot and nondominant foot in 3 out of 5 attempts with or without assistance.
2. Yellow	Student dribbles with inside of each foot through 10 cones located 7 feet (2.1 meters) apart, up and back, with control in 3 out of 5 attempts.
3. Orange	Student dribbles fast with outside of each foot through 10 cones located 7 feet apart, up and back, with control in 3 out of 5 attempts.
4. Green	Student dribbles fast with inside and outside of each foot through 10 cones located 5 feet (1.5 meters) apart, up and back, without losing the ball 75 percent of the time.
5. Blue	Student dribbles against a defender with inside and outside of foot for 30 yards (27.4 meters).
6. Purple	Student dribbles against two defenders for 30 seconds within a 20-yard (18.3-meter) radius using the inside and outside dribble without losing the ball 75 percent of the time.

Passing	
Task	Student performs an exact pass using the inside or outside of the foot to a standing or moving partner.
Scale components	(a) Form, (b) number of performances, (c) motion

Rubric level and color	Rubric descriptors
1. White	Student passes with dominant foot or nondominant foot in 3 out of 5 attempts with or without assistance.
2. Yellow	Student passes with inside of the foot to a partner standing 10 feet (3 meters) away using each foot 10 times.
3. Orange	Student passes with outside of the foot to a partner standing 10 feet away using each foot 10 times.
4. Green	Student passes with inside or outside of the foot to a partner standing 20 feet (6.1 meters) away 10 times (5 with the inside foot and 5 with the outside foot).
5. Blue	Student passes with only the inside of the foot to a partner moving up and down the field and has control most of the time.
6. Purple	Student passes with only the outside of the foot to a partner moving up and down the field and has control most of the time.
7. Brown	Student passes to a partner 20 yards up field, leading the receiver on the run, and keeping ball within 5 feet (1.5 meters) of the receiver's foot 8 out of 10 times.

> continued

Table 6.1 > *continued*

Game Play	
Task	Student is an active participant in a soccer game.
Scale components	(a) Dribbling, (b) passing, (c) defense, (d) shooting (all performed consistently during a scrimmage or game)

Rubric level and color	Rubric descriptors
1. White	Student participates in a 3-on-3 game, demonstrates a dribble and a pass when on offense, and shows knowledge of defense when his or her team is on defense.
2. Yellow	Student participates in a 3-on-3 game, consistently demonstrates a dribble and a pass when on offense, and consistently shows knowledge of defense when team is on defense.
3. Orange	Student participates in a 5-on-5 scrimmage, consistently demonstrates a dribble and a pass when on offense, and consistently shows knowledge of defense when team is on defense.
4. Green	Student demonstrates all previous skills, cuts for a pass, and shoots on goal 50 percent of the time when a shot is available.
5. Blue	Student demonstrates all previous skills, consistently cuts for a pass, and consistently shoots on goal 80 percent of the time when a shot is available.
6. Purple	Student participates in a full-field soccer game with consistent offensive and defensive skills for at least 10 minutes.
7. Brown	Student participates in a full-field soccer game with consistent offensive and defensive skills for at least 15 minutes.

to test youth ages 10 to 17 on their fitness skills. The Brockport test has criterion-referenced fitness standards and computer applications to assist the physical educator in designing intervention programs for the individuals with specific disabilities.

Leisure Skill Inventory

Complementary to the creation of the health-related physical fitness goals is an assessment of the student's leisure interests and abilities. School recreation therapists are rarely found. These specialists are now in community parks, recreation settings, and in hospitals and outpatient clinics. So, reviewing assessment tools for leisure skills interests have expanded to meet more community and clinical needs. A book commonly referred to as the big red book is the two-inch-thick, red-bound *Assessment Tools for Recreational Therapy and Related Fields, Third Edition* (Burlingame & Blaschko, 2002), where the assessments Leisurescope Plus and Teen Leisurescope Plus are described (pp. 276-300), which can be used for the transitional IEP.

Leisure skills inventories are being created by those who are responsible for the IEP team transi-

tion goals in leisure and recreation. The inventory is designed with the student's community in mind. The checklists are administered to the student and their parents or caregivers. The critical issue addressed is: To create a checklist, ascertain what is available in the community for physical recreation activity. A list is drawn up, and the physical educator, special education teacher, or paraprofessional can administer the checklist. Sometimes this has to be pictorial both for the activity and the response categories. When the student and family have determined what is feasible to include in the training for the transitional IEP, then the skill content is identified, and a task analysis of the skills involved is developed so that instruction can be initiated. An ecological task analysis can be outlined, including where the student will participate and what level of assistance, if any, the student needs. For example, if swimming is the student interest and there are resources in the community, then a task analysis of training can begin. Will the student need lessons? Is a facility available? The student must learn how to enter the changing room, change, use the locker, shower, and come out to the pool area. A form can easily be created for this use.

Where is the validity and reliability with these self-constructed checklists or questionnaires? There is social validity if parents look at the results of the assessment and the final evaluation and say, "Yes, that is my child!" *and* if students can communicate in some form that they are pleased with their choices. Additionally, if the assessments are formed into evaluation reports, and the reported plan of action results in a student who obviously has skills for leisure and knows how to use the associated environment successfully, the checklist has contributed to additional social validity.

Observations

All evaluation techniques involve observation. Both technological and nontechnological observations are used to capture the student's performance.

Recording performance in physical activity permits the assessor to enlist the aid of other professionals to analyze the student's skill level. Further recording of student performance at periodic intervals provides an effective means of evaluating skill improvement over time. Parents, too, find a visual recording an informative experience. They can see progress and engagement, which helps them understand the importance of physical education and its contribution to overall development.

As a tool in the assessment process, an observation is best done with emphasis on a systematic approach, with a reasonable number of observations made across repeated physical activity events or classes. In this manner, GPE and APE teachers can provide more validity to their observations of repeated examples of movement performance for parents and members of the IEP team.

Nontechnology-oriented observations include systematic observations of how the student is performing in their class. The teacher can observe for a specific amount of time, note the time, and then describe what skill is being performed by the class and how the target student is performing. In this case, the observer makes nonjudgmental descriptive statements—for example, "The class was running laps around the gymnasium. Most of the students ran for five minutes. Sam ran for two minutes and stopped and rested." In the case cited, the teacher may observe that Sam has lower cardiovascular endurance than his peers. A sample format is provided in figure 6.9. Visual recording of the student's performance, including a thoughtful analysis provided by the teacher, in combination with other sources of valid test data (e.g., interviews) provides

a powerful and helpful communication device.

Self-evaluation is an important skill for students. To institute self-evaluation in a traditional program, the teacher can encourage the student to develop the objectives to be evaluated. If not, the student should at least be clear about what the objectives for the self-evaluation are.

Once the objectives have been identified, the student is then provided with a checklist on which objectives listed for the student to accomplish in a unit. The decision as to whether the objective has been met is made by the student based on the criterion identified for each objective. Although various rating scales can be used, a popular system is to have the student place a plus sign by those objectives that are completed and a check by those requiring more teacher assistance. A zero or a star suggests that more practice is required. Lieberman and Houston-Wilson's examples in their book on inclusion make good references for this type of self-evaluation (Lieberman & Houston-Wilson, 2009).

Interviews

An increasingly popular assessment tool is the use of interviews to obtain complementary information about a student's performance capabilities and interests. An interview is a nonstandardized tool and is valid for use in data gathering for an IEP. As an illustration, parents have valuable information about their child. Open questions in an interview add to the IEP creation. Examples include: "What would you like me to know about Joshua in physical education or activity?" and "What does he particularly like doing for physical activity?"

As the student progresses in the education system, interviews with the parents are helpful in considering the family values and desired physical activity for their child. In addition, the student may be interviewed. Eventually, the student engages in the transitional IEP beginning at age 16 (required under IDEA [2004]), with an eye toward graduation. APE and GPE staff and other staff work to create a transitional IEP with the student and their family. If the family knows and trusts the physical education staff, the whole process for the transitional IEP is positive teamwork.

In this manner, there is time to formulate plans for teaching the necessary skills as well as working with the reality of engaging in those activities in the community. Lists of leisure activities for the parents provide team feedback. Leave space for open-ended questions such as, What else are you concerned about for Joshua's leisure time activity once he leaves high school?

//

Physical Education Observation Form

Student name: _____ Birth date:_____ Date observed: _____

Observer name: (print)_____ Title:_____

Reason for observation: *Michael is new to this school district. There is concern with his GPE teacher that he is struggling in the class. Are there interventions to increase Michael's time on task?*

Description of setting: *Class is held in a small gym. Stations are set up on the sides of the gym. Balls are out of view. The center area has mats laid out in one large circle.*

Observer signature: _____

Time	Class activity	Target student behavior
10:00 a.m.	Sit in a circle in the center of the room on mats. Warm up to music: walk twice around the room, jog or walk three times. Return to mats and sit.	Michael refused to sit with the class and went to a bench on the side of room. No other students were there. Walked twice and sat down on the bench. No other student sat there.
10:15 a.m.	Stations for kick to target, five stations (three at a station) At each station different activities with different skill levels representing easy to difficult. Special group today are students in blue T-shirts. This group is always told which station. The target student has a blue T-shirt. A gong sound indicates students should and move to the next station to the right. Two stations are for jogging between cones, with three students at each of these stations.	Michael went to the first kick station, which is the middle challenge. He missed a broad goal 10 feet away most of the time. The teacher switched this student to kicking to a wall from 10 feet. Michael stayed on task for the whole time. Michael jogged between cones once and sat down on a bench. No other student joined him.
Summary	Michael, the target student, enjoyed the class today. He was smiling and laughing, while watching teacher instructions half the time. His motor skill and stamina were less than those of his classmates. His station for kicking was successful at the lower skill level.	
Recommendations	Michael is functioning below his age peers today in cardiovascular activity and is in the lower half of his class for the skill of kicking. Michael needs an RtI plan to determine what interventions can be devised, focusing on increasing skill performance, stamina, and attention to task. Presently he is not on an IEP in motor/physical education. An RtI is required first before referral to Special Education Services.	

//

FIGURE 6.9 Sample observation form of a target student's performance in a physical education class.

Currently, students who are capable can and do participate in their own IEP. The student's input at an IEP meeting can be a valuable addition to the team and, when possible, should be encouraged. An interview with the student prior to the meeting does focus the student's thoughts. They can be interviewed to obtain their perceptions of their physical fitness levels and physical activities in class or what they are particularly enjoying in class.

Pictures are other methods of obtaining input from the student. They can be cut out from magazines, drawn by the student, or collected from cell phone albums. Student assessments for interests in the community can be performed by a recreation therapist or specialist. Information brought to the meetings can be copresented with the student if appropriate.

Curriculum-Based Assessment

Figure 6.4 earlier in the chapter is a simple example of part of a curriculum to be used as a curriculum-based assessment. Report percentiles for what the student could do (expected for grade) within the curriculum is very understandable to parents and allows the rest of the IEP team to know how to provide supports and an appropriate placement for the child. Most school districts have standards for their curriculum by grades to identify what is taught and how progress is measured for student learning.

Evaluation Communication

Explaining an assessment to parents or legal guardians is appropriate when the assessor remembers that parents do not necessarily use such terms like *locomotion skills*. Use family-friendly language. Name the skills such as running, jumping, hopping, or sliding. Also, with games and sports skills, describe them in terms of family, peer, or friends' interests if that has been discussed. It helps to talk to the parents about the physical education program and broaden their knowledge of what their child feels they can do. It allows them to see what activities their child enjoys.

Positive communication is essential to managing a cadre of interdisciplinary individuals and the student's parents or other caregivers in a meeting to discuss and plan the educational goals (Diliberto & Brewer, 2012). Communication examples include the following:

- *Positive:* "I agree with the information you have presented on April. Can you help me understand how we can bring the necessary resources within the school to meet the goal?"
- *Negative:* "I can't see how *that* will happen in April's school!"

Setting an openness for communicating throughout the year that will set the tone for positive communication between the parents or caregivers and the educators and clinicians who can contact one another in a variety of ways. Some families need to understand special education and separate meetings and activities can be offered.

Six tips have produced positive communication within an IEP meeting.

1. Use a preplanning meeting. Here professionals don't predetermine the goals for the

student but instead involve the parent at every step to discuss the student's strengths, needs (e.g., a plan for teenage social skill development through PE), and goals.

2. Identify a meeting facilitator who runs the meeting, keeps to the agenda, and reminds people of the rules of engagement, allowing all to participate; another person records.

3. Develop an agenda several days ahead of the IEP meeting.

4. Post the ground rules with a sample outline of an agenda that includes an opening, then introduction of members, explanation of the ground rules, summary of assessment data; review of the current status of the student's strengths and needs, development of the IEP, and a closing statement (Diliberto & Brewer, 2012).

5. Turn team members' knowledge of data into goals. Remember that no one knows the student better than a parent or caregiver. Being realistic about what can be accomplished in a school year is a consideration for all team members.

6. Use friendly language in the discussions. This increases communication by avoiding discipline-specific jargon that might not be understood by families or other disciplines. For example:

   ○ "John is happy in the gym and we want to teach him more locomotor and object control skills."

   ○ "John loves his PE time, and we will continue to teach him more skills like skipping and hopping to use in games, as well as throwing and kicking a ball."

Only those disciplines necessary for the student's education should participate in IEP meetings. For example, a district's physical therapist might be present for a student with cerebral palsy, whereas that person may not be needed for a student with intellectual disability. Care should be taken to report the success and to advance the learning. Age comparisons are not reported or emphasized. It is devastating to hear that a child is functioning years below their age expectations. Rather, it is much better to communicate "This where we are, and this is where we want to go." The parents know their child is receiving services because they are behind and need more assistance to succeed. The legal communication is covered physical activity.

Summary

Assessment of the skills and activities for APE is essential in creating evaluation reports that are valid and thus lead to an appropriate qualification for APE service and the creation of the IEP for children and youth or an individualized family service plan for infants and toddlers. Assessment is the collection of numbers about performance, and evaluation is a set of judgments about the numbers collected. Each state determines its own eligibility requirements for APE services. To have a disability does not mean that the student receives services in APE, or that they receive it in all academic areas addressed under special education. If the student cannot be successful in the GPE program without needing modifications or adaptations, they are referred for consideration for APE service. RtI is a prereferral approach to intervention for special education consideration. In some states, this is required before referring a student for a full special education referral. Types of tests used in assessment for APE service are norm referenced, criterion referenced, task analysis, self-evaluation, interviews, observations, checklists and rubrics, and curriculum-based assessment. Interviews produce qualitative data, and observations can produce both numbers and qualitative data. Selection of an instrument for assessment is based on the age of the student and the type of information needed. Parents or caregivers provide valuable information in the IEP meetings about the child. Discipline professionals must use friendly language in IEP and individualized family service plan meetings.

Intellectual Disability

Halfpoint Images/Moment RF/Getty Images

CHAPTER OBJECTIVES

After completing this chapter, you will be able to do the following:

- Define intellectual disability, considering intelligence quotient and adaptive functioning criteria.
- Describe levels of support for individuals with intellectual disability.
- Understand the application of chronological age and developmental age with instructional strategies for adapted physical education and activity for those with intellectual disability.
- Identify the learning characteristics of individuals with an intellectual disability and the associated teaching strategies.
- Identify prompts and their use with instructional strategies for individuals with intellectual disability.
- Understand behavior modification programming and the use of the antecedent, behavior, and consequences in mapping out an intervention.
- Describe the differences in the sports programs of Special Olympics, Unified Sports of Special Olympics, and Motor Activity Training Program of Special Olympics.
- Describe the Mobility Opportunities Via Education curriculum and the instructional strategies for individuals with severe and profound intellectual disability in physical activity.

The understanding of who has intellectually disability (ID) is not straightforward. This chapter begins with a history of what was understood and describes where we more appropriately provide physical activity environments and experiences for those with intellectual disability. Physical activity engagement for children and youth with intellectual disability has positive effects on both their physical and psychosocial health (Kapsal et al., 2019). This engagement is offered in physical education, adapted physical education, community recreation, and local and international sports programs like Special Olympics. Educators, clinicians, and volunteers are involved in supporting quality physical activity participation for those with ID.

The American Association on Intellectual and Developmental Disabilities (AAIDD) is *the* advocacy group in the United States for individuals with ID. Founded in 1887 as the Association of Medical Officers of American Institutions for Idiotic and Feebleminded Persons, and despite what are now considered dehumanizing terms, these early members were *advocates* for those with ID. Today that advocacy legacy continues and influences both educational and clinical services.

Until the AAIDD's advocacy succeeded, intelligence quotient (IQ) was the *only* score considered for diagnosis of ID. Today, diagnostic assessments include measures of IQ *and* adapted functioning. Two broad areas are considered for a diagnosis of ID: that the person's IQ is significantly below the average on standardized testing and the adaptive functioning is below what would be expected given the individual's age and sociocultural context.

The AAIDD's other main contribution was to define the support required for individuals to function well intellectually and behaviorally. The AAIDD's descriptions of these supports are a prime resource for educators to formulate learning strategies and environments for physical activity participation. These supports become operational in physical activity when applied to communicating directions, teaching skills, tracking interventions, modifying a curriculum, designing game adaptations, and focusing on the goal of well-being and health for those with intellectual disabilities at their school, at home, and within their community.

Causes and Prevalence

In a study of children ages 3 to 17 years, the prevalence of ID in the United States was reported at 3.2 percent per 1,000 in data collected in 2016 (McGuire et al., 2019). Other studies have noted an increase in incidence from 2000 to 2019. However, estimates are replete with the use of terminology that compounds the overall misunderstanding of incidence. For example, in special education, some of the children are initially placed in a category of developmentally delayed (DD) and later receive a more precise diagnosis of ID. Causes of intellectual disability include:

- *Genetic conditions:* Such conditions include Down syndrome (chromosomal disorder), fragile X syndrome and phenylketonuria. If one or both biological parents have an ID, the intellectual capabilities of their child are most likely affected.

- *Problems during pregnancy:* Use of alcohol during pregnancy is the leading preventable cause of ID, resulting in fetal alcohol spectrum disorders (Mayo Clinic, 2023). ID is also caused by malnutrition, exposure of the mother to certain environmental toxins (lead), and illnesses of the mother during pregnancy (such as measles, toxoplasmosis, or cytomegalovirus).

- *Problems during birth:* Oxygen deprivation for too long at the time during birth (anoxia) and a premature birth are risk factors for ID.

- *Illness and injury:* Illness of the child (meningitis, encephalitis, measles, whooping cough, chicken pox) and injury (severe head injury, near-drowning, extreme malnutrition) may lead to brain damage. Severe abuse and neglect can cause irreparable damage of the brain.

- *Severe poverty and cultural deprivation:* Being raised in poverty is a high-risk factor for malnutrition, disease, environmental health hazards, and inadequate access to health care—all contributing to risk for ID. Severe understimulation results in intellectual disability during childhood where there is lack of affection, an unsafe and chaotic home, being ignored by parental figures, and having nothing to play with.

Down Syndrome

The medical classification of a disability or disease is sometimes named after the researcher who first identified it. The British physician Dr. John Langdon Down delivered a talk in 1866 entitled "Observation on the Ethnic Classification of Mongoloid Idiots," making Dr. Down the first to publicly identify the condition. Today the term *mongoloid idiot* is abhorrent. In the 1970s, the World Health Organization replaced the term *mongoloid idiocy* with *Down syndrome* (Pitetti et al., 2013).

Down syndrome is the most common of all genetic disorders. It has three types; the most common is trisomy 21, caused by an extra chromosome; less frequent are mosaic trisomy and Robertsonian translocation. All the individuals with these conditions have some degree of ID. It is estimated that approximately one in 700 infants born in the United States (6,000 births per year) has Down syndrome (March of Dimes, 2020). The diagnosis of Down syndrome is made based on blood tests and the following physical characteristics:

- Facial features include a flat nose with slanted eyes.
- The head, ear, and mouth are small.
- The tongue can protrude.
- The hands are small and square.
- Hair is usually sparse and fine.
- The person being diagnosed might have one or more impairments in speech.
- The person being diagnosed is likely short and stocky.

Fragile X Syndrome

Fragile X syndrome is genetically inherited and refers to a mutation of the FMR1 gene on the X chromosome. The mutation obstructs the production of a protein that supports brain development and other functions. In the history of understanding what has come to be called fragile X syndrome, the first children studied had presented with ID. In 1947, scientists James Purdon Martin and Julia

Bell linked ID to an X chromosome. Following Martin and Bell's research, Hubert Lubs reported a genetic mutation—a fragile site on the lower part of an X chromosome in 1969. In 1991, the name fragile mental retardation 1 (FMR1) was given to the genetic mutation.

Not all individuals with a mutation of the FMR1 gene have fragile X syndrome due to differences in the amount of FMR1. Individuals with fragile X syndrome have enough mutation of the FMR1 gene's production of a protein (fragile mental retardation protein) to share the conditions for fragile X syndrome. This lack of protein is thought to effect changes in brain development. FMR protein assists the brain in getting rid of weaker connections in the brain known as synaptic pruning. Healthy brains prune well to establish strong neuronal pathways for healthy neurologic function.

According to the Eunice Kennedy Shriver National Institute on Child and Human Development, the diagnosis for children eventually identified with fragile X syndrome is typically developmental disorder in infancy and toddlerhood. A genetic test can be conducted if fragile X is suspected. Fragile X syndrome is noticed physically in puberty when the individual's face elongates, the forehead widens, the head and ears are large, and the feet are flat (figure 7.1). These individuals have difficulties in cognitive capacity and are classified in a range from mild to severe ID. Learning disabilities are reported, especially in mathematics, and hyperactivity, language processing problems, and lack of impulse control

are also reported. These symptoms lead to testing to establish an IQ. Socially, the children are shy where lack of eye contact is compounded by high anxiety, particularly in adolescence. According to the National Human Genome Project, the prevalence is higher in boys, with reports of 1 in 4,000, and the prevalence for girls is at 1 in 8,000.

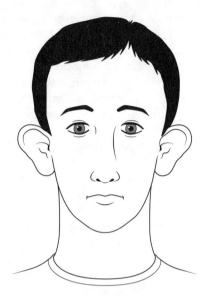

FIGURE 7.1   Adolescent with fragile X syndrome exhibiting the common features.

Fetal Alcohol Spectrum Disorders

Fetal alcohol syndrome and fetal alcohol effect are two conditions associated with prenatal alcohol exposure. After 60 years of research, there is a greater delineation of prenatal exposure to alcohol, and because of this, *fetal alcohol spectrum disorders* is the umbrella term now encompassing a spectrum of diagnoses resulting from the mother drinking alcohol during pregnancy (Mayo Clinic, 2018). The umbrella term and consequent diagnoses reveal the expanded terms in the field of prenatal alcohol exposure. From the Mayo Clinic (2018), the following diagnoses on the spectrum are defined:

- *Alcohol-related neurodevelopmental disorder:* Intellectual disabilities or behavioral and learning problems caused by drinking alcohol during pregnancy.
- *Alcohol-related birth defects:* Physical birth defects caused by drinking alcohol during pregnancy.
- *Fetal alcohol syndrome:* The severe end of the fetal alcohol spectrum disorders, which includes both neurodevelopmental disorder

and birth defects caused by drinking alcohol during pregnancy.

- *Partial fetal alcohol syndrome:* Presence of some signs and symptoms of fetal alcohol syndrome caused by drinking alcohol during pregnancy, but the criteria for the diagnosis are not met.
- *Neurobehavioral disorder associated with prenatal alcohol exposure:* Problems functioning due to neurocognitive impairments, such as problems with mental health, memory, impulse control, communication, and daily living skills, caused by drinking alcohol during pregnancy.

According to the Centers for Disease Control and Prevention (CDC, 2022), children with fetal alcohol syndrome present with abnormal facial features, such as a smooth (flat) ridge between the nose and upper lip (figure 7.2). They also have a small head, short stature, low body weight, poor coordination, hyperactive behavior, difficulty with attention, poor memory, learning disabilities, speech and language delays, intellectual disability, poor reasoning and judgment skills, vision or hearing problems, and problems with the heart, kidneys, or bones. Fetal alcohol syndrome is always associated with intellectual disability.

FIGURE 7.2   Facial features with fetal alcohol spectrum disorder: eye width is narrow, upper lip is narrow, and the space above the lip is flat.

According to the CDC, there are treatment options for children with fetal alcohol spectrum disorders, including behavior therapy, parent training, and special education for children experiencing difficulties with learning or behavior. Referring to protective factors, the CDC lists the following to reduce the effects of fetal alcohol spectrum disorders: diagnosis before six years of age, stable home environment during the school years, absence of violence, and involvement in special education and social services (2022).

Prematurity

The classification of premature as the completion of gestation before 37 weeks is now the consensus of the World Health Organization, the American Academy of Pediatrics, and the American College of Obstetrics and Gynecologists (Barfield & Lee, 2020). This was announced in 2020 and is important for understanding treatment and improvement of care for the young babies and their mothers. These early ages, days, and weeks are defining times. Every moment, every ounce, and subsection of the ounce counts.

The World Health Organization has used categories of moderate to late preterm (32-37 weeks), very preterm (28-32 weeks), and extremely preterm (<28 weeks) as of 2022 (WHO, 2022). Also, classifications of prematurity intersect with classifications of risk by weight .These are babies born small by weight. Very low birth weight is <1,500 grams, and extremely low birth weight is <1,000 grams (Cutland et al., 2017).

One of the risks of prematurity is a diagnosis of ID later in the development of the premature baby. Babies born prematurely continue to grow their lungs, brain, and other important parts of their body outside of the womb to their full nine months of gestational age.

Classification and Diagnosis

Categorizing intelligence has been fraught with debate and has severely limited the societal engagement of people with ID. Assessment of intelligence is traced back to Alfred Binet in 1905. Binet was a French psychologist who developed a screening tool to identify children struggling in school. The test was attractive because it assigned a number to intelligence. According to the scholars Kliewer, Binken, and Peterson (2015), Binet believed that his test measured intelligence, yet importantly ". . . he himself understood this to be neither a fixed nor innate construct" (p. 3). In fact, he felt that it was deplorable to believe a person's intelligence was fixed. He referred to a notion of fixed intelligence as empirical and hierarchical *nothingness*. Unfortunately, Binet died in 1911, ending a positive outlook on intelligence that was quickly replaced by pessimism grounded heavily in eugenics.

Intelligence Quotient

The American psychologist Henry Goddard used Binet's work to sort out those individuals whom he considered mentally defective. His measure used a mental age correlation, and he created the term *moron*. Kliewer and colleagues (2015) report that Terman worked off Goddard's eugenics philosophy and developed the Stanford-Binet Intelligence Scales in 1916. In the United States, this test's chronological age correlations were described and later accepted by scholars as a ". . . predictive statistic that falls along a bell-shaped curve . . . Those who scored poorly or who were deemed to have *less* intelligence were . . . possessing an objective and measurable disconnectedness from valued citizenship and full humanness" (p. 5). Even into the 1960s, this resulted in pediatricians recommending commitment of infants with Down syndrome to a state institution for life.

In the 1990s, American psychologists argued for models of intelligence based in social and multiple cognitions where intelligence is considered fluid and multidimensional, flowing across relationships that take in people, materials, opportunities, and expectations. In 2005, Gardner wrote that "intelligences . . . do not function in isolation but exist . . . across an individual's mind and between the mind and the social realm" (Kliewer et al., 2015, p. 5).

In both educational and clinical settings, assessment for intelligence is conducted by a qualified professional who individually administers comprehensive measures that are considered culturally appropriate and having sound psychometric properties to measure intelligence (APA, 2022; IDEA, 2004). Individuals with intellectual disability typically have scores greater than two standard deviations or more below the population mean (IQ below 70), including a margin for measurement error calculated as the standard error measurement (SEM). The SEM is calculated to be plus or minus five points for most IQ assessment tools. Given this, a person with ID can obtain an IQ score of 75 upon testing (Greenspan & Woods, 2014). Medically, additional neuropsychological testing can be conducted when there is question about results; for example, when there is a very low functional skill and higher than typical IQ to make the diagnosis of ID (APA, 2013). There are currently no screening tools that are sufficiently valid or reliable enough to identify children with a probable ID (McKenzie & Megson, 2012).

Intelligence quotient is typically assessed using the Wechsler Intelligence Scale for Children, Fifth Edition (Wechsler, 2014) or the Stanford-Binet Intelligence Scales, Fifth Edition (Roid, 2003). Figure 7.3

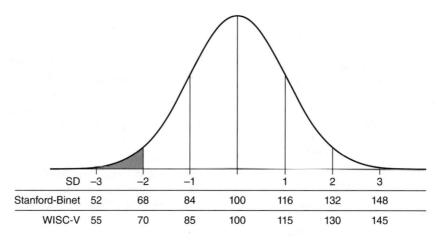

SD	-3	-2	-1		1	2	3
Stanford-Binet	52	68	84	100	116	132	148
WISC-V	55	70	85	100	115	130	145

FIGURE 7.3 Theoretical normal distribution of IQ and scores for Standard-Binet and Wechsler Intelligence Scale-Revised under that distribution. As previously noted, while SD is never a negative value it is typically expressed as such to show directionality when below the mean.

depicts the IQ for both tests of intelligence across the normal curve. Note that an IQ that is two or more standard deviations below the mean meets part of the criteria in educational law for ID.

Infants, toddlers, and preschoolers are diagnosed with disabilities much differently than children over the age of five years. An early diagnostic term in education services is *DD*. In medical services, the term is *general developmental delay*. In early childhood, the domains of development like motor and cognition are intertwined so much so that motor is often the first sign of delay in development, indicating a delay in cognitive functioning suggesting ID (e.g., Hadders-Algra, 2021). Accurate diagnosis takes time even when the infant presents with identifiable conditions associated with ID like Down syndrome and most types of cerebral palsy.

Professions serving those with ID in the early ages cross the education and medical fields. Early intervention teams in the community generally encompass early childhood special education teachers, pediatric occupation and physical therapists, and speech and language pathologists. Clinical professionals include pediatricians and developmental pediatricians, pediatric nurses, pediatric occupational and physical therapists, child psychologists, pediatric neurologists, and audiologists and ophthalmologists.

Screening and comprehensive assessments are stipulated by the American Academy of Pediatrics, particularly at 9, 18, 24, and 30 months of age. A standardized developmental screening test is required for all children at the 9, 18, and 30-month visits (clinical or community) and particularly for those with delayed or disordered development.

Adaptive Functioning and Levels of Support

How a person with an ID managed their life was ignored when IQ was the sole emphasis in diagnosis. The AAIDD fought to have an assessment of adaptive functioning added to the determination of ID to clearly identify the supports needed to meet determined societal expectations to manage life. The AAIDD has defined *adaptive behavior* (see sidebar) and laid out *levels of support within those behaviors* (Schalock et al., 2010).

Regarding adaptive functioning, it is understood that expectations vary for different age groups. During infancy and early childhood, significant delays in motor skills, communication skills, self-help skills, and sensory-motor activities are potential indicators of ID. During childhood and early adolescence, the primary focus is on the ability to learn basic academic skills, which includes physical education. As the student enters high school ages, a gradual focus shifts to making a living and to handling oneself and one's affairs. What level of support is needed in what areas? Is it continuous or is it episodic?

The Diagnostic Adaptive Behavior Scale is an assessment tool for individuals ages 4 to 21 years (Tassé et al., 2016). This tool aligns perfectly with the adaptive skills advocated for assessment by the AAIDD. These adaptive skills are listed for conceptual, social, and practical skills in the sidebar. An individualized education program (IEP) for a four- or five-year-old will address social skills and will address practical skills related to personal care (use of the bathroom and handwashing) often

Adaptive Behavior Defined by the AAIDD

Adaptive behavior is the collection of conceptual, social, and practical skills that are learned and performed by people in their everyday lives.

- *Conceptual skills:* These include language and literacy; money, time, and number concepts; and self-direction.
- *Social skills:* These include interpersonal skills, social responsibility, self-esteem, gullibility, naïveté (i.e., wariness), social problem-solving, and the ability to follow rules and obey laws and to avoid being victimized.
- *Practical skills:* These include activities of daily living (personal care), occupational skills, seeking and receiving healthcare, conducting travel, maintaining schedules, being safe, using money, and using the telephone.

From: American Association on Intellectual and Developmental Disability (AAIDD). Available: www.aaidd.org/intellectual-disability/definition.

expanding on those skills emergent in the earlier individualized family service plan (IFSP).

The Vineland Adaptive Behavior Scales, Third Edition (Sparrow et al., 2016) is another standardized tool for assessing adaptive functioning. Used with individuals from birth to age 90, the tool assesses communication and daily living. Many of these assessment results find their way into the IFSP for the youngest children and the IEP for those aged at least into first grade.

The AAIDD has assessment tools for determining the level of support required for a child or an adult to be successful in the home and community (Thompson et al., 2002). Supports Intensity Scale-Children's Version (AAIDD, 2016) is appropriate for ages 5 to 16. In part I of the tool, focus is on specific medical conditions and behavioral concerns potentially requiring support. Part II assesses activities for home living, community and neighborhood, school participation, school learning, health and safety, social activities, and advocacy. The adult version of the scale (AAIDD, 2015) measures support needed for success in home living, community living, life-long learning, employment, health and safety, social activities, and protection and advocacy.

The levels of support are used in APE and GPE environments to distinguish what is needed for the student with ID to learn. The *support level* runs on a continuum from intermittent to pervasive, from settings that are selective to nearly all settings, and with varying amounts of professional assistance. Table 7.1 is, therefore, a necessary guide to apply to the implementation of an IEP in the student's physical education placement.

The relationship between a deficit in adaptive function and the support needed (table 7.1) is critical to understand. Effective matching of these realities equals program engagement in physical activity for the student with ID.

Educational Model

For classifying a disability or impairment, there is an educational model and a clinical model. The educational model uses criteria in federal education law, IDEA (2004). The clinical model is guided by the criteria of the American Psychiatric Association's

TABLE 7.1   AAIDD Levels of Support for Intellectual Disabilities

Level of support	Amount of professional assistance
Intermittent	Consult: occasional Monitor: occasional
Limited	Contact: occasional/regular
Extensive	Contact: regular weekly
Pervasive	Contact: continuous Monitor: continuous

Adapted from Schalock et al. (2010).

Diagnostic and Statistical Manual of Mental Disorders, Fifth Edition, Text Revision (2022). Both models use assessments of intelligence and adaptive function to determine the eventual classification of ID for the individual. Federal educational law for individuals with disabilities is concerned with appropriate classification to support the educational performance of the individual. When the individual is assessed in a medical setting, a diagnosis of ID is made to establish proper medical care. Meeting classification criteria allows students to be served in special education, following formulas for federal and state allocation of monies.

Under federal educational law in the United States, "intellectual disability means significantly sub-average general intellectual functioning existing concurrently with deficits in adaptive behavior and manifested during the developmental period that adversely affects a child's educational performance" (IDEA, 1997, § 300.7). In October 2010, President Barack Obama signed Rosa's Law, changing federal statutes to use the term *intellectual disability* rather than *mental retardation*.

To determine an educational classification of ID, the individual's IQ score performance is studied in relationship to their adapted functioning. Then classification of mild, moderate, severe, or profound ID is made by qualified personnel (figure 7.4). Levels of support are assessed to determine need per settings. These levels of support are not found in the federal educational law, but they can profoundly influence how a student with ID can learn. See figure 7.5 for the educational terminology used across classification of ID that includes intellectual function and adaptive behavior's level of support.

There are many pieces of information to follow as the flow of information is initiated from assessment of the intellectual quotient to adaptive functioning to application for a student into an adapted along with their classifications and then into levels of support leading eventually into the application for adapted physical education and general physical education's curriculum. Figure 7.5 illustrates this.

Clinical Model

Clinically, intellectual disabilities are characterized by intellectual difficulties as well as difficulties in conceptual, social, and practical areas of living that begin in childhood (Patel et al., 2022.).. Specific IQ criteria include deficits confirmed in areas such as reasoning, problem-solving, and academic learning. "Deficits in adaptive functioning result in failure to meet developmental and sociocultural standards for personal independence and social responsibility" (Patel et al., 2022, p. S25.). Without ongoing support, the deficits limit functioning *across multiple settings* with skills like communication, social participation, and independent living.

For a diagnosis of ID, an individual's IQ is studied in relationship to the individual's skills in adaptive functioning. The clinical terminology is

---

The AAIDD levels of support are not specified in IDEA (2004). Nonetheless, they have influenced IDEA assessment choice and evaluation reports leading to educational plans and instructional strategies.

Intelligence Quotient	Classification of Intellectual Disability
55-70*	Mild
40-55	Moderate
25-40	Severe
<20-25	Profound

Adaptive Functioning

Conceptual

Social

Practical

*Considering an SEM of five, the IQ can go up to 75 (Colarusso et al., 2017).

FIGURE 7.4   Education considerations for classification of intellectual disability.

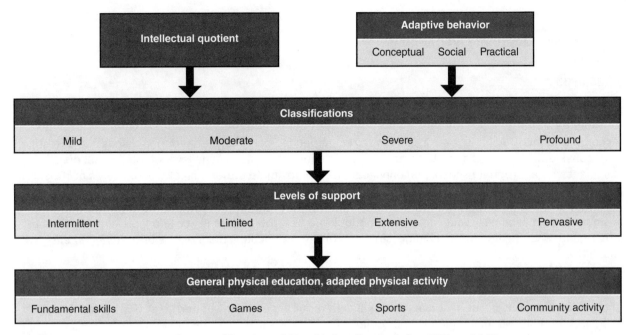

FIGURE 7.5 Assessments for classification of ID with implications for GPE and APA.

laid out in figure 7.6, which looks very similar to figure 7.4. Today there is more similarity than dissimilarity. Note that the medical diagnostic terms for level of severity of ID are mild, moderate, severe, and profound. In adapted functioning, the AAIDD influenced both the medical and educational criteria, resulting in the same categories of assessment across the conceptual, social, or personal domains. Levels of support have a different categorization than the educational domain. In the *Diagnostic and Statistical Manual of Mental Disorders, Fifth Edition*, the levels of support are driven by the adaptive functioning (conceptual, social, practical), the age of the individual with an ID, and the severity. These levels of support are retained in the *DSM-5-TR* (2022).

Intellectual disability may also be concomitant with mental disorders, as described by the American Psychiatric Association in its *Diagnostic and Statistical Manual of Mental Disorders, Fifth Edition, Text Revision* (known as *DSM-5-TR*; APA, 2022). The medical term *comorbidity*, meaning existing with, is used for individuals who have an ID and a mental disorder. The *DSM-5-TR* uses the term *intellectual disability disorder* (IDD) to match the World Health Organization classification. Educational settings will still rely on IDEA (2004) definitions and use the term *intellectual disability* (ID) in special education services. We will use *ID* in this and subsequent chapters. Reports from clinical settings may use *IDD*.

Evaluation and the IEP

With the diagnosis of ID, the student will be assessed by the IEP team. As the child grows and matures, the status of support may shift, and the specifics of the goals change. The IEP in physical education changes with the curriculum by grade of the student.

Instructional Considerations

Students with ID have learning characteristics in common with their peers without ID and vary greatly in the extent to which they demonstrate specific characteristic behaviors. Learning characteristics and corresponding considerations for students with ID include the following:

- The total amount of learning does progress yet is less than age peers without ID.
- The rate of learning is less than age peers without ID, yet it does progress.
- Attention is short compared to age peers without ID.
- Needed processing time (e.g., instructions, decisions) to performance takes longer compared to age peers.
- Instructions should be presented in short, concrete terms, avoiding abstract thought compared to some age peers.

///

Intelligence Quotient Overlapping

50 to 75

35 to 55

20 to 40

Up to 25

According to the APA, full-scale IQ scores are recommended and interpreted during discussion of testing, with consideration for social, cultural, and linguistic contexts. To determine level of intellectual disability, clinicians and appropriate school personnel can use approximate rather than absolute scores of IQ, and if needed, additional assessment of a cognitive profile with neuropsychological testing occurs. For individuals with an IQ of 70 to 75, those clinicians and school personnel can substitute the cognitive profile for a single IQ test especially when adaptive functioning is very low and IQ is above a typical range. On the other hand, when testing for IQ is impossible or extremely difficult, a diagnosis is *unspecified intellectual disability*.

Adaptive Functioning

If significant deficits occur in at least one skill area requiring ongoing support to perform adequately, a diagnosis of adaptive functioning is appropriate. The skill areas include the following:

Conceptual

Social

Practical

Severity Classification of Intellectual Disability

Mild

Moderate

Severe

Profound

Level of Support

Adaptive functioning determines level of support across the life span, including preschool, school age, and adulthood. At each level, given the age and the adaptive function deficit category (conceptual, social, practical), support is explained.

Term from *DSM 5*, American Psychiatric Association (2022).

///

FIGURE 7.6   Medical considerations in classification of intellectual disability.

- Teachers should employ short instructions versus long verbal narratives, incorporating physical, visual, or verbal prompts:
  - Teachers can prompt behavior using a hierarchy from most to least intrusive—physical (most intrusive), visual, and verbal (least intrusive).
  - Teachers can combine prompts when necessary, such as verbal and physical or verbal and visual.
- Generalizability is difficult for individuals with ID. Have the students practice the skills in the setting for which the skills are used.
- Social skills for an activity are learned. Teach the social skills expected in the physical activity environment.
- Applied behavior analysis helps students learn particularly if it is used consistently across settings in the student's day. Applied behavior analysis is more effective if the same strategies are used across all settings in school, at home, and in the community.
- In education, use the behavior plans of the IEP team in physical activity settings.

- Analyze movement skills for the activity rather than relying on typical motor development progressions. Use a task analysis approach to understand the current functional level in movement and how the program content will build skills toward an expected competency for the youth.

- Opportunities to repeat or rehearse the same activities is supportive of learning.

Social Skills

Children and youth with intellectual disability benefit from being taught social skills for physical activity participation, particularly with social rules and result of their actions; teach social skills associated with team performance, good sports behavior with a team defeat, and personal hygiene connected to social presence in sports.

Recess is a difficult time for many children because this time is typically unstructured free play. Rules for social engagement in these situations are not easily learned for a student with ID. There are social skills for using the equipment on the playground and participating in the group games that children and youth repeatedly enjoy during recess. Therefore, helpful strategies such as cuing when recess is ending smooths the transition for *all* children and especially for students with ID. If recess is indeed fun, no one likes it have it end. An agreed-upon sign helps children anticipate a change in their time in recess. Positive staff comments toward the student with ID help reinforce the learning of social skills associated with play. Examples include "Hey Martin, you looked good out there giving high fives to your friends" and "Angela, great tossing of the ball to your teammate." Having more equipment available for recess structures activity, and teachers and paraprofessionals can be mindful of their role to suggest a game and manage behavior from the positive.

McConnell (2000) promotes the use of the naturalistic behavioral interventions to teach social skills. This means that an intervention is more effective when conducted in the setting in which it will be used and where natural rewards and consequences are in place. For example, in the general physical education class, a student may have trouble following the direction to "give a high five to a classmate and line up by the wall." The teacher observes that Mateo has had trouble doing this in the past. The teacher instructs *all* the students to use the high-five technique. Then the teacher points out how well Mateo did the high five, as well as how Kali, Mira, Hiram, and others did. The teacher

then asks these students to give a buddy a high five. This is a natural positive consequence, and it is immediate and brief.

In a study, reciprocal imitation training improved the social engagement of a group of adolescents with intellectually disabilities (Ingersoll et al., 2013). In another study, student social skills improved by using video prompting and modeling (Canella-Malone et al., 2013). A child can learn social skills when specific imitation is targeted, introduced, commented on, and repeated. An example of the use of reciprocal imitation training with very young children is the classic use of a mirror. Young children like to look at themselves in a mirror. For example, a therapist might say to her young client, Madeline, "Wave bye-bye." Madeline and her therapist look in the mirror and both the therapist and Madeline wave bye-bye.

In a clinical setting if social skills are problematic, the therapist can discuss a strategy with the parent that is being used in the school. For some children

Bold Stock/age fotostock

with ID a therapy session is new and needs explanation and descriptions of when the child is doing well with a social skill or putting out a positive effort.

Lag in Expression of Skills

For a young child with ID, there is often a noticeable lag in the expression of expected age-appropriate physical, social, emotional, and communication skills. Parents may first see a real developmental lag in early age group gatherings (birthday parties or family gatherings) and then in early school-aged classes. Their child's age peers take on more complicated tasks. Sometimes this is heartbreaking for parents. Yet, children with ID with appropriate supports flourish in their classrooms. They are happy and well placed in the motor room and enjoying recess. They have friends, and their developmental lags are accommodated. Approximately 42 states and the District of Columbia have kindergarten programs (Education Commission of the States, 2018) that are either full or half day.

Less Physically Active

Children with ID have shown to consistently score lower than age peers on measures of strength, endurance, agility, balance, running speed, and flexibility. The degree to which this affects physical activity participation is individual. Children without ID can score low on any of the number of measures for any number of reasons. Understanding and applying the AAIDD level of support measures for children with ID, in combination with data from physical skills assessed, will result in modifications and adaptations to increase capacity for GPE and APE participation and thus bump up physical activity engagement. Yet it is important that the student enjoy being active and is positively regarded for the individual they are. Lifting weights is fun for some teens and if there is no competition with who lifts the most weight, the fun continues and the student gains in their strength.

In a large data set in the United States, obesity prevalence for children and youth with ID ages 10 to 17 were found to be twice that as compared to their age peers when corrected for poverty (Segal et al., 2016). According to Collins and Staples (2017), children with ID and children with autism and ID in Canada are less physically active than their age peers and lag on their performance of fundamental movement skills. Difficulty in skill performance may be attributed to failure to understand the movement skill, limited attention and comprehension skills, low fitness level, or an overall lack of access to community activities. Collins and Staples, as well as Segal, reported that offering a 90-minute physical activity program for 35 children with ID, ages 7 to 12 years of age, once a week for 10 weeks, focusing on fundamental skills related to a sport or lead-up game by age, improved the children's physical fitness as measured by the Brockport Physical Fitness Test (Winnick & Short, 2014). This program was heavily staffed (one university student for every three participants) and instruction was in small groups. It exemplifies the fact that access to physical activity engagement in the community with trained staff and program modifications was successful in improving fitness for the children.

Down Syndrome

Differences in physical fitness for children with Down syndrome may be due to their challenges with cardiovascular response (Pitetti et al., 1992). Recent improvements in cardiac surgery and the neonatal care of infants with Down syndrome has resulted in healthier babies (Versacci et al., 2018). Those with Down syndrome tend to gain weight in their early teens after they reach their maximum height (Glaze, 1985). Upper respiratory infection is also very prevalent among individuals with Down syndrome. Yet, these individuals do well and improve through physical activity engagement and training programs (Jeng et al., 2017).

Individuals with Down syndrome may have a condition known as atlantoaxial instability, which is decreased movement and malalignment of the "first [atlas] and second [axial] cervical vertebra joint articulation" (Tomlinson et al., 2020, p. 293). These are vertebrae in the upper spine (neck) under the base of the skull. The joint *between* the first cervical vertebra (C1, atlas) and second cervical vertebra (C2, axis) is called the atlanto-axial joint. Those with Down syndrome have lax ligaments connecting to the muscles in that area and "bony abnormalities of the atlantoaxial joint" (p. 293). In people with Down syndrome, the ligaments connecting to muscle are "lax" or floppy. This results in less stable vertebrae, which makes the joint vulnerable to damage and can lead to damage to the spinal cord (Massachusetts General Hospital, 2019). If it is not known that the student has atlantoaxial instability, damage to the spinal cord can occur during physical activity. Atlantoaxial instability exists in approximately 17 percent of all individuals with Down syndrome. In the past, X-rays of the vertebral column were recommended for everyone with Down syndrome who participated in physical activity. This is no longer recommended for those with Down syndrome who do not have symptoms of atlantoaxial instability (Tomlinson et al., 2020). Rather, Tomlinson and colleagues recommended that three questions be asked by the clinician who knowns the student to detect if the student has this instability: Is there (1) any evidence of muscle weakness progressing, (2) any evidence of poor head or neck muscle control, and (3) at the point when the neck is in flexion, does the chin rest on the chest? To test question 2, have the person lie on their back, legs out straight, and pull them to a sitting position. When the head lags back as the body is brought forward, this is a marker for atlantoaxial instability. Persons with Down syndrome should be examined by a health care professional for easy fatigability, difficulties in walking, neck pain, head tilt, incoordination and clumsiness, spasticity, hyperreflexia, clonus, and a few other neurological signs of atypical motor performance (Tomlinson et al., 2020).

It is noted that forward or backward bending of the neck, which is common in some sports such as gymnastics, may dislocate at the atlas (figure 7.7). *In the absence of medical clearance*, students with Down syndrome should be restricted from participating in gymnastics, diving, butterfly stroke in swimming, high jump, pentathlon, and any warm-up exercise placing pressure on the head and neck muscles. If diagnosis confirms atlantoaxial instability, the student should be permanently restricted from these activities and other activities should be selected that are enjoyable and pose less risk.

Age Correction for Prematurity and Development

An infant's chronological age needs to be corrected for prematurity. Chronological age is age in real time. A baby born at *full term* is born at 9 months, and after 12 months on Earth they are 1 year old. If a baby is born at 6 months' gestation, they are 3 months early (not having developed yet to 9 months). In testing in clinics and early intervention (EI) services, this infant has a chronological age that needs to be adjusted for prematurity. It is inappropriate to test a premature infant who has only been on this earth for few months. The baby's community clinicians will wait for them to reach full gestational age to further assess and begin their interventions. If not, any testing of their development is asking them to do skills that are months ahead of their developmental age. They will fail, and their skills will be underestimated. All developmental testing requires assessors age correct for prematurity until around 3 years of age.

Referral to early intervention (EI) services for premature infants does not begin right after birth. They may spend time in the hospital and then grow in strength and age at home. When the referral is made to EI the premature infant qualifies under the category of DD or possibly an orthopedic impairment (cerebral palsy) if there are developmental delays (Greene & Patra, 2016). If the family has access to an interdisciplinary neonatal follow-up clinic, the

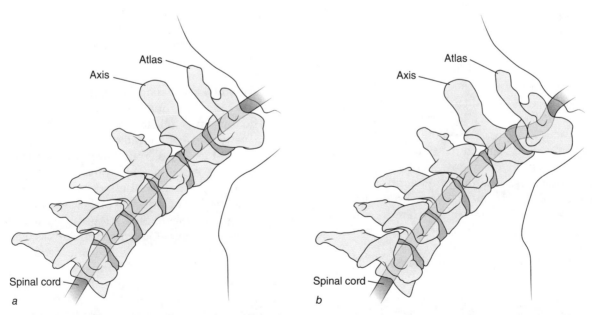

FIGURE 7.7   Head flexion with stable cervical spine position (*a*), versus with atlantoaxial instability (*b*). Dislocation of the atlas (C1) would injure the spinal cord.

infant and family are followed from discharge from that clinic by a team of specialists including occupational therapy, neonatology, child psychology, and nursing. The neonatal intensive care unit team will initiate the referral for the community-based services of EI. In this program, the infant and their parents are visited by occupational or physical therapy and other specialists as needed. Sometimes premature infants do not qualify for EI services in their state because when tested they do not meet criteria for a certain percent delay (e.g., 30% below the mean on standardized developmental testing). Greene and Patra's research (2016) reported that EI services were more highly available in their state (Illinois) for babies born weighing <1,000 grams than those born weighing >1,000 grams, dispelling the myth that all infants born premature automatically enter EI services.

Developmental age is a calculated age of maturation based on skill performance in specific domains (physical, cognitive, language) on standardized tests. Early intervention services use standardized tests, or developmental checklists if standardized tests with norms are not possible. The CDC has posted a developmental checklist, Act Early, for parents or caregivers, teachers, and clinicians (www.cdc.gov/MilestoneTracker) working with young children. Activities are recommended for each age group.

For example, a toddler with a 20-month chronological age and a skill set of 10 months developmentally in one or more domains has a definite 10-month lag; hence the child continues to qualify for services under DD within the mandates of IDEA (2004). Regarding their home or center-based physical activity, this child is to be involved in content of a 20-month-old (running on the playground, digging in the sandbox, building structures) with the instruction geared to their developmental age of 10 months. As the child matures into early school programs, this guide is easier to understand. When it is time to go through the stations for throwing, the child with a delay goes right along and there are adaptations waiting. In general, rather than talk about developmental and chronological age to parents, it is more appropriate to communicate what their child is doing in physical activity ("Arthur loves to kick the ball") and then explain where the next goals will be ("Next he will kick to a wide goal").

A simple mantra of instruction: *Content is geared to chronological age, and instruction is geared to developmental age.* This becomes more important as the child advances in the educational system. There is a practicality in this approach. A child cannot perform a movement skill for which their body is not yet mature enough, yet their interests can be age appropriate. A high school student who has a cognitive developmental age of a younger child still wants to dance and play sports more appropriate for their age group. An adapted and interdisciplinary approach to their physical activity is what is needed using the same mantra.

Program Placement and Focus

Infants and toddlers learn their movement skills differently than school-age children, whether they are typically or atypically developing. With young children, arranging the environment is the key to having infants begin exploring and learning movement activities. These young children do not form lines to perform, nor do they wait in lines. Infants, toddlers, and preschoolers with ID make progress in learning their early movement skills, though there is developmental lag. Much more information on these young ages and their early movement, development, and instruction is contained in chapter 5.

Infancy Through Preschool

Planning the adapted physical activity program begins at birth for infants referred into EI if they have an ID and meet federal and state criteria for the program. Down syndrome is an example of a disability that can be diagnosed at birth and qualifies for EI services then. Some babies lag in developmental milestones across domains but are too young for a specific diagnosis. As explained, those infants carry a diagnosis of DD and can begin receiving EI if they qualify in their state.

The EI team is to listen to the parent's goals for their baby and collaborate to begin the infant's active life (Pletcher & Younggren, 2013). The cognitive, social, emotional, and physical domains of early development are all intertwined. The physically active infant builds a strong structure for positive growth (Shonkoff, 2011) because when they move, they are developing physical skills as well as all other domain-specific skills. Babies who do not move, do not develop well for many reasons. Special attention is paid to tracking the changes taking place within months, as well as years, as the child with ID grows from infancy to toddlerhood. Early intervention serves the child and family in infancy and toddlerhood, and then early childhood special education takes over in most states for preschool and kindergarten.

The home is the first place of intervention for infants with intellectual disabilities. A member of their intervention team, along with the parent, develops an individual family service plan (IFSP). Some teams are transdisciplinary, meaning that they can carry out IFSPs across disciplines. Some visit by discipline need; therefore, a physical therapist would work with the baby on positioning and strengthening lax muscles. Babies with Down syndrome have floppy muscles and are behind their peers for executing skills like rolling over, pulling to stand, crawling, and walking.

Dr. Dale Ulrich developed a baby treadmill that exposes young children with Down syndrome, who are delayed in the onset of walking, to walking experiences to give them more opportunities for walking with support (Ulrich et al., 2001). He has shown that toddlers who use this device do begin walking earlier than expected. Others have used the baby treadmill to investigate benefits to early walking (Lloyd et al., 2010), and this treadmill is found in some pediatric rehabilitation centers. This has been exciting for many parents and is an opportunity for the infant to be upright and begin to strengthen muscles for walking.

Physical and occupational therapists work with the parents and caregivers on how to position infants and toddlers with ID in play to facilitate the developmental milestones (for example, independent sitting, reaching, grasping and releasing, and pulling to stand) and how to position the infant to progress them along these expected skills. Not all movement in these ages is considered therapy, but it is important that these young infants and toddlers are playing and in the correct positions for that play, although this correctness takes time to facilitate without being intrusive for the child.

The W-sit is a sitting position that babies and toddlers with Down syndrome prefer, but it is a very harmful position for the hips and knee joints and is therefore detrimental to their development. In this position, the child sits on their bottom with their legs bent towards their back and splayed out (figure 7.8). The physical therapist helps with a repositioning intervention by assisting the child and the IFSP team members, including parents. Pediatric physical therapists can make the transition out of a W-sit *fun*. After gradual coaching, the child typically gives up the position for the appropriate position. This position is seen in young children without disabilities and with other disability areas. In each case, it *requires* intervention.

FIGURE 7.8 The W-sit.

Over time, infants with ID or DD need opportunities to practice early movements skills. The EI teams of occupational and physical therapy, speech and language pathology, and others will choose a person to come to the home and remain as the case manager to listen to what the family wants for their baby and to support their concerns and the development of their baby.

Toddlers with ID or DD can be served in the home or in a program. Toddlers are known for increasing mobility over infancy, particularly with the onset of walking. The walking skills of toddlers with ID are delayed by as much as two years. The range of the onset of walking for a typically developing peer is from 8 months to 18 months. The child with ID may still be crawling at this time. That means covering a lot of distance with crawling and exploring their environment and family members. This is appropriate, and in due time, the child will walk. Physical therapists and others can encourage the home or center facility to have tunnels (boxes) to crawl through, things to crawl around and over, and to climb up and descend. This is developmentally appropriate and will strengthen muscles for initiating pull-to-stand, cruise, and later walk. To encourage more moving and more upper body activity, balls of various sizes for throwing, catching, pushing, and rolling should be provided for play.

School Age

As children reach school age, children with ID continue to lag in motor ability and in physical fitness (Faison-Hodge & Porretta, 2004; Pitetti & Fernhall,

2004). Gains in skill can be made when appropriate programs are provided (e.g., Bryce, 2021). Engaging in the general physical education class with input from the IEP team is known to improve self-concept and general emotional development. The younger child's understanding of concepts, such as shape, size, and color can be reinforced while developing motor skills. When the same concepts are presented across settings, learning takes place for children with ID. APE and GPE teachers working with special education teachers coordinate activities and share information. Some children are in small-group APE.

In preschool, the child enters the three-year-old group and is supported by the special education team. Some states do not have preschool. Kindergarten is part of K12 education. The student with ID is placed in an integrated or segregated classroom or in a combination of integrated and segregated classrooms. The makeup of the child's placement is devised based on the desires of the parent, the classrooms available, and the assessment data.

Instructional Strategies

In early childhood classrooms, the classroom teacher may be the instructor for the physical activity room because IDEA (2004) only stipulates "qualified person." Who advises this teacher on the children with intellectual disabilities who have an IEP or an IFSP? Most likely, if there is an adapted physical education person on the IEP or IFSP team, that person will help the classroom teacher. If not, then the physical therapist or occupational therapist will assist. Legally, this can get confusing because IDEA (2004) does not require physical education for the children with disabilities if the children without disabilities do not have physical education in the school. Some states do not. Therefore, the team would not write an IEP or IFSP in adapted physical education. They would help the classroom teacher with adaptations for learning in the classroom like computer skills and using the bathroom and moving around the school.

At these early ages, accuracy in movement is not the goal of the movement for any child. Time to explore the movements and have many opportunities to repeat the skills is the goal. With this type of exploration, the young child begins to bring together many different systems (e.g., auditory, neurological, muscular, visual) and learns specific movements.

In GPE or APE, the child with ID may have a paraprofessional in the class with them. Preteach-ing is a solid strategy for some students to have an opportunity to understand the activity and understand directions and social skill. Use the assessment data, observe what the child can do, and adapt from there.

Developmental Approach

At very young ages, it is appropriate to consider a bottom-up developmental approach for teaching children with intellectual disability in physical activity. In the bottom-up approach, skills are taught in a sequence where prerequisite motor skills are required before moving on to the next skill (Burton & Miller, 1998), especially for fundamental skills like kicking, throwing, running, and striking. Later in their education and if the student is not progressing, this approach is not appropriate for two reasons: (1) children with intellectual disability may skip steps thought to be requisite; and (2) the child does gain in skill, but the program progresses into age-appropriate games and activities with the introduction of games with more rules, team play, and the need for quick responses. Therefore, these activities are adapted. Adapted activity allows children with intellectual disability to play games and sports and pursue individual age-appropriate physical activity. It is boring and discouraging to stay focusing on how to swing a bat using the developmental approach when the student is older or when younger and others have mastered it and moved on. Instead, adapt either the equipment, the rules, or the environment, or accept a different type of swing.

One exception to a developmental approach in the younger ages is where the disability will not allow a traditional understanding of prerequisite motor skills. An example would be that children who use a wheelchair for ambulation will not run with their legs but will use their arms to propel themselves in their chair in games and activities.

Environment and Equipment

For many children, particularly those with ID, conducting classes in a large space may interfere with their skill development. These children are easily distracted, and the presence of equipment usually found in the gymnasium will compete with the teacher's ability to hold the attention of the students. Small groups for instruction are beneficial to learning. As the participants become proficient in the skill, opportunities should be provided to utilize the new skills within the larger environment of the playground or gymnasium.

Physical education teachers should strive to maintain a class size conducive to learning (although often they don't have a choice). The ratio of teacher to student will vary according to the motor skill level of the youngsters, the ability of the teacher, and the presence of educational assistants. Children with severe ID can require a one-to-one adult-to-student ratio. For others, the class size can be 1 to 10 or even higher with trained educational assistants. Using trained peer tutors can provide an invaluable resource to the classroom teacher and provide beneficial experiences for students with and without ID (Houston-Wilson, 1993). Paraprofessionals are used in the APE and GPE class to teach skills and activities under the supervision and training of the teacher. If assistants are used in the clinical setting, they must be trained and supervised.

An insufficient amount of equipment reduces the maximum number of practice trials available to any student. In the schools, there should be enough equipment for each activity. Having enough equipment allows for exploration of the use of that equipment, which is critical in the learning process of students with ID. It also increases the opportunity to respond that is so important to learning the skill itself. To maintain the involvement of all the students with varied skill levels, the availability of a variety of equipment is desirable to match skill levels. Large balls are recommended for young children learning to catch, and small balls that match their hand size are recommended for throwing. Various sizes and weights among these are helpful. These recommendations are also in line with universal design for learning in physical education (Lieberman et al., 2020).

Student Motivation and Interest

Predictable structure of the class is a big motivator in GPE or APE classes for students with ID. As time goes on, the student knows what to expect, and their confidence expands and anxiety lowers. A younger student's schedule might be: circle time or warm-up, skill focus, stations or game, and cool down. Content for those time slots change, and teaching strategies are aligned with skill progressions. Students with intellectual disabilities need to be alerted that there will be a switch in activity within the class. Using time-oriented warnings is accepted even with younger students who don't understand time concepts but do understand that something will change. Use a signal the teacher has developed for the students. Then announce "Five minutes to stop time," and hold up a hand with five fingers. Later, "Three minutes," while holding up three fingers. Finally, "OK, stop." After this, there is a routine of picking up the balls, putting them

away, coming to the center of the room, and sitting or standing in the center circle.

Interest and motivation are also developed for the student with intellectual disability as the physical activity classmates understand that they are all doing their personal best. The concept of developing a personal best is repeatedly used. "Raise your hand if you did your personal best!" Everyone will likely raise their hand. It really doesn't matter. The point is that everyone is different, but everyone is trying their personal best. Those in clinical settings can ask the same question.

Interests of the student with an ID (and really any student) are important to observe and use in physical activity in the school and clinical program. Observe what they are attracted to and like, such as books, toys, athletic figures, movie figures, sports teams, family outings, or equipment preferred in the gym or on the playground. Listen to what they talk about. Tell them that you like their green T-shirt. Tell them you saw one of them on the swings and noticed how hard they were pumping! Comment on how happy they looked running in the gym or playing a game.

Ask the students in middle school to name their team or group. For younger students, ask them the name of a person in a story that they like. Then use that as a team name. These are all ways to bring "positives" of the students' lives into the physical activity programs. Conveying words for affirmative emotions when students are physically active gives them positive associations with movement.

Direct Method

The direct method is successful for instructing students with ID in physical activity. This method uses concrete materials that are interesting, age appropriate, and relevant to the student. Present information and instructions in small, sequential steps as espoused in task analysis and review each step frequently. Provide cues and immediate feedback when building skills, and provide opportunities for success.

Level of Prompts

Instructions are based on determining what level of prompt to use with the student. There is a hierarchy to these prompts that is classically defined as being on a continuum from most intrusive to least intrusive. Plan a prompt as a form of instruction that moves the instruction forward. Understanding the level of prompts is very important in instructing students with ID. Refer to chapter 5 on instruction for a complete description.

Physical Prompts

The level of a prompt is selected by where the student can use to be successful. For example, in a high school class practicing yoga, a student with an ID might need a physical assist when first assuming the position of downward dog. Over time, the teacher may only need to use a verbal prompt "downward dog" to assist the student. With young children, a physical prompt is initiated with a verbal cue: "I'm going to help your racket arm." Then, if it is OK with the child, use physical assistance and move them through the swing. In figure 7.9, the adult is demonstrating a physical assist.

Physical assistance can be employed when teaching a child to ride a tricycle. The child may not understand the action required to pedal the tricycle until the teacher uses kinesthesis with the child's feet on the tricycle pedals. Sometimes a teacher adds the verbal cue "Push." Rhythmically saying push while physically assisting the child can lead to the trike moving. Later, the instructor can use only the verbal prompt, *push*. In the early phase of physical assistance, the hold taken on the child should be reassuring to promote confidence in attempting the movement. As the need for physical assistance fades, a light touch may be all that is needed.

FIGURE 7.9   Eye contact with physical assistance holding the torso in place helps the child learn the correct body position.

If the physical assistance seems to be overly extensive while teaching a skill or recreation activity, choose a lower level skill. For example, given the previous situation, overly extensive physical assistance might be lifting the child onto the scooter, then pushing the feet physically, then assisting with the direction of the handlebars. Instead, the teacher or therapist might start by having the child use a scooter without pedals. With the scooter, the child just pushes their feet off the ground to give the scooter a forward movement (alternating feet to push off or using both feet together to push off the ground for a forward movement). Some children like pushing the back of the scooter without even getting on it. Nowadays, there are lots of little bicycles without pedals, so the next step up the task analysis might be a bike with two wheels. It depends on the child's interests.

Visual and Verbal Prompts

Visual assistance and verbal prompts are often used together when teaching students with ID. The teacher points so the student knows where to start the obstacle course, or sets up arrows in cones, or sets pictures into cones in a gym of the activity, or after explaining the rules briefly uses red and green flags with the game of Red Light, Green Light.

A picture exchange communication system (PECS) is a very specific communication system that takes advantage of visualization and is tied to a behavioral modification system (Frost & Bondy, 2002). It was designed to help young children with autism communicate and develop functional language. Frost and Bondy, two speech psychologists, found their tool effective with others with developmental disabilities (2002). Instructors and therapists can use this system and its pictures to help with physical activity instructions, especially when a student with ID is already working with a picture exchange communication system. Basically, in APE or GPE classes, pictures are used with the student that represent the physical activities of the class. Sometimes they are ordered in the time sequence of the class—like having a schedule on the wall that includes a simple picture per activity can help individuals understand the equipment and structure of the class. Sometimes these activities are on a chart in the class for the student; other times teachers or paras put the pictures on cards and have them on a lanyard around their neck to show the student. Teachers and the student can devise the pictures. There are commercial pictures and there are more do-it-yourself pictures. For example, maybe a soccer ball represents the game in the class. There are many ways to devise a PECS. The SLP can assist as the student may be using the system in other educational settings.

Other examples of visual prompts that help students with ID are cues for track starts and colored lines painted on the gymnasium surface for specific common points of reference. Visual and verbal prompts could also be used together, such as saying "over there" while pointing to a cone marker or a track start.

Verbal prompts can be used in much the same way in instructing students with ID as with students without disabilities. The difference is in using more simple verbal prompts such as *sit*, *hold*, or *step over*, related to the skills, games, and sports they are learning. If appropriate, use the word alone or in a simple, short sentence.

Research by Hans van der Mars has shown that overreliance on long verbal instructions in physical education class is not optimal for engaging the students in activity. Most students need short and simple instructions. Care must be exercised to avoid providing students more information than they can process during a given time. Others have reported that overreliance on the use of verbalization with students who have communication disorders has definite limitations. It is not uncommon to observe a response delay of several seconds in students with ID.

Consistency in the instructional environment—using similar cues—is helpful in establishing gains in GPE/APE classes for the student with ID. Likewise, in the instruction of any task, it is essential for the teacher's directions to be as specific as possible. Providing exact visual or verbal prompts results in students being able to perform the task because they understand what is expected of them. It may take a little time for them to follow the prompt but they will.

Task Analysis

Instructional efforts should be directed toward providing success-oriented experiences for the participants. Recognition of this teaching strategy is especially critical for teachers, coaches, and clinicians of students with intellectual disabilities. Breaking skills down into their subcomponents and listing them in a hierarchical sequence is referred to as task analysis. Addressed in chapter 6, each component has a behavioral statement whereby criterion levels may then be developed so that all will know when to advance to the next step.

Staff Participation

Because students with ID are easily distracted, class observers (e.g., extra adults in the gym) should be kept to a minimum or be participants in class activities. Physical education is an *educational class*. It is not time for other teachers to take a break in the gymnasium while their students are in there. If the teachers, a coach, or an allied health professional is in the gym, participation is encouraged in the play and fitness activities of these students. An exception applies if any one of these professionals is performing an observation for a specific purpose.

Positive feedback for the student with ID in the form of sincere praise during skill or game execution increases satisfaction and fun for the student. The attempt may not result in successful performance, but the student's effort should be commended by the teacher, coach, or allied health professional. Use the student's name and be specific, in a few words, about what you are praising. Examples include the following:

- "Marcus, you did that leap so far out!"
- "Henry, your team didn't win today, but you shot toward the goal!"
- "Jhumpa, what a great teammate you were today with your smiles and hard work."
- "Winston, thanks for picking up all the extra balls on the floor today."

Games, Pacing, and Peer Tutors

Individuals with ID perform best the first few times they do a skill. Consequently, it is to their advantage to end practice after a few attempts. After the skills of a game have been mastered, they should be reviewed with a few words for a brief amount of time each time before the game is played. These periods should be just long enough to refresh the students' memories.

Because some individuals with ID have low physical vitality, they fatigue easily. This has important implications for the teaching situation. First, it means that new and complex activities should be planned for the early part of the period while the students are fresh and alert. Then, too, a greater chance of injury exists after fatigue sets in, so it is important for the instructor to watch for signs of fatigue. Research supports that fitness levels can be significantly improved if opportunities and proper training supervision take place (Lavay & McKenzie, 1991; Pitetti & Tan, 1991).

In some instances, GPE and APE teachers have obtained the assistance of high school students who volunteer to provide individual attention for youngsters with ID. Also, students without disabilities in the same age class as the student with an ID, can assist as a peer tutor. Both the high school program

and the peer tutoring have proven to be worthwhile learning experiences for students with or without a disability. To utilize program volunteers effectively, they must be trained, and the teacher and parents must provide a written program for each student emphasizing the skills to be learned (Houston-Wilson et al., 1997). A concerted effort must be made to monitor the efforts of the volunteers, correcting and reinforcing them when appropriate.

Behavior Plans

A prearranged behavior plan is recommended for students with ID who may have problems that result in disruptions in a physical activity class, therapy, or sport training session. It needs to be discussed with the student using concrete examples in a short amount of time with less verbiage. There are many resources for this situation. One of the best strategies is to try to figure out the antecedent, behavior, and consequences of the situation. (Chapter 10 on behavior disorders has more information on this and other behavioral issues.) What happened just before the event (the antecedent)? What happened (the behavior)? What happened for the student after the behavior took place (consequence)? This is discussed with those at the school who can help devise an intervention plan. The student's parents or caregivers can also be recruited for a discussion. Sometimes students are asked to pick their consequence for not performing the expected behavior.

Physical Activities

GPE teachers are skilled in differentiated instruction where there is a lesson for the whole class and accommodations for students in their class. Communication with the student with ID may involve a paraprofessional, peer instruction, or volunteer who is trained to assist in the GPE or APE class. Some students will only be in the GPE setting for part of the time. For example, hockey may be a highly valued activity in the community and the GPE program, but neither the student nor the student's family are interested in this activity. Another activity can be substituted and offered at the same time, hopefully with a few other students interested in the same activity.

Basic Motor Skills

The young child with ID lags in the development of their motor skills compared to their age peers. They do progress given instruction and opportunity to respond to practicing skills. Basic skills for play

kali9/E+/Getty Images

are running, hopping, jumping, skipping, kicking, hanging, catching, and throwing. These are part of the school's physical education curriculum by grade. To include the student with ID with their peers in both adapted physical education and general physical education settings, modifications might be made to the curriculum while the activities in the activity environment might be adapted.

Pretend Play

Any pretending can require that the instructor be specific and *concrete* with young children with intellectual disabilities. If the children are to pretend to be farm animals, then someone like the classroom teacher should have introduced them to animals via songs (such as "Old MacDonald Had a Farm"), stories, or pictures of animals. The APE or GPE teacher can ask them to pretend they are animals, and the children can quack like ducks as they walk, hop like bunnies, and walk softly on tiptoes like kittens. Instructors and children can try these movements before doing them as a group. (Farm animals resonate in the rural farming communities!) Imitating the actions of people can also be used; this is best done where the actions reflect the people of the community. Pretend play may be difficult for

some children with ID, but if the child with ID has familiarity with a related story and instructions are simple, pretending will more potentially be successful. It might take time and it might take a peer-buddy.

Lead-Up Games

For grade school children with ID, activities such as relays (not necessarily races), parachute play, and simple games are part of the curriculum for their grade. A very simple game is one in which

- the space is relatively small,
- choices are few,
- some positions are fixed,
- the quality of performance brings no penalties or privileges,
- the possible directions of movement are restricted,
- personnel remain the same, and
- motor skill requirements are limited/identified.

For the adolescent with ID who has successfully participated in activities meeting these criteria, opportunities to learn lead-up games such as kick-ball and line soccer are fun. The student with ID may require learning the game task analyzed as may the other peers in the class. Social skills associated with the lead-up games must be taught, and the focus should be on students' personal best if easily applied here.

Rhythmic Activities

Like most children, individuals with an ID enjoy music and often like dance and rhythmic activities. Improvement in rhythm may also lead to improvement in performance of skilled movements (Chatzihidiroglou et al., 2018; Ekins et al., 2019). Extensive dance activities, ranging from simple movements to more complex could be included in the physical education program. There is always that popular YMCA song and its accompanying movements. Some cultures have songs that all ages know, and all ages participate in the movements on the dance floor!

Team Sports and Special Olympics

Instructors of students with ID hear a number of their students recall the names of local and national sport heroes. Most of these students are familiar with sporting events as a result of attending local contests and watching sport events on television. As students with ID learn lead-up games, APE and GPE programs direct teaching to the team sports, to engage in more vigorous activity essential to physical fitness. And some don't like team sports at their school, preferring Special Olympics.

APE and GPE teachers plus coaches provide the instruction for those interested students with ID to compete against other teams. Competitive athletics for those with intellectual disabilities is offered in the Special Olympics program that began in 1968 (Special Olympics, 2021). Many individuals with ID enjoy competition of this nature and desire it for the personal satisfaction and the social engagement that it brings them.

Special Olympics is a large international organization for individuals with intellectual disabilities. Offices and programs can be found in nearly all states in the United States, as well as in many countries throughout the world (Special Olympics, 2021). The website for Special Olympics (specialolympics.org) is filled with materials to use to train athletes who stay local and those who go on to international competition. These training programs are time tested and the videos are exciting.

Special Olympics began as a segregated sports program for those with intellectual disabilities and now offers Special Olympics Unified, an integrated program for athletes with ID and those without ID, training in their home community and later competing in their home country's competition and in international competition. Special Olympics is detailed more fully in Adapted Sport (chapter 16).

Special Olympics is reaching to children with ID ages 2 to 7 years in a program called Special Olympics Young Athletes. These children join in play with children without ID. Research reports that the children with ID gained in their motor skills, sometimes as much as twice that of children not in motor activities (Special Olympics, 2018). The program exposes these young children to early movement skills such as running, throwing, catching, and playing simple games. All the training materials are free and found on the website. We don't actually refer to children as young as 2 years of age as athletes. In this case, they are participating in a play program that is developmentally appropriate for their ages with content in fundamental movement skills known to build on the skills they will someday use, if they so choose, to be a Special Olympics athlete or a Special Olympics Unified athlete.

Serving Students With Severe or Profound ID

Of all individuals with ID, those in the category of severe or profound are small in numbers. Only 3 to 4 percent of the individuals have severe ID, and 1 to 2 percent have a profound ID. The overall consideration here is that these categories are not that prevalent within ID. IDEA (2004) does not specify IQ levels for severe or profound ID.

In reviewing the medical reference *DSM-5*, the student with severe ID needs "caretakers [who] provide extensive supports for problem solving throughout life" (APA, 2013, p. 36). These caretakers provide a level of support described in the DSM-5-TR (2022) as *continual*. The students often use augmentative communication or know simple vocabulary for social communication. There is an understanding of simple speech and gestures. The APE can take advantage of these attributes in communicating with the student. The physical activity program is one to one with assistance from paraprofessionals. The adapted physical education teacher may be acting as a consultant to oversee the content and the progressions in skills and recreational opportunity or may work directly with the student.

Students may understand simple instructions or gestures. They enjoy relationships with well-known family members, caretakers, and familiar others, such as their APE teacher. Recreation activities can include listening to music, watching movies, going out for walks, participating in swim/water activities, and attending special seasonal events in the community.

Program Considerations

In 1990, Croce implemented a well-structured physical education class for students who were institutionalized that resulted in gains in physiological and behavioral changes. This contrasts with a history of leaving these students sitting or lying down for hours. In many ways, the role of the APE teacher is similar for both categories of students with severe and profound ID. Both students require one-to-one supervision and support, and students have ways of communicating and showing enjoyment and displeasure. In a 13-year follow-up study, the fitness levels of those with ID are low (e.g., Graham & Reid, 2000); yet, a pilot study of peer-mediated treadmill walking for individuals with moderate and severe ID resulted in increased compliance (Vashdi et al., 2007). These students learned. A generally accepted goal in physical activity for students with severe and profound levels of ID is to facilitate activity that challenges the physical activity level. Physically active individuals do better on all measures than inactive individuals.

Students learn with proper supports in place. The youth with ID can be assisted in enjoying activity in the home and in the community. Transition planning at the later ages must include a recreation activity assessment and training for being out and enjoying their community.

Motor Activity Training Program

According to the Special Olympics organization, the Motor Activity Training Program (Special Olympics, 2021) is for those athletes with ID at the severe or profound level who have never been able to compete in Special Olympics.

> "The Motor Activity Training Program is designed to prepare athletes—including those with severe or profound intellectual disability and significant physical disabilities—for sport-specific activities appropriate for their ability levels."
>
> Special Olympics (2020).

The program trains these athletes for sport-specific activities that match their abilities. Some APE teachers might be interested in the training manual for the Motor Activity Training Program as a resource for activities and planning at their school. All the training manuals are free and available on the Special Olympics website. The assessments are accessed online at no cost. Also included are training programs that include a class session of warm-up, skill stations, group games, and a final relaxation exercise. Many APE teachers are already involved in this program.

Sensory Processing

Occupational therapists often have training to determine the sensory processing attributes of individuals. According to extensive study by the scholar Dr. Winnie Dunn, sensory processing is unique for each individual (Dunn, 1997, 1999, 2002, 2006). Dunn

Severe and Profound Disability Without ID

Those children and youth who are without an ID and are intensely affected physically by their disability need support for being physically active. Medically the level of support is associated with severe and profound disability (APA, 2022). Children with certain forms of cerebral palsy who are very impacted by the motor impairment but who have normal and above normal intelligence fall into this medical group. Looking into adulthood, some disabilities involving the neurological system are progressive, meaning the person doesn't get better, and their systems decline with age. At some point, they need continuous support, yet they can be employed, married, and active in their community. A famous example of this situation was the physicist Dr. Stephen Hawking of the University of Cambridge, who had amyotrophic lateral sclerosis, often referred to as Lou Gehrig disease. At age 40, the doctors told him he would have six years to live. At the time of his diagnosis, he was ambulatory. At age 78, he had far surpassed those six years, but he was completely dependent on a continuous level of support, although in theoretical physics, he remained intellectually brilliant. He died in March 2018 having predeceased his adult children.

has analyzed the sensory system processing (e.g., visual, touch, and sound) and people's pattern of responses to determine thresholds and regulation. Dunn conceptualizes sensory processing as having a neurological threshold of response that is on a continuum from high to low and self-regulation from passive to active. This is not to be confused with sensory integration work, which is also found in the field of occupational therapy. Processing is about an awareness of how an individual's sensory system reacts and how this information can be used to increase learning and satisfaction in life. A person cannot change how they process sensory information. But they can be aware of where they are sensitive and how the threshold can be controlled.

When working with individuals with ID with severe and profound disability , be aware of how the person responds to sensory stimuli. Many physical education programs for young children with these levels of disability have included what is termed *sensory experiences* in the educational day of the student. For example, arms are rubbed arms with fabric or brushes. If this is part of the IEP for the individual, the textures the student likes (e.g., soft towels, fleece fabrics, and soft brushes) would be identified and why they are being used would be explained. It is the responsibility of the occupational therapist to work with the IEP team and explain this.

In addition to using tactile stimulation to ready the student for engagement, the APE can ask the IEP team about sound and visual responses to determine what is stimulating and what is over-stimulating for the student (Dr. Dunn's thresholds). For example, for some children who have a seizure disorder along with ID, seizures can be brought on by the flashing lights in the backboards when the ball goes into the hoop. Not every student is going to like flashing lights and musical responses. Work closely with the occupational therapists as well as with the classroom teacher, who may have many ideas about what motivates the student and their thresholds for stimulation, what should be avoided, or what should be pursued.

The skills of reaching, grasping, holding, and releasing do not develop typically for individuals with severe ID. They must be taught. Therefore, opportunities for these individuals to play with textured toys should be provided when they are younger. Finger, hand, and arm movements may also be elicited using materials such as water, sand, and clay. Again, an occupational therapist is to be a consultant to develop these educational units as the student with ID matures.

Fundamental Motor Skills

In addition to the sensory-motor experiences, the physical education curriculum for individuals with severe ID should include activities that develop basic everyday skills, such as lifting the feet over objects. Additional examples of the basic activities that can be included in the program and the techniques most frequently used for teaching them appear in the following list. Demonstration is usually suggested in the following list, but if the student has issues with vision, then this may not be helpful. Sometimes just repeating the demo does help. Sometimes a slow, rhythmic verbalization goes well with some of these skills, like "up, down, up, down"; "sit, stand, sit, stand"; or "down, up, down, up." Because of the individual variation found within this population, the techniques listed are suggestions and do not preclude the use of other techniques. The Mobility Opportunities Via Education program deals with many of these basic movements for individuals who are not young. The skills suggested in the following list all have a functional application for students. In addition, they keep the student agile and moving.

- *Rolling:* Demonstration, physical assistance
- *Sitting:* Demonstration, physical assistance (external supports such as straps, if necessary)
- *Standing (with and without assistance):* Demonstration, physical assistance
- *Walking:* Demonstration, physical assistance (use parallel bars and weighted pushcart, if necessary)
- *Bending at the waist to pick up a favorite toy or object:* Demonstration, physical assistance
- *Bending at the knees to pick up a favorite toy:* Demonstration, physical assistance
- *Stair climbing:* Demonstration, physical assistance; one-foot lead possibly needed before getting to an alternating pattern
- *Balancing:* Physical assistance (two strips of tape on the floor a set distance apart with a target object at the end; assist the student; and use a wide beam on the floor; assist student along the wide beam)
- *Stepping over and into objects:* Physical assistance (use hula hoops, boxes, beams)
- *Jumping from object:* Physical assistance (use an object or beam no higher than one foot in the beginning; start by pulling the student off balance)

- *Climbing:* Physical assistance (use a ladder)
- *Running:* Demonstration, physical assistance (guide by the hand or use rope around the waist)
- *Throwing:* Physical assistance (use an eight-inch or larger ball and a hula hoop on the ground or garbage can as a target; student starts by dropping the ball; gradually increase the distance from the target)
- *Catching:* Physical assistance (use an eight-inch ball; in the beginning use short distances and place the ball into the hand; use a count of "ready, 1-2-3!")
- *Kicking:* Demonstration, physical assistance; use large, soft rubber balls or medium beach balls, kicking to nothing with beach balls, then kicking soft rubber balls into medium cardboard boxes and eventually to large pop bottles that make a noise when they fall over

The way in which these activities are presented by the teacher is extremely important in achieving positive results. As pointed out previously, instructing students with severe to profound intellectual disabilities is usually one on one or in a very small group. The APE can train peers to teach skills and participate with the students. The program needs to be age-appropriate.

Participation should be of short duration. After leaving one activity, the teacher may return to it in a few minutes or at some time before the period is over. The same activities should be presented every day until a goal has been reached. After the skills of one activity have been mastered, new activities may be introduced; but the skills already learned should be reviewed briefly from time to time. An obstacle course in which students climb stairs, duck under bars, step over ropes, and step into and out of tires and hoops provides a good warm-up and a means of quickly reviewing important activities.

Most adapted physical education instructors understand that improvement comes in small increments. Effort by the student should be acknowledged with indications of approval. Heward and Orlansky (1992) recommend that a behavioral approach with the following elements be employed:

1. Aim to have the student perform the target behavior repeatedly during a session.
2. Provide immediate feedback in the form of positive reinforcement.
3. Use cues that help the student respond from the very beginning and systematically withdraw these as appropriate.
4. Help the student generalize the newly learned skill to different environments.

Withdrawing the identified prompt supports the next step in learning the movement skill or game. Students requiring more support to be physically active will always need assistance, so if it is not advisable or appropriate, the cue is not withdrawn.

Behavior Modification

Verbal praise is used with those students with severe and profound ID differently because many of the students do not comprehend a great deal of spoken words. But there are emotions expressed and individual ways to demonstrate pleasure and displeasure. Professionals and volunteers working in these programs become very familiar with their students and very sensitive to their emotions and expressions. Behavior modification used in teaching is effective when used properly so the students learn.

With behavior modification used in APE, there are selected reinforcers to weaken, maintain, or strengthen behaviors for students with severe and profound ID. Although there are several behavior modification techniques, the two most successfully employed with those with severe and profound ID have been demonstration and positive reinforcement: demonstrate the skill and reward the movement. The demonstration is for smaller actions with few steps of instruction for an activity. Physically assisting a movement is common with a reward.

Several types of reinforcers may be employed. These include manipulatable reinforcers such as toys and hobby items; a not-so-quickly applied reward are the visual and auditory stimuli such as films, records, and animations but a case can be made for a seasonal reinforcement within the class. More immediate rewards also include social stimuli such as verbal praise and attention (Dunn, 1975). Selection of the appropriate reinforcer must be determined for each person. For some students, praise or knowledge that the attempt was successful is sufficient reinforcement. The time between the reinforcement and the desired behavior must be as short as possible; otherwise, the student is not always certain what he or she is being rewarded for.

Educational Health Care Providers

The expertise of educational health care providers like occupational therapists, physical therapists, speech and language pathologists, and child psychologists is utilized for children with intellectual disabilities at various times in their educational life. For example, young children with Down syndrome often need occupational and physical therapy to help with positioning for sitting. Listed here are health care professions and samples of their work focus with students with ID.

Occupational Therapy

- Reach, grasp, and release in early movement
- Reach, grasp, release in school classrooms including physical education, and use of adapted equipment in physical activity

Physical Therapy

- Moving in and out of positions for physical activity
- Moving fast . . . suggestions or contraindications for physical activity
- Sitting in story time for young children
- Alternatives to W-sitting
- Placing toys to encourage initial sitting, pulling to stand, standing, safe initial walking, safe walking
- Adaptations for older student participation if using adapted equipment in physical activity

Speech and Language Pathology

- Basic social greetings
- Communication interventions specified in the child's IFSP or the IEP of a student
- Communication board for physical activity class (e.g., PECS)
- Use of some prompt that says "Well done!" or "Great" used by all staff in physical activity with the student with ID

School Psychology

- Behavior issues; working with the IEP team to document a behavior issue and to deter-

mine the target problem and intervention plan; also to determine data collection, rewards, and consequences
- Any variety of observational needs for interventional work
- Family issues impacting the child's learning

Summary

Those with an ID are diagnosed based on both an IQ and their adaptive functioning. It is essential to determine the level of support for learning a child with ID requires in the physical activity and education setting. Instructional strategies stress that students with ID do learn; yet compared to their peers without ID, the amount of learning is less, the rate at which they learn is less, their attention span is shorter, and generalizability is a huge challenge requiring that skills are taught, if possible, where the skill is performed. Social skills need to be taught for physical activities. Instruction employs a prompt hierarchy from physical or visual to verbal, and it uses task analysis. Content in physical education is directed at the student's chronological age, and instruction is based on the developmental age. A prearranged behavior plan is recommended for students with ID who may have problems that result in significant disruptions in a physical education, therapy, or sport training session. Special Olympics is a popular sports program for those with ID. Unified Special Olympics is a program where teams are integrated—teams include those with and without ID. Young Athletes is a new Special Olympics program for the youngest of children with ID to play with their peers without ID. Students with severe and profound levels of ID can be assessed for their physical education program using the Mobility Opportunities Via Education curriculum and can also participate in the Special Olympics Motor Activity Training Program.

CHAPTER 8

Autism Spectrum Disorder

CHAPTER OBJECTIVES

After completing this chapter, you will be able to do the following:

- Identify the main characteristics of students with autism spectrum disorder.
- Describe instructional strategies used in working with students with autism spectrum disorder in general physical education (GPE), adapted physical education (APE), and other clinical settings.
- Understand the individualized education program (IEP) in communication for the student with autism spectrum disorder including when and how to use it in the GPE or APE program.
- Describe the varied reasons for the use of a predictable structure for a student with autism spectrum disorder in the general physical education, adapted physical education, or clinical setting.
- Describe approaching assessment for GPE or APE for a student with autism spectrum disorder with particular attention to what helps the student more comfortably perform.

In this chapter, the term autism spectrum disorder (ASD) is used. In 2022, the American Psychiatric Association (APA) released its newest revision of the Diagnostic and Statistical Manual of Mental Disorders, Fifth Edition, Text Revision (*DSM-5-TR*; APA, 2022), using this term, although under IDEA (2004), the term *autism* is used, not *ASD*, and it has its own disability category. The placing of this cate-gory of disability in the amendments of this law has reflected the known science of its etiology.

In 1975, under the Education for All Handi-capped Children Act (Public law 94-142), the etiol-ogy of autism was thought to be emotional and thus categorized under seriously emotionally disturbed. In later reauthorizations of the law, advocacy influenced the placement of autism in other health impaired (EAHCA, 1984). In the reauthorization in the 1990s, autism was allotted its own category. Yet, some people still confuse autism with an emotional disturbance or health impairment.

For children and students with autism, IDEA (2004) focuses on deficits of development in communication and social interaction that affects learning (Colarusso et al., 2017). IDEA (2004) states the following:

> Autism means a developmental disability significantly affecting verbal and nonverbal communication and social interaction, generally evident before age three, that adversely affects educational performance. Other characteristics often associated with autism are engagement in repetitive activities and stereotyped movements, resistance to environmental change or changes in daily routines, and unusual response to sensory experiences. Autism does not apply if a child's educational performance is adversely affected primarily because the child has a serious emotional disturbance.
>
> IDEA (2004, § 300.8[c][1]).

There is a range of features of autism; hence a spectrum is expected for children. An individual student with autism has specific and unique strengths and weaknesses in the educational setting. This reality has ramifications for the assessment method and the resulting interventions for learning within the physical activity and physical education programs of general physical education (GPE) or adapted physical education (APE). Understanding the communication and social skill level of the child is essential to creating a place where they learn how to move and have fun in physical activity.

Causes and Prevalence

Autism spectrum disorder (ASD) is considered a neurobehavioral disorder (*neuro* meaning the neurologic system; *behavioral* meaning the day-to-day actions and interactions of the individual). The neurologic system of the child or youth with ASD functions differently, which baffles many educators and clinicians unfamiliar with ASD. Some feel there is purposeful ignoring of instruction or class directions. This isn't usually the case (although, of course, at times it might be); it's that the brain of someone with ASD responds differently, and this is observed in their behavior. Basic science research is engaged in understanding why this occurs. Some of this research is conducted by tracking changes in the brain's electrical activity to investigate the core deficits within the brain of individuals with ASD (Jeste & Nelson, 2009; Varcin & Nelson, 2016). Studies such as these conclude that there are "... likely impairments in higher level auditory and visual processing, with prominent impairments in the processing of social stimuli" (Jeste & Nelson, 2009, p. 495). In addition, structural imaging of the brain, called functional magnetic resonance imaging (fMRI), has reported atypical symmetries in the brain linked to more language impairment (e.g., Lindell & Hudry, 2013).

According to prevalence data from the Centers for Disease Control and Prevention, in 2000, 1 in 150 eight-year-old children were diagnosed with ASD; in 2010 it increased to 1 in 68, and in the latest survey in 2018, findings were 1 in 44 (CDC, 2022). The increase in the incidence of autism spectrum disorder has fueled an intense debate. Autism does not go away, but having early knowledge of autism and early application of useful interventions helps the family and child develop a positive developmental trajectory that avoids a cumulative effect of challenging behaviors (Wetherby, 2012).

Classification and Diagnosis

In the DSM-5-TR (APA, 2022), the APA changed the diagnostic criteria of autism spectrum disorder by clarifying that children with ASD meet all the criteria rather than just any of the criteria laid out in the manual. The DSM-5 (APA, 2013) had removed some of the subclassifications of autism, specifically Asperger disorder, Rett syndrome, childhood disintegrative disorder, and pervasive developmental disorder-not otherwise specified and replaced these and other delineations with autism spectrum disorder. These past subclassifications still appear in school and medical records. The changes made were driven by the need for effective interventions for those who are given a diagnosis (Happe, 2011). Numerous diagnostic labels within autism produced idiosyncratic labeling and interventions, and individuals could receive a different diagnosis from different diagnosticians. Importantly, many on the DSM-5 committee felt that the diagnosis did not effectively inform intervention (Wetherby, 2012). The DSM-5-TR panel for APA felt that the diagnosis could be strengthened if all the criteria—not just some—were met, thus changing the diagnostic name to autism spectrum disorder.

The diagnosis of autism spectrum disorder is typically made by a pediatrician or interdisciplinary team within a medical context (Colarusso et al., 2017). Some states have their own professionals in special education who qualify children for educational services under autism spectrum disorder. When the child enters the school system with a diagnosis of ASD, educators follow the Individuals with Disabilities Education Improvement Act (IDEA, 2004) to design educational services. And diagnosis early in a child's life helps with interventions that keep the child and family from avoiding cumulative risk (Koegel et al., 2014). If behaviors are not addressed early, they compound over time making interventions much more difficult later in the child's life.

Understanding the common behavioral characteristics of individuals with ASD is helpful for physical educators as well as for clinicians. Educators and clinicians can reference the DSM-5 (APA, 2013) clinical diagnostic criteria as well as the criteria in IDEA (2004) for special education. How these criteria affect the student's participation in a physical activity class depends on the unique individual, because the diagnosis of autism spectrum disorder broadly encompasses many children who uniquely express their personal characteristics. The DSM-5 describes three levels of severity with ASD (table 8.1). These levels remain in the DSM-5-TR (APA, 2022). The panel makes available a clinical-rated severity of autism spectrum and social communication disorders measure.

Reviewing the table can help the physical educator understand which interventions need to be in place. For instance, a common characteristic with ASD is inflexibility, the severity of which varies. This is why interventions in the literature make clear that this student needs to understand the GPE or APE program and the interventions being used in that program (Menear & Smith, 2008; Obrusnikova & Dillon, 2011; Todd, 2012). The program has to be predictable, and when the student needs to make a change, that has to be dealt with proactively. Also, one main diagnostic attribute of ASD is deficits in social skill and communication expected for age. Many professionals new to working with students with ASD are taken aback by the nonresponsiveness, as if the student were purposely ignoring them (which could sometimes be the case but mostly is not). The lack of eye contact, lack of a language repertoire expected for their age, and sometimes odd behaviors are characteristics of ASD although striking for some physical educators and school clinicians. Today we know a great deal about how to engage students with ASD in physical activity experiences.

Characteristics

Physical educators and some clinicians are not trained in the diagnosis of autism but may be called upon to submit information to the diagnosticians. There are special teams of clinicians in the schools and in the medical community who are trained to diagnose autism spectrum disorder. Children with ASD perform repetitive behaviors beyond a typical age expectation (APA, 2013), have limited social

TABLE 8.1   Autism Spectrum Disorder Severity and Support Levels

Level of support needed based on severity	Communication and social deficits	Repetitive behaviors and other behaviors
Level 1. Very substantial support	Severe. Very limited initiation and minimal response. Few words. Unusual approaches to meet needs and responds to only very direct social approaches.	Inflexible. Extreme difficulty with change. Repetitive behavior interferes with functioning. Great distress with changing focus.
Level 2. Substantial support	Marked deficits. Speaks in simple sentences. Odd nonverbally. Limited initiation, narrow interests.	Inflexible. Use of repetitive behaviors interferes in a variety of functions.
Level 3. Support	Can speak in full sentences but conversations fail. Attempts at friendships are odd.	One or more contexts where inflexibility interferes with functioning. Difficulty switching activities. Independence hampered by problems with organization and planning.

Adapted from American Psychiatric Association (2022).

engagement, like routine, and like collecting things but relate to the parts of the things. In sum, because of the complexities in brain function, an individual with ASD has difficulty with social interaction and communication either verbal or nonverbal (Autism Speaks, 2018).

Specialists diagnosing ASD in a child must examine what is within the range of typical development for the child's age. Children with ASD have limited social engagement for age (e.g., limited eye contact or no eye contact). Typically developing children may also use little eye contact (e.g., being shy) or not be very verbal. But the child with autism begins this pattern very early in life, and this stands out first in the family setting and later, of course, in the school setting. There is difficulty with change in a routine. The child lacks transition skills for age compared to their peers. For example, typically developing children may like sameness. But for a child with ASD, this need blurs the events for the child and upsets them if the sameness isn't there. Huge behavioral outbursts can occur when a new skill or activity is introduced in the GPE or APE class or if an instructor is absent from a home classroom. Typically developing children may collect sticks, straws, and wrappers. But for the child with ASD, there is an attachment to these collectibles. .They relate more to an object's parts than the object. When they play with a truck, the truck's wheels are more fascinating than the whole truck.

Motor Deficits

Regarding deficits of the children with ASD, neither the DSM-5 nor IDEA (2004) lists motor deficits as criteria for identification of autism. Yet, there is little doubt that in the presence of this neurological disorder, motor performance can be affected. Given the social and communication deficits of ASD, without adaptations to tasks and use of focused instructional strategies, learning will be a challenge for the child.

Lee and Porretta (2013) noted motor deficits of those with ASD compared to peers. Case studies and anecdotal sharing abound in this area, and researchers have documented delays in fundamental motor skills (Berkeley et al., 2001) as well as lack of coordination (Provost et al., 2007). Research is amassing documentation that a child with ASD can learn fundamental motor skills, games, and sports. Research has already reported success in aquatic programs (Lee & Porretta, 2013), surfing clubs (Cavanaugh et al., 2013), and fitness circuits (Hovey, 2011). These studies assist adapted physical educators (APE) and others with the strategies that worked for a specific group of children in a specific activity.

Instructional Considerations

As stated, the hallmarks of diagnosis of ASD are marked deficits in communication and social skills (Wetherby, 2012). Children with autism spectrum disorder range from nonverbal skill to functional verbal skill. Communication skill impacts the interventions for the development of social skills.

For those children who are nonverbal, a functional communication system for physical activity needs to be built so that the student can choose equipment, interact with other people, follow procedures, and participate in classroom discussions (Green & Sandt, 2013). The physical educator works with the educational team to understand how the student communicates. The speech and language pathologist (SLP) contributes an evaluation report detailing a plan for communication within the individualized education program (IEP). It is important that these interventions for communication in the adapted physical education class or the general physical education class are used in every educational setting with the student with autism spectrum disorder. The SLP report of the IEP informs the instructional strategies for all educational settings. Fittipaldi-Wert and Mowling have reported success with visual prompts for instructing and organizing the class for the child with ASD (2009) and have included visuals in their article on the topic. Students with autism have told these researchers that they like visuals in the classroom.

Kline (1996) reported that students with ASD need direct instruction in

- interpreting the behaviors of others,
- monitoring their own social skill interactions,
- using eye contact, gaze, and gestures in interpersonal communication, and
- understanding practical aspects of language.

To help with these recommendations, Temple Grandin, a professor of agriculture who has been diagnosed with autism spectrum disorder, has been an advocate of understanding the ways that children with ASD learn. She recommends

- using concrete visual methods in teaching,
- avoiding long verbalizations,
- whispering (because for some children loud verbal sounds are distressing), and
- using realistic drawings in visual communication rather than line drawings (Grandin, 2002).

Groft and Block (2003), as well as Houston-Wilson and Lieberman (2003) also recommend that the teacher keep an even, calm tone in the voice that is predictable and matter of fact, and interprets the body language and nonverbal cues for the student if misinterpretations occur.

This interpretation is like some skills used in counseling, whereby the professional describes to the client what has happened, such as "Juliet was waving at you to say hello when she came into the gym today." It communicates the *wave* and the reason for the wave to the student with ASD, who may have misunderstood the gesture. The misunderstanding may have been observed by the instructor or paraprofessional. David (a student with ASD) may have watched it blankly or felt bothered by it. Juliet was disappointed and started to come across the gym to say hello again. The paraprofessional felt compelled to clarify. Interestingly, researchers found that a group of autistic children ages 5 to 17 scored similarly to their age peers in identifying emotions (Peterson et al., 2015). This finding reminds us that each child with ASD is unique.

Social Skills Training in Young Children

Research has been building regarding interventions employed to help children with ASD succeed socially in classrooms. Kennedy and Shukla reported that "(a) social interactions can be taught and learned, (b) social interventions in typical settings can be successfully accomplished, and (c) substantial positive outcomes accrue" (1995, p. 21).

Boyd and colleagues (2013) compared the TEACCH and LEAP programs for efficacy in promoting social skill improvement in young children with autism (three to five years of age). They were compared to comprehensive treatment models used in special education.

TEACCH

TEACCH strategies include accommodations to the environment such as visual schedules and work systems to promote child learning (Hume & Odom, 2007; Mesibov & Shea, 2010). Attention is given to the physical structure of the classroom. For the student, schedules are visual and depict where, when, and what the activity is. A schedule contains visual information for the learning tasks. Schools usually offer the TEACCH program in segregated classrooms away from typically developing peers. When physical educators have used the TEACCH approach, they work across ages and reorganize the environment in a small group situation and provide teacher-directed workstations for instruction in physical activity (e.g., Todd, 2012).

LEAP

The LEAP instructional program is offered in an inclusive educational program where same-age peers typically mediate the social instruction and intervention. Focus is on systematic efforts to increase the target child's on-task behavior, their use of appropriate language (versus echolalia, threats, and name-calling), and their positive interactions with peers (e.g., sharing materials, assisting one another, and engaging in verbal exchange). Additional focus is on decreasing deviant behavior (e.g., hitting, self-injury, screaming). The essential element of this program is reinforcement contingencies. Although the goal differs in a lesson for the peer helpers (typically developing children) from the lesson for a child with ASD, both are rewarded for meeting their goals. Both the peer helper and the peer with ASD receive instruction on eliciting appropriate responses.

Comprehensive Treatment Model

The comprehensive treatment model is a program using accepted practice in early childhood special education. TEACCH, LEAP, and the comprehensive treatment models were all reported to meet high standards for competence in the respective program. Boyd and others (2013) found no significant differences among the programs; all produced positive gains in social skill for the children. In their study, all the children made gains over the school year with each group showing significant positive change by decreasing ASD severity and increasing communication and fine motor skills. In the end, the researchers reported that the teachers were all highly qualified in special education and employed similar practices found to effective when educating children with ASD.

Leading researchers in ASD report that early intervention is imperative to increase social and communication skills (Wetherby, 2012). Waiting to intervene in social skills for children with ASD only compounds the problems. A simple skill of a mother gaining a two-year-old's attention when talking with the child briefly can relieve the cumulative negative risk in the development of communication for that toddler. Cumulative risk is known to derail development if risk factors in development are not identified and addressed (Bronfenbrenner, 1977).

Autism Resources

Autism Navigator and Baby Navigator are free resources on training on a comprehensive understanding of intervention with children with autism spectrum disorder and their families (autism-navigator.com). Most of the children who begin intervention under 24 months of age with their family go on to fully integrated kindergarten. The program was developed by Dr. Amy Wetherby at Florida State University with other top researchers. The site maintains excellent video clips with friendly language for both families and professionals. Over 400 clips provide side-by-side views of a peer and a child with ASD filmed over time to make developmental comparisons of supports for the child with ASD. A physical educator watching the many, many free clips, can observe how the development differs from what is typical and what interventions are used to develop language and thus meet child needs, leading to more typical behavior. Applying this, the general physical education (GPE) and adapted physical education (APE) instructors have a model for engaging the child in physical activity. These strategies observed are what the speech and language pathologist (SLP) recommends to the IEP team.

The Baby Navigator website (babynavigator.com) has a handout with 16 signs of early ASD at 16 months of age (2020). Both of these resources can be used for staff training by an SLP or by knowledgeable adapted physical educators and the school allied health professionals and community clinicians. The federal government provided seed monies for the development of these training films. The content is state of the art. This information adds a knowledge base used with instructional strategies backed by extensive research.

Social Skills Training in School-Age Children

In the past, IEP teams have placed the student with autism in physical education to develop their social skills. Deficits in social skills are diagnostic markers for ASD, and therefore social skills are not the strength of students with ASD. With children with ASD, social skills for physical activity in their school and community are actively taught.

When working to instruct in social skills, there is debate as to whether social skills need to be taught separate from the motor skills. Such separation is advocated by researchers at the Frank Porter Graham Child Development Institute at the University of North Carolina. In an integrated setting, supports need to be in place to teach the movement skills, the routines of the class, and the specific activity. Some basic communication skills and social skills may be added to the learning of the motor skills used in a game. Even with typically developing children, we often break down an activity by first learning the motor skills. Games demand social skill. In time, the child with ASD can use his or her social skills for the game. For example, the student can use a high-five gesture instead of verbalizing "Good job" to their teammates. Coordinate with the SLP and the special education teacher to design the social skill expectations in PE for the student.

The most effective way for the student with ASD to learn the social skill is to have it taught in the context of the naturally occurring environment of the skill—where the student would use it in their day, in their activity. That said, the student may do better if preteaching a specific skill is conducted before the skills are used in the general physical education class or other physical activity environment. Due to neurological differences in processing of visual information for the student with ASD, observing others use the skill in a game doesn't carry over to the student with ASD using the social skill.

The skills can be taught if they are presented in a concrete manner. For example, when using the term *good friend*, instruct about specific behaviors that demonstrate being a good friend in a given situation. Demonstrate and give ample opportunity to repeat the skill. There could be a gym poster that says "Everyone is a good friend when . . ." Then, list three actions that demonstrate this.

Program Placement and Focus

Peer tutors are often used in the APE and GPE setting to cue the student with ASD for specific skill movements. The key to using peer tutors is to train them in that cue and what is expected of the student with ASD in performance. This would include a consistent use of a key word or phrase (one, two, three, jump), employment of the positives that are being used across settings (in the classroom, at recess, and at home if possible), and any consequences to shape behavior. In other words, the trained peer tutor most likely needs to know the behavioral plan for the student while in a physical activity. Teachers can periodically observe the tutor with the student.

Instructional Strategies

Within the structure of an adapted physical education or general physical education class or other physical activity experiences, the activities and units change. Alexander and Schwager (2012) describe a multiactivity model in general physical education whereby the classes are predictable with warm-up, skill practice, game play, or time for more skill acquisition. The units are 3 to 4 weeks long, amounting to 9 to 12 lessons. Students without ASD like the variety. For the student with ASD, this amount of time might be too short for learning the skills. In playing games, the student with ASD may be confused by changes in rules (e.g., handle a soccer ball

with the feet, not the hands; handle a basketball with the hands, not the feet) and by changes in positions that require a different performance.

The following have helped the success of students with ASD in physical activity (Grenier & Yeaton, 2011; Menear & Smith, 2008, 2011; Sherlock-Shangraw, 2013; Todd, 2012):

- Using visual prompts
- Outlining the class activities in a short story or visual schedules
- Using the student's picture or realistic pictures, if possible, in a story or chart
- Using a poly spot to mark a student's place
- Using one color for the student for a vest, wall spots, floor spots, and all activity equipment
- Marking off boundaries for each activity
- Taking advantage of the child's interests (such as planets or cars) and placing visual representations on cones within an obstacle course or on their personal visual prompt cards

- The teacher raising their hand, then all students raising a hand and looking at the teacher (avoids loud noise in gym)
- Using the picture exchange communication system to progressively increase the engagement of the nonverbal student (for a detailed description, see Green & Sandt, 2013)
- Using whiteboards for visual representation of a skill sequence or using the personal visual prompts for the student
- Setting class goals and posting them with checkoffs for stages accomplished.

The inclusion of students with ASD in GPE is more prevalent today than in the first decade of the millennium. Now the curriculum is assessed for modifications for a particular student and the necessary adaptations like visual cues are applied as per that student's IEP. If the student is placed in a separate, APE class for some units, even then the following can apply. Each student with ASD is unique, and their placement for physical education will be unique unto them.

Motor Planning and Learning

- Use stations with a variety of choices of equipment.
- Use whole-part-whole to teach specific skills.
- Have a time-out activity so the student can exit if needed; for example, they could sit on a large exercise ball or use a stationary bike.
- Pair with partners in athletic practice and use corresponding cue terms, such as *plant*, *kick*, and *follow through*.
- Teach noncompetitive activities such as rowing, stationary or regular biking, running, skating, bowling, and swimming.
- Present a social story about not winning to develop the individual's social skills with losing.
- Present a social story about the physical activity to develop interest in a new activity.
- The instructor or another person writes social stories for the student. The story can be something as simple as saying to the student "I have written this story for you. It is about kicking a red ball. Let's read it together now." The story is concrete and is composed to help the student understand an emotion, an activity, or any other aspect of the class. The story can contain pictures.

Environmental aspects to consider when instructing (Groft & Block, 2003; Houston-Wilson & Lieberman, 2003) include the following:

- Giving a predictable beginning, middle, and end to the class.
- Developing routines in the class for the skills taught. For example,
  - place the ball on the t-stand;
  - pick up the bat;
  - hold the bat over your shoulder;
  - swing the bat at the ball;
  - when the ball is off the tee, put the bat down; and
  - run to first base.
- Forewarning about transitions (e.g., a verbal cue: "Five minutes until stations switch" or holding up a flag of a color other than red).
- Providing additional alerts as the time draws near to initiate another activity.
- Allowing students to indicate choice (e.g., a simple verbal response, a picture board, a sign).
- Using a token economy to increase participation (e.g., stars and checks can be accumulated for a special event or object).
- Having more preferred activities than non-preferred ones.
- Explaining to the student the organized space for PE.
- Explaining where activities are performed (the gym, the track, and the pool).
- Explaining where things are located (balls in bins, rackets on hooks).
- Establishing boundaries using cones.
- Training support staff when setting up additional instruction and practice time in motor skills, or to be of assistance in the use of equipment or routines.

Goals in PE for those with ASD focus on functional activity that is beneficial for a lifetime (e.g., Hovey, 2011; Pan et al., 2011). This includes recreational activity, as well as activity in GPE or APE. This is positive for both fitness and social skill development. Pan and colleagues reported that adolescents with increased levels of physical activity in a GPE class had increased social interaction during that time (2011). This increase was attained by arranging the environment for success. They recommend content attractive to participants, use of the outdoors (which increased physical activity in their study) and the presence of peers to enhanced social engagement.

Physical Activities

Hovey (2011) lists six steps in developing a fitness circuit for individuals with ASD. These steps take into account many of the instructional strategies for executing fitness activities with the student with ASD.

1. Select a task. Use stations for a fitness circuit. Base the selection of activities on the known components of fitness (e.g., cardiorespiratory endurance), developmental level of the students (for the level of activity intensity), and the interests of the students (taking into account the chronological age of the students and the available equipment). List the activities for the students. Survey interests and orient the program to activities of teenagers. Ask for input from teachers and parents about what the student is best at or what he enjoys the most.

2. Use visual markers to lay out the circuit (e.g., cones and directional arrows). Be attentive to the flow of the circuit. Adjust if overcrowding at a station occurs. Use the treadmill and elliptical machines to work cardiorespiratory endurance. Label each station. Use a picture of an individual performing the task at the station. Use preteaching or previewing to demonstrate the circuit.

3. Match the skill levels for success. Pretest on the circuit for more than just one day.

4. Individualize the program for each student based on assessment. Find out what supports the student is using for task completion. If possible, use that approach. For example, attach small task cards to a clipboard for the student if it is compatible with the student's support system in other classes.

5. Identify and train the student's paraprofessional. Describe the motor tasks. Indicate the level of prompting and motivational strategies for their student. Seek the paraprofessional's input on this.

6. Evaluate how the circuit is working. Adjust.

Assessment and Evaluation

When assessing the motor development and fitness of children with autism spectrum disorder, the particular characteristics of the child, the environment, and the task need to be considered (Reed & O'Connor, 2003). This is a broad statement that can

be filled in to guide the APE or GPE assessor and the clinician in assessment. Children with ASD do learn new skills in physical activity (e.g., Pitett et al., 2006).

Standardized assessment tools may not produce valid results for children with ASD. The normative population may not have included children with autism spectrum disorder. Students with ASD may not be successful with the standardized protocols that use physical demonstrations and a preponderance of spoken language. In addition, the protocols limit the number of demonstrations and verbal content provided to the student (e.g., Ulrich, 2020). These aspects of testing are difficult and often contraindicated when communicating with a child with autism spectrum disorder.

Many students with ASD

- can perform the skill but do not understand what is expected of them;
- may not understand what a testing situation is;
- will feel disrupted in their routine school day if a testing situation is not anticipated;
- will do better with advanced repeated visual and verbal cues to indicate a change in schedule;
- will have less anxiety and fewer distractions to overcome with acclimatizing to being tested (Block et al., 1998);
- can also have an intellectual disability (Allen et al., 2017), which will influence the presence of a motor delay (Green et al., 2009);
- will find that the gymnasium with lots of activity, noise, sounds, and people is a great challenge (Grandin, 2002), thus affecting performance in physical activity experiences; and
- should always have the preferred communication strategy used in their testing situations.

When adaptations are made to a standardized test, list them in the evaluation report and do not report the norms—for example, "John could perform all the items with an average of five prompts and a time lag of at least a minute between repeated prompts."

Testing Younger Children

Numerous articles attested to the validity and reliability of the Test of Gross Motor Development-3 (Ulrich, 2020) and its use with children with ASD. Using the Test of Gross Motor Development-3, researchers used extra picture cards, short verbal prompts, and extra physical demonstrations with

Transitional IEP

Older students with ASD follow the same assessment focus and testing needs as other students with disabilities for their transitional IEP in physical activity. Many students with ASD do not like group sports but would rather participate in stationary biking, running, skating, swimming, or bowling. Exposing the student to these activities or investigating the student's experience in these activities is appropriate. The team must discuss with the family their interests for their child (a youth) after high school graduation. For some families, this begins in the sophomore year of high school. Will the student work in a sheltered workshop or in their general community, head on to postsecondary school? How does the high school program support the family's plan and the plan of the individual student for postgraduation? Depending on the level of support needed (intermittent or continual) students with ASD might be more interested in the present than in activities they believe are farther off in their life. This takes time for them to fathom but is not to deter an ongoing description of activities in their community and the training. If the training is enjoyable there is more motivation to participate and then gradually over the years put together why. After all, it does mean a change in their daily routine, which is conceptually difficult.

their students with ASD, as well as with their control group. The children with ASD performed better with the addition of the extra cues than without. Researchers recommended visual prompts to be simple and that the prompter be attentive to the age of the child.

Curriculum-based measures, as described in chapter 6, are highly recommended for a student

Courtesy of Michael Beets.

with ASD. This is helpful to determine the supports needed for the student to participate in the GPE expected for age.

Testing Older Students

Alexander and Schwager noted that sensory difficulties will impact the fitness scores of some students with ASD (2012). The progressive aerobic cardiovascular endurance run of the Brockport Physical Fitness Test sounds a rhythmic beat to cue the performance, which can distract and overwhelm a student with ASD. A gentle voice of someone familiar to the student may facilitate data collection. This is a simple modification, and although it is not part of the protocol, it may provide data for the GPE or APE instructor to establish a fitness component in class. Sometimes, though, data cannot be obtained. For example, touching the board for a sit and reach test or having the feet held in a sit-up, might elicit an emotional response that precludes any data collection (Alexander & Schwager, 2012). In another test situation, the texture of the ball being thrown may distract the student. In this situation, provide some choices and observe which ball the student chooses. Use that ball to assess throw. Repeat this selection for catching.

In ongoing assessments, the instructor can assist the individual student with adjustments to the task required, and the environment where the activity is being offered. Some students have a pictorial board outlining the class. Use this card with the student when the activity is going to change. Other students with ASD need visual cues to know what to do at a given station. For some students, the teacher has cue cards nearby (such as on a lanyard), and for others they are at the station where other students benefit from the visual cue as well. The use of physical assistance is problematic in that many students with ASD do not like to be touched. The GPE or APE or OT can assess this to understand to what lengths physical assistance could be used to instruct during class, if at all.

Summary

Students with autism spectrum disorder have a significant difference in communication and social skill compared to their age peers without ASD and typically developing. Despite initial motor deficits, the children learn and are active. When instructing, use concrete visual methods, avoid long verbalizations, use realistic drawings, and speak in a calm voice. Teach social skills of an activity separate from teaching the motor skill, then teach the motor skill, and later combine them and instruct as needed. Social skills training for young children with ASD was successful with well-trained special education teachers using individualized goals for each student. Videos from Autism Navigator and Baby Navigator are excellent free resources for training on communication skill development with students with ASD. Apply the SLP recommendations of an IEP to the GPE or APE program. In physical activity settings, it is recommended to instruct the motor skill separate from the social skill, then combine them later. In a concrete manner, teach social skills in the context used. Standardized assessment tools are a challenge for children with autism spectrum disorder, and examiners should be sensitive to difficulties when a person administers a test to the student; children need to be familiar with the activities, and the environment for testing should have limited distractions and soft lighting. Use the child's preferred communication strategy. Add visuals to help with directions. Curriculum-based measures are more highly recommended than other assessments. Taking longer to assess is sometimes necessary. Fitness circuits can be modified for the student with ASD. Offer visual supports ahead of program changes. Routines are essential, and transition warnings within the class structure and forewarnings for program changes are helpful.

CHAPTER 9

Specific Learning Disabilities and Attention-Deficit/ Hyperactivity Disorder

CHAPTER OBJECTIVES

After completing this chapter, you will be able to do the following:

- Define the term *specific learning disabilities* and what leads to a diagnosis under IDEA (2004).
- Explain how receptive language deficits impact learning in physical activity environments for students.
- Explain how expressive language deficits impact learning in physical activity environments for students.
- Describe the transitional considerations for the IEP team and the student with SLD.
- Describe the main features of attention-deficit/hyperactivity disorder (ADHD).
- Describe contraindications in physical activity environments for students with ADHD.
- Recognize instructional strategies in physical activity with students with ADHD.

Specific learning disability (SLD) is a condition under special education services that differs from attention-deficit/hyperactivity disorder (ADHD). SLD has its own category under IDEA (2004), and ADHD does not, but it is included under the definition of other health impaired. Having SLD does not mean that the individual has ADHD. But in some cases, individuals do have both, which is referred to as concomitant or comorbid.

As with most aspects of the diagnosis of disability and physical activity for students age 3 to 21 years, there is the federal educational law IDEA (2004) and its categories of disability, and there is the clinical diagnostic manual, the American Psychiatric Association's *Diagnostic and Statistical Manual of Mental Disorders, Fifth Edition, Text Revision* (*DSM-5-TR*; APA, 2022) and its disorders. Therefore, with learning difficulties, a student might have a *disability* according to educational law criteria, and the same student might have a *disorder* according to a clinician. Both will allow the student to be considered for special education services. Assessments are not done in infancy and toddlerhood for a specific learning disability or disorder. Assessments can begin at age three years. Physical educators do not diagnose, but they do need the diagnostic information to develop individualized education programs (IEPs) for adapted physical education (APE) and the ongoing instruction of the student.

Students with SLD do not have an intellectual disability. That is one of the exclusion criteria for educators and school allied health in the diagnosis of SLD in IDEA (2004) and according to the *DSM-5-TR*. This means that a diagnosis of SLD cannot be made if a student has an intellectual disability with deficits assessed based on their intellectual quotient and adaptive skills. Taken together, the assessments result in an evaluation that meet criteria for intellectual disability (see chapter 7). Students with intellectual disability receive special education services based on their intellectual disability, not SLD and the consequent appropriate interventions continuum with general physical education (GPE) or adapted physical education (APE) under a continuum of placement options.

Causes and Prevalence

The cause of SLD continues to be discovered through scientific studies state Fletcher and colleagues (2018), who warn that those seeking knowledge about SLD should stay away from testimonials, nonreplicated clinical reports, and anecdotal statements. Experts in SLD note that students with SLDs drop out of school at a greater rate than students with more obvious disabilities. In 2019 to 2020, of the 53,836 students with SLD in high school, 32,784 dropped out, which is 60 percent of those with SLD (U.S. Department of Education, 2022). The overwhelming evidence is that these students fail academically by the end of high school.

The greatest percent of students ages 3 to 21 with disabilities who were served under IDEA in 2020 to 2021 were those with SLD, at 30 percent of all students served, with the total number of students receiving special education services being 7.3 million in 2020 to 2021 (NCES, 2022). Students with ADHD ages 3 to 17 are prevalent, at a rate of 6 to 16 percent across the United States with 58 to 92 percent of those receiving some type of treatment or interventions (CDC, 2021). ADHD occurs in most cultures in about 5 percent of the children (APA, 2022).

Athletic Success

Tim Tebow, a former outstanding college football player, has dyslexia, which is a specific learning disability (SLD). Magic Johnson, an outstanding basketball player of his time, has dyslexia, as does Gabrielle Daleman, a Canadian Olympic skater. Michelle Carter won gold in the Olympics for the shot put and has dyslexia. The legendary boxer Muhammad Ali had dyslexia. Michael Phelps, an Olympic gold medalist in swimming, has attention-deficit/hyperactivity disorder (ADHD). Simone Biles, an Olympic gold medalist in gymnastics, has ADHD. Justin Gatlin, an Olympic gold medalist in the 100-meter sprint, has ADHD as does Cammi Granato, an Olympic gold medalist in women's hockey who was inducted into the hockey hall of fame.

All these athletes have stories of their struggles in school and their advantageous entry into elite athletic competition. In some cases, as with Michael Phelps, the athletic competition took him to early personal heights of accomplishment and helped him to succeed in school. Needless to say, many very accomplished individuals have an SLD or ADHD.

Classification and Diagnosis

The complexity of classifying and diagnosing SLD and ADHD is compounded by the reality that many of their associated symptoms are exhibited by children for many different reasons. For example, high activity levels can be associated with anxiety in children and not solely because the child might have ADHD. Similarly, inattention in the classroom can be due to an undiagnosed SLD rather than ADHD. It takes highly trained education specialists or school allied health working with teachers and parents to make the diagnosis.

Specific Learning Disabilities

Students with specific learning disabilities are eligible for federally funded special education programs. Under IDEA (2004), the term is *specific learning disability* (SLD) and is defined as

> . . . a disorder in one or more of the basic psychological processes involved in understanding or in using language, spoken or written, that may manifest in the imperfect ability to listen, think, speak, read, write, spell, or to do mathematical calculations, including conditions such as perceptual disabilities, brain injury, minimal brain dysfunction, dyslexia, and developmental aphasia. Specific learning disability does not include learning problems that are primarily the result of visual, learning or motor disabilities, or mental retardation, or emotional disturbance, or environmental, cultural, or economic disturbance, or of environmental, cultural, or economic disadvantage.
>
> IDEA (2004, § 300.8[c][10]).

In writing or speaking about SLD according to IDEA (2004), understand that the main category is specific learning disabilities, and with a single disability it is referred to as specific learning disability. Under the *DSM-5-TR*, the correct specific learning disorder is found under neurodevelopmental disorders.

Discrepancy

The educational approach considers services under SLD based on a significant discrepancy between what the student is achieving in the classroom and what the student is expected to achieve based on what capabilities they have.

Under the guidelines of IDEA (2004), a multidisciplinary team must be used to establish that a severe discrepancy in one or more areas exists between the student's actual and expected levels of achievement based on the individual's age and ability. At a minimum, a team must include the student's parents, the general educator, and a professional qualified to conduct diagnostic testing (e.g., psychologist) (Colarusso et al., 2017). Areas in which the severe discrepancy between ability and achievement may be found are

- oral expression,
- listening comprehension,
- written expression,
- basic reading skill,
- reading fluency,
- reading comprehension,
- mathematical calculation, and
- mathematical problem-solving.

Each state has the discretion to determine the eligibility criteria of severe discrepancy for service under specific learning disability. The evaluation team must determine that the reason for the severe discrepancy between achievement and ability cannot be attributed to other conditions or sociological factors.

Response to Intervention

In IDEA (2004), there must be evidence of the outcome of a response to intervention, whereby a systematic attempt has been documented to work with the student to improve academic performance. This is true with students suspected of SLD. If the data show, despite the use of teaching strategies based in the science of the discipline (e.g., reading, mathematics, or physical education), the student does not improve, then other reasons may exist for the student's lack of achievement. Interventions often exceed three months, and may be adjusted for another three months. Thus, a total of six months may have accumulated where the student is not progressing despite interventions. After this attempt, if there is no progress, the process for special education service is initiated. Regarding general physical education (GPE) and response to intervention, if the interventions need to stay in place (because the student flounders when they are taken away) then the student obviously needs to be referred for consideration for APE.

Clinical Diagnosis

Specific learning disorder is placed in a category under neurodevelopmental disorders within the *DSM-5-TR* (APA, 2022). This implies a neurologic basis for the disorder, whereby a list of disorders with areas like reading, mathematics, and writing were all combined under SLD. Note this is a medical disorder.

Main Features of Specific Learning Disorder (APA, 2022)

- The student reads words slowly and inaccurately.
- The student does not understand what is read.
- The student uses incorrect spelling, with omissions, additions, and other errors.
- The student's expression in writing is poor.
- Number facts, or calculation magnitude is difficult for the student.
- Solving quantitative problems is difficult for the student.

The Centers for Disease Control and Prevention (CDC, 2020) lists a few of the more common learning disorders:

- *Dyslexia:* Difficulty with reading
- *Dyscalculia:* Difficulty with math
- *Dysgraphia:* Difficulty with writing

The CDC also lists some of the symptoms of learning disorders, some of which seem to have a direct link into a physical education class. The following symptoms are selected out of a list of difficulties of students with SLD as they might cause complications for achievement in physical activity experience (CDC, 2020).

- Difficulty telling right from left
- Difficulties recognizing patterns or sorting items by size or shape
- Difficulty understanding and following instructions or staying organized
- Difficulty remembering what was just said or what was just read
- Lacking coordination when moving around
- Difficulty doing fine motor tasks with the hands, like writing, cutting, or drawing
- Difficulty understanding the concept of time

Many authorities have recognized that some students with learning disabilities do experience motor deficiencies. (Fawcett & Nicolson, 1995; Iversen et al., 2005; Lyyrunen et al., 2001). Children with dyslexia did better in experimental test situations of postural sway when given additional information (Razuk et al., 2020). Initially the children with dyslexia did poorly compared to their peers without dyslexia but their sway decreased with additional visual cues. This supports the multimodality approach when teaching these students in physical activity and education.

Attention-Deficit/Hyperactivity Disorder

The main features of ADHD are inattention, hyperactivity, and impulsivity (sometimes written as *hyperactivity-impulsivity*) that interfere with developmental functioning. Everyone experiences these behaviors at one time or another, but the diagnosis of ADHD requires that the symptoms be inappropriate for the person's age, and that they are excessive, long term, and pervasive (observed across different settings) (APA, 2022). Many authorities consider ADHD a disorder and refer to it as developmental, acknowledging a neurobehavioral basis. The American Academy of Pediatrics encourages children with ADHD to be screened for mental health issues like depression (Wolraich et al., 2019). *DSM-5-TR* features of ADHD are as follows: combined presentation, predominantly inattentive presentation, predominantly hyperactive or impulsive presentation; and other specified attention-deficit/hyperactivity disorder, unspecified attention-deficit/hyperactivity disorder. These are presented here to familiarize an educator or various school allied health with evaluation report terminology.

Interestingly, IDEA (2004) does not have a definition for ADHD and, therefore, federal education law relies on the medical or psychiatric classifications for meeting service qualifications in special education. Under IDEA (2004), the students are served under other health impaired, emotional disturbance, or SLD as determined by the eligibility team (Colarusso et al., 2017). Students with ADHD who do not meet any of the IDEA (2004) classifications mentioned can be served under Section 504 of the Vocational Rehabilitation Act of 1973 if they are in need of interventions to support learning. If the student receives services under a category of IDEA (2004), then there will be an IEP. If they receive accommodations under the Vocational Rehabilitation Act, Section 504, they will be in the general education program with accommodations.

The three main features of ADHD are inattention, hyperactivity, and impulsivity. Much has been written about these features with comparisons with age peers showing definite difficulties affecting motor performance and fitness (Harvey & Reid; 2003). All these features of ADHD can be well addressed (Barkley, 2000) in general and specifically in the physical education setting given expertise by professionals. Children with ADHD are on-the-go (APA, 2022) and for the most part enjoy being physically active. Teaching can be aligned for these students to be successful in a physical activity class.

The feature of inattention for students with ADHD is described as an inability to filter out unnecessary stimuli; hence, the person attends to everything (Kline & Silver, 2004). It would be a common misunderstanding to believe that these students do not attend. They do. The problem is that their neurological system attends to everything, and, in attending to everything, the individual has a hard time getting organized and sequencing. This is a problem for the students both at home and in school life.

Hyperactivity can be a on spectrum of personality for a typically developing child, and it can also be a developmental step. There are children by nature who are active. These children go beyond physical activity levels that are culturally expected for their age group. Yet, they do not fall behind socially, emotionally, or functionally because of their activity level. Developmentally young children are highly active walking and running around or using their wheelchairs or other adapted devices to move around a lot. As they mature, they have more focus with their physical activity. These attributes distinguish a child who is typically developing from a child who is atypically developing regarding activity.

The symptom of impulsivity is observed in ADHD when a stimulus is given, and the student responds without thinking. For example, the hand goes up before the teacher finishes the question. They run into the gym and grab the basketball before hearing the instructions. This is evidence of how their neurologic system is wired.

Diagnosis

The diagnosis of ADHD is made by clinical personnel such as a psychologist or developmental pediatrician, child psychiatrist, neurologist, or school psychologist, with input from parents, the classroom teacher, and others as deemed necessary. Many of the primary symptoms of inattention and impulsivity seen in children with ADHD are also symptoms of other problems, such as depression or anxiety. Input from family history, observations by the classroom teacher concurrent with standardized testing, and direct observations and interviews with the student are important components of the diagnostic procedure (see Barkley, 2000). The guidelines in the *DSM-5-TR* (APA, 2022) are used to diagnose ADHD with symptoms that must appear prior to age seven years and persist for at least six months. Many of these characteristics can be summarized as developmentally inappropriate degrees of inattention, impulsiveness, or hyperactivity. Very young children can attend only for a short period of time. This is not inattention but is developmentally expected, although there are younger children who can be diagnosed as ADHD by a well-qualified professional working with their families.

Myths of ADHD have proliferated: the child is lazy; the child is just a kid who will get over it; the child should receive medication and get off it as quickly as possible; they can focus on the video games, so they don't have ADHD; it's just poor parenting (Reiff & Tippins, 2004). The reality is that these are myths. Children with ADHD can become very downtrodden. They would like to succeed. They will not outgrow out ADHD, but some symptoms are modified in adulthood—the symptoms look different as they grow older. Being able to focus on video games is not as challenging as focusing on academic material.

The goal, of course, is to ensure that students with ADHD are recognized as individuals who may need special assistance and to provide the appropriate intervention. Many of the ideas and suggestions presented in this chapter will provide useful information in developing meaningful and positive physical activity programs for students with ADHD. Teaching strategies employed with children with behavior disorders are useful with students who have ADHD because the behavior exhibited can be similar, although the etiology can be vastly different.

Medication

Medication has been helpful for some children with ADHD. The mechanisms of the medicine vary, and the choice of which to use is best left to parents and physicians. Typically, parents and clinical personnel work together to understand how and what type of medication can best assist the child with ADHD. The CDC (2022a) has incorporated the recommendations of the American Academy of Pediatrics that for children ages six years and under, behavior therapy including parent training *precedes* medication management. When behavior therapy is not successful for very young children, medication can be considered by the parents and health care practitioner. For children six years through adolescence, medication and behavioral therapy can be used. Behavioral training includes

- parent training in behavior management,
- behavioral interventions in the classroom,
- peer interventions that focus on behavior, and
- organizational skills training. (CDC, 2022a)

Medications can help some children focus on the academic tasks and therefore increase academic success, social acceptance, and self-acceptance. Medication alone is not considered the silver bullet for solving all the difficulties faced by students with ADHD and their families. Instead, a multipronged approach is recommended. This approach includes the CDC-recommended behavioral strategies as well as medicine. In some cases, it is helpful for teachers to know if a student is taking medicine, particularly if there are side effects. Sometimes teachers are asked to help assess whether the medicine is helping the student. Caution is recommended when interpreting the behavior of the student. Sometimes a behavior is attributed inappropriately to a student's confirmed ADHD, even if the behavior is really reasonable given the situation and not necessarily due to the ADHD diagnosis.

Qualifying for Special Education

The student with ADHD will qualify for special education services in physical education if they struggle to understand instructions without attention to the necessary modifications and adaptations. They may or may not be motorically delayed, although some children are lagging or are on the low end of the typical for age. Without specific instructional strategies in place in PE, the student risks failing to learn (Lieberman et al., 2021; Lieberman & Houston-Wilson, 2000).

Concomitant Developmental Coordination Disorder

Some children with ADHD have problems with movement skill performance, and some do not (Harvey & Reid, 2003). The attribution of movement problems with a diagnosis of ADHD is compounded by the prevalence of comorbidity with other disorders. It is difficult to separate whether the move-

ment problems are caused by SLDs, developmental coordination disorder, depression and anxiety, or other problems (see NIMH, 2003).

Some students with SLD are clumsy, and some are not. Historically, the term *clumsy child syndrome* was used. Later, the term *dyspraxia* (*dys*, meaning not or breakdown; *praxia*, meaning action) was developed in the medical community. Then the diagnostic term *developmental coordination disorder* was put forth by the American Psychiatric Association (2022), identifying four diagnostic components needed for the disorder:

1. Motor coordination substantially below expectation for age and intelligence
2. Interference with academic achievement
3. Not due to a medical condition
4. In the presence of an intellectual disability, a lack of motor coordination in excess of expectations for age

In the medical community, developmental coordination disorder and dyspraxia are considered synonymous (Gibbs et al., 2007). Gibbs and colleagues recommend a brief and practical summary of the child's coordination difficulties to assist in diagnosis and develop interventions for physical education participation. Practically, this diagnosis is best made by the school or clinic-based physical therapist. Zimmer and colleagues (2020) noted that close relationships with the teacher helped children with developmental coordination disorder cope with being bullied and with the difficulty they felt in performing the activities in physical education. In addition, the researchers found that the children perceived teachers more positively when the activities were based on child preferences and competencies and gave them a sense of challenge and fun. Importantly these teachers also listened to the children and their negative feelings finding them as valid given the demands in PE.

Instructional Considerations

The start of this chapter discussed students with SLD or ADHD who struggled academically as young children and excelled in a physical activity. Their experiences gradually led to a sport that influenced their whole life. For these athletes, once diagnosed, academics improved as strategies were applied in the classroom. Michael Phelps' mother is a teacher. When he became interested in swimming, she used books about swimming to encourage reading, which was not his strong suit. Math was also not a strength for Phelps. His mother used swim times (e.g., splits) to have him solve math problems. When he first entered the water, he didn't like getting his face wet, so she had him on his back, and then he tried his side. Soon, he flipped over and the rest eventually became Olympic history! Physical educators will see a task analysis in his early swim experiences.

Students with SLD typically participate in inclusive physical activity programming. Educational experts are now interested in accurate observations of the academic area and in determining which interventions will be successful for the student with SLD. In the past, physical educators relied on the classic approach to these learners, which was based on the belief that the person could not translate visual and auditory images into meaningful symbols, and this led the teachers to try to improve perceptual motor ability for these students. Today, concurrent with other educators, the physical educator is encouraged to seek the benefits of engaging students with SLD in physical activity with their peers and connect interventions where appropriate to assist the student in learning.

The student will qualify for special education services in physical education if they struggle to understand instructions without modification and adaptation to the curriculum, not as if they are motorically delayed (although as stated, some children are lagging, or on the low end of what is typical for age). The goal is for the student to know and enjoy the physical activity environments that offer a wide variety of exposure so they can learn about their preferences, skill level, and how to use their community resources.

Language

Because effective teaching is based upon adequate communication, it is imperative that physical educators and school allied health be cognizant of individual differences among children in ability to receive auditory information (receptive language) and to use language to express themselves (expressive language). With a receptive language deficit, the student can't receive the auditory input. With expressive language deficit, the student can't verbally explain what was just said. Classroom teachers should expect physical educators and school allied health to employ the instructional strategies used in the classroom to ensure that students with SLD are learning in the physical activity environment. Asking a child with SLD who has a receptive language deficit to respond to the question "What did I just say?" is problematic. Given only a verbal

set of instructions, deficits in expressive language will also be impede an appropriate response. Their neurologic system doesn't work typically.

Receptive Language

Receptive language is the ability to comprehend words (receive them) and to remember their sequences. Teachers should assume that the student with SLD and a reception language deficit is unable to understand information shared in an auditory mode. Unfortunately, students with learning disabilities whose condition is not correctly diagnosed as a receptive language deficit can develop compensatory behaviors. These behaviors are protective behaviors that the child uses (such as being boastful, showing off, wandering off, or humiliating others) that often alienate others, causing trouble with family, teachers, and peers.

Using a multimodality approach to instruction, the teacher obtains eye contact from the student and provides a visual prompt along with auditory information. The teacher could use the direction "Go to the corner of the gym where the red cone is," while pointing to the specified corner where the red cone is placed. Realistically, this helps both the student with receptive language deficits and others in the class. This is an example of universal design for learning in PE, which was discussed in chapter 5 (Lieberman et al., 2021).

Expressive Language

Auditory expressive language deficits refer to verbalizing. In a physical education class, students may understand but be unable to verbally explain what is required. Or they may struggle to ask a question about a task in the physical activity environment. This is where the physical education teacher can coordinate with the speech and language pathologist to understand the strategies that are being employed with this student for communicating wants, needs, and academic material. If a student has expressive language deficit, then responding to "What are we doing first at the station?" is problematic. In the end, the speech and language pathologist is the best resource to know how this student is communicating throughout the school day and can adapt this to the physical education class.

Perception

Sometimes students with learning disabilities have problems understanding laterality (e.g., identifying the right and left hand; an awareness of two sides of the body) or directionality (e.g., concepts of over and under). Thus, they may have poor body awareness. Some of these deficits just persist throughout their life (Fawcett & Nicholson, 1995). Such was the instance of an architect in a group aerobics class. The instructor was in the center with the class circled around her, and he could not rhythmically follow her with an alternate kick forward and clapping his hands under the extended leg. As the music played on, he stopped. Architects deal with space and dimensions but not their body in relationship to those concepts.

Visual Perception

A child with a genuine problem with visual perception will be consistent across physical activity sessions until an intervention is devised. Visual perception may be due to difficulty in one or more of the following: visual discrimination, figure–ground discrimination, depth perception, object constancy, and object identification (visual agnosia). Children whose visual perception is affected by inadequate visual discrimination have difficulty in determining the size, shape, color, and texture of an object. In physical education, they may be unable to distinguish a large ball from a small ball, a blue beanbag from a red beanbag, or rough ground from smooth ground. There are very few games and activities that do not require some degree of discrimination

in size, form, color, and texture. Consequently, intervention will facilitate success and pleasure in play. The occupational therapist on the student's IEP team may be consulted for recommendations based on testing.

Figure–Ground Discrimination

The ability to visually differentiate a specific object from a complex background is minimal in young children, and it develops slowly to reach its peak during adolescence. In children with faulty visual perception due to poor figure–ground discrimination, this development is impaired. Such children lack the ability to identify and focus attention upon a single object or figure in a cluttered or complex background. They may, for example, become so confused by the various players that form the background for a game of tag that they cannot locate the one who is *it*. Inability by some children to follow the aerial path of a thrown ball is another illustration of the figure–ground problem. It may be that additional cues (colored stripes on the ground, brightly colored balls) are needed to increase the performance of many activities in the physical education program.

Depth perception is the term given to the ability to judge distances between near and far objects. Those who have problems determining the distance of an object have difficulty placing their bodies in

Kali9/E+/Getty Images

the proper relationship to the object. In catching a ball, for example, they overreach or do not reach far enough, and they miss catching the ball. Any activity that requires judgment of distances is difficult, if not impossible, for students with this visual perception deficit.

Object consistency is the ability to identify an object regardless of the direction from which it is viewed. Students lacking this ability become lost in a maze of unrecognizable objects as they move about. For example, such children will not be able to recognize an item of play equipment when viewed from any side other than the one from which they learned to identify it. Such a deficit in visual perception obviously creates many difficulties in physical education. Encouraging children to walk all the way around the equipment assists in this difficulty. In line with universal design for learning PE, have *everyone* do this in pairs. Often this is advantageous beginning at the younger ages.

Self-Esteem

It is widely known that students with learning disabilities are at high risk for developing low self-esteem. Studies report that students were in the lower third of their class, and avoidance and lack of motivation were present (Shapiro & Ulrich, 2001; Sideridis & Tsorbatzoudis, 2003) while survey data report dropout rates as high (Fletcher et al., 2018). Yet, children with SLD, like their peers, have the capacity to understand and show insight into the meaning of their own behavior. Students with learning disabilities need to start early to form meaningful and satisfactory relationships with others, with some researchers some suggesting before the age of eight years old (Gresham et al., 2001). Having fun contributes to engagement in youth sports with obvious offshoots into friendships (Gould & Walker, 2019). Working with the school psychologist or school counselor may help to better strategize about interventions if depression is more than typical for a teen (Kline & Silver, 2004). Teens like to be recognized, have a friend, succeed in their classes, and have parents be proud of them. Without needing feedback from the student with an SLD, PE teachers can recognize effort or outright accomplishment in class, use buddy systems to facilitate learning motor skills, and encourage friendships. They can also point out when a buddy team was exceptional not just in winning but in other attributes like cooperation and respect, and they can report to parents the positive side of their child's participation in GPE or APE. They can keep doing this. Often, the student with SLD is *not* familiar with positive feedback, yet hopefully this can become their reality.

Program Placement and Focus

Program placement for students with learning disabilities runs the full array of possibilities in GPE and APE. Some students only need accommodations for an expressive or receptive language deficit impacting the ability to follow instructions by the teacher. These students, like the elite athletes featured in the opening of this chapter, do not lag in their motor skills or games and sports participation. In fact, they excel. Other students may need more support in the GPE with consultation from the APE and the occupational therapist, physical therapist, or speech and language pathologist. Follow the curriculum focus for that grade and school district.

Instructional Strategies

Physical education for students with SLD has the potential to affect the positive development of social and emotional health and to help them feel good about themselves despite difficulties they may have in movement or at school. A much more functional approach to getting the student into the curriculum for their age and doing their personal best is being advocated to engage the student with SLD in PE activity.

For years the instructional approach taken with students with SLD was developmental. Instead of taking a developmental approach, it works better to use the top-down assessment described in chapter 6, which makes observations about the student's performance within the curriculum. Here the student with a learning disability progresses along with his peers, through a large array of physical activity in the school years, and he is not singled out. What needs to be modified are equipment, rules, environment and the instruction (e.g., Lieberman & Houston-Wilson, 2000).

It does little good to implore students with ADHD to pay attention. They would if they could. Their distractibility is of a neurological origin. It requires other teaching strategies. Some students with ADHD have problems with perseveration on a task. Perseveration is the ability to stay on task. The student cannot shift with ease from one activity to another. The child would like to follow directions, but they simply cannot respond immediately and appropriately to stop-and-start activities. Teachers in general and in adapted physical education often use class signals in preparing students for a change in activity. This is sometimes called a warning. Some teachers use time, as in "In five minutes, we will switch stations." Watching a clock is not the important message. The message is that things will change soon. Even younger children learn that concept. Without doing this sort of preparation, disaster often awaits. Often, the child is enjoying the activity! It is hard to have them stop and then prepare to start another activity. For instance, watch a young child being removed from a swimming pool with the prompt "We have to go now" while simultaneously being lifted out of the pool. The child is fully engaged in playing in the pool, they burst into tears, screaming and kicking. In addition, if the child was highly active, jumping, swimming, or playing with a friend, that arousal needs calming down before a successful shift takes place. In a PE class, after a signal to the whole class, the teacher can add, "Phillipo and Pippa, you look like you having so much fun! In a few minutes you can say 'See you soon! Bye.'"

Multimodality for SDL

Students with SDL can be successful in physical education settings when instruction is provided using a multimodality approach. The primary one of these approaches is a visual prompt with auditory instructions. Point to the direction the group needs to run in a game versus using an auditory description. Using other components of teaching in APE such as task analysis and ecological task analysis will also help. But remember, there is no need to remediate the issues with perception or language. However, there is a need to accommodate students with instructional strategies supportive of the learning of the movement activities. This is not to say that if repeated practice would help the student, then place the student with some others who could also use more practice time. Have the

smaller groups of children perform different skills repeatedly and then switch. This way, the students who need extra practice are worked into the lesson without being made to stand out. Many students need more practice time on skills. Buddy systems are popular when teaching physical activity skills. It increases socialization and learning without stigmatizing the student with SLD. It's fun, too. For example, if mathematics is important to a game, use a buddy system where one is the wizard, and the other is the ruler of the land. The wizard advises the ruler of the land especially if the ruler has an SLD in math.

Clumsiness

Clumsiness is seen often with students with SLD. It is not a reason for them not to have fun in physical activity. Clumsiness will not completely disappear or improve markedly, although practice increases confidence (Sigmundsson, 2005). The instructor can praise performance attempts of all the children. They can use names when praising, such as "Sam, good effort." One parent explained to their son's GPE teacher that their son didn't need to play in the game, but they wanted him to be recognized as being on the team. Their son had told his parents he wanted his team to win, and he decided that sometimes he wasn't going to play. The GPE teacher disagreed and said their son would *always* play. The teacher's philosophy was that winning wasn't the goal of playing the game.

The aim for a child who appears clumsy in the physical activity environment is to be functional in performing the age-appropriate skills considering a range of typical performance for age. Balance can be particularly challenging, but it can be normal enough. The student may be awkward in move-

Caregiver Communication

Parents and caregivers of the children with SLD hear often that their child is developing atypically. It would be a great benefit to hear from the GPE teacher and school allied health that their child is enjoying a certain physical activity and making a friend or has friends in the class. Stay away from describing at length perceptual motor difficulties. (The occupational therapist can address any concerns that impact an IEP with a thrust on intervention within the class setting.) Instead, the emphasis should be on the child's strengths in the curriculum. Taken out of the context of perceptual motor problems, the strengths are translated into phrases such as "likes soccer," and the weaknesses are described in such words as "providing more practice time with the soccer skills," or "The performance is this student's personal best." In other words, given the extra assistance in PE, a student with a learning disability might have a great time in their physical education classes. Having a great time in physical activity environments translates into *having fun*, which the sport psychologists have identified as the reason youth stay involved in sports (Gould & Walker, 2019).

Transitional IEP

The transitional IEP in high school guides the student with SLD into physical activities based on their strengths, interests, community resources, and the family interests. Bicycling, running, walking, hiking, swimming, and using a fitness club are activities that potentially can be performed successfully whether a person is highly coordinated, can read or do mathematics well; or understands verbal-only directions or whether none of these is true. If the student has been involved in a team sport and desires to continue participating, the IEP team can look for opportunities for involvement in the community. This recommendation is for both ends of the spectrum regarding physical performance of the student with SLD. With proper intervention through the transitional IEP, the student with SLD can remain physically active after graduation.

ment performance and in the lower quadrant by standardized testing, but if they are functional, then the teacher can consider no further testing and adapting and add positive regard and multimodality instructions. A referral to the school physical therapist can be made if the child is always running into things in the classroom or physical activity environments—and getting injured by doing so. There is a possibility that the child may have concomitant problems that match a school psychologist's expertise.

Task Analysis

Ecological task analysis considers the unique aspects of the individual, the unique way a task is presented to the performer, and the unique environment in which the task is performed (Davis & Burton, 1991). If the student with SLD is struggling in a physical activity, work must be done to analyze how these aspects—*performer*, *task*, and *environment*—contribute to their movement performance. Modifications to the curriculum and adaptations to the activities need attention while taking in the unique aspects of the performer and environment.

Teachers should identify the motor skills where the student is experiencing problems, and when needed, analyze the skill into small units; provide direct instruction and reinforcement; and allow for sufficient repetition and practice. Other students can join in the repetition, understanding that many children benefit from more practice time. If the task analysis of skill isn't successful, it might be important to consider a top-down approach to assessing that skill. The top-down approach is used when more complex physical activities or games are part of the curriculum. Instructions should be delivered in a multimodality manner rather than just verbally. Teachers can group the student with SLD with other students who need more practice time; thus, making every attempt to not single out any student.

ADHD Engagement

To effectively engage children with ADHD in physical education classes is to understand the difficulty they have with attention and that they will be impulsive as well as highly active.

The following instructional strategies have been found to be helpful for children with ADHD: behavior management, cognitive behavior techniques, and being clear with instructions/direct teaching (CDC, 2022b; Reiff & Tippins, 2004). For the physical educator, this requires the interventions that are being employed in the general education settings to be implemented in the physical education classes.

The modifications and adaptations that are needed for a student with ADHD are not necessarily with the movement skills but rather with the instructional delivery and the organization of the activities. Sometimes poor movement skills performance is due to lack of opportunity to respond, lack of ability to understand the instructions due to impulsivity, and a high activity level. Some children with ADHD can also have SLD. It is important for physical education teachers and school allied health to understand whether auditory processing is compounding the problems of being highly active.

Facility Modification for ADHD

Facilities may need modification to accommodate the inattention, hyperactivity, and impulsivity of the student with ADHD. The following should be considered:

• *Consistency in structure:* Teaching stations and the placement of equipment are recommended to be consistent from day to day. Because children with ADHD are often described as lost in space, the instructional environment should be highly structured with as little as possible left to chance. In a highly structured physical education program, the children always enter the gymnasium through the same door, go to the same floor spot, participate in warm-up activities, and start individualized instruction at the same teaching station. The direction of rotation between stations is uniform from day to day, as are the stop and start signals employed by the teacher. If or when the student shows less distractibility, structure can be gradually lessened.

• *Floor markings:* The number of lines on the floor and markings on the wall should be minimized for students with attentional problems. It is recommended that floor spots in the form of simple geometric shapes or other relevant symbols be placed on the floor to assist young children in finding their own space and to assure that the distance between students is sufficient to eliminate body contact.

• *Reduction of space:* For classes, reduce the space for instruction through the use of partitions or the identification of small rooms within the school that can be used for physical activity purposes. Placing sturdy tumbling mats vertically on an easily designated but effective cubicle creates an instructional setting for students who are easily distracted. When children play outdoors, it is especially important that small areas be roped off or marked off with cones so that space boundaries are carefully defined.

• *Sufficient teaching stations and equipment:* Children with ADHD don't do well waiting in line and are enthusiastic about getting involved in the specified activity. Keep all the students moving if they're at stations. When one throws to a target, others pick up the balls. Similarly, when kicking to a target or rolling to the pins, those who aren't kicking or rolling are collecting the balls. Have lines for students to stand behind. Having more than one line might help with distance from the target. Students might impulsively pick one line too close or too far. Have the paraprofessional help them with their next choice. For youth, use the same techniques for lead-up game activities. Keep students from just standing around waiting. Skilled students in a sport can sometimes be the coach at a station to assist with key prompts for the others. They would need to be trained and *not* held to this position throughout class.

• *Opportunities to view self:* With media so replete and with permission by parents, for individual or group viewing have the student observe their team's recorded performance.

Contraindicated Practice

Many practices in physical activity environments that traditionally have been thought of as desirable are sometimes contraindicated for children with ADHD and those with learning disabilities. Some of these are presented in table 9.1.

Courtesy of Michael Beets.

TABLE 9.1 Physical Education Practices for Students With ADHD

Traditionally beneficial in physical activity but contraindicated for students with ADHD	Beneficial for students with ADHD
Opportunities to develop leadership–followership qualities through membership on many kinds of teams with different students serving as leaders each time.	Frequent changes in group structure often confuse students with ADHD. They should be allowed to play with the same small group throughout the year (or a season) with as few changes in leadership as feasible.
Opportunities to let off steam and to develop fitness through freedom to run, jump, and shout in an optimal amount of space.	Letting off steam tends to heighten hyperactivity. Time should be spent on the mastery of skills and activities that are designed primarily for cardiovascular development. Experiment with variations in speed and distance to determine which kinds of fitness activities are best for everyone.
Emphasis upon the development of speed through awards for track and field events and the association of winning with the fastest team. Students skilled in competition can qualify to join school or community sport teams.	Many students with ADHD need assistance in learning how to perform at their best and not comparing themselves to others. Decrease the emphasis on competition with others and develop the skills and the notion of cooperation with the team, and doing the best that they can.
Pick a countable activity and ask students to see how many times they can do in five minutes.	Use goal-setting techniques. Students set a goal and see how close they come to their goal. At the end of the allotted time, prompt with: "Raise your hand if you did your best" and "Say 'yeah' if you got close to your goal." There is no competition and more practice. Figure 9.1 shows a picture drawn by the student to illustrate their attempts at making a basket. The teacher can ask children to draw a picture of themselves.
Without a warning, tell the class it is time to go, and they need to line up to leave.	Use a warning cue (something that the whole class knows signals the class will end shortly). Then it is also very important to use cool-down activities after heightened physical activity.

FIGURE 9.1 A student's picture of their goal of making a basket. A playful approach to learning how to set goals.

Cues and Prompts

Effective diagnostic techniques enable the physical educator or clinician to teach to the level of student success. For different reasons, it is helpful for the teacher or clinician to determine which is the best way the student with ADHD learns: verbally, visually, or kinesthetically. The accepted practice is to emphasize the use of those senses that are unaffected rather than to attempt to remedy the disability. This implies that some individuals must be taught mainly through the visual and kinesthetic modalities while others must receive instruction chiefly via the verbal (auditory) and kinesthetic modalities. Overall, the approach is to teach to the student's strength, whatever sensory medium is strongest for the student.

ADHD Behavioral Risks and Interventions

In the intermediate and secondary grades, when emphasis is more on individual and dual activities, students with ADHD can be taught using the top-down approach to performance. Some students will be highly motivated to learn these activities, and their impulsivity will get the best of them. Use the strategies in table 9.2 to address impulsivity when bringing out equipment and giving information to students. Structure in the class is important to all to build the physical skills for the activity. Use positive reinforcement to shape behavior. And of course, some of these students will be very talented motorically. Table 9.2 will help physical education students with a full range of talent levels.

TABLE 9.2   ADHD Features With Physical Education Students' Behavioral Risks and Selected Interventions

Features	Behavioral risks	Instructor strategies
Primary features		
Inattention	• Can process instructions and rules for the game but not all at once. Distracted by equipment and other children. • Wandering off or being a poor team player.	• Keep instructions short and simple. Multimodality delivery. • Keep equipment, if possible, out of the visual line until in use. • Do not give equipment to a student and ask them to hold it and listen. • Keep the class structured and predictable. • Provide signals to begin and end activities and make transitions.
Impulsivity	• Action before thinking, calling out repeatedly, using equipment before their turn, difficulty waiting in line for their turn, and difficulty staying on task. Results in negative consequences for student.	• Have students stand behind lines on the floor for tasks. • Regard the student in positive terms whenever possible, reflecting to the student without needing a response. • Use the term *personal best* for differences in performance. • Have the student use high fives to others for positive regard. • Encourage the student's skills in self-evaluation and setting realistic goals. Reset unrealistic goals. "Let's try again." • Outside class, have students draw goals. See figure 9.2. Use drawings as the beginning of training around goal setting. This is not a rigid task, but rather talk about the drawings with the student. • Keep stations with equipment in place. Use short instructions and very little waiting to engage in the activity. Paraprofessionals assist and are trained.

Features	Behavioral risks	Instructor strategies
Primary features		
Hyperactivity	• Difficulty moderating arousal and will become very active beyond what is expected for age level. No reduction in hyperactivity based on a normal range of vigorous physical activity. Neurologically hard to transition out of a pleasurable activity once active.	• Younger children use marked spots for arrival places. Older students have a predictable routine structure. There is a beginning, a middle, and an end to class. • Meet with the student outside class one to one to explain that the student is a good mover and that you are excited to have them in the class. Then simply explain how the class is run and what is expected. Keep the meeting short. • Use warnings to transition to the next activity. Use this pattern: *warn*, wait, *warn*, transition. • High-arousal activities will need teacher-mediated structure to decrease the arousal. • Provide cooldowns before ending the PE class.
Secondary features		
Low self-esteem	• Has a low tolerance for negative feedback, losing, or facing failure.	• Provide positive regard to the student even if it is not about the physical activity, such as complimenting a T-shirt. • Do not argue with the student about the positive feedback. State it and let it go. • Prioritize the behaviors you will work on with the student and let the others go unless physical harm ensues. • Have the student describe a reward for doing well. Examples might be extra jump rope, more time shooting baskets, or leading students out of the gym.
Lack of age-appropriate social skills	• Does not know how to be a leader but wants to be. • Does not know how to be positive and give positive feedback to peers, take turns easily, or cooperate with team activities.	• Teach the social skills associated with the game or sport. • Use short and simple instructions. • Use a multimodality approach.
Low frustration tolerance (anger and temper control)	• Quick to become upset if called "out" during a game, is on the losing team, feels that a rule is unfair, and consequently does not perform well in class. • Can have temper tantrums or meltdowns.	• Explain that sometimes life is unfair but that they did their best in the game or activity. • Catch the student when they could have gotten angry and did not, and point out that you noticed they were successful in keeping their cool. • Notice that a student's behavior is about to escalate and intervene before the student loses it. Use proximity, standing close with a positive verbal regard.

FIGURE 9.2 A student's drawing of their social skills of being positive and how many times they will do this.

Physical Activities for Children With ADHD

Children with ADHD in the primary grades are like their peers who do not have inattention, impulsivity, and difficulty with hyperactivity. They want to be physically active. They need to be physically active with the guidance of a teacher or clinician who understands how to manage and engage them. It is a myth that just running around will slow them down. In part, yes, they eventually do get tired, but probably not in the time to return to the next class! The more they learn the structure of a class, the more control they feel in the class.

Younger children will be developing basic movement patterns—running, jumping, hopping, throwing, catching, striking, and kicking. Engagement in all the activities for their grade is appropriate with behavior plans in place. Physical educators and school allied health can work with the classroom teacher and use the behavior plans from their classroom in the gym and other areas of physical activity. If all the teachers are using similar approaches, it will help the student, especially if the management techniques are focused on the positive. These children are used to being negatively approached in so many settings that hearing something positive often comes as a shock; sometimes they deny it. If that happens, the teacher should repeat this and not get into a discussion.

Instruction in individual and dual sports should begin as early as third grade but more likely begins a little later. Most important, competence in individual activities (e.g., swimming, track events, roller skating, or hiking) and dual activities (e.g., badminton, pickleball , or table tennis) enhances self-esteem and serves to compensate for any inability to participate successfully in team activities, if that is the case. Early acquaintance with developing these lifetime sports also contributes to family unity and may lead to closer parent–child relationships when, for instance, parents and children can bowl, swim, hike, play table tennis, or play badminton together.

The primary grades in physical education may play a major role in the development of language and the enrichment of vocabulary about their body and its ability to move. PE teachers and school allied health can impart a vocabulary about physical activity at school, using terms such as *up* and *down*, *over* and *under*, *below* and *above*, *forward* and *backward*. They can also enable students to describe their experience kinesthetically (unless if they have expressive language problems). Body parts and the terms for different kinds of movements and positions are easy to share. The physical education class is an apt setting for the child with ADHD to learn given the combined verbal and kinesthetic input for these words and what they mean.

Cooper Neill/Getty Images for Liberty Mutual Insurance

Assessment and Evaluation for Children With SLD

For the student with SLD, assessing skills will aid the teacher in knowing whether additional teaching strategies are required. In assessing children who have SLD for physical activity, note the impact their disability might have when using standardized protocols. For example, some standardized testing will limit the prompts to the extent that verbal language is given without physical cues. Overall, there are limits on the number of demonstrations or attempts with the skill. This could underestimate the student's skills. Standardized testing may have to be modified to increase the student's understanding of what is being asked. If testing is modified, then follow instructions for reporting in chapter 6.

The Test of Gross Motor Development-3 (TGMD-3; Ulrich, 2020) can be used with children ages 3 to 10 years with autism spectrum disorder needing extra cues (see the instructor's manual of the TGMD-3). This might be explored for use for children with SLD. In the evaluation report, note that the TGMD-3 was used as adapted and is valid for children with autism spectrum disorder who need extra cues and verbal

instructions. Since there is not literature yet on the validity of using the TGMD-3 with children with SLD and adding extra cues, the assessor can use the test and add cues but not use the standard scores. It can be reported as a checklist. This data can be very helpful to parents, caregivers, and the IEP team.

Curriculum-based measurement, as explained in chapter 6, is used with children who have SLD to assess for inclusion in the physical activity experiences (Burton & Miller, 1998; Deno, 1997, 2002; Deshler & Bulgren, 1997). Through this process, a reasonable idea is developed regarding the student's movement skills and how that fits in with the expected physical activity experiences for them. Instructional supports tend toward multimodality.

Educational Health Care Providers

Expect that the school occupational and physical therapists, as well as the speech and language pathologist will be contributing to the development of the student's IEP for both students with ADHD and SLD. The evaluation findings used by these professionals directly affect physical activity engagement. Occupational therapists and physical therapists can assist with assessments that affect the execution of movement skills and participation in games and recreational sport. The speech and language pathologist will be particularly interested in how instructions are given, so the student can act appropriately. If a student has a receptive or expressive language deficit, the GPE and APE teachers must know and make accommodations. Sometimes an instructor will think a student is noncompliant, when in fact the student's disability has been affected by verbal-only instructions. Multimodality instructions are important.

Students with ADHD will often be taking medication to help them during school hours. Educators can expect to give feedback to the school nurse or to the parents or caregivers when they ask. It is very helpful if these individuals let the teachers know when a medication is being changed (increased, decreased, discontinued, newly prescribed) and what to expect. Clinical personnel are part of these students' lives, and in working together with the family, the GPE and APE can provide important evidence of a student's well-being.

Summary

SLD, a category of disability in IDEA (2004), is defined as a significant discrepancy between student achievement in the classroom and what the student is expected to achieve in oral expression, listening comprehension, written expression, basic reading skill, reading fluency, reading comprehension, mathematical calculation, and mathematical problem-solving. Each state sets its own criteria for defining *discrepancy*. According to the *DSM-5-TR*, SLD is a neurodevelopmental disorder resulting in difficulties in reading, math, or written expression (APA, 2022). Issues to be aware of for physical activity engagement are how the student uses expressive and receptive language. Multimodality instruction helps the children learn and have fun. Physical educators and school allied health are encouraged to share positive behavioral observations with parents and caregivers. Observational statements can be simple as "Joshua likes swimming." The problems of the child with SLD are neurologically based and are to be accommodated rather than heavily ameliorated. The main features of attention-deficit/hyperactivity disorder (ADHD) are inattention, hyperactivity, and impulsivity. These children want to be physically active. Instructors enable the students to succeed in physical education environments with interventions for the individual child and class management regarding symptoms of ADHD. Secondary features of low self-esteem and low frustration tolerance require instructor skills in providing positives to the child and catching the child ahead of outbreaks and using behavior management techniques as needed.

CHAPTER 10

Behavior Disorders

CHAPTER OBJECTIVES

After completing this chapter, you will be able to do the following:

- Identify the characteristics of emotional behavioral disorders (EBD) in children and youth as defined in IDEA (2004) under emotional disturbance (ED).

- Appreciate the diagnoses made by mental health specialists when children carry behaviors that cannot be ignored because of their serious inappropriateness and emotional reactions resulting in interference in their learning.

- Understand the importance of analyzing the frequency, intensity, and duration of a behavior that is disruptive in physical education participation.

- Understand broad characteristics of disorders and how to engage the student in physical education.

- Describe teaching strategies to increase participation in physical activity for students with behavior disorders.

The term *behavior disorder* that is used in this chapter is not a category under IDEA (2004). Under IDEA (1997) the category was seriously emotionally dis- turbed, but intense pressure resulted in *seriously* being dropped in federal education law (Colarusso et al., 2017). Some states continue to use *seriously emotionally disturbed.* The term *emotional disturbance* is often used with the umbrella term *behavior disorder* found in much of the literature on children and youth. According to special educators Colarusso and colleagues (2017), there is controversy in the usefulness of the term *emotionally disturbed* in the federal law's (IDEA, 2004) definition. An advocacy group has formed in which researchers and authors use the terms *emotional and behavioral disorders (EBDs).*

Individuals with an EBD qualify for special education services not necessarily because of significant motor deficiencies but rather because their behavior prevents them from learning and being successful in physical environments and experiences. With behavior interventions in place, these students can participate well in inclusive physical activity environments.

Causes and Prevalence

In the study of child development, risk factors contribute to negative developmental outcome. When children become depressed and anxious, they may act out and not follow societal expectations for age in the home, community, and school. Other perspectives consider the construct of psychopathy that identifies emotional and interpersonal features

leading to severe, violent, and chronic antisocial behavior; but it is very controversial (Frick, 2022).

Of children 3 to 17 years of age in the United States, during a national survey ending in 2019, approximately 8.9 percent have a diagnosed behavior problem, 9.4 percent have an anxiety disorder, and 4.4 percent have depression (Bitsko et al., 2022). With depression, 73.8 percent also had anxiety, and 47.2 percent had behavior problems. These data have probably increased since survey data ended in 2019 and the COVID-19 pandemic began in 2020 by the CDC timeline (2021). This ultimately resulted in school closures, disrupting children's day-to-day life, and mental health issues were apparent with survey research reporting "…anxiety, depression, loneliness, stress, and tension" (Theberath et al., 2022, n.p.).

Children living in poverty are especially affected by mental health conditions of depression and anxiety. The CDC found that these conditions increase over time for these children, with most having both conditions (Bitsko et al., 2022). Among children living 100 percent below the federal poverty level, more than one in five (22 percent) had a mental, behavioral, or developmental disorder with one in six children aged two to eight years (17.4 percent) diagnosed for these (Cree et al., 2018).

Acting out in aggressive ways is among the symptoms of posttraumatic stress disorder (PTSD). Across the United States, emotional trauma in children has increased the incidence of posttraumatic stress disorder where 12.5 percent of children in vehicle accidents and 43 to 63 percent in sexual assault have posttraumatic stress disorder (AAP, 2020). This stress contributes to the percentage of children with posttraumatic stress disorder posited to have stress-induced abnormal neurodevelopment that increases reactivity and emotional dysregulation as they age. This leads to acting out in school, home, and community. Herringa theorized that ". . . youth with PTSD are subject to multiple or repeated traumas that interact with genetic vulnerability to alter neurodevelopment over the course of childhood and adolescence" (Herringa, 2017, p. 6). In a 2021 report on medical claims and the effect of the COVID-19 pandemic on teens in the United States, anxiety was up by 93.6 percent, depression by 83.9 percent, self-harm by 333.9 percent, and adjustment disorder 89.7 percent (FAIR Health, 2021). Early stress with food scarcity and family homelessness was and is impacting young children as are the experiences of violence in the home and community. In 2020, Cohen and Bosk reported that,

COVID-19 has likely increased the already elevated risks for LGBTQ, maltreated, and homeless youth, as well as youth with substance use disorders and youth in foster care, because of a complex combination of potentially negative family interactions, economic uncertainty, the stress and anxiety of living through a pandemic, and more limited access to resources.

Cohen & Bosk (2020, p. 2).

The Center on the Developing Child at Harvard is adamant that young children living in stress need interventions as soon as possible (CDCH, n.d.). If intervention begins in the younger ages or as soon as possible, it can mediate negative effects the stress has on the developing brain, and parents learn soon how to interact with their children to promote positive developmental trajectories.

Classification and Diagnosis

To provide guidelines for the identification and education of students with behavior disorders, IDEA (2004) stipulates that the student have a condition exhibiting one or more of the following characteristics over a long period of time and to a marked degree, which adversely affects educational performance:

1. An inability to learn that cannot be explained by intellectual, sensory, or health factors

2. An inability to build or maintain satisfactory interpersonal relationships with peers and teachers

3. Inappropriate types of behavior or feelings under normal circumstances

4. A general, pervasive mood of unhappiness or depression

5. A tendency to develop physical symptoms or fears associated with personal or school problems

Most authorities agree that childhood behavior disorders involve behavior that is extreme for the age and social and cultural expectations. It is beyond the scope of this text to diagnose psychiatric disorders of children that fit the category of behavior disorder. This work is done by specialized medical personnel such as child psychiatrists and psychologists. In reports that come to the schools, disorders of childhood are found under two categories: mood disorders and anxiety disorders (APA, 2022). Mood disorders include bipolar disorders and depressive disorders, and anxiety disorders include separation anxiety and panic disorder, general anxiety disorder, obsessive compulsive disorder, body dysmorphia disorder, and trauma and stress disorders. In the *Diagnostic and Statistical Manual of Mental Disorders, Fifth Edition, Text Revision* (*DSM-5-TR*; APA, 2022) disruptive mood dysregulation disorder is found when children are sad and irritable, which significantly affects their ability to function well.

Under IDEA (2004), students with behavior disorder have average to above average learning capabilities and their school-related problems are not the primary result of any intellectual inadequacy, rather their behavior is getting in the way of learning. There is also an inability to interact positively with peers and teachers. Regarding this, it is possible to track the frequency, intensity, and duration of their behavior patterns. These are very important to understand to set up interventions for learning.

- *Frequency* refers to how often the behavior is performed. All children cry, get into fights, and at times respond aggressively. Exhibiting these behaviors, however, does not constitute a behavior problem unless the specific behavior—fighting, for example—occurs frequently. Although the student who is disturbed exhibits inappropriate behaviors like those of other children, for them this response is frequent.

- *Intensity* describes the magnitude of a given behavior. Although many people occasionally respond angrily in a loud voice, individuals with behavior disorders frequently rely on a high-volume voice as the medium to express all their demands. There are also students with EBD who express themselves too softly to be heard. The concept of magnitude may be applied to many behaviors, such as the intensity with which a child fights, slams a door, verbally abuses others, or picks on others. The intensity can be physically harmful to themselves or others. An example would be throwing chairs at other students or a teacher.

- *Duration* is a measure of how long a student engages in a behavior. The amount of time students with behavior disorders act unacceptably is different from that of their peers without EBD. For example, although many younger children experience temper tantrums lasting a few seconds to a few minutes, the student with severe behavior problems may have outbursts for a period approaching one hour or longer.

Familiarity with aspects of the clinical categories is important so that physical educators, coaches, and other school and clinical personnel will be able to communicate with parents and the various mental health specialists. There are characteristics of the students with EBD that teachers and coaches will observe during the school day of importance to such practitioners and the student's parents. The following are samples of some of the diagnostic classifications of children with behavior disorders.

Disruptive Mood Dysregulation Disorder and Oppositional Defiant Disorder

Children with disruptive mood dysregulation disorder have frequent extreme reactions of angry outbursts. They are chronically irritable. Previously the student could have been diagnosed as bipolar. Treatments are new and include working with knowledgeable healthcare personnel. In time, this disorder may change, leading the student to become anxious and depressed.

In the *DSM-5-TR* (APA, 2022), disruptive mood dysregulation disorder now encompasses oppositional defiant disorder for some children. They often coexist. Other children will only carry the diagnosis of disruptive mood dysregulation disorder. It is not the job of school personnel to diagnose mental health disorders, but physical educators and coaches are in good positions to communicate with

parents and medical personnel about the behavior of a specific child, thus assisting in their care. Medical personnel know that the earlier the child and family get involved in interventions, the better the adjustment can be for the child.

The Mayo Clinic (2020), explains that inherited and environmental differences contribute to oppositional defiant disorder.

- *Inherited:* This refers to the way the brain's neurologic processes work, as well as the temperament of the child.
- *Environment:* The environment for child-rearing is without supervision, inconsistent, harsh in punishment, or abusive and neglectful.

Overall, children with disruptive mood dysregulation disorder or oppositional defiant disorder have a pattern of anger and irritable moods—losing their temper or being easily annoyed, angry, and resentful. The children are also argumentative and defiant in their behavior, including arguing with adults, actively refusing to comply with requests or rules, deliberately annoying others, and blaming others for their mistakes. A child with one of these disorders has likely shown vindictiveness at least twice in the past six months. The level of oppositional defiant disorder is considered mild if it occurs in only one setting or severe if the behavior occurs in three or more settings (e.g., home, school, and community). Symptoms usually occur during preschool.

Conduct Disorder

A student with a conduct disorder has behaviors that oppose societal rules and violate others' basic rights. The student may be aggressive toward people and animals, destroy property, seriously violate rules, be deceitful, or engage in theft. Some of the following aggressive behaviors are present: bullying, threatening, intimidating, fighting, harming someone with a weapon, being physically cruel, engaging in forceful sexual activity, and stealing.

Regarding the developmental course of conduct disorder, with an early onset in preschool and middle childhood, the prognosis is dire. Environmental risk factors include parental rejection, neglect, inconsistent child-rearing practices, harsh discipline, physical or sexual abuse, lack of supervision, early institutional living, frequent change of caregivers, parental criminality, peer rejection, and neighborhood exposure to violence. If the onset is in adolescence, these individuals can achieve, adjust, and have adequate social and occupational functions.

Bipolar Disorder

Much more delineation of why someone is experiencing a bipolar episode has been addressed in the *DSM-5-TR* (APA, 2022). This disorder includes both a depression and a mania. In the *DSM-5-TR*, this includes bipolar I disorder, bipolar II disorder, cyclothymic disorder, substance- or medication-induced bipolar and related disorder, bipolar and related disorder due to another medical condition, other specified bipolar and related disorder, and unspecified bipolar and related disorder.

Depression

A depressed student is sad, withdrawn, and may be experiencing lethargy, low self-esteem, poor concentration, feelings of hopelessness, sleep problems, and changes in appetite (over- or undereating) (APA, 2022). Students who have major depression exhibit characteristics for at least two weeks with behaviors that include loss of interest, loss of pleasure, or irritability.

The mania with depression results in a lack of sleep and brings on a feeling of increased sense of self. The individual's speech is rapid, they have racing thoughts, and they are distractible with movement and psychological agitation.

Anxiety Disorders

Anxiety disorders are seen in students who exceed normal levels of anxiety and fear. Interestingly, anxiety and depression in children often have similar symptoms, which makes it difficult for teachers to recognize what is going on. There are many different types of anxiety disorders, but general symptoms include dread, fear, worry, school avoidance, withdrawal, sweating, nausea, shaking, and tremors. Diagnosis is aided by observing which symptoms are present, as well as where they occur. Children with high anxiety can also be very active or very subdued.

Instructional Considerations

Educators and coaches who work with students who have EBD recognize the value that positive physical education and activity experiences have for the students. Not only do students have an opportunity to learn skills related to health and fitness, but they also have the opportunity to blow off steam in a day that can be filled with challenges. Although numerous studies verify that the unstructured nature of recess time is troublesome for students with behavior problems, Lavay believes this can be addressed through more supervision and increased choices on the playground (2019), thus gaining the benefits that recess has for children and youth. The American Academy of Pediatrics believes recess is crucial for a child's development (2013). It affords critical play and unstructured social opportunities for the adolescents, and they gain from breaks in structured academic work, returning to class to perform better on cognitive tasks.

Restricting students from engaging in physical activity such as recess or physical education is an inappropriate consequence for poor school behavior in another class. Physical education is an academic area and holding a student back from an academic area as a punishment for poor behavior (e.g., on the bus or at lunch time) is not appropriate. The exception is if physical harm to self or others is happening or anticipated. If a student is throwing a desk in a class, or pushing violently, they need to be removed and school protocols followed.

Limited Knowledge of Games and Activities

Students with EBD have often been left out of play and recreational activity. They may have been kicked out of physical education classes, being out of class more than in it. They may have little experience with family or a neighborhood affiliation with age-appropriate physical activity. The result is limited knowledge of the games and activities of their peers. Some older students claim they know how to play basketball, but they have only had access to a hoop and shot baskets. Therefore, skills practice can be a bridge into knowledge of the game and the intricacies of the sport. They really do not know the rules of basketball. Younger children are completely at a loss, especially if they have expressive and receptive language disorders. These children do not know the social skills associated with the physical activity and games. The physical education teacher may have to do more teaching of the physical activity than expected. Using classic instructional methods, teachers may need to demonstrate, from a multimodality standpoint, social skills; cue the skill within an activity, repeat, and practice the skill in an activity (Block et al., 2016). For other skills, the student may need checklists, picture schedules, and someone working with them on anger control and problem-solving.

Fear of Losing

Students with EBD do not want to lose. If there is a possibility that they will lose, then there will be acting out. This can best be handled before the students get angry and out of control. Lead-up games are a way to increase knowledge and skill in a sport.

Not keeping score in these games is recommended until there is a sense that winning is not the goal of the game; effort and fun are the goals.

Inexperienced in Fun

Here is an example of a six-year-old child who was inexperienced in fun. The child was in day treatment. During testing of his movement skills, the child got on all fours, growled, and clawed at the ground. The social worker later explained to the assessor that his biological mother put him outside in the dog kennel when he misbehaved. When he got stressed, he assumed this posture. He had fascinations with dead animals and burials. Other members of the team explained that his biological mother had him participate in burials in group worship and buried him alive. Eventually, he was in a day treatment program for children EBD and living with foster parents. After more than a year, his biological mother was deemed not able to care for her son, and the foster parents adopted him. He asked that his name be changed so that his mother could never find him. It was. During his year in the treatment program, he grew into a little boy who loved school, recess, and

Christopher Futcher/Getty Images/iStockphoto

physical activity. The team that cared for him saw his social skills with his peers increase. He left the treatment program and its school and went on to a school in his community near the home of his new parents and family and his new name.

This child's early life is an example of the extreme reality of many children with EBD who do not trust and have found ways to compensate for the rejection and abuse they have experienced. Their compensatory behaviors are what has kept them alive, but they should not have had to develop those behaviors. When that happens, they have skills that are socially unacceptable and that leave them isolated—just what they don't need. But they do not have anything to replace those unacceptable skills. Yet.

In the RTC, there are special educators, childcare workers, and case workers (full-time) and professionals (full-time, part-time, or consultants) in speech and language pathology, adapted physical education, child psychology, child psychiatry, and social work. The teams meet and review assessments, create plans for individualized education programs (IEPs), and review progress. They meet with the children individually as well as with their parents and make recommendations as the child's plans progress. Children and youth in this program do carry diagnoses compatible with more specialized care. Once they leave the RTC or day treatment program, most plan to participate in their community school.

Program Placement

Children and youth with behavior disorders can be in the general education program in a community school. But if they need much more structure and expertise brought to their educational placement, they can be placed in a residential treatment center (RTC), in a day treatment facility within an RTC, or in a stand-alone day treatment program. Hellison's model for physical education was used successfully in tough, inner-city Chicago schools many decades ago and is applied successfully to physical education programs in settings today (2011). Hellison's method is discussed later in this chapter. If treatment goals established in RTC or day treatment are followed through each classroom setting including physical education, then students can be successful in PE. Hellison's model is complementary to most treatment goals. Highly active children with EBD need to be managed well in the gym and other venues for games and sport.

Instructional Strategies

Educators and clinicians are providing quality experiences for students with behavior challenges through interventions for increasing participation in physical activity classes and teaching social, communication, and self-control skills within physical activity (Alstot & Alstot, 2015; Bambara et al., 2015; Lavay et al., 2016). Educational programs have improved dramatically with particular emphasis on positive behavior supports (Block et al., 2016).

Physical Activity Environment

A physical education class for students with EBD must be predictable and structured. For many of these students, life is often unpredictable. If these children are anxious or depressed, predictable structure will assist them in their day and allow them to learn in PE classes.

Intervention Development

Behavior change always takes time to replace the unacceptable behavior with a socially acceptable behavior. Sometimes the negative behavior increases. Sometimes it takes at least three sessions for a change to begin. The following aspects of working with students with EBD will support the change the student needs to enjoy physical activity and develop much needed skills both physically and socially. In the process of developing an intervention:

- Collect the data and review it to identify the behavior being targeted by using the ABC approach (Lavay, 2019).
- Part of the intervention is to determine an appropriate positive reinforcement schedule.
- Track the data and evaluate the status of progress. Remember it isn't easy to change behavior, but bringing all the data collected to the behavior, in a proactive approach, allows the teacher and coach to securely make decisions.
- Meet to review the data and evaluate whether the intervention is positive in changing the student behavior.

Predictability in the physical education class offers the student the opportunity to learn the expected skills needed in physical education, including not only the physical activity but also the skills for being social and behaving within age expectations emotionally. Predictability is related to the way the teacher works with students, is consistent with rules (shaped in a positive form, e.g., what students will do as opposed to what they will not do), divides up the class time, and teaches skills. The students need to be informed as to what the content will be for the class and when it will change (e.g., swimming is next in two weeks). Since many students with EBD do not have age-appropriate experiences with physical activity, it is helpful to inform them ahead of time about the *content* of the next activity. For instance, with swimming, an encouraging description of learning to be in the water with a flotation device, kicking while holding onto a board and playing water games. Before the transition to swimming, bring some of the kick boards and some of the balls and things used in games in the pool. Stay away from swim races and timed events for students with EBD because they are not typically able to handle defeat well, nor is this type of event necessary to develop a liking of swimming nor being in the water safely.

It is important to offer structured choices in class. Stations are good to set up and have students rotate for skill practice. Teachers can let students choose a station and rotate them through the stations. Regarding games, the students can develop a list of games they know or want to know. As time passes, either they or the teacher chooses from that list. As students develop their knowledge and skill in other games, those games can be added to the list.

Challenging behaviors in a physical education class require a created behavior plan. Block and colleagues (2016) have a systematic approach to developing a behavior plan. The sidebar in this section depicts a proactive approach with time well spent on positively moving toward decreasing, if not eliminating, the challenging behavior. These behaviors get in the way of the student's learning in class and disrupt class for other students. The end results negatively affect a physical educator's or coach's time with students. Many of the interventions are a part of commonly held teaching strategies: stand closer to the target student, plan on buddying up the student and all the other students, and change the activity. The created behavior plan is drawn up by a team of people most familiar with the student.

Determine the function of the behavior (Alstot & Alstot, 2015; Block et al., 2016). What does the student need that they are getting out of the inappropriate behavior? Do they need the teacher's attention? Are they angry at something going on in their life? This might take some discussion with other professionals in a group team meeting. Four areas of function for inappropriate behavior in the physical education class are shown in the following list. In the first three, the teacher inadvertently facilitates the student to obtain what they want (Alstot & Alstot, 2015).

1. *Attention:* In this area, the behavior helps the student obtain attention from the teacher or peers.
2. *Access:* In this area, the child obtains access to a tangible object, activity, or event.
3. *Escape:* The behavior gets them out of the class, an unwanted activity, away from social attention, or helps them escape discomfort.

Basics for Creating a Behavior Plan for a Student With Challenging Behavior

1. Describe *the student behavior* in objective and measurable terms.
2. What is happening *before* the behavior occurs, including where and when?
3. Examine what *function the behavior* might serve for the student, such as seeking attention, indicating pain or discomfort, or needing help.
4. What were the immediate or delayed *consequences* of the behavior, and how did the student react?
5. What *simple interventions* might reduce or prevent the behavior such as rearranging the environment, changing the activity, partnering the student, or regrouping the class?
6. Write up the specific plan, including what the behavior is and the plans for reducing negative behavior. Discuss with the student concerns about the behavior and the consequences.

Adapted from Block et al. (2016).

4. *Sensory stimulation:* These are behaviors that feel good to the senses yet are socially intrusive in the physical education class. There is no purposeful need to get out of an activity with behaviors such as hand flapping, staring at lights, humming, and pacing. It just feels good to the child.

If a behavior becomes full blown and dangerous to the student or others in a class, a teacher must act quickly for safety. This is not a time to discuss the situation. Follow whatever strategy the school or the team has planned for these situations.

Developing Social Responsibility

Dr. Don Hellison devoted his physical education expertise to working with students classified as at risk for behavior problems, even if they have not actually engaged in that behavior (Hellison, 2011). Hellison's philosophy was that teaching physical education is not about disciplining students but rather about using specific skills and strategies with

that student in class. He also believed that being a physical education teacher has a spirit that provided a moral compass along with a sense of purpose and a vision. He felt passionately that kids needed an imaginative, creative teacher who created more dots for them versus just connected them.

Hellison trained physical education teachers to develop social responsibility in students with very difficult lives. While working in the inner city of Chicago where poor children in poor schools needed help, he posed questions during a reflective time in physical activity: Did you help someone today? Hurt someone? Waste your time? Did anything about yourself come up in volleyball today? His method is a progression for the students that grows their sense of self as a responsible person. The levels he developed began with a student showing no responsibility and ended with a caring individual (figure 10.1). He trained his students through a tight physical education program with predictable structures and reflective questions aimed at listening to the student (Hellison, 2011).

Level IV, Caring

Students at Level IV, in addition to respecting others, participating, and being self-directed, are motivated to extend their sense of responsibility beyond themselves by cooperating, giving support, showing concern, and helping.

Level III, Self-Direction

Students at Level III not only show respect and participation but also are able to work without direct supervision. They can identify their own needs and begin to plan and carry out their physical education programs.

Level II, Participation

Students at Level II not only show at least minimal respect for others but also willingly play, accept challenges, practice motor skills, and train for fitness under the teacher's supervision.

Level I, Respect

Students at Level I may not participate in daily activities or show much mastery or improvement, but they are able to control their behavior enough that they don't interfere with the other students' right to learn or the teacher's right to teach. They do this without much prompting by the teacher and without constant supervision.

Level Zero, Irresponsibility

Students who operate at Level Zero make excuses, blame others for their behavior, and deny personal responsibility for what they do or fail to do.

FIGURE 10.1 The levels presented as a cumulative progression.

Adapted by permission from D. Hellison, *Teaching Personal and Social Responsibility Through Physical Activity*, 3rd ed. (Champaign, IL: Human Kinetics, 2011), 6-7.

Positive Behavior Management

A student's behavior can get in the way of the student being able to learn. Managing these behaviors challenges the teacher, but when the teacher can address them effectively, positive teaching outcomes result (Lavay, French, & Henderson, 2016). Lavay speaks from personal experience when he says that you cannot teach if you cannot manage and motivate your students (2019). Students with identified behavior disorders that go beyond just challenging behaviors add an intensity to the challenge because of the frequency, intensity, and duration of those behaviors. Nonetheless, there are interventions that have borne positive results.

Group participation in play activities is highly desirable because it makes social contacts possible. Some students experience considerable strain in social adjustment, so it may be necessary to work gradually toward group activities. For some students it may be necessary to progress from spectatorship to one-to-one instruction and eventually to small-group activity. As the students become accustomed to small-group play, more peers can be taken into the group to increase the scope of social contacts. Their inclusion in the activity also provides an incentive for approved social conduct, but the instructor should monitor carefully to ensure that certain students do not dominate the game or detract in any way from the successful performance of any of the students.

Again, revert to Hellison's levels of physical education participation. It is up to the student to show they can be introduced to the levels and advance. Then it is up to the teacher to create a class with activities that will meet the social and physical skills that the student has now. The promise is that the skill engagement will advance, and the configuration of the level will increase. This is probably done more easily in a residential or day treatment physical education program. However, people have developed cards with Hellison's levels on them and discussed them with the student to begin engaging a student in a physical education class. Then they moved them along as skills increased.

In an inclusive physical education program and in an RTC, close attention to positive behavior management in physical activities is paramount (Lavay et al., 2016). This is part of being proactive.

> Being proactive means taking the time to consider the strategies you need to establish to help participants understand what is expected of them. Because you are more likely to encounter disruptive behavior during management time than during instruction or activity time, it is important to develop a proactive management plan . . . Effective physical activity professionals are not reactive but rather are good managers of behaviors, who anticipate problems before they occur and go into the setting with a proactive prevention plan. Proactive management works best if you carefully consider and integrate your own teaching, coaching, or leadership style; your unique individual and group needs; and the instructional environment.
>
> Lavay et al. (2016, pp. 28-29).

Understanding the antecedent-behavior-consequence (ABC) method of positive behavior management has led to successful participation for students in physical activity (Lavay et al., 2016). The elements of the method follow.

- *Antecedent:* What was happening in the physical activity class and with the student *just before* the challenging behavior took place?
- *Behavior:* Describe is the challenging behavior.
- *Consequences:* What were the consequences of this behavior? What happened just after the behavior? What did the student get or what did they need? (Alstot & Alstot, 2015)

Antecedent

It is critical to know what happened just *before* for the student's challenging behavior. If a student erupts and begins kicking and screaming, what was happening just before that happened? If a student shoves teammates, what was going on in the class just before this happened?

Sometimes the plan results in a simple solution. In the case of the little boy who resorted to growling and clawing at the ground while being tested for his movement skills, it was clear in a discussion with the social worker that this behavior communicated that he was stressed. Going forward, the assessments were shortened to about 10 minutes, and he came and went happily to and from his classroom as the assessments were paced. With more complex interventions, the plan would be created with input from the individualized education program team.

Behavior

Measuring the behavior for frequency and duration will provide baseline data to set up target behaviors in the intervention plan. Count the frequency of a behavior within a specific time frame (such as the number of negative remarks to classmates during the first 15 minutes of class) and as well as measuring the duration of on-task behavior during stations such as kicking a ball in a net. Then realistic goals can be set for increasing the positive remarks and on-task behavior.

Consequence

Sometimes it takes a while to figure out what the student is getting out of the behavior. Then it is time to ask for help (Lavay et al., 2016). What do parents or guardians think about the behavior? In the school, are there behavior plans of which the physical educator or coach should be aware? Does this happen in other settings at school or at home? Are there family, cultural, or emotional factors to be considered? Do other professionals know of any related issues or conditions? In each case, the physical education teacher or coach can ask for suggestions for increasing effectiveness with the student.

Physical Activities

The comprehensive program of physical activity experiences for students with classic behavior disorders incorporates movement skill development, exercise, fun through games, individual and team sport activities, as well as leisure time physical activities and social skills training. Research has helped to dispel a common myth that exercise programs tend to excite students with behavior disorders, and in turn, inhibit their performance upon returning to the classroom. Physical inactivity is negatively associated with the poor mental health of youth (Biddle & Asare, 2011). For graduating seniors who partici-

pated in short bouts of physical exercise during the day, there was a marked increase in on-task behavior in classes and reported feelings of vitality (Mavilidi et al., 2020)—very positive for graduating seniors. Physical and verbal aggression decreased using Hellison's work on teaching personal and social responsibility in the physical education class with over 200 students ages 10 to 12 years (Pérez-Ordás et al., 2020).

Assessment and Evaluation

The assessment of movement skills for children and youth with EBD is more an issue of behavior management than of their skills. Any of the age-appropriate tools described in chapter 6 can be accessed for assessment and evaluation of these children. Often their individualized education program for PE is not motor based but rather behavior based. It is critical to obtain valid data during a well-managed assessment session. Any assessor must be aware of all educational assessments noting if there is a learning disability or attention-deficit/hyperactivity disorder that would necessitate addressing these issues and other multimodality instructional cues during the assessment. Note if the student has been assessed by the school psychologist for any diagnosis and what the recommendations for learning might be. Does the occupational therapist have any further recommendations? Often the student has age-appropriate basic movement skills but lacks social skills. These data might be better obtained by a systematic observation of a PE class, interviews with a general physical education teacher, or the student's classroom teacher. The student might need to broaden their knowledge of themselves in games and sports. In grade school and high school, a student's athletic prowess can be turned into a positive for exploring other games and sports or as a reward for time in other activities of general physical education.

Assessment ABC

Hannah, age 11, was hitting a few of her classmates 10 times in the first half of the class. Hannah had low social skills due to environmental deprivation. The function of her behavior was felt to be a compensatory behavior to get a reaction from her classmates and attention from her teacher. The intervention behavior was for Hannah to use high fives with classmates five times in the first half of class. To set a tone, the teacher decided he would initiate a high five to Hannah and a few other students in the class. This would provide a model of intensity (no slapping) and would provide Hannah with attention from the teacher. As this target behavior (goal) was reached, further social skill in physical education for Hannah could be developed.

Educational Health Care Providers

Professionals who engage with children and youth with challenging behaviors are coaches, physical educators, adapted physical educators, and the allied health professionals of occupational and physical therapy, nursing, and speech and language pathologists. They assist with ongoing needs in motor skills in a physical activity environment. They consult on handwriting and use of computer for learning in the classroom, medicine management while at school, and communication skills within the learning environment. These professionals help parents with ongoing concerns. Administrators of RTC benefit from this information as their staff are supervised and programs developed for these children and youth.

It takes a team approach to manage the behavioral intervention plans of children who deviate to a marked extent from what is generally accepted as appropriate behavior (Lavay et al., 2016). Challenging behavior in a physical activity class ranges from violent and destructive acts to withdrawn and sullen behavior. For these participants, cooperating with teachers and parents, making friends, accepting themselves, and exhibiting prosocial behaviors are extremely difficult. Terms such as *socially maladjusted* and *emotionally handicapped* have been ascribed to these students (Doroshow, 2016). Doroshow explains that in the 1940s and 1950s, children with unruly behavior were living in RTCs, and the term *emotionally disturbed child* arose. Such children pushed mental health reform because they could not be treated in the community. Eventually a subgroup of very seriously ill children was identified in the RTCs in the later 1950s.

Summary

Challenging behavior in physical activity environments ranges from violent and destructive acts to withdrawn and sullen behavior. Individuals with EBD qualify for special education services in physical education not necessarily because of significant motor deficiencies but rather because their behavior prevents them from being successful in physical activity environments. They can be placed in the inclusive physical education setting with behavioral interventions such as Hellison's method or using the ABC method of ascertaining what the student is getting out of their behavior in class. Educational programs for students with EBD emphasize positive behavior supports. IDEA (2004) stipulates that the student have a condition over a long period of time to a marked degree that adversely affects educational performance. Tracking the frequency, intensity, and duration of the behaviors will assist the instructor in knowing what behavior is getting in the way of learning, what is motivating it, and how to reward the student and shape their behavior toward acceptable behavior for the physical education program. Follow the ABC path to determine what came before the target behavior, what the behavior was, and what the consequence was for the student. Teachers need a predictable and structured class that offers choices with the activities and a behavior plan created to address the problematic behavior. There must be an intervention plan in place.

CHAPTER 11

Sensory Impairments

vgajic/E+/Getty Images

CHAPTER OBJECTIVES

After completing this chapter, you will be able to do the following:

- Appreciate the changing perspective of physical activity for individuals with visual impairments.
- Recognize the various communication techniques utilized with students with visual impairments to benefit from adapted physical activities.
- Identify the instructional strategies used with students with visual impairments as they participate in a motor development program.
- Identify the instructional strategies used with students with visual impairments participating in sports while in grade school and high school.
- Describe how goalball and baseball are played for students with visual impairments.
- Describe how swimming is adapted to enable individuals who are blind to participate in training and competition.
- Identify the instructional techniques used with Deaf students when in the physical education program.
- Identify and describe a general approach to instructing Deafblind students in physical education programs.

In the 1830s, three schools for children with visual impairments were founded in the United States, providing the first educational opportunities for these children. One of these schools, Perkins Institute in Boston, had as its director a medical doctor who was an enthusiastic advocate of the benefits of physical exercise for his students. He organized a program of vigorous physical activity that included playing outdoors, swimming in the ocean, and working on gymnastic apparatus. His program was far in advance of the physical education in the public schools of his day. Other special schools for those with visual impairments were gradually established.

Today, physical education programs at these special schools offer a variety of activities, including intramural and interscholastic sports. Dr. Charles Buell, a physical educator who was blind and a former athletic director at the California School for the Blind, was instrumental in formulating many of the ideas used in physical education classes for students with visual impairments in the United States. Today, students with visual impairments, who in former years would have been enrolled in special schools, attend public schools and participate in general physical education (GPE) or adapted physical education (APE).

Causes and Prevalence

Sensory impairment refers to sight and hearing that is not considered to be typical. The discussion in this chapter includes visual and hearing impairments and a combination of the two referred to as dual sensory impairment. The Deaf community prefers a capitol D for Deaf and Deafblind when these terms are used before any noun, unlike other areas of disability. The capitalized D is cultural, otherwise it can be written as deaf or deafblind.

Visual Impairments

The primary function of the eye is to receive visual input and to transmit this information to the brain via the optic nerve. This is a complicated procedure in which the eye collects light reflected from objects in the visual field and focuses these objects on the retina. First, light focuses on the cornea; then it passes through a watery liquid. Next, light passes through the pupil, a circular hole in the center of the eye that contracts or expands according to the amount of light reaching the eye. The light then enters the lens, which is curved to reflect the light more before the light enters a jellylike fluid. The retina is in the back of the eye globe. A clear image finally reaches the retina and is transmitted to the brain via the optic nerve. Visual impairment (VI) is a generic term that includes a range of visual acuity (Bloomquist, 2003b).

Approximately one child out of every four or five has some significant deviation from the accepted norm of good vision. A large majority of these have slight deviations that are not extremely detrimental to the child or that are remediable either medically or by wearing prescribed lenses. For these children, no special educational provisions need be made.

Hearing Impairments

The ear is a complex organ, capable of discriminating the intensity and frequency of various sounds. Sound is first received by the outer ear and transmitted to the middle ear before it finally reaches the inner ear, where it is transferred to the brain via the auditory nerve. The function of the outer ear is to collect sound waves and transmit them via the auditory canal to the middle ear. In the middle ear, the sound passes from the tympanic membrane to the ossicular chain, where the vibrations created by the motion of the stapes, incus, and malleus move the sound from the outer to the inner ear. The inner ear is divided into two sections, the vestibule and the cochlea. The cochlea is the critical element in hearing. As the stapes bone moves, the oval window moves, transmitting the sound from the middle ear to the fluid-filled cochlea. Inside the cochlea are thousands of tiny hair cells that are set in motion. Movement of the hair cells in turn causes electrical impulses to be sent to the brain. Also located in the inner ear are three small loops called the semicircular canals. Although the semicircular canals do not contribute to the hearing process, they are extremely important in maintaining balance.

Hearing disabilities are usually structural in origin, and damage to any part of the ear can result in a hearing loss. The three types of hearing loss are classified as conductive, sensorineural, or mixed. Conductive hearing loss is caused by a physical obstruction to the conduction of the sound waves to the inner ear. The deafness is never total. A hearing aid improves hearing loss due to conduction difficulties. The other cause of conductive hearing loss is otitis media (infection of the middle ear) due to colds, sinus infections, allergies, or blocked eustachian tubes (Bloomquist, 2003a). Sensorineural hearing loss is usually a more serious condition. These children have a cochlear implant and not a hearing aid. The hearing loss is caused by damage to the cells or nerve fibers that receive and transmit the sound stimuli. The loss of hearing may be mild or profound (total). Some degree of sensorineural deafness is common among older adults. In children and young adults, the most frequent cause of sensorineural deafness is congenital—the nerve having been damaged before or during birth. This damage does not allow the cochlear nerve to function well and transmit sound vibrations hitting the eardrum (tympanic membrane). By hitting the eardrum, those vibrations are converted into electrical signals that the cochlear nerve carries to the brain (Healthline, 2023).

Prolonged loud sounds of any spectra can produce a temporary threshold shift (auditory fatigue); recovery usually takes place within a day. The more intense the sound, the shorter the exposure time needed before temporary fatigue takes place. *Continual exposure eventually produces a permanent hearing loss.* The ears should only be exposed to sounds over 130 decibels (units of loudness) momentarily.

Of those individuals 6 to 19 years old, 12.5 percent of them have a hearing loss due to listening to loud music (HLAA, 2018). The loss is at the higher frequency ranges. Also, in the United States, 1 in 10 individuals has a hearing loss that includes 1 in 5 teens and 2 to 3 people per 1,000 born with a hearing loss (HLAA, 2018). Hearing loss is on a spectrum. Individuals who have some functional hearing are referred to as people who are *hard of hearing*. Those with more severe loss are referred to as Deaf people. People who are hard of hearing can use amplification to hear. Individuals who are hard of hearing outnumber Deaf individuals (Lieberman, 2011).

Dual Sensory Impairments

Some diseases acquired by the mother while pregnant result in deafblindness. Babies who are born prematurely, exposed to drugs in utero, or contract meningitis can acquire deafblindness. In the literature this is often spelled Deafblind.

There are two relatively new syndromes associated with deafblindness. Usher syndrome is a congenital disability whereby the onset can be at birth or later in adolescence. CHARGE syndrome is a newer identified genetic disorder of complex multisensory impairment with primary hearing loss that affects balance and kinesthetic control (Hilgenbrinck et al., 2020). CHARGE is an acronym for several of the features common to this disorder: coloboma, heart defects, atresia choanae (or choanal atresia),

growth retardation, genital abnormalities, and ear abnormalities. Children with CHARGE syndrome have multiple anomalies at birth, including those of the eyes, heart, genitalia, brain, and ears. A great percentage of the children with the syndrome are Deaf, and many are visually impaired. CHARGE was first reported in 1979.

Classification and Diagnosis

IDEA (2004) definition:

> Visual impairment, including blindness, means an impairment in vision that, even when corrected, adversely affects a child's educational performance. The term includes both partial sight and blindness.
>
> IDEA (2004, § 300.8[c][13]).

Deaf individuals or those who are hard of hearing have a hearing loss, depending on the degree of loss and, to some extent, on the communication ability of the individual. Deafblindness is a loss of both hearing and sight but the greater portion of children have some sight and hearing (Hodge et al., 2012). Thus, only a very small percentage of students with Deafblindness are completely blind and Deaf.

Visual Impairments

Visual acuity, the ability to clearly distinguish forms or discriminate details, is commonly measured by a chart of progressively smaller letters or symbols. The person being tested reads the chart from a specific distance. Visual acuity is expressed in a numerical ratio. For example, a ratio of 20 to 200 indicates that the person being tested had to stand 20 feet from the chart (the first number in the ratio) to see what someone with normal vision can see from 200 feet (the second number).

The degree to which students are impaired is determined largely by how much their vision deviates from normal. Those with visual acuity of 20/200 or less with glasses are considered legally blind, and most have some useful sight. They may be able to perceive light, form, or movement and are considered partially sighted. It is now common practice that students with visual impairments (VIs) are enrolled in public school systems in their community. Sometimes their instruction is provided in classes with a teacher trained in methods of instructing students who are partially sighted and with equipment designed for their needs. In other situations, the students are accommodated in the general education classroom.

VI is currently defined functionally by the degree to which the vision loss affects the person's ability to perform tasks in their daily life (Lieberman et al., 2013). In general, *blind* means no functional vision and *low vision* means there is functional vision that cannot be corrected to normal with glasses. According to IDEA (2004), both blind and low vision are included in the overall term *visually impaired*.

Knowing when the individual became visually impaired is important (age at onset). Those children and youth who have congenital blindness (since birth or slightly thereafter) differ in their use of visual memory. Those with adventitious blindness (blind later in life) have knowledge of sight and the consequences of a life with vision. Those born with visual impairment do not have the advantage of having "seen" life. This affects instructional methods.

Hearing Impairments

The term *deaf* may be used to encompass all forms of hearing loss as is common among groups such as the American Athletic Association for the Deaf. Within educational settings, it is common to make a distinction between the terms *deaf* and *hard of hearing*.

As pointed out, hearing loss may also be described in terms of its age of onset. The child who is deaf from birth will not be able to learn to speak spontaneously. The needs of this student are very different from those of a child who acquired a hearing loss after the age of seven, when speech and language are well developed. Frequently, the terms *prelingual* and *postlingual* are used to distinguish the impact of a hearing loss on the ability of the student to speak. Those with a prelingual hearing loss cannot speak normally because the hearing loss

occurred before they heard any spoken language. Those with a postlingual hearing loss retain the ability to speak normally with special assistance. Their hearing loss occurred after they learned to speak and had hearing.

Deafblindness

IDEA (2004) refers to deafblindness as concomitant hearing and visual impairment where the loss cannot be accommodated in special education programs *solely* for students with either deafness or blindness. Typically, teachers use a multimodality instructional approach, selecting the modality most accessible by the student. Yet with Deafblind students, strategies for neither students who are solely blind nor Deaf students who are solely Deaf will be effective. Both areas are significantly impaired. The students may have some sight or hearing ability, but together there is a cumulative effect of the loss that is greater than the sum of its parts. Yet, they can succeed. Helen Keller, who was profoundly both Deaf and blind, is an outstanding example. Some argue she had success because of the determination she brought to learning and her dedicated teacher by her side through most of her life.

Note that *deafblindness* is spelled without any hyphenation (*not* deaf-blind). This spelling has been advocated to connote the cumulative effect of the disability (Smart, 2009). However, IDEA (2004) uses a hyphen.

CHARGE syndrome is very rare form of deafblindness, and physical educators are gathering more information on assessing these children and serving them in the schools (Hilgenbrinck et al., 2020). Testing them requires extra physical demonstrations, input from the entire multidisciplinary team of the individualized education program (IEP), and most importantly, strategies with behavior, skills, and knowledge of motivational factors and interests for use at school.

Acute Development of Other Senses

There is no evidence to support the concept that students with visual impairments have an unnatural or mystical gift that enables them to perform activities that would seem possible only for the seeing. The adroitness with which a student without sight walks down the crowded sidewalk avoiding other walkers and obstacles, negotiates the curb, and crosses with the light may seem amazing to those with full sight. Behind the skill of this walker is a developed kinesthetic training, the ability to listen closely to auditory clues, and extensive experience in the interpretation of the various stimuli to the other senses. The person's sixth sense is simply appropriate training and practice.

Instructional Considerations

It is important to consider people-first language in writing or making addresses about individuals with sensory impairments. It is not considered appropriate to use terms such as *the blind*. Rather, we should use words such as *the individual*, *the child who is blind*, or *the student with VI*. Other methods are to name the student and if necessary, given the context, name the disability. For example, when talking with a paraeducator, you might say, "Isaiah, who is blind, needs a peer partner this week when we are running on the track. You know his peer tutor and you know how to coach him to assist Isaiah. Thanks for taking the lead on this."

Preteaching for VI

For a student who is visually impaired, in any placement, preteaching may be required (Lieberman et al., 2013). A responsible person reviews the plan for an activity or activities with the student ahead of the physical education class time. Preteaching can include using a tactile model made up of the basics of the room for an activity in the GPE program (soccer goals, basketball hoop, videos) with the student. Students are also oriented to the activity space (walking around using verbal descriptions and physically touching the space) and to the equipment (e.g., feeling it and hearing a description of how the equipment will be used in the activity). The preteaching can be conducted by any number of responsible individuals including a teacher for students with VI, trained peer tutors, an older trained

student, or the paraeducator. Time for preteaching might be before the unit at school, a few minutes before each class, or a prearranged time during the school day. It is recommended that preteaching be specified in the student's IEP.

Adapted Physical Activity Environment

Students who are blind should have a thorough verbal introduction to an unfamiliar physical activity environment before they are allowed to participate and engage with others. They should know the size and shape of the area and the nature of the boundaries. To orient the students, the teacher or trained paraeducator should walk with them around the area, including the locker room facility, describing the essential details and, when appropriate, having the student feel an area or object. Specific areas—such as entrances, exits, and other permanent fixtures—are to be identified for the student. Doors remain open. These permanent fixtures, commonly referred to by individuals who are blind as anchor points, serve as valuable reference points for orientation. In the play area, a few simple games or contests might be played to help the students gain familiarity with the playing area before engaging in strenuous play.

To guide children with VI in running activities and to give them greater security, guide ropes and rings that are grasped may be attached from primary wires strung across the gymnasium well above the heads of the participants. For outside running events, guide ropes can be placed along the path of

Camp Abilities

Camp Abilities is a sport camp for children with sensory impairments that takes place on the campus of the State University of New York at Brockport (SUNY Brockport) (Furtado et al., 2017). Since 1996, over 2,209 children with visual impairments in the United States have attended the camp, and now the model has expanded to over 20 states and internationally. The camp keeps an active web presence with videos and photos of the campers at Camp Abilities, and World Camp Abilities (2021). The campers experience what most consider the time of their life, playing and enjoying one another while at camp. Dr. Lauren Lieberman reported from World Camp Abilities, "They told me they were best friends. I asked how long they had known each other. They answered, 'Since Friday'" (2021) The staff are composed of physical educators, adapted physical educators, special education teachers, teachers who specialize in sensory impairment, and orientation and mobility specialists. Martha Ruether, a former Camp Abilities sport participant, competed in swimming at The Paralympics in Rio in 2016. When interviewed, she explained that in grade school, she wasn't allowed to play soccer because it was thought to be too risky. Totally blind in one eye from the time of her premature birth, any errant ball hitting her head could cause even more damage to her one partially sighted eye. She turned to competitive swimming on the advice of a coach.

the runners to guide them as in a track. The runners will need some type of warning at the finish line; this may be a knot tied at the end of the rope, an auditory signal such as a whistle, or the presence of a person using a verbal or physical prompt.

The play area, indoors and outdoors, should be a large, uncluttered space. As a safety precaution, the play area should be free of nonessential equipment and unnecessary obstructions. For outdoor playing fields, hedges and shade trees are considered desirable boundaries rather than walls or fences, which present a certain element of danger for all students. Boundaries for games can be indicated by varying the composition of the court as, for example, having the in-bounds area composed of asphalt or an all-weather surface and the out-of-bounds area of sand or grass. Players will then be able to tell by foot sensitivity when they have stepped out of bounds. Newspaper tightly secured to mark the out-of-bounds area on a floor or field is an inexpensive method to achieve this effect.

Boundaries in the indoor playing area should be painted in white for the benefit of those students able to distinguish white. The gymnasium should be well lighted to present the best possible seeing conditions for perceiving light. Rope taped to the floor is also a cheap and safe way to distinguish boundaries.

Children who are visually impaired can memorize the location of the permanent fixtures but cannot avoid superfluous equipment that has been left in their way. Tethers and auditory aids are invaluable in participating in several physical activities. These are demonstrated in the videos discussed in this chapter.

Playground Area

Playground equipment for younger children with VI may be the same type found on any playground, including swings, jungle gyms, and teeter-totters; however, the child with a VI must exercise greater care in locating them to avoid injury. Swings should be constructed with no more than two swings on the stand; a third swing, in the center, is difficult to reach without danger when the other two swings are occupied. The use of guard rails or ground markers is a necessary safety precaution to prevent youngsters from bumping into equipment or being hit by flying swings.

Culturally Responsive Teaching

Despite the common perception of hearing loss as a condition that isolates people, Deaf individuals argue that deafness is not a disability. They offer that Deaf people constitute a subculture and that they comprise a linguistic minority. Deaf people argue that treatment and educational programs should not focus on fixing them, but rather they should be recognized and accepted as unique and culturally different. Hence, as pointed out in the introduction, the term *Deaf* capitalized precedes the individual, not the other way around as is typical for disability regard. This is part of their identity. While this view of the Deaf person as an ethnic minority is not universally accepted, the movement has led to some rethinking of educational and treatment programs for Deaf and hard-of-hearing individuals. This includes important questions of where, what, and how to teach this population. Issues of inclusion in community schools have challenged the notion that this truly is the least restrictive environment in which Deaf students learn. Supporters of the Deaf culture suggest, too, that Deaf individuals are best reared and educated in settings with members of their own culture. Given that 90 percent of Deaf children are born to hearing parents, this creates some challenging concerns for parents and educators. The goal is not only to assist Deaf people and people hard of hearing in learning, but to recognize their unique sociocultural perspective.

It is no longer considered correct to use the term *hearing impaired* in reference to students, although IDEA (2004) uses it as a category. The term *hard of hearing* is used instead of *hearing impaired* and means that the person has a hearing loss making it more than difficult, if not for some impossible, to process spoken language through their ears. These people need amplification with hearing aids or other audiology assistance. This is the most common category of hearing loss. *Deaf* means the person has a profound hearing loss and cannot hear enough to process language with or without hearing aids. The community of Deaf people do not feel they are impaired or deficient. Deaf culture prefers use of American sign language *only*, and does not favor cochlear implants. People hard of hearing mostly use a hearing aid.

Gallaudet University's students and faculty advocate for an uppercase *D* when referring to deaf. And their preferred term is *Deaf person* because, according to the university culture, Deaf culture is a shared culture and a shared language more than a medical condition. This perspective represents the reality of Deaf people who do not consider themselves disabled. This should be kept in mind when working in special education, where the federal government *does* consider Deaf and hard of hearing a disability category by which students receive support in their education programs.

Communication

American Sign Language (ASL) is the preferred communication by the Deaf community in the United States (Lieberman, 2011). As more people learn ASL, the communication will increase with the Deaf community and others. Deaf persons who could not speak verbally were once taught signing as the sole means of communication, but Deaf children are now being taught to speak by the technique of properly utilizing the mouth and vocal cords in the production of sounds, as well as speech reading. Communication preference for Deaf people is influenced by their parents, speech therapy, and educational background (Hodge et al., 2012). Signed Exact English is signing exactly what is being said while the person speaks. This is also referred to as total communication. ASL uses facial expression, hands, and body behavior to communicate. According to experts, ASL signs are native English words used in a syntax that is particular to ASL. Pidgin Sign English is a method of communication that combines Signed Exact English with ASL. Pidgin

Sign English mixes the rules for ASL and Signed Exact English. All in all, it is advised to explain what you as the physical education (PE) teacher will use in the gym. Some ASL signs are probably the easiest way to proceed, placing a picture of the sign up and trying to use it in the class with spoken English (at least in the United States).

Students with a hearing loss will not pick up incidental learning. For example, if the teacher is giving feedback in a lesson to a group of students near the student with a hearing loss, the student with a hearing loss won't incidentally pick up that information. Instead, the instructor must *face* the student and communicate. Even the most skilled individuals in ASL say that they make mistakes in class! Do expect that it will take time to communicate but that a sincere approach will work well. As with most students, a rapport will develop between the physical educator, any paras working in the classroom, and the student. A high five or a thumbs up does communicate positive feedback in many situations. See figure 11.1 for signs used in physical activities.

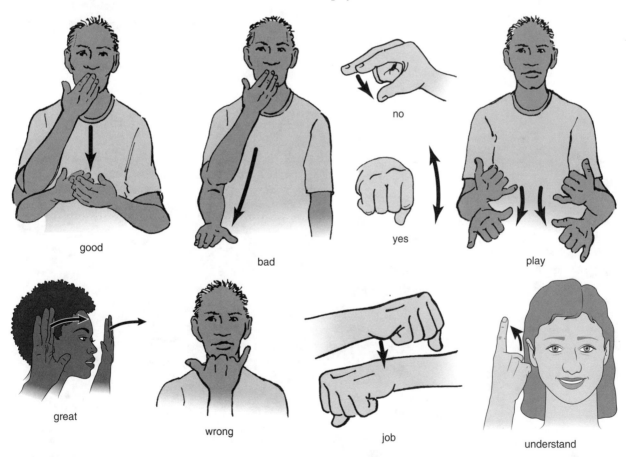

FIGURE 11.1 Signs commonly used for instruction in physical activity environments.

Reprinted by permission from J.P. Winnick and D.L. Porretta, *Adapted Physical Education and Sport*, 6th ed. (Champaign, IL: Human Kinetics, 2017).

> *continued*

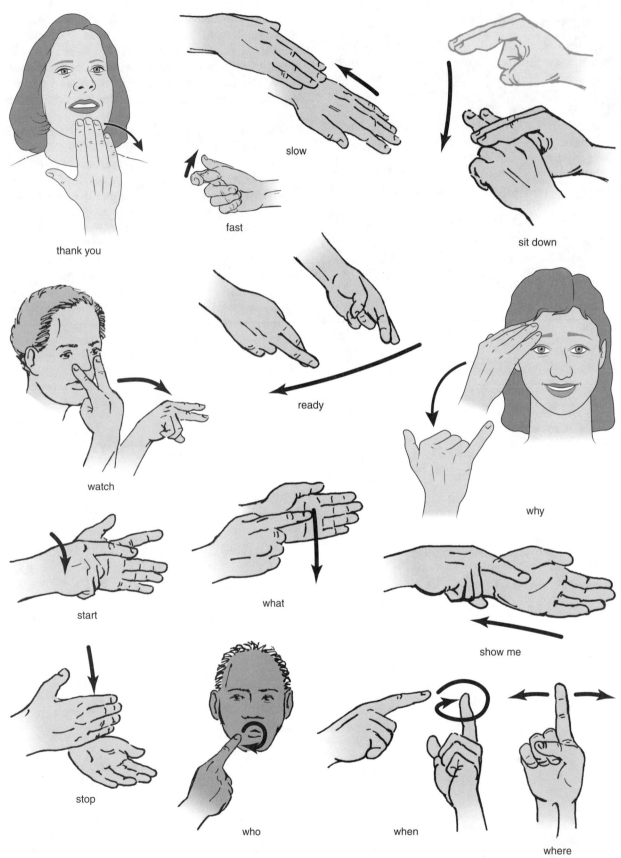

thank you

slow

fast

sit down

watch

ready

why

start

what

show me

stop

who

when

where

FIGURE 11.1   *(continued)*

Reprinted by permission from J.P. Winnick and D.L. Porretta, *Adapted Physical Education and Sport*, 6th ed. (Champaign, IL: Human Kinetics, 2017).

Columna and Lieberman (2011) have a resource to help teachers of physical education teach peer sign language: *Promoting Language Through Physical Education*. In addition, there are other resources for learning ASL (Schultz et al., 2014).

Hearing Aids

Students with a hearing loss often have residual hearing, and many find a hearing aid invaluable. Their hearing loss is conductive. The purpose of the hearing aid is to amplify sound. Contrary to the generally held concept, hearing aids do not make speech and sound clearer; those who hear distorted sounds will still experience distortion with a hearing aid. The value of hearing aids lies in enabling children with severe hearing impairments to learn to recognize the sound of their own name or in assisting those with a moderate loss to hear their own speech.

There are many different types of hearing aids worn in areas like behind the ear or in eyeglasses. Students should be encouraged to wear their hearing aids throughout the day. It is important that they learn how to use the aid to help them interpret conversation. In the physical education setting, the hearing aid should be worn as much as possible.

Given the noise level in the gymnasium and the inability of the hearing aid to selectively filter certain sounds, some students will choose to remove the hearing aids on occasion. Students also will need to remove the hearing aids for certain activities, such as swimming. The physical education teacher should be cognizant of when the student is or is not wearing the hearing aids and adjust the process for communicating accordingly. Without this assistance to the individual's auditory perception, the student will again be disadvantaged in the amount of verbal direction they can comprehend. The teacher must anticipate this and be prepared to help the student make the necessary adjustment.

For calling roll or giving preliminary instruction to the class before the activity begins, the teacher should place the student with a hearing loss where the student will be in the best position to watch the instructor's face. During actual play, when the need to comment arises, the teacher may move close to those students well before speaking. Or the students may be granted privileges to move about freely to a position at which they are better able to hear the speaker.

Cochlear Device

A cochlear implant (CI) works by bypassing damaged portions of the ear to deliver sound signals to the auditory nerve (Mayo Clinic, 2022). There is an outside part of the device and an inside part that is surgically placed. The outside has a microphone with a battery to pick up sound and a processor that sends sound as electrical signals to the inner ear's surgically placed mechanism (Bowdich, 2023a). This device is used with a student with a sensorineural hearing loss. CI device hearing enhances learning of spoken language (Sharma et al., 2020). Sharma and colleagues reported that this benefited students up to high school for whom 75 percent of those with early childhood CI are in mainstreamed education without supports. The CI is not a hearing aid, "which stimulates the ear with amplified acoustic information," but rather it is used by "people with significant hearing loss to hear sounds and understand speech via electrical stimulation of the inner ear" (Bowdich, 2023a).

After receiving a cochlear implant, learning to interpret the sounds takes time to then speech read, recognize sound, and discriminate some words (Mayo Clinic, 2022; Silverstein et al., 1992). In physical education or physical activity environments, the student who has a cochlear implant may have to be mindful of their participation (Hilgenbrinck et al., 2004). Sports that could result in a blow to the head should be avoided or modified. Activities where the person could lose balance and strike their head are also to be avoided. Or, if the individual does participate, they could remove the device and wear a helmet. In swimming activities, students can place a waterproof device over the external part of their CI (Bowdich, 2023b). The student's audiologist can obtain this cover. The CI device is often described as waterproof, meaning during activity producing excessive sweating, it will still work properly until the increased moisture increases unwanted noise. Headbands help some students. If at any point the student removes the external device, they will be without hearing and the teacher must use other means of communication with the student. Those students with hearing aids must take them out for swimming and will not have enhanced hearing.

Social and Emotional Development

There are several factors that mediate social and emotional adjustment problems of Deaf children and youth. These include:

- level of parental acceptance,
- availability of appropriate role models,
- reduction in level of communication and interaction, and
- limited school and extracurricular activities.

Parents of Deaf children can be overprotective, thus limiting the skills for developing adaptive behavior (Papadopoulos et al., 2011). Researchers reported slow development of social cognition and less mobility and independence that also contributed to less competence in adaptive behaviors for age. Others have encouraged parents to participate in education programs and counseling and all involvement in programs for young Deaf children. If the Deaf child is using sign language and the more others in their environment use it, the greater the conversations.

The early childhood literature recognizes that play is critical to the development of a healthy personality and physical education teachers are in a unique role to foster the social and emotional development of Deaf and hard-of-hearing children and youth. First and foremost is the need to create an educational environment in which Deaf youth feel they are part of and welcome in the physical education setting. Second, it is essential to develop success experiences so that Deaf and hard-of-hearing students feel they are progressing and enjoying the opportunity to participate in and learn various concepts related to movement. Third is the need to expand the ability of the teacher to communicate so that the student recognizes that their form of communication is accepted and valued. Additional tips for teaching students who are Deaf and hard of hearing are found later in the chapter.

Without the orientation of the auditory background and the symbols and warnings that are customarily provided by sound perception, Deaf individuals are prone to frustrations and anxieties. This is particularly true in cases in which hearing is lost in adolescence or adulthood. The longer a person has had full hearing, the more difficult is the adjustment to a severe hearing loss. The loss of background sounds contributes also to inaccuracy in the recognition of space and motion, and consequently, the movements of Deaf individuals are often vague and distorted.

Motor Performance of Deaf and Hard-of-Hearing Persons

Studies have been conducted since the 1930s to examine the motor performance of Deaf and hard-of-hearing persons. These investigations have focused primarily on measures of balance, fine and gross motor skills, and motor ability. Efforts have also been made to compare the performance level of Deaf and hard-of-hearing individuals to those without a hearing loss. For the most part, the studies conducted are not definitive because of the

failure to control for factors such as the cause of the hearing loss and the level of hearing loss. Presently, accepted generalizations about Deaf students and those students hard of hearing are that they are similar motorically except for balance. When differences are present, it could be from lack of experience. A pertinent conclusion of motor development studies of young Deaf children was:

> Delay in motor development in Deaf children is not necessarily the result of deafness or vestibular problems, but individual, environmental, and exercise factors are also involved. Providing appropriate educational opportunities for these children, training specialized teachers and parents, and holding training courses for hearing specialists can help promote motor development in these children.
>
> Vieskarami & Roozbahani (2020, p. 10).

Generally, these findings suggest that Deaf and hard-of-hearing students should be engaged in physical activity. Successful experiences will require teachers willing to develop sufficient communication skills to assist the Deaf student to benefit from the instruction offered. Most Deaf and hard-of-hearing students can successfully participate in general physical education classes with minimal modifications.

Program Placement and Focus

Students with VI should be placed in the GPE program with necessary supports *unless* the education team determines this not appropriate (Columna et al., 2010). The placements a school offers should not be just GPE and segregated physical education, but rather a continuum of placements. This continuum includes a smaller modified class, a segregated class, and a combination of placements (Lieberman & Houston-Wilson, 2009).

Some units of the GPE curriculum may have to be modified with supports, including appropriate activity adaptations. Some variables to be considered when placing a student with VI in the GPE setting are the sensory effect of the acoustics on the student, the size of the class that may affect performance, the student's motor and fitness skills, and the student's ability to work independently and with others (Lieberman et al., 2013).

The Expanded Core Curriculum was instituted as a curricular approach to make sure children with VI have the support they need for their educational needs (Sapp & Hatlan, 2010). The physical educator can infuse Expanded Core Curriculum components into the PE classes using the team of professionals who work with the students with VI (e.g., teachers of students with VIs, and orientation and mobility instructors) (Lieberman et al., 2014). The components of Expanded Core Curriculum include compensatory or access skills, orientation and mobility skills, social interaction skills, independent living skills, recreation and leisure skills, career education, use of assistive technology, sensory efficiency skills, and self-determination. Reading the article by Lieberman and colleagues will elaborate clearly the Expanded Core Curriculum and its components (Lieberman et al., 2014). Using this article, the PE teacher will have many ideas for the PE program's essential contribution for student learning in the Expanded Core Curriculum. The sidebar on videos includes the Expanded Core Curriculum.

Nearly all the varieties of activities offered to sighted students in the GPE curriculum can be presented to youngsters who are blind in that program. Some require more adaptation than others, but children who are visually impaired enjoy and need participation in the same games, sports, and physical activities as their age peers. Therefore, students with VI participate with their sighted peers. When special instructional assistance is needed, it is in addition to general instruction in physical education. As noted, preteaching, or preparing the student for the expected activities and environment, is imperative.

Exercise for individuals with a VI produces the same positive psychological benefits as it does for those without such an impairment, including

- more opportunities to improve socialization skills;
- practice and improvement in balance skills, which may be low;
- improvement in self-image, confidence, and spatial orientation;
- improvement in cardiovascular fitness; and
- decrease in obesity. (Bloomquist, 2003b, p. 325)

According to Lieberman and Coward (1996), games help students with VI to refine their movement skills and engage in physical activities that produce health benefits. The following guidelines are recommended for implementing games (Lieberman & Coward, 1996):

- Locate age-appropriate games that meet the needs of all students in a class.
- Only make the needed modifications.
- Implement and monitor the game.
- Provide positive feedback, adjust the game if necessary, or make a mental note to adjust in the future.

The educational placement for Deaf and hard-of-hearing students has generated considerable attention. The National Association for the Deaf (NAD, 2023) points out that there is already a vast array of schools for Deaf students: residential, charter, day schools where sign language is used, day schools for Deaf children that emphasize *spoken* language only, and neighborhood schools with programs for Deaf and hard of hearing students.

In general, Deaf students' success in integrated settings depends on adequate support services. In this respect, the Individuals with Disabilities Education Act (IDEA, 2004) emphasizes that, if needed, Deaf students should be provided interpreters. This need is determined by the IEP team. The National Association for the Deaf emphasizes that Deaf students learn best visually and recommend that parents with hearing learn sign language and that school personnel learn some signs, too. Physical educators have a unique opportunity to combine many aspects of the visual in teaching of Deaf and hard-of-hearing students. Demonstrations of movement complemented with some basic sign use and physical movements of approval are all at their disposal.

IEP

The IEP team may have members from special education for students with sensory impairments, including a certified orientation and mobility specialist. The APE may be an advocate for inclusion for the student, recruiting supports for the student in the GPE classes. The IEP team must be informed if there are any contraindications for physical activity participation. Some types of disability resulting in low vision (e.g., glaucoma) have a risk factor for further deterioration if the student is hit in the head or eye during physical activity. Determine if there are contraindications for the student regarding physical activity both in the classroom and while participating in physical education activities. Follow the district policy on whether the parent or medical personnel should provide this information to the IEP team.

Instructional Strategies

Teaching students with sensory impairment requires attention to what is impaired (vision or hearing) and then teaching with known practices that enhance learning for that student. Fortunately, physical activity is dynamic, and a teacher's positive grasp of how kinesthetics and cueing support learning leads to positive experience for students and is a big step to support these students' learning in physical activity. The information provided herein applies to students taught in various educational or clinical settings. The introduction of new skills requires a kinesthetic approach. Teaching gross motor skills to children with VI is demonstrated in Camp Abilities videos referenced in the sidebar. (These videos are invaluable resources and provided to us graciously by Dr Lauren Lieberman, Director at Camp Abili-

ties.) Here you will see how to accompany a student from point A to point B, to use preteaching and the whole-part-whole approach to instruction, and to provide physical assistance that is preceded by the student's permission. Note that it takes time to teach basic skills. Yet, these skills are essential and provide confidence in participation for sport, games, and leisure and recreational pursuits.

Environmental Modifications for VI

What modifications and adaptations are important to enable the student with a VI to be physically active in physical education? How does this student play the games, learn their movement skills, have fun, make friends, and socialize and understand what they like in PE? The following are validated

Camp Abilities Instructional Videos

Video demonstrations of instructional strategy can be found on the Camp Abilities website from the State University of New York at Brockport, www.campabilities.org (under Instructional Materials). All videos are excellent examples of instructional strategies (Camp Abilities, 2022). Play them repeatedly to fully grasp the terminology and watch the instructors interact with the students. The videos demonstrate proper ways to physically assist in teaching a skill: use of whole-part-whole, task analysis, tactile modeling, and other invaluable techniques to use when teaching children with VI. The following videos discuss motor development, staff training in physical education and athletics, and how the children themselves feel when they are included in physical education and extracurricular activity:

- *Teaching Gross Motor Development to Children With Visual Impairments:* This video informs teachers on how to instruct motor skills for children with VI (i.e., jumping, skipping, galloping).

- *Staff Training for Physical Education for Children With Visual Impairments:* This video provides instructional strategies on how to assist children with VIs in athletics and physical education.

- *I Feel Included:* Children with VIs share their feelings on when they feel included in their physical education class or extracurricular activity.

- *Sports videos:* Several videos on teaching and coaching various sports for those with a VI are provided. In the swimming video, the introduction is by an athlete of the RIO 2016 Paralympics, and the content provides resources for swim competitions. Guiding techniques and demonstrations for track and cross country running include a guide wire, an auditory runner, a radio runner, and tethering using a guide runner. The sports are as follows: volleyball, goalball, tennis, soccer, basketball, track, cross country (XC) running, swimming (this also includes resources for swim competitions), and wrestling (Camp Abilities, 2022).

Pay close attention to the number of ways the person with VI grasps onto the sighted person, how far ahead the sighted person should walk or run next to a person with VI, and the role of the sighted person in verbal and tactile instructions. Other students in class should be shown the proper way to walk with their classmates who are visually impaired. This will provide the student with VI an opportunity to practice trailing with different guides and provide the student with sight skills for assisting others with VI in their home and community.

Videos created in cooperation with the Lavelle Fund for the Blind, Inc; The State University of New York College (SUNY) at Brockport; Camp Abilities (Dr. Lauren Lieberman, director); and the Institute of Movement Studies for Individuals with Visual Impairments at Brockport. Permission courtesy of Camp Abilities, 2022.

techniques and modifications to the playing field and equipment for students with VI (Lieberman et al., 2013):

- *Enhance the usable vision in physical activity:* By placing colored tape of a contrasting color on a goal or a ball, students with VI might be able to participate more easily in a game. Also changing the ball to a larger size enhances visual acuity for play.

- *Illumination:* Adjusting the light available in an area where physical activity is taking place requires attention to how much light helps and how much actually contributes to glare, and thus is not helpful. If the students are blinking because of the increased light source, it is a glare. The angle may be adjusted to avoid it. The use of sunglasses can be helpful for those with oversensitivity to light. A hat or a visor helps some children to be more comfortable playing given their oversensitivity to light.

- *Contrast:* Assess the activity for any need to contrast surfaces such as the plate and bases for playing a game of kickball or tee ball. Use a contrasting-colored tape to indicate the end of a balance beam. Place dark mats under light-colored weight benches. Put orange tape on the volleyball. A yellow acetate sheet can go over signs in the physical activity to make the print stand out; yellow filters enhance and change blues, grays, and purples to black.

- *Size:* Increasing the size of the ball normally used in an activity may help the student with a VI participate in the game. Use a colorful volleyball for a softball or a beach ball instead of a volleyball.

- *Balls:* In addition to using a larger size ball, it is recommended that balls used by students with VI be softer than regulation balls. They are usually yellow or white, which makes them more easily seen by those with some vision. Bells, rattles, or buzzers inside the balls help to indicate their location to players who are blind. Placing a plastic bag over a soccer ball also works as it rustles somewhat. Putting a sock over a tennis ball slows it down for developing the skill of catching.

- *Touch techniques:* Adding touch to the activity itself increases participation. To help students feel the boundary for a game, place cords under the tape at the out-of-bounds markers. To increase the physical sense of space, have the students run in the space in which they will be playing to learn the parameters. Also, some students can pace the playing field with their long cane to gain a physical sense of what the game area is like.

When exploring by touch, use the whole hand versus just the tips of the fingers to scan the surface. Students can scan on the equipment for skill-building activities played with a ball, a bat, and a hockey stick. These approaches help develop muscle memory, whereby the muscles and joints of the body are activated repeatedly so that learning takes place (e.g., Latash & Singh, 2024). This muscle memory is similar when participating in a sport that hasn't been played for a long time. A player might be rusty at first, but as time goes on, the player improves! In due time, the muscle memory kicks in, and the individual gradually remembers how to play.

Touching a portable aluminum rail is a useful aid for bowling. The rail may be used on bowling alleys or on the gymnasium floor when plastic bowling sets are being used.

- *Sound devices:* Hearing is often an aid in learning physical activity. Sound-emitting devices that indicate the location of a piece of play equipment helps students with a VI participate in the game. Sound-emitting devices are found in an array of balls, basketball backboards (referred to as a beacon device), and soccer goal areas (again a beacon device). In these cases, the sound may be powered by a battery that emits a sound constantly or when the equipment is in motion. Bells are also embedded in balls of all sorts.

A beacon device with a human voice projected by a portable radio can also be used. This adaptation considers the frequency and pitch of the beacon or sound-emitting device and the ambient noise present in the activity. Because of this, the pool area and the gymnasium may lose the sound particularly if it is high pitched. In the end, the student may be using more than just sound to play the game. For example, they may be drawing on touch to find the boundaries and the training in specific moves (muscle memory) to aid them in the game.

- *Tethers:* Tethers are what joins a student to another (e.g., a band of nylon rope). Use tethers to guide the student in a space or in a locomotor activity like a run. Tethers are exemplified in the video on teaching. There are many ways that tethers are used in many different activities in PE.

Special equipment for the physical education program can be obtained through the American Foundation for the Blind. In 1879, a federal law was passed to promote the education of those who were blind, with particular attention to textbooks. American Printing House, established around the 1850s, is a government agency that provides free equipment and materials to educate children with VIs, with a certain amount of funding allotted per student each year. Additionally, there are federal quota-eligible materials available, which includes equipment for physical activity.

Teaching the Whole-Part-Whole Method for VI

A student who cannot see or cannot see well (has low vision) will perform basic locomotor skills and object control skills (Ulrich, 2020) differently and later than their age peers. They need to be taught the skills. Competency in fundamental skills prepares the student for participation in age-appropriate games and later in sports activities (Burton & Miller, 1998). When assessed on six locomotor and six object control tasks of the Test of Gross Motor Development-2 (Ulrich, 2020), 23 children who were blind (ages 6-12 years of age) were significantly delayed in all skills as compared to 28 sighted peers matched for age and gender (Wagner et al., 2013). The skills that were particularly hard for these students with VI were the running, leaping, kicking, and catching. The authors reported the practical implication for employing a whole-part-whole teaching strategy to initiate instruction.

Using the whole-part-whole method of teaching, first expose the student to the whole skill and then break it down into parts for instruction. Use tactile modeling whereby a student with sight (peer student) performs the whole skill (e.g., jumping) while the student with the VI feels the peer student in movement. As the model performs, the teacher can describe what the model is doing, such as bending their knees, pushing up, and bending the knees to

soften the landing. The student with VI feels this action in the model. Then do the same with the arms. If the student has a bit more vision, have the peer student perform the skill within the area the student with VI can see (Lieberman et al., 2013). In time, the teacher can adapt this general approach for the student with VI if there are finer points of the jump like a task analysis, and it can be embellished as needed. The horizontal jump can be taught next using all the teaching components described. Then other fundamental skills can be taught. Sum: feel the whole skill performed.

Sometimes, the student needs to have physical assistance by adding teacher guidance. A natural example is the fundamental skill of throwing a tennis ball. In addition to the whole-part-whole method of instruction, the teacher stands behind the student with their hand over the hand that has the ball. The teacher can use words to cue the student as they move the throwing arm. (Many GPE teachers have their own shortcut narratives for these skills that are used with their classes.) In due time, the physical assistance is reduced and only the verbal cues are used. Finally, the student can perform the skill without physical assistance or cues. The student can enjoy many attempts with this skill as the process of learning progresses. In time, most note that their skill performance is on par with their sighted peers.

When teaching an age-appropriate game or sport, the fundamental skills are combined and enhanced.

For example, the game of kickball combines both kicking and running. The teacher can use the whole-part-whole method in addition to enhancing the ball (adding a bright color) and adding a sighted peer to run with the student to the base, or have a radio playing at first base, or have a person using a constant verbal cue to the runner, such as "Here Melissa here! Keep running to the base. Keep going!" The videos from Camp Abilities define and demonstrate the whole-part-whole method (see sidebar).

Before the student with VI plays a game, the rules and game strategies are explained to the student in simple terms, a little at a time. (The brevity is due to the human brain's inability to easily hold a lot of new information with many steps.) Preteach. For example, have the student walk or run the bases (use the assistance appropriate for that game, for that student), walk the playing field, and swing the bat off the t-stand. During this time, it is necessary to verbally explain the indoor or outdoor space.

Instructional Prompts for VI

Instructional strategies always include information on the levels of prompts using verbal, visual, and physical prompts. These apply to children with VI and will need to be modified to be effective.

- *Verbal:* Describe a room, a space, a game, a path while running, advising that the path turns. Use precise language and not slang. Review body parts with the child; the teacher can use these terms in teaching, reminding the student to bend their knees and to put their hands and arms up and above their head and shoulders.

Verbal cues are used alongside the physical and the visual cues whenever teaching. Keep verbal cues short when teaching actions. Describing spaces as in preteaching is not a cue per se. Verbal cuing will continue for many reasons not common to teaching a student without VI.

- *Visual:* Take advantage of any sight that the student has and enhance the visual as described earlier. Use physical and auditory modifications to the environment and adaptations to the activity to engage the student in the activity.

- *Physical:* With permission from the student, move the parts of their body that needs to move and use all the different techniques (explained earlier) to touch the equipment. For example, ask if it is OK to move the student's arm to show them the throw. Use tactile boards

of game layouts (for soccer or basketball) and space setups (soccer goals, basketball hoops). Then walk around a play space or around a pool or walk in the pool if the pool is shallow. Use a combination of touch, feel, move, and repeat to enable the student to grow in their understanding of where the activity is taking place and what the activity is.

As the lessons continue and the student has given permission to be physically touched, then repeat the assistance of the throw or other motion. You may gradually withdraw the physical assist as the student gets a sense of the action. Continue with the verbal instruction. There will be a lot more teaching for the student who is visually impaired. In an underhand throw, the student may have to feel the teacher throw the ball by placing their full hand on the arm of the teacher, or the leg of the teacher to feel the step forward.

Peer Tutoring for Students With VI

Peer tutoring is an effective method of instruction in a general physical education class for individuals with VI (Lieberman & Houston-Wilson, 2018). Training the peer tutor to assist the individual with VI is

critical to the success of this instructional method for learning movement skills, games, and sports. Use kid terms to explain VI when training peer tutors and with inclusion in the general physical education classes. These include explaining the following (Lieberman, 2017a):

- Children will have difficulty seeing.
- They have this disability because of a birth accident, an accident after birth, or a sickness.
- Some kids can see a little bit and walk around by themselves; some kids can see a little bit but need some help getting around; and some kids cannot see anything and need help in getting around.
- With practice and a cane or a guide dog, kids may be able to walk around school and their neighborhood by themselves.
- These kids can use their utensils and find the items for a meal by using the clock system. You can tell them their milk is at 12:00, which means their milk is at the very top of their tray, and their fork is at 9:00, which means their fork is just to the left of their plate.
- They can dress themselves, and they know which clothes are which color by brailling the color on the tag of the shirt.
- They find out what is happening in their environment, who is around them, and where they are going by having people tell them.
- Do not be afraid to use the words *see* or *look* in a sentence. They will use these words and you can too.

Older students with vision have reported a reciprocal benefit from participating in leisure activities such as cross-country running or training for competitions with the individual with a VI. Inclusion in kids' language (Lieberman & Houston-Wilson, 2018) includes these ideas:

- You can guide your classmates by allowing them to grab your elbow and walk one step behind you. This will allow them to let go if they want to.
- You can describe their environment to them, such as who is in the room, what the weather is like, and what equipment is around the gym.
- You can answer their questions and make sure they are included in conversations.
- If you are a peer or buddy with them in class, do not ever leave a room without telling them you are leaving. They may want to talk to you and not know you are gone, and this is embarrassing.
- You can make sure they are included in games and activities in your neighborhood on the playground. Modify the equipment, the playing area, or the rules. You can ask your PE teacher for help too.

Sample Softball Unit Modification for VI

It is important for the educator or clinician to ascertain how well the student can see. Use the IEP team for information. Also, if the student is older, the teacher can ask the student about their visual abilities. With this knowledge about the student, the teacher can make simple modifications in the activities to accommodate the student in the games of the class.

For example, assume that a student with partial vision is to be integrated into a softball unit with sighted students. The teacher would first identify the tasks involved in the game of softball and

Understanding Cooperation

In the lower grades where the play is less dependent upon vocal directions and rulings, the Deaf child is usually a considerably successful student. Clear explanations directed at the student and careful demonstrations of the skill to be performed should alleviate the misunderstandings if it is obvious that the student misunderstood. It is the teacher's responsibility to make sure that students understand what is expected, including how to play selected games and sports. Students who are hard of hearing may demonstrate a lack of cooperation in class activities mostly due to their failure to have understood the directions or rules of the game. Students who hear will understand a Deaf student's need to understand the directions and rules otherwise they get confused. Bullying should not be tolerated in any physical education class, which should be in line with the school's policy in any class or on the campus.

then systematically explore ways with the student the various tasks could be modified. Softball, for instance, requires students to hit, run bases, pitch, field, catch, and throw. Modifications for the task of hitting might include having the student hit using a batting tee; hit with a larger bat; use a larger, brightly colored ball; swing at a pitched ball with the verbal assistance of the teacher or a classmate; or use an audible ball. Each of these modifications must be studied carefully with a view to identifying the one most closely approximating the original task that can be performed successfully by the student. A substitute batter should be used only if none of the other options were successful. Modifications for other softball skills are given in table 11.1 and offer an example of the way in which games can be adapted for participation by players with a VI.

Students without disabilities must come to know the student with a VI as a valued asset rather than a liability for the team. Utilization of modifications like those suggested promotes the development of such recognition. The teacher sets the tone for how the student with VI is received. If the teacher is overly protective and solicitous of the student in the class, such will be the general attitude displayed by the class. Acceptance of the students for who they are, with an appreciation of the talents and abilities they display, will be the response of the class with this attitude demonstrated by the instructor.

Modifications for Deaf Students

Visual aids for teaching Deaf students in physical education include videos (tablet or YouTube demonstrations), pictures, demonstrations, written announcements, posters with instructions, and whiteboard drawings with explanations for the activity like the placement of players (Schultz et al., 2014).

Research-validated instructional and coaching strategies for working with hard-of-hearing or Deaf students in both segregated and integrated settings include the following (Hodge et al., 2012):

- Give instructions for activities with easily understood visual cues and demonstrations.
- Use trained peer tutors to increase the time the target student is active in physical education.
- Give start and stop signals that are clear and known to both the teacher and the student.
- When playing a game, use a visual scoreboard and timer.
- As an instructor, face the student in good light where the student has a good view of your face and lips.
- The teacher should *not* stand with the sun behind them.
- Ask if the student understands the game and assist with instruction if it is apparent they do not.
- Provide choices.

TABLE 11.1   Modifications for the Game of Softball

Task	Modification
Hitting the ball	• Use a larger, bigger bat • Use a larger, brightly colored ball • Use a batting tee • Use an audible ball • Swing at a pitched ball with the verbal assistance of the teacher
Running the bases	• Follow a guide rope • Use the natural contrast of a worn base path to the grass field • Shorten the distance between bases • Run with a partner • Run to a sound provided by an audible device or a teammate's coaching
Fielding a ball	• Use the buddy system for assistance • Modify the rule so that if a player who is visually impaired picks the ball up before a runner reaches base, the runner is out • Modify the rule to allow for an out when the ball is thrown to the closest player or base • Use an audible ball

- With hearing peers, identify the hard of hearing or Deaf student as the captain or leader.

In addition, the following guidelines are also recommended:

- Good eye contact must be maintained. This means that the teacher will need to be in a position that enables the student to see the instructor's face. It may be necessary for the teacher to kneel or sit down on the floor when talking with young children.

- The teacher must speak clearly but avoid talking slowly or overemphasizing words. When it is apparent that the student did not understand the teacher's directions, repeat the instructions but use simpler words and phrases. (Some other students probably didn't understand either.)

- Instructors must explain sport jargon to the student with a hearing loss if they are not familiar with the sport. Sport terms are frequently difficult for a young Deaf student to follow.

- A whiteboard may help in the gymnasium. This aid allows the instructor to draw diagrams and use key words. The teacher's ability to maintain eye contact while speaking and drawing helps all students to follow directions.

- When outside during group instruction, teachers should avoid standing in the shadow of buildings or trees or stationing themselves with the sun at their back and with students looking into the sun. Shadows that descend over the face of the instructor interfere with the Deaf student's ability to speech read or follow instructions.

- Some students with hearing loss find long verbal instructions very fatiguing. This is attributed to the intense listening effort that some must maintain to follow the class discussion. Teachers, therefore, should recognize this special need and provide for frequent rest periods as well as employ alternative methods of providing information to Deaf students.

- When teaching Deaf students, it is important that the teacher ask frequent questions to ascertain whether the student is following the specific lesson. It is also important that only one question be asked at a time to avoid confusion.

- Other students must be reminded that they should look at their Deaf student classmate when asking or answering a question. The teacher can repeat the classmate's question so it is clear to the Deaf student as well as others in the class.

- If possible, a student with hearing should be assigned to serve as a peer aide for the student with a hearing loss. The aide's responsibilities include helping in the orientation to new activities and providing visual signals when required during play in team games. A weekly or monthly rotation of the peer aide is recommended to avoid overdependence. Caution must be exercised, too, to ensure that the aide assists only when it is necessary. Peers tutoring has generally helped younger students with VI in integrated PE classes. By the time the student reaches adolescence, they report not wanting an assigned peer tutor unless they ask for one. Instead, they prefer that friends help them (Haegele et al., 2022).

Transitional IEP

In high school, the student with an IEP in physical education begins the transition phase of physical activity into their home community. The student needs to spend time experiencing different leisure-based physical activities. For example, the student may be very familiar with swimming and like it but have no knowledge of age-appropriate leisure activities such as hiking, camping, aerobic dance, and yoga. Again, all the possible adaptations outlined in this chapter may need to be explored to facilitate both learning and ongoing involvement in the activity in their next home community.

Modifications for Deafblindness

The student with deafblindness needs to be taught everything. There is no incidental learning by being in the same space where an activity is performed. To communicate, if the student has some sight, the instructor working one to one with the student signs in front of the person. If not, then signing is done in the hand. The aim of working with the students is to focus on a quality of life where they have the opportunity ". . . to learn every sport and activity that is taught to their same-age peers" (Hodge et al., 2012, p. 305, figure 10.3).

When teaching Deafblind students, the physical educator can use the recommendations for teaching students who are blind or have low vision, as well as teaching Deaf students. Research also supports other recommendations for teaching Deafblind students (Hodge et al., 2012):

- Promote movement: swimming, swinging, biking, climbing, side lying.

- Use the student's preferred mode of communication. Get to know them and what they are communicating.
- Use a multimodality approach to teaching: tactile modeling, physical assistance, demonstration (where appropriate with established tactile procedures), and explaining in a way that communicates effectively.
- Offer choices in equipment and activity (for example, they can choose the size or hardness of the ball).
- Use trained peer tutoring to expand the social opportunities the student who is deafblind has.
- Teach both the word for the activity and the purpose of the activity.

Like the individuals who are blind or Deaf, the Deafblind child needs to develop the unimpaired senses as well as learn to utilize fully any residual sight or hearing. Deafblind students must rely heavily on their tactile, kinesthetic, vestibular (inner ear balance), and olfactory sensations as stimuli for movement. The educational environment should provide opportunities for experiences that encourage such use.

The formation of a positive self-concept is important to normal social development. Knowledge of one's physical self, the body image, is necessary for the development of a concept of the self. Because they have great difficulty in learning to move about in their world, Deafblind children have limited opportunities to develop an awareness of their body and to integrate their observations with other information to form a concept of themselves as persons. One of their most essential needs, therefore, is to have greatly expanded opportunities to utilize their bodies in movement.

Movement-related activities should be encouraged from birth with the goal of associating cues (visual, auditory, tactile) with various forms of movement. Van Dijk (1966) developed a system of teaching communication through movement. In this system, which consists of several stages, the teacher uses close body contact with the student to imitate various movements. As the student progresses, the amount of body closeness between teacher and student can be reduced. Throughout the instructional program, the goal is to introduce language by associating movement with cues that can be understood by the student.

Experiences that create tactile and social awareness and control of the body in gross and fine motor movements need to be provided. The total movement experience for Deafblind children must be varied enough to help them understand their potential in movement and to provide the means to realize this potential.

The physical education activities that can be presented to Deafblind students depend upon their age and upon the degree of deafness and blindness and the extent to which movement has been learned. Movements that are taught should be presented in such a manner that they contribute to the communication skills of the person. To accomplish this, the physical education teacher must learn body signs for general communication from the teacher who works with the student so that the same signs can be used in physical education. Other signs will need to be developed to convey certain concepts of movement peculiar to physical education. The signs developed for this purpose should be used consistently, and additional signs should be introduced only when the previously learned signs are inadequate in instructing the child in a new motor movement.

One system that has been successfully employed with Deafblind students with intellectual disability is to rely on kinesthetic cues to communicate. For instance, in teaching to reach for a ball, the teacher, with the student in a seated position, would tap the student's elbows as a signal to reach for the ball. If the student fails to reach as requested, the instructor would then take the Deafblind student's hands and physically assist the child to reach the ball (or start the task with physical assistance to reach from a seated position). Additional feedback would be provided by moving the student's head to indicate yes (up/down) or no (side to side) with the physical assistance agreed upon prior to use.

The teacher must also develop a daily routine so that the Deafblind student will know what to expect each day. The lesson should begin with the teacher identifying themselves to the student. A watch or ring that is normally worn every day is useful for this purpose; the child can feel it on the teacher and associate it with the GPE teacher. Following the introduction, a review of previously taught movements is desirable. The same order should be used in each review. After practice of the previously taught movements, a new movement can be introduced, and the child allowed to experiment and practice it. The lesson may end with a familiar activity or game that the child particularly enjoys. Although the idea of sameness might appear boring or limiting to some teachers, it is essential that the program for Deafblind students follow a consistent routine.

Physical Activities

The ability of a student with VI to move about independently is one of the goals of the student's educational development. Mobility refers to the ability to move from one point to a second point. Orientation refers to the ability of students with VI to use their remaining senses to relate their body position to other objects. Both skills contribute to an independent student with VI. Instructional strategies for soccer, basketball, swimming, and tennis are found in the videos discussed in the Camp Abilities Instructional Videos sidebar.

There are few restrictions on the age-appropriate activities that may be offered to Deaf students or those with hearing loss in the general or an adapted physical education class in their neighborhood school or a special school for Deaf students. These students need to be social rather than limited by their Deafness or hard-of-hearing status.

Primary Grade Activities for Students With VI

Activity in physical education helps the understanding of how the body moves through space and navigates an environment for young students with VI. Not only do they play and have fun, but they also begin to apply their orientation and mobility skills in larger group settings. The tactile models within the preteaching of skills and the space for learning are directly applied with input from their orientation and mobility instructor. Within the context of physical education, overall movement skill development is both introduced and reinforced through the play and games.

Fundamental skills of locomotion are rolling, crawling, walking, running, and jumping, and variations of these. Exploration of these skills helps children learn the variety of ways the body can be moved from place to place. When teaching these skills, it is important to clearly identify for the student with VI, a stationary point where all movement skills begin and end (e.g., the mat, the peeping marker, the large bright yellow line). This will help students to feel secure and confident as they engage in various movement activities.

Activities for Older Students With VI

There are many games suitable for middle and high school students with VI that need no modification. Some games lend themselves more easily than others to adaptation for students who are visually impaired. Although the needs of those with VI are like those of the sighted, special attention must be directed toward the physical fitness of these students. They are overall lower than their peers with vision (Brian et al., 2019). Without engagement in fitness activity, the individual loses stamina, strength, and flexibility. Rowing, cycling, dance aerobics, and cross-country skiing are all activities promoting fitness. All have known modifications for participation of those with VI.

Bloomquist (2003b) recommends that when testing individuals for exercise, manual and visual orientation of all testing equipment and facilities should be conducted as should keeping the facility clear of clutter. Individual sports such as swimming, weight training, dance, track and field, golf, and aerobics can be assessed for participation and benefit from Bloomquist's recommendations. That said, goalball and beep ball are both very popular games played by students with VI and without! There are a plethora of instructional materials available including skill assessments.

For middle school and high school students with VI, the United States Association for Blind Athletes sponsors many activities across the United States. Camp Abilities is offered in many states and abroad. This program enables the student to try or continue activities with expert instruction. And in general, individual sport activities for students with visual impairments include track, cross-country, field events, aquatics, wrestling, judo, rowing, and tandem bicycling. Training tips are found through the United States Association of Blind Athletes (USABA, 2021). Lieberman (2017a) has been influential with instruction for students with VI in middle school and high school.

Activities for Deaf Students

Those who are Deaf and hard-of-hearing may be underdeveloped physically, owing to a lack of opportunity or their withdrawal from vigorous play. Poor coordination is also observed for some due to the lack of sound orientation. Yet, there are elite athletes who are deaf like the following (AI media, 2022): basketball superstar Tamika Catchings, Singaporean-British para-equestrian competitor Laurentia Tan, former NFL star Derrick Coleman, South African swimmer and Olympic medalist Terence Parkin, champion Women's Motocross athlete Ashley Fiolek, and accomplished American volleyball player and Olympic gold medalist David Smith.

Balance is often challenged with Deaf students. Training in all games and sport activities encourages the development of better balance. Deaf students need opportunities to be included in activities along with hearing students. Pull out programs are not appropriate in PE. After-school sport programs are encouraged. All individual and team sports may be learned by Deaf and hard-of-hearing individuals. Many segregated schools field basketball, baseball, and football teams that compete successfully against teams of hearing players. Deaf students enjoy competitive play and play to win, but more important is the social contacts provided by the game and the acceptance of equality by hearing opponents.

There are, of course, some hazards to the safety of the Deaf and hard-of-hearing in competitive play because they are unable to hear signals and other warning sounds. As a precautionary measure, certain visual signals should be arranged. For example, the waving of colored flags for specific rules within a game is necessary with the instructor explaining each signal before play begins. Check to understand that the athletes understand the flags' meanings. If the opponents are also deaf, the signals should be agreed upon and understood by both teams. If the opponents can hear, they should be alerted to the need for the visual signals and for their cooperation in preventing accidents to Deaf and hard of hearing players.

Fencing, archery, bowling, tennis, golf, and badminton are other sports with demonstrated appeal for students. Team play is often emphasized over individual sport to teach the give and take of com-petition. Individual sports like bowling have a spot in the transitional IEP if a student is drawn to them.

Bloomquist (2003a) recommends the removal of hearing aids before contact sports, gymnastics, self-defense, and aquatics programs. With the aquatics program participation, earplugs should be used by students who have tympanic tubes. To prevent electrostatic discharge, students with cochlear implants should avoid mats, plastic ball pits, or plastic equipment. Train individuals with hearing loss to be visually aware of nearby moving vehicles during activities such as cross-country running, cycling, and jogging. In case of an emergency in the school facility, use strobe fire alarms.

Water play and swimming are enjoyed by Deaf and hard-of-hearing students as much as by other active students. Although some may experience balancing difficulties in the water, nearly all progress like other children in learning swimming skills. A modified stroke that permits the head to remain above water will be necessary for those who cannot get water in the ears or who become disoriented when their heads are submerged. If warranted, use peers in swimming to increase social opportunity and skill development. Long sticks held by a coach or teacher that can reach the swimmer from the pool deck are often used to signal the swimmer (e.g., end of the lane when swimming laps). Also when swimming laps in a pool with lane markers, the student can be trained to use the physical contact to know where they are in the pool or lane.

Courtesy of Michael Beets.

The sports included in USA Deaf Sports Federation competition include badminton, baseball, basketball, bowling, curling, cycling, golf, hockey, martial arts, orienteering, shooting, skiing, snowboarding, soccer, swimming, tennis, table tennis, team handball, track and field, triathlon, volleyball, water polo, and wrestling. Teaching lead-up games and activities related to these sports is especially important if a student doesn't want to be competitive but rather recreational in these activities or is too young to play the sport (Lieberman, 2017b).

Activities for Deafblind Students

Students with CHARGE syndrome were found to do well in physical education with support from staff, a teacher's aide, or a paraeducator (Lieberman et al., 2012). Parents reported that there was success with activities such as swimming, scooters, bowling, t-ball, dancing, floor hockey, and gymnastics. Fundamental motor skills were the most challenging. Each student is typically considered unique and requiring individualized programming with trained support staff. Parents of these children highly value physical education for their child yet found that many PE teachers struggled in their instruction and inclusion (Lane, 2019).

Each activity should be given a specific body sign that the teacher gives before an activity starts, so that the student with CHARGE syndrome can become aware that this sign refers to the activity that follows. The activities are listed in order of difficulty of performance for most children. However, because of experience or interest, some children may perform the most difficult skills more easily than the skills preceding them. The order also reflects the increased communication skills that are developed as the activities progress.

In some way, obtain the student's permission to be moved into these positions. These are positions taken to engage in physical activity.

- *Kneeling:* Help the child take a position on their knees with their buttocks resting on the back of the legs. Have the student lift their buttocks off the legs to raise the trunk to the upright position.

- *Rolling down:* Help the child into place on an incline mat and move the body so that it rolls forward and down the incline. Help child shift weight so that body rolls without assistance.

- *Rolling on the level:* Help the child to take a prone position. Move one leg over the other. Cross the arm on the same side over the body. Push the child over onto the stomach. Move the leg that was moved when the child was on the back over the other leg; pull the same arm across the back until the body turns onto the back.

- *Pushing and pulling:* Put the child's hands on the object to be pushed or pulled (for pulling, the fingers are placed around the object). Push or pull the arms until the object moves.

- *Running:* Holding hands, run at a slow pace with the child. As the child gains confidence, run together, each holding opposite ends of a short length of rope.

- *Running (unaided):* The child holds a guide rope while running. This is a suspended rope that the runner can hold onto for running in an area like a gym or long open space for track. Physically assist the hand placement and walk the area with the student before running.

- *Running (aided):* The runner uses a rope or string that is also held by a sighted person. Together they run side by side. Walk the area before running when first learning to run aided.

- *Rebounding in a jump:* Physically assist the child to balance on an inner tube or a jouncing board. Lift at the waist or under the shoulders. Move the legs from flexion to extension in coordination with the lift and return. A helper will be needed.

- *Jumping:* Put the child in a standing position and indicate that knees are to be flexed. Lift up and down, simultaneously helping the legs to flex or extend as in rebounding. A helper will be needed.

- *Rolling:* While standing, place the child's hand on an object to be rolled forward. Lead the arms through a push. When the object is released without aid, move the arm through the push more vigorously to achieve forward movement of the object and then cue a release. Preteach the release.

- *Pushing:* Have the child sit with feet out forming a *V* with the legs, and a light playground ball between the legs, and push it away to a wall or to a person. Repeat to get the back and forth of a game.

- *Striking:* When introducing new equipment, such as the ball and bat, it is essential that the student be provided an opportunity to orient to the equipment by feeling and touching it. Let the child feel the bat and the tee. Set a large ball on a batting tee. Let the child feel it in relationship to the tee. Standing behind the child, place the bat in the hands of the child enclosing the child and holding the bat with the child's hands around it. Practice the swing together. Have a helper retrieve the ball. Repeat many times. As skill improves, move the bat farther from the ball.

- *Catching:* Place the child's hands in the proper position for catching: hands waist level and out from the body, cupped near one another. Drop a ball onto the hands and immediately bring the arms up to entrap the ball between the arms and chest.

- *Moving to a drumbeat:* Place a large drum near enough to the child to enable the vibrations to be felt. Beat the drum with one hand and move parts of the child's body in time to the beat. Have the child beat the drum! Depending on the size of the drum, have the child beat and move!

- *Playing games:* Physically assist the child in feeling the equipment and walking the play area if the game involves space to another. Try the action using physical assistance. Then the student can do scooter rides, hula hoop play, beanbag tossing at various targets, jumping on the trampoline, bouncing a ball, catching and rolling a ball, goal kicking, and moving through an obstacle course.

Older students will be able to participate with assistance in many activities, among them bowling, golf, shuffleboard, archery, weight training, track and field events, dancing, wrestling, and swimming. Look at the functional value of the activities—particularly fitness—as the child ages. Any of these activities and others, particularly running, dancing, swimming, bowling, or weightlifting, can become lifetime leisure activities.

Research with individuals with CHARGE syndrome reports these students enjoy a number of activities such as swimming, tee-ball, dancing, and floor hockey. These activities need modifications based on the individual student. The nature of the physical activity program is to improve the quality of life of Deafblind students. The modifications are a joint effort of the student and specialists working with the educational team and the paraeducator. Some students have enjoyed weightlifting, hiking, goalball, roller skating, and canoeing. The sports competitions for those who are blind are also open to Deafblind athletes. (Look for these organizations on the Internet: United States Association of Blind Athletes and the United States of America Deaf Sports Federation.)

Assessment and Evaluation

The Physical Activity Barriers Questionnaire-Visual Impairments is used with youth (Armstrong et al., 2020). The respondent is asked to rate their perceived barriers to being physically active (PA) that are categorized as personal, social, and environmental. These barriers were found to distinguish adequately across ages and severity of VI (Martin et al., 2021). A sample statement from the questionnaire addressing environment is: "My school has PA equipment for people with visual impairment (e.g., bell balls, beep balls, and guide wires)." A sample personal statement is "I like how my body looks or feels when I do PA" (p. 588). This tool seems to be a good fit for the transitional IEP as well as generally reviewing individual motivation for engaging in PA.

See chapter 6 on the myriad of assessment tools and their adaptations for providing valid data for ongoing IEP goals and inclusion strategies.

Educational Health Care Providers

Physical educators ask their students to execute mobility skills near constantly within the context of the development of skills for games and sports. Certified orientation and mobility specialists are a part of the IEP team for the student with VI. They have expertise in how the student with VI can use their school and community to navigate well. These professionals are adept at interpreting medical and rehabilitation reports for IEP development as well as ongoing health care needs and mobility. As such, they assist the teachers of PE and APE, as well as the coach when educating this student, and they work within the occupational therapy and physical therapy goals when students have multiple disabilities. One important aspect of moving around the physical activity space is to know what is *not* typical for the student with VI compared to the typical way the students with vision move in the classroom, school, or community. Teachers can train the student to move and move safely after they understand the challenges of architecture, of activity demands, and of the student's own unique personality and development.

It is imperative that communication between instructor and Deaf student is in place for an inclusive setting in PA. Deaf children and youth are served in the schools in consultation with speech and language pathologists or other specialist in alternative communication. These individuals train the student to communicate in school including with the GPE and APE teacher. In some states, special education teachers have certifications for working with Deaf students and are very knowledgeable in communication techniques in school. The use of peer tutors trained by any of these professionals enhances socialization and learning in the PA activities. Students who are not deaf are known to enjoy the role of peer tutor with their Deaf classmate. The peer trained by the APE or PE teacher uses a speech and language pathology consultant in whatever system the student is using to communicate in school as identified in the IEP. In the spirit of universal design in PE, try a form of signing where the whole class uses signing or specific sign symbols during activity or particular games. Make it a privilege to be a peer tutor. Train them. Have more than one student as a trained peer tutor, thus encouraging more potential friendships for Deaf students. These professionals as speech and language pathologist, special education teacher, GPE, and APE with experience in communication with Deaf students are invaluable resources in the education of Deaf students and those hard of hearing.

Summary

Visual impairment is a term that refers to a range of visual acuity. When engaging in instruction, ascertain what a student with visual impairment can see. Instructional techniques for those with VI involve kinesthesis (i.e., tactile modeling)—assisting the student's body to learn movement. It also takes advantage of a developed auditory awareness by using PA equipment with sounds. Games that are played with auditorily enhanced equipment have been developed. In other situations, sound-emitting devices indicate the location of a piece of equipment enabling students with a visual impairment to participate in the game (i.e., hoops emitting auditory signals). The benefits of physical activity are similar for both visually impaired and sighted individuals. Assist students in physically feeling the boundary for a game. Walk the student who is blind around the room, feeling the walls, floors, and doors. Always leave a door open in the gym. Preteaching is always recommended; it is conducted ahead of the physical activity engagement whereby a responsible person reviews the plan for an activity or activities with the student. Many activities of the PA classes are pretaught to encourage comfort with equipment, rules of the game, and the physical space. Use auditory and kinesthetic cues and prompts to assist when the student is visually impaired. Deaf students can be in inclusive physical activity environments with support. Use visual and kinesthetic cues to assist where the auditory sense is impaired. Terminology regarding Deaf students is the exception to person-first language. The Deaf community prefers the adjective *Deaf* placed before the noun, not afterwards. They consider themselves a community, not disabled. Do not use *the blind* or *the Deaf*, but rather say *the individual who is blind* and *the Deaf person*.

Orthopedic Impairment and Traumatic Brain Injury

FatCamera/E+/Getty Images

CHAPTER OBJECTIVES

After completing this chapter, you will be able to do the following:

- Identify the main reasons why an individualized education program (IEP) would need to be developed for a student with an orthopedic impairment such as cerebral palsy.
- Understand how to provide physical activities with a life course perspective and interdisciplinary approach consistent of educational and clinical experiences for those with an orthopedic disability.
- Given a spinal cord injury, identify the relationship of the spinal cord injury to the nerves and vertebrae and the relevance for physical activity engagement.
- Explain the application in creating an IEP given the difference between a term like *quadriplegic* and a term like *quadriplegia* and its application in creating the student's IEP.
- Describe a traumatic brain injury and how to assess for engagement in the physical education program.
- Describe cerebral palsy and how a student with cerebral palsy might be served in physical education.
- Describe the multidisciplinary aspect of engaging a student with an orthopedic impairment in their physical activity programs of school and community.

Physical activity engagement makes one of its most significant contributions to the well-being of those who have disabilities. As such the role of physical activity and sport participation is a powerful aspect of life for those with orthopedic disabilities. It also helps them to move well. For most children, play and early games provide the incentive for the improvement in basic motor skills. When more complex game skills are achieved, or in cases when movement skills are reacquired after an injury or hospitalization, self-esteem is reestablished and children and youth look forward with greater confidence and reassurance to being a physically active person!

The information on the identified orthopedic impairments and adapted physical activity of this chapter is organized under the headings of causes and prevalence, classification and diagnosis, and instructional strategies. Under each heading then follows information for each of the selected disabilities for this chapter. Therefore, the reader will encounter all the chapter's identified impairments under specific headings throughout the whole chapter.

The adapted physical educator plays a huge role in facilitating the physical education program for children and youth with orthopedic impairment. They work closely with their colleagues in the schools and examples of this proliferate in this chapter. This happens as the student is in their appropriate physical education placement. As the narrative refers to GPE or APE keep in mind the complexity and specificity that this entails!

Causes and Prevalence

Families coming to understand their child and any disability might ask, "What caused this?" Children might have a false understanding themselves. Researchers often place findings in the context of "why" and "how often." Professionals need context to fully engage a child or youth in physical activity. Understanding why is useful.

Cerebral Palsy

Cerebral refers to brain and *palsy* refers to lack of muscle control (CDC, 2022d). The overall hallmark of cerebral palsy is a disorder in motor function. Clinically, cerebral palsy is considered an umbrella term for motor impairment due to lesions or anomalies in the brain development caused by an injury before, during, or after birth (Rosenbaum et al., 2002). The impairment is considered nonprogressive in that it does not lead to death although the motor impairment of cerebral palsy can change functionally over the course of time (Wood & Rosenbaum, 2000).

Spastic cerebral palsy results from a lesion in the motor cortex (figure 12.1). The motor cortex forms tracts that originate in the upper central portion of the cerebrum and proceed downward through the brain into the spinal cord. In figure 12.1, the damaged area of the brain is highlighted and results in diplegia, hemiplegia, and quadriplegia in cerebral palsy. The information going to the spinal cord results in disruptions in the signal for voluntary muscle use and muscle tone, hence the difficulty with performance of movement skills. Because of the insult to the brain, the student with cerebral palsy can also have an intellectual disability and impairments of vision, hearing, and speech.

The spasticity in a body part affects mobility and its responsible muscles. For example, a scissors gait causes a smaller base of support and thus balance and locomotor activities are difficult, with a jerky movement. The wrist can be flexed rather than extended, compromising skills for games and play. The main trunk of the body has muscles that tighten, too.

Rosenbaum and colleagues (2002) explain that when parents first hear the diagnosis of cerebral palsy, they want to know whether their child will walk. In these early ages (birth to 16 months), the ability to predict function across the child's life has not been validated. Part of the difficulty in prediction is the varying clinical types of cerebral palsy and the ineffective links among early reflexes, early developmental milestones, and walking (Rosenbaum et al., 2002). Assessment of function across time as the child ages is advocated to assist the family and the child. This approach recalibrates the understanding of what the child's abilities are in gross motor function.

It is estimated that 1 in 345 children have been diagnosed with cerebral palsy in the United States (CDC, 2022c). Cerebral palsy does not appear to be related in any way to socioeconomic structures. Of these children with cerebral palsy, 90 percent are in the general classroom, the special education classroom, or a combination. Of those affected, about 10 percent have more severe disabilities requiring a different type of intensive care.

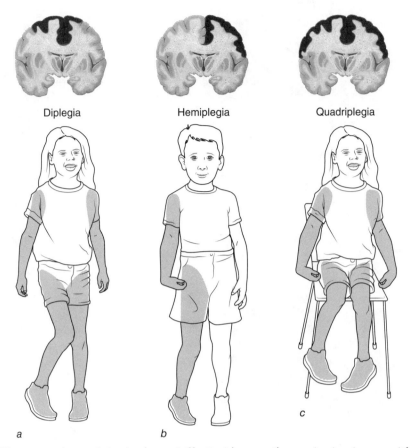

Diplegia   Hemiplegia   Quadriplegia

a   b   c

FIGURE 12.1 Different regions of the brain are affected in spastic cerebral palsy, resulting in a presentation of *(a)* diplegia (both arms or both legs), *(b)* hemiplegia, and *(c)* quadriplegia.

Spina Bifida

Spina bifida is a group of conditions affecting the spinal column and happens to the fetus before the mother even knows she is pregnant. The condition is a neural tube defect. The bones of the vertebrae surround and protect the nerves in the spinal column. In spina bifida, this has not formed correctly (figure 12.2).

In some infants, there is a visible protrusion in their back along the spinal column area. This lumbar area is affected where the protrusion exists. These children will have varying degrees of difficulty with movement because of where the nerves are interrupted in carrying signals from the body to the brain. Sometimes there is paralysis in the lower limbs that results in loss of bladder and bowel control. Those with the condition often use both a wheelchair and crutches for ambulation. They may also have braces on their legs to aid them in movement. In the United States, prevalence is 1 in 2,758 births (Mai et al., 2019). According to the Spina Bifida Association (2023a), 90 percent of babies born with spina bifida now grow up to lead full lives,

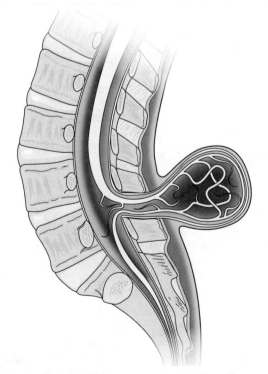

FIGURE 12.2 The visible protrusion in the spinal cord in spina bifida.

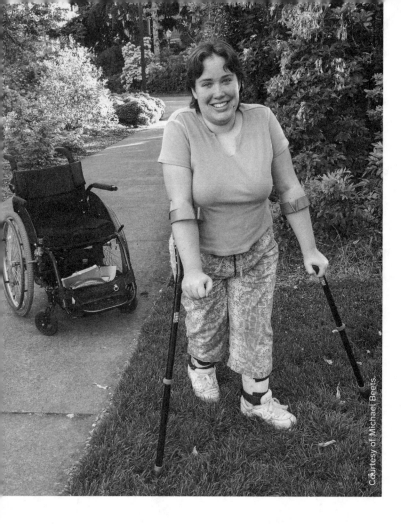

Courtesy of Michael Beets.

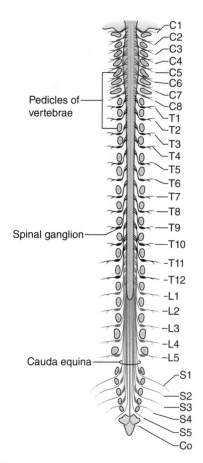

Spinal ganglion

Cauda equina

C1
C2
C3
C4
C5
C6
C7
C8
T1
T2
T3
T4
T5
T6
T7
T8
T9
T10
T11
T12
L1
L2
L3
L4
L5
S1
S2
S3
S4
S5
Co

80 percent have normal intelligence and do well in school, and about 75 percent play sports and do other enjoyable physical and recreational activities.

Spinal Cord Injury

The spine consists of a spinal cord surrounded by bony structures called vertebrae. The spinal cord is segmented, and spinal nerves exit the spinal cord at each segment. These nerves carry movement signals to and from the brain. The spinal segments, vertebrae, and nerves are numbered. The relationship of the spinal cord segments and nerves to the surrounding protective vertebrae is seen in figure 12.3.

The spine is divided into cervical (C), thoracic (T), lumbar (L), and sacral (S) segments. The tailbone is also called the coccyx. The spinal cord segment is not always collocated at the similarly numbered vertebra (the spinal cord is shorter than the vertebral column). To understand a spinal injury, it is important to know the injured spinal cord segment and spinal nerve roots, as well as the vertebral injury.

Spinal injuries are described in terms of spinal cord levels, not vertebral levels. For example, the neurologic injury resulting from a significant fracture of the T12 vertebra is not necessarily limited to the T12 spinal segment and nerves. The injury may involve lumbar and sacral neurologic levels.

FIGURE 12.3 The spinal cord and vertebral column. As the spinal cord is shorter than the vertebrae, nerves emerging (for example, at S1) are located further up the vertebral column.

Figure 12.4 indicates where specific nerves innervate specific areas of the body. If there is injury to that nerve, the damage to function is either complete or partial. An extreme example is if the injury to the spinal cord at C3 is complete, it typically means death; if partial, there is paralysis from C3 on down the spinal column, and the person is quadriplegic. The physical activity instructor will be most interested in how this injury affects functional use of muscles and the resulting ability to perform movements and have fun in a physical activity program.

Spinal cord injury (SCI) can be the result of sudden traumatic blow to the body resulting in a fracture, dislocation, crushing, or compression of the vertebrae. It can also be from a gunshot or knife wound severing the spinal cord. In some cases, it is the result of nontraumatic events like cancer and the degeneration of disks.

Overall causes of SCI are from motor vehicle accidents (nearly 50 percent), falls (31 percent), other violence (13 percent), sports and recreation participation (10 percent), and alcohol use (which is involved

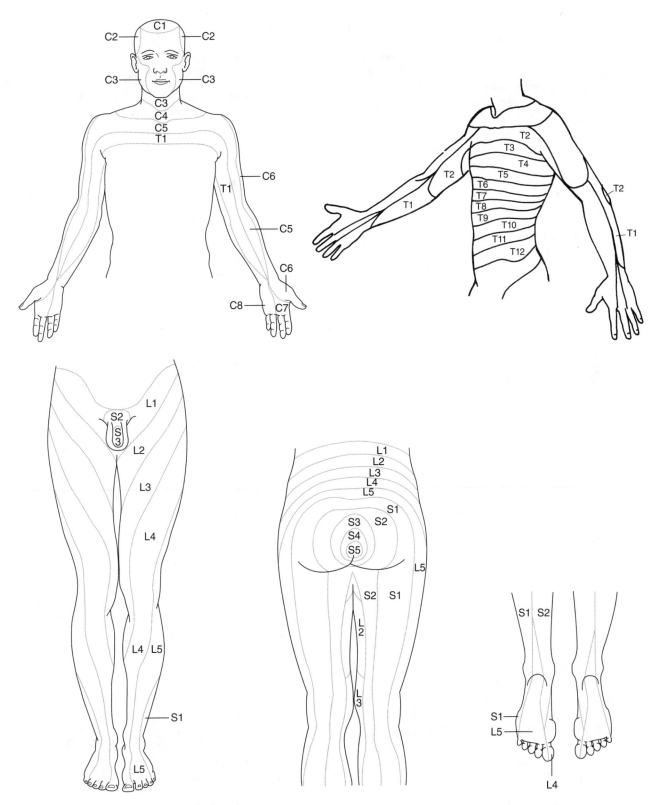

FIGURE 12.4   Cutaneous distribution of spinal nerves. The letters labeled throughout the pictures are correlated with the area affected in the spine.

in one out of four spinal cord injuries). For children eight years old and under, the most common causes of SCIs are motor vehicle accidents, falls, and child abuse. For children eight years and older, SCI usually occurs due to a motor vehicle accident or and sports injury. Twenty-five percent of children with an SCI are delayed in symptoms from 30 minutes to 4 days (Moo, 2022). Therefore, any child who has been in a motor vehicle accident, fallen from a height of three meters or greater, or been submerged should be examined for a spinal cord injury.

Traumatic Brain Injury

The Centers for Disease Control and Prevention (CDC) indicates a traumatic brain injury (TBI)

> . . . is caused by a bump, blow, or jolt to the head that disrupts the [typical] function of the brain. Not all blows or jolts to the head result in a TBI. The severity of a TBI may range from "mild" (i.e., a brief change in mental status or consciousness) to "severe" (i.e., an extended period of unconsciousness or memory loss after the injury).
>
> CDC (2022a).

Most TBIs that occur each year are mild, commonly called concussions (CDC, 2022a; Dean et al., 2012). The concussion does persist six months after the initial incident, but to what degree seems to be debatable depending on the classification system and functional assessments employed (Voormolen et al., 2018). Like spinal cord injuries, TBI can be caused by traffic accidents, falls, or child abuse, and they can be sport-related injuries. TBI can also be caused by other situations with a loss of consciousness.

The CDC (2022b) reported children, birth to 17 years old, had 16,070 TBI-related hospitalizations in 2019, and in 2020 there were 2,774 TBI-related deaths. Of those children and youth who died in this age span during 2018 and 2019, the "most common mechanisms of injury for TBI-related deaths were motor vehicle crashes (average annual rate of 1.0 per 100,000) and homicide (average annual rate of 0.9 per 100,000)" (CDC, 2022b, p. 10).

Classification and Diagnosis

Orthopedic impairment is defined by IDEA (2004) as a

> . . . severe orthopedic impairment that adversely affects a child's educational performance. The term includes impairments caused by a congenital anomaly, impairments caused by disease and impairments from other causes.
>
> IDEA (2004, § 300.8 [c][8]).

Traumatic brain injury has its own category in IDEA (2004). TBI is defined by IDEA (2004) as an

> . . . acquired injury to the brain caused by an external physical force, resulting in a total or partial functional force disability or psychological impairment, or both, that adversely affects the child's educational performance. The term applies to open or closed head injuries resulting in one or more areas, such as cognition; language; memory; attention; reasoning; abstract thinking; judgement; problem solving; sensory, perceptual, and motor abilities; psychological behavior; physical functions; information processing; and speech. The term does not include brain injuries that are congenital or degenerative, or brain injuries induced by birth trauma.
>
> IDEA (2004, § 300.8 [c][12]).

Cerebral Palsy

Cerebral palsy encompasses a broad array of atypical movement patterns resulting in impairments.

Children with cerebral palsy (CP) will exhibit stiff muscles (spastic CP), uncontrolled movements (dyskinetic CP), or poor balance and coordination (ataxic CP). Cerebral palsy is classified based on the dominant type of cerebral palsy, because no individual has just one type of cerebral palsy. The three main types are spastic, dyskinetic, or ataxic (CDC, 2020c).

According to the CDC (2022c), some individuals have more than one dominant type of cerebral palsy. The United Cerebral Palsy Association only uses three classifications. Mixed type is not used for competition in athletics.

Spastic Cerebral Palsy

With spastic cerebral palsy, the suffix -plegia is not to be confused with paralysis from a spinal cord injury. For example, a person who has spastic cerebral palsy can have quadriplegia when all four limbs are affected. This person can move, but the affected muscles have spasticity. A person who is quadriplegic from a severed SCI cannot move the four limbs; they are paralyzed. For this reason, clinicians prefer the suffix *-paresis* rather than *-plegia* when referring to movement and cerebral palsy (Oczkowski & Bodzioch, 2021). Be aware of the setting in which the suffix is being used. The suffix *paresis* may be found in medical reports for individuals or in clinical settings, while in schools and communities the typical suffix used is *-plegia*. The following are explanations of common terms.

• *Hemiplegia and hemiparesis: Hemi* means half. Children with hemiplegia have a brain impairment that affects movement on one side of their body. Physical educators will hear a term like *right-sided hemiplegia*. In this case, the involvement is on the right side of the body and is affecting that side's leg, arm, and some of the trunk. These students have various degrees of involvement in the affected areas (figure 12.5).

Children and youth who have spastic cerebral palsy and are hemiplegic find tasks difficult if they require that both sides of the body work together to perform a task. These activities include writing, self-care (such as dressing and grooming), catching balls, grasping a parachute, and more.

The clinical treatments sometimes recommended for these children are to wear splints or braces to stretch the muscles and or improve the function of the arm and hands. Sometimes, they have injections to reduce the muscle tightness in specific muscles. They may take some medicines to manage seizures.

• *Diplegia and diparesis: Di* means two in Latin. The impairment is primarily in both legs, and sometimes there is slight involvement in the arms. In clinical terms, this is referred to as spastic diplegia.

• *Quadriplegia and quadriparesis: Quad* means four. In quadriplegia, movement is affected in all four limbs. The muscles of the neck, face, mouth, and throat can also be affected.

Characteristics of spastic cerebral palsy include

• persistent and increased hypertense muscle tone;

• movement that is usually restricted, jerky, and uncertain, with inconsistent control; and

• limbs that respond to the slightest stimulation.

Terminology used in reports and in discussions can include all the aforementioned areas. In the end, though, the physical educator wants to see the child, know the child, engage them in movement, and refer to the student by name and not the diagnosis.

People who have spastic cerebral palsy have increased muscle tone (hypertonia) resulting in muscles that are stiff. Various parts of the body can be affected as follows:

• *Spastic diplegia or diparesis:* Muscle stiffness in the legs (some in the arms) that makes it difficult to walk. This results in what is termed a scissors gait (figure 12.6). Note some arm involvement in this figure.

• *Spastic hemiplegia or hemiparesis:* This involvement is seen on one side of the body (figure 12.5).

FIGURE 12.5   The walking pattern of a person with a right-sided hemiplegia.

FIGURE 12.6   Typical scissors gait of an individual with spastic cerebral palsy.

- *Spastic quadriplegia or quadriparesis:* This type of cerebral palsy can often be the most severe type because it affects all four limbs. The student usually cannot walk and uses a wheelchair for locomotion (figure 12.1).

Dyskinetic Cerebral Palsy

This type of cerebral palsy was formerly referred to as athetoid. But now according to the CDC (2020c), athetoid cerebral palsy has been subsumed under the larger category, *dyskinetic.* Also included under dyskinetic cerebral palsy are choreoathetoid and dystonic cerebral palsy. Dyskinetic cerebral palsy is complex, and the CDC is only now parsing out its definition. Again, we can leave these subtle aspects of diagnosis to the clinical diagnosticians. But it is important for the physical educator (APE or GPE) to understand what they are observing with the student with cerebral palsy. The overarching type of cerebral palsy has ramifications for the physical education program participation.

The prominent feature of dyskinetic cerebral palsy is the predominance of uncontrolled movement that is either writhing or rapid and jerky. The muscle tone can change from day to day and within a single day, from lax tone to very high tone. A student with dyskinetic cerebral palsy may also have facial grimacing, difficulty with head control, and difficulty controlling salivation. The lack of head control affects perception and accuracy in physical activity.

The student also has difficulty speaking. The speech and language pathologist (SLP) provides strategies for communication in the classroom, which need to be carried into the physical activity settings.

Ataxic Cerebral Palsy

Students with ataxic cerebral palsy have severe balance and coordination problems. This type of cerebral palsy is rare. These students are unsteady when they walk, find quick movements difficult, and have problems in controlling hands and arms when reaching. They are also hypotonic, having very lax muscle tone. These children and youth often use walkers or wheelchairs for locomotion. Their fine motor skills are challenged, which means that some of the object control skills will need input from the occupational therapist for the physical education class. From a gross motor aspect, they often move too far or not far enough in executing a required movement.

Spina Bifida

Spina bifida is a neural tube defect (CDC, 2020d). In the developing fetus, the neural tube encases the spinal cord as development progresses. In the United States, 1 in 1,427 babies born in a year is born with spina bifida (CDC, 2020d). When development goes awry resulting in spina bifida (SB), the neural tube doesn't enclose completely, and the spinal cord and the nerves are damaged (figure 12.2). The severity is dependent on location and the size of the opening on the spine and whether the spinal cord and the nerves are affected (CDC, 2020d). Depending on this damage, intellectual and physical disability are possible. Due to the initiation of folic acid intake among women of childbearing age in the United States, there was a reported reduction of at least 1,300 babies born around 2011 without SB (Williams et al., 2015). This number was reported after initiation of the use of folic acid intake during pregnancy and statistically calculated for woman at risk for having a baby with SB.

Three diagnostic classifications of the most common forms of SB are listed in terms of order of their severity. Diagnosis is made at birth for myelomeningocele and meningocele due to the visible nature of the opening and the bulge of the sac. Diagnostic classifications include the following:

- *Myelomeningocele:* This is pronounced *my-low-ma-nin-jo-seal.* It involves an opening in the baby's back that contains a sac of fluid with a damaged spinal cord and damaged nerves.
- *Meningocele:* This is pronounced *ma-nin-jo-seal.* It involves a bulge caused by a sac of fluids, but there is no spinal cord in the bulge.
- *Spina bifida occulta:* This features a small gap in the spine with no opening of the skin, therefore it is not visible to the naked eye and is often diagnosed later in childhood or in adulthood.

Open spina bifida is another term for myelomeningocele and can be surgically corrected before the baby is born, if a specialty surgical team is available (CDC, 2020d). More adults than children now live with SB in the United States, most likely due to increased prevention initiatives particularly with increasing folic acid intake during a pregnancy or while a woman is expecting to become pregnant. The CDC now recommends childbearing women to consume daily 400 mcg of folic acid and add iron-rich foods to the diet (2020d). Other risk factors leading to SB are obesity and diabetes. Pregnant women are also to avoid overheating (e.g., hot tubs and saunas).

The multidisciplinary model is highly recommended to medically manage individuals with SB (Thibadeau et al., 2020). The multidisciplinary model

> . . . utilizes skills and experience from practitioners belonging to various disciplines, each treating patients from a specific clinical perspective. The Spina Bifida Association (SBA) supports and recommends that clinical care for people with SB be provided in specialty clinics of which the MCM [multidisciplinary model] is an example; that care be coordinated; and that there be a plan for transitional care.
>
> Thibadeau et al. (2020, p. 100,883).

Transitional care is care from childhood to adulthood. The greatest focus is to be on children in pediatric care.

Spinal Cord Injury

Spinal cord injury (SCI) can be to vertebrae, ligaments, or disks of the spinal column; and to the spinal cord (Mayo Clinic, 2020). *Low typical* is the lowest typical place on the spinal cord (e.g., C4, T5). *Severity* is the completeness of the injury. With a complete injury to the spinal cord, there is no feeling or movement control below that level of the injury. If there is feeling and movement below the level of injury, then the injury is incomplete. The neurological level and completeness of the injury is conducted by the individual's health care team.

Spinal cord injuries have a clinical basis in terms of diagnosis and how impactful the trauma is on the neurologic capabilities. These neurologic capabilities translate into movement potential and are part of classifying individuals for elite sports (chapter 16) and leisure pursuits with a competitive recreational focus (chapter 14).

The clinical team for those with spinal cord injuries includes the orthopedic surgeon, or physiatrist from a rehabilitation program, who evaluates movement paralysis. The physical and occupational therapists focus on functional skills of movement by age-appropriate activities beginning early in life

and extending to old age. Engagement with these clinical people is episodic. When the child begins school, the adapted physical educator observes and conducts assessments given the curriculum. As the student begins the transitional individualized education programs (IEPs) in high school, the physical activity interests of the student and their community resources account for their physical education goals. The adapted physical educator can consult with the school physical therapist and occupational therapists to provide adaptations to movement performance or modifications to the curriculum, avoiding assumptions that a student could perform a movement if they tried harder.

The understanding of how an SCI affects movement performance is complex. From a clinical standpoint, the following are considered:

- The areas of injury in the spine
- Whether the nerve roots have been damaged, and whether the cord is intact
- Whether the head was concussed, resulting in cognitive impairment
- Whether the eyes were damaged, resulting in impaired vision
- Whether there are problems affecting bowel and bladder function

Spinal cord injuries and spina bifida are similar in that both involve a lesion in the spinal cord that cause a paralysis of the limbs. Paralysis levels are the following:

- *Quadriplegia:* This involves a loss of sensation and movement in the four limbs of the body plus the trunk. This is usually from an injury at T1 or above.
- *Paraplegia:* This involves a loss of sensation and movement in two sides of the body, often at T1 or below.
- *Triplegia:* This involves a loss of sensation and movement in one arm and both legs. It is often caused by incomplete SCI.

Traumatic Brain Injury

Traumatic brain injury (TBI) has a range from mild to severe. If the status is mild, there is no rehabilitation program referral for the individual from the hospital. This person still needs to be watched and followed by clinical personnel. Those with a severe TBI will be referred from the hospital to a rehabilitation program before returning to home. TBI and orthopedic injuries can occur together for the same individual and require family support for the individual to recover well-brain function (Narad et al., 2017). This includes a combination of TBI and SCI.

Instructional Considerations

Sensitivity to the student with orthopedic impairments or traumatic brain injuries includes the reality that for some of the students, their emotional well-being is challenged in the school setting. They can experience social rejection or excessive sympathy because of their motor difficulties, communication differences, and appearance. With a proper atmosphere of acceptance, these students have a better chance of developing good self-concept and feelings of adequacy. For example, we met a young man with spastic cerebral palsy who is an engineer in a large federal agency. He is married, known among his colleagues for competent work and a great sense of humor. His birth was in the very early days of special education, and he did not have early childhood services. Yet, his parents were known to be supportive of him from a young age, including him in all family and community life. His parents most likely impressed the same upon the teachers to enable them to extend positive regard and to adapt what was needed for him to be successful in his educational pursuits.

Cerebral Palsy Terminology

Clinical terminology abounds when working with students with cerebral palsy. As a member of the educational team, the physical educator will hear this terminology and can incorporate this knowledge into the physical education activities. Clinical terminology can be used in reports by occupational and physical therapy, as well as speech and language pathology. (Muscles are involved in vocalizing, and the impairment affects some students' production of speech.) The student and their family have most likely worked with clinical specialists including pediatric neurologists, orthopedists, rehabilitation medicine physicians (physiatrists), nurses, an audiologist, an adaptive equipment specialist, a child psychologist, a social worker, and more. There are clinical terms for the tone of the muscles and the movement patterns. Diagnostic terms for the classification of cerebral palsy reference the parts of the body involved. All the terms are used at times when working with the student who has cerebral palsy.

To assist the physical educator with clinical terminology and aid in an understanding of the atypical movements seen in cerebral palsy, the following is presented based on CDC (2020c) information.

Atypical Muscle Tone Terms

- *Spasticity:* This describes muscles that are extremely tight, resist movement, and tend to spasm. A spasm is a sustained muscle contraction or a sudden movement seen in the student (e.g., an arm thrusts out, a head jerk to the side). This tightness typically increases when the student tries to move quickly (e.g., go quickly from A to B) or is moved too quickly by someone else.
- *Hypertonic:* Spastic muscle tone is also referred to as hypertonic because of the high tone in the muscles.
- *Hypotonia: Hypo* means low. *Hypotonic* means low muscle tone with arms and legs that seem floppy.
- *Rigidity:* The muscles are extremely tight whether the child is moving quickly or slowly.

Involuntary Movement Terms

- *Ataxia:* The movement results in an unbalanced way of walking, which looks unsteady and with shaky movements and tremors.
- *Dyskinetic:* All over the body, the movement is slow with uncontrolled writhing extra movements. These writhing movements are not like those seen in a seizure but rather a continuous movement of the body that is uncontrolled. Some describe this as looking like a butterfly dance. The student exhibits this involuntary movement at rest, and this also increases when a student attempts to move. When moving from point A to B, the movement pattern is as described.
- *Dystonia:* Muscles sustain an involuntary contraction. This results in a twist or a repetition of atypical postures.

Hospitalization and IEP

What happens when a student with an orthopedic impairment is hospitalized? By federal educational law IDEA (2004), they are to have access to special education if they are on an IEP. They may have been on an IEP before they entered the hospital, or they may be placed on one because of their health problems. The category of other health impairment of federal educational law may be applied. If they are not able to qualify under that category, they may qualify under Section 504 of the Rehabilitation Act of 1972. But what is more likely is that the child will be served by physical therapy in the hospital. The extension of physical therapy programs will be transferred to the home-visiting team or to the school physical therapist. The physical educator will then coordinate any new information into the child's IEP.

Concerns regarding the transition back into school after hospitalization should be addressed in the IEP meeting, at which time parental input can be obtained. Physical therapy (PT) is most likely involved with the transition back to the school. Occupational therapy (OT) is also involved in many cases. The general physical educator, the adapted physical educator, and the PT must coordinate medical information into adapted physical education.

Assistive Devices

Students with cerebral palsy and those with spina bifida often use assistive devices to support their gross motor movement. For example, a common support for students with classifications of cerebral palsy is a plastic ankle–foot orthosis. These are inserted into a shoe for land-based physical activity and removed for swimming. Children who use an ankle–foot orthosis can also use mobility devices like the forearm support crutch. Some physical education equipment can be attached to both a crutch and the walkers and wheelchairs used in the PE class. Sometimes the students are physically in and out of these supports in the physical education classes depending on the activity.

The physical educator and the paraprofessional need to know how and when these supports are used, as well as how the student moves in and out of the wheelchair. Most adapted physical educators are experts in these areas. PTs are often eager to educate teachers and family members about these transfer skills. With wheelchairs, there may be straps needing adjustment, enabling the student to be in the wheelchair with maximum support for an activity. If needed, OT and PT can consult on wheelchair use and positions for activities. Adapted tricycles and bicycles are used by children with cerebral palsy, as are scooter boards with longer lengths that enable a child to get out of a wheelchair or away from the walker to participate in an activity within a class.

Wheelchair User Fitness Levels

The fitness level of individuals in wheelchairs is generally low and often attributed, in part, to the unnec-

essary activity restrictions for and by those who use wheelchairs (Hansen et al., 2021). There are physical barriers as well as interpersonal barriers whereby lack of confidence or knowledge can severely hamper a person's participation. Hansen and colleagues found that those that who finished high school and were not obese where more physically active in their community (2021). Exercise programs can be geared to improving the fitness level of the individual, as well as their functional independence. The activities to include in the program vary according to the level of functional skills of the individual.

With young children in physical education, the medical specialist's information will help the physical educator understand what to engage the student in within the physical education curriculum, when modifications are needed, and when an activity needs adaptations. The educational physical and occupational therapist can assess based on the curriculum of the student and provide support for participation in the physical education program. For example, if a student cannot engage in a volleyball unit because of quadriplegia, then curriculum modification is recommended.

Transitional IEP

When working with the transition programs of the IEP, teachers can use resources and NCHPAD recommendations for adults starting an exercise program. The NCHPAD recommends choosing a facility that is staffed with personnel knowledgeable about physical activity from a wheelchair (NCHPAD, 2020a).

Precautions for Students With Spina Bifida

The protrusion of the spinal cord creates complications for the flow of the cerebrospinal fluid that requires a shunt. According to the Spina Bifida Association (2023b), with excess of flow of fluid to the head, the head enlarges, and during a surgical procedure a shunt is placed to drain the fluid, emptying into the abdomen, to prevent brain damage. Participation in physical activity must consider the sensitivity to the shunt area in the head. Confer with the family about any restrictions, like with swimming activity.

The student with spina bifida likely has typical intelligence and exceeds in verbal intelligence quotient test items (CDC, 2013). The verbal intelligence quotient has been predictive of academic performance over other aspects of intelligence quotient testing. Some students with SB have difficulty with perceptual motor skill, can be hyperactive, and find sequencing and memory challenging for them. They can also start a growth spurt early, which then levels off. Many children with spina bifida are of short stature. Students with spina bifida may start puberty early and be misjudged for being older than they are. If needed, Spina Bifida Association has resources on intimate relationships (2023c, 2023d) that could be useful with this early maturity.

Bowel and bladder control are addressed before the child enters school, with clinical training of the child in clean intermittent catheterization to help completely empty the bladder. The procedure is described in detail for both boys and girls on the website of the American Academy of Pediatrics noted in the references list. There is information on the academy's website on how to deal with going to camp and on overnight outings for older children (AAP, n.d.). The emphasis is to be prepared with necessary supplies, have the privacy that is needed, and conduct all the procedures with good hygiene. Before going on outings, students are encouraged to find assistance if they need it by alerting a friend or an adult on how they can help. The APE and GPE teachers will work closely with the student and the family to handle these issues on an individual basis. Every effort must be made to respect their needs while engaging the student fully in age-appropriate physical activity.

The NCHPAD (n.d.c) encourages people with spina bifida to monitor their urinary cycle and empty their bladder *before* exercise. Thermoregulation difficulties make it imperative that individuals with spina bifida wear appropriate exercise clothing for the weather and drink fluids as necessary. Those with spina bifida need to check the skin for pressure sores when engaged in wheelchair sports and regularly perform wheelchair pushups to alleviate pressure from sitting (while sitting in their chair, they raise themselves up for a few seconds). Trained individuals assist individuals with spina bifida for transfers from the wheelchair to accessible exercise machines. Stretching spastic muscle groups is recommended to avoid increasing an excessive spastic condition. If swelling occurs in feet and legs, elevated the legs. If this swelling persists, see a doctor.

The Spina Bifida Association (2023a) estimates that more than 73 percent of those with spina bifida have latex allergies. They should avoid latex products from birth and instead use items made from silicone, plastic, nitrile, or vinyl. In physical education classes, this includes balls, bungee cords, play pits, balloons, playground surfaces, toys, water

toys, beach caps, goggles, and zippered storage bags or other plastic bags (plastic and PVC are okay as is nylon swimwear). An allergic reaction to latex consists of watery or itchy eyes, wheezing, hives, flushing or a skin rash, itching, or swelling. In severe reactions, the person goes into anaphylactic shock, where breathing becomes difficult, and the throat and tongue become swollen. Students who are allergic are encouraged to wear a medical alert bracelet, and the family needs to make clear the arrangements for medical assistance. The student's doctor can be consulted about injectable epinephrine that is made available in all environments (e.g., at school, at home, in vehicles, and at childcare facilities).

Precautions for Students With Spinal Cord Injury (SCI)

Instructors should be sensitive to the reality that the interruption in communication between the body and the brain may affect the ability of the individual with an SCI to adjust to changes in blood pressure and heart rate during exercise. Careful observation of the student is recommended, as well as assisting the student in recognizing the need to pace in a physical activity.

The NCHPAD (n.d.a) recommends that the individual with an SCI stay hydrated, change positions slowly, and, if necessary, wear compression stockings to encourage more typical circulation of the blood throughout the body. Skin integrity is challenged when the sensations of pain are disrupted by an SCI. Therefore, skin breakdown can occur in areas subjected to prolonged pressure (e.g., hips, heels, and tailbone). Hypotension, or lowered blood pressure, can cause dizziness or light-headedness during exercise in the individual with an SCI; this is referred to as orthostatic hypotension. Some individuals with an SCI also have respiratory involvement, which makes them at risk for infections, congestion, and either shortness of breath or rapid breathing. The physical educator can obtain information on these and other conditions from the family and clinical personnel, physical therapist, or speech therapist. Thus appropriate exercise exertion happens without causing the individual distress, and it is known what actions to take if the individual is in distress.

Precautions for Students With TBI

For children with a TBI, the overall engagement in GPE is individualized based on the assessments from the IEP team. The adapted physical education teacher (APE) and the PT and OT are key members contributing to understand the IEP in physical education placement and content.

Functional assessments for curriculum activity contribute to engaging the student in their physical education classes (see chapter 6). The adapted physical educator assesses and the IEP team members of occupational and physical therapy contribute their expertise. Each student is unique. Given these assessments, modifications to curriculum and adaptations to activities are arranged. Younger children enter the movement skill development activities and age-appropriate games. Adapted activities such as swimming, bowling, and stationary biking (in various forms) are considered for youth and their transitional IEP considerations.

The brain can take its time recovering as the individual works with specialists and gets involved in their life again. The recovery of language and cognition takes time, as does concentration, communication, and memory. In a hospital setting, youth sometimes sit endlessly crying out for something and seemly inconsolable. Months later they are walking down the hall of the rehab unit, nodding pleasantly to staff, pleased to be leaving with bags over the shoulder and headed to the exit!

Program Placement and Focus

Some orthopedic disabilities are obvious at birth, and infants with those disabilities can begin early intervention. Their early movement skills are delayed because the disability gets in the way of execution of skills. For example, maybe there is too much or too little tone in the muscles. The infant may try to go across the floor space but can't move in the desired direction. With early intervention, pediatric PTs and OTs work with infants and children and the family to arrange environments for play that offer opportunities for learning and practice. When children with orthopedic disabilities enter kindergarten, the educational system takes over services with combined school-based OT and PT, and physical educators engage the student in physical activity and a multitude of environments.

A student returning to school after hospitalization with an orthopedic impairment may display no apparent aftereffect; others may exhibit a mild or severe movement disorder. Although there may be no visible debility, the physical educator should receive medical recommendations as to the amount of activity in which the student should engage, the kinds of activities that will prove most beneficial, and those that should be monitored carefully. With this knowledge, the adapted physical educator and general physical educator will be able to plan the kind of program that will help students increase their general level of fitness and motor efficiency to meet the physical demands of daily life. They can also seek input from PT and OT.

The returning student who has a moderate or severe disability may need considerable help in achieving maximum physical efficiency. Students who have considerable residual paralysis or a limb amputation are also likely to need help in making a satisfactory adjustment to their disability. Because of their possible concern about their appearance and their inabilities to perform motor skills, they may experience more anxieties about physical education class than about other phases of their school life. The physical educator can help alleviate their fears by assisting them to find a solution that is satisfying to them concerning dressing and showering in the presence of others, and by preparing them to meet the challenges of their restrictions.

Instructional Strategies

Many students with orthopedic impairment achieve a high level of motor efficiency in physical education. Special instruction for them may need only to be directed toward refinement of movement patterns and the introduction of new skills. Other youngsters, however, require the same kinds of physical education programming considerations as those with recently acquired orthopedic disabilities.

Students With Cerebral Palsy

The greatest shift in understanding and working with children and youth with cerebral palsy is the focus on function: What is the child's ability? And what functions are expected of this student for their age? Enormous efforts by a cadre of clinicians have produced easy-to-use assessments on functional ability (Rosenbaum et al., 2002), and families and children have benefited from the positive therapeutic approach. This approach is making its way into the educational setting and matches well the spirit of federal education law that espouses the least restrictive environment for learning (IDEA, 2004).

Because the student with spastic cerebral palsy may also have an intellectual disability, chapter 7 on intellectual disability can be referenced for teaching strategies.

The student with spastic CP will need adaptations when learning and executing a movement skill and when using skills in games, sports, and fitness activities. The students may walk with a scissors gait (figure 12.5). Running is difficult but not impossible. Activities requiring *great* agility and *fast-moving actions* performed in competition with typically developing children are to be avoided. Although our students in these photos would probably disagree! Noncompetitive activity and running around is fine.

The occupational therapist can suggest modifications for activities like throwing and catching, where grip is necessary. Sometimes, the body must be stabilized on the opposite side for the child to gain some control to execute the skill performance. Also, the physical therapist may have some helpful modifications to address motor planning in physical education. Sometimes, the student with dyskinetic cerebral palsy needs frequent rest. Their energy output may be greater than would typically be expected.

Jerry Holt/Star Tribune via Getty Images

In the learning of fundamental skills like grasping, the adapted physical education teacher or the general physical education teacher may need to use accessories with the equipment like clips, hook-and-loop fasteners, and tape. Here are more adaptations that assist in engaging the student in physical activities:

• *Equipment:* Use a larger or lighter bat, a larger goal or target, and scoops for catching; mark positions on the playing field; lower the goal or target; and vary the size, weight, color, and texture of the balls.

• *Rules prompts and cues:* Demonstrate the activity, provide partner assistance, disregard time limits, use oral prompts, arrange for more space between students, eliminate outs or strikeouts, allow the ball to remain stationary (versus a moving ball coming toward the student), allow the batter to sit in a chair, and place the student with disability near the teacher.

• *Boundaries and playing field:* Decrease distances, use well-defined boundaries, simplify patterns, and adapt the playing area by removing obstacles and making the field or court smaller.

• *Actions:* Change locomotor patterns, modify grasps, modify body positions, reduce the number of actions, and use different body parts.

• *Time:* Vary the tempo, slow the activity pace, lengthen the time, shorten the time, and provide frequent rest periods.

Physical activities for older students should continue to view the present with the future in mind. We want to know what types of activities this student wants to learn, leading them to being physically active as they leave high school. What adaptations are required for participation? Here is a list of some adaptations needed for age-appropriate activity in high school:

• *Bowling:* Reduce the number of steps; have the student use two hands instead of one, have them remain in a stationary position or use a ramp (this is attached to a wheelchair to improve accuracy of the ball as it moves to the pins, see chapter 15), have the student use a partner, and give students continuous verbal cues.

• *Basketball:* Use various balls (differing in size, weight, texture, and color), allow traveling, allow two-handed dribbling, disregard the three-second lane violation, use a larger or lower goal, slow the pace especially when first learning. If a student uses a wheelchair, allow him to hold the ball on his lap while pushing the wheelchair.

- *Softball:* Use hook-and-loop balls and mitts, use larger or smaller bats, use a batting tee, reduce the distance between bases, use training baseballs or softballs, and shorten the pitching distance. If an individual is in a wheelchair, allow them to push the ball off a ramp, off their lap, or from tee. Provide a peer to assist. Players without disabilities play regular-depth defense. Students without disabilities count to 10 before tagging out the person with disability.

Spastic Cerebral Palsy

When using the teaching strategy of physically assisting a student with spastic cerebral palsy through a skill (e.g., throwing), a different approach is required. The muscles of a student with spastic cerebral palsy atypically contract with sudden touch. A sudden unexpected movement of a limb can result in a sudden contraction followed by repeated jerks (this is called clonus). Instead, instructors need to use a gentle, slow movement of the limb. Both the physical educator and the paraprofessionals in the physical activity program must use this strategy when providing a physical assistance.

For some students, external stimuli must be controlled. Loud noises and sudden movements will cause the student to become tense and go into extension, with their legs and arms rigidly extended and their head back. If the student has gone into extension, he or she can return to a less hypertonic state given time and gentle touch. When instructing, it helps to focus on continuously repeated movements, which are easier to perform for those with spasticity in their muscles.

Any child with cerebral palsy must be exposed to learning the fundamental movement skills and the games of young children, typically with modifications. The curriculum must be analyzed to determine what activities are appropriate for the student's physical education program. Input on which activities to include in the IEP comes from the IEP team, the parent, and, if appropriate, the student. The IEP team can assist with input for participation on a case-by-case basis and an activity-by-activity basis. See figure 12.7 for an example of a tag game with options for adaptations listed for equipment, rules, environment, and instruction. When this checklist is completed, it will look different even if two children share the same diagnosis. The Lieberman and Houston-Wilson handbook (2018) is a resource for any child, especially for the student with cerebral palsy who wants to be involved in the activity.

An assessment of the student's home community is important, too. Do they live near a swimming

Tag Game Modifications and Adaptations

Equipment	Rules	Environment	Instruction
— Poly spots	— Have spots on floor	— Constant movement	— Make student calm self before starting
— Soft, long objects	— Must use soft object	— Bright boundaries	— Peer tutoring
— Time-out chair	— Same locomotor activity	— Rough boundaries	— "It" students do different skill
— Pinnies	— Use first names	— Check understanding	— Direct
— Scarves	— Everybody is "it"	— Big smile to class	— Indirect
— Sponge balls	— Steal teammates' scarves	— Ice arena	— Small group
— Cones	— If tagged, 5 push-ups	— Mats	— Physical assistance
— Whistle	— Gender rule	— Flat surface	— Feedback
— Carpet squares	— Touch rule	— Mirrors	— Positive role model
— Scooters	— Bumpers up	— Remove leg rest	— Demonstration
— Radio	— Airplane space	— Large area	— Verbal cues
— Hula hoops	— Partner tag	— Boundaries	— Brailling assistance
— Pillow polo stick	— Animal walk	— Circles	— Nonverbal cues
— Bean bags	— 10-second rule	— Lines	— Quality movement
— Hard scarves	— Start/stop signal	— Music	— Stress cooperation
— Different size balls	— Activity book	— Smaller lines	— Instruction feedback
— Bright color objects	— After tag do a skill	— Smaller distance	— Proximity
— Tagging objects	— More than 1 person	— Flags	— Verbal cues
— Wands	— Practice moving safely	— Safety zone	— Peer runners
— Nerf balls	— Use soft stick to tag	— Goals	— Command style
— Tape	— Clap 4 times then run	— Groups for tag	— No time factor
— Wiffle balls	— Partner is "it"	— Uncluttered	— Task analyze
	— Walk, no running	— No confusing sounds	— Speak naturally
	— Tag on body parts	— Good lighting	— Braille tags
	— Blindfold partner	— Level surface	— Preorient child
	— Change locomotion	— Large movement	— Utilize all senses
	— Run on balls of feet	— Movement friendly	— Guided discovery
	— Tag softly	— Outside on grass	
	— Don't throw at face	— Cooperative	
	— Freeze when tagged		
	— Follow the leader		

FIGURE 12.7   Considerations for modification and adaptation in low-organized and tag games.

Reprinted by permission from L.J. Lieberman and C. Houston-Wilson, *Strategies for INCLUSION: A Handbook for Physical Educators* (Champaign, IL: Human Kinetics, 2009).

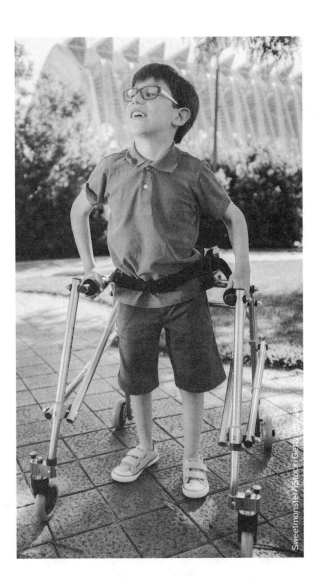

Sweetmonster/iStock/Getty Images

pool? Do they like wheelchair sports? Does their community have sponsorship of adapted sport teams? This analysis keeps the program functional for the student as they enter high school and the transitional IEP begins. In many cases, a modification of the equipment will enable participation in physical activity. Physical therapists who provide clinical care for the student outside of the school program are often available to help the physical education teacher design modifications for games and sport participation. To contact them, parental permission is usually required. Often, these physical and occupational therapists have worked with a child for years and know the child and family well.

Dyskinetic Cerebral Palsy

The student with dyskinetic cerebral palsy may be using a wheelchair for mobility. Motor planning is a challenge for these students. When movement is executed, the body has a great amount of over-

flow. In attempting voluntary movements (e.g., picking something up, striking an object, and finding their place on the floor), they overshoot or undershoot the target. The student requires many attempts and lots of time in an activity of kicking a ball. If target accuracy is expected, provide extra time and a relaxing atmosphere, and increase the target size.

Ataxic Cerebral Palsy

A child with ataxic CP will present with uncoordinated jerky movements. These are not the movements of spastic CP. If the young child with ataxic cerebral palsy is in an inclusive setting, they will benefit from trying all the fundamental skills and participating with adaptations in games. Partnering with an older student or with an age peer may be fun for the child. The child should be encouraged to participate as much as they can. Adults should avoid doing activities for the child in physical education. These young children will often be receiving therapeutic support in clinical settings outside of the school setting. So, the opportunity to play and have some fun with peers is a plus for them in physical education. It is important to remember that physical education is *not* therapy. It is an academic area.

Students With Spina Bifida

The activity guidelines from the Spina Bifida Association (2023a) for children are part of meeting the intentions of best practice in adapted physical activity. Parents and caregivers should be informed, work together with medical personnel as well as the school and coaches, to facilitate participation for their child that is safe and enjoyable. This is the recommended guideline summary:

- Use appropriate assessments to identify medical risks and select modifications to ensure participation.
- Use activity adaptations to minimize risk and promote safety.
- Take precautions when children with shunts and ambulatory limitations are being active.
- Balance their involvement with the child's need for independence when they participate in physical activity.
- Use PTs and OTs to ensure fitting mobility equipment to maximize physical activity participation.
- Work with the children to address personal barriers such as bowel and bladder care,

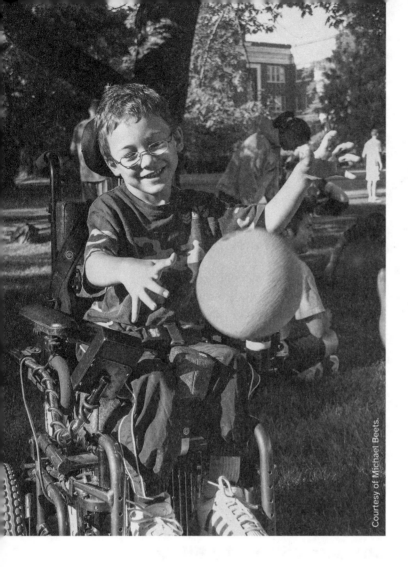

Courtesy of Michael Beets.

medical events, assistive devices, and environmental factors.

- Encourage parents and caregivers to advocate for physical activity goals to be added to their child's IEP or Section 504 plan.

The kinds of motor activities chosen for those with spinal injuries, including spina bifida, depend on the severity and level of the lesion. The physical educator will need to assess the movement potential of each student, utilizing knowledge of the level of injury and the resulting paralysis, and observing the student moving plus working with OT and PT. The physical educator must attend to the ways in which the student manages their body to perform daily routines.

Overall, the children and youth with spina bifida are to exercise like their peers without SB, following recommendations to be physically active daily, including aerobic fitness and skills development for inclusion in their class at school with their IEP developed and carried out (Spina Bifida Association, 2018). NCHPAD endorses the importance of being physically active and has a teen video of an exercise class, Teens on the Move (n.d.f).

Physical Activities

The activities of the program for those with orthopedic disabilities will be determined by the nature and extent of the impairment and general ability. The student with a disability should be included in the activities of the general physical education classes, allowing for inclusion. The IEP team makes the decisions as the student progresses in the educational system.

"Life on Wheels" (NCHPAD, n.d.b) is a resource on exercise in general and working out for those who use wheelchairs for physical activity. For school age, this resource applies to teens as well as the transitional IEP preparation into community facilities. NCHPAD, in cooperation with Beneficial Designs, Inc., also produced *Discover Accessible Fitness: A Wheelchair User's Guide to Using Fitness Equipment* (2014).

Students With Cerebral Palsy

The older student with spastic cerebral palsy must be involved in physical activities that are age appropriate. Even when the student has an intellectual disability, their program must be age appropriate. Swimming, soccer, bowling, bocci, and cycling are age-appropriate and have potential for the pursuit of lifelong leisure activities. Many of these activities will be of interest to the student and their family and match their community resources. If recreational therapists are hired in the school district, they can assess the leisure interests of the student for use in the transitional IEP. Physical educators can also create lists of leisure activities found in their community and use them as a checklist with the student to build the student's physical activity knowledge and skill.

Knowing the resources in the community helps the physical educator train the student in the physical education class and points the family to community engagement opportunities for their child. For example, in Minnesota, there is an active group of physical educators and other volunteers that work to enable youth to participate in Adapted Athletic Programs-Minnesota High School League. Competitions are held in the fall for soccer, in the spring for softball and bowling, and for floor hockey in the winter.

Those with spasticity ought to engage in range-of-motion (ROM) exercises because the spasticity in their muscles can lead to rigid joints. An adult may move them through the range. The exercises involve moving the body through its typical range. For an example, an arm is moved gently and

American Association of Adapted Sports Programs

For children and youth with physical disabilities (e.g., cerebral palsy, spina bifida, spinal cord injury, sensory impairment) the American Association of Adapted Sports Programs (AAASP, n.d.) is an active group in interscholastic adapted sport that sponsors programs in extracurricular adapted athletics cooperating with the states' education services throughout the country (local education agencies, state high school associations, state departments of education). This group's website has detailed information on their programs and program development with downloads for coaching and ball skills and wheelchair use for sports. Competition sports are wheelchair basketball, football, track and field, hockey, and, for those with sensory impairment, beepball.

slowly through its range of up, out, backward, forward, and down. Often, the physical therapist is consulted for demonstration of these exercises. Both the student and whomever does the ROM exercises with the student benefit from these demonstrations. The physical therapist might work with the student toward independence in moving in an appropriate range. As they get older, students may do these exercises as preparatory to sport participation or as a part of a fitness program or in a group home setting. Avoiding range-of-motion exercises results in development of contractures, so moving becomes painful for their body. This begins to restrict students' overall activity participation.

Weightlifting is a great, popular age-appropriate activity for teenaged boys and girls. The student with cerebral palsy can do this alongside their peers as everyone has different weightlifting programs in any give gym. The NCHPAD website (NCHPAD, 2023a) on weightlifting and resistance training notes that modes for resistance exercise consist of three general categories: free weights, portable equipment (i.e., elastic bands, tubing), and machines. For individuals with low levels of strength, gravity-resistant exercises may be what an individual can perform. Others can use more resistance. Here are some guidelines and advice from the NCHPAD (2023a, 2023b):

- Occasionally, the person may experience muscle spasms. These are often transient and should not present a problem in resistance training routines unless they are occurring often. They can often be stopped by gently placing the limb (arm or leg) in an extended position.

- Avoid quick movements that may increase spasticity or cause a muscle spasm. Use slow, controlled movements.

- High-intensity training is to be avoided in spastic muscle groups.

- When training spastic muscle groups, emphasize slow and fluid movements within the person's capability. Understand that it may be impossible for some clients to move the limb in a completely smooth fashion due to high levels of muscle tone.

- To improve or maintain muscle balance between flexors and extensors, strengthen muscle groups that oppose the spastic muscle. For example, if the biceps have a high level of spasticity, work on strengthening the triceps.

- Remember, tight muscle groups (spastic) are not necessarily strong and also need to be strengthened.

Additionally, pay attention to the position that the individual uses to perform the exercises. In many cases, seated may be better than supine positions. This lessens the difficulty in working against gravity, which is difficult for individuals with spastic cerebral palsy.

Swimming and bicycling are activities where students with dyskinetic cerebral palsy can succeed. These activities can be taught at younger ages and expanded in high school to leisure education in the community. Stationary biking is very popular in recreation centers and private clubs to promote cardiorespiratory fitness activity.

Swimming is also a wonderful activity for children with ataxic cerebral palsy. The water is buoyant and allows for much more freedom for the child compared to being on land. Students can practice walking in the water, which is a fitness activity for them. When they are surrounded by toys and others, being in the water can be social and fun. They may need flotation devices to help them in the water.

Activities that have been successfully taught to youth with ataxic cerebral palsy include bowling, table tennis, horseshoes, and, of course, swimming.

Students With Spina Bifida

The Spina Bifida Association (SBA, 2018) advocates the practical importance in fitness activity for individuals across the lifespan. For young children, physical fitness activities are those engaged in when they are playing games and playing in a neighborhood open space such as a park or playground. Specific activities in the physical education program for fitness for older students with spina bifida should be age appropriate. And with spina bifida, weight control and preventing deconditioning are important as the individual ages. Like their peers without spina bifida, engaging in physical activity contributes on many levels to healthy living.

SBA (2023b) recommends that the 2018 Physical Activity Guidelines (USDHHS, 2018) published by the U.S. government are for *all people*, including those with spina bifida, unless an activity is unsafe clinically. The physical activity guidelines for children ages 6 to 17 are stated:

- Children should engage in 60 minutes or more of physical activity each day.
- Aerobic activity should make up most of the youth's physical activity each day; vigorous-intensity aerobic activity should be done at least three days per week.
- Muscle strengthening activities should be done at least 3 days per week as part of the 60 or more minutes.
- Bone-strengthening activities should be done at least 3 days per week as part of the 60 or more minutes.

For younger children, catching and throwing games are easily devised; target games using beanbags are also readily developed. Bouncing balls off walls is another activity that is possible for a child in a chair. Even a game of modified handball is possible; the child bats the ball so that it returns to them or to a partner, who in turn bats it to the wall. A ball suspended from the ceiling with a heavy cord makes an excellent piece of equipment for teaching catching and throwing skills to the child who uses a wheelchair. In addition, the suspended ball can be used for various activities, such as throwing at a target drawn on a board or at empty milk cartons or plastic bottles standing on a table (Webster et al., 2001). After using the suspended ball, explore using an unsuspended one!

The child in a wheelchair can also take part in parachute play, including exchanging places with another player while the parachute is in the air by using wheeling in their chair for walking and running. The same substitution is possible in most basic skill games.

Older students can be offered many of the activities included in the general education program, with only such modifications as are necessitated by the need to remain in the chair. The top-down assessment approach is recommended (Burton & Miller, 1998). Given the curriculum, the physical educator can observe the individual in the activity and decide what, if any, modifications are needed to successfully engage in the activity. The way in which the skills are performed usually requires some adaptations; specific suggestions for these are made in the chapters on various activities, and Lieberman and Houston-Wilson (2002, 2018) have provided a good framework for making adaptations for many activities. Options for modifications of game regulations and equipment are identified. For example, the playing area for games and sports is usually reduced in size, playing equipment is lighter, and frequently the handles of rackets and mallets are extended to increase the range of the reach. In team games, the area that each player must cover is reduced, the assignment of duties is made based on the players' abilities, or two people (peers) with different abilities share an assignment. For rhythm and dance activities, the size of the formations is increased to accommodate the wheelchair in the maneuvers.

Swimming is an especially good activity for total physical conditioning. Students with bowel- or bladder-control problems prepare as planned in their IEP. Today some individuals use anal plugs for swimming only. For individuals with paraplegia, fitness is important to achieve and maintain. Activities that strengthen the arms and shoulder girdle are especially important because the continuous use of upper extremities with wheelchair use leads to muscle fatigue, which slows the movement down (Qi et al., 2021).

For individuals with paraplegia, weight training can be used to develop muscular strength. The NCHPAD (n.d.c) recommends strength training using free weights, weight machines, a medicine ball, a wall pulley, and exercise bands. Wheelchair push-ups can be performed beginning at 10 minutes each day and held for 30 to 60 seconds. The elbows must be bent slightly on the extension. Strength training is usually three days per week (in line with the SBA), and exercises should be varied to avoid overuse of the muscles.

Several organizations promote sport competition on local, national, and international levels for persons who have paraplegia and quadriplegia. Through the school physical education program, young athletes can be encouraged to compete in local events such as archery, bowling, basketball, table tennis, swimming, weightlifting, shooting, and tennis. More information can be found in chapter 15, Leisure Activity.

Students With SCI

It is important that the physical educator focus on the activities of physical education and avoid setting a one-to-one exercise program only. The individual with an SCI needs access to the general physical education curriculum to the extent possible. If the individual is interested, participation in community physical activity in recreation programs and specialized athletic competitions are often fun and help with fitness and self-esteem. Today, more competitive programs are available for individuals with spinal cord injuries. The activities of the exercise program depend on the level of functional ability. NCHPAD has listed their table of function (n.d.e). For those with access to equipment, rowing machines and treadmills adapted for wheelchairs are used. Muscle strength training and endurance exercises are also recommended by the NCHPAD. Here the individual increases the intensities of the weight to gain strength and varies the muscle groups trained to avoid overuse injuries. Lifting through the full range of movement is important even if physical assistance is necessary. Muscle endurance is measured by the number of times the individual can lift moderate weights. For the person who uses a wheelchair, this endurance is critical for health and mobility. Two pieces of equipment are used in weight workouts: the equalizer bars and a weight exercise machine. Easily transportable equipment includes elastic tubing, free weights, and weights attached with hook-and-loop fasteners to the wrists and ankles.

Flexibility is maintained by range-of-motion exercises and helps to protect the individual from pain or injury. It also enhances the integrity of the joint. If the student is interested in a competitive approach to activity outside of the school setting, coordination with community physical therapy can be facilitated by the family. Sports and recreation program involvement can be incorporated into the life of an individual with an SCI for physical and psychological well-being and considered in the transitional IEP, where PT can be involved too.

Athletes who compete in sports are classified by functional ability to create equity in the competition. The classification systems, or functional profiles, vary for different sports. Youth in high school can be introduced to these sports through their physical education program and in their transitional IEP goals. After they leave high school, they can participate in competitive athletic programs available for adults with spinal cord injuries, such as basketball, tennis, swimming, downhill skiing, and floor hockey. For recreational athletics, local city and county recreation departments should be contacted.

Assessment and Evaluation

Today, the functional assessment of those with cerebral palsy points to more accurate information on what the capabilities are for students now and

Athletic Inspiration

Athletes with injuries or disabilities can be invited to schools to talk with all students and demonstrate their skills. Often soldiers injured in the recent wars have been introduced to adapted sports through rehabilitation, with encouragement from their OT or PT. If they had been an athlete prior to their injury, they may be highly motivated to welcome sports into their life again, though some can be skeptical of participation. Since the Gulf Wars, Paralympics volleyball and basketball competitors had histories associated with injuries from their military combat. Testimonials abound on the Internet of the positive experience competitive sports, adding companionship and competition on the playing field.

Other testimonials come from athletes whose SCI was due to recklessness. Although talking to youth about this association with SCI might fall on deaf ears, it is a positive experience to share how someone's life turned around with involvement in sports after a tragic accident with involvement in sports.

as they grow and change (Eliasson et al., 2006; Rosenbaum et al., 2002). Functional assessment is also used for sport competition for athletes. This assessment equalizes the playing field so that athletes can play against those with a similar level of ability. Top-down assessment within the physical education curriculum is appropriate.

The Gross Motor Function Measure (GMFM) reflects research on the functional ability of children with cerebral palsy and tracks that function over time (Rosenbaum et al., 2002). These children are unique and most therapists like this tool because a child can be compared to themselves to check their basic functional ability, making sure it is stable and not slipping as the child grows. The whole tool is free, including scoring sheets and instructions, and housed at McMaster University in Canada under *CanChild* (GMFM, n.d.). This functional assessment is typically administered by the physical therapist with an evaluation shared with the IEP team, which may also assist in the adapted physical activity for children. This system has been expanded since the early days. The paper-and-pencil approach is the GMFM-88 and GMFM-66; an app is accessed on the CanChild website under GMFM (n.d.). Tabulated reference percentiles are also available for clinical use of the GMFM-66 (Hanna et al., 2008).

For assessing the use of hands, the Manual Ability Classification System (Eliasson et al., 2006) can be provided by the occupational therapist with recommendations for the physical educator. This classification can lead more easily to determine the skill adaptations for physical activity. For example, if a child is at level III because they do tasks slowly and handle the object with difficulty, the APE or GPE teacher and OT can adapt where necessary in a game that requires the use of balls and bats.

TBI

A student returning to school with a traumatic brain injury (TBI) needs an approach to functional assessment in physical education that acknowledges the transition from rehabilitation to school. Medical guidance and physical activity participation should have followed the student with their discharge plans. The parents should be contacted to obtain this information and solicited as a member of their child's IEP team regarding an adapted physical education. Since TBI encompasses language and cognitive function, the IEP team must discuss cognitive capacity with the school psychologist or other qualified professional. The SLP can assist in an understanding of communication skill for

the student. These levels of skill are worked into the IEP, and the APE day-to-day interactions will reflect these.

The APE program will need to protect the student from sustaining impact to the head, therefore some curriculum modifications will probably be made. It is advised to obtain interests that the student has for physical activity. For some children, they may just want to be back with their classmates. Or they might want to take it slowly back into PE. With that in mind, assessment of activity is a top-down approach: see how much of the activity the student can perform. Younger children will be learning their fundamental skills, older students more games and leisure physical activities. It's probably prudent not to try games with many players and lots of rules. Instead, find activity where frequent reminders and verbal cues are easy to impart and use some task analysis to teach skills. Other students in the class most likely can also benefit from this. Create places for them to repeat practice time. Some students do well with color-coding for activity. Use colored flags or place colored cards in cones to indicate a location for an activity. Instructions may need to be repeated over a unit's execution. Directions benefit from simplicity and brevity. A para trained in the specific needs of the student can be there for these prompts but needs to allow the student opportunity to be as independent as possible. The brain heals in time, but it takes time. Allow the student some RnR within the classes. If needed, create an assistant role for some of the activities of PE where there is proximity to a less active role. With all the instructional strategies, an educator needs to give the approaches time but be sensitive to the student who needs more direction or another plan. In this way, assessment flows into evaluation, and on into the physically active student who happened to have sustained a traumatic head injury.

Educational Health Care Providers

An orthopedic surgery residency is a most sought-after placement following medical school. A hundred people can apply for six openings in a residency program. Many of these women and men are themselves athletes with a lifetime of participation in sports as recreational or elite athletes. Physical therapists share a similar history and passion for exercise and graduate eager to begin working with individuals needing rehabilitation or school-based services under special education. As their training advances, orthopedists and physical therapists, along with their colleagues in occupational therapy, begin to identify pediatric, adolescent, adult, or geriatric subspecialties. There are also sub-specializations by anatomy: knees or hips, hands, arms or shoulders, backs, ankles and feet, and others. Some individuals go into acute care in the hospital; some enter rehabilitative medicine in clinics and inpatient units; and some enter private practice. These professionals do relish the fact that individuals with an orthopedic impairment can be assisted in becoming physically active and to enjoy their life.

In the educational settings, the pediatric professions of occupational therapy, physical therapy, speech and language pathology, and school nursing; the adapted physical educator and general physical educator; and the coaches are all focusing on engaging children and youth with orthopedic impairments in physical activity. They consult, teach, coach, direct, and provide the programs for physical activity engagement at school, in the community, and at home.

Summary

Orthopedic impairment includes cerebral palsy (CP) with three dominant types. Under IDEA (2004) orthopedic impairment also includes spinal cord injuries (SCI) and spina bifida. TBI is its own category under IDEA (2004). *Paraplegia* is the term used to identify an area of the body affected by CP. Cerebral palsy is a movement and motor disorder that does not paralyze the body so much as effect atypical movement patterns by lesions in the brain. With SCI, the impact of the spinal cord injury is observed across the body. Nerve distributions affect various parts of the body, and there is loss of function (paralysis). Persons with all these impairments and injuries benefit from engagement in physical activity for health, socialization, fitness, and enjoyment. Numerous examples of physical activity adaptations and program modifications are provided. The physical therapist, occupational therapist, and speech and language pathologist are particularly solid members of the IEP teams and partners with the general physical educator and the adapted physical educator.

Other Health Impairment

CHAPTER OBJECTIVES

After completing this chapter, you will be able to do the following:

- Describe the IDEA (2004) category of other health impairment.
- Describe the approach to including a student with obesity in physical activity environments.
- Understand the need for safe participation in physical activity and environments by working with the student with epilepsy and their family.
- Understand the role of exercise for a student with diabetes and employing coordination with their family in the development of the student's physical education program.
- Discuss physical education participation for students with sickle cell anemia.
- Discuss physical education for students with HIV or AIDS.
- Understand the risk of bleeding for those with hemophilia and the selection of physical activity experiences.

Children who need supports in their education because of health issues are addressed under IDEA (2004), in the category other health impairment (OHI). The law defines OHI as follows:

> Other health impairment means having limited strength, vitality or alertness, including a heightened alertness to stimuli, that results in limited alertness with respect to the educational environment, that is due to chronic or acute health problems such as asthma, attention deficit hyperactivity disorder, diabetes, epilepsy, a heart condition, hemophilia, lead poisoning, leukemia, nephritis, rheumatic fever, and sickle cell anemia; and adversely affects a child's educational performance.
>
> IDEA (2004, § 300.8[c][9]).

The category of OHI is not limited to the medical conditions mentioned in the law. By using *such as* in the definition of OHI, there can be other conditions included. Every effort should be made to ensure that appropriate physical education experiences are provided for students with health impairments who qualify under IDEA (2004). Students with a categorical disability found in IDEA (2004) and who are very overweight will most likely qualify for special educational services under that disability rather than under OHI. The disability category is their primary disability, and they happen to also carry extra weight.

Obesity

Obesity is one of those "such as" conditions not specifically named under the category of OHI but that fit all the criteria for impairment because of limited strength, vitality, or alertness. Of course, there are children who are obese who present as energized and may require adaptations to manage physical activity participation. Our focus is on those for whom the classic definition of OHI fits.

It is normal for children to gain weight at different rates and times during their childhood. One of the best things that educators and clinicians can do is to encourage children to celebrate their individual strengths and abilities. It is important to teach students that their most important qualities are not physical appearance (this is very hard for many reasons but especially for the teens). This is a hard line to walk for some physical educators who want their students to look healthy. Although it is important to be healthy, slender people are not always healthy.

Causes and Prevalence

Physical appearance is influenced by genetics, as well as the degree to which the child likes, has access to, and participates in physical activity. It is natural for children to vary in appearance across ages and stages of development. Sometimes children are obese because they live in a food desert severely limiting access to fresh fruits and vegetables, nor do they have anyone in the home who cooks with them or for them. In adolescence, children can put on weight when they depressed and become sedentary.

Emphasis in physical education should never be placed on body type, weight, or size. Body shapes and sizes vary for many reasons. At the same time, a child's weight will fluctuate with growth spurts and patterns. Genetics also play a part in appearances. Bone size and overall body shape is inherited. In all situations, judgment should never be passed on a child's shape or size. Person-first language must be employed, as should treating all students with the same courtesy, respect, and tact.

Since the early 1990s, the number of children who are overweight has more than doubled among 2- to 5-year-olds and more than tripled among 6- to 11-year-olds. According to data using statistics to 2017-2018, the prevalence of obesity was 19.3 percent and affected about 14.4 million children and adolescents (CDC, 2018a):

- Obesity prevalence was 13.4 percent among 2- to 5-year-olds, 20.3 percent among 6- to 11-year-olds, and 21.2 percent among 12- to 19-year-olds. Childhood obesity is also more common among certain populations.

- Non-Hispanic White children's percent of obesity is 16 percent for boys and 24 percent for girls. Non-Hispanic Black children's percent of obesity is 14 percent for boys and 29 percent for girls.

Regarding prevalence of children with disabilities who are obese:

- Twenty percent of children 10 through 17 years of age who have special health care needs are obese compared with 15 percent of children of the same ages without special health care needs (CDC, 2007). This is an old statistic but currently being used by the Centers for Disease Control and Prevention (CDC). We can assume it is much higher now, recognizing the trend in obesity in children across the decades and the adverse influence of the COVID-19 pandemic on access to school and safe physical education classes.

It cannot be overemphasized that a child's growth in height and weight may not always be proportional. It is reasonable to expect that all children will have periods when they grow out in weight before they grow up in height. As a physical educator, it is important to consider a child's growth over time and to consistently encourage healthy habits, before becoming concerned that a child is too heavy or too thin. Growth rate charts for boys and for girls ages 2 to 20 are published as a PDF on the CDC website (2020a, 2020b).

Body Mass Index and Diagnosis

Body mass index (BMI) may not be a reliable tool in children with certain health conditions. For example, some conditions influence bone size, body fat, and muscle distribution; this could make the use of the reference data for body composition inappropriate for certain children. In another example, BMI-for-age may not identify overweight in some children who are overfat because of decreased muscle mass. Yet, BMI is the most used way to estimate body fat. The Centers for Disease Control and Prevention provides useful calculations of BMI for children and teens, ages 2 to 19 years of age (2021b). Those in high school or who are age 20 and older use the CDC's adult BMI calculation (2021a). There is also a tool on the CDC website for home use calculation of the height and weight of a child or teen (2021c). It can be used when justifying services under OHI.

A BMI less than the 5th percentile means a child is underweight. A BMI between the 5th and 85th percentile is considered normal and healthy for most children. A BMI greater than the 85th percentile, but below the 95th percentile, means the child is at risk for being overweight. A BMI more than the 95th percentile means that the child is obese. BMI is generally lowest in children who are four to six years old. The BMI then increases from these ages into adulthood. For children, it is best to have a BMI for age in the normal range, not a specific BMI number as is advised for adults. Children usually gain fat, then they grow outward, and then grow in height. In general, unless a child (up to age 18) has a BMI more than the 95th percentile for age, we encourage the child to maintain weight and not lose weight.

Obesity in children needs to be approached differently than it is in adults. Weight loss is typically indicated only for children over seven years of age with a BMI greater than the 95th percentile for age. When weight loss is indicated, it is done under close medical supervision. This means that the physical educator should not direct a weight loss effort. It is not a part of the individualized education program (IEP). Instead, the IEP for these children is engagement in the curriculum. This must be reasonably paced as with any component of an IEP. It is child centered and begins where the child is successful.

Program Placement and Focus

Children should be encouraged to maintain weight by making good, healthy choices about food and physical activity. If the physical education (PE) teacher is also teaching about healthy foods, they should do so in a way that the information is fun for students. Fun is a great motivator and may lessen the social stress for children who are overweight.

IEP

The physical educator is *not* responsible for weight loss but rather in aspects of engagement in adapted physical activity. The IEP in adapted physical education does not reflect weight loss. To meet criteria for IDEA (2004), this would be necessary for the ability of the student to learn. The school would also pay for the clinical services required, justifying that weight loss will increase the student's ability to learn. Instead, the school has an obligation to recognize low stamina and alertness and its contribution to learning. Low stamina can be addressed in the school setting by a universal design for learning in PE approach whereby the adaptations are ones in which most students participate. Potentially, being physically active will increase alertness as stamina increases. The IEP for the student who is obese addresses modifications and adaptations to curriculum activity allowing for pacing, for choice, and of the task analysis of skills and PE activities for age.

At each developmental level, physical activity should be part of normal daily life. All children, whether they overweight or not, can benefit from developing healthy physical activity habits as well as nutritional intake. Educators set positive examples with their own habits and provide an environment that empowers their students to make positive decisions. Yet, regarding nutrition, we realize many children do really suffer from food insecurity (starvation), food deserts (full grocery stores are too far from their home), and social situations that contribute to being overweight.

Instructional Strategies

Within the educational setting, physical educators have the greatest control and sphere of influence over the child's access and attitude toward age-appropriate or condition-appropriate physical activity. The greatest hurdle to overcome for a student who is obese is often low self-esteem and low motivation to participate where failure is obvious and stamina is taxed. No other academic area is so visible for failure as the gymnasium or playground. Based on accepted practice with students who need specialized attention in physical education settings, the following is recommended when working with children who are very overweight:

- Get to know the child's interests outside of physical activity. This provides a way for the teacher to talk with the child about his or her interests not related to weight or motor skill. This establishes rapport with the child and gives the teacher a fuller picture of who the child is.

- Recognize and correct the bias against body weight that may exist with the physical education staff, paraprofessionals, or other teachers. Check negative attitudes at the door and provide discussion time with staff members to encourage an attitude that allows each child to gain physical activity skills, knowledge, and success.

- Adapt activities for an overweight child as needed and include other children in the adaptation. Oftentimes other children in a physical activity class will also be interested in the alternative activity. Making adaptations for intensity and duration of the activity may increase the number of children who willingly participate and increase the social circle for the child who is overweight.

An example would be pairing all students with a buddy for the week. Make a list of things that the students need to find out about their buddy during walking: middle name, favorite ice cream, favorite older person in their family. This conversation could slow down the walking pace.

- Carrying excess weight while being physically engaged in physical activity stresses the body's systems, and individuals who are overweight need monitoring.

- Establish realistic goals for an activity. Have classmates make goals, too—not just the children who are overweight. Many children can use a pacing approach (universal design for learning in PE), which is very important to the child who is obese. Observe closely for overexertion and pace the child.

- Focus on the personal best of each child and being positive. Only allow positive comments among children and explain that each person in the class has a personal best that is their unique time, distance, or skill. Positives can come in the form of comments like "Hey, great green T-shirt today!" Everyone enjoys positive feedback. The child without weight issues often participates in a physical activity for social reasons (fun and friends). The child with weight issues needs to be in the class for the same reasons. Therefore, a teacher can balance the focus on physical participation with the social aspects of physical activity by saying things such as "Hey, Greg, nice job being a friend there with Tom!"

- Continue to expose the child to a variety of activities. However, be sensitive to the differences in an individual sport (e.g., bowling or physical activity stations) versus a team sport (e.g., basketball or a simple game of tag) where physical fitness is a key component to success. For older children, a dual sport such as table tennis is appropriate. (Chapter 16 discusses activities that are recreational and can be enjoyed as a teen.)

- Specialists working in clinics for children who are overweight recommend getting the child interested in any physical activity. Typically, the child has very little experience in physical activity and therefore little knowledge of themselves being physical.. This recommendation aligns with other recommendations from the American College of Sports Medicine on extreme sedentary behavior and from the 2018 *Physical Activity Guidelines* of the Department of Health and Human Services: *Just Move!* The exception is for those children who are very heavy but who have been active—a new group being studied now.

- Stay away from a traditional fitness focus in the child's physical education program. Do not take the child out of classes to work on fitness goals. Rather, adjust class activities on a universal design for learning in PE and use buddies and stations for moving children through learning activities.

- Do not allow any bullying in classes. Proactively address this as a rule of the class. In this regard, guide the children to come up with this idea.

- Focus on social skill development. These children have low self-esteem and need to be taught how to engage. Make it a game with some themes if possible. Teachers can spot times when the student who is obese exhibits social skills, by saying things like "Hey, Mark, nice *hey* to your teammate!" Be aware of rewarding students who are obese for their self-deprecation. This is often a compensatory

FS-Stock/iStock/Getty Images

behavior to avoid being made fun of. For example, to boost self-esteem, the teacher might say, "Gabby, I'd say you are just a really good friend to have in PE today!"

• Find ways rewards in natural ways expected in the class for every student. Perhaps the child who is obese can be allowed to line up first. Match favorite teaching strategies with the target child. Teacher helpers are selected from the class and given duties. This is a privilege.

Diabetes Mellitus

Diabetes mellitus is a disease where the body cannot properly use the starches and sugars that it ingests. Type 1 diabetes results when the body loses its ability to produce insulin, and type 2 diabetes results from a combination of resistance to the action of insulin and insufficient insulin production. Type 1 diabetes affects young individuals normally before the age of 24, and type 2 is more common among those over the age of 40; yet the incidence of type 2 diabetes is now being reported in children under 20 years of age, and the number is rising each year (Divers et al., 2020). In fact, both type 1 and 2 are rising each year among children ages 20 years and younger.

Diabetes is a major health epidemic that affected more than 34 million Americans in 2020, up from 20.9 million in 2011 according to the American Diabetes Association (2020). The prevalence of the disease is increasing in children; 210,000 children under the age of 20 years have diabetes. In 2014 there were only 23,200 children with the disease (ADA, 2020). Much of the increase attributed to obesity is now more prevalent in children's lives and with an onset much earlier than in the past (Divers et al., 2020). Physical activity engagement is very much a part of controlling diabetes. All ages of students can participate in their physical activity environments and enjoy a huge variety of experiences the same as their peers without diabetes. Controlling diabetes within the activity setting involves the student, their family, and those professionals who are instructing skills and coordinating activities.

Treatment and Warning Signs

With diabetes, each person has a medical plan of intervention when the blood sugar is too high or too low. They should know what to look for and then what to do. The school, the family, and the student need to share what needs to be done in an emergency. This should be clear to the physical educator and all teachers working with the student, as well as any paraeducators in the classroom. The student in all positive scenarios takes proper care of him- or herself. Yet, depending on many circumstances, serious medical situations do arise, and action needs to transpire as soon as possible.

Treatment of the disease is handled with attention to nutritional intake, insulin, and exercise. The educational team must know how to handle the student with diabetes in school. The following questions need to be addressed, documented, and shared with all teachers and paraeducators at the school. Everyone in a position to monitor the student must know what to do.

• Does the student take medicine orally, or are there injections?

• Are there dietary restrictions or dietary needs regarding exercise?

• What is to be done if the student has an episode of insufficient insulin or too much insulin?

Type 1 Diabetes

In type 1 diabetes, the body by itself has no insulin. Treatment of the disease is handled with attention to taking insulin, dietary control, and exercise. The student needs to know what blood sugar level they need to maintain. If the blood sugar is too high in the blood, and there are symptoms of hyperglycemia (too much blood sugar), then staff must implement the student's plan. This plan must be determined ahead of time and distributed to all teachers. Prepare to call 911 if the student's symptoms put them in a dire situation.

Symptoms of high blood sugar are excessive urination, excessive thirst, nausea and vomiting, abdominal pain, drowsiness, sweet (acetone) breath, rapid pulse, and coma.

Type 2 Diabetes

In type 2 diabetes, the body does not metabolize well what insulin the body has. Treatment could include insulin medication (by pill or injection), exercise, and a specific daily nutritional intake. The student, teacher, and school nurse must understand the student's insulin management. The physical education teacher can work with the student to understand what the student needs in case of a hyperglycemic response (high blood glucose) or hypoglycemic response (low blood glucose).

Symptoms of low blood sugar are shakiness, dizziness, sweating, hunger, fast heartbeat, inability to concentrate, confusion, irritability and moodiness, anxiety (nervousness), and headache.

For low blood sugar, foods such as raisins, sugar cubes, fruit, or crackers are recommended to be nearby. The student should have a plan if an injection of insulin is needed prior to exercising and what monitoring of blood sugar levels may need to take place.

Instructional Considerations

Exercise is an essential component in the effective treatment of diabetes. In many ways, life depends on the way a person handles physical activity. People who exercise have less risk for becoming diabetic or obese (Cleven et al., 2020). Some of the advantages of a vigorous exercise program that were outlined by Leon (1993) have stood the test of time. Exercise can improve insulin and weight control and effect an increased sense of well-being.

Exercise Precautions

Each person is unique, and they will be cared for medically by their doctor. This person is the conduit for safe medical management of the student during the school day. In physical activity note the following:

- *Muscle site:* There are some exercise precautions that should be considered when working with the student who is diabetic. The muscle site in which the student injects insulin is important because the absorption rate of working and nonworking muscles is very different at the site. Some have reported that the absorption rate of working muscles might be twice as fast as that of the nonworking muscles. Therefore, if the legs and arms are to be heavily used (e.g., javelin throw), the preferred injection site might be the abdomen. This decision requires articulation with the student's physician.

- *Buddy up:* An individual who is diabetic should not exercise alone and should make certain that a partner is aware of the possibility of a hypoglycemic response. Adequate fluid during and after exercise is also important to avoid dehydration.

- *Feet:* Diabetes is associated with peripheral vascular disease and tendency for infection. Circulation to the extremities is different for those with diabetes. Proper footwear and good foot hygiene are important to the diabetic involved in an exercise program. Care must be taken to avoid blisters and other foot problems, which can become serious problems with this population.

Aspects of teaching students with diabetes that school personnel and the physical education teachers should consider include the following:

- Service providers need to be aware they have a student with diabetes in their class. Pertinent information that should be obtained from the parents and provided to teachers includes whom to call in an emergency, the name of the student's physician, signs and symptoms prior to an insulin reaction, the time of day the student is most likely to experience an insulin reaction, and the kinds of sweets used to reverse insulin shock. What should staff do in case of insulin shock? Who administers insulin? How? Obtain contact information for the parents, including their names and address. Record this and date it with parental signature.

- Individuals with diabetes are expected to test their blood for the presence of sugar. The teacher must provide support for testing.

- Efforts must be extended to assure other students that diabetes is not infectious.

- Service providers understand what insulin shock looks like for their student. Have on hand dextrose tablets, candy bars, or soft drinks available to them to administer in case a student experiences an insulin shock. This protocol should be in writing and signed by a parent.

• The individual who is diabetic, when engaging in vigorous activity, will on occasion find it necessary to stop activity to eat sweets to compensate for the increased metabolic state, thus avoiding an insulin reaction. Fortunately, many individuals with diabetes recognize the early signs of a low glucose level. Teachers should reinforce a student's decision to stop his or her activity rather than to tough it out.

• The individual with diabetes is particularly susceptible to infection, and great care must be practiced to avoid cuts, abrasions, blisters, and fungus infection. Although it is probably a challenge, the physical education teacher can help the student monitor this.

Physical Activity

Students need to be encouraged to be active and to learn the important relationship between nutritional intake, medication, and exercise early in life. A strong immersion in their age-appropriate physical activities allows them to choose the activities they like now and hope to continue engagement. They can also have confidence to seek other new physical activities as they age.

IEP

When questions of possible limitations to participation arise, the individualized education program planning process can be effectively utilized to ensure that the input of all parties is received before imposing unnecessary restrictions. The real need with a student's IEP will be the coordination of medical needs throughout the day and especially during physical education, recess, and any athletic extracurricular programs offered by the school in which the student participates.

Many doctors emphasize the importance of muscular activity in the lives of individuals with diabetes. Exercise is important not only because it decreases the need for insulin but also because it contributes to general body health. Moreover, exercise helps to keep the body weight under control, given a tendency toward obesity over time. Exercise also improves glucose tolerance even in the absence of insulin. Some find it helpful to eat a snack prior to exercise and at regular intervals throughout the exercise period. In general, during the school day

any deviation from the regular eating, exercise, and medication pattern needs monitoring by the student if mature enough or by appropriate school member (e.g., classroom teacher, GPE or APE).

Individuals with diabetes don't stand out with common features of their body. Motor function may be very typical for age and therefore they do not usually experience social-emotional problems at the same level of those with more obvious disabilities. Unsatisfactory adjustment found in those with diabetes can be overprotection or overindulgence by the parents during childhood. It is not uncommon to have parents be fearful and want to protect their child.

Individuals with diabetes have excelled in every conceivable sport and activity. From the United States, North and South America, and across Europe, there are 96 elite athletes with type 1 diabetes listed under 20 different sports (Wikipedia, 2023). Historically, athletes with diabetes such as Ty Cobb, Jackie Robinson, Billie Jean King, and Arthur Ashe achieved superstar status as professional athletes. For the young person with diabetes, this means that the physical education program should be well rounded and include all the same activities available to other students. The aim of the physical education experience for those with diabetes is to (1) foster within students an appreciation for the value of exercise as an important factor in the management of diabetes, and (2) develop a deep love for physical activity. Exercise will always be essential for their quality of life.

Asthma

Asthma is the common term used for the condition of bronchial asthma. It is a disease of the bronchi characterized by swelling of the mucous membrane lining the bronchial tubes, excessive secretion of mucus, and spasms of the bronchial tubes. Symptoms of asthma are dyspnea (breathlessness), coughing and wheezing, and a feeling of constriction in the chest. Typically, an attack of asthma is characterized by a coughing stage, followed by dyspnea and wheezing. The attack usually terminates with the coughing up of a large amount of thick sputum.

People afflicted with asthma tend to overuse the intercostal muscles in breathing at the expense of the diaphragm. Also, there is a tendency to tighten the abdominal muscles during inspiration, which further reduces the action of the diaphragm. The reduction in action causes a decrease in the amount of air that is inhaled. Continual reliance on the upper chest muscles for breathing results in a gradual loss of flexibility of the diaphragm.

Asthma is a chronic disease in which periodic attacks are followed by periods of remission of the symptoms. Attacks vary greatly in severity and duration; they may range from a slight period of wheezing to a prolonged period of coughing accompanied by severe shortness of breath. Attacks can be triggered by breathing very cold air, breathing air that has a high content of moisture, or by experiencing respiratory infections. Extrinsic asthma is caused by the reaction of the body to the introduction of a foreign substance to which the body is sensitive. Usually this substance, called an allergen, is suspended in inhaled air; however, the offending substance may also be ingested in the form of food or drugs. The most common allergens are plant pollen, dust, molds, and animal fur.

Asthmatic attacks may be induced by exercise. This condition is frequently referred to as exercise-induced asthma. Fatigue and emotions are also factors in attacks. The tolerance level for exercise of those subjects to exercise-induced asthma varies from person to person but is related to physical condition; those who are in good physical condition usually have a higher tolerance than those who are not. Attacks also strike different people at different times. In some people, the symptoms occur during exercise; in others, the symptoms manifest themselves several minutes after the end of the activity.

An as-yet-undefined relationship exists between asthma and the emotions. Some cases are thought to be chiefly due to emotional stress because they have no extrinsic causes, and the symptoms disappear when the emotional tension subsides. Thus, extrinsic asthmatic cases often become worse in times of emotional distress.

Asthmatic attacks that are neither extrinsic in nature nor primarily caused by emotional reaction are thought to be related in some way to a deficient cellular function that affects the sympathetic nervous system, which, in turn, alters the tonus (continuous and low-level contraction) of the bronchial tube linings.

Of children in the United States, a little over 8 percent have asthma. Of those children, there is a greater representation in the Black community followed by the Hispanic and then Caucasian (Pate et al., 2021) communities. Poor people often cannot afford to purchase their medications. Despite the reality that there is no exact cause of asthma, attacks can be controlled by staying away from the triggers. Each person has their unique triggers such as air pollution, dust, or mites (CDC, 2020c).

LSOPhoto/iStock/Getty Images

Asthma Action Plan

The CDC recommends that in addition to avoiding the individual triggers, medications that have been prescribed need to be used exactly as indicated. Medications are either breathed in or taken in pill form. These medications are in two types: quick relief and long-term control. The quick-relief medication is used in the event of an attack. The long-term medication controls the incidences of attacks and is taken continually. The CDC guidelines now emphasize that an individual can control their asthma using their healthcare providers' help and devising an Asthma Action Plan, which can be documented on a form available on its website. This is developed with the student's physician to show the student their daily treatment and how to handle an asthma attack. The plan explains when to call the doctor or go to the emergency room (CDC, 2022). The CDC encourages the parents to share the asthma action plan with all those caring for their child including schools.

Physical Activities

Ongoing participation in physical activity has a positive effect on the lives of children and youth with asthma (Dimitri et al., 2020). Children and youth have more asthma-free days and a better quality of life with increases in cardiovascular fitness and physical capacity. The American Academy of Pediatrics issued a statement recommending that children with asthma be encouraged to participate in physical education and sport programs. The American Academy of Pediatrics supports physical activity involvement for individuals with asthma.

In elite competition, asthma is more highly represented than in the population in general and even more so in the long endurance training athletes (Mulić et al., 2020). This led Mulić and colleagues to report that "[with] good disease control athletes can play and compete undisturbed for many years" (p. 209).

Exclusions from physical education programs must be avoided for the student with asthma. Individualized physical education goals must be developed for health-impaired children, including those with asthma. In more severe cases, consultation with the parents, physician, child, and other school personnel within the format of an IEP meeting is essential.

Epilepsy

Epilepsy is not a specific disorder but rather a result of an electrical–chemical imbalance within the regulatory mechanism of the brain. The abnormality of brain function causes seizures. Individuals with intellectual disability, cerebral palsy, or both can have epilepsy. In some cases, the term *developmental disabilities*, for instance, is used to describe those who have cerebral palsy, epilepsy, intellectual disability, or a combination of these conditions.

Many persons diagnosed with epilepsy respond so effectively to treatment that they live remarkably unhindered lives because their seizures are controlled. In others, however, the seizures are not entirely controlled. This appears to be particularly true of those with severe disabilities. Educators and clinicians must be knowledgeable about the student's epilepsy, thus responding to the students' needs and communicating with others while engaging them in a physically active life.

Seizure Types

Seizures are divided into groups depending on where they start in the brain (onset), whether a person's awareness is affected, and whether seizures involve other symptoms, such as movement (Epilepsy Society, 2022). Several different classifications are used for the types of epilepsy. The World Health Organization (WHO, 2019) divides seizures into two major categories: focal and generalized. This classification notes the part of the brain where the disturbance occurs that results in the seizure. This classification system is endorsed by the Epilepsy Foundation of America. The Mayo Clinic also uses this classification (2022).

Focal Seizures

Focal seizures are those where one area of the brain has abnormal activity.

- *Focal seizures without loss of consciousness:* There is no loss of consciousness. The person may have involuntary jerking of one body part, some tingling, or dizziness. Sometimes they see flashing lights. The seizures may alter emotions or change the way things look, smell, feel, taste or sound. Some people experience déjà vu.

- *Focal seizures with impaired awareness:* The person may experience a loss of consciousness or awareness, and it may seem like they are having a dream. Impaired awareness occurs during the seizure, with the person staring into space and not responding normally to the environment or performing repetitive movements, such as hand rubbing, chewing, swallowing, or walking in circles.

Generalized Seizures

Seizures that appear to involve all areas of the brain are called generalized seizures. Six types of generalized seizures exist.

1. *Absence seizures:* These seizures typically occur in children. The child stares into space with or without subtle body movements (such as eye blinking or lip smacking). The seizure typically lasts 5 to 10 seconds. The person has a brief loss of awareness, happening as often as 100 times per day.

2. *Tonic seizures:* Tonic seizures cause stiff muscles and may affect consciousness. These seizures usually affect muscles in the person's back, arms, and legs and may cause them to fall to the ground.

3. *Atonic seizures:* Atonic seizures, also known as drop seizures, cause a loss of muscle control. Since this most often affects the legs, it often causes the person to collapse or fall down.

4. *Clonic seizures:* Clonic seizures are associated with repeated or rhythmic, jerking muscle movements. These seizures usually affect the neck, face, and arms.

5. *Myoclonic seizures:* Myoclonic seizures usually appear as sudden brief jerks or twitches and usually affect the upper body, arms, and legs.

6. *Tonic-clonic seizures:* Tonic-clonic seizures, previously known as grand mal seizures, are the most dramatic type of epileptic seizure. The person experiences abrupt loss of consciousness and body stiffening, twitching, and shaking. The seizures sometimes cause loss of bladder control or biting the tongue.

A tonic-clonic seizure includes three phases: tonic, clonic, and sleep:

1. *Tonic (stiff):* During the tonic phase, the individual will stop all activity, lose consciousness, experience a generalized body stiffening, and fall to the ground. As the muscles tighten, air may be forced from the lungs resulting in a piercing and sometimes frightening cry.

2. *Clonic (jerking):* Following the tonic phase, the individual will experience a clonic (jerking) phase during which various uncontrolled body movements will occur, such as frothing of the mouth and excessive saliva building up due to the interference with the mechanics of swallowing.

Regular respiration is also inhibited, characterized by blueness of the skin due to lack of oxygen, which is temporary.

3. *Sleep:* After the seizure, a general sense of confusion takes over as well as headache symptoms. Sleep occurs from a few minutes to several hours after the seizure.

Seizure Action Plan

Status epilepticus is a seizure lasting more than five minutes without any slow-down. It is just continual seizure activity with difficulty breathing (stiffness, jerking, and repeat). This is a medical emergency. To manage status epilepticus, call 911. Do not attempt to transport the child in a car. The school must have detailed written instructions on how to proceed when this type of seizure occurs.

If the seizure stops before five minutes and the child is breathing normally, there is no need to call 911. The parents must be contacted, and the plan set out by the doctor must be followed. Usually, the child is tired after the seizure. Let them rest and follow the doctor's orders for postseizure.

A *Seizure Action Plan* form is published on the website of the Epilepsy Foundation (2020). It is recommended that the physical education teacher have access to this form, understands it, and reviews it with the school nurse and the parent. This should guide the coordinated action when a student has a seizure. The following are general ways to assist when a student has a seizure:

1. It is important for you to remain calm and for you to ask any other adults to remain calm also. The children will then follow suit. Children and youth who have seizures typically have the same type of seizure repeatedly. The protocol will become familiar with the students and a discussion with all the class will help when a seizure takes place. If the student is old enough, they can also talk to their classmates at this time. Epilepsy is a medical condition. It is not a disability.

2. Do not attempt to restrain the person, but you can loosen anything tight that would restrict the person's breathing.

3. To help keep the airway clear, you can gently turn the person on their side. They cannot swallow their tongue, and it is *not* recommended to put a finger or object in the person's mouth.

4. Clear the area around the person for anything sharp or hard that would hurt the person if they moved over or into it.

5. You can place something soft and flat under

the person's head. Be sure that there is little elevation of the head.

6. Be aware of when the seizure starts and stops. This will be helpful to medical personnel if the seizure goes on for longer than five minutes. If it does, call 911.

7. When the seizure is over, the person will likely begin breathing normally. In this case, there is no need to do any resuscitation unless the person is not breathing. Then call 911 and follow any procedures set up with the student, family, and medical doctor.

8. Once the convulsions have stopped, place an item such as a blanket or shirt over the student to eliminate the possibility of embarrassment if the individual has soiled him- or herself.

9. If the student is hazy following the seizure, move him or her to a quiet place to rest or sleep. The student should be kept warm and be permitted to rest as long as necessary.

10. After class, the teacher should report the seizure to the appropriate school official. In some school systems this may be the nurse, a health officer, or the principal. Reporting the incidence to a central source assures that the total number of seizures within a day or specified time will be accurately recorded. This is particularly important for those students who are experiencing a change in the dosage of their medication. Communication should be clear between the school and the family regarding any medication change. The educational team can work with the family on school–family communication about management of seizures.

Physical Activities

Students with seizures that are under control need no special consideration and can participate in the activities of the general physical education program without modification but with consideration made for high-contact sports, as would happen for any child (Webb Pennington & Pennington (2020). If activities are particularly risky (such as rock climbing) then caution (such as lowering the attainable height in rock climbing) is recommended or another activity is substituted. The Penningtons go on to elaborate that fitness is low for individuals with epilepsy, yet exercise normalizes the brain's electrical function while increasing overall fitness levels. Their recommendations to increase participation and inclusion in general physical education are:

- *Modifications:* High-risk activities that may include falling (such as rock climbing and horse-

back riding) require more educator attention and supervision. Decrease the space of play to increase supervision. Note and adjust the activity location or offering, as heat and humidity affect seizure incidence.

- *Safety:* Be aware of equipment or surfaces above the head during physical activity. Obtain approval from parents or guardians and the student's doctor for risky activity. Have the student use a helmet. It is important when participating in physical activity near or in water to have the student wear supportive gear. Be aware of the student's medications and their side effects.

Good seizure control has allowed athletes with epilepsy to participate in sports (Webb Pennington & Pennington (2020). The important phrases here are *good seizure control* and *controlled seizures*. As far

back as 1974, it has been the policy of the American Medical Association that individuals with good seizure control could participate in basketball, soccer, wrestling, football, ice hockey, and lacrosse. WHO, along with others, has advocated for inclusion of persons with epilepsy in sports (Carter & McGrew, 2021). They, along with others, find that participation is open for persons with controlled seizures given direct supervision with trained professionals. This includes permitting swimming under supervision but not swimming in open waters alone. Sports on the ground like bowling and cross-country skiing have no restrictions for the participant. Activities considered moderate risk are ones like ice hockey, surfing, windsurfing, skateboarding, water skiing, and weightlifting. Carter and McGrew (2021) have created a valuable list of sports risk to the participant and bystanders if the participant had a seizure.

IEP

Information about the student's medication should be discussed in the IEP meeting. When the seizures are not controlled, the family should be prepared to consult with the team on which sports the student can participate in and what to do when a seizure occurs. Otherwise, the PE program can proceed as usual. The student needs to learn age-appropriate physical activities. In addition, PE is a positive social outlet in the educational environment.

Human Immunodeficiency Virus

Acquired immune deficiency syndrome (AIDS) is the last stage of human immunodeficiency virus (HIV), which is also referred to as Stage 3 HIV. With AIDS, the acquired virus has severely damaged the immune system and brutal diseases called opportunistic infections take over the body. The most common illnesses of those with AIDS are a lung infection called *Pneumocystis jiroveci* pneumonia and a cancer, Kaposi's sarcoma. Evidence shows that the virus may also attack the nervous system, causing damage to the brain.

AIDS was first diagnosed in 1981, and then in the early days of AIDS without the protection of the immune system, most individuals with AIDS died. Some people did and do remain well but are able to infect others. Others can develop a disease referred to as AIDS-related complex. Signs and symptoms of AIDS-related complex include loss of appetite, weight loss, fever, night sweats, skin rashes, diarrhea, tiredness, lack of resistance to infection, or swollen lymph nodes. Today the use of antiretroviral therapy medicines has allowed individuals with HIV to live long lives given their overall health. It has transformed care and led to a push for AIDS prevention.

The disease affects those who have sexual relationships with same sex partners, bisexual partners, straight partners, the babies of women who are affected, and those using intravenously administered drugs. Young men are statistically at much higher risk than young women for developing AIDS. If they do not seek medical care with their HIV status, they run the risk of getting AIDS. If they do not know if they have HIV but have participated in known risky behavior for HIV, they should be tested. The transmission of HIV is from another person with HIV via needle behaviors and exchange of body liquids. According to the CDC (2020a), these fluids must contact a mucous membrane or damaged tissue or be directly injected into the bloodstream (from a syringe used by someone who has the disease) for transmission to occur. Mucous membranes are found inside the rectum, vagina, penis, and mouth.

According to the CDC (2020a), the estimated cumulative number of those HIV cases in the United States would be 1.2 million, which includes those age 13 and older. Adults ages 20 to 24 with HIV are 69 percent gay men, 24 percent heterosexual and 7 percent drugs users. In the heterosexual group, 16 percent are women and 7 percent are men. In 2019, young people accounted for 21 percent (7,648) of all new HIV diagnoses, with young gay and bisexual men accounting for 83 percent (6,385) of these diagnoses in people aged 13 to 24 in that year (CDC, 2020b).

Adapted physical education has always promoted the use of person-first language to recognize the dignity of the children and youth served across the United States. The *2020 HIV Primary Care Guidelines* from the HIV Medicine Association of the Infectious Diseases Society of America stated that they were using people-first language to place the person before the disease and acknowledge the dignity of people with HIV, and they were using gender-neutral language where appropriate. They cited that ". . . optimal care outcomes are dependent on a stigma-free and welcoming care environment" (Thompson et al., 2021, p. e3573). They recognized the structural societal barriers to engaging the individuals in their own health care: inadequate transportation; health system barriers to engagement; food or housing insecurity; stigma and discrimination based on HIV status, race, and ethnicity; gender identity; sexual orientation; disability; and immigration status. This is a lot to grapple with in education systems.

HIV and 504 Plans

Students with HIV or AIDS may share their medical status with the school, but the school is not obliged to share it other than an alert in the medical file regarding a blood condition. This is a legal issue, a right to privacy according to the Health Insurance Portability and Accountability Act. If, however, the student needs support because of weakness or failing health, then there would be a determination of how they would be served. They could be served on a 504 plan, and if a student meets criteria in their state for OHI, they can receive services there. Most states prefer the 504 plan. If someone who has HIV participates in an extracurricular contact sport, then the school has a medical alert to a blood issue in the student's file. If the student with HIV is pregnant, then support would be provided by the usual means for pregnant teens in the school district.

Inclusion and Legal Protection

Some school districts have argued that children with HIV or AIDS pose a health threat to teachers and other students. These worries are unfounded. Scientific evidence has repeatedly demonstrated that HIV is hard to transmit and is passed only during intimate sexual behavior, the sharing of intravenous drug needles, and from an infected woman to her fetus. The virus cannot be transmitted through casual contact such as eating with or touching a person with AIDS. While it is true that the AIDS virus has been found in tears and saliva, the amount of virus in these fluids is very small, and there have been no reported cases where the virus was passed through these fluids.

Early in the AIDS epidemic, several authorities articulated that those students with AIDS and those with HIV should be received positively in educational programs. Surburg (1988) cautioned that students with AIDS should not be viewed as a potential problem but as pupils who deserve an appropriate physical education program.

For these reasons, students with AIDS are covered under the provisions of federal law and should be enrolled in school and encouraged to participate

in all activities of which they are capable. From the U.S. Department of Education, Office of Civil Rights (1991), the following legal guidance was issued:

Most children with AIDS can attend school in the regular classroom without restrictions. There has been no medical evidence disclosed to show that AIDS is contagious in the school setting. According to the latest medical information, there have been no reported cases of the transmission of the AIDS virus in schools. The Surgeon General and other health authorities, such as the Centers for Disease Control and the American Medical Association, have reinforced this position stating that there is no significant risk of contracting AIDS in the classroom.

U.S. Department of Education (1991, n.p.).

Instructional Considerations

In general, students with HIV or AIDS should be allowed to participate to the extent their medical condition will permit. Contrary to what some might argue, no one has caught AIDS from the water in the swimming pool. In addition, these students should be encouraged to participate in normal childhood activities, with modifications as appropriate.

Some individuals with HIV remain healthy, with no apparent symptoms of illness. Those who have AIDS-related complex must be carefully weighed and appropriate modifications in activities made because of skin rashes, diarrhea, tiredness, or lack of resistance to infection. The goal is to include students with AIDS and HIV in as many activities as possible.

Because of the possibility of injury and blood loss in a physical education class, many questions have surfaced concerning first aid procedures. Although the risk of contracting HIV by giving first aid is extremely small, the risk can be further minimized by adhering to the following guidelines when giving first aid to a person with a bleeding injury:

1. Wear disposable plastic or latex gloves.
2. Clean any blood spills with soap and water and use a disinfectant, such as bleach, afterwards.
3. Put blood-soaked items that need to be laundered or thrown away in a plastic bag.
4. Wash your hands with soap and water when finished.

Sickle Cell Anemia

In sickle cell anemia, the blood hemoglobin does have enough healthy red blood cells to carry oxygen to the body as it should. Sickle cell disease is an inherited disorder more prevalent in the African American population, but some Caucasians whose ancestors are from the Mediterranean area, the Middle East, and parts of India may also have the disease. All babies born in the United States are screened for sickle cell anemia, but young adults can be carriers and not know their status. Sickle cell trait occurs when one parent has the trait for sickle cell and the other does not. If their children do not have symptoms of the disease, they carry the trait. During vigorous exercise, a crisis trigger can occur and become life threatening if a person is unaware of their status.

There is no drug therapy for sickle cell anemia, only treatment for symptoms. Anticoagulants have had some success in dislodging the clumps of sickle cells, and ice packs can relieve swelling of the joints. Some physicians recommend blood transfusions to relieve the symptoms, but relief is only temporary. Those with sickle cell anemia must avoid high altitudes and other situations in which there is less oxygen available in the air than normal.

Children with sickle cell anemia are medically compromised. Hostyn and colleagues found that in the six-minute walk, nine-year-olds were functionally slower walkers than their peers (2013). Children with sickle cell disease must be monitored very carefully during participation in physical education. It is possible that these students could experience a vaso-occlusive crisis by lowering the oxygen level slightly. Physical education teachers must offer experiences, therefore, that require a minimal supply of oxygen. Motor skill activities should be provided to develop agility, coordination, balance, and the ability to manipulate objects. Physical fitness, particularly cardiovascular activities, must be developed cooperatively with the assistance of qualified medical personnel.

Generally, children with sickle cell trait can participate fully in all school activities, including some vigorous physical education activities. Hydration is important throughout the day, especially with physical activity, and children can participate in most activities of childhood as long as they are not overdoing it and resting when tired (CDC, 2020d). Swimming has not been recommended for those with severe sickle cell because of the risk of triggering a vasoconstriction resulting in vaso-occlusive pain. This most likely results from the inability of many programs to heat the pool water warm and facing a transition from cold to hot or vice versa.

Cold water triggers vasoconstrictive reactions for those with sickle cell. Narcisse and colleagues (2018) reported on summer camping programs for children with sickle cell that accommodated the children during hot days for swimming by heating the pool and having drying huts.

In all physical activities, the student should take breaks when needed; mild, moderate, and vigorous participation have been allowed depending on the medical status of the student. More typical is the mild to moderate level of participation. At these levels, students should take frequent breaks, stay hydrated, and stay warm enough (Hostyn et al., 2013).

The National Association for the Advancement of Colored People recommends that all athletes be tested for sickle cell. The National Collegiate Athletic Association Committee on Competitive Safeguards and Medical Aspects of Sports' position is that the likelihood of a sickle crisis is very remote and that the athlete with sickle cell trait should not be restricted or limited in their participation in sport. It does caution, however, that athletic trainers and others should carefully monitor athletes with sickle cell trait to ensure that they do not become dehydrated during practice sessions or while playing or practicing (Howe & Boden, 2007).

IEP

The IEP of a student with sickle cell anemia is infused with the status of the disease as documented by the student's physician. Bringing the medical information into the physical education program is best addressed in the IEP meetings with this medical advice presented to inform the team. Family PE goals for the child must be heard. As the child grows, this document should be updated, and the IEP should follow suit. A physical education teacher can be sensitive to when the student is avoiding engagement in the class and can help the student with pacing and removal as needed to manage the sickle cell response.

Hemophilia

Hemophilia is a blood disorder resulting in the inability of the blood to coagulate properly. There are different forms of hemophilia. Physical educators need to be clear on what the child's participation in activities is like given their age and disease. Hemophilia effects the muscles and joints (there is bleeding there) and thus the physical fitness of the student. In the 1970s, it was not recommended that students with hemophilia participate in physical education and have a physically active life. But today that is not the stance. Physical activity engagement increases muscle endurance and bone development, which supports the joints better and thus controls bleeding better. Factor replacement therapy has paved the way for more opportunity for a less sedentary life.

Physical therapist Hernandez and colleagues organized over 100 physical activities by risk for bleeds over various body areas for those with hemophilia (2018). They created an interactive chart called Activity Intensity Risk, which is published online at the back of their publication (2018). These physical therapists came from centers for hemophilia care, and this data can potentially be very useful in assisting physical educators making decisions about physical activity participation.

The chart lists where the risks for bleeds are per activity, so the identified body part can be left out of the movement, or the activity can be modified to reduce stress. A list of low-risk activities for bleeds has been provided. The physical educator, coach, parent, or caregiver can use this to reassure themselves that the activity is not expected to cause a bleed. It also provides a broad array of activities for program development by the physical educator particularly for youth and later in the transitional IEP.

Children with hemophilia have a medical health care specialist and clinic to care for them. Risk is known to change with age. The physical educator

must work using the most current information for physical activity from the health care specialist. Hernandez and colleagues (2018) provide the following forms in their article's appendix to gather information:

- Agreement for sports participation
- Activity intensity risk tracker
- Planning guide for parents

IEP

The adapted physical educator (or GPE) works with forming the IEP with an assessment of what the student can currently perform relative to grade curriculum (curriculum-based assessment). This would assist the school-based allied health members on the level of involvement in activities. Because of more advance medical therapies, these students can participate in physical environments and activity and benefit in controlling the body's predilection for bleeds. They can learn fundamental motor skills and the games of their age group. They can also participate in selected activities that are low risk for bleeds. As the children age, the IEP in physical education will need adjustment to better match the medical status.

Temporary Conditions of Disability

Children and young people with and without disabilities have health crises, accidents, injuries, and surgeries. Most often they want to be with their friends at school during stages of treatment and recovery. The laws in education allow for that and the support needed for it to be successful! Students with temporary conditions that effect their participation in physical education can either be served under OHI or a 504 plan in the following situations:

- *504 plan:* In the case of injuries resulting in surgery, a 504 plan can be initiated to provide accommodations in education while the student recovers.

- *Existing IEP:* If a student already has an IEP and has surgery or an illness, then the team reconvenes and adds notes for the student's IEP in either general physical education or adapted physical education, arranging modifications and adaptations.

- *OHI:* Under the category of OHI, if a student becomes sick with cancer, then they can receive the modifications they need in academic areas including physical education. This applies to other illness that may persist or cause the student ill health while attending school during part or all their treatment.

A school has at its disposal both OHI as part of IDEA (2004) and a 504 plan to make accommodations for the student's access to their education. It depends on the student's condition and the state's interpretations of guidelines. Physical therapy and occupational therapy can be brought into an IEP or 504 plan only to the extent that the services are needed related to learning in the school setting. This is compatible with federal law for related services.

Summary

Other health impairment is a category of IDEA (2004). It particularly targets those diseases or medical conditions that limit strength, vitality, and alertness in education. If students with other health impairments are not already served under any category of special education, then they may qualify under the category of OHI. Children who are obese do not have an IEP that targets losing weight but rather engages the child in the activities of PE for their age or grade. Systematic observation of the target child in physical education can assist knowing the level at which the student can participate. The goal is to start where the child is successful and then move them forward. Diabetes is a serious disease, and students must have a plan for emergencies when there is too much blood sugar or no blood sugar. Otherwise, they can participate in general physical education. Epilepsy is not a disease but a medical condition where there is abnormal electrical activity in the brain and the individual has seizures. There must be a plan for what is to be done in general physical education in the case of an emergency. Children with epilepsy can participate in physical education with attention to breaks and hydration. Children and youth with asthma benefit from being physically active. A plan of action is recommended for control of asthmatic events. General physical education participation is recommended for children with hemophilia to strengthen muscles and protect joints from bleeds. PE teachers can work with the medical team, particularly physical therapists, regarding risk for bleeds by activity. Low-risk bleed activities are published. Sickle cell anemia is a disease that effects the stamina of young children. They can participate well in PE with managed care. Overall, engaging in physical activities benefits children and youth with medical conditions that can be managed successfully by positive communication with clinical and educational personnel. The students benefit enormously.

PART III

Adult Adapted Physical Activity

CHAPTER 14

Health-Related Fitness

BraunS/E+/Getty Images

CHAPTER OBJECTIVES

After completing this chapter, you will be able to do the following:

- Provide a contemporary definition of health in relationship to disability.
- Describe health-related fitness (HRF) as opposed to performance-related physical fitness.
- Understand the collaboration of a variety of professionals required for adults with disabilities to participate in HRF physical activity experiences in their community.
- Describe the new paradigm of aging for people with disability as applied to supporting participation in HRF adapted physical activity.
- Describe the rating of perceived exertion and the relationship to HRF for adults who are aging.
- Understand why *just move* is an appropriate recommendation in physical activity for older adults who are aging.
- Understand HRF guidelines of some common diseases of aging.

What is health? The World Health Organization defined health in 1948 as "a state of complete, physical, mental and social well-being and not *merely the absence of disease or infirmity*" (WHO, 1948). The implication is that if one had a disease or infirmity, one was not healthy. This definition has influenced research in aging. Molton and Yorkston (2017) are adamant that this is ableism: ". . . in some ways this focus on avoidance of disability in later life embodies ableism, a set of beliefs that assign superior worth to people without disability" (p. 291). Importantly, population studies do not support the notion that old age is not "without appreciable deterioration in health or function" (p. 291). Krahn and colleagues (2021) report that defining health has advanced over the past 70 years. The perfect complete state of health—perfect health—is unattainable. Instead, *adaptation interacts with resilience.* Social determinants of health profoundly affect people's health in negative ways when living with resource-poor environments, systemic racism, racial bias, and chronic stress. Krahn and colleagues propose a new definition of health: "Health is the dynamic balance of physical, mental, social, and existential well-being in adapting to conditions of life and the environment" (p. 3).

Expanding on this, the authors elaborate on the following understanding of what is health in contemporary times.

1. Health is dynamic, not static, and therefore it is on a continuum.

2. Health is multidimensional, including existential, as well as physical, mental, and social well-being. (Existential means in the present; here and now.) Existential well-being is living one's values, also understood as with one's purpose in life.

3. Health is distinct from function. Good health can exist in the presence of limitations. Health systems are accountable for promoting the health of persons with disabilities.

At times, during the initial wave of the COVID-19 pandemic, medical settings had to allocate scarce resources based on whether a patient could benefit from the intervention. Assessments used where overtly biased against those with disabilities. Krahn and colleagues reported that "A year in the life of a person with a disability is worth less than year of an able-bodied person" (Krahn et al., 2021, p. 4).

4. Health is determined by balanced adaptation. Balance is within oneself and the social and physical environment. Adaptation includes making change and accepting change—the new normal with modification in lifestyle.

5. Health adaptation is deeply influenced by an individual's ability to handle the environmental context of the physical, social, and political. For example, racism and ableism are two realities that intersect and impact on a political reality.

Krahn and colleagues provide their definition of disability in the context of contemporary health:

> . . . *disabilities* as experienced limitations in body function, activities, or participation in major life activities due to a health condition that occur in the context of one's environment and are influenced by personal factions.
>
> . . . *chronic diseases* as primarily noncommunicable diseases with duration of at least one year that may require ongoing medical attention; and
>
> *chronic conditions* to include long-term disabilities as well as chronic diseases that may or may not be associated with functional limitations.
>
> Krahn et al. (2021, p. 1).

These contemporary definitions of health, disability, and chronic disease and conditions are applied when engaging individuals in health-related fitness (HRF) at every point of engagement and performance. It is particularly important to understand Krahn and colleagues' emphasis that good health can exist in the presence of limitations is revolutionary. The conventional wisdom has been that good health was without limitations. In reality, the natural process of aging cannot avoid limitation. Those limitation can be addressed and good health experienced. This is dynamic living, which is attributed to encompassing the ecology of physical activity participation by involving interdisciplinary professionals of care and is done by individuals with disabilities (Kennedy et al., 2021).

The application of HRF for adults aging *with* disabilities and those aging *into* disabilities is the focus of this chapter, thus we continue to follow and elaborate on the contemporary model of aging and disability (Molton & Yorkston, 2017). We begin with the components of health-related fitness and performance-related fitness (Winnick & Porretta, 2022).

Health-Related Fitness

- Muscular strength
- Muscular endurance
- Aerobic functioning
- Flexibility
- Body composition

Performance-Related Fitness

- Agility
- Balance
- Coordination
- Speed
- Power
- Reaction time

Performance-related fitness is exemplified watching the giant slalom of the Paralympics, Olympics, or Special Olympics. These athletes work with coaches to improve the performance of fitness components essential to their competitive edge, such as power and speed. HRF is physical activity engagement with a focus on functional health modalities such as completing important tasks or physical activity engagement in such activity as walking, jogging, swimming, biking, dancing, gardening, or dancing. HRF is the basis for the 2018 *Physical Activity Guidelines for Americans* from the United States Office of Health and Human Services (USDHHS, 2018). Functional health is the individual's physical capability *to perform and sustain important tasks independently* such as leisure physical activities and activities of daily living. Health-related fitness contributes ". . . to a person's capacity to enjoy life and withstand challenges" (USDHHS, 2018, p. 21).

As more adults in the late 1980s began to experience injuries related to their fitness activities, the Cooper Clinic initiated research looking at HRF activity; reporting that less intense exercise was very beneficial to life. Swimming activity improved cardiac output (e.g., Chase et al., 2008), and adults who participated in 30 minutes of walking, at a moderate level, five times a week, had a 30 percent lower all-cause risk for mortality (they were not going to die younger than would be expected for age) (Haskell, 2007). These adults could spend 30 minutes walking while being able to talk. Back in 1993, using large data sets of the Cooper Clinic (more than 10,000 data sets), 51 percent of men who went from sedentary to physically activity had a 51 percent lower all-cause risk for mortality (Blair, 1993). In addition to these types of studies, adults were reporting their ability to run had diminished. They wanted to run, but maybe not so intensely or as far. These data impacted the notion that intense, vigorous physical activity was *not* the guard against an early death and a promotion of healthy life. Instead, an HRF approach was potent, dynamic, flexible to assessment modalities and individualized implementation, and physically tolerable and enjoyable.

Components of Health-Related Fitness

The components of HRF—muscular strength, muscular endurance, aerobic functioning, flexibility, and body composition—have a relation to healthful functioning of the body. Muscular strength and endurance allow a wide range of activities to be undertaken with decreased incidents of muscle strains and sprains. Flexibility also reduces the chances of the occurrence of these conditions, especially in the low back and hamstring muscle groups. The health benefit of aerobic functioning is improved primarily by a reduced heart rate and enhanced ability of the heart to move blood as well as produce more efficient respiratory patterns. The relationship between the reduced capacity of the cardiorespiratory system and a variety of cardiovascular degenerative diseases is becoming widely accepted by the medical profession. Body fatness has been implicated in a variety of poor health conditions, including high blood pressure, heart disease, and diabetes.

Muscular Strength

Repeatedly lifting a toddler is a challenge to an adult's muscle strength in multiple areas of the

Daniel Tardif/Photodisc/Getty Images

body. Muscle strength is the maximal amount of force that a muscle or functional muscle group can exert. It is usually measured in pounds or kilograms. It is quite possible to be strong in one muscle group and weak in another. Consequently, the muscles involved in the action should be specifically tested. Balance is supported by strong muscles. Fall prevention is paramount in the aging of adults. The development of muscle strength is extremely important to individuals with disabilities and those who are aging as it supports most of the capacity for physical tasks, including the activities of daily living, physical activity for health-related fitness, sport, and leisure.

In all the recommendations for adults exercising, working weekly on muscle strength is recommended (USDHHS, 2018). It is one system of the body that is easiest to improve upon even in oldest ages. No matter how sedentary a person is, working out to improve muscle strength is productive. Equipment can be free weights, resistance bands, weight machines, or even bottles filled with water or cans of food.

Muscular Endurance

Engaging in distance walking (half-marathons) allows one to experience muscle endurance and muscle strength. But training is necessary; a novice, won't make it to the finish line if they have not trained and their muscles can't take the load. The capacity to sustain repeated muscular contractions is muscle endurance, which depends on the ability of the muscle to get and use oxygen and to rid itself of waste. Muscle endurance is measured by the number of times a given movement can be performed, carrying a load that is a given percentage of the strength of the muscles before fatigue causes cessation.

A person can possess exceptional muscle endurance without being especially strong. The leg muscles of the marathon runner may not be nearly as strong as those of the football player, but they possess far greater endurance capacity. As is true of strength, each muscle possesses a degree of endurance and must be tested separately to determine its capacity to sustain repeated contractions.

Aerobic Functioning

The heart is a muscle that needs exercising as much as the other muscles of the body. A strong heart pumps blood well. A quality of health-related physical fitness is determined by the amount of oxygen that the heart and lungs (cardiorespiratory endurance) can deliver to working muscles. Improved cardiorespiratory endurance enables persistence at physically demanding tasks and decreased recovery time, a definite benefit in performing any activities requiring continued large-muscle exercise. In addition, efficient aerobic functioning offers substantial health benefits. Running a mile and shuttle runs are examples of aerobic functioning.

Flexibility

Many adults age into arthritis. After surgery for a total knee replacement (TKR) because of arthritic knee joints, the physical therapist (PT) works on flexibility to get that knee joint to fully *extend* to an appropriate degree. To begin, the knee is swollen and sore; the extension's flexibility is limited. Working on this joint's flexibility is essential to recover from the total knee replacement. The capacity to move a joint through a range of motion is termed *flexibility*. It is usually measured in degrees of joint rotation. Some joints have 360 degrees of rotation. Certainly, a knee joint does not. Some people are more flexible than others. Some diseases require a daily routine of range of motion exercises (e.g., neuromuscular), as does recovery from some injuries until the joint is healed. A person can be flexible in some joints but not others. Differences can also be noted from one side of the body to the other. Stretching joints with their associated muscles is beneficial to maintaining and increasing flexibility, preventing injury in physical activity participation, and contributing to relaxation.

Body Composition

Body composition is popularly understood as the percent of the total body weight that is fat. There are percentages calculated that indicate a healthy percent. One measurement is to calculate a body mass index (BMI) based on a person's height and weight. Another indicator of body composition and health is to measure waist circumference. The CDC (2020b) cautions that neither one of these measurements stands alone to indicate a healthy weight or a disease risk, but rather they should be interpreted in the presence of a health history and individual consultation with the person's health care practitioner. The Cooper Institute (2022) and the CDC (2020b) both provide BMI calculators on their websites. Both these measures are considered screeners. It is also well known that muscular athletes are not measured well with the BMI calculation; it does not distinguish between lean tissue and fat tissue, and athletes have more lean tissue, so their BMIs might indicate they are in the obese range (Hall, 2005).

Current percentages based on BMI calculations classify the following in relation to obesity (CDC, 2020c):

- BMI less than 18.5 is considered underweight
- BMI of 18.5 to 24.9 falls within the normal or healthy weight range
- BMI of 25.0 to 29.9 it falls within the overweight range
- BMI of 30.0 or higher is considered obese

Adults with any body composition, no matter whether underweight, normal, overweight, or obese, can participate in physical activity for health. Trained professionals and others can offer activity programs that aid in becoming healthy if a person's weight is unhealthy. The main contribution is increasing physical activity participation. Other specialists such as nutritionists are part of the medical team managing issues of obesity. Unhealthy weight is a risk factor for so many diseases including diabetes and heart disease. Nutritionists are part of many Medicare Advantage health insurance plans for older adults, sometimes at no cost. Weight loss is commonly thought to be dependent on a balance of nutrition and exercise, a strong contributor to healthy living. More research is addressing issues like the contributions of psychological health, disordered eating, and weight management.

Exercise Intensity

Understanding how exercise intensity is measured helps us describe to one another how we are meeting the intensity levels provided in the U.S. Department of Health and Human Services (USDHHS) guidelines on physical activity (2018). Someone ambling along on a two-mile walk is getting exercise, but someone walking briskly for those miles is getting more health benefit in absolute terms. One common and easy way of measuring how intense an exercise is for someone is to ask them to rate their exertion.

These are typically based on the rating of perceived exertion (RPE), developed by Swedish researcher Gunar Borg (1982, 1998), who devised a system whereby the individual could report their sense of exertion. With his work, application was made to output by major systems in the body that were engaged while exercising—a remarkable feat in its simplicity. The Borg scales (1998), often referenced simply as RPE, provide a numerical measure of

... how hard it feels that the body is working based on the physical sensations that the subject experiences, including increased heart rate, increased respiration or breathing rate, increased sweating and muscle fatigue.

Norton et al. (2010, n.p.).

When using the RPE, the one exercising simply looks at the chart numbers and indicates the number they feel represents how they are feeling.

Sample Rating of Perceived Exertion Scale

1. Nothing at all (resting)
2. Extremely little
3. Very easy
4. Easy
5. Moderate
6. Somewhat hard (starting to feel it)
7. Hard
8. Very hard (making an effort to keep up)
9. Very, very hard
10. Maximal effort (cannot go any further)

The American College of Sports Medicine (ACSM) has published accepted objective and subjective measures, from the field of exercise physiology, that correlate with the intensity categories. Table 14.1 describes the intensity levels from a functional standpoint and provides practical information on accounting for energy expenditure. Fortunately, the talk test (TT) and frequency, intensity, time, and type (FITT) can account for an individual's metabolic expenditure (MET) using ACSM data applied to Norton's descriptions (Norton et al., 2010). Norton and colleagues felt that there was too much ambiguity for the terms of light, moderate, vigorous, and heavy used to define exercise intensity and proposed a standard definition. Their research included the use of the Talk Test (TT), meaning that a person can exercise and still talk to someone, and the MET as a calculation of a person's weight and a measurement of their oxygen expenditure after one minute of exercise. One MET indicates the person is at rest. A person who is 154 pounds (70 kg) can expect to expend around five METs when walking at a moderate intensity (Healthline, 2023). The following levels of intensity are assigned up to six METs, with one and a half being the lowest on the scale:

- *Light:* Barely detectable change in breathing, untrained 60 minutes or more; one and a half to three METs.
- *Moderate:* Can pass the talk test, breathing and talking 30 to 60 minutes; three to six METs.
- *Vigorous:* Can't pass the talk test; untrained person 20 to 30 minutes; six to nine METs.
- *Heavy:* Heavy breathing; untrained person engaged for <10 minutes; more than nine METs.

Sometimes ratings of moderate-to-vigorous physical activity (MVPA) are reported. METs account for

> . . . energy demands and, therefore, represent the gradient in metabolic and neurohumoral [hormones and nervous system] responses during activity. These "stress" responses are not linear as the intensity of exercise increases. Many physiological responses, or disturbances in homeostasis, show an accelerating pattern as intensity increases. Small increases in exercise intensity can lead to relatively large increases in the physiological and metabolic demands of the body.
>
> Norton et al. (2010, n.p.).

According to the ACSM (Moore et al., 2016), light-intensity physical activity occurs when the individual exhibits no change in breathing when engaged in the physical activity.

Functionally, individuals often report that they are exercising too hard or not very hard (heavy or light) using the RPE. Instructors are encouraged to communicate to their class about the RPE. Attenuate them to its meaning. Keep it simple. Many instructors working in health clubs are ACSM certified with degrees in exercise physiology. They are more than qualified to monitor their class members.

Researchers find that this practical assessment of exertion by self-report is as simple as the talk test (TT) (Sørensen et al., 2020). TT is related to MVPA and is easy to conduct with verbal individuals because respiration isn't getting in the way of conversing. Although respiration is interacting with other systems, affecting the ability to exercise, the TT remains a functional overall measure of intensity. If the person is not verbal, then, can the person still indicate their RPE? Is it appropriate for a professional to observe the person slowing down and breathing heavily and make a judgment? Is the person perspiring more than normal and breathing heavily? Physiologic changes observed complement the RPE ratings. The validity without the participant reporting the exertion is in question, but some level of exertion can be observed by an instructor or accompanying supportive adult when the individual with a disability is not verbally communicating (Sørensen et al., 2020). Sørensen and colleagues explain that one way to obtain an RPE via TT is to have a supportive adult exercise with the person

TABLE 14.1   Descriptions of Intensity Ratings of Physical Activity

Intensity category	Description
Sedentary	Activities have *little movement* and require low additional energy. Sitting or lying.
Light	*Aerobic activities* can be sustained for at least 60 minutes. Light-intensity physical activity. No change in breathing when engaged in physical activity. Untrained person. At one and a half to three METs.
Moderate	Aerobic activity conducted while being able to maintain a *continual conversation.* May last 30 to 60 minutes (TT). Untrained person. TT with FITT. At three to six METs.
Vigorous	Aerobic activity that cannot sustain a constant conversation. May last about 30 minutes. Can't pass the TT. At six to nine METs.
High	Aerobic activity sustained for <10 minutes and cannot be sustained longer. At more than nine METs.

METs = The ratio of working metabolic rate relative to resting metabolic rate. One MET is an individual's resting rate (basal metabolic rate).

Adapted from Norton et al. (2010). Adapted from Moore et al. (2016).

with intellectual disability, explaining that talking while exercising is one of the goals. Experiment with a fast gait, then a slower gait. The supportive adult observes the differences and discusses these in simple terms with the person with intellectual disability. To monitor intensity and observe is a safety measure and accepted practice when working with aging adults exercising across the age spectrum, especially those starting an exercise program.

Achieved levels of intensity change for individuals over time. When starting an exercise activity for HRF, the pace may be slower. After a while, the person's

The FITT Principle

FITT stands for frequency, intensity, time, and type of exercise people with and without disabilities will do. FITT is part of what ACSM believes is an important principle for their members to follow for helping people to participate in an active lifestyle safely and effectively. Beyond ACSM membership, the wider community of professionals involved with direct involvement with both fitness and HRF programs also follow this principle. The components of FITT are defined as follows:

- *Frequency:* How often to exercise? This is typically referenced as a number of days per week.
- *Intensity:* In common terms, this refers to low, moderate, or high demand on the body.
- *Time:* This indicates how long the exercise session will last. It might also identify the time of day.
- *Type:* This refers to the kind of exercise. It might be aerobic, strength training , or some other component of HRF. These might be termed *cardio* and *weights* in a brochure or on a website.

FITT principles can be communicated to help the participant pick up the vocabulary.

body adjusts to the activity, and they can bump up the pace to stay at MVPA. An activity that once was easy for conversation sometimes gets hard, and an adjustment is needed to keep physical activity at a moderate level of intensity. In these ways, people can exercise safely. If there is medical concern during a bout of exercise, the person stops and rests, and has some sips of water. There are multiple reasons for a sudden onset of a change in response to intensity of exercise. After an analysis, if needed, consider a visit with the participant's primary care provider; of course, in extreme cases, call 911.

The 2018 *Physical Activity Guidelines for Americans* states that regular physical activity is one of the most important things people can do to improve their health (USDHHS, 2018). These benefits are applicable to individuals with disabilities across the life span. The FITT principle is a guide for recommending physical activity parameters (see sidebar). *The type and amount of physical activity should be determined by a person's abilities and the severity of the chronic condition.* For many chronic conditions, physical activity provides therapeutic benefits and is part of recommended treatment for the condition.

Exercise Recommendations

The United States Office of Disease Prevention and Health Promotion is responsible for the programs of Healthy People and the *Physical Activity Guidelines for Americans*. The overall department in the federal government responsible for both is the USDHHS.

Healthy People 2030 details all the current federal goals and objectives for Americans and their health across the life span. The Healthy People website (see references) is filled with important information based on the status of Americans' health since Healthy People 2020. A section of Healthy People 2030 (2021) is devoted to physical activity for health, giving statements about people with disabilities and goals and objectives for their participation in physical activity, access to programs, development of programs, and more. The 2018 *Physical Activity Guidelines for Americans* (USDHHS, 2018) still hold at the time of the publication of this text.

The 2018 *Physical Activity Guidelines for Americans* (USDHHS, 2018) names intensity levels to indicate their recommendations, categorizing the health benefits gained due to exercise, followed by recommendations grouped for adults of all ages, including adults with chronic conditions and disability.

Adults Exercising

Adults with early acquired disability and later acquired disability benefit from adapted physical activity (APA). The Health and Disability section later in the chapter notes many of the avenues

Delayed-Onset Muscle Soreness

Experiencing pain when starting an exercise program is common. When working with adults, share information about delayed-onset muscle soreness (DOMS) (ACSM, 2011; Minnis, 2020). This is the pain experienced about 12 to 24 hours after exercising and is the result of loading the muscles beyond what the individual typically has been doing. It lasts three to five days, and one experience of this (one bout) develops protection given similar muscle demand. The pain is accompanied by swelling in the joints, stiffness, tenderness, and reduced strength. The pain is part of the repair process of the muscle fibers, not the build-up of lactic acid (which was previously held as fact but has been debunked).

Activities prone to DOMS are strength training, walking downward, jogging, and step aerobics. Participants new to exercise need to be advised of this, and in some cases older people and those with disabilities need this type of information in very simple terms. When DOMS occurs, stop the activity for a few days and apply ice, gentle massage, and oral pain relief. Some PTs recommend heat or heat alternating with ice. These measures control the symptoms. Return to the activity pacing comfortably (ACSM, 2011) including a reduction in the repetitions, the weight level, or the tension level. Then build to the first desired goal knowing that the muscles have repaired. Most active people have experienced DOMS. It doesn't require stopping the activity forever. It means that the muscle was overloaded. Preventative measures when starting a new exercise program include slow-paced progressions. Sometimes it takes a case of DOMS or two to determine that overload occurred. Sitting in a bath or taking a shower, although it does not speed up DOMS recovery, is comforting.

for engagement. This next section will address the recommendations for HRF as an individual enters adulthood and moves through to through the oldest of ages. These guidelines for physical activity engagement are explicitly laid out by federal government agencies and national professional organizations.

The USDHHS explains the degree of health benefit from aerobic and muscle-strengthening physical exercise. *Some* health benefits are gained by adults who sit less and do *any amount* of moderate-to-vigorous physical activity. There are *substantial* health benefits gained by adults who do at least 150 minutes to 300 minutes a week of moderate-intensity physical exercise, or 75 minutes to 150 minutes a week of vigorous-intensity aerobic physical activity, or an equivalent combination of moderate-to-vigorous-intensity aerobic activity. Aerobic activity is preferred to be spread throughout the week. Reasonably so, *additional* health benefits are gained by engaging in physical activity beyond the equivalent of 300 minutes of moderate-intensity physical activity a week. Muscle-strengthening activities of moderate or greater intensity that involve all major muscle groups on two or more days a week are recommended.

Regarding moderate-intensity aerobic exercise, an option is to engage in aerobic exercise 5 days a week for 1 hour to equal 300 minutes for the week. A measure of moderate physical activity addressed earlier is the talk test (TT), where conversation can be maintained while exercising (Sørensen et al., 2020). This could be walking, wheelchair walking, hiking, using a stationary bike, or swimming for half an hour and walking for half an hour. The activity can be 30 minutes to a destination and back to the start. One could also do 30 minutes on a stationary bike and then take a 30-minute walk, possibly breaking it up into 15 minutes to the destination and then back. These examples all build to 300 minutes a week in physical activity if they are done five times a week.

For muscle strengthening, recommendations by an exercise specialist are to use of free weights, machines in a gym, or exercise bands. Strong muscles help with balance and in executing activities of daily living, as well as increasing the safety of a broad range of physical activities for leisure enjoyment.

Older Adults Exercising

Older adults are now receiving research attention because they need to move as they age. There is a range of health and disability status in older adults that includes those who are sedentary and wanting or needing to begin to exercise. The Get Up, Stay Up, Move rubric was designed to assist these individuals in safely beginning to exercise by targeting the muscles that need strengthening (Schlicht et al., 2021). The rubric progresses from rising from a seated position (get up), to stand (stay up), to ambulating (move). The muscles targeted for training are:

- *Get up:* Triceps brachii, gluteus maximus, quadriceps
- *Stay up:* Rectus abdominis, erector spinae, hip abductors
- *Move:* Tibialis anterior, hip flexors

Schlicht and colleagues (2021) allow aerobic activity after the individual has more strength and functional balance. Hence, the need to progress across the rubric sequentially.

The CDC program Move Your Way (2021b) recommends that older individuals *just move*. For those who are not moving, ". . . moving more and sitting less will benefit nearly everyone" (Piercy et al., 2018, p. 2020). There is no emphasis on frequency, intensity, or duration. Move Your Way options include gardening, playing with children, a yoga class; and strolling by foot, walker, or wheelchair. None of these activities has to be in a grand amount. Gardening can include a few pots of flowers and herbs or a small patch of some favorite perennials. Just walking or strolling by wheelchair is enough movement to count in Move Your Way. The focus is on moving, in and of itself, rather than quantifying moving by intensity or any other measured way.

The *least* amount of aerobic exercise recommended for older adults is 150 minutes cumulative in a week. That is half an hour a day for 5 days. Then, work with weights. An easy way for people to accomplish this is to join a strength and balance class. Online classes may afford access right into the home or other location. The instructor guides the individual through their muscle groups: arms, upper legs (quadriceps and hamstrings), back (upper, lower, and long muscle groups), and buttocks. The instructor can individualize weights, suggesting how many repetitions at a given weight the person could try; if the person can't do that, the weight can be lowered. Referrals by an individual's health care practitioner (HCP) to physical therapy (PT) offer strength and balance assessments to be used in a home exercise program.

Chronic Medical Conditions

The Centers for Disease Control and Prevention defines chronic medical conditions "as conditions that last 1 year or more and require ongoing medical attention or limit activities of daily living or both" (CDC, 2021a, n.p.). Examples are cancer, heart disease and stroke, diabetes, and arthritis. A secondary condition is a medical condition that results from the primary condition. For instance, type 2 diabetes is secondary to obesity. Obesity is the primary medical condition because if the person is overweight, they have developed type 2 diabetes. (Not every person who is obese develops diabetes, but it is considered a risk factor of obesity, especially if the person leads a sedentary lifestyle.)

Research has shown that a physician's interest in their physical activity is a powerful motivator for individuals; a "prescription" is even more motivating. Physicians working to engage their adult sedentary patients in physical exercise now have available resources through an initiative of the American College of Sports Medicine (ACSM) and the American Medical Association (AMA) called Exercise is Medicine (EIM) (ACSM, n.d.). One resource is a Health Care Providers' Action Guide with outlines, pictorials, and forms, and details on how to address physical activity with patients in a medical practice (ACSM, 2021). And another is specific HRF physical activity sheets a physician can give to their patient (ACSM, n.d.), part of the Exercise is Medicine program. There are HRF sheets for conditions like hypertension, heart failure, osteoarthritis, cancer, and many more. Next time the patient has an office visit, a discussion about physical activity has context!

Adults Exercising With Chronic Health Conditions and Disabilities

Those with chronic conditions should understand whether and how their conditions affect their ability to do regular physical activity safely. The sidebar lists those conditions. Adults with chronic conditions or disabilities, who are able, should do at least 150 to 300 minutes a week of moderate-intensity, or 75 to 150 minutes a week of vigorous-intensity aerobic physical activity, or an equivalent combination of moderate- and vigorous-intensity aerobic activity. Preferably, aerobic activity should be spread throughout the week. When older adults cannot do 150 minutes of moderate-intensity aerobic activity a week because of chronic conditions, they should be as physically active as their abilities and conditions allow. They should also engage in muscle-strengthening activities of moderate or greater intensity that involve all major muscle groups on 2 or more days a week.

If adults with chronic conditions or disabilities are not able to meet the above key guidelines, they should engage in physical activity according to their abilities and avoid inactivity. Adults with chronic conditions or symptoms should be under the care of an HCP and consult with them and obtain referrals to PT and licensed or certified physical activity specialists. These professionals can advise moving based on the types and amounts of activity appropriate for their abilities and chronic conditions.

If the referral from the HCP can be for six months, the PT has time to engage the client every few weeks and then monthly to evaluate and encourage them while updating the interventions before discharge into the home and community. Best practice in PT is to refer to community resources for physical activity. Attending classes at the YMCA, health clubs, senior centers, or municipal recreation programs is sometimes more motivational for adults.

The American College of Sports Medicine (ACSM) analyzed the *Physical Activity Guidelines for Americans* (USDHHS, 2018) for older adults and adults with chronic conditions and disabilities and modified the guide (Moore et al., 2016). The recommendations of ACSM are lowered. They advise the following as their basic special activity scenario:

- 150 minutes per week of MVPA
- 150 minutes per week of light-intensity physical activity for those who can't do MVPA
- Strength training exercises such as sit to stand, step-ups, and arm curls (around 4 lb [1.8 kg] to 8 lb [3.6 kg] weights)

Strength training is individualized based on FITT. Sit-to-stand may be two complete sets: sit and stand, then sit and stand. *Step-ups* refers to steps on a stairway. If two complete steps is too much, it can be as low as the person needs. In all cases, find the baseline data for step-ups. Sometimes therapists will add a chair for the individual to use during the exercise execution until the individual is stronger.

Health-related fitness requires continued attention to be maintained particularly as people age. HRF is dynamic, and the activities, while staying true to the components, should be enjoyable. A well-skilled professional working with a physically active adult should focus on HRF and enjoyment. This is appropriate along the spectrum of physical activity engagement from the beginning of an exercise program to trying out new activities or making changes in one's life necessitated by changes in physical activity participation. Making it enjoyable takes interest and commitment.

With chronic disease and disability that effects the person's physical activity, it is important for individuals to engage in regular exercise with guidance (Moore et al., 2016).

The basic CDD4 (Chronic Diseases and Disabilities 4th ed.) exercises of the American College of Sports Medicine are to be followed when the individual is not able to perform using the 2018 *Physical Activity Guidelines for Americans* (Moore et al., 2016). Figure 14.1 is the ACSM's basic CDD4 exercise recommendations, which is recommendations for chronic disease and disability. These are followed for specific conditions and at specific stages in a condition. Diseases of older age such as multiple sclerosis, type 2 diabetes, and Alzheimer's disease can benefit from the basic CDD4 exercises when capacity is limited for exercise. Otherwise, use the 2018 *Physical Activity Guidelines for Americans* (USDHHS).

Oldest Old

In reviewing the guidelines for physical activity and adults with chronic health conditions and disabilities, some of these people and the oldest old need special attention. Published recommendations may be unrealistic and instead "a greater emphasis on reaching levels of physical activity that are practically possible to achieve (relative to an individual's current physical performance and capacity) . . . would allow older people to preserve their independence" (Levinger et al., 2021, p. 8).

Aerobics

Suggestions are to walk, swim, do water aerobics, bike, or garden at a frequency of 4 to 5 days a week. The duration is as tolerated, with a goal of around 40 minutes. The intensity is started at the self-selected intensity of the talk test (amble, stroll, or walk slowly). Progress with this over 4 weeks in a self-selected pace to 40 minutes with increased intensity as tolerated.

Strength

Begin the exercise session by having the client sitting in a chair and rising to stand (sit-to-stand), doing at eight repetitions, which equals one set. Then have them perform eight repetitions per set of arm curls using small cans of food. Gradually build to tolerance; for curls, start with one set and over eight weeks build to two sets. Do this two to three times a week. Functional gravity exercises are also recommended and do not involve any equipment. Check with an exercise professional.

Flexibility

The hips, knees, shoulders, neck are targeted for flexibility. Check with an exercise specialist for stretches. Stretches should be done 3 days a week for a 20-second stretch. When stretching, start the stretch without pain and never go to the point of pain. Ease up if there is pain. The length of a stretch varies by body part.

Warm Up and Cool Down

Have the person doe some activity requiring easy exertion (interpreted as an RPE at or below three) before and after each workout session for 10 to 15 minutes.

FIGURE 14.1 Basic CDD4 exercise recommendations from the ACSM.

Adapted from Moore et al. (2016).

Extreme Sedentary Aging

For the adult who is in extreme sedentary aging, moving just as little as 10 minutes a day lowers mortality risk (Saint-Maurice et al., 2022). Older adults with intellectual disabilities, who were considered extremely unfit, gained a 0.3 percent lower mortality risk for every 0.6 miles (1 meter) on the shuttle walk test, and higher speeds resulted in 35 percent lower mortality risk in increments of 0.6 miles (1 km; Oppewal et al., 2020).

Ekelund and his colleagues from across five countries (Norway, Sweden, England, United States, and Australia) studied more than 44,000 individuals for physical activity (2020). The men and women who were most sedentary, compared to their peers who exercised 30 minutes most days at MVPA, were 260 percent more likely to die early (Ekelund et al., 2020). The comparison group's time at MVPA (30 minutes) was lower than has ever been reported to gain a mortality benefit. Recently, adding those minutes a day to an individual's activity level, no matter how active the individual, lowered a risk of premature death (Saint-Maurice et al., 2022). These realities are encouraging for professions responsible for promoting the physical activity of adults when someone is at the lowest end of fitness or even just the lower end of minutes in MVPA. The reality is that people abandoning some of their sedentary ways live longer.

Doctors are now seen as critical in facilitating healthy engagement in physical activity for their patients. They can now communicate that ". . . even small amounts of physical activity are beneficial and reductions in the risk of disease and disability occur by simply getting moving" (Thompson & Eijsvogels, 2018, p. 1983).

Instead Levinger and colleagues recommend that the oldest adults be as active as possible (as the USDHHS recommends), pursuing activity that is of meaning to them (the "existential well-being" of Krahn et al., 2021, p. 3) and in consultation with their health care professional, coordinating with a therapeutic recreation specialist of their care facility or any other exercise specialists such as exercise physiologists or PTs. Walking can begin at 5 minutes a day weekly progressing to 15 minutes a day over months. They can add a few minutes of strength and balance exercises twice per week with a goal

Ftwitty/E+/Getty Images

of 40 minutes eventually. Outdoor activities such as gardening, using outdoor exercise equipment, receiving pet therapy outdoors, and engaging in childcare partnerships are recommended.

Health and Disability

The current paradigm in disability and aging research is dichotomous, describing those aging *with* a disability and those aging *into* disability. Those aging with a disability are identified early in life at birth or some time relatively soon in early childhood (such as those with cerebral palsy); whereas those aging into disability are identified after middle age (beginning at 40 years of age) (Molton & Jensen, 2010; Molton, & Yorkston, 2017). This paradigm is a product of the evolution in defining disability over the years (Krahn et al., 2015). It is a functional disability model recognizing that impairment affects the carrying out of life's activities (Drum, 2009). A person who has had a disability since early in life is understood to be a different group of persons than the person who later in life encounters disability and must understand themselves anew. This is considered to radically influence the type of services and support a person could need. Thus, it has potential to influence the professional involvement in kinesiology, particularly how to motivate and continue support of individuals to engage safely in adapted physical activity. This reality is expected to influence disciplines like exercise physiology, sport psychology, recreation therapy, and others. Positive experiences in physical education and adapted physical education (APE) in grade school and high school are potentially potent in contributing to positive engagement in APA in aging.

Using this aging model, researchers were eager to further explore the potential relationships within the dichotomous groups. Using the National Paralysis Survey, they applied the paradigm of aging *with* a disability and aging *into* a disability to study the self-report of an individual's health status (Dixon-Ibarra et al., 2016). They discovered an unexpected difference in how these two reported their health status. In their survey, individuals were chosen for their paralysis functionally defined as having difficulty or being unable to move upper or lower extremities. Disabilities represented included spinal cord injury, cerebral palsy, spina bifida, stroke, traumatic brain injury, and others. Both groups were of similar ages. Those aging with disability reported better overall health, despite secondary health problems. Those aging

into disability reported a less healthy life and had a higher incidence of chronic health problems. This finding begs the question, *Why?* The authors speculated that those aging with disability had a repertoire of resiliency strategies as defined by Resnick and colleagues (2011). Having dealt with these issues since early childhood, they were more capable of adjusting to adversity, hardship, and life stressors than those just now aging into their paralysis in older age. The researchers felt that the group aging with disability of paralysis fit the disability paradox, whereby those who had serious disabilities did not report themselves as having poor health, despite the fact that others regarded them as such (Albrecht & Devlieger, 1999). Other researchers added that "The differences in health outcomes are critical when planning for health professional training, services, medical needs, and understanding optimal aging among these two distinct populations with disabilities" Dixon-Ibarra et al., 2016, n.p).

Why the good health report from those aging with disability? What does the effect of adapting in physical activity from early ages have on aging? Just this attention and facilitation may have strengthened an early resolve that those aging with disability in the Paralysis study are successful. Adapting is a part of life. By the time the people in the Paralysis study have graduated from high school, those aging with disability could have had a maximum of 22 years' experience with APA.

Table 14.2 depicts engagement in adapting in physical activities for those aging with and into disability (Molton & Jensen, 2010; Molton & Yorkston, 2017). Better health is traditionally associated with a physically active life for older adults, with immediate improvements in sleep, lessening anxiety, lower blood pressure; and long-term effects of reduced risk of dementia, depression, stroke, diabetes, risk for cancers, weight gain, falls, and improved bone health (CDC, 2020a). Thus, it is important to understand the differences that adults bring to their aging by virtue of when they began living with a disability. This has ramifications for understanding the total ecological context of engagement, program development, and the interdisciplinary nature of APA (Kennedy, 2021).

Table 14.2 also presents APA engagement based an individual's status. Current definitions of health and disability are applied. Krahn and colleagues (2021) defined health as "the dynamic balance of physical, mental, social, and existential well-being in adapting to conditions of life and the environment" (p. 3). They further defined disabilities as "experienced limitations in body function, activities, or participation in major life activities due to a health condition that occur in the context of one's environment and are influenced by personal factions" (p. 1). These distinctions are important to apply to the provision of HRF activity—to the full ecological context for engagement (Kennedy, 2021).

Recalibration is used as the dynamics of health and disabilities elements are confronted and rearranged to promote an existential well-being, thus the person readjusts to create for themselves a sense of being in the here and now and feeling good. This recalibration, because it is dynamic, involves many systems and is a full ecological context detailed

TABLE 14.2   Considered Influences in APA Engagement Using a Dichotomous Model of Aging

Aging with disability	Aging into disability
Grade school through high school	
• **Early identification of disability** and services in education if they qualify. Some participate at birth. See chapter 3. • APE with specific fitness curriculum beginning around age 10, including fitness for sports and HRF activities. Some children participate in general physical education. • *Assessments:* Individualized education program (IEP) assessments and development for APE engagement. In high school, the transitional IEP begins with training and plans for APA in the student's community postgraduation. • *Community:* Possible experience in the community, neighborhood, or municipal recreation if programs were adapted and safe. • *Legal precedent for APA:* Federal law for ages 3-22 in 1975; ages 0-2 in 1985. By graduation, the person might have had 14 to 22 years of APA.	• **No disability at early age.** • General physical education with fitness curriculum. • 504 plan for temporary disability and access to APE possible. • *Assessments:* School district assessments for general physical education per grade. • *Community:* No adaptations for potential physical activity experience in the community, neighborhood, or municipal recreation. • *Legal precedent for APA:* 504 plans, Section 504 of the Rehabilitation Act (1973). By graduation, potential for one year or less of APA (depending on injury or illness).
Post–high school	
• **Continued management of conditions of early disability.** • Transitional IEP follow-through with appropriate supports in place. • *Community:* Participation in specialized and inclusive programs. • *Employment or higher education:* Accessible gyms, fitness centers, classes, activities, and employee workout rooms.	• **No disability.** Predominantly no need for APA. • May sustain an injury or have an illness requiring APA or a rehabilitation clinic. • *Community:* Predominantly no need for APA. • *Employment or higher education:* Access to gyms, fitness centers, campus recreation programs, and employee on-site workout rooms.
Middle adulthood	
• **Disabilities of childhood plus medical conditions of aging.** • May need and want recalibration for APA. Engaged in HRF based on years of understanding of self in APA. • By middle age, have experienced potentially 40-50 years of APA. Potentially positive effect on APA engagement.	• **Medical conditions of aging.** • Engages in physical activity. • Illness and injury may require recalibration. APA is a newer concept for the individual. May need a clinic for rehabilitation services. • By middle age, a new engagement in APA. Potential psychological struggle. Need for supportive specialists in clinic and community.

across time in table 14.2. The considered influences for APA engagement vary for each group until the groups merge more at older and oldest ages. No one can deny the sense of psychological weight felt by each group in their advanced ages. It is striking to note the change and loss at oldest adulthood. Krahn and colleagues (2021) have given us a dynamic perspective from which to explore this question, and others related to health and disability across aging. APA engagement can support individuals as they recalibrate again and again with an interdisciplinary thrust attempting for that engagement again and again.

Dr. Lee, a rheumatologist who places value on physical activity for his patients with severe conditions, comments on his role in facilitation of that:

Aging with disability	Aging into disability
Middle adulthood *(continued)*	
• Aging process has a natural impact on the whole self—the physical, mental, social, and existential self. • Onset of medical conditions associated with aging requiring health care interventions. • Intervention if not engaged in APA: Guided by trusted professional(s) in medicine and exercise to engage in APA understanding the whole self. Develop a personal skills knowledge of existential self. Join health clubs, Silver Sneakers, or Silver & Fit (Medicare insurance benefit), use municipality, neighborhood spaces, and so on. Rehabilitation clinic outpatient activity.	
Older adulthood	
• Continued management of health conditions of disability, aging conditions, and potential chronic disease. • HCP, as well as other clinicians recognize the ongoing familiarity of adapting life activity for the individual.	• Greater effect of disabilities on health, with continued aging conditions, and potential chronic disease. • HCP, as well as other clinicians recognize the newness of dealing with APA for the individual.
• Need for encouragement in life balance and assistance toward APA. • Interventions include continuing with HCP evaluations to support APA; and referrals to specialists if needed. • If engaged in APA, continue support from HCP, occupational therapy (OT), PT and community activity leaders for participation and medical management of pain, injury, disease. The individual recalibrates APA. • If not engaged in APA, the HCP needs to *encourage* the individual and make referrals to PT or OT to assess and treat overall functional capacity for APA. HCPs encourage the individual to return to evaluate APA activity and medical needs to continue. • The person may need a rehabilitation clinic. A physiatrist, OT, and PT provide direct care toward APA.	
Oldest adults	
• Prior status with medical conditions of older adulthood remain for both early acquired disability and later acquired disability with individual recalibration continuing for APA, or not. • Change of residence or support in the home. The person may move to an assisted living center, nursing home, or other new home. Some of the oldest old remain in their home with supports allowing continued residence. • Engagement in APA for residents through a therapeutic recreation program. APA follows guidelines for oldest adults exercising. • Those not engaged in APA lead a sedentary life. • What changes are occurring in the personal life because of disability and disease? What APA fits for this person at this time? Common elements are change of residence, significant others, or friends due to death or disability, family consolations, finances, or physical capacity. Enjoyable APA activity contributes to health.	

Examples of medical conditions of aging to age 50: hypertension, arthritis, high cholesterol, obesity, depression, vertigo, vision changes, and hearing loss.

Aging model: Molton & Jensen (2010); Molton & Yorkston (2017).

> For my patients with arthritis and chronic disease, I strongly believe exercise and physical activity can improve health and quality-of-life. If needed, I refer to physical therapy to assist with evaluating and formulating a home exercise program and connecting to resources in the community. Otherwise, I make recommendations and I particularly like water/pool-based exercises. There are numerous studies in the medical literature showing the benefits of exercise in patients with arthritis and chronic disease. Unfortunately, I find that it can be hard for my older patients to find transportation for community physical activity.
>
> Dr. Lee (personal communication).

In order for individuals with disabilities to take advantage of health-related fitness opportunities, Rimmer wrote nearly 20 years ago about the need for fitness professionals to strengthen their skills in health promotion and disability, to have rehabilitation professionals embrace the concept of extending their services into community-based fitness centers, and to have Medicaid and Medicare, insurance companies, and managed care organizations be willing to pay for the membership and the consultative services of physical therapists who would work alongside fitness professionals in delivering health promotion programs to people with disabilities (1994). Today these concerns are making a positive shift. For example, classically recognized bastions of sport and fitness are offering training for those needing APA. As such, the ACSM has an extensive program to train people to work with individuals in APA who are on the autism spectrum. Many fitness centers include classes specifically geared to those needing lower impact exercises or advertise them as a Silver Sneakers class. Medicare does support access to free APA classes within clubs and community programs through programs like Silver Sneakers or Silver and Fit. Hospital community education programs offer guidance on being physically active in older ages or with specific illness like cancer, arthritis, or heart disease. Kennedy and colleagues are promoting the use of community facilities within the clinical goals of people in outpatient PT programs (2021).

There is need for interdisciplinary coordination with the medical care of those with disabilities. The individuals need to be encouraged and supported by their clinical care team to find and to engage with professionals in the community at health clubs and municipalities. As this gradually happens, professionals will be following the person in their care and their physically active life or their sedentary life.

The need for program development is apparent in reviewing table 14.2. No matter how old the adult is, finding qualified leaders and programs that are inclusive of disability are very important. The Commit to Inclusion Initiative (Kraus & Jans 2014) provides information for disability inclusion in physical activity, nutrition, and obesity programs and policies. Pertinent in this initiative's report are these points that support program development for physical activity engagement:

- People with disabilities (and their family and other caregivers and experts with disabilities) are involved in every aspect of program development and implementation, as well as evaluation of that program.
- The program clearly states objectives of inclusion of people with disabilities.
- The program should include outreach to those with disabilities for program engagement.
- Accessibility includes physical, social, behavioral, and communication aspects.
- The program makes accommodation for participants, tailoring for their needs and supports.
- Costs for support staff, staff training, and special equipment must be budgeted.
- Programs should be affordable for those with a disability and their attendants.
- Evaluations are process oriented; collected from participants, attendants, and family; and reported as outcomes of the program using measures of disabilities.

Exercise Initiation

As individuals begin an exercise program, the National Center on Health Physical Activity and Disability (NCHPAD, 2023) recommends that adults with disabilities discuss a program with their HCP and review their medications for effects on exercise (dehydration, dizziness), be tested for their current level of fitness and work with a trained exercise professional to obtain an individualized exercise prescription. They emphasize that strong muscles help avoid falls in the home. They also recommend being attentive to risk by installing handrails where needed and clearing clutter on the floor. Clothing and shoes need to fit. Individuals should carry a cell phone or other alert system if possible. Many adults are enjoying exercise classes offered on the Internet and coming into their home. These recommendations will support exercising at home as well as in the community. See the sidebar where PTs are expanding their understanding of community engagement while their patients are in clinical treatment.

Those coming out of a rehabilitation program should have a very good idea of their physical capacity. If not, before discharge, they should ask pointed questions about a home fitness program. They can also contact the NCHPAD for resources in their state. Health clubs employ professionals with certificates from the ACSM, making the professionals very capable of individualized exercise prescription for activities to try at various levels. At clubs, there typically is a free general introduction to their programs. Sometimes the introduction to the facilities is all an individual needs. Individualized sessions for an exercise prescription typically have a fee above the monthly fee. If a club member is new to a piece of equipment, it is customary to ask a staff person to demonstrate how it is used. There is no cost to those types of inquiries. Municipalities employ individuals who are specially trained for recreation and APA for those with special needs. See chapter 15 for much more detail.

A trained exercise professional is one who has a degree or an advanced degree in movement sciences with a certification from an exercise association. The ACSM is one of many exercise associations. If possible, check on the association to determine just how much training is required to qualify for a certificate. If it is only an online certificate with no education requirement, it is not appropriate for adults with disabilities. Universities and colleges around the country offer bachelor of science, master of science, and doctor of philosophy in kinesiology with an emphasis in that degree in exercise physiology. Other degrees are associated with physical activity, exercise, or public health. A doctorate noted as DPT is a doctor of physical therapy indicating they are a highly trained academic or practitioner.

Considerations for Selected Conditions

Parkinson's disease and arthritis are diseases acquired later in life and have special exercise considerations. Those aging with cerebral palsy also have special considerations.

Parkinson's Disease

Parkinson's disease is a progressive nervous system disease that occurs later in life. Symptoms include appearance of slowed movement (bradykinesia), tremor in the arms or hands, stooped posture, balance difficulties, soft-spoken speech, rigid muscles, difficulty writing, a masklike facial expression, and depression (Mayo Clinic, 2022b). This disease has variability in presentation and changes with medications and time. The masklike facial expression and the soft voice make it hard for instructors to interpret the RPE. People with Parkinson's disease have trouble regulating temperature. During exercise, experts do need to monitor for the individual's exaggerated response to being too hot and too cold, potentially without the person complaining. Individuals with Parkinson's disease greatly benefit from a class just for their condition with an instructor specialized in their disability as they lead, monitor, and supervise.

For those with Parkinson's disease, exercise is recommended to increase social opportunities and to use the body that is challenged by the disease.

Physical Therapy Interventions in the Community

Physical therapists are surveying their colleagues' comfort and skill with interventions that combine treatment in the clinic with extension into the client's community (e.g., Rethorn et al., 2021). Professional standards in physical therapy consider this best practice. Rethorn's study reported that PTs rated themselves with high confidence in making referrals for physical activity in the community, yet they struggled to screen with their patients for their community involvement in physical activity. Furthermore, they felt they were aware of national guidelines for physical activity; but when tested, most were not accurate. The authors believe studies like this, when followed with continuing education, will greatly assist physical therapy professional organizations in boosting their members' skills for meeting not only a standard but, most importantly the HRF engagement of their clientele.

Hoehn and Yahr developed a scale (one to five) for the progression of Parkinson's disease (1967). For those rated at level one or two on Hoehn and Yahr's scale, the ACSM (Moore et al., 2016) recommends the general *Physical Activity Guidelines for Americans* (USDHHS, 2018) for exercise. Exercise has been shown to reduce the risk of falls, decrease motor symptoms, improve motor performance balance and gait, and produce positive repercussions in quality of life (Cristini et al., 2021; Flynn et al., 2019; Koop et al., 2019; Schootemeijer et al., 2020). Fitness activity at level three on this scale should be individualized and can include walking, biking, stretching, group classes, and weights. Supervision is important with balance issues, even providing extra support on the treadmill.

Arthritis

Arthritis is a common disease of adults ages 65 and older (31 percent of those in this age group are afflicted; NCOA, 2021). The most common form of arthritis is osteoarthritis. With all arthritis forms, the joints swell and are tender. In osteoarthritis, the cartilage that covers the ends of the bones begins to break down (Mayo Clinic, 2022a). Rheumatoid arthritis is more serious and is caused by the immune system attacking the joint lining first followed by progressing the attack. Exercise can relieve pain if done correctly with low-impact activities, stretches, and strength training (Mayo Clinic, 2022a). Exercise also helps with weight management, which, in turn, aids in pain relief with arthritis, so the National Council on Aging (NCOA) recommends staying within the recommended weight for height (2021). Calculations show that losing one pound (0.4 kg) can remove four pounds of pressure (0.3 kg per cm^2) on your knees; less pressure on the knees leads to less pain in the joint. Follow the individual's HCP's advice given life conditions and total health status.

With osteoarthritis, follow the *Physical Activity Guidelines for Americans* (USDHHS, 2018), and when the disease progresses, use the ACSM's basic CDD4 recommendations (figure 14.1). The key is not to exacerbate the joint by repetitive use that goes beyond tolerance. Gentle is good, so resistance on stationary bicycling is paced. Water exercise supports the body and is highly recommended, and pacing oneself in the classes allows the body to adjust to the activity. DOMS will be present when starting and can be managed. There is a paradox that orthopedists find, preparatory to considering joint replacement due to osteoarthritis, that some people have very narrow joint space in the knees (bone on bone) and *have no pain*; others have more space in the joint, yet report *more pain*. The doctors don't know why this paradox occurs, but no pain typically means no surgery.

Use the CDD4 guide for those who have rheumatoid arthritis at later stages, as they can still exercise. Also, a PT or OT can work with the individual on a home program if it is preferred or needed (Moore et al., 2016). Even at the CDD4 level, the activities of gardening or cycling are recommended, as is water exercise (which, for many, means the pool of a club or municipal program—warmed if possible). Exercise does improve symptoms of arthritis such as pain, stiffness, physical function, balance, a sense of well-being, and improved sleep. Pain with arthritis can be episodic, thus fluctuating. To avoid downregulation of exercise due to pain, modify the program of exercise (back off some), and if need, consult the health care provider or exercise specialist. In most cases, backing off allows the body to recover, and after a week or more, the person can gradually resume the exercise and increase the frequency or intensity until reaching the level attained prior to the bout of pain. Those with rheumatoid arthritis are likely to benefit from exercise that would reduce their risk of heart attacks due to overall inactivity and low fitness (Metsios et al., 2020).

Cerebral Palsy

Cerebral palsy (CP) is a broad term for a motor disorder as a result of damage to the developing brain or after birth (see chapter 12). It is diagnosed in early life. Therefore, it is an early acquired disability and the person reaches aging having life with their disability for a long time (Molton & Yorkston, 2017). Many individuals with CP use assistive devices like a wheelchair, walker, or crutches. These same individuals have a long history of sport competition, physical fitness activity, and playing with their peers as children and youth in the school systems. Upon graduation from high school, the challenge increases to secure community programs and facilities with personnel to support participation. The transition from high school to community for physical activity engagement should have been handled in the transitional IEP.

HRF is important for adults with CP to maintain mobility, decrease sedentary time, and increase quality of life. Including physical activity in a care plan for adults sometimes is ignored, especially in facilities where the care is fragmented. Many of these individuals had a physically active life when they were young due to engagement in an APE program. Entering the community is hard for these individuals as they live, work, attend college or university, find ways to exercise, and socialize.

Heller and colleagues found that adults with CP who did exercise were not living in residential care and had an available, accessible facility for working out. They had a higher ability to care for themselves and were in better health with fewer limits on mobility. Their care provider understood that exercising was important in their care (2002). The most influential factor was the positive attitude of the care provider.

Those with CP who do not have an accessible workout facility, using the basic CDD4 can be recommended exercise. They don't need expensive equipment or even a gym as exercise can be undertaken in the neighborhood (if it is safe) and at home. If a care provider understands the value of exercise, the leisure activities the person with CP engages in can be socially based (see chapter 15).

For those with CP that walk with and without the support of assistive devices, 25 percent have pain as they age, becoming more easily fatigued leading to a decline in use (Moore et al., 2016). The energy required to walk is greater for them than for those without CP because of the greater demand for syncopation of the body's systems for ambulation. Never doubt that they are working hard to get from place to place. They are, and this effort leads to fatigue.

The ACSM recommends HRF activities for adults while relying on the Gross Motor Function Classification System (Palisano et al., 1997) (figure 14.2). It recommends that all individuals start with the basic CDD4 activities with the understanding that adaptations will be made on a case-by-case basis (Moore et al., 2016). The ACSM suggests that to stave off boredom, the person can add a walking partner, a graphic that monitors the activity and the progress, or make it into a game.

Adults with CP in level I and II can use basic CDD4 exercises as a starting point. The basic CDD4

resistance activities do help individuals with CP, especially when performed slowly to avoid quick, jerky moves inducing a reflexive response. If one occurs, just wait, let the limbs relax, and begin again.

According to the NCHPAD, the exercise session for someone with CP can decrease fatigue by offering:

> . . . short intervals and relaxation and stretching sessions throughout the training sessions . . . Types of aerobic activity can include arm cycling, chair aerobics, dancing, jogging, leg cycling, rowing, swimming, walking, water aerobics, and wheeling. Resistance training for persons with cerebral palsy is important because it helps to increase their strength without an adverse effect on muscle tone . . .
>
> NCHPAD (2010, n.p.).

Adults in level III (wheeled mobility) with CP can use light to moderate aerobic exercise working up to 150 minutes a week (Moore et al., 2016). The talk test (TT) is a good measure of intensity if the person's baseline conversation is familiar to the instructor as speech production is sometimes affected by CP. If the usual production is pressed, then expect the same as the exercise intensity increases but to a greater degree. More importantly, ask the person how they feel. If the person is in an enclosed space, use the RPE chart (having familiarized the person to the chart's use). Err on the side of caution.

Level III still involves the muscle-strengthening and flexibility recommendation of basic CDD4 (Moore et al., 2016). There are more exercises from a seated position, and there is often equipment fit for wheelchairs in gyms. An instructor at the gym can be engaged for advice. Free weights can

Level	Description
I	Walks without support
II	Walks with support sometimes
III	Uses wheeled mobility in the community
IV	Uses powered mobility or is pushed in a manual chair
V	Is transported in a wheelchair at all times

FIGURE 14.2 Gross Motor Function Classification System (GMFCS).

Adapted from Palisano et al. (1997).

build strength slowly, and as stability increases the weights can increase.

Adults in level IV with CP engage in light-intensity physical activity of 150 minutes per week with some of the activity out of the wheelchair on mats or in a swimming pool. This needs to be fun. Maybe the person can be a part of an aerobics class, using the flotation vests of the class, moving the legs and arms to the music if possible. When in the pool, the person could push some equipment like a soccer ball into a goal area against the wall. Care must be taken for the person to be supported if they are a nonswimmer.

Adults in level V with CP engage their whole 150 minutes per week out of their wheelchair. They could be side lying on a mat, listening to music, moving to music that they like. Try some stretches to some music. There must be some fun in this so as not to be seen as therapy but as HRF. Water activity is excellent for the support the water provides, but care must be taken to support the person in the water with vests and head supports if necessary.

The ACSM (Moore et al., 2016) recommends adaptations to daily flexibility exercises for levels III through V, as people with CP tend to get stiff. Examples include the following:

- Exercises are performed from the wheelchair with the brakes on and the belt on.
- The person sits in a chair and reaches right, then reaches left (sit and reach).
- Do not stretch beyond tolerance nor to the point of pain in the shoulders particularly.

Summary

HRF differs in components from physical fitness and performance-related fitness. HRF is believed to contribute to a person's capacity to enjoy life and withstand challenges. Today, *health* is defined not as the absence of disease or infirmity but rather as a state of physical, mental, and social well-being. Health is dynamic, multidimensional, and distinct from function. A person can have a disability and be healthy as determined by balanced adaptation. Intensity of exercise is critical in managing participation in HRF activity. The *Physical Activity Guidelines for Americans* (USDHHS, 2018) are presented with ACSM adaptions for those with disabilities and chronic conditions. Aerobic physical activity along with muscle endurance are critical for engaging in based on recommendations. For some clinical populations, balance is needed in their HRF program no matter what. The paradigm of aging *with* disability and aging *into* disability is employed to present APA engagement across the life span.

Leisure Activity

CHAPTER OBJECTIVES

After completing this chapter, you will be able to do the following:

- Understand the progression for participating in community-based physical activities after various types of rehabilitation program engagement.
- Identify the interventions in the case of extreme sedentary lifestyle regarding physical activity engagement.
- Identify the extension of levels of support from adapted physical education activity for the adults aging *with* disabilities in community engagement in leisure.
- Discuss the considerations for facilitation of those adults aging *into* disability to engage in community physical activity.
- Discuss a variety of leisure physical activities with their adaptations for a variety of disability considerations.

Leisure can be deeply satisfying when it is understood to be important to one's life. Leisure exists in a time and it is activity (Hurd & Anderson, 2011). Leisure studies include serious leisure, casual leisure, and projects-based leisure (Stebbins, 2020); however, for our purposes, it is simply leisure. It is activity free from *obligation* of tasks of subsistence. It is enjoyable, restorative activity.

Leisure in adulthood may be negatively associated with a life of forced retirement, unemployment, failing health, loss of self-esteem, and a lack of access to enjoy leisure activities. Recognizing that these life circumstances do negate the satisfaction and joyfulness of leisure activity, we emphasize two points. One is that these situations can be addressed by working across disciplines to offer adapted physical activity to individuals to be enjoyed in leisure. Two, there is always a one-on-one aspect of working to engage an individual in adapted physical activity. Chapter 2 provided examples of the dialogue with the person with a disability in different systems (e.g., primary care, community agencies, and private health clubs). Leisure activities can result in a positive change in health status across aging for those aging *with* disability and *into* disability.

This chapter addresses leisure and the engagement in adapted physical activity across the ages of adulthood. Enjoyment is emphasized because with enjoyment, the participant is motived to return to it (Jin et al., 2018).

Leisure and Disability

In approaching leisure, we recognize that those adults who had a transitional individualized education program had training in their pursuit of adapted physical activity upon graduation. These activities took place at a higher education campus or in the person's own neighborhood after work, or while seeking work, or within a new living situation. Those in general physical education in high school didn't have years to prepare for their leisure after high school that included any discussion of a disability. Their understanding of themselves in adapted physical activity was potentially years off as they entered adulthood with a late-acquired disability.

On college campuses, there are typically recreation centers offering specific activity classes, open gyms and pools, weight rooms with exercise machines, and specialty sport courts. These campus recreation centers are also social activity centers.

Students find it is easy to meet people who share similar interests or make acquaintances by saying *hello* to the same people repeatedly after a workout.

If these programs are operating with inclusion in mind, the classes and the facility are accessible. If not, the National Center on Health, Physical Activity and Disability (NCHPAD, 2022) recommends creating an inclusive program by having an inclusion coordinator on staff; establishing a connection with the office of students with disability services; highlighting links to the campus recreation website on accessibility and inclusion so they are easy for users to find; and having rentals or loaning equipment that makes participation easier. Furthermore, the NCHPAD suggests providing staff training on pertinent topics such as interacting with those with disabilities, explaining the similarity of their needs and exercise interests to those of their peers without disabilities. Finally, if there are architectural barriers to accessibility, plan to remove them and implement new construction to comply with ADA standards.

Working adults with disabilities potentially have leisure. We say "potentially" because many report that outside of work, they arrange meals, clean, sleep, and take care of other necessities. For retired adults both with and without disabilities, leisure may be plentiful, but the individuals do not know what activities to undertake. They need their health care provider (HCP) to ask, "What are you doing for physical activity in your leisure?" The experts believe this is vital to ask (see chapter 4), because practitioners play a role in asking and finding resources for the individual. Importantly, the benefits of participating in physical activity as adults include reduced risk for

all-cause and cardiovascular mortality, cardiac and cerebrovascular events, hypertension, type 2 diabetes, lipid disorders, and cancer of the bladder, breast, colon, endometrium, esophagus, kidney, stomach, and lung.

Thompson & Eijsvogels (2018, p. 1984).

Those adults with and without disabilities who have not retired but are unemployed are sometimes experiencing depression from the lack of work. Depression is a necessary area of assessment from clinical colleagues, as this information is linked to finding enjoyment in adapted physical activity during leisure. Physical activity engagement is highly recommended to increase a positive mood during depressive episodes (Giandonato et al., 2021).

In midlife, around age 40, disease onset results in the beginning of adapting physical activity in leisure. This is aging into disability time. Heart disease (particularly hypertension), type 2 diabetes, breast cancer, and osteoporosis are leading diseases of those age 40 (Johns Hopkins, 2023). Hypertension or type 2 diabetes might be a new disease related to an existing health issue. Breast cancer mediates physical activity involvement by interruptions to daily life for interventional therapies and side effects including depression. Osteoporosis can be painful and requires adjustments to formerly enjoyed physical activity. Some physical activities are abandoned completely, some are adapted, and for some people there is initiation into a new physical activity. The risk at this juncture is that compensatory behavior begins, resulting in not being as physically active. And, gradually socialization is not associated with physical activity. Those who are aging with disability in midlife add disease and injury to their understanding of themselves in leisure activities.

Community and Professional Resources

In rehabilitation programs, retirement homes, and assisted living and nursing homes recreation therapists conduct assessments of their clients. They assess to determine attributes that impact participation in leisure activity such as interests, value of leisure, and barriers to leisure. Program planners need to know just what activities the individual likes and to get a sense of what they may now like to try. Sometimes residents (or inpatients) are provided with lists of recreation activities to use as a discussion point for those coordinating care or life in the new home. Each type of assessment the recreation therapist or activities director conducts yields information that is useful to the process, potentially engaging the individual in enjoyable activity during leisure.

Residential homes for adults have individuals both aging with disability and into disability. These homes can be a safe place to live with increased socialization and activities offered in the facility and in the surrounding communities and countryside. They generally employ a person to direct recreation activity who has training in therapeutic recreation and is licensed by the state.

Municipal recreation agencies employ personnel referred to as inclusion specialists when mindful of serving their whole community. These therapeutic recreation personnel supervise or coordinate with other recreation staff and volunteers. For example, they might help people like a young adult with intellectual disability who has grown tired of Special Olympics get involved in parks and recreation dances and summer camp for adults.

In municipal programs, the person's interest alone often is enough to allow entry for participation. In rehabilitation programs, the outpatient time of the program is primed to engage the individual in adapted physical activity (APA) in their community,

and the best rehab programs include the transition into APA in the patient's home and community. Referrals are made to programs and specific people who greet the individual and enroll them comfortably in a selected class or activity. Then the individuals participate and provide feedback to the rehab personnel—including the physiatrist, the recreation therapist, the physical therapist (PT), and the occupational therapist (OT). This exchange of feedback has value in enhancing APA participation. If one's time is negative, a problem-solving discussion results.

In rehabilitation, individuals might need the attention of a physiatrist. If they're not in rehabilitation, they might need their HCP. In addition, the PT can check individuals' progress in walking and balance issues, discuss considerations for some adaptive equipment like the use of a cane or walker, and watch for depression. Occupational therapists help with any self-care for physical activity engagement or adaptations of recreational equipment (gardening tools) or any ADLs encountered in physical activity.

The American College of Sports Medicine (ACSM) and many physical activity experts suggest finding a friend or friends to walk with or to attend exercise class together. Dogs are also recommended as an exercise partner (Moore et al., 2016)!

Leisure Activity Checklist

It is important to find out what a person likes to do, or liked to do, and what they are interested in now.

A leisure activity checklist, conducted verbally or in writing, can simply be composed of physical activities from the community in which the person resides. For example, small towns on the Oregon and Washington coast might include clamming, walking on the beach, searching for sand dollars or agates, and attending activities of the local recreation or art center in a nearby town. Leisure activity in larger urban cities might include walking around the lake, hiking in a city park, playing pickleball, social dancing, or activities at senior centers and private health clubs. Seniors can also join hiking clubs and venture out into the foothills of the nearby mountain ranges for the day. These trips are sponsored by the municipal recreation program as well as special interest groups, private clubs, and residential centers.

In creating an assessment tool that lists activities by community, people can give suggestions of activities that were not included. This list in has social validity. Interviewees can answer in the following ways:

- No, do not want to participate.
- Yes, would like to participate.
- I don't know.
- Other (comment):

or

- Like
- Don't like
- Don't know
- Other (comment):

Step It Up!

The United States Surgeon General's office issued a call to action, Step It Up! to promote walking and to create safe and accessible communities *for all* (CDC, n.d.). This effort was enhanced by findings that physical activity engagement increases health outcomes for all, reduces risk factors for different diseases of older age and positively affects an individual's mental health (Lee & Buchner, 2008; Martin-Diener et al., 2014; USDHHS, 2018). According to the Centers for Disease Control and Prevention (CDC), four main goals were targeted to enact the call to action:

1. *Accessibility:* Create access to places for walking and to encourage use of these places such as public parks; health, fitness, and recreational facilities; schools, colleges, and universities; malls; senior centers; and work sites.

2. *Focus on social interventions like friendships to support walking:* Use buddy systems and contracts with others to complete specified levels of physical activity or walking groups.

3. *Individually adapted health behavior programs:* Set physical activity goals, monitor progress toward these goals, seek social support, and use self-reward to reinforce progress.

4. *Community-wide campaigns:* Seek media coverage, risk factor screening and education, community events, and policy or environmental changes.

The Step It Up! resource is free online and contains information that elaborates on each of these points. Wheelchair rolling is included as an adaptation for bipedal walking.

When reviewing the information, the interviewer follows up on activity the person liked to do in the past, and what other activity they listed. The survey provides the person with an opportunity to remember and to think about the present time.

If the person is exploring a health club, looking over the offerings ahead of time or together with the professional is beneficial to building involvement. The person can pick one activity to try and the professional can encourage the individual to report back their likes and dislikes. Herein is the beginning of a process and relationship to address concerns, solve problems, and share success. This can lead to the increasing confidence in making another choice for physical activity involvement or being even more engaged in their current choice.

Aging and Disability

Those who are aging with disability need ongoing attention to the level of support needed for community participation. Intellectual disability and autism

Leisure and Adapted Physical Activity Participation

Through middle age, chronic conditions expand for some people, and others begin experiencing chronic conditions such as arthritis, Parkinson's disease, Alzheimer's disease, cardiovascular disease, cerebral vascular accident (stroke), more hypertension, chronic obstructive pulmonary disease, obesity, cancers, type 2 diabetes, osteoarthritis, osteoporosis, and diseases of the eyes (cataracts and macular degeneration) (NCOA, 2021). These require medical care, and may necessitate an adaptation of physical activities with assistance to begin or continue a physically active life in leisure. There are two steps they might take to improve their ability to be active.

Step 1: Health Care Provider Assessment and Guidance

Evaluation from an HCP or one or more clinical specialists may result in a referral for APA.

- *Option A:* The person might be directed to attend a rehabilitation program before clearance to engage in HRF or leisure activities.
- *Option B:* The person has been cleared for participation in selected leisure activities and receives referrals for them.

For many people with chronic conditions resulting in a medical emergency, the initial phase in participating in physical activity during leisure may begin as the various members of the clinical team initiate the patient's discharge from acute stabilizing care. This can be casual ("Start back slowly on your walking when you get home.") or more formal with referral into outpatient rehabilitation programs or more intense inpatient rehab programs. Outpatient rehabilitation programs are reported to be fun for some participants. For example, exercise specialists in community pools conduct aquatic exercises for those having had cardiac surgery or heart attacks, and they are supervised by medical personnel. Music is provided, and socialization is greatly encouraged. Due to the length of the program, participants can form social groups. This can lead to friendships outside of rehab. Also, the progressive nature of the exercises builds confidence in taking up exercising without fear of a medical incident. Overall, there is a lessening of the fear and depression that typically follows heart attacks or surgeries.

Step 2: Leisure Engagement

If one does not need a rehabilitation program, they enter option A, described next. These programs are adjusted with an instructor. To foster communication, the individual shares class concerns with the instructor and shares success and concerns with the HCP or their OT or PT during health care visits.

- *Option A:* The person participates in leisure activities in the community based on interest and available supports and resources. As personality and social skill dictates, they can engage socially before, during, or after activity classes. However, sometimes people choose an activity for solitude.
- *Option B:* If they have an *extremely* sedentary lifestyle, they can be directed to *just move* in any capacity (explained in chapter 14).

spectrum disorder are two disability areas where the degree of impairment is indicated by the level of support the person needs for daily tasks and other activities of their life (APA, 2022). Their physical education in the schools was provided with supports to ensure success (see chapter 7 and chapter 8). Their level of support may not change and must be continued into adulthood. If a person needs support to dress appropriately for physical activity, then this will continue as an adult. Also, their health status changes with aging. For instance, in adulthood, individuals with intellectual disability may be diagnosed with Parkinson's disease (Palat et al., 2018). Their physical activity participation needs a level of support that was begun in adapted physical education and now is applied to their aging and health status.

Aging with and into disability and pursing leisure activity engagement necessitates working with the health care professional (Kennedy et al., 2021). The ACSM (Moore et al., 2016), the CDC (n.d.), and the U.S. Department of Health and Human Services 2018 *Physical Activity Guidelines for Americans* (USDHHS, 2018) are all adamant that health care practitioners work with their patients to be physically active.

People aging into disabilities often enter leisure physical activity by starting with an assessment with their HCP (see the Leisure and Adapted Physical Activity Participation sidebar). By definition, they are experiencing a disability that has an impact on physical activity engagement.

See table 15.1 for conditions regularly seen by a cardiologist when cardiac conditions bring up many

Leisure Activity Case Study

Teri, 75 years old

In junior high, I learned I was unathletic because I was always chosen last for softball and volleyball teams. I tried—skiing, tennis, riding a 10-speed bike. They were hard, and that meant I was not an athlete and never would be. I did little activity in high school and college. Sedentary life was impacting me. In pregnancy, I gained more weight, and even walking was difficult. We joined a gym, and I started swimming again. A Jazzercise studio opened nearby and I and other neighborhood women signed up. I felt better. I got a better bike and went back to teaching in a grade school and was on my feet all day—a lot of walking and moving kids around!

But into my 50s I found myself single and dealing with weight gain, and I took a class in nutrition offered by a nearby hospital. I then determined I needed to consider lifting weights. I hired a personal trainer who taught me the basics of free weights until he recommended that I join a gym. I made my son join to help me work the machines and ease into the gym culture. I did get comfortable and have lifted weights for over 20 years, not always consistently, but I regularly return to them. Now that I'm in my 70s, I particularly notice the benefits, as I am able to garden and lift things that my younger friends cannot.

I took up golf, which I had tried earlier in life, but found it difficult and honestly getting off the first tee, terrifying—everyone waiting silently, watching as you miss the ball, sighing. I was about to quit when a friend invited me to join her group of duffers. I did and it was fun, but I needed help. Her husband built clubs for me to fit my height (I'm tall) and gave me lessons. He told me I had a natural swing. What? I might have some athletic ability? I stayed with it for a few years 'til arthritis messed with my hands. I have hired trainers to take me to new levels of exercise. Too much sitting during COVID put me into physical therapy to deal with new pain and movement issues. Now my pursuits include walking, and I belong to a great gym through the Silver Sneakers program.

I learned a lot about aging body parts and the need for regular movement to avoid pain from lack of movement. I do my exercises, knowing that without them, I am limited. Pain still lingers as arthritis finds new joints to settle into; one knee is likely to need surgery, and my back—that's been a problem since I was 25—is more persistent with its pain. I am coming to grips with the reality that OTC pain meds make a difference, not occasionally like it was years ago, but regularly as this is the new state of my body. I keep walking, doing PT, and lifting weights; and if an over-the-counter pain med makes it all more tolerable, I accept it and go forward. All things considered, I am quite mobile and am grateful for that. The challenge is to embrace my aging.

TABLE 15.1   Cardiac Conditions, Programs, and Leisure Physical Activity Recommendations

Cardiac condition and symptoms	Program	APA
Heart failure: • Shortness of breath with activity • Chronic fatigue • Decreased exercise capacity	*Cardiac rehabilitation.* After a post-cardiac event and on referral from the cardiologist, this program lasts for a duration of 12 weeks, one to two sessions per week, which is covered by insurance. Many people feel nervous about beginning to exercise again after a cardiac event, and cardiac rehab is a safe, medically supervised program designed for just such people. During this program of medically supervised physical activity, people are carefully monitored and given homework for physical activity in their home, neighborhood, or community. When program participation is completed, they receive recommendations for structured physical activity programs or activities that can be done at home or in their community. Physical activity engagement is for leisure physical activity outside or inside, with or without equipment.	APA is focused on aerobic exercise, muscle strength, and endurance and flexibility. For this reason, many individuals like yoga, Pilates, and tai chi. Rating of perceived exertion (RPE) is followed in classes. Warm-up and cool-down, including stretches, are recommended. In the aerobic section, use RPE if possible. Walking goals of 30 minutes a day might be indicated. Remain at 30 minutes a day for most days. If a training effect is the goal (increasing capacity for walking), increase the time walking; or with the same time, walk up a hill as part of the 30 minutes (increasing the intensity). It should be fun. People can participate at their local YMCA, municipal recreation programs, or health clubs. They can also take advantage of outdoor activities of the community for walking. In inclement weather, have them walk in enclosed shopping centers, inside a health club, or on treadmills. Stationary bicycles could also be used.
Coronary artery disease with chronic angina • Limiting activities of daily living • Dizziness • Fatigue • Nausea • Shortness of breath • Sweating • Chest pain	Insurance will not cover a referral to a cardiac rehabilitation program. Cardiologists can prescribe medications, perform stenting to dissipate the blockage, and refer the patient for surgical procedures. Research has reported that stenting is equal to surgery in forestalling a heart attack. Some people use a nitroglycerin tablet before they exercise. Others use it in the event of an onset of symptoms to which they are accustomed. The tablet goes under the tongue.	In their APA program, have them begin slow and slow down or stop and rest if necessary. They can follow RPE. For example, if one decides to mow the lawn, then they should do it in stages rather than the doing whole lawn at once. They should mow a section and then rest. They should take as many sessions as comfortable to complete the job. Research has shown that exercise increases branching in the heart muscle, which is positive for creating more capacity for flow of the blood within the heart.
Peripheral artery disease: Claudication (pain in the legs) disabling the individual	Insurance companies will pay for cardiac rehabilitation for people with peripheral artery disease. At first, they require a regimented walking program through cardiac rehabilitation. After this, the person can participate using their home or community for physical activity.	In rehab, patients first start walking two minutes per session, being mindful of the RPE. The next session may be three minutes. The important focus is to use the legs. This will benefit collateral branching in the legs, thus increasing blood vessels for circulating blood to the legs. This can be fun, especially as the person graduates from rehab into community activity.

questions for physical activity. The cardiologist can make referrals for programs and recommend physical activity. The focus of table 15.1 is on three cardiac conditions resulting in the question, *What APA can this person do in leisure?* A consulting cardiologist for us has described the program workings and recommended the following APA for each condition. These leisure activities can be enjoyable for the individual within the parameters of their heart condition. Rather than be sedentary, depressed, scared, or tired, these individuals can look forward to these leisure activity pursuits.

Leisure Activity Recommendations

Amireault and colleagues advocate for "likable physical activity" based on a study conducted with older adults resulting in praise for dancing, walking, swimming, biking, and doing water activities to music (2019). There are physical activities that are commonly referred to by community recreation instructors, cardiologists, rehabilitation physicians, and health club instructors and reported to be enjoyable with older people such as aquatic or water-based activity, tai chi, and yoga. Some activities are access dependent, such as gentle hikes, gardening, and skiing. Paddleboarding is also popular for those with upper body strength and functional balance. People in their 70s often participate in cross-country skiing and snowshoeing in Oregon! It is easy to do in retirement and when the mountains are close by.

For those in the *just move* category of physical activity engagement, it is now appropriate to consider attending outdoor events or strolling by rivers, lakes, or other urban areas. Each involves a rest and watch, which just might not be wasting time (Hampl, 2019). For those who need to just move, low-intensity physical activity for very short periods of time is doable. Those who are not needing to just move, social activities are critical for maintaining mental health. Appropriate activities include going to art museums or small galleries, walking short distances with friends at their homes, visiting open spaces to sit outside and observe people, volunteering to help children read, teaching English to adults, or helping in an election. Those with a more adventuresome spirit and more economic means can travel, visit distant relatives, visit an historical site, or go to national forests. These activities require that people move in and out of a car, bus, or airplane. All the mentioned activities enhance life and constitute an important step toward a healthier life.

Leisure activities pursued for their aerobic benefit combined with those for strength and adding balance are now recommended for young adults to oldest of old adults (CDC, 2022). And, adults with disabilities may need to be monitored for level of support in community activities, and for some those supports need to be in their home activities. Individuals with certain disabilities cannot be unsupervised in the community.

Walking

Walking cannot be overlooked as a cost-effective way of taking part in physical activity, either independently or assisted by a mobility device. Joining with other persons makes it social. Setting up a schedule for the activity is advantageous as it becomes routine. Groups can start a recreation monthly calendar and discuss activities and try them out. In creating this calendar, try the following:

- Scan community programs and special events.
- Attend an outdoor festival, walking, or moving along in a wheelchair. This is enjoyable, as there are people and things to observe, and it is a fun, inclusive environment.
- Find a local track and set a goal (such as two to three laps). Set a lap goal and then reset the goal when it is time to increase the number of laps. Let the participants determine the goal.
- Map out a neighborhood walk of a certain mileage. Use a smartphone with a free app that counts steps and displays miles. Some find this motivating.
- Invite people to join in a walking group for a designated time, such as a four-week group, and maybe give the group a name like Winter Walkers or Spring Stompers.
- Use seasons and seasonal special events for physical activity. In some communities with snow, festivals have ice sculpture competitions to view, as well as snowshoeing and sit-skiing. Warm climates have their water-oriented adapted activities like surfing, paddleboarding, or canoeing. Community recreation programs offer hikes through the mountains labeled easy, moderate, or challenging. The U.S. Forest Service now lists its trails that are accessible by wheelchair.

The ACSM, the CDC, and the USDHHS all recommend walking as a form of low-cost exercise that is easily executed at intensities monitored by the frequency, intensity, time, and type for adults across all ages, even to oldest adults. Some like group walking, and others like a solo walk. Health care professionals can safely recommend walking to their clients to benefit their health. Wheel walking for those using a wheelchair for ambulation is also beneficial. Many older people using their walkers to take a walk in their neighborhood, in a park, or on accessible trails. They can amble slowly, which still expends a lot of energy for them.

Walking is an individual lifetime activity with worldwide participants. Noncompetitive walking events and permanently established walking courses or trails can be found. The American Volkssport Association conducts periodic events, typically 10-kilometer walks (2022). There is typically a window of 6 to 10 hours when walkers will be on the course. Some participants prefer a solitary walk, while others walk in groups and stop for lunch or to sightsee. Avid participants keep a log and commemorative pins or patches for each walk. In some cities and rural areas, the courses are permanently marked and may be completed at any time. Many of the courses are suitable for strollers and wheelchairs (thus walkers), so the entire family may participate.

The course length may need to be modified for individuals who use assistive devices (wheelchairs, walkers) or might include more resting along the way. Although many individuals with sensory impairments walk independently, the opportunity to be with others in group outings is particularly enjoyable. Individuals who use assistive devices can now check online for accessible trails and routes both in the city and in the federal parks system. Bring a cell phone when walking with a friend or family member. If going for a short walk, people should take a drink of water ahead of time and bring along water for longer walking experiences.

Nordic Walking

According to Dr. Aaron Baggish, director of the Cardiovascular Performance Program at Harvard-affiliated Massachusetts General Hospital, Nordic walking is the rage in Switzerland, where the train station is filled with older people carrying their poles, heading up the mountain to walk (Harvard, 2022). Nordic walking was birthed in Finland and is now very popular around Europe, especially with older people (Kunysz-Rozborska & Rejman, 2019). Many report it is catching on in the United States because of the low equipment cost of two poles (relative to other recreational equipment) and its overall excellent fitness benefits of cardio and muscle endurance as well as flexibility and an overall an improvement in the quality of life. It also results in a reduction of fat mass, low-density lipoprotein cholesterol, depression, and anxiety. It can be conducted on a multitude of surfaces such as mountain trails, city sidewalks, along a beach, around or by a lake, through the woods, along country roads, in city parks on the grass or around

Ariel Skelley/Getty Images/Getty Images

the track, and in neighborhoods. Duration can be short or long, and everything in between depending on the frequency, intensity, time, and type. Expert Tom Rutlin says if you can hug someone or shake their hand, you can stride out with your poles and "exerstride" (Rutlin, 2022).

> When you walk without poles, you activate muscles below the waist. When you add Nordic poles, you activate all of the muscles of the upper body as well. . . . You're engaging 80% to 90% of your muscles, as opposed to 50%, providing a substantial calorie-burning benefit.
>
> Harvard (2022, np).

The poles for Nordic walking are designed a bit differently at the handle than cross country ski poles and hiking poles and are purchased at sporting goods stores and online. There are specially designed tips, call paws, small rubber booties that face backwards on the tips, and larger rubber ones for people with balance issues. Some tips resemble a regular rubber tip of a hiking pole that can be removed for use on ice. Poles with a handle curved to fit the hand with a rest at the bottom can assist in stability. The equipment tips are modified for the type of terrain. Those with balance issues can use a larger tip to assist with balance.

One of the main features of this exercise is that it accommodates a range of balance skill. Some disability areas like Deafness, autism, learning disability and attention-deficit/hyperactivity disorder could adapt to this activity well. Those with mild obesity might find this enjoyable, especially if they start slowly and feel they are coordinated.

There are many different techniques for Nordic walking, but most recommend starting slow and gaining speed later. Participants should let the arms and legs swing naturally. They should begin by placing the poles out and striking the ground with the pole at the same time as the foot goes out into a stride. Nordic walkers swing the full arm (shoulder to hand) into position for a handshake (Rutlin, 2022).

Participants should remember to squeeze the pole handle lightly and feel the muscles contract in the arm, back, and in the abdominal area. Then they release and repeat on the other side and continue back and forth in this manner until they feel comfortable with the movement.

Nordic walkers must remember to hydrate ahead of time or bring water with them based on the planned length of their walk. They should start slow as a warm-up and end slow as a cool-down. Loose clothes allow for arm swing, and sturdy shoes appropriate for the surface and weather provide security and support.

Some people want to do Nordic walking on a treadmill. Treadmills are constructed to accommodate legs and arms in forward motion, not the addition of extra widths to either side of a person where arms with poles are moving forward. It is not safe for Nordic walking!

Hiking

Those with disabilities can obtain a free accessibility pass for hiking in U.S. national parks on-site or online. Even if trails are deemed accessible by wheelchair, users should know that snow and ice are still deterrents to accessibility. U.S. national parks having better accessible travel are: Grand Canyon National Park, Arizona; Sequoia National Park, California; Great Sand Dunes National Park and Preserve, Colorado; Everglades National Park, Florida; Acadia National Park, Maine; Glacier National Park, Montana; Zion National Park, Utah; and Yellowstone National Park, predominantly in Wyoming.

People with disabilities have organized to offer accessible hiking resources (maps, directions, pictures), including groups such as Access Recreation in Portland, Oregon, and Global Opportunities Unlimited in New Mexico (Morris, 2022). The Access Recreation guide identifies numerous trails and emphasized that photographs of trail details substantially help people select a hiking location.

When trails are accessible to people with disabilities the whole family can benefit. Children and other family members with aging-related mobility issues can find a free and clear passage to fun.

Handcycle equipment for hiking is expensive. The GRIT Freedom group has worked hard to enable people to use their chair and get out into the outdoors. Likewise, Global Opportunities Unlimited in New Mexico provides these types of handcycles for free use in their area (Morris, 2022).

Local parks and recreation departments often offer hiking for seniors. Hikes are not necessarily labeled beginners, intermediate or advanced; instead, they will be identified with terms like *rambles* and *walks*. Walks have little elevation if at all, the surface is flat, and the walk can be short (maybe an hour). Sometimes hikers on a walk decide to sit and rest, or rest and wait until the others reach their destination, turn around, and meet up with them. Sometimes hikers start with the walks, gain in strength and endurance, and advance to rambles. Ramblers continue for years or months and return to walks to accommodate additional health issues. Hikers are advised to bring water and stay hydrated, pack snacks, and be sun smart (e.g., hats, sunglasses, sunscreen lotion).

Boots that give support over the terrain are recommended. There is nothing like feeling small rocks on the bottom of the foot throughout the hike! One or two hiking sticks (poles) are a must for those with balance issues and not at all uncommon on the hiking trail across ages! To determine pole height, stand in hiking boots with the pole gripped where the elbow is bent at a 90-degree angle and brought in close to the body. Hikers should make sure their shoulders are in a relaxed position with the poles at 90 degrees to the ground. If the shoulders are hunched up, then the poles are too long. Tips can be covered with a rubber tip.

Tai Chi

Tai chi is another leisure activity often referred for its benefits of stress reduction, as well as increasing flexibility and muscle endurance. Tai chi was born in China as a fighting art in 700 AD to 1,500 AD. Over the years, it has retained a smoothness, and the movements stretch in full range where the spine is continually turning. Tai chi requires no equipment and is low impact. Research confirms the benefits of tai chi are decreased stress, anxiety, and depression; improved mood, improved aerobic capacity, increased energy and stamina, improved flexibility, balance and agility, and improved muscle strength and definition (Mayo Clinic, 2022). Qualified instructors can often be found through classes at a senior center, health club, or community center. If that isn't possible, to look for videos in the library.

The yang style of tai chi is the most popular in the United States, particularly among older adults. Breathing is important when moving through the forms and bringing focus into the physical movements. In an intervention study that significantly reduced falls after 6 months, the yang style of tai chi focused on "multidirectional weight shifting, awareness of body alignment, and multisegmental (arms, legs, and trunk) movement coordination . . . [and] Synchronized breathing" (Li et al., 2004, p. 2048).

One true modification to tai chi is to use a chair. Skilled instructors can add this adaptation for their students or the whole class. Guide participants to start with a beginning level class, learning the complexity in combining the positions and then adding the speed. Instruction in tai chi often follows the classic motor learning paradigm of presenting the material as whole-part-whole.

Yoga

Yoga is a very popular leisure activity for increasing strength and flexibility for adults and maintaining relaxation; performed alone or in classes, modified and adapted for disabilities across the ages of adulthood. Yoga is explained by Madhivanan and his colleagues referencing its ancient roots going back to more than 1,000 years BCE with material written for postures (asanas), breath control connected to meditation, and spiritual practices. Hatha is a popular contemporary practice of the physical aspects (Madhivanan et al, 2021). Besides hatha yoga, other practices popular in the United States are vinyasa, Iyengar, ashtanga, and kundalini (Madhivanan et al., 2021).

Yoga can be adapted for disability, particular with the popular gentle chair yoga (Park et al., 2017), and it is favored as an intervention for health benefits across disabilities because adaptations can be made to the poses with expert instruction (Madhivanan et al., 2021).

Yoga instructors will reference the following poses (possibly with their own adaptations): mountain pose, lotus pose, child pose, tree pose, downward facing dog, upward facing dog, and warrior. For many, the most beloved of all poses at the end of class is Savasana. This pose is described as lying on the back, hands by the sides slightly away from the body, with eyes closed, letting everything relax and just breathing.

Equipment for yoga includes blankets, mats, rollers, blocks, and straps, depending on the type of yoga, modifications made, or specific adaptations needed. This equipment is to make it easier to get into or hold poses, and then safely move out of the pose. During yoga sessions, some people are opposed to wearing shoes, some socks with traction are used, and casual clothes allow for movement.

Well-trained instructors teach gentle yoga with a chair or beginners' yoga, which usually means there could be chair use if one needs it. Gentle yoga poses offered are seated eagle, seated pigeon, chair mountain, chair cat, and cow. Some adults begin with the gentle yoga and gain in strength and flexibility and move on to beginner or even intermediate yoga classes.

Dance

Dancing is considered a likable physical activity. In retirement homes, slow dance means touching another person, which many elderly people miss. Dancing can be with partners, friends, or alone. The enjoyment of music is a motivational component, bringing back memories of the times when a particular piece was popular. Organizationally, dance doesn't require more than a speaker, access to music, and a clear area. Dance organizers can use themes or reflect on the holidays and special events of the community, such as St. Patrick's Day, Valentine's Day, Easter parade with a bunny hop, Lamba, *Día de los Muertos*, and Diwali. Square, country line, and swing dances are familiar to those from rural communities and city dwellers alike. The waltz is a dance that is easily adapted. In some communities an adapted tango, rumba, and salsa are popular as adults age.

Those in wheelchairs can be on the dance floor and be social. Give them a scarf to wave to the rhythms of the music. If those using a chair need assistance to move, the pusher can bring the person to others on the dance floor or dance with them. Those that use walkers can move around the floor, too, or sway either while standing or sitting. Be sure to provide water as the dancing continues.

Water Aerobics

Water aerobics can be very social, with people chatting before, during, and after, and sometimes singing along to the provided music. Instructors are certified and can offer a class that begins with a warm-up, has a more intense aerobic plus muscular endurance middle section, and then a slow-down before concluding the class. Water is buoyant and easy on the body, protecting the joints from weight-bearing. The sore and older body can move easier in a pool of water. The water temperature is between 83 and 88 degrees Fahrenheit for most water exercise classes (Mayo, 2022). If the class is specifically for those with arthritis, warmer temperatures of around 92 degrees Fahrenheit are considered.

The Aquatic Exercise Association (AEA, 2022) recommends pools that range in depth from three and a half to five and a half feet (1.7 m) for shallow-water aerobics and a depth of at least six and a half feet (2 m) for deep-water classes. RPE is to be used to judge intensity and exertion. Instructors should be certified in lifesaving techniques, including cardiopulmonary resuscitation especially if a lifeguard is not present.

Exercise clothing in the water might be more supportive than a swimsuit (AEA, 2022). In deep water, flotation devices (belt or vest) are necessary, as are shoes. An aquatic shoe for water aerobics is like the shoes used in outdoor water activities. In general this shoe is recommended particularly for those who are pregnant, obese, diabetic, and those who have musculoskeletal disorders. Wearing this type of shoe also helps when walking on the pool deck and in the locker room. Wearing aquatic shoes in the water helps with alignment of the body because the grip is better on the floor of the pool. Street shoes are not

10'000 Hours/Digital Vision/Getty Images

worn in the pool area. Have participants prepare for the sun in outdoor classes with sunglasses, hats or visors, and sunproof sunscreen and sun-protective clothing. Drink water before, during, and after class (AEA, 2022).

Handheld flotation devices like Styrofoam noodles and kickboards or hand bars are used in classes but if the water is too deep for the participant and they let go, a water rescue might ensue. Most of the moves in the class should have the arms submerged, no tight grips on the equipment. There are deep water aerobics classes where competency as a swimmer are required for participation.

Swimming Laps

Those who enjoy lap swimming for exercise in their leisure activity are also considered in referrals for swimming. This is a solitary activity, which is a draw for many people as is the support the water gives to the older body. Kickboards are often used during the warm-up or cool-down, and laps can be combinations of the crawl stroke (freestyle), backstroke, butterfly, and breaststroke. The sidestroke is a resting stoke as well as a flutter kick lying on the back. Goggles are a must for handling the chlorine or saline solutions of the water. Some programs are able to advertise saline pools, which have much less chlorine. Kickboards can be used for strengthening the legs, and foam wedges for strengthening the arms cut the boredom of laps.

Swimmers who are blind use their same means of guidance to find the edge of the pool and enter the water and can swim by staying close to the lane markers. Much of the information in chapter 11 on sensory impairments regarding orientation also applies to the swimming pool, pool space, and locker rooms. Encourage the swimmer who is blind to swim with another person or let someone know they are going to the pool to swim.

In public pools, people who use wheelchairs will find some form of a mechanical lift or a gradual entry with a handle to transfer into the pool. The Americans with Disabilities Act requires accessibility in public buildings.

Adults with intellectual disabilities should have their needed level of support to use the pool facilities appropriately, swim in their lane, join in a class, find their way to the locker room, shower, and dress (level of support, chapter 7). If any of these tasks need to be learned, use a task analysis. With the actual skill of swimming, those with early acquired disability could have learned to swim in the APE classes and many people with intellectual disability learned to swim for Special Olympics competition.

Canoeing and Rowing

The feeling of independence generated by moving a boat or canoe through the water is perhaps the number one reason many individuals with disabilities enjoy boating activities. Rowing requires the use of the upper extremities, making this a particularly beneficial activity for individuals with lower body paralysis.

In canoeing and rowing, the major adaptations relate to the how the person gets into the canoe or boat. Although there is much individual variation and preference, the most common method used by boaters with mobility disabilities is to transfer into the canoe or boat from a mat placed on the deck next to the canoe. The boater with a disability then leans back and, using the arms for support, drops the buttocks into the boat, landing on a soft mat. Next, the legs are lifted by pulling on the pant cuffs and placed into position one leg at a time. PTs can individualize a transfer if needed, or a seasoned canoeing professional working in inclusive programs can do the same.

Rowboats and canoes require little modification for individuals with disabilities. Some individuals will use a shorter paddle or oar to compensate for their limited shoulder and arm mobility. Seats that are contoured are also desirable for those who require support while sitting.

The individual with a disability uses the same basic bow stroke taught to all beginning canoers. With this stroke, the upper arm pushes forward and across the front of the body while the lower arm pulls. The paddle should be pulled backward until the bottom hand reaches the hip and the upper arm is fully extended with the hand over the water. An effective technique for teaching individuals with paralysis proper stroke technique is to have them practice paddling in shallow water while seated in their wheelchair.

Safety is a critical factor in the design and implementation of a boating program for all participants, including those with disabling conditions. The American Red Cross requires that participants with physical disabilities perform the following skills prior to participation in one of the organization's courses:

- Be able to pitch or fall, fully clothed, into the water and recover to the surface.
- Swim one minute without a personal flotation device.
- After being thrown a United States Coast Guard-approved personal flotation device, remain afloat an additional four minutes, progressing a minimum of 20 feet through the water.

It is recommended that boaters with disabilities, particularly those with orthopedic impairments, make a checklist of any special needs they should prepare for while boating. In addition to a personal flotation device, some will require special medication. Care should also be taken to analyze and prepare for the effects of weather on specific disabilities prior to long boating trips. Wilderness Inquiry does involve people in wheelchairs on its canoe trips (2022).

Rowers with limited shoulder mobility may require oars that have been shortened and adjusted to ensure proper balance. Rowers with visual impairments should be provided an opportunity to examine the oar or paddle with the hands as it is taken through several complete cycles of the stroke. This can be accomplished with the assistance of a sighted partner and the placement of the boat in shallow water. In the open water, the paddler with visual impairments will assume the front position with the sighted partner in the rear, or stern, responsible for controlling the general direction of the canoe.

Depending on the nature of a person's disability, some modification to the canoe may be necessary. A person with lower body amputations or atrophy needs some bracing to prevent him or her from sliding forward in the seat. Individuals with poor trunk balance may need additional support for balance and padding to prevent pressure sores or other injuries. Individuals with cardiorespiratory problems should be taught to monitor their pulse rate to establish an oar or paddle cadence consistent with their functioning level.

Researchers exploring paddle boarding for those young adults with disabilities needing physical and psychological support found there was low program availability as well as administrative concerns over risk management policies and leisure funding. Yet, paddlers reported fun, exercise, and relaxation (Merrick et al., 2021).

Bicycling

Bicycling is one of the most useful lifelong skills for a person. Not only is riding a bike fun, but it is an activity that promotes leg strength and cardiovascular endurance and has enhanced the quality of life for many individuals. A bicycle is transportation to and from leisure activities, and riding one is an activity in and of itself. This skill may or may not have been learned in the APE or GPE. Young adults can learn to ride on a two-wheeled road bicycle. Those in middle age and older can consider three-wheeled bicycles. These are popular, especially when attachments include baskets to carry things and pets.

The fit of the bicycle is important. If the person is riding with a two-wheeled road bicycle, have them straddle the bike with feet flat on the ground and their crotch a few inches above the frame—not above the seat. With someone holding the bike, have the person mount the bike and lean forward to grab the handlebars, lengthen the legs, which should be slightly bent (about 80-90 percent of a full extension of the leg). Adjust the seat if the leg length is not correct for pedaling. When the rider is reaching across to grab the handlebars, the arms should be shoulder-width apart and approximately at 90 degrees to the torso. If the handlebars are too far away, the bike may be too big. If the person's reach is too low or high, raise or lower the seat. The seat itself should be parallel to the ground. Because of back problems, some people need to have their handlebar designed for being upright while biking.

If a three-wheeled bike is used, get a good fit with leg length and the rotation of the pedals as you would with a two-wheeled bicycle. Recumbent bicycles have their own fit and the legs thrust out ahead of the body, but the rotation of the legs is similar to that of a person seated upright on a two- or three-wheeled bike. Recumbent and hand-cranked bicycles are three-wheeled. The propulsion on a hand-cranked bike is from the arms and not the legs. Tandem bicycles enable cyclists with visual impairments to enjoy the experience of biking. It is a fun experience to cycle in this manner with another person and may have been a mode of biking from childhood for those with disabilities.

There are different types of three-wheeled bikes, including the following:

- *Upright:* This is the classic tricycle for adults where the person sits on a three-wheeled implement that looks like a larger trike.
- *Upright tandem tricycle:* This type of bicycle is expensive, but it might be what someone wants. One person is in front of the other.
- *Recumbent:* This bike is low and allows the individual stretch out the legs and support the back. There is also a hand cycle version for those with impairment of the legs or a preference to use the arms.

If possible, a physical therapist or a rehabilitation staff member may be able to help with recommendations for a bicycle for an adult known to them.

Safety is a must with cycling, and in adulthood it needs to be assessed for some disability areas. In some cases, the individual is only going to ride with others in their family or within a program, and safety will be monitored. Bicycle and motorcycle helmets must comply with mandatory federal safety standards of the Consumer Protection and Safety Commission. Individuals with intellectual impairments must be monitored for traffic signals, warning signs, and traffic patterns. This is where an instructor or therapist can use a tandem bicycle to practice traffic skills with the student in a safe and controlled manner. One type is a side-by-side bike with independent controls. On another type, one sits in the front the other in the back. Individuals with visual impairments can benefit from a tandem bike where the sighted person provides information on terrain and directions. This has been employed in road races.

Bowling

Bowling is an extremely popular game among people who use wheelchairs and have the use of at least one arm. Bowling is not an aerobic activity, but it encourages muscle flexibility and strength with the picking up and thrusting of the ball down the alley. It is also social as players wait around their lane for their turns, encourage one another, and get something to eat. Bowlers with visual impairments are usually successful in their efforts at bowling; they do need someone to tell them which pins are left standing after the first ball and to record their scores when automatic scoring is not used.

In addition to providing equipment for bowling instruction when regular alleys are not available, polyethylene pins and balls are excellent for those individuals who, because of their disabilities, lack the strength and coordination to use the heavier, regulation bowling balls. The grip on the ball is taken at the first joints of the fingers rather than the second joints, which are used in gripping a regulation bowling ball.

Individuals with muscular weakness in the arm and hand may find the use of a specially designed bowling ball with a retractable handle a valuable piece of equipment. The handle enables the bowler to grasp the ball with all of the fingers of the hand similar to the action used to carry a bucket. As the ball is released, the handle retracts completely so that the ball rolls smoothly. A bowling ball holder—a ring that attaches to a chair—is a helpful device for a wheelchair user who prefers not to have the ball rest in the lap when positioning or moving to the line.

A light metal rack is also a good modification in the game. It provides a track for the ball to travel down from the lap of the holder to the floor of the alley. The ball is placed on the track and the track is aimed toward the pins. The ball is released, and it rolls down the track and onto the alley toward the pins These ramps are really essential for many people who use wheelchairs to experience bowling as a lifetime activity. A resource for a bowling ramp is listed in the references (Bowling ramp, 2022). Prospective bowlers can also review commercial products online on their own.

To bowl from a wheelchair when the metal rack isn't needed, the bowler must place the chair to face the pins. The body is moved as far as possible to the side of the chair from which the ball will be released. The player leans over the side of the chair to permit the arm to swing freely in delivering the ball. To compensate for the lack of approach in the delivery, a preliminary swing may be taken. The ball swings back, then forward without touching the floor, back again, and in another forward swing, the body is leaned farther to the side so that the ball can be released smoothly on the floor. Unlike ambulatory bowlers, the arm swing for the bowler in a wheelchair must be a straight, pendulumlike swing. A firm grip on the nonthrowing side of the wheelchair will prevent the bowler from falling out of the chair. Some bowlers equip their chairs with a reinforced brake to increase the holding power of the brake during the release phase.

If the wheelchair is too high for the bowler, a chair without arms may be used. A chair might also be used by bowlers on crutches or others with limited locomotion. An adaptation for those who are able to stand but are unable to make the necessary steps in the approach is to permit them to stand at the foul line to make the delivery.

All bowlers who lack strength in the arm and shoulder should use the lighter polyethylene ball and pins. In using this ball, only the straight ball may be thrown, because the ball is not easily controlled in a spin; otherwise, the ball responds like a regulation bowling ball.

Bowlers with visual impairments orient themselves by feeling the sides of the alley or using a rail if one is provided. The accuracy of the aim may be determined by the number of pins knocked down, which is told to the bowler by a sighted person.

Bowlers who have intellectual disability will need special assistance and additional practice to ensure that they perform the approach, delivery, and release correctly if they have not played before. The use of footprints to remind them of the proper foot placement can be a very helpful aid. For some individuals it may be best to teach and practice the release first, then the release and one step, and so on, before introducing the full approach with four steps. In essence, the skill is taught in a backward sequence.

Bocci

The Italians call it *bocci*, the French call it *petanque*, and the English refer to it as lawn bowling. In the United States, bocci (sometimes spelled *bocce*) is played on both public and private lawns and on sandy beaches—anywhere that the balls will eventually stop in the playing field (not on a shined, hard surface). It is adaptable for people using wheelchairs, where the grass can be cut close to allow mobility with the chair. If the throwing distance is a challenge for some, the court can be shortened for the fun of the game.

Two teams of one, two, or four players use four balls each, and there is one target ball (a *pallina* in Italian). There is a foul line in the middle of the playing field. Balls are delivered down the court to get closer to the *pallina*, knocking the other team's ball away from the *pallina* or hitting the *pallina* so that it ends up closer to your team's ball. A free resource on rules is available (World Bocce League, n.d.).

Summary

Leisure is free from obligation of tasks of subsistence and is enjoyable activity participated in for restoration. The paradigm of aging with and into disability is applied to leisure by illustrating the timing of onset of disease, injury, or illness affecting physical activity pursuit in leisure. There is an expectation that the HCP will ask, "What are you doing for physical activity?" The progression of engaging in physical activity for adults aging with and into disability are that some adults require a specific rehabilitation program before participating in the community; others can go directly from their HCP's office to an activity. Deciding who assesses for leisure activity interests varies but often it is a recreation therapist or the OT or PT. Assessments are helpful to adults in senior housing, residential care, and nursing homes and are required by most state's laws. For some disability areas, the level of support for engaging in physical activity must carry on into leisure activity in the community as they age. Leisure activities need to be likable. Research reports that individuals like participating both solo and with others. Concluding the chapter are physical activities with adaptations to pursue in leisure.

CHAPTER 16

Adapted Sport

CHAPTER OBJECTIVES

After completing this chapter, you will be able to do the following:

- Describe the current aging paradigm as it applies to adapted sport.
- Explain why the health care professional is a gatekeeper to opportunities in physical activity.
- Discuss the history of athletic participation in adapted sport.
- Discuss an ecological approach in understanding a professional's role in facilitating health with adult adapted sport.
- Describe the Paralympics, their athletes, and examples of sport competition.
- Describe Special Olympics by their athletes and where their presence is felt in the United States.
- Discuss a variety of considerations for equal participation in adapted sports of athletes and recreational users regardless of disability conditions or category.

Sports participation for those needing a modification or an adaptation to participate is referred to as adapted sport. As competitions ensued, associations developed to promote the sports. Deaf students in 1870 played baseball at the Ohio School for the Deaf, and they played American football in 1885 in Illinois at the state school for Deaf people (Winnick, 2017). These programs spread to other schools for the Deaf, and in 1924 the International Silent Games were held in Paris. In 1945, the American Athletic Association for the Deaf was established. Those with visual impairments began competition in Baltimore in 1907. The Stoke Mandeville Games began in the 1940s; the games were organized by Dr. Ludwig Guttmann, who believed that sport was an important part of rehabilitation from injuries of war. The University of Illinois held the first wheelchair basketball competition in 1949. Associations founded to expand opportunities for sport were the National Wheelchair Athletic Association (1950s) and the National Wheelchair Basketball Association. Disabled Sports USA was started by a small group of Vietnam veterans in the 1960s. Their athletes have disabilities including orthopedic, spinal cord, neuromuscular, and visual impairments. Athletes with intellectual disability are associated with Special Olympics, formed in the late 1960s. Athletes with cerebral palsy, closed head injury, stroke, dwarfism, and others have disability-specific adapted sport program organizations presently.

International competition in adapted sport has also flourished with the International Paralympics that follow each Olympic competition using the same sites and facilities. The United States Olympic Committee is a national governing body, that along with other governing bodies and federations, is dedicated to sanctioning sport competition and certifying their officials to nominate athletes to compete in the U.S. Olympics, Paralympics, and other international multisport games. The International Sports Organization for the Disabled works in coordination with associations and federations that are disability specific such as BlazeSports America, Disabled Sports USA, the Dwarf Athletic Association of America, Special Olympics, the United States Association of Blind Athletes, USA Deaf Sports Federation, and Wheelchair and Ambulatory Sports, USA (Davis, 2017). All these organizations are affiliated with the Paralympics except for Special Olympics, although they offer World Special Olympics), and the USA Deaf Sports Federation offering Deaflympics.

Most people know that countries bid to hold the Olympics. Now, according to Davis (2017), the proposals are judged, in part, by how well the country includes athletes with disabilities in transportation and housing. The Paralympics always follow the Olympics at the same site. The Warrior Games are sponsored by the United States Paralympics for injured veterans to train in sport. This includes an adaptive sport reconditioning program with partic-

ipation in regional games. Events include archery, cycling, sit volleyball, swimming, and track and field. Davis points out that the Wounded Warrior Project *is not* the same as the Warrior Games and is not connected to sports. The Invictus Games are organized for injured men and women veterans and those serving in their military career. Prince Harry established the games in 2014 in London after attending the Warrior Games in the United States. In September 2023, the U.S. team roster includes 59 athletes competing in Düsseldorf, Germany.

The mission of Special Olympics is to provide year-round sports training and athletic competition in a variety of Olympic-type sports for children and adults with intellectual disabilities, giving them continuing opportunities to develop physical fitness, demonstrate courage, experience joy, and participate in a sharing of gifts, skills, and friendship with their families, other Special Olympics athletes, and the community (Special Olympics, 2021).

The reach of Special Olympics is an international competition with 200 countries, and it is deeply embedded in the United States sports scene. Special Olympics reports there are over 5 million athletes in the United States, and over 200 million athletes worldwide. The program Unified Fitness comprises mixed teams of participants with intellectual disability and their age peers without intellectual disability. Every U.S. state offers Special Olympics.

Ongoing engagement in sports competition and the additional programs offered by Special Olympics change the health status of these athletes who are at high risk for heart disease and obesity. With involvement in exercise, positive reductions in blood pressure and weight were reported for 383 participants with intellectual disability (Rubenstein et al., 2020).

Participation in adapted sports for the recreational and competitive athlete with a disability begins with the early opportunities to engage in physical activity as a youth. A quality educational experience that provided opportunities to develop foundational movement skills and grant exposure to successful engagement in physical activity were paramount.

Adapted sport entry is for those who played a sport, were injured, wanted to continue in the sport, and found an adapted version. Wheelchair tennis and basketball are good examples of popular sports adapted for those who were injured. They work with professionals other than adapted physical educators to pursue their adapted sports, unless of course, these APE professionals volunteer or are on staff for the sport. Athletes work with the adult tennis instructor, an exercise instructor, or an exercise physiologist. These individuals are aging into disability, adapting, and participating in competitive sport.

Access and Marketing

Too many people do not know of the programs in physical activity for people with disability (Thomas et al., 2020). Often the printed language is not of the people and can result in confusion. Health care practitioners need well-written materials on sports programs in the community. A simple recommendation has been to test printed and online materials with end users (the athletes themselves). Department of Veterans Affairs' hospital outpatient services should recruit from the inpatient services for sport competitions, have athletes visit rehabilitation programs to initiate the process of becoming an athlete, and do small-group presentations.

In community recreation centers and health clubs, there is a need to have open gym times for wheelchair basketball play and to include in their regular offerings training programs for the adapted sports of competitive racquetball, volleyball, pickleball, tennis, and basketball. For sports in these areas, they should consider offering a mixed team, unified of those with and without disabilities. Agencies can co-sponsor competitions in the local community. Many significant marathon races, such as the Portland Marathon and the Boston Marathon, include athletes with disabilities.

People with training in adapted physical activity need to be employed by health clubs and municipalities to integrate people with disabilities into sport programs. Outreach can be enhanced by getting persons with disabilities on the governing boards and councils of these agencies to provide a representative voice to program development. They can speak, guide, encourage, and bring in a broad array of ages and voices from the community to join in the efforts for engagement in adapted sports.

Experience and Training

There is a vast number of adapted sports, and learning how to play those sports often started in high school for those in special education and potentially adapted physical education (Davis, 2017).

- *Parallel:* Some athletes participated in sports as a student while in high school. Their physical education program provided skill development (e.g., in soccer or basketball), and the coach for the school team either provided a parallel experience while building skills in practice or was able to move the student into competition. When the coach felt the student's skills matched game-skill level, they entered the game. Otherwise, the student could still build skills and continue to progress with his social activity associated with his sport group.

- *Segregated:* Some athletes lived in states where there were sport competitions solely for those with a specific disability, such as Special Olympics for those with an intellectual disability.

- *Unified:* These programs in high school are a mix of athletes with and without disabilities. Athletes join in playing tennis, swimming, or playing side-by-side sports that take advantage of the mix of athletic classifications. In high school, these programs are typically held in schools or with other schools. Legally, if a sport program in the school is offered to students, those students with a disability *who are qualified* must also be able to participate.

- *General:* These sport programs are offered to athletes with disabilities under the law, whereby reasonable accommodation is made to engage the student in sport play. For instance, competitors look for cue cards from the sideline for plays, or a tennis player uses colored cards to communicate the serve is out. Another example is sighted runners participating with a runner who is blind. Students with disabilities are participating along with their peers without disabilities.

In early adulthood, an athlete with a disability can continue their athletic endeavors through the previous work of the transitional individualized education program team's focus on physical activity in the community. If the student attends a community college, college, or university, the sport resources should have been explored with the transitional individualized education program work. Facilities at these institutions of higher education almost always have recreation facilities where athletes train. If a student has an interest in a sport, there are typically student physical activity programs where exploration of inclusion can occur.

If the student wants to explore a new sport, they can reach out to staff at the recreation center or kinesiology faculty, review the offerings of the recreation center and observe classes, or work with the disabilities office for the college or university. Outside of higher education, sources for adapted sport are municipal recreation programs, private health clubs, and community athletic organizations. For all individuals, the National Center for Health, Physical Activity and Disability wants to be contacted to determine where programs are located close to the residence of the individual.

Adapted Sport in Adulthood

The aging model that dichotomizes into aging *with* disability and aging *into* disability has ramifications for adapted sport participation and how we understand many aspects of the promotion of physical activity, collaboration with health care professionals, and the training across professional disciplines to foster competitive physical activity for those with disability.

Respecting the dichotomy of aging with and aging into disability, herein we can identify points at which educational and clinical professionals can facilitate the person's participation in adapted sports (table 16.1). We can understand better how the person engaged in adapted sports or did not engage as they aged; and we can understand supports for participation for both groups. Table 16.2 expands the model of aging with and aging into disability with a broad ecological perspective: individual, interpersonal, organizational, community, and public policy.

Professional Support

Health care professionals are gatekeepers to opportunities for physical activity for persons with disabilities (Kennedy et al., 2021). These professionals include primary care physicians, community health nurses, and specialists of disability such as physiatrists, orthopedists, neurologists, urologists, and endocrinologists. Some of these professions have been *traditionally* ill trained on advising and guiding individuals with disability into being physically active (Thomas et al., 2020). These professions are probably lesser advocates for their patients in adapted competitive sport programs. Exceptions are the physiatrist directing a rehabilitation unit and the staff there—volunteers from the health care professions associated with Special Olympics and Paralympics, and the many other disability-specific

TABLE 16.1   Model of Aging in Adult Adapted Sport Participation

Roles and stages	Aging with disability	Aging into disability
Athlete	Coming into adapted sports competition as a young person. Additional factors of aging, injury, or illness are part of one's adapted physical activity (APA) around middle age through old age and maybe oldest ages.	Coming into sport participation without adaption in youth. Begins APA around middle age through old and possibly oldest ages.
Sport entry and continued participation	Either segregated or integrated high school or college sports APA. Enjoys sport. In adulthood: Given disability and sport history, membership in disability-specific sport associations and elite participation in competitions. Recreational APA sport participation.	High school or college sports participation most likely segregated. Enjoys sport. In adulthood: Illness, injury, and aging condition requiring adaptations for sport participation. Membership in recreational sport participation that could progress to elite sport competitions or elite sport participation that shifts to recreational sport participation due to issues of aging.
	Scope: Competition at levels that are local, state, regional, national, and world.	
Professional support and health care team	Knowledgeable people who can *refer* the individual to community sport programs or to disability-specific sport associations: rehabilitation team, primary care provider or other health care provider (HCP), occupational therapist, physical therapist, exercise physiologists in health services, orthopedist, neurologist, family, friends, and other athletes involved in sport.	Knowledgeable people to *refer* individual to adapted sports: rehabilitation team, primary care provider or other HCP, occupational therapist, physical therapist, exercise physiologists in health services, orthopedist, neurologist, family, friends, and other athletes involved in sports.
	In ongoing health care visits, check-ins regarding sport participation should be conducted. Encourage *self-advocacy*—discussing sport participation and health care issues of pains, fatigue, and pacing with their health care professional, raising any health care issues linked to sport participation.	
	Psychological support: Health care professional in follow-up or ongoing medical care should stay interested in the individual's sport participation and to offer encouragement. Document sport participation in the medical chart for psychological follow-up.	
Exercise and sport professionals	Individuals to coach individuals and teams for sport participation should be well trained.	
	Expertise: Given the disability, know the physiological considerations for competitive athletics and training. How to train the individual given their disability and their additional common aging disabilities. How to modify and adapt the sport choice for the athlete. Where to play the sport.	Expertise: How to modify and adapt the activity for continued participation, such as having senior divisions, age-bracket awareness. Training to avoid injury or negative physical consequences from sport participation. How to modify and adapt the sport for participation. Where to play the sport.
	Develop programs for athletes addressing barriers to participation.	

Model of aging adapted from Molton & Jensen (2010); Molton & Yorkston (2017).

TABLE 16.2   Ecological Model of Health Behavior in Aging and Adult Adapted Sport

Ecological level	Aging with disability	Aging into disability
Individual level: concerns knowledge, attitudes, and skills directly related to the individual	It is important to consider the individual's disability identity and provide support tailored around this identity regarding sport and physical activity.	The individual may be attempting to identify their connection to their disability depending on the onset. Education and providing resources to assist with this is pivotal in the context of sport and physical activity.
Interpersonal level: concerns exchanges and interactions within an individual's network; both primary and secondary groups that are larger and broader	Connecting with the individual's established network is key, as well as being able to educate the established networks. It is important to provide connections to others if needed.	Connecting with the individual's established network is key. However, be ready to provide information related to new networks depending on how the individual's current support network functions.
Organizational level: focuses on social institutions that serve as established authorities and offer generally recognized and accepted purposes	The individual may be a part of organizations that support adapted physical activity. As an advocate, connect with those organizations and incorporate them in working with the individual. You may also need to provide alternatives or other organizations that have access to other types of sport or assist with transitioning to a sport appropriate to physical capacity.	The individual may need assistance with continuing to be a part of various sport organizations. There may be opportunities to adapt participation. The individual needs preparation for alternative organizations that support them in sport activity.
Community level: includes relationships that organizations form with each other, which commonly exist in coalitions and conglomerates	The individual's community or network of organizations may already be established, but it is important for an advocate to be able to communicate with the community and continue to provide support. The individual may also need to assist in establishing community.	The individual may need assistance with navigating their community and vice versa. The individual's community may need to help in adapting its function to support the individual as they age into disability sport. Support may be needed at both ends.
Public policy level: contains all regulatory legislature, spanning from local municipalities to the federal government	It is important to be aware of the current policies that support or place barriers for people with disabilities. You may need to provide education on these to the individual.	It is important to be aware of the current policies that support or place barriers for people with disabilities. You may need to provide education on these to the individual.

You = the professional working with the individual.

Adapted from Kennedy et al. (2021).

adapted sport associations. Special Olympics is exemplary in its marketing and recruitment of volunteers, many of whom come from the allied health fields as well as kinesiology and special education. The rehabilitation community is gaining an audience with the Paralympics as they become aware of the adapted sport competitions, particularly for clients with competitive sport history. And these highly successful athletes are reaching out to local sport programs to discuss, with all honesty, the road to elite competitions.

Other supporters of adapted sport are the many adapted physical educators, general physical educators and coaches who supported sport participation for their students from grade school and high school, including Special Olympics, Unified Sport, Deaflympics, and other sport participation. These athletes were young when they started and eventually are aging adults in competitions. These individuals were also potentially involved in disability-specific sport competitions at younger ages with groups like the Spina Bifida Association and Disability Sport, USA, because their teachers, or their health care professionals were aware of the programs.

As these athletes age, the key to their sport participation is staying healthy and participating in check-ins with their health care team. This should be motivational for the athlete by providing an essential opportunity for the athlete to self-advocate with the HCP around issues affecting participation like pain, fatigue, and pacing. These areas need attention, and unless the athlete brings them to the attention of HCP, they may not be addressed. All athletes need to be able to advocate for themselves, to not be intimidated by the HCP, and to reason that their health is important to competition. To get answers and avoid extending the appointment time, athletes are encouraged to develop strategies for the office visit. One strategy is to make a list of questions for the visit with the HCP. Eventually, the HCP knows to say, "What is on your list today?" The list strategy is particularly true for specialties like orthopedics and neurology. They are a wealth of information in physical activity, but an athlete must ask about sport-life concerns, unless that is the reason for the visit. Athletes should ask about a knee that is painful during practice, or the timing of medications on game day. Be specific. Also, share athletic outcomes with the HCP ("We won that game

I was telling you about!").

The field of kinesiology has a long history of promoting sports engagement for persons considered aging with disability. As mentioned, there are special interest groups that have cultivated sports competition for their members across a variety of sports such as Special Olympics, the Dwarf Athletic Association of America, the National Sports Center for the Disabled, and U.S. Paralympics. There are also disability-specific groups such as the National Beep Baseball Association, the National Wheelchair Basketball Association, the United States Handcycle Federation, the Handicapped Scuba Association, the Adaptive Sports Center (skiing), the International Tennis Federation, and Wheelchair Tennis under the International Tennis Federation. Some of the athletes are persons who were born with a disability and hence are aging with that disability (e.g., intellectual disability, dwarfism, and orthopedic impairment) and some are athletes who experienced an accident or injury and are experiencing a disability later in life (e.g., spinal cord injury).

Does it really make any difference in sports to know the etiology of onset of disability? Epidemiological studies like the Paralysis Study have discovered that using the term *adults with disabilities*, without the modern paradigm dichotomy and

PHILL MAGAKOE/AFP via Getty Images

subcategories with their definitions elaborated on, leads to erroneous conclusions. Therefore, we have presented an application of this paradigm and assert that it does make a difference in how an athlete experiences their participation in adult adapted sports if they have always been around adapted physical activity (aging with disability) versus one who was an athlete and now is not participating in that sport because of a chronic medical condition or an accident (aging into a disability) and needing APA to participate?

For some individuals who are aging into disability, it is depressing. They want their youth and their game to be same. Others readily acknowledge they can't do certain things anymore. They stop. They might gain weight. They might enter competition that is geared to their age group and their skill level, or change the sport entirely. Whichever way they go, there needs to be professionals who support the engagement in competitive athletics if the individual is capable. In some cases, there are definite physiological considerations to bring to the competition from the individual's health care practitioner. For example, an athlete with diabetes most likely needs to confer with their nutritionist to determine how to maintain proper insulin levels during workouts and competition. For others it might be working with pain or a limb injury with a physical therapist or occupational therapist. For others, pacing might be the discussion between coach and experts for a specific sport within those disability-specific sport teams.

Classifications for Adapted Sport

The overall need for classification systems is to ensure "… that the athlete's impairment minimizes the impact on the sport performance" (Davis, 2017, p. 54). By using a classification system, an event can have fair competition for athletes with different abilities. Measurement is made of their impairment in muscle power, passive range of motion, limb deficiency, leg-length difference, short stature, hypertonia, ataxia, athetosis, vision impairment, and intellectual impairment (Busse, 2014). Then their competition record is analyzed for consideration into the games before competition and during competition. After competition, additional evaluations conducted.

Classes are designated categories to organize athletes into competitive groups that best serve their functional ability. These are very specific.

Some textbooks have taken great care to list all the classes for athletes. All the classifications for the Paralympic events are published on its website (2018), and all the rules and regulations per sport are also published there (2021b) with a note that they are subject to change. In fact, everything about Paralympics is on its website, where one can look up who has qualified for the competitions, in what classification, and from which country (2021a).

It is recommended that classifications be examined through each organization (e.g., Wheelchair & Ambulatory Sports, USA). We recommend the current specifics on sport classifications in the many chapters on adapted sport in Winnick & Porretta (2022). For example, Wheelchair Ambulatory Sports, USA–sponsored classed divisions in track and field events are as follows:

Seated classes include T31, Y32, T33, T51. T52, T53 and T54 for track events and F31, F32, F33, F34. F51, F54, F55, F56 and F57 for field events. Standing athletes compete in track as T35, T36, T37, T38, T42, T44, T45, T46 and T47 and in field events as F35, F36, F37, F38, F40, F42, F44, F45, and F46. T/F11, T/F12, and T/F13.

Winnick & Porretta (2022, p. 524).

Numbering and lettering classification can be found on the Paralympic website (www.paralympic.org). For example, adapted track (T) is delineated by these categories:

- T11 to T13 (vision impairment)
- T20 (intellectual impairment)
- T35 to T38 (coordination impairments such as hypertonia, ataxia and athetosis
- T40 to T41 (short stature)
- T42 to T44 (lower limb competing without prosthesis affected by limb deficiency, leg length difference, impaired muscle power, or impaired passive range of movement)
- T45 to T47 (upper limb or limbs affected by deficiency, impaired muscle power, or impaired passive range of movement)
- T61 to T64 (lower limb or limbs competing with prosthesis affected by limb deficiency and leg length difference)

Using this Paralympic list and the Wheelchair & Ambulatory Sports, USA information prior to that, athletes classified as T35 through T38 would have coordination impairments and would stand for their track events by the Wheelchair & Ambulatory Sports, USA.

Individual Sports

The most popular individual sports of the Paralympic Games are alpine skiing, track and field, and individual swimming events. Other individual sports are bocci, track and road cycling, judo, archery, equestrian, biathlon, cross-country skiing, snowboarding, and wheelchair curling. Each of these sports will have a classification system for competition, as well as modifications and adaptations for performing the sport based on the needs of the athlete to obtain the best performance. For the Paralympics, these are governed by the International Olympic Committee and well-known to the athletes who are participating. For example, in cross-country skiing, there is classification for physical impairment and visual impairment. There are standing events for those with impairments of arms or legs; seated events with all leg impairments, and skiers with visual impairments. Standing skiers use conventional skis and poles, and seated skiers use a sit-ski that is a chair placed over a pair of skis. The skis ride in a track and the skier is secured to the chair with strapping. Those athletes with visual impairments compete with a sighted guide.

Alpine Skiing

In parts of the United States where skiing is popular, downhill skiing is an adapted sport in which adults with a disability participate. Those most likely to be competing are younger adults. Sometimes these athletes were great alpine skiers or snowboarders; injury occurred, and they thrived on the chance to be competitive again. There are those with childhood disabilities like visual impairment who were also competitive as alpine skiers in their childhood.

These skiing programs for those with disability refer to adapted sport as *adaptive* sport in their marketing materials. Names like Oregon Adaptive Sports and the Adaptive Adventure Sports Coalition reflect this trend. There are at least 10 U.S. states with adapted ski programs: Ohio, Oregon, Utah, California, Wyoming, Colorado, Montana, Vermont, Maine, and New York. In some cases, 10 sponsors are the financial backbones of one program. Those sponsors range from municipalities, health insurers, ski resorts, foundations, and cell phone companies. All the adapted sport's programs appear to have multiple funding sources with paid and volunteer staff.

The configuration of ski equipment for a person with a disability who is participating in adapted skiing is described as four-track, three-track, two-track, mono-skiing, and bi-skiing.

- *Four-track:* Two skis, two hand-held outriggers
- *Three-track:* One ski, two hand-held outriggers
- *Two-track:* Two skis with the use of tethers, spacers, ski bras, and the like on the skis for stability
- *Mono-skiing:* A bucket style seat with a single ski underneath it; handheld outriggers
- *Bi-skiing:* A bucket style with two skis underneath; handheld outriggers or an assistant with fixed outriggers and tethers

A skier with below-knee amputation should consult with their prosthetist first to determine the best type of components for their intended skiing activity. The prosthetist must recognize the force the skier may be applying to their prosthetic knee.

Paralympics has alpine skiing with 12 physical impairment classes that represent stand-up skiers and mono-skiers plus 3 visually impaired classes. The ski events of the Paralympics are downhill, super-G, giant slalom, and super combined, with each event having a sit, stand or visual impairment category. Adaptive snowboard was added in 2014, with classes for participation. Snowboard classification is new to the Paralympics, and athletes are classified as upper extremity involvement or lower extremity involvement. Athletes get into competitive alpine skiing and snowboarding through the programs offered under Team USA (2022). There are affiliations across the country in states like Colorado, Utah, and Vermont that offer connections to training and understanding of qualifications for the Paralympics as a registered athlete.

Special Olympic competition is offered to athletes with intellectual disability in alpine events of the super G, giant slalom, and slalom. Nordic events include distance races of 500 meters, 1 K, 2.5 K, 5 K, 7.5 K, and 10 K, as well as a 4 × 1 K relay, and one with a unified team (mixed members with and without intellectual disability.

Track and Field

Track and field events are opportunities for individuals with disabilities to participate in competitive sports. Some of these athletes compete through disability-specific sport competition such as the Dwarf Athletic Association of America, Special Olympics,

Inc., the United States Association of Blind Athletes, the USA Deaf Sports Federation, and Wheelchair & Ambulatory Sports, USA.

Those with upper limb disabilities can participate in running and jumping events; those with lower limb disabilities are able to participate in throwing events. Students with visual impairments will be able to take part in throwing events without much modification, but some adaptation will be needed to enable them to participate in the running events. Individuals who perform track and field activities from a wheelchair need additional adaptations. To participate in jumping events, slight adaptations in style are necessary for individuals with upper arm amputations.

Running Events

Wheelchair racing events consist of the 50-meter and 5,000-meter events and a slalom race in which the racers must negotiate an obstacle course that tests their strength and ability to maneuver the wheelchair.

Competitive track events for runners with visual impairments include various distances, including short races of 100 meters, middle distances, and marathons. In the dashes, the runner with a visual impairment uses guide wires stretched 100 meters along the track without intervening supports. Alternatively, a continuous sound is made by someone standing at the finish line to guide the runner in the right direction (see chapter 11). In sanctioned meets sponsored by the United States Association of Blind Athletes, the international caller system is used for athletes with limited vision (B-1 and B-2) in the 100-meter dash. Runners compete individually against the clock, following an auditory signal, usually a number representing the lane in which they are running. If the runner swerves off-course, the number being yelled is changed to indicate that the runner is off-course. Participants with greater sight (B-3) are not allowed any modifications. For races of longer distance, the runner who is blind runs with a sighted partner using a tethered rope of less than 50 centimeters (approximately 19 inches), which is held by both runners. Sighted runners are not permitted to run in front of their partner. Below-the-knee amputees are now using prosthetic devices designed to improve running technique. The Flex-Foot (figure 16.1a) enabled runners in the early days of prosthetic assistance. Today there are three new running feet: Cheetah Xcel for sprinting, Cheetah Xpanse for long jumping, and Cheetah Xceed for distance (Ossur, 2022).

Jumping Events

The two most popular events in field competition are the long jump and high jump. However, in some schools, the triple jump or hop, step, and jump is also

FIGURE 16.1   Adapted equipment. *(a)* Marlon Shirley was the world's fastest amputee, using the Flex-Foot Cheetah in 2003. *(b)* Cheetah-Exceed for explosive short distance sprints.

(a) ARIS MESSINIS/AFP via Getty Images; *(b)* Diarmuid Greene/Sportsfile via Getty Images

included. The participant with a visual impairment and the student with a single leg can perform both the high jump and the long jump from a stationary position. The former can also execute the triple jump from a stationary start. The high-jump participant who is blind stands at the point of takeoff, swings the lead leg back and forth to gain momentum, and then springs from the takeoff leg. A jumper with one leg performs in the same way without the swinging of the leg to generate momentum.

Participants missing or without the use of one or both arms must alter the style of the high jump to compensate for the lack of the use of the arms in maintaining balance as they go over the bar. The takeoff point for the standing long jump and triple jump would be the start of the long jump or triple jump for athletes with visual impairments or leg amputations.

Throwing Events

The shot put, discus, and javelin are the main field events of most track and field meets. Athletes who use wheelchairs and whose limitations affect only the lower body can participate in all three of these field events. Each participant must adapt a style of throwing based on personal capabilities. If trunk maneuverability is possible, the participant can use the twisting of the trunk to help generate power in the throw; otherwise, they must rely completely on the arm and shoulder. In throwing events, the wheelchair must be made secure to prevent its turning over.

Throwing events require little modification for participants with limited vision. In the javelin event, they must usually decrease the distance they run before making the throw to a few steps so they will not run over the foul line; or they throw from a stationary position.

Swimming

Swimming competition is held at the games of the Paralympics and Special Olympics games. The Summer Paralympic Games in 2021 saw American Jessica Long (S8, SB7, SM8) take the silver in the 300-meter breaststroke. Before the games, she trained with gold medal swimmer Michael Phelps, whom she credited with giving Paralympic swim athletes credibility with the media, who had seemed to push these athletes aside until Phelps personally encouraged his colleague and friend, Long (2021). According to Long, she was born without fibula bones, ankles, or heels, and when she was 18 months of age, her legs were amputated below the knees (2021).

Swimming events of the Paralympics are the butterfly, backstroke, breaststroke, and freestyle, with their various classifications. Distances range from 50 meters to 400 meters. The modifications to the competition include the starting position whereby the swimmer sits on the platform (if they can sit) or standing in the water. If the athlete is blind, they can have tappers who stand at the end of the pool and tap when the athlete reaches near the wall to turn or end the race.

Special Olympics offers competition in butterfly and breaststroke (25 and 50 meters), backstroke (25, 50, and 100 meters), and freestyle (23, 50, 100, 200, and 400 meters), plus a 100-meter medley. Diving is also an event.

If the athlete desires to compete with other athletes with disabilities, the USA Deaf Sports Federation is another resource, as is the Dwarf Athletic Association of America. Deaflympics (2022) offers swimming and many Olympic-style competitions for deaf athletes.

Dual Sports

Any of these sports in which individuals compete as elite athletes in either the Paralympic or Special Olympic can be played at local levels. Both elite and recreational athletes need access to coaches, facilities, and other athletes. (Recreational sports are addressed in chapter 15). One key is to connect with disability-specific sport programs and any of their connections into municipal recreation programs, health clubs, and coaches. Another avenue is the unified program entry, which involves joining a mixed team of those with and without disabilities. Special Olympics has unified programs across the United States and abroad.

Tennis

Adapted competitive tennis is an exciting game of athleticism. Singles and pairs wheelchair tennis is an event of the Paralympics. It is adapted for those with an impairment of the lower body. Athletes use specially designed wheelchairs. The ball can bounce two times, and the second bounce can be outside of the court. Rackets and balls remain the same as in tennis without adaptation or modification. The International Tennis Federation governs rules of competition, and the National Foundation of Wheelchair Sport develops and sponsors competition. Adapted tennis is a widely popular sport.

Adapted tennis is played in the Special Olympics by athletes with intellectual impairment competing in singles, doubles, mixed doubles, unified doubles, and mixed doubles. Athletes who are deaf also play tennis in singles, doubles, and mixed doubles in the Deaflympics.

Table Tennis

Table tennis has been a competition in the Paralympic games since 1960 in Rome. The International Table Tennis Federation governs the sport. Wheelchair athletes were the first to compete in the 1960 Paralympics, and standing athletes started competing in 1976. According to the current classifications, there is a diverse group of athletes competing in table tennis. To serve, players place the ball on their elbow or at the end of the paddle rather than tossing it. All other basic rules are similar to those in the Olympics for equipment, scoring, and match process. The motto of the International Table Tennis Federation is "TABLE TENNIS. FOR ALL. FOR LIFE." As such their involvement is with the Paralympics and they have separate committee work on gender and diversity plus ongoing competitions organized for athletes' impairments (ITTF, n.d.). ITTF reported that for the 2020Paralympics, there were 11 classes according to the impact of impairment on athletes' performance. Classes 1 to 5 are for those in wheelchairs, classes 6 through 10 are the standing competitors, and class 11 is for those with intellectual impairment.

Team Sports

Team sports for those competitive athletes with disabilities are again described here from the Paralympics and Special Olympics. Other *recreational* sports activities for individuals, duos, and teams are addressed in chapter 15.

Ice Sledge Hockey

Ice sledge hockey is an exciting hockey game played by athletes with a physical impairment of the lower limbs. They sit in a double-blade sledge and use two sticks where one end is spiked for pushing and one end is bladed for shooting. Rules are determined by the International Ice Hockey Federation, with modifications. It is a fast game and is played by men and women. Steven Cash is a recently retired outstanding American player, having won a gold medal in the sport (2021). He became an amputee of one leg when he was three years old due to osteosarcoma. In his playing days in the Paralympics as a goalie he faced 33 shots and stopped them all.

Sitting Volleyball

There is little difference in stand-up volleyball and sitting volleyball with the exception that in sitting volleyball, players must keep their pelvis in contact with the ground at all times, the net is lowered, and

Jordan Mansfield/Getty Images for Invictus Games

the court is smaller. Men and woman play this fast-paced game. In the Rio Paralympics, 192 players composed the 8 teams. Recently, young veterans who lost limbs in wars have played this game.

Goalball

Goalball is another very popular game played by athletes with VI. The goalball has a sounding device in it. It is played on the ground with the players attempting to throw the ball into the opponent's goal basket (like a hockey net). All team members wear opaque shades over their eyes. The game is played all over the world and it is governed by the International Blind Sports Federation, which sponsored competitions in the off-Paralympic years.

Wheelchair Basketball

Wheelchair basketball started in the United States after World War II, when men who were athletes were injured and still wanted to play basketball. It has since greatly expanded in the United States and throughout the world and includes a broad array of impairment and ages of athletes. The wheelchair sport is the same as the stand-up sport, although there are a few adaptations. It is played on the same size court, using the same point system. Dribbling has an adaptation whereby the player rests with the ball, or holds it in the hand; they can take up to two pushes of the wheelchair and then dribble the ball. The player can repeat this as many times as desired in the game. Fouls are committed by making illegal contact of an opponent's wheelchair, which is considered a part of the player.

Summary

The current definition of aging *with* disability and *into* disability broadens the understanding of adapted sport participation. Those who are aging with disability can begin their life in adapted sport earlier, whereas those who are aging into disability because of aging, injury, or illness begin adapted sport around the adult time of an injury or in middle age. These distinctions are important as the individual interacts with sports organizations and their own medical supports. Pain, fatigue, and pacing are attended to by the individual in conjunction with health care supports. Health care professionals are gatekeepers to participation in adapted physical activity during aging. The key to an athlete's sport participation is checking in with their health care team. Just what role is played within the ecology of adapted sport participation by the individual and those that interact with them is described in detail. Special interest groups sponsor adapted sport. This includes Special Olympics for individuals with intellectually disability, the Dwarf Athletic Association of America, the National Sports Center for the Disabled, and the U.S. Paralympics. There are also disability-specific groups such as the National Beep Baseball Association, the National Wheelchair Basketball Association, the United States Handcycle Federation, the Handicapped Scuba Association, the Adaptive Sports Center (skiing), the International Tennis Federation, and Wheelchair Tennis of the U.S. Tennis Association.

CHAPTER 1

Agiovlasitis, S., Yun, J. K., Jin, J., McCubbin, J. M., & Motl, R. W. (2018). Physical activity promotion for persons experiencing disability: The importance of interdisciplinary research and practice. *Adapted Physical Activity Quarterly, 35*, 437-457. https://doi.org/10.1123/apaq.2017-0103

Anderson, W. L., Armour, B. S., Finkelstein, E. A., & Wiener, J. M. (2010). Estimates of state-level health-care expenditures associated with disability. *Public Health Reports, 125*, 44-51. https://doi.org/10.1177/003335491012500107

Anderson, W. L., Weiner, J. M., Khatutsky, G., & Armour, B. S. (2013). Obesity and people with disabilities: The implications for health care expenditures. *Obesity, 21*, E798-E804. https://doi.org/10.1002/oby.20531

Atkinson, M., Rees, D., & Davis, L. (2015). Disability and economic disadvantage: Facing the facts. *Archives of Disease in Childhood, 100*, 305-307. https://doi.org/10.1136/archdischild-2014-307463

Bassett, D. R., John, D., Conger, S. C., Fitzhugh, E. C., & Coe, D. P. (2015). Trends in physical activity and sedentary behaviors of United States youth. *Journal of Physical Activity and Health, 12*, 1102-1111.

Bedell, G., Coster, W., Law, M., Liljenquist, K., Kao, Y., Teplicky, R., Anaby, D., & Khetani, M. (2013). Community participation, supports, and barriers of school-age children with and without disabilities. *Archives of Physical Medicine and Rehabilitation, 94*, 315-323.

Belcher, B. R., Berrigan, D., Dodd, K. W., Emken, B. A., Chou, C., & Spruijt-Metz, D. (2010). Physical activity in U.S. youth: Effect of race/ethnicity, age, gender, and weight status. *Medicine & Science in Sports & Exercise, 42*, 2211-2221.

Berry, J. G., Bloom, S., Foley, S., & Palfrey, J. S. (2010). Health inequity in children and youth with chronic health conditions. *Pediatrics, 126*, S111. https://doi.org/10.1542/peds.2010-1466D

Booth, M. L., Bauman, A., & Owen, N. (2002). Perceived barriers to physical activity among older Australians. *Journal of Aging and Physical Activity, 10*, 271-280. https://doi.org/10.1123/japa.10.3.271

Bureau of Justice Statistics (BJS). (2021). Crime against persons with disabilities, 2009–2019—statistical tables. U.S. Department of Justice, Office of Justice Programs, accessed November 4, 2021. https://bjs.ojp.gov/content/pub/pdf/capd0919st.pdf

Carroll, D. D., Courtney-Long, E. A., Stevens, A. C., Sloan, M. L., Lullo, C., Visser, S. N., Fox, M. H., Armour, B. S., Campbell, V. A., Brown, D. R., & Dorn, J. M. (2014). Vital signs: Disability and physical activity—United States, 2009-2012. *Morbidity and Mortality Weekly Report, 63*, 407-413.

Centers for Disease Control and Prevention, National Center on Birth Defects and Developmental Disabilities, Division of Human Development and Disability. (n.d.). *Disability and health data system (DHDS) data.* Accessed June 29, 2020. https://dhds.cdc.gov

Drum, C. E. (2009). Models and approaches to disability. In C. E. Drum, G. L. Krahn, & H. Bersani (Eds.), *Disability and public health* (pp. 27-44). American Public Health Association.

Halfon, N., Houtrow, A., Larson, K., & Newacheck, P. W. (2012). The changing landscape of disability in childhood. *The Future of Children, 22*, 13-42.

Johnson, M., Stoelzle, H., Foss, S., Finco, K., & Carstens, K. (2012). ADA compliance and accessibility of fitness facilities in western Wisconsin. *Topics in Spinal Cord Injury Rehabilitation, 18*(4), 340-353. https://doi.org/10.1310/sci1804-340

Kann, L., McManus, T., Harris, W. A., Shanklin, S. L., Flint, K. H., Queen, B., Lowry, R., Chyen, D., Whittle, L., Thornton, J., Lim, C., Bradford, D., Yamakawa, Y., Leon, M., Brener, N., & Ethier, K. A. (2018). Youth Risk Behavior Surveillance—United States, 2017. *Morbidity and Mortality Weekly Report: Surveillance Summaries, 67*(8), 1-114. https://doi.org/10.15585/mmwr.ss6708a1

Khavjou, O. A., Anderson, W. L., Honeycutt, A. A., Bates, L. G., Razzaghi, H., Hollis, N. D., & Grosse, S. D. (2020). National health care expenditures associated with disability. *Medical Care, 58*, 826-832. DOI: 10.1097/MLR.0000000000001371

Kinne, S. (2008). Distribution of secondary medical problems, impairments, and participation limitations among adults with disabilities and their relationship to health and other outcomes. *Disability and Health Journal, 1*, 42-50. https://doi.org/10.1016/j.dhjo.2007.11.006

Kinne, S., Patrick, D. L., & Doyle, D. L. (2004). Prevalence of secondary conditions among people with disabilities. *American Journal of Public Health, 94*, 443-445. https://doi.org/10.2105/ajph.94.3.443

Krahn, G. L., Walker, D. K., & De-Araujo, R. C. (2015, February 17). Persons with disabilities as an unrecognized health disparity population. *American Journal of Public Health*, e1-e9.

Kraus, L., Lauer, E., Coleman, R., & Houtenville, A. (2018). *2017 disability statistics annual report.* University of New Hampshire. https://disabilitycompendium. org/sites/default/files/useruploads/2017_Annual Report_2017_FINAL.pdf

Mattson, G., Kuo, D. Z., & AAP committee on psychosocial aspects of child and family health, AAP council on children with disabilities. (2019). Psychosocial factors in children and youth with special health care needs and their families. *Pediatrics, 143,* e20183171. https://doi. org/10.1542/peds.2018-3171

McDonald, C. M. (2002). Physical activity, health impairments, and disability in neuromuscular disease. *American Journal of Physical Medicine and Rehabilitation, 81,* S108-S120. https://doi.org/10.1097/00002060- 200211001-00012

Palisano, R. J., Rezze, B. D., Stewart, D., Freeman, M., Rosenbaum, P. L., Hlyva, O., Wolfe, L., & Gorter, J. W. (2018). Promoting capacities for future adult roles and healthy living using a lifecourse health development approach. *Disability and Rehabilitation.* https://doi.org/ 10.1080/09638288.2018.1544670

Reid, G. (2003). Defining adapted physical activity. In R. D. Steadward, G. D. Wheeler, & E. J. Watkinson (Eds.), *Adapted physical activity* (pp. 11-25). University of Alberta Press.

Rimmer, J. H. (1999). Health promotion of people with disabilities: The emerging paradigm shift from disability prevention to prevention of secondary conditions. *Physical Therapy, 79,* 495-502.

Rimmer, J. H., Chen, M., & Hsieh, K. (2011). A conceptual model for identifying, preventing, and managing secondary conditions in people with disabilities. *Physical Therapy, 91,* 1728-1739. https://doi.org/10.2522/ ptj.20100410

Rimmer, J. H., & Lai, B. (2017). Framing new pathways in transformative exercise for individuals with existing and newly acquired disability. *Disability and Rehabilitation, 39,* 173-180. https://doi.org/10.3109/09638288. 2015.1047967

Rimmer, J. H., Padalabalanarayanan, S., Malone, L. A., & Mehta, T. (2017). Fitness facilities still lack accessibility for people with disabilities. *Disability and Health Journal, 10,* 214-221.

Rimmer, J. H., Rauworth, A., Wang, E., Heckerling, P. S., & Gerber, B. S. (2009). A randomized controlled trial to increase physical activity and reduce obesity in a predominantly African American group of women with mobility disabilities and severe obesity. *Preventive Medicine, 48,* 473-479. https://doi.org/10.1016/ j.ypmed.2009.02.008

Rimmer, J. H., Riley, B., Wang, E., Rauworth, A., & Jurkowski, J. (2004). Physical activity participation among persons with disabilities: Barriers and facilitators. *American Journal of Preventive Medicine, 26,* 419-425.

Rimmer, J. H., & Rowland, J. L. (2008). Physical activity for youth with disabilities: A critical need in an under-served population. *Developmental Neurorehabilitation, 11,* 141-148.

Rimmer, J. H., Rowland, J. L., & Yamaki, K. (2007). Obesity and secondary conditions in adolescents with disabilities: Addressing the needs of an underserved population. *Journal of Adolescent Health, 41,* 224-229. https:// doi.org/10.1016/j.jadohealth.2007.05.005

Rose-Jacobs, R., Fiore, J. G., de Cuba, S. E., Black, M., Cutts, D. B., Coleman, S. M., Heeren, T., Chilton, M., Casey, P., Cook, J., & Frank, D. A. (2016). Children with special healthcare needs, supplemental security income, and food insecurity. *Journal of Developmental and Behavioral Pediatrics, 37,* 140-147. https://doi.org/10.1097/ DBP.0000000000000260

Santiago, M., & Coyle, C. (2004). Leisure-time physical activity and secondary conditions in women with physical disabilities. *Disability and Rehabilitation, 26,* 485-494. https://doi.org/10.1080/09638280410001663139

Swanson, M., & Bolen, J. (2011, November 29). *CDC's life course model for children and young adults with chronic conditions (Episode 2)* [Webinar]. AAIDD and AAHD: The Unique Role of CDC's Division of Human Development and Disability, Centers for Disease Control and Prevention.

U.S. Department of Health and Human Services (USDHHS). (2005). *The surgeon general's call to action to improve the health and wellness of persons with disabilities.* Office of the Surgeon General.

U.S. Department of Health and Human Services (USDHHS). (2010a). Disability and health: Objectives. HealthyPeople.gov. https://wayback.archive-it. org/5774/20220414161601/https://www.healthy-people.gov/2020/topics-objectives/topic/disability-and-health/objectives

U.S. Department of Health and Human Services (USDHHS). (2010b). *Rethinking MCH: The life course model as an organizing framework: Concept paper.* www. mchnutritionpartners.ucla.edu/sites/default/files/ images/Kotelchuck%20paper_Rethinking%20MCH.pdf

U.S. Department of Health and Human Services (USDHHS). (2018). *Physical activity guidelines for Americans* (2nd ed.). U.S. Department of Health and Human Services.

U.S. Department of Health and Human Services (USDHHS). (2022). *2019-2020 children and youth with special health care needs.* Health Resources and Services Administration, Maternal and Child Health Bureau. U.S. Department of Health and Human Services. https://mchb.hrsa.gov/sites/default/files/mchb/ programs-impact/nsch-data-brief-children-youth-special-health-care-needs.pdf

United States Government Accountability Office (U.S. GAO). (2010). *Students with disabilities: More information and guidance could improve opportunities in physical education and athletics.* U.S. Government. www.gao.gov/ products/GAO-10-519

Ward, M. J. (2009). Models and approaches to disability. In C. E. Drum, G. L. Krahn, & H. Bersani (Eds.), *Disability and public health* (pp. 45-63). American Public Health Association.

World Health Organization. (2003). *Constitution of the World Health Organization*. www.who.int/governance/eb/who_constitution_en.pdf

CHAPTER 2

American Association of Nurse Practitioners. (n.d.). Starting your nurse practitioner (NP) career. https://www.aanp.org/student-resources/starting-your-np-career

Americans with Disabilities Act (ADA), U.S. Department of Justice, Civil Rights Division. (n.d.). *Introduction to the Americans with Disabilities Act*. https://www.ada.gov/topics/intro-to-ada/

Centers for Disease Control and Prevention (CDC). (2021). *Child development specific conditions*. http://cdc.gov/ncbddd/childdevelopment/conditions.html

Dunn, W. (2017). Strengths-based approaches: What if even the 'bad' things are good things? *British Journal of Occupational Therapy, 80*(7), 395-396.

Kurtzman, E. T., & Barnow, B. S. (2017). A comparison of nurse practitioners, physician assistants, and primary care physicians' patterns of practice and quality of care in health centers. *Medical Care, 55*(6), 615-622.

Stroke Camp. (n.d.). *Stroke Camp*. https://strokecamp.org/

Wilson, W. J., Theriot, E. A., & Haegele, J. A. (2020). Attempting inclusive practice: Perspectives of physical educators and adapted physical educators. *Curriculum Studies in Health and Physical Education, 11*(3), 187-203. https://doi.org/10.1080/25742981.2020.1806721

CHAPTER 3

Centers for Disease Control and Prevention (CDC) National Center on Birth Defects and Developmental Disabilities, Division of Human Development and Disability. (2000). *Disability and health overview*. https://www.cdc.gov/ncbddd/disabilityandhealth/disability.html

Centers for Disease Control and Prevention (CDC) National Center on Birth Defects and Developmental Disabilities, Division of Human Development and Disability. (2020). *Frequent mental distress among adults with disabilities: An easy-read summary*. https://www.cdc.gov/ncbddd/disabilityandhealth/easy-read-frequent-mental-distress

Deal, A., Dunst, C., & Trivett, C. (1989). A flexible and functional approach to developing individualized family support plans. *Infants and Young Children: An Interdisciplinary Journal of Special Care Practices, 1*(4), 32-43.

Education of All Handicapped Children Act of 1975 (PL 94-142), 20 U.S.C. 1401.

Education of All Handicapped Children Amendments Act of 1984 (PL 99-457).

Individuals with Disabilities Education Act (IDEA). (2004). http://idea.ed.gov

Leonardi, M., Bickenbach, J., Ustun, T. B., Kostanjsek, N., & Chatterji, S. (2006). The definition of disability: What is in a name? *The Lancet, 368*(9543), 1219-1221.

Lieberman, L. J., & Houston-Wilson, C. (2009). *Strategies for inclusion: A handbook for physical educators*. Human Kinetics.

Lieberman, L. J., & Houston-Wilson, C. (2018). *Strategies for inclusion: A handbook for physical educators* (3rd ed.). Human Kinetics.

McKeever, A. (2020). How the Americans With Disabilities Act transformed a country. *National Geographic*. www.nationalgeographic.com/history/article/americans-disabilities-act-transformed-united-states

Sameroff, A. J., & Chandler, M. J. (1975). Reproductive risk and the continuum of caretaking causality. In F. D. Horowitz, M. Hertherington, S. Scarr-Salapatec, & C. Siegel (Eds.), *Review of child development research* (pp. 187-244). University of Chicago.

Shonkoff, J. P., & Phillips, D. A. (Eds.). (2000). *From neurons to neighborhoods: The science of early childhood development*. National Research Council/Institute of Medicine. National Academy Press.

Turnbull, R., Huerta, N., & Stowe, M. (2009). *The Individuals With Disabilities Education Act as amended in 2004* (2nd ed.). Pearson.

U.S. Department of Education, Office for Civil Rights. (2013, January 25). *Dear colleague letter: Students with disabilities in extracurricular athletics*. https://www2.ed.gov/about/offices/list/ocr/docs/dcl-fact-sheet-201301-504.html

White House. (2010, July 26). Remarks by the President on 20th anniversary of the Americans with Disabilities Act [Press release]. https://obamawhitehouse.archives.gov/the-press-office/remarks-president-20th-anniversary-americans-with-disabilities-act

Winnick, J., & Porretta, D. L. (2017). *Adapted physical education and sport* (6th ed.). Human Kinetics.

World Health Organization (WHO). (2021). *World report on disability. What is disability?* www.who.int>disability.report

CHAPTER 4

Adolph, K. E. (1997). Learning in the development of infant locomotion. *Monographs of the Society for Research in Child Development, 62*(3), Serial No. 251.

Agiovlasitis, S., Yun, J. K., Jin, J., McCubbin, J. M., & Motl, R. W. (2018). Physical activity promotion for persons experiencing disability: The importance of interdisciplinary research and practice. *Adapted Physical Activity Quarterly, 35*, 437-457. https://doi.org/10.1123/apaq.2017-0103

Álvarez-Bueno, C., Pesce, C., Cavero-Redondo, I., Sánchez-López, M., Garrido-Miguel, M., & Martínez-Vizcaíno, V.

(2017). Academic achievement and physical activity: A meta-analysis. *Pediatrics, 140*(6):e20171498.

American Academy of Pediatrics (AAP). Council on School Health. (2013). The crucial role of recess in school. *Pediatrics, 131*(1), 183-188.

American College of Sports Medicine (ACSM). (2009). American College of Sports Medicine position stand. Exercise and physical activity for older adults. *Medicine & Science in Sports & Exercise, 41*, 1510-1530.

Anaby, D. R., Campbell, W. N., Missiuna, C., Shaw, S. R., Bennett, S., Khan, S., Tremblay, S., Kalubi-Lukusa, J.-C., Camden, C., & GOLDs (Group for Optimizing Leadership and Delivering Services). (2019). Recommended practices to organize and deliver school-based services for children with disabilities: A scoping review. *Child: Care, Health and Development, 45*(1), 15-27.

Ball, L., Lieberman, L., Haibach-Beach, P., Perreault, M., & Tirone, K. (2021). Bullying in physical education of children and youth with visual impairments: A systematic review. *British Journal of Visual Impairment.* https://doi.org/10.1177/02646196211009927

Barnett, D., Clements, M., Kaplan-Estrin, M., & Fialka, J. (2003). Building new dreams: Supporting parents' adaptation to their child with special needs. *Infants & Young Children, 16*(3), 184-200.

Bauer, U. E., Briss, P. A., Goodman, R. A., & Bowman, B. A. (2014). Prevention of chronic disease in the 21st century: Elimination of the leading preventable causes of premature death and disability in the USA. *The Lancet, 384*(9937), 45-52.

Bills, K. L. (2019). The direct relationship between bullying rates and extracurricular activities among adolescents and teenagers with disabilities. *Journal of Social Welfare and Human Rights, 7*, 2.

Bills, K. L. (2020). Helping children with disabilities combat negative socio-emotional outcomes caused by bullying through extracurricular activities. *Journal of Human Behavior in the Social Environment, 30*(5), 573-585.

Bronfenbrenner, U. (1977). Toward an experimental ecology of human development. *American Psychologist, 32*(7), 513-531. https://doi.org/10.1037/0003-066X.32.7.513

Bronfenbrenner, U., & Morris, P. (2006). The bioecological model of human development. In *Theorectical models of human development* (pp. 793-828). Wiley.

Campos, J. J., Anderson, D. I., Barbu-Roth, M. A., Hubbard, E. M., Hertenstein, M. J., & Witherington, D. (2000). Travel broadens the mind. *Infancy, 1*, 149-219.

Center on the Developing Child. (2007). *The science of early childhood development.* National Scientific Council on the Developing Child. www.developingchild.net

Center on the Developing Child. (2019). *5 steps for brain-building serve and return.* www.developingchild.net

Center on the Developing Child at Harvard University. (2010). *The foundations of lifelong health are built in early childhood.* http://www.developingchild.harvard.edu

Centers for Disease Control and Prevention (CDC) Disability and Health Promotion. (2014). *Increasing physical activity among adults with disabilities.* https://www.cdc.gov/ncbddd/disabilityandhealth/pa.html

Centers for Disease Control and Prevention (CDC) Disability and Health Promotion. (2020). *Barriers to participation experienced by people with disabilities.* https://www.cdc.gov/ncbddd/disabilityandhealth/disability-barriers.html

Centers for Disease Control and Prevention (CDC) National Center for Chronic Disease Prevention and Health Promotion (NCCDPHP). (2022). *About chronic disease.* https://www.cdc.gov/chronicdisease/about/index.htm

Cioni, G., Ferrari, F., Einspieler, C., Paolicelli, P. B., Barbani, T., & Prechtl, H. F. (1997). Comparison between observation of spontaneous movements and neurologic examination in preterm infants. *The Journal of Pediatrics, 130*(5), 704-711.

Colarusso, R. P., O'Rourke, C. M., & Leontovich, M. A. (2017). *Special physical education for all teachers* (7th ed.). Kendall Hunt.

Corbin, C. B., Kulinna, P. H., & Sibley, B. A. (2020). A dozen reasons for including conceptual physical education in quality secondary school programs. *Journal of Physical Education, Recreation & Dance, 91*(3), 40-49.

Cunningham, C., O'Sullivan, R., Caserotti, P., & Tully, M. A. (2020). Consequences of physical inactivity in older adults: A systematic review of reviews and meta-analyses. *Scandinavian Journal of Medicine & Science in Sports, 30*, 816-827. https://doi.org/10.1111/sms.13616

Delprato, D. J., & Midgley, B. D. (1992). Some fundamentals of B. F. Skinner's behaviorism. *American Psychologist, 47*(11), 1507-1520. https://doi.org/10.1037/0003-066X.47.11.1507

Dunn, J. M., & Leitschuh, C. A. (2014). *Special physical education* (10th ed.). Kendall Hunt.

Eagen, T. J., Teshale, S. M., Herrera-Venson, A. P., Ordway, A., & Caldwell, J. (2019). Participation in two evidence-based falls prevention programs by adults aging with a long-term disability: Case-control study of reach and effectiveness. *Journal in Aging and Health, 31*(10 Suppl), 39S-67S. https://doi.org/10.1177/0898264318808918

Emerson, E., Fortune, N., Llewellyn, G., & Stancliffe, R. (2021). Loneliness, social support, social isolation and wellbeing among working age adults with and without disability: Cross-sectional study. *Disability and Health Journal, 14*(1), 100965.

Emery, C. F., Truong, E. A., & Oliver, K. N. (2022). Physical activity/exercise and cardiovascular disease. In *Handbook of cardiovascular behavioral medicine* (pp. 379-409). Springer.

Erickson, K. I., Hillman, C., Stillman, C. M., Ballard, R. M., Bloodgood, B., Conroy, D. E., Powell, K. E., for 2018 Physical Activity Guidelines Advisory Committee.

(2019). Physical activity, cognition, and brain outcomes: A review of the 2018 physical activity guidelines. *Medicine and Science in Sports and Exercise, 51*(6), 1242.

Erikson, E. (1950). *Childhood and society.* Norton and Co.

Erikson, E. (1968). *Identity, youth and crisis.* Norton and Co.

Erikson, E. H. (1978). *Adulthood: Essays.* Norton.

Erikson, E., Erikson, J., & Kivnick, H. (1994). *Vital involvement in old age.* WW Norton & Company.

Ferretti, L. A., & McCallion, P. (2019). Translating the chronic disease self-management program for community-dwelling adults with developmental disabilities. *Journal of Aging and Health, 31*(10 Suppl): 22S-38S. https://doi.org/10.1177/0898264318822363

Fletcher, G. F., Landolfo, C., Niebauer, J., Ozemek, C., Arena, R., & Lavie, C. J. (2018). Promoting physical activity and exercise: JACC health promotion series. *Journal of the American College of Cardiology, 72*(14), 1622-1639.

Frawley, P., & O'Shea, A. (2020). "Nothing about us without us": Sex education by and for people with intellectual disability in Australia. *Sex Education, 20*(4), 413-424.

Gerber, M. (2002). *Dear parent: Caring for infants with respect* (J. Weaver, Ed.). Resources for Infant Educarers (RIE).

Grove, L., Morrison-Beedy, D., Kirby, R., & Hess, J. (2018). The birds, bees, and special needs: Making evidence-based sex education accessible for adolescents with intellectual disabilities. *Sexuality and Disability, 36*(4), 313-329.

Haegele, J. A., Hodge, S. R., Zhu, X., Holland, S. K., & Wilson, W. J. (2020). Understanding the inclusiveness of integrated physical education from the perspectives of adults with visual impairments. *Adapted Physical Activity Quarterly, 37*(2), 141-159. https://doi.org/10.1123/apaq.2019-0094

Halfon, N., & Forrest, C. B. (2018). The emerging theoretical framework of life course health development. In N. Halfon, C. B. Forrest, R. Lerner, & E. Faustman (Eds.), *Handbook of life course health development* (pp. 19-43). Springer.

Halfon, N., & Hochstein, M. (2002). Life course health development: An integrated framework for developing health, policy, and research. *The Milbank Quarterly, 80*(3), 433-479.

Haywood, K. M., & Getchell, N. (2019). *Life span motor development* (7th ed.). Human Kinetics.

Hodge, S. R., Lieberman, L. J., & Murata, N. M. (2017). *Essentials of teaching adapted physical education: Diversity, culture, and inclusion.* Routledge.

Houtenville, A. J., Paul, S., & Brucker, D. L. (2021). Changes in the employment status of people with and without disabilities in the United States during the COVID-19 pandemic. *Archives of Physical Medicine and Rehabilitation, 102*(7), 1420-1423.

Jin, J., Yun, J., & Agiovlasitis, S. (2018). Impact of enjoyment on physical activity and health among children with disabilities in schools. *Disability and Health Journal, 11*, 14-19.

Kim, J., Lee, S., Chun, S., Han, A., & Heo, J. (2017). The effects of leisure-time physical activity for optimism, life satisfaction, psychological well-being, and positive affect among older adults with loneliness. *Annals of Leisure Research, 20*(4), 406-415.

King, S. P., & Mason, B. A. (2020). Myers-Briggs type indicator. *The Wiley Encyclopedia of Personality and Individual Differences: Measurement and Assessment, 315-319.*

Krahn, G. L., Walker, D. K., & De-Araujo, R. C. (2015, February 17). Persons with disabilities as an unrecognized health disparity population. *American Journal of Public Health,* e1-e9.

Lavay, B. W., French, R., & Henderson, H. L. (2016). *Positive behavior management in physical activity settings.* Human Kinetics.

Lear, S. A., Hu, W., Rangarajan, S., Gasevic, D., Leong, D., Iqbal, R., Casanova, A., Swaminathan, S., Anjana, R. M., Kumar, R., Rosengren, A., Wei, L., Yang, W., Chuangshi, W., Huaxing, L., Nair, S., Diaz, R., Swidon, H., Guptam, R., … Yusuf, S. (2017). The effect of physical activity on mortality and cardiovascular disease in 130,000 people from 17 high-income, middle-income, and low-income countries: The PURE study. *Lancet, 390*(10113), 2643-2654.

Lieberman, L., Grenier, M., Brian, A., & Arndt, K. (2020). *Universal design for learning in physical education.* Human Kinetics.

Lieberman, L. J., & Houston-Wilson, C. (2018). *Strategies for inclusion: A handbook for physical educators* (3rd ed.). Human Kinetics.

Maeng, H., Webster, E. K., & Ulrich, D. A. (2016). Reliability for the Test of Gross Motor Development-Third Edition (TGMD-3). *Research Quarterly for Exercise and Sport, 87*(S2), A38.

Masten, A. S., & Garmezy, N. (1985). Risk, vulnerability, and protective factors in developmental psychopathology. In B. B. Lahey & A. E. Kazdin (Eds.), *Advances in clinical child psychology* (Vol. 8). Springer. https://doi.org/10.1007/978-1-4613-9820-2_1

Masten, A. S., & Wright, M. O. D. (1998). Cumulative risk and protection models of child maltreatment. *Journal of Aggression, Maltreatment & Trauma, 2*(1), 7-30.

McCarty, K., Dixon-Ibarra, A., & MacDonald, M. (2022). Evaluation of the Special Olympics team wellness health promotion program for individuals with intellectual disabilities. *Journal of Intellectual Disabilities, 26*(1), 109-120.

McLeod, S. A. (2018, May 3). *SimplyPsychology: Erik Erikson's stages of psychosocial development.* www.simplypsychology.org/Erik-Erikson.html

McWilliam, R. A. (2010). *Routines-based early intervention. Supporting young children and their families.* Brookes.

Minnesota Developmental Adapted Physical Education (MNDAPE). (2023). *MNDAPE Active learning guide.* https://mndape.org/active-learning-guide

Molton, I., Cook, K. F., Smith, A. E., Amtmann, D., Chen, W. H., & Jensen, M. P. (2014). Prevalence and impact of pain in adults aging with a physical disability: Comparison to a U.S. general population sample. *The Clinical Journal of Pain, 30,* 307-315. https://doi.org/10.1097/AJP.0b013e31829e9bca

Molton, I. M., & Yorkston, K. M. (2017). Growing older with a physical disability: A special application of the successful aging paradigm. *The Journals of Gerontology, 72*(2), 290-299. https://doi.org/10.1093/geronb/gbw122

Molton, I. R., & Ordway, A. (2019). Aging with disability: Populations, programs, and the new paradigm an introduction to the special issue. *Journal of Aging and Health, 31*(10 Suppl), 3S-20S.

Odom, S. L., & Pungello, E. P. (Eds.). (2012). *Infant and toddler poverty.* Guilford Press.

Oliver, C. (2021). *Muscles do matter: Aging well—Aging strong.* eBookIt.com.

Oppewall, A., Maes-Festen, D., & Hilgenkamp, T. I. M. (2020). Small steps in fitness, major leaps in health for adults with intellectual disabilities. *Exercise and Sport Sciences Reviews, 48*(2). https://doi.org/10.1249/JES.0000000000000216

OSEP TA Community of Practice: Part C settings. Workgroup on Principles and Practices in Natural Environments. (2008, March). *Agreed upon mission and key principles for providing early intervention services in natural environments.* http://ectacenter.org/~pdfs/topics/families/Finalmissionandprinciples3_11_08.pdf

Pedro Ángel, L. R., Beatriz, B. A., Jerónimo, A. V., & Antonio, P. V. (2021). Effects of a 10-week active recess program in school setting on physical fitness, school aptitudes, creativity and cognitive flexibility in elementary school children. A randomized-controlled trial. *Journal of Sports Sciences, 39*(11), 1277-1286.

Pletcher, L. C., & Younggren, N. O. (2017). Developing an individualized family service plan. *The Early Intervention Workbook: Essential Practices for Quality Services.* Brookes Publishing.

Posner, M. I., & Rothbart, M. K. (2007). Relating brain and mind. In M. I. Posner & M. K. Rothbart (Eds.), *Educating the human brain* (pp. 25-53). American Psychological Association. https://doi.org/10.1037/11519-002

Pushkarenko, K., Causgrove Dunn, J., & Wohlers, B. (2021). Physical literacy and inclusion: A scoping review of the physical literacy literature inclusive of individuals experiencing disability. *Prospects, 50*(1-2), 107-126.

Putnam, M. (2014). Bridging network divides: Building capacity to support aging with disability populations through research. *Disability and Health Journal, 7,* S51-S59. https://doi.org/10.1016/j.dhjo.2013.08.002

Putnam, M. (2017). Extending the promise of the Older Americans Act to persons aging with long-term disability. *Research on Aging, 39,* 799-820. https://doi.org/10.1177/0164027516681052

Quennerstedt, M., McCuaig, L., & Mårdh, A. (2021). The fantasmatic logics of physical literacy. *Sport, Education and Society, 26*(8), 846-861.

Rimmer, J. H. (2015). The nexus of rehabilitation and exercise: Where and why the two shall meet. *Kinesiology Review, 4,* 85-90.

Rimmer, J. H., & Lai, B. (2017). Framing new pathways in transformative exercise for individuals with existing and newly acquired disability. *Disability and Rehabilitation, 39,* 173-180. https://doi.org/10.3109/09638288.2015.1047967

Rothbart, M. K., Senter, M., & Shiner, R. (2012). Advances in temperament: History, concepts, and measures. In M. Senter & R. Shiner (Eds.), *Handbook of temperament* (pp. 3-20). Gilford Press.

Rowe, D. A., Sinclair, J., Hirano, K., & Barbour, J. (2018). Let's talk about sex . . . education. *American Journal of Sexuality Education, 13*(2), 205-216.

Sahono, M. N., Sidiastahta, F. U., Shidik, G. F., Fanani, A. Z., Nuraisha, S., & Lutfina, E. (2020, September). Extrovert and introvert classification based on Myers-Briggs Type Indicator (MBTI) using support vector machine (SVM). In *2020 International seminar on application for technology of information and communication (iSemantic)* (pp. 572-577). IEEE. DOI: 10.1109/iSemantic 50169.2020.9234288

Scanlan, T. K., & Simons, J. P. (1992). In G. C. Roberts (Ed.), *Motivation in sport and exercise* (pp. 199-215). Human Kinetics.

Shonkoff, J. (2011). Protecting brains, not simply stimulating minds. *Science, 333*(6045), 982-983.

Shonkoff, J. P., & Phillips, D. A. (Eds.). (2000). *From neurons to neighborhoods: The science of early childhood development.* National Research Council and Institute of Medicine. Committee on Integrating the Science of Early Childhood Development. Board on Children, Youth, and Families, Commission on Behavioral and Social Sciences and Education. National Academy Press.

Shonkoff, J. P., Slopen, N., & Williams, D. R. (2021). Early childhood adversity, toxic stress, and the impacts of racism on the foundations of health. *Annual Review of Public Health, 42,* 115-134.

Singh, A. S., Saliasi, E., Van Den Berg, V., Uijtdewilligen, L., De Groot, R. H. M., Jolles, J., Andersen, L. B., Bailey, R., Chang, Y., Diamond, A., Ericsson, I., Etnier, L. L., Fedewa, A. L., Hillman, C. H., McMorris, T., Pesce, C., Pühse, U., Tomporowski, P. D., & Chinapaw, M. J. M. (2019). Effects of physical activity interventions on cognitive and academic performance in children and adolescents: A novel combination of a systematic review and recommendations from an expert panel. *British Journal of Sports Medicine, 53*(10), 640-647.

Skinner, B. F. (1938). *The behavior of organisms.* Appleton-Century-Crofts.

Skinner, B. F. (1974). *About behaviorism [by] BF Skinner.* Knopf.

Strong, W. B., Malina, R. M., Blimkie, C. J. R., Daniels, R. K., Dishman, R. K., Gutin, B., Hergenroeder, A. C., Must, A., Nixon, P. A., Pivarnik, J. M., Rowland, T.,

Trost, S., & Trudeau, F. (2005). Evidence based physical activity for school-age youth. *The Journal of Pediatrics, 146*(6), 732-737.

Team USA. (n.d.). *Athletes.* www.teamusa.org/athletes?pg=2#SearchBtn

Thompson, P. D., & Eijsvogels, T. M. H. (2018). New physical activity guidelines: A call to activity for clinicians and patients. *JAMA, 320*(19), 1983-1984.

Trost, S. G., Owen, N., Bauman, A. E., Sallis, J. F., & Brown, W. (2002). Correlates of adults' participation in physical activity: Review and update. *Medicine & Science in Sports & Exercise, 34*(12), 1996-2001.

Ulrich, D. A. (2000). *Test of Gross Motor Development* (2nd ed.). PRO-ED.

Ulrich, D. A. (2017). *Test of Gross Motor Development* (3rd ed.). PRO-ED.

U.S. Department of Health and Human Services (USDHHS). (2005). *The surgeon general's call to action to improve the health and wellness of persons with disabilities.* USDHHS, Office of the Surgeon General.

U.S. Department of Health and Human Services (USDHHS). (2018). *Physical activity guidelines for Americans* (2nd ed.). U.S. Department of Health and Human Services. https://health.gov/sites/default/files/2019-09/Physical_Activity_Guidelines_2nd_edition.pdf

U.S. Department of Health and Human Services (USDHHS). (2023). *Move your way. Walk. Run. Dance. Play. What's your move?* https://health.gov/moveyourway

Vader, K., Doulas, T., Patel, R., & Miller, J. (2021). Experiences, barriers, and facilitators to participating in physical activity and exercise in adults living with chronic pain: A qualitative study. *Disability and Rehabilitation, 43*(13), 1829-1837.

Webster, E. K., & Ulrich, D. (2017). Evaluation of the psychometric properties of the Test of Gross Motor Development-Third Edition. *Journal of Motor Learning and Development, 5*(1), 45-58. https://doi.org/10.1123/Jmld.2016-0003

Winnick, J. (2017). Program organization and management. In J. Winnick & D. L. Porretta (Eds.), *Adapted physical education and sport* (6th ed., pp. 23-57). Human Kinetics.

World Health Organization (WHO). (2019). *Global action plan on physical activity 2018-2030: More active people for a healthier world.* World Health Organization.

Wright, J. A. (2008). Prenatal and postnatal diagnosis of infant disability: Breaking the news to mothers. *The Journal of Perinatal Education, 17*(3), 27-32.

Yang, Y. C., Boen, C., Gerken, K., Li, T., Schorpp, K., & Harris, K. M. (2016). Social relationships and physiological determinants of longevity across the human life span. *Proceedings of the National Academy of Sciences, 113*(3), 578-583.

Yen, H. Y., & Lin, L. J. (2018). Quality of life in older adults: Benefits from the productive engagement in physical activity. *Journal of Exercise Science & Fitness, 16*(2), 49-54.

CHAPTER 5

Baker, P. C., & Mott, F. L. (1992). *Following children over time: Child development and its linkages with family social and economic transitions.* Presented at Statistics Canada Symposium on Design and Analysis of Longitudinal Surveys. Ottawa, ON, Canada.

Block, M. E., Henderson, H., & Lavay, B. (2016). Positive behavior support of children with challenging behaviors. In M. E. Block (Ed.), *A teacher's guide to including students with disabilities in general physical education* (4th ed., pp. 304-332). Paul H. Brooks.

Bronfenbrenner, U. (1977). Toward an experimental ecology of human development. *American Psychologist, 32*(7), 513-531. https://doi.org/10.1037/0003-066X.32.7.513

Bronfenbrenner, U., & Morris, P. A. (2006). The bioecological model of human development. In R. M. Lerner (Ed.), *Handbook of child psychology (Vol. 1). Theoretical models of human development* (pp. 793-828). Wiley.

Burlingame, J., & Blaschko, T. (2002). *Assessment tools for recreational therapy and related fields* (3rd ed.). Idyll Arbor.

Burton, A. W., & Davis, W. E. (1996). Ecological task analysis: Theoretical and empirical foundations. *Human Movement Science, 15*, 285-314.

Chubbuck, S. M. (2010). Individual and structural orientations in socially just teaching: Conceptualization, implementation, and collaborative effort. *Journal of Teacher Education, 61*(3), 197-210.

Chubbuck, S. M., & Zembylas, M. (2016). Social justice and teacher education: Context, theory, and practice. *International Handbook of Teacher Education: Volume 2*, 463-501.

Collier, D. H. (2017). Instructional strategies for adapted physical education. In J. P. Winnick & D. L. Porretta (Eds.), *Adapted physical education and sport* (6th ed., pp. 121-149). Human Kinetics.

Council for Exceptional Children (CEC). (2008). *CEC's position on response to intervention (RTI): The unique role of special education and special educators.* https://exceptionalchildren.org/sites/default/files/2020-08/RTI_FIXED.pdf

Davis, W., & Burton, A. (1991). Ecological task analysis: Translating movement behavior theory into practice. *Adapted Physical Activity Quarterly, 8*, 154-157.

Delprato, D. J., & Midgley, B. D. (1992). Some fundamentals of B. F. Skinner's behaviorism. *American Psychologist, 47*(11), 1507-1520. https://doi.org/10.1037/0003-066X.47.11.1507

Donohue, B., Gavrilova, E., Strong, M., & Allen, D. N. (2020). A sport-specific optimization approach to mental wellness for youth in low-income neighborhoods. *European Physical Education Review, 26*(3), 695-712.

Dunn, J. M., Morehouse, J. W., & Fredericks, H. D. (1986). *Physical education for the severely handicapped.* PRO-ED.

Fuentes, M. A., Zelaya, D. G., & Madsen, J. W. (2021). Rethinking the course syllabus: Considerations for promoting equity, diversity, and inclusion. *Teaching of Psychology, 48*(1), 69-79.

Gibson, J. J. (1979). *An ecological approach to visual perception*. Houghton Mifflin.

Goldberger, M., Ashworth, S., & Byra, M. (2012). Spectrum of teaching styles retrospective 2012. *Quest, 64*(4), 268-282. https://doi.org/10.1080/00336297.2012.706883

Greenwood, C. R., Maheady, L., & Delquadri, J. (2002). Classwide peer tutoring programs. In M. R. Shinn, H. M. Walker, & G. Stoner (Eds.), *Interventions for academic and behavior problems II: Preventive and remedial approaches* (pp. 611-649). National Association of School Psychologists.

Guttentag, C. L., Landry, S. H., Williams, J. M., Baggett, K. M., Noria, C. W., Borkowski, J. G., Swank, P. R., Farris, J. R., Crawford, A., Lanzi, R. G., Carta, J. J., Warren, S. F., & Ramey, S. L. (2014). "My Baby & Me": Effects of an early, comprehensive parenting intervention on at-risk mothers and their children. *Developmental Psychology, 50*(5), 1482-1496. https://doi-org.ezp2.lib.umn.edu/10.1037/a0035682

Halfon, N., & Forrest, C. B. (2018). The emerging theoretical framework of life course health development. In N. Halfon, C. B. Forrest, R. Lerner, & E. Faustman (Eds.), *Handbook of life course health development* (pp. 19-43). Springer.

Halfon, N., & Hochstein, M. (2002). Life course health development: An integrated framework for developing health, policy, and research. *The Milbank Quarterly, 80*(3), 433-479. https://doi.org/10.1111/1468-0009.00019

Hall, T. E., Meyer, A., & Rose, D. H. (Eds.). (2012). *Universal design for learning in the classroom: Practical applications*. Guilford Press.

Harrison, J. M. (1987). A review of research on teacher effectiveness and its implications for current practice. *Quest, 39*, 36-55.

Hirschfeld, S., Goodman, E., Barkin, S., Faustman, E., Halfon, N., & Riley, A. W. (2021). Health Measurement Model—Bringing a life course perspective to health measurement: The PRISM model. *Frontiers in Pediatrics, 9*, 605932. https://www.frontiersin.org/articles/10.3389/fped.2021.605932/full

Hodge, S. R., Lieberman, L. J., & Murata, N. M. (2017). *Essentials of teaching adapted physical education*. Routledge.

Houston-Wilson, C., Dunn, J. M., van der Mars, H., & McCubbin, J. A. (1997). The effect of peer tutors on motor performance in integrated physical education classes. *Adapted Physical Activity Quarterly, 14*(4), 298-313.

Houston-Wilson, C., Lieberman, L., Horton, M., & Kasser, S. (1997). Peer tutoring: A plan for instructing students of all abilities. *Journal of Physical Education, Recreation & Dance, 68*(6), 39-44.

Johns Hopkins All Children's Hospital. (2021). *Sexual attraction and orientation*. www.hopkinsallchildrens.org/patients-families/health-library/healthdocnew/sexual-attraction-and-orientation

Kennedy, W., & Yun, J. (2019). Universal design for learning as a curriculum development tool in physical education. *Journal of Physical Education, Recreation & Dance, 90*(6), 25-31.

Lavay, B. (2019). Behavior management: What I have learned. *Journal of Physical Education Recreation and Dance, 90*(3), 5-9.

Lerner, R. M., Theokas, C., & Jelicic, H. (2005). Youth as active agents in their own positive development: A developmental systems perspective. In W. Greve, K. Rothermund, & D. Wentra, *The adaptive self: Personal continuity and intentional self-development* (pp. 31-47). Hogrefe & Huber.

Lieberman, L. J., Grenier, M., Brian, A., & Arndt, K. (2021). *Universal design for learning in physical education*. Human Kinetics.

Lieberman, L. J., & Houston-Wilson, C. (2009). *Strategies for inclusion: A handbook for physical educators*. Human Kinetics.

Lieberman, L. J., & Houston-Wilson, C. (2018). *Strategies for inclusion: A handbook for physical educators* (3rd ed.). Human Kinetics.

Masten, A. S. (2015). *Ordinary magic: Resilience in development*. Guilford Publications.

Meyer, A., Rose, D. H., & Gordon, D. T. (2014). *Universal design for learning: Theory and practice*. CAST Professional Publishing.

Mosston, M., & Ashworth, S. (2002). *Teaching physical education* (5th ed.). Benjamin Cummings.

National Center for Heath, Physical Activity and Disability (NCHPAD) and National Consortium of Physical Education for Individuals With Disabilities (NCPEID). (n.d.). *Laying the foundation for universal design for learning in physical education: An interactive infographic*. www.nchpad.org/fppics/Universal%20Design%20for%20Learning%20in%20PE.pdf

Newell, K. M. (1986). Constraints on the development of coordination. In M. G. Wade & H. T. A. Whiting (Eds.), *Motor development in children: Aspects of coordination and control* (pp. 341-360). Martinus Nijhoff.

Pisha, B., & Coyne, P. (2001). Smart from the start: The promise of universal design for learning. *Remedial and Special Education, 22*(4), 197-203.

Positive Behavioral Interventions and Supports. (2018, June 24). *OSEP Technical Assistance Center*. www.phis.org/training/technical-guide

Rogers, S. J., Toby, L., Menaghan, P., & Menaghan, E. G. (1991, June). The effects of maternal working conditions and mastery on child behavior problems: Studying the intergenerational transmission of social control. *Journal of Health and Social Behavior, 32*(2), 145-164.

Rogers-Shaw, C., Carr-Chellman, D. J., & Choi, J. (2018). Universal design for learning: Guidelines for accessible online instruction. *Adult Learning, 29*(1), 20-31.

Roth, K., Zittel, L., Pyfer, J., & Auxter, D. (2016). *Principles and methods of adapted physical education & recreation*. Jones & Bartlett Learning.

Schellenberg, J. A. (1978). *Masters of social psychology: Freud, Mead, Lewin, and Skinner.* Oxford U Press.

SHAPE America. (n.d.). *Physical education.* www.shape america.org

Shonkoff, J. P., Slopen, N., & Williams, D. R. (2021). Early childhood adversity, toxic stress, and the impacts of racism on the foundations of health. *Annual Review of Public Health, 42,* 115-134.

Skinner, B. F. (1938). *The behavior of organisms: An experimental analysis.* Appleton-Century.

Skinner, B. F. (1976). *About behaviorism.* Vintage.

Skinner Quotes. (n.d.). BrainyQuote.com. https://www.brainyquote.com/quotes/b_f_skinner_676462

Turnbull, R., Hureta, N., & Stowe, M. (2009). *The Individuals with Disabilities Education Act as Amended in 2004* (2nd ed.). Pearson.

U.S. Bureau of Labor Statistics and U.S. Census Bureau. (2021). *Analysis by Zippa.* http://Zippa.com

CHAPTER 6

Allen, K. A., Bredero, B., Van Damme, T., Ulrich, D. A., & Simons, J. (2017). Test of Gross Motor Development-3 (TGMD-3) with the use of visual supports for children with autism spectrum disorder: Validity and reliability. *Journal of Autism and Developmental Disorders, 47*(3), 813-833.

Bayley, N., & Aylward, G. P. (2019). *Bayley scales of infant and toddler development—4.* Pearson.

Bidabe, L., & Lolar, J. M. (1990). *Mobility opportunities via education.* Office of Kern County Superintendent of Schools.

Brian, A., Taunton, S., Lieberman, L. J., Haibach-Beach, P., Foley, J., & Santarossa, S. (2018). Psychometric properties of the Test of Gross Motor Development-3 for children with visual impairments. *Adapted Physical Activity Quarterly, 35*(2), 145-158.

Bricker, D., Dionne, C., Grisham, J., Johnson, J., Macy, M., Slentz, K., & Waddell, M. (2021). Assessment, evaluation, and programming system for infants and children (3rd ed.). Brooks.

Brigance, A. H. (2020). *Early childhood online management system.* http://brigance.com.au/earlychildhood/Early_Childhood_Admin_Guide.pdf

Bruininks, R. H., & Bruininks, B. D. (2005). *Bruininks-Oseretsky test of motor proficiency* (2nd ed.). AGS.

Bryce, C. J. C. (2021). School based motor skill interventions for developmentally delayed and non-delayed children. *Global Pediatric Health.* doi: 10.1177/2333794X211057707

Burlingame, J., & Blaschko, T. M. (2002). *Assessment tools for recreational therapy and related fields* (3rd ed.). Idyll Arbor, Inc.

Burton, A. W., & Miller, D. E. (1998). *Movement skill assessment.* Human Kinetics.

Centers for Disease Control and Prevention (CDC). (2021). *Child development specific conditions. Developmental monitoring and screening for health professionals, developmental screening.* https://www.cdc.gov/ncbddd/childdevelopment/screening-hcp.html

Colarusso, R., O'Rourke, C., & Leontovich, M. A. (2017). *Special education for all teachers* (7th ed.). Kendall Hunt.

Davis, W., & Burton, A. W. (1991). Ecological task analysis: Translating movement theory behavior into practice. *Adapted Physical Activity Quarterly, 8,* 154-177.

Diliberto, J. A., & Brewer, D. (2012). Six tips for successful IEP meetings. *Teaching Exceptional Children, 44*(4), 30-37.

Dykeman, B. F. (2006). Alternatives strategies in assessing special education needs. *Education, 127*(2), 265-273.

Folio, M. R., & Fewell, R. R. (2023). *Peabody developmental motor scales* (3rd ed.). PRO-ED.

Individuals with Disabilities Education Act (IDEA). (2004). http://idea.ed.gov

Jírovec, J., Musálek, M., & Mess, F. (2019). Test of motor proficiency second edition (BOT-2): Compatibility of the complete and short form and its usefulness for middle-age school children. *Frontiers in Pediatrics, 7,* 153.

Johnson-Martin, N., Attermeir, S., & Hacker, B. (2007). *Carolina curriculum.* Brookes.

Lieberman, L. J., Grenier, M., Brian, A., & Arndt, K. (2021). *Universal design for learning in physical education.* Human Kinetics.

Lieberman, L. J., & Houston-Wilson, C. (2009). *Strategies for inclusion: A handbook for physical educators.* Human Kinetics.

Lieberman, L. J., & Houston-Wilson, C. (2011). Strategies for increasing the status and value of adapted physical education in schools. *Journal of Physical Education, Recreation and Dance, 82*(6), 25-28. https://doi.org/10.1080/07303084.2011.10598641

Lieberman, L. J., & Houston-Wilson, C. (2018). *Strategies for inclusion: A handbook for physical educators* (3rd ed.). Human Kinetics.

Lipkin, P. H., & Macias, M. M. (2020). Council on Children with Disabilities, Section on Developmental and Behavioral Pediatrics. Promoting optimal development: Identifying infants and young children with developmental disorders through developmental surveillance and screening. *Pediatrics, 145*(1), e20193449.

Parent Training and Information Centers (PTIs). (2021). *Evaluation.* www.parentcenterhub.org/evalution/

Parks, S. (1992/2006). *Inside HELP: Administration and reference manual for HELP birth-3 years.* VORT Corporation.

Parks, S. (1992/2013). *HELP strands.* VORT Corporation.

Special Olympics. (n.d.). *Motor activity training program.* https://www.specialolympics.org/what-we-do/sports/motor-activity-training-program#:~:text=The%20Motor%20Activity%20Training%20program%20(MATP)%20is%20designed%20for%20those,and%20participation%20rather%20than%20competition

Squires, J., & Bricker, D. (2018). *Ages and stages questionnaires* (3rd ed.). https://agesandstages.com/asq-online/

Ulrich, D. A. (2000). *Test of Gross Motor Development* (2nd ed.). PRO-ED.

Ulrich, D. A. (2020). *Test of Gross Motor Development* (3rd ed.). PRO-ED.

Winnick, J., & Porretta, D. L. (2022). *Adapted physical education and sport* (7th ed.). Human Kinetics

Winnick, J., & Short, F. (1999). *The Brockport physical fitness test manual.* Human Kinetics.

CHAPTER 7

American Association on Intellectual and Developmental Disability (AAIDD). (2015). *Supports Intensity Scale—Adult Version (SIS-A).* https://www.aaidd.org/sis

American Association on Intellectual and Developmental Disability (AAIDD). (2016). *Supports Intensity Scale—Children's Version (SIS-C).* https://www.aaidd.org/sis

American Association on Intellectual and Developmental Disability (AAIDD). (2021). *Defining criteria for intellectual disability.* www.aaidd.org/intellectual-disability/definition

American Psychiatric Association (APA). (2013). *Diagnostic and statistical manual of mental disorders* (5th ed.). American Psychiatric Association.

American Psychiatric Association (APA) (Ed.). (2022). *Diagnostic and statistical manual of mental disorders* (5th ed., Text Revision). American Psychiatric Publishing.

Barfield, W. D., & Lee, K. G. (2020, January 15). Late term infants. *UpToDate.* Wolters Kluwer.

Bryce, C. J. C. (2021). School based motor skill interventions for developmentally delayed and non-delayed children. *Global Pediatric Health.* doi: 10.1177/2333794X211057707

Burton, A. W., & Miller, D. E. (1998). *Movement skill assessment.* Human Kinetics.

Canella-Malone, H. I., Fleming, C., Chung, Y., Wheeler, G. M., Basbagill, A. R., & Sing, A.H. (2013). Teaching daily living skills to seven individuals with severe intellectual disabilities: A comparison of video prompting to video modeling. *Journal of Positive Behavioral Interventions, 13*(3), 144-153.

Centers for Disease Control and Prevention (CDC). (2022). *FASDs: Training & education.* https://www.cdc.gov/ncbddd/fasd/training.html

Chatzihidiroglou, P., Chatzopoulos, D., Lykesas, G., & Doganis, G. (2018). Dancing effects on preschoolers' sensorimotor synchronization, balance, and movement reaction time. *Perceptual and Motor Skills, 125*(3), 463-477.

Colarusso, R., O'Rourke, C. M., & Leontovich, M. A. (2017). *Special education for all teachers* (7th ed.). Kendall Hunt.

Collins, K., & Staples, K. (2017). The role of physical activity in improving physical fitness in children with intellectual and developmental disabilities. *Research in Developmental Disabilities, 69,* 49-60.

Croce, R. V. (1990). Effects of exercise and diet on body composition and cardiovascular fitness in adults with severe intellectual disability. *Education and Training in Intellectual Disability, 25,* 176-187.

Cutland, C. L., Lackritz, E. M., Mallett-Moore, T., Bardají, A., Chandrasekaran, R., Lahariya, C., Nisar, M. I., Tapia, M. D., Pathirana, J., Kochhar, S., Flor, M., Muñoz, F. M. , & The Brighton Collaboration Low Birth Weight Working Group. (2017). Low birth weight: Case definition & guidelines for data collection, analysis, and presentation of maternal immunization safety data. *Vaccine, 35*(48 Pt A), 6492-6500.

Dunn, J. M. (1975). Behavior modification with emotionally disturbed children. *Journal of Physical Education and Recreation, 46*(3), 67-72.

Dunn, W. (1997). The impact of sensory processing abilities on the daily lives of young children and families: A conceptual model. *Infants and Young Children, 9*(4), 23-35.

Dunn, W. (1999). *The sensory profile.* Psychological Corporation.

Dunn, W. (2002). *The infant toddler sensory profile.* Psychological Corporation.

Dunn, W. (2006). *The sensory profile school companion.* Psychological Corporation.

Eberhard, Y., & Eterradossi, J. (1990). Effects of physical exercise in adolescents with Down syndrome. *Adapted Physical Activity Quarterly, 16,* 281-287.

Ekins, C., Wright, J., Schulz, H., Wright, P. R., Owens, D., & Millder, W. (2019). Effects of a drums alive kids beats intervention on motor skills and behavior in children with intellectual disabilities. *Palaestra, 33*(2), n.p.

Faison-Hodge, J., & Porretta, D. L. (2004). Physical activity levels of students with intellectual disability and students without disabilities. *Adapted Physical Activity Quarterly, 21*(2), 139-152.

Frost, L., & Bondy, A. (2002). *The picture exchange communication system training manual.* Pyramid Educational Products.

Glaze, R. E. (1985). *Height and weight of Down syndrome children as compared to normal children aged ten to eighteen* [Unpublished master's study]. Illinois State University, Normal.

Graham, A., & Reid, G. (2000). Physical fitness of adults with an intellectual disability: A 13-year follow-up study. *Research Quarterly for Exercise and Sport, 71*(2), 152-161. https://doi.org/10.1080/02701367.2000.10608893

Greene, M., & Patra, K. (2016). Part C early intervention utilization in preterm infants: Opportunity for referral from a NICU follow-up clinic. *Research in Developmental Disabilities, 53,* 287-295.

Greenspan, S., & Woods, G. W. (2014). Intellectual disability as a disorder of reasoning and judgement: The gradual move away from intelligence quotient-ceilings. *Current Opinion in Psychiatry, 27*(2), 110-116.

Hadders-Algra, M. (2021). Early diagnostics and early intervention in neurodevelopmental disorders—age-dependent challenges and opportunities. *Journal of Clinical Medicine, 10*(4), 861.

Heward, W. L., & Orlansky, M. D. (1992). *Exceptional children: An introductory survey of special education.* Merrill.

Houston-Wilson, C. (1993). The effect of untrained and trained peer tutors on the opportunity to respond (OTR) of students with developmental disabilities in integrated physical education classes [Unpublished doctoral dissertation]. Oregon State University, Corvallis.

Houston-Wilson, C., Lieberman, L., Horton, M., & Kasser, S. (1997). Peer tutoring: A plan for instructing students of all abilities. *Journal of Physical Education, Recreation & Dance, 68*(6), 39-44. https://doi.org/10.1080/07303084.1997.10604964

Individuals with Disabilities Education Act (IDEA). (2004). http://idea.ed.gov

Ingersoll, B., Walton, K., Carlsen, D., & Hamlin, T. (2013). Social intervention for adolescents with autism and significant intellectual disability: Initial efficacy of reciprocal imitation training. *American Journal of Intellectual and Developmental Disabilities, 118*(4), 247-261.

Jeng, S., Chang, C., Liu, W., Hou, Y., & Lin, Y. (2017). Exercise training on skill-related physical fitness in adolescents with intellectual disability: A systematic review and meta-analysis. *Disability and Health Journal, 10*(2), 198-206.

Kapsal, N. J., Dicke, T., Morin, A. J., Vasconcellos, D., Maïano, C., Lee, J., & Lonsdale, C. (2019). Effects of physical activity on the physical and psychosocial health of youth with intellectual disabilities: A systematic review and meta-analysis. *Journal of Physical Activity and Health, 16*(12), 1187-1195.

Kliewer, C., Biklen, D., & Petersen, A. (2015). At the end of intellectual disability. *Harvard Educational Review, 85*(1), 1-28.

Lavay, B., & McKenzie, T. L. (1991). Development and evaluation of a systematic run/walk program for men with mental retardation. *Education and Training in Mental Retardation, 333-341.

Lieberman, L., Grenier, M., Brian, A., & Arndt, K. (2020). *Universal design for learning in physical education.* Human Kinetics.

Lloyd, M., Burghardt, A., Ulrich, D. A., & Angulo-Barroso, R. (2010). Physical activity and walking onset in infants with Down syndrome. *Adapted Physical Activity Quarterly, 27*(1), 1-16. https://doi.org/10.1123/apaq.27.1.1

March of Dimes. (2020). *Down syndrome.* www.marchofdimes.org/find-support/topics/planning-baby/down-Syndrome#:~:text=About%201%20in%20700%20babies,live%2060%20years%20or%20more

Massachusetts General Hospital. (2019). *Atlanto-axial instability (AAI): What you need to know.* www.massgeneral.org/children/down-syndrome/atlantoaxial-instability-aai#:~:text=Atlanto%2Daxial%20instability%20(AAI),are%20%E2%80%9Clax%E2%80%9D%20or%20floppy

Mayo Clinic. (2023). *Fetal alcohol spectrum disorders.* www.mayoclinic.org/diseases-conditions/fetal-alcohol-syndrome/diagnosis-treatment/drc-20352907

McConnell, S. R. (2000). Interventions to facilitate social interactions for young children with autism: Review of available research and recommendations for educational interventions and future research. *Journal of Autism and Developmental Disorders, 32*(5), 351-365.

McGuire, D. O., Tian, L. H., Yeargin-Allsopp, M., Dowling, N. F., & Christensen, D. L. (2019). Prevalence of cerebral palsy, intellectual disability, hearing loss, and blindness, National Health Interview Survey, 2009-2016. *Disability and Health Journal, 12*(3), 443-451.

McKenzie, K., & Megson, P. (2012). Screening for intellectual disability in children: A review of the literature. *Journal of Applied Research in Intellectual Disabilities, 25*(1), 80-87.

Patel, D. R., Cabral, D. M., Ho, A. & Merrick, J. (2022). Clinical primer on intellectual disabilities. *Translational Pediatrics, 9*(Suppl 1), S23-S35. https://tp.amegroups.com/article/view/36118/pdf

Pitetti, K., Baynard, T., & Agiovlasitis, S. (2013). Children and adolescents with Down syndrome, physical fitness, and physical activity. *Journal of Sport and Health Science, 2*(1), 47-57.

Pitetti, K. H., Climstein, M., Campbell, K. D., Barrett, P. J., & Jackson, J. A. (1992). The cardiovascular capabilities of adults with Down syndrome: A comparative study. *Medicine and Science in Sports and Exercise, 24*, 13-19.

Pitetti, K. H., & Fernhall, B. (2004). Comparing run performance of adolescents with intellectual disability, with and without Down syndrome. *Adapted Physical Activity Quarterly, 21*(3), 219-228.

Pitetti, K. H., & Tan, D. M. (1991). Effects of a minimally supervised exercise program for mentally retarded adults. *Medicine & Science in Sports & Exercise, 23*(5), 594-601.

Pletcher, L. C., & Younggren, N. O. (2013). *The early intervention workbook: Essential practice; Essential practice for quality services.* Paul H. Brookes.

Roid, G. H. (2003). *Stanford-Binet intelligence scales* (5th ed.). Riverside Publishing.

Schalock, R. L., Borthwick-Duffy, S. A., Bradley, V. J., Buntinx, W. H., Coulter, D. L., Craig, E. M., Gomez, S. C., Lachapelle, Y., Luckasson, R., Reeve, A., Shogren, K. A., Snell, M. E., Spreat, S., Tasse, M. J., Thompson, J. R., Verdugo-Alonso, M. A., Wehmeyer, M. L., & Yeager, M. H. (2010). *Intellectual disability: Definition, classification, and systems of supports.* American Association on Intellectual and Developmental Disabilities.

Segal, M., Eliasziw, M., Phillip, S., Bandini, L., Curtin, C., Kral, T. V. E., Sherwood, N. E., Sikich, L., Stanish, H., & Must, A. (2016). Intellectual disability is associated with increased risk for obesity in a nationally representative sample of US children. *Disability and Health Journal, 9*(3), 392-398.

Shonkoff, J. (2011). Protecting brains, not simply stimulating minds. *Science, 333*(6045), 982-983.

Sparrow, S. S., Cicchetti, D. V., & Saulnier, C. A. (2016). *Vineland adapted behavior scales* (3rd ed.). Pearson.

Special Olympics. (2018). *Young athletes.* www.specialolympics.org/our-work/inclusive-health/young-athletes?locale=en

Special Olympics. (2020). *Motor activity training program.* www.specialolympics.org/our-work/sports/motor-activity-training-program

Special Olympics. (2021). *Special Olympics.* http://specialolympics.org

Tassé, M. J., Schalock, R. L., Thissen, D., Balboni, G., Bersani, H., Jr., Borthwick-Duffy, S. A., Spreat, S., Widaman, K. F., Zhang, D., & Navas, P. (2016). Development and standardization of the diagnostic adaptive behavior scale: Application of item response theory to the assessment of adaptive behavior. *American Journal on Intellectual and Developmental Disabilities, 121*(2), 79-94.

Thompson, J. R., Hughes, C., Schalock, R. L., Silverman, W., Tassé, M. J., Bryant, B., Craig, E. M., Campbell, E. M. (2002). Integrating supports in assessment and planning. *Mental Retardation, 40*(5), 390-405.

Tomlinson, C., Campbell, A., Hurley, A., Fenton, E., & Heron, N. (2020). Sport preparticipation screening for asymptomatic atlantoaxial instability in patients with Down syndrome. *Clinical Journal of Sport Medicine, 30*(4), 293-295.

Ulrich, D. A., Ulrich, B. D., Angulo-Kinzler, R. M., & Yun, J. (2001). Treadmill training of infants with Down syndrome: Evidence-based developmental outcomes. *Pediatrics, 108*, 7.

Vashdi, E., Hutzler, Y., & Roth, D. (2007). Compliance of children with moderate to severe intellectual disability to treadmill walking: A pilot study. *Journal of Intellectual Disability Research.* https://doi.org/10.1111/j.1365-2788.2007.01034.x

Versacci, P., Di Carlo, D., Digilio, M. C., & Marino, B. (2018). Cardiovascular disease in Down syndrome. *Current Opinion in Pediatrics, 30*(5), 616-622.

Wechsler, D. (2014). *Wechsler Intelligence Scale for Children* (5th ed.). Pearson.

Winnick, J. P., & Short, F. X. (2014). *The Brockport Physical Fitness Test* (2nd ed.). Human Kinetics.

World Health Organization (WHO). (2022). *Preterm birth.* www.who.int/news-room/fact-sheets/detail/preterm-birth

CHAPTER 8

Alexander, A. G. F., & Schwager, S. M. (2012). *Meeting the physical education needs of the child with autism spectrum disorder.* National Association for Sport and Physical Education.

Allen, K. A., Bredero, B., Van Damme, T., Ulrich, D. A., & Simons, J. (2017). Test of Gross Motor Development-3 (TGMD-3) with the use of visual supports for children with autism spectrum disorder: Validity and reliability. *Journal of Autism and Developmental Disorders, 47*(3), 813-833.

American Psychiatric Association (APA). (2013). *Diagnostic and statistical manual of mental disorders* (5th ed.). American Psychiatric Association.

American Psychiatric Association (APA) (Ed.). (2022). *Diagnostic and statistical manual of mental disorders* (5th ed., Text Revision). American Psychiatric Publishing.

Autism Speaks. (2018). *What are the symptoms of autism?* www.autismspeaks.org/what-are-symptoms-autism

Baby Navigator. (2020). *16 by 16: 16 early signs of autism by 16 months.* https://babynavigator.com/16-early-signs-of-autism-by-16-months/

Berkeley, S. L., Zittel, L. L., Pitney, L. V., & Nichols, S. E. (2001). Locomotor and object control skills of children diagnosed with autism. *Adapted Physical Activity Quarterly, 18*(4), 405-416.

Block, M. E., Lieberman, L. J., & Connor-Kuntz, F. (1998). Authentic assessment in adapted physical education. *Journal of Physical Education, Recreation & Dance, 69*(3), 48-55.

Boyd, B. A., Hume, K., McBee, M. T., Alessandri, M., Gutierrez, A., Johnson, L., & Odum, S. L. (2013). Comparative efficacy of LEAP, TEACCH and non-model specific education programs for preschoolers with autism spectrum disorders. *Journal of Autism and Developmental Disorders.* https://doi.org/10.1007/s10803-013-1877-9

Bronfenbrenner, U. (1977). Toward an experimental ecology of human development. *American Psychologist, 32*(7), 513-531. https://doi.org/10.1037/0003-066X.32.7.513

Cavanaugh, L., Rademacher, S., Rademacher, J., & Simons, R. (2013). Planning and implementing a surf camp for students with autism spectrum disorder. *Palaestra, 27*(1), 17-22.

Centers for Disease Control and Prevention (CDC). (2022). *FASDs: Training & education.* https://www.cdc.gov/ncbddd/fasd/training.html

Colarusso, R. P., O'Rourke, C. M., & Leontovich, M. A. (2017). *Special physical education for all teachers* (7th ed.). Kendall Hunt.

Education of All Handicapped Children Act of 1975 (PL 94-142), 20 U.S.C. 1401.

Education of All Handicapped Children Amendments Act of 1984 (PL 99-457).

Evans, G. W., Li, D., & Whipple, S. S. (2013). Cumulative risk and child development. *Psychological Bulletin, 139*(6), 1342-1396.

Fittipaldi-Wert, J., & Mowling, C. (2009). Using visual supports for students with autism in physical education. *Journal of Physical Education, Recreation & Dance, 80*, 1-58. https://doi.org/10.1080/07303084.2009.10598281

Grandin, T. (2002). *Teaching tips for children and adults with autism.* Center for the Study of Autism.

Grenier, M., & Yeaton, P. (2011). Previewing: A successful strategy for students with autism. *Journal of Physical Education, Recreation & Dance, 82*(1), 28-43. doi: 10.1080/07303084.2011.10598558

Green, A., & Sandt, D. (2013). Understanding the picture exchange communication system and its application in physical education. *Journal of Physical Education, Recreation & Dance,* 33-39. https://doi.org/10.1080/07303084.2013.757190

Green, D., Charman, T., Pickles, A., Chandler, S., Loucas, T. O. M., Simonoff, E., & Baird, G. (2009). Impairment in movement skills of children with autistic spectrum disorders. *Developmental Medicine & Child Neurology, 51*(4), 311-316.

Groft, M., & Block, M. (2003). Children with Asperger's syndrome: Implications for general physical education and youth sports. *JOPHERD, 74*(3), 38-43.

Happe, F. (2011). Criteria, categories and continua: Autism and related disorders in *DSM-5. Journal of the American Academy of Child & Adolescent Psychiatry, 50*(6), 540-542.

Houston-Wilson, C., & Lieberman, L. J. (2003). Strategies for teaching students with autism in physical education. *JOHPER, 74*(6), 40-44.

Hovey, K. (2011). Six steps for planning a fitness circuit for individuals with autism. *Strategies,* 12-15. https://doi.org/10.1080/08924562.2011.10290946

Hume, K., & Odum, S. (2007). Effects of an individual work system on the independent functioning of students with autism. *Journal of Autism and Developmental Disorders, 37,* 1166-1180.

Individuals with Disabilities Education Act (IDEA). (2004). http://idea.ed.gov

Jeste, S. S., & Nelson, C. A. (2009). Event related potentials in the understanding of autism spectrum disorders: An analytical review. *Journal of Autism and Developmental Disorders, 39,* 495-510. https://doi.org/10.1007/s10803-008-0652-9

Kennedy, C. H., & Shukla, S. (1995). Social interaction research for people with autism as a set of past, current, and emerging propositions. *Behavioral Disorders, 21*(1), 21-35.

Koegel, L. K., Koegel, R. L., Ashbaugh, K., & Bradshaw, J. (2014). The importance of early identification and intervention for children with or at risk for autism spectrum disorders. *International Journal of Speech-Language Pathology, 16*(1), 50-56.

Lee, J., & Porretta, D. L. (2013). Enhancing the motor skills of children with autism spectrum disorders. *Journal of Physical Education, Recreation & Dance,* 41-45. https://doi.org/10.1080/07303084.2013.746154

Lindell, A. K., & Hudry, K. (2013). Atypicalities in cortical structure, handedness, and functional lateralization for language in autism spectrum disorders. *Neuropsychological Review.* https://doi.org/10.1007/s11065-013-9234-5

Menear, K. S., & Smith, S. (2008). Physical education for students with autism: Teaching tips and strategies. *Teaching Exceptional Children, 40*(5), 32-37.

Menear, K., & Smith, S. C. (2011). Teaching physical education to students with autism spectrum disorders. *Strategies,* 21-24. https://doi.org/10.1080/08924562.2011.10590929

Mesibov, G. B., & Shea, V. (2010, May). The TEACCH program in the era of evidence-based practice. *Journal of Autism and Developmental Disorders, 40*(5), 570-579. doi: 10.1007/s10803-009-0901-6

Obrusnikova, I., & Dillon, S. R. (2011). Challenging situations when teaching children with autism spectrum disorders in general physical education. *Adapted Physical Activity Quarterly, 28*(2), 113-131.

Pan, C.-Y., Tsai, C.-L., & Hsieh, K.-W. (2011). Physical activity correlates for children with autism spectrum disorders in middle school physical education. *Research Quarterly for Exercise and Sport,* 491-498. https://doi.org/10.1080/02701367.2011.10599782

Peterson, C., Slaughter, V., & Brownell, C. (2015). Children with autism spectrum disorder are skilled at reading emotion body language. *Journal of Experimental Child Psychology, 139,* 35-50.

Pitett, K. H., Rendoff, A. D., Grover, T. G., & Beets, M. W. (2006). The efficacy of a 9-month treadmill walking program on the exercise capacity and weight reduction for adolescents with severe autism. *Journal of Autism and Developmental Disorders.* www.nchpad.org

Provost, B., Lopez, B. R., & Heimerl, S. (2007). A comparison of motor delays in young children: Autism spectrum disorder, developmental delay, and developmental concerns. *Journal of Autism and Developmental Disorders, 37,* 321-328.

Reed, G., & O'Connor, J. (2003). The autism spectrum disorders: Activity selection, assessment, and program organization—Part II. *Palestra, 19,* 20-27, 58.

Sherlock-Shangraw, R. (2013). Creating inclusive youth sport environments with the universal design for learning. *Journal of Physical Education, Recreation & Dance,* 40-46. https://doi.org/10.1080/07303084.2013.757191

Todd, T. (2012). Teaching motor skills to individuals with autism spectrum disorders. *Journal of Physical Education, Recreation & Dance,* 32-48. https://doi.org/10.1080/07303084.2012.10598827

Ulrich, D. A. (2020). *Test of Gross Motor Development* (3rd ed.). PRO-ED.

Varcin, K. J., & Nelson, C. A., III. (2016). A developmental neuroscience approach to the search for biomarkers in autism spectrum disorder. *Current Opinion in Neurology, 29*(2), 123.

Wetherby, A. (2012, September 20-21). *Improving outcomes for children with ASD.* Autism Society of Minnesota workshop, St. Paul, MN. www.ausm.org

Winnick, J. (2010). *Adapted physical education and sport* (5th ed.). Human Kinetics.

CHAPTER 9

American Psychiatric Association (APA) (Ed.). (2022). *Diagnostic and statistical manual of mental disorders* (5th ed., Text Revision). American Psychiatric Publishing.

Barkley, R. A. (2000). *Taking charge of ADHD* (Revised ed.). Guilford.

Burton, A. W., & Miller, D. (1998). *Movement skill assessment*. Human Kinetics.

Centers for Disease Control and Prevention (CDC). (2020). *ADHD treatment recommendations.* www.cdc.gov/ncbddd/adhd/guidelines.html

Centers for Disease Control and Prevention (CDC). (2021). *ADHD.* www.cdc.gov/ncbddd/adhd

Centers for Disease Control and Prevention (CDC). (2022a). *Treatment of ADHD.* https://www.cdc.gov/ncbddd/adhd/treatment.html

Centers for Disease Control and Prevention (CDC). (2022b). *ADHD in the classroom.* https://www.cdc.gov/ncbddd/adhd/school-success.html

Colarusso, R., O'Rourke, C. M., & Leontovich, M. A. (2017). *Special education for all teachers* (7th ed.). Kendall Hunt.

Davis, W. E., & Burton, A. W. (1991). Ecological task analysis: Translating movement behavior theory into practice. *Adapted Physical Activity Quarterly, 8*, 154-177.

Deno, S. L. (1997). Whether thou goest . . . Perspectives on progress monitoring. In J. W. Lloyd, E. J. Kameenui, & D. Chard (Eds.), *Issues in educating students with disabilities* (pp. 77-99). Lawrence Erlbaum.

Deshler, D. D., & Bulgren, J. A. (1997). Redefining instructional directions for gifted students with learning disabilities. *Learning Disabilities, 8*(3), 121-132.

Fawcett, A. J., & Nicolson, R. L. (1995). Persistent deficits in motor skill of children with dyslexia. *Journal of Motor Behavior, 27*, 235-240.

Fletcher, J. M., Lyon, G. R., Fuchs, L. S., & Barnes, M. A. (2018). *Learning disabilities: From identification to intervention.* Guilford Publications.

Gibbs, J., Appleton, J., & Appleton, R. (2007). Dyspraxia or developmental coordination disorder? Unravelling the enigma. *Archives of Disease in Childhood, 92*(6), 534-539. https://doi.org/10.1136/adc.2005.088054

Gould, D., & Walker, L. (2019). Youth sport: Meeting unique development needs of young athletes for preventing dropout. *Psychology of Sport and Exercise, 10*(1), 87-95.

Gresham, F. M., Sugai, G., & Horner, R. H. (2001). Interpreting outcomes of social skills training for students with high-incidence disabilities. *Exceptional Children, 67*(3), 331-344.

Harvey, W. J., & Reid, G. (2003). Attention deficit hyperactivity disorder: A review of research on movement skill performance and physical fitness. *Adapted Physical Activity Quarterly, 20*, 1-25.

Individuals with Disabilities Education Act (IDEA). (2004). http://idea.ed.gov

Iversen, S., Berg, K., Ellerstsen, B., & Tonnessen, F. E. (2005). Motor coordination difficulties in a municipality group and in a clinical sample of poor readers. *Dyslexia, 11*, 217-231.

Kline, F. M., & Silver, L. B. (2004). *The educator's guide to mental health issues in the classroom.* Brookes.

Lieberman, L. J., Grenier, M., Brian, A., & Arndt, K. (2021). *Universal design for learning in physical education.* Human Kinetics.

Lieberman, L. J., & Houston-Wilson, C. (2000). *Strategies for inclusion.* Human Kinetics.

Lyyrunen, H., Ahonen, T., Eklund, K., Guttorum, T. K., Laakao, M., Laakso, M., Leionen, S., Leppanen, P. H. T., Lyytinen, P., Poikkeus, A., Puolakanaho, A., Richardson, U., & Viholainen, H. (2001). Developmental pathways of children with and without familial risk for dyslexia during the first years of life. *Developmental Neuropsychology, 20*, 535-554.

National Center for Education Statistics (NCES). (2022). Students with disabilities. *Condition of Education.* U.S. Department of Education, Institute of Education Sciences. https://nces.ed.gov/programs/coe/indicator/cgg

National Institute of Mental Health (NIMH). (2003). *Attention-deficit/hyperactivity disorder.* www.nimh.nih.gov/publicat/adhd.cfm

Razuk, M., Lukasova, K., & Bucci, M. P., & Barela, J. A. (2020). Dyslexic children need more robust information to resolve conflicting sensory situations. *Dyslexia.* Whiley online. doi.org/10.1002/dys.1641

Reiff, M. I., & Tippins, S. (2004). *ADHD: A complete and authoritative guide.* American Academy of Pediatrics.

Shapiro, D. R., & Ulrich, D. A. (2001). Social comparisons of children with and without learning disabilities when evaluating physical competence. *Adapted Physical Activity Quarterly, 18*(3), 273.

Sideridis, G. D., & Tsorbatzoudis, C. (2003). Intragroup motivational analysis of student with learning disabilities: A goal oriented approach. *Learning Disabilities: A Contemporary Journal, 1*(1), 8-19.

Sigmundsson, H. (2005). Disorders of motor development (clumsy child syndrome). *Neurodevelopmental Disorders,* 51-68.

Ulrich, D. A. (2020). *Test of Gross Motor Development* (3rd ed.). PRO-ED.

U.S. Department of Education, Office of Special Education Programs. (2022). *Individuals With Disabilities Education Act (IDEA): Section 618 data products; State level data files.* https://data.ed.gov/dataset/idea-section-618-data-products-state-level-files

Wolraich, M. L., Hagan, J. F., Allan, C., Chan, E., Davison, D., Earls, M., Evans, S. W., Flinn, S. K., Froehlich, T., Frost J., Holbrook, J. R., Lehmann, C. U., Herschel, R. L.,

Okechukwu, K., Pierce, K. L., Winner, J. D., & Zurhellen, W. (2019). Clinical practice guideline for the diagnosis, evaluation, and treatment of attention-deficit/hyperactivity disorder in children and adolescents. *Pediatrics, 144*(4), e20192528.

Zimmer, C., Dunn, J. C., & Holt, N. L. (2020). Experiences in physical education for children at risk for developmental coordination disorder. *Adapted Physical Activity Quarterly, 37*(4), 385-403.

CHAPTER 10

Alstot, A. E., & Alstot, C. D. (2015). Behavior management: Examining the functions of behavior. *Journal of Physical Education, Recreation and Dance, 86*(2), 22-28.

American Academy of Pediatrics. (2013). The critical role of recess in the schools. *Pediatrics, 131*(1), 183-188.

American Academy of Pediatrics. (2020). www.aap.org

American Psychiatric Association (APA). (2013). *Diagnostic and statistical manual of mental disorders* (5th ed.).

American Psychiatric Association (APA) (Ed.). (2022). *Diagnostic and statistical manual of mental disorders* (5th ed., Text Revision). American Psychiatric Publishing.

Bambara, L. M., Janney, R., & Snell, M. E. (2015). *Behavior support* (3rd ed.). Brookes Publishing.

Biddle, S. J., & Asare, M. (2011). Physical activity and mental health in children and adolescents: A review of reviews. *British Journal of Sports Medicine, 45*(11), 886-895.

Bitsko, R. H., Claussen, A. H., Lichtstein, J., Black, L. J., Everett Jones, S., Danielson, M. D., Hoenig, J. M., Davis Jack, S. P., Brody, D. J., Gyawali, S., Maenner, M. M., Warner, M., Holland, K. M., Perou, R., Crosby, A. E., Blumberg, S. J., Avenevoli, S., Kaminski, J. W., & Ghandour, R. M. (2022). Surveillance of children's mental health—United States, 2013-2019. *MMWR, 71*(Suppl-2), 1-42.

Block, M. E., Henderson, H., & Lavay, B. (2016). Positive behavior support of children with challenging behaviors. In M. Block (Ed.), *A teacher's guide to adapted physical education: Including students with disabilities in sports and recreation* (4th ed.). Brookes Publishing.

Center on the Developing Child at Harvard (CDCH). (n.d.). *A guide to toxic stress.* https://developingchild. harvard.edu/guide/a-guide-to-toxic-stress/

Centers for Disease Control and Prevention (CDC). (2021). *CDC timeline.* https://www.cdc.gov/museum/timeline/index.html

Cree, R. A., Bitsko, R. H., Robinson, L. R., Holbrook, J. R., Danielson, M. L., Smith, D. S., Kaminski, J. W., Kenney, M. K., & Peacock, G. (2018). Health care, family, and community factors associated with mental, behavioral, and developmental disorders and poverty among children aged 2-8 years—United States. *MMWR, 67*(5), 1377-1383.

Cohen, R. I. S., & Bosk, E. A. (2020). Vulnerable youth and the COVID-19 pandemic. *Pediatrics, 146*(1). https://doi.org/10.1542/peds.2020-1306

Colarusso, R. P., O'Rourke, C. M., & Leontovich, M. A. (2017). *Special physical education for all teachers* (7th ed.). Kendall Hunt.

Doroshow, D. B. (2016). Residential treatment and the invention of the emotionally disturbed child in twentieth-century America. *Bulletin of the History of Medicine, 90*(1), 92-123. https://doi.org/10.1353/bhm.2016.0023

FAIR Health. (2021). *The impact of COVID-19 on pediatric mental health.* https://s3.amazonaws.com/media2. fairhealth.org/whitepaper/asset

Frick, P. J. (2022). Some critical considerations in applying the construct of psychopathy to research and classification of childhood disruptive behavior disorders. *Clinical Psychology Review,* 102188.

Hellison, D. (2011). *Teaching personal and social responsibility through physical activity.* Human Kinetics.

Hellison, D., & Wright, P. (2003). Retention in an urban extended day program: A process-based assessment. *Journal of Teaching in Physical Education, 22*(4), 369-381.

Herringa, R. J. (2017). Trauma, PTSD, and the developing brain. *Current Psychiatry Reports, 19,* 69. https://doi.org/10.1007/s11920-017-0825-3

Individuals with Disabilities Education Act (IDEA). (2004). http://idea.ed.gov

Lavay, B. (2019). Behavior management: What I have learned. *Journal of Physical Education Recreation and Dance, 90*(3), 5-9.

Lavay, B. W., French, R., & Henderson, H. L. (2016). *Positive behavior management in physical activity settings* (3rd ed.). Human Kinetics.

Mavilidi, M. F., Mason, C., Leahy, A. A., Kennedy, S. G., Eather, N., Hillman, C. H., Morgan, P. J., Lonsdale, C., Wade, L., Riley, N., & Heemskerk, C. (2020). Effect of a time-efficient physical activity intervention on senior school students' on-task behaviour and subjective vitality: The 'burn 2 learn' cluster randomised controlled trial. *Educational Psychology Review, 33,* 299-323.

Mayo Clinic. (2020). *Oppositional defiant disorder (ODD).* www.mayoclinic.org/diseases-conditions/oppositional-defiant-disorder/symptoms-causes/syc-20375831

Pérez-Ordás, R., Pozo, P., & Grao-Cruces, A. (2020). Effects on aggression and social responsibility by teaching personal and social responsibility during physical education. *Journal of Physical Education and Sport, 20*(4), 1832-1838.

Theberath, M., Bauer, D., Chen, W., Salinas, M., Mohabbat, A. B., Yang, J., Chon, T. Y., Bauer, B. A., & Wahner-Roedler, D. L. (2022). Effects of COVID-19 pandemic on mental health of children and adolescents: A systematic review of survey studies. *SAGE Open Medicine, 10,* 20503121221086712.

Wolraich, M. L., Hagan, J. F., Allan, C., Chan, E., Davison, D., Earls, M., Evans, S. W., Flinn, S. K., Froehlich, T., Frost, J., Holbrook, J. R., Lehmann, C. U., Herschel, R. L., Okechukwu, K., Pierce, K. L., Winner, J. D., & Zurhellen,

W. (2019). Clinical practice guideline for the diagnosis, evaluation, and treatment of attention-deficit/hyperactivity disorder in children and adolescents. *Pediatrics, 144*(4), e20192528.

CHAPTER 11

AI Media. (2022). *Famous deaf people: 15 athletes who are deaf or hard of hearing.* ai-media.tv/ai-media-blog/famous-deaf-people-15-athletes-who-are-deaf-or-hard-of-hearing

Armstrong, E., Lieberman, L., Guerrero, M., & Martin, J. (2020). The development of a physical activity barriers questionnaire for youth with visual impairments. *Pamukkale Journal of Sport Sciences, 11*(1), 23-36.

Bloomquist, L. E. C. (2003a). Deaf and hard-of-hearing. In J. L. Durstine & G. E. Moore (Eds.), *ACMS's exercise management for persons with chronic diseases and disabilities* (2nd ed., pp. 320-324). Human Kinetics.

Bloomquist, L. E. C. (2003b). Visual impairment. In J. L. Durstine & G. E. Moore (Eds.), *ACSM's exercise management for persons with chronic diseases and disabilities* (2nd ed., pp. 325-328). Human Kinetics.

Bowdich, S. (2023a). *John's Hopkins Medical. Cochlear implants.* https://www.hopkinsmedicine.org/health/treatment-tests-and-therapies/cochlear-implants

Bowdich, S. (2023b). *John's Hopkins Medical. Living with cochlear implant.* https://www.hopkinsmedicine.org/health/treatment-tests-and-therapies/cochlear-implants/living-with-a-cochlear-implant

Brian, A., Pennell, A., Haibach-Beach, P., Foley, J., Taunton, S., & Lieberman, L. J. (2019). Correlates of physical activity among children with visual impairments. *Disability and Health Journal, 12*(2), 328-333.

Burton, A. W., & Miller, D. E. (1998). *Movement skill assessment.* Human Kinetics.

Camp Abilities. (2022). *Instructional materials.* www.campabilities.org/instructional-materials.html

Columna, L., Davis, T., Lieberman, L. J., & Lytle, R. (2010). Determining the most appropriate physical education placement for students with disabilities. *Journal of Physical Education, Recreation and Dance, 81*(7), 30-37. https://doi.org/10.1080/07303084.2010.10598506

Columna, L., & Lieberman, L. J. (2011). *Promoting language through physical education.* Human Kinetics.

Furtado, O. L., Lieberman, L. J., & Gutierrez, G. L. (2017). Sport summer camp for children and youth with visual impairment: Descriptive case study of Camp Abilities. *British Journal of Visual Impairment, 35*(2), 154-164.

Haegele, J. A., Ball, L. E., Nowland, L. A., Ally Keene, M., & Zhu, X. (2022). Visually impaired students' views on peer tutoring in integrated physical education. *Sport, Education and Society,* 1-14.

Healthline. (2023). *Cochlear nerve.* https://www.healthline.com/human-body-maps/cochlear-nerve#1

Hearing Loss Association of America (HLAA). (2018). *Hearing loss facts and statistics.* https://www.hearingloss.org/wp-content/uploads/HLAA_HearingLoss_Facts_Statistics.pdf

Hellman, S. A., Chute, P. M., Kretschmer, R. E., Nevins, M. E., Parisier, S. C., & Thurston, L. C. (1991). The development of a children's implant profile. *American Annals of the Deaf, 136*(2), 77-81. doi: 10.1353/aad.2012.1077

Hilgenbrinck, L., Lieberman, L. J., & Cavanaugh, L. (2020). Gross motor assessment results and placement in physical education of five students with CHARGE syndrome. *Palestra, 34*(3), 26-35.

Hilgenbrinck, L., Pyfer, J., & Castle, N. (2004). Students with cochlear implants: Teaching considerations for physical educators. *Journal of Physical Education, Recreation and Dance, 75*(4), 28-33.

Hodge, S. R., Lieberman, L. J., & Murata, N. M. (2012). *Essentials of teaching adapted physical education.* Holcomb Hathaway.

Individuals with Disabilities Education Act (IDEA). (2004). http://idea.ed.gov

Lane, K. J. (2019). Parental perspectives on physical education services for children with CHARGE syndrome. *Kinesiology, Sport Studies, and Physical Education Synthesis Projects,* 64. https://digitalcommons.brockport.edu/pes_synthesis/64

Latash, M. L., & Singh, T. (2024). *Neurophysiological basis of motor control* (3rd ed.). Human Kinetics.

Lieberman, L. J. (2017a). Visual impairments. In J. P. Winnick & D. P. Porretta (Eds.). *Adapted physical education and sport* (6th ed., pp. 235-252). Human Kinetics.

Lieberman, L. J. (2017b). Hard of hearing, deaf, or deafblind. In J. P. Winnick & D. P. Porretta (Eds.). *Adapted physical education and sport* (6th ed., pp. 253-269). Human Kinetics.

Lieberman, L. J., Columna, L., Haegele, J., & Conroy, P. (2014). How students with visual impairments can learn components of the Expanded Core Curriculum through physical education. *Journal of Visual Impairments and Blindness, 108*(3), 239-248.

Lieberman, L. J., & Coward, J. F. (1996). *Games for people with sensory impairments.* Human Kinetics.

Lieberman, L. J., Haibach, P., & Schedlin, H. (2012). Physical education and children with CHARGE syndrome: Research to practice. *Journal of Visual Impairment and Blindness, 106*(2), 106-119.

Lieberman, L. J., & Houston-Wilson, C. (2009). *Inclusion.* Human Kinetics.

Lieberman, L. J., & Houston-Wilson, C. (2018). *Strategies for inclusion: A handbook for physical educators* (3rd ed.). Human Kinetics.

Lieberman, L. J., Ponchillia, P. E., & Ponchillia, S. V. (2013). *Physical education and sports for people with visual impairments and deafblindness: Foundations of instruction.* AFB Press.

Martin, J. J., Snapp, E. E, Whitney, E., Moore, E., Lieberman, L. J., Armstrong, E., & Mannella, S. (2021). Factor structure of the barriers to physical activity scale for youth with visual impairments. *Adapted Physical Activity Quarterly, 38*(4), 585-604.

Mayo Clinic. (2022). *Cochlear implants.* mayoclinic.org/tests-procedures/cochlear-implants/about/pac-20385021

National Association of the Deaf (NAD). (2023). *Deaf kids.* https://www.nad.org/deaf-kids/

Papadopoulos, K., Metsiou, K., & Agaliotis, I. (2011). Adaptive behavior of children and adolescents with visual impairments. *Research in Developmental Disabilities, 32*(3), 1086-1096. https://doi.org/10.1016/j.ridd.2011.01.021

Sapp, W., & Hatlan, P. (2010). The Expanded Core Curriculum: Where we have been, where we are going, and how we get there. *Journal of Visual Impairments and Blindness, 104*(6), 338-348.

Schultz, J. L., Lieberman, L. J., Ellis, M. K., & Hilgenbrinck, L. C. (2014). Ensuring the success of deaf students in inclusive physical education. *Journal of Physical Education, Recreation and Dance, 85*(5), 51-56.

Sharma, S. D., Cushing, S. L., Papsin, B. C., & Gordon, K. A. (2020). Hearing and speech benefits of cochlear implantation in children: A review of the literature. *International Journal of Pediatric Otorhinolaryngology, 133*, 109984.

Silverstein, H., Wolfson, R. J., & Rosenberg, S. (1992). Diagnosis and management of hearing loss. *Clinical Symposia, 44*(3), 32.

Smart, J. (2009). *Disability, society, and the individual* (2nd ed.). PRO-ED.

Ulrich, D. (2020). *Test of Gross Motor Development* (3rd ed.). PRO-ED.

United States Association of Blind Athletes (USABA). (2021). *Home page.* www.usaba.org

Van Dijk, J. (1966). The first steps of the deaf-blind child towards language. *International Journal for the Education of the Blind, 15*(4), 112-114.

Veiskarami, P., & Roozbahani, M. (2020). Motor development in deaf children based on Gallahue's model: A review study. *Auditory and Vestibular Research, 29*(1), 10-25.

Wagner, M. O., Haibach, P. S., & Lieberman, L. J. (2013). Gross motor skill performance in children with and without visual impairments—research to practice. *Research in Developmental Disabilities, 34*, 3246-3252.

World Camp Abilities. (2021). *Home page.* www.campabilities.org

CHAPTER 12

American Academy of Pediatrics (AAP). (n.d.). *Clean intermittent catheterization.* Healthychildren.org

American Association of Adapted Sports Programs (AAASP). (n.d.). *Off the sidelines and into the game.* https://adaptedsports.org

Burton, A. W., & Miller, D. E. (1998). *Movement skill assessment.* Human Kinetics.

Centers for Disease Control and Prevention (CDC). (2020a). *Cerebral palsy: 11 things to know about cerebral palsy.* www.cdc.gov/ncbddd/cp/index.html

Centers for Disease Control and Prevention (CDC). (2020b). *Health issues & treatments for spina bifida.* www.cdc.gov/ncbddd/spinabifida/treatment.html#Open-Spina-Bifida

Centers for Disease Control and Prevention (CDC). (2020c). *Types of cerebral palsy.* www.cdc.gov/ncbddd/cp/facts.html

Centers for Disease Control and Prevention (CDC). (2020d). *What is spina bifida.* www.cdc.gov/ncbddd/spinabifida/facts.html#myelomeningocele

Centers for Disease Control and Prevention (CDC). (2022a). *Get the facts on traumatic brain injury.* https://www.cdc.gov/traumaticbraininjury/get_the_facts.html

Centers for Disease Control and Prevention (CDC). (2022b). *Surveillance report of traumatic brain injury related deaths by age group, sex, and mechanism of injury, United States 2018–2019.* https://www.cdc.gov/traumaticbraininjury/pdf/TBI-surveillance-report-2018-2019-508.pdf

Centers for Disease Control and Prevention (CDC). (2022c). *Cerebral palsy. Data and statistics for cerebral palsy.* cdc.gov/ncbddd/cp/data.html

Centers for Disease Control and Prevention (CDC). (2022d). *What is cerebral palsy?* https://www.cdc.gov/ncbddd/cp/facts.html

Dean, P. J., O'Neill, D., & Sterr, A. (2012). Post-concussion syndrome: Prevalence after mild traumatic brain injury in comparison with a sample without head injury. *Brain Injury, 26*(1), 14-26.

Eliasson, A., Krumlinde-Sundholm, L., Rösblad, B., Beckung, E., Arner, M., Öhrvall, A., & Rosenbaum, P. (2006). The Manual Ability Classification System (MACS) for children with cerebral palsy: Scale development and evidence of validity and reliability. *Developmental Medicine and Child Neurology, 7*, 549-554. https://doi.org/10.1017/S0012162206001162

Gross Motor Function Measure (GMFM). (n.d.a). *CanChild Center.* https://www.canchild.ca/

Gross Motor Function Measure (GMFM). (n.d.b). *Resources.* https://canchild.ca/en/resources/322-gmfm-other

Gross Motor Function Measure (GMFM). (n.d.c). *Scoring.* https://www.canchild.ca/en/resources/321-gmfm-scoring; https://www.canchild.ca/system/tenon/assets/attachments/000/003/355/original/gmfm-88_and_66_scoresheet-V4.pdf; https://canchild.ca/en/resources/322-gmfm-other

Hanna, D. E., Bartlett, D. J., Rivard, L. M, & Russell, D. J. (2008). *Tabulated reference percentiles for the 66-item Gross Motor Function Measure for use with children having cerebral palsy.* www.canchild.ca

Hansen, R. K., Samani, A., Laessoe, U., Larsen, R. G., & Cowan, R. E. (2021). Sociodemographic characteristics associated with physical activity barrier perception among manual wheelchair users. *Disability and Health Journal, 14*(4), 101119.

Individuals with Disabilities Education Act (IDEA). (2004). http://idea.ed.gov

Lieberman, L., & Houston-Wilson, C. (2002). *Strategies for inclusion: A handbook for physical educators.* Human Kinetics.

Lieberman, L. J., & Houston-Wilson, C. (2018). *Strategies for inclusion: A handbook for physical educators* (3rd ed.). Human Kinetics.

Mai, C. T., Isenburg, J. L., Canfield, M. A., Meyer, R. E., Correa, A., Alverson, C. J., Lupo, P. J., Riehle-Colarusso, T., Cho, S. J., Aggarwal, D., & Kirby, R. S. (2019). National Birth Defects Prevention Network. National population-based estimates for major birth defects, 2010-2014. *Birth Defects Research, 111*(18), 1420-1435. https://doi.org/10.1002/bdr2.1589

Mayo Clinic. (2020). *Spinal cord injury.* https://www.mayoclinic.org/diseases-conditions/spinal-cord-injury/symptoms-causes/syc-20377890

Moo, G. (2022). *Spinal cord injury in children.* Merck Manual, www.merchmanuals.com

Narad, M. E., Treble-Barna, A., Peugh, J., Yeates, K. O., Taylor, H. G., Stancin, T., & Wade, S. L. (2017). Recovery trajectories of executive functioning after pediatric TBI: A latent class growth modeling analysis. *Journal of Head Trauma Rehabilitation, 32*(2), 98-106.

National Center on Health, Physical Activity and Disability (NCHPAD). (n.d.a). *Discover fitness: A wheelchair user's guide for using fitness equipment.* https://www.nchpad.org/discoverfitness/files/inc/084021749b.pdf

National Center on Health, Physical Activity and Disability (NCPHAD). (n.d.b). *Life on wheels.* https://www.nchpad.org/fppics/Life%20on%20Wheels%20final%20version%20web.pdf

National Center on Health, Physical Activity and Disability (NCHPAD). (n.d.c). *Spina bifida. Important considerations when exercising.* https://www.nchpad.org/222/1445/Spina~Bifida

National Center on Health, Physical Activity and Disability (NCHPAD). (n.d.d). *Spinal cord injuries.* www.nchpad.org/55/403/Spinal~Cord~Injury

National Center on Health, Physical Activity and Disability (NCHPAD). (n.d.e). *Spinal cord injury location and function of major muscle groups (Table 4).* https://www.nchpad.org/94/754/Resistance~Training~for~Persons~with~Physical~Disabilities

National Center on Health, Physical Activity and Disability (NCHPAD). (n.d.f). *Teens on the move!* https://www.nchpad.org/416/2237/Teens~on~the~Move~~An~Exercise~Video~for~Teens~with~Spina~Bifida

National Center on Health, Physical Activity and Disability (NCHPAD). (2004). *Spina bifida—Physical activity guidelines factsheet.* https://www.nchpad.org/222/1445/Spina~Bifida~-~Physical~Activity~Guidelines

National Center on Health, Physical Activity and Disability (NCHPAD). (2023a). *Resistance exercise guidelines for persons with physical disabilities.* https://www.nchpad.org/94/730/Resistance~Training~for~Persons~with~-Physical~Disabilities

National Center on Health, Physical Activity and Disability (NCHPAD). (2023b). *High intensity weight training.* https://www.nchpad.org/24/173/High-Intensity~-Weight~Training~for~People~with~Disabilities

Oczkowski, W., & Bodzioch, M. (2021). Muscular weakness (paresis and paralysis). *McMaster textbook of internal medicine.* Medycyna Praktyczna. https://empendium.com/mcmtextbook/chapter/B31.I.1.21

Qi, L., Guan, S., Zhang, L., Liu, H. L., Sun, C. K., & Ferguson-Pell, M. (2021). The effect of fatigue on wheelchair users' upper limb muscle coordination patterns in time-frequency and principal component analysis. *IEEE Transactions on Neural Systems and Rehabilitation Engineering, 29,* 2096-2102.

Rosenbaum, P. L., Walter, S. D., Hanna, S. E., Palisano, R. J., Russell, D. J., Raina, P., Wood, E., Bartlett, D. J., & Caluppi, B. E. (2002). Prognosis for gross motor function in cerebral palsy: Creation of motor development curves. *JAMA, 288*(11), 1357-1363.

Spina Bifida Association (SBA). (2018). *Spina bifida your guide to a healthy life: Physical activity life for ages 0-18+.* https://www.spinabifidaassociation.org/wp-content/uploads/Physical-Activity-Guidelines.pdf

Spina Bifida Association (SBA). (2023a). *What is spina bifida?* https://www.spinabifidaassociation.org/resource/spina-bifida/

Spina Bifida Association (SBA). (2023b). *Adapted physical education.* https://www.spinabifidaassociation.org/resource/adapted-physical-education/

Spina Bifida Association (SBA). (2023c). *Let's be frank about relationships and intimacy for men with spina bifida.* https://www.spinabifidaassociation.org/resource/lets-be-frank-relationships-and-intimacy-for-men-with-spina-bifida/

Spina Bifida Association (SBA). (2023d). *SB-YOU Women & relationships.* https://www.spinabifidaassociation.org/resource/sb-you-women-relationships/

Thibadeau, J., Walker, W. O., Castillo, J., Dicianno, B. E., Routh, J. C., Smith, K. A., & Ouyang, L. (2020). Philosophy of care delivery for spina bifida. *Disability and Health Journal, 13*(2), 100883.

U.S. Department of Health and Human Services (USDHHS). (2018). *Physical activity guidelines for Americans* (ODPHP Publication No. U0036). U.S. Department of Health and Human Services. www.health.gov/paguidelines

Voormolen, D. C., Cnossen, M. C., Polinder, S., Von Steinbuechel, N., Vos, P. E., & Haagsma, J. A. (2018). Divergent classification methods of post-concussion syndrome after mild traumatic brain injury: Prevalence rates, risk factors, and functional outcome. *Journal of Neurotrauma, 35*(11), 1233-1241.

Webster, J. B., Levy, C. E., Bryant, P. R., & Prusakowski, P. E. (2001). Sports and recreation for persons with limb deficiency. *Archives of Physical Medicine and Rehabilitation, 82*(3), S38-S44.

Williams, J., Mai, C. T., Mulinare, J., Isenburg, J., Flood, T. J., Ethen, M., Frohnert, B., & Kirby, R. S. (2015). Updated estimates of neural tube defects prevented by mandatory folic acid fortification—United States, 1995-2011, CDC. *Morbidity and Mortality Weekly Report, 64*(1), 1-36.

Wood, E., & Rosenbaum, P. (2000). The Gross Motor Function Classification System for cerebral palsy. *Developmental Medicine & Child Neurology, 42*(5), 292-296. https://doi.org/10.1111/j.1469-8749.2000.tb00093.x

CHAPTER 13

American Diabetes Association (ADA). (2020). *Statistics about diabetes.* www.diabetes.org/resources/statistics

Carter, J. M., & McGrew, C. (2021). Seizure disorders and exercise/sports participation. *Current Sports Medicine Reports, 20*(1), 26-30.

Centers for Disease Control and Prevention (CDC). (2000a). *Growth rate chart for boys.* www.cdc.gov/growthcharts/data/set1clinical/cj41l023.pdf

Centers for Disease Control and Prevention (CDC). (2000b). *Growth rate chart for girls.* www.cdc.gov/growthcharts/data/set1clinical/cj41l024.pdf

Centers for Disease Control and Prevention (CDC). (2007). *Children with disability and obesity.* www.cdc.gov/ncbddd/disabilityandhealth/obesity.html

Centers for Disease Control and Prevention (CDC). (2018a). *Childhood obesity facts.* www.cdc.gov/obesity/data/childhood.html

Centers for Disease Control and Prevention (CDC). (2018b). *Prevalence of overweight, obesity, and severe obesity among children and adolescents aged 2-18 years: United States, 1963-1965 through 2017-2018. Table 3.* www.cdc.gov/nchs/data/hestat/obesity-child-17-18/obesity-child.htm#table3

Centers for Disease Control and Prevention (CDC). (2020a). *Diagnoses of HIV infection in the United States and dependent areas, 2018 (updated).* https://www.cdc.gov/hiv/pdf/library/reports/surveillance/cdc-hiv-surveillance-report-2018-updated-vol-31.pdf

Centers for Disease Control and Prevention (CDC). (2020b). *HIV basic statistics.* www.cdc.gov/hiv/basics/statistics.html

Centers for Disease Control and Prevention (CDC). (2020c, February). *Moving the needle on asthma control: Examining context, promising practices, and innovation.* Centers for Disease Control and Prevention, National Center for Environmental Health, Division of Environmental Science and Practice, Asthma and Community Health Branch.

Centers for Disease Control and Prevention (CDC). (2020d). *Living well with sickle cell disease.* https://www.cdc.gov/ncbddd/sicklecell/healthyliving-living-well.html

Centers for Disease Control and Prevention (CDC). (2021a). *BMI for adults.* www.cdc.gov/healthyweight/assessing/bmi/adult_BMI/english_bmi_calculator/bmi_calculator.html

Centers for Disease Control and Prevention (CDC). (2021b). *BMI for children and teens.* www.cdc.gov/healthyweight/bmi/calculator.html

Centers for Disease Control and Prevention (CDC). (2021c). *Measuring height and weight at home for children and teens.* www.cdc.gov/healthyweight/assessing/bmi/childrens_BMI/measuring_children.html

Centers for Disease Control and Prevention (CDC). (2022). *Asthma.* www.cdc.gov/asthma/asthmadata.htm

Cleven, L., Krell-Roesch, J., Nigg, C. R., & Woll, A. (2020). The association between physical activity with incident obesity, coronary heart disease, diabetes and hypertension in adults: a systematic review of longitudinal studies published after 2012. *BMC Public Health, 20*(1), 1-15.

Dimitri, P., Joshi, K., & Jones, N. (2020). Moving more: Physical activity and its positive effects on long term conditions in children and young people. *Archives of Disease in Childhood, 105*(11), 1035-1040.

Divers, J., Mayer-Davis, E. J., Lawrence, J. M., Isom, S., Dabelea, D., Dolan, L., Imperatore, G., Marcovina, S., Pettitt, D. J., Pihoker, C., Hamman, R. F., Saydah, S., & Wagenknecht, L. E., (2020). Trends in incidence of type 1 and type 2 diabetes among youths—Selected counties and Indian reservations, United States, 2002-2015. *MMWR Morbidity and Mortality Weekly Report, 69*, 161-165. https://doi.org/10.15585/mmwr.mm6906a3

Epilepsy Foundation. (2020). *Epilepsy seizure action plan.* www.epilepsy.com/sites/default/files/atoms/files/SCHOOL%20Seizure%20Action%20Plan%2020-April7_FILLABLE.pdf

Epilepsy Society of the United Kingdom. (2022). *Types of seizures.* https://epilepsysociety.org.uk/about-epilepsy/epileptic-seizures

Hernandez, G., Baumann, K., Knight, H., Purrington, H., Gilgannon, M., Newman, J., Tobase, P., Mathew, S., & Cooper, D. L. (2018). Ranges and drivers of risk associated with sports and recreational activities in people with haemophilia: Results of the activity-intensity-risk consensus survey of US physical therapists. *Haemophilia, 24*(57), 5-26. https://doi.org/10.1111/hae.13623

Hostyn, S. V., Carvalho, W. B., Johnston, C., & Braga, J. A. (2013). Evaluation of functional capacity for exercise in children and adolescents with sickle-cell disease through the six-minute walk test. *Jornal de Pediatria (Rio J), 89*(6), 588-594. https://doi.org/10.1016/j.jped.2013.04.005

Howe, A. S., & Boden, B. P. (2007). Heat-related illness in athletes. *American Journal of Sports Medicine, 35*(8), 1384-1395.

Leon, A. S. (1993). Diabetes. In J. S. Skinner (Ed.), *Exercise testing and exercise prescription for special cases* (2nd ed., pp. 115-133). Lea and Febiger.

Mayo Clinic. (2022). *Epilepsy.* www.mayoclinic.org/diseases-conditions/epilepsy/symptoms-causes/syc-20350093#:~:text=Epilepsy%20is%20a%20central%20nervous,and%20sometimes%20loss%20of%20awareness

Mulić, M., Lazović, B., Dmitrović, R., Jovičić, N., Detanac, D., & Detanac, D. (2020). Asthma among elite athletes, mechanism of occurrence and impact on respiratory parameters: A review of literature. *Sanamed, 15*(2), 209-213.

Narcisse, L., Walton, E. A., & Hsu, L. L. (2018). Summer camps for children with sickle cell disease. *Ochsner Journal, 18*(4), 358-363.

Pate, C. A., Zahran, H. S., Qin, X., Johnson, C., Hummelman, E., & Malilay, J. (2021). Asthma surveillance—United States, 2006-2018. *MMWR Surveillance Summaries, 70*(SS-5), 1-32. https://doi.org/10.15585/mmwr.ss7005a1

Surburg, P. R. (1988). Are adapted physical educators ready for students with AIDS? *Adapted Physical Activity Quarterly, 5*(4), 259-263.

Surgeon general's report to the American public on HIV infection and AIDS. (1993). Centers for Disease Control and Prevention, National Institute of Health.

Thompson, M. A., Horberg, M. A., Agwu, A. L., Colasanti, J. A., Jain, M. K., Short, W. R., Singh, T., & Aberg, J. A. (2021). Primary care guidance for persons with human immunodeficiency virus: 2020 update by the HIV Medicine Association of the Infectious Diseases Society of America. *Journal of Clinical Infectious Diseases, 73*(11), E3572-E3605.

U.S. Department of Education, Office for Civil Rights. (1991). *Placement of school children with acquired immune deficiency syndrome (AIDS).* ED/OCR92-2R. www2.ed.gov/about/offices/list/ocr/docs/hq53e9.html

van Leeuwen, J., Koes, B. W., Paulis, W. D., Bindels, P. J., & van Middelkoop, M. (2020). No differences in physical activity between children with overweight and children of normal-weight. *BMC Pediatrics, 20*(1), 1-7.

Webb Pennington, L. M., & Pennington, C. G. (2020). Inclusive physical activity and physical education for students with epilepsy. *Journal of Physical Education, Recreation & Dance, 91*(2), 52-53.

Wikipedia. (2023). *Athletes with diabetes.* https://en.wikipedia.org/wiki/List_of_sportspeople_with_diabetes

World Health Organization. (2019, August 21). *Epilepsy.* www.who.int/news-room/fact-sheets/detail/epilepsy

CHAPTER 14

Albrecht, G. L., & Devlieger, P. J. (1999). The disability paradox: High quality of life against all odds. *Social Science & Medicine, 48*(8), 977-988.

American College of Sports Medicine (ACSM). (n.d.). *Rx for Health series: A series on today's most common chronic conditions and their exercise prescriptions.* https://www.exerciseismedicine.org/eim-in-action/health-care/resources/rx-for-health-series/

American College of Sports Medicine (ACSM). (2011). *Delayed onset muscle soreness.* www.acsm.org/docs/default-source/files-for-resource-library/delayed-onset-muscle-soreness-(doms).pdf?sfvrsn=8f430e18_2

American College of Sports Medicine (ACSM). (2021). *Health care providers' action guide.* https://www.exerciseismedicine.org/wp-content/uploads/2021/02/EIM-Health-Care-Providers-Action-Guide-clickable-links.pdf

Blair, S. N. (1993). 1993 CH McCloy research lecture: Physical activity, physical fitness, and health. *Research Quarterly for Exercise and Sport, 64*(4), 365-376.

Borg, G. A. (1982). Psychophysical bases of perceived exertion. *Medicine Science Sports and Exercise, 114*, 377-381.

Borg, G. A. (1998). *Borg's perceived exertion and pain scales.* Human Kinetics.

Centers for Disease Control and Prevention (CDC). (2009). *The prevalence of physical inactivity in adults with and without disabilities, BRFSS.* www.cdc.gov/ncbddd/disabilityandhealth/documents/physical-inactivity-tip-sheet-_phpa_1.pdf

Centers for Disease Control and Prevention (CDC). (2020a). *Benefits of physical activity for adults.* www.cdc.gov/physicalactivity/basics/adults/health-benefits-of-physical-activity-for-adults.html

Centers for Disease Control and Prevention (CDC). (2020b). *BMI calculator.* www.cdc.gov/healthyweight/assessing/bmi/adult_bmi/english_bmi_calculator/bmi_calculator.html

Centers for Disease Control and Prevention (CDC). (2020c). *Healthy weight.* www.cdc.gov/healthyweight/assessing/index.html

Centers for Disease Control and Prevention (CDC). (2021a). *Chronic disease.* www.cdc.gov/chronicdisease/about/index.htm

Centers for Disease Control and Prevention (CDC). (2021b). *Move your way: What's your move?* https://health.gov/sites/default/files/2021-02/PAG_MYW_FactSheet_OlderAdults_508c.pdf

Centers for Disease Control and Prevention (CDC). (2022). *Physical activity basics.* https://www.cdc.gov/physicalactivity/basics/index.htm

Chase, N. L., Sui, X., & Blair, S. N. (2008). Comparison of the health aspects of swimming with other types of physical activity and sedentary lifestyle habits. *International Journal of Aquatic Research and Education, 2*(2), Article 7. https://doi.org/10.25035/ijare.02.02.07

Cooper Institute. (2022). *Calculate BMI.* www.cooperhealth.org/services/bariatric-and-metabolic-surgery-center/why-choose-bariatric-surgery/obesity-and-body-mass-index

Cristini, J., Weiss, M., De Las Heras, B., Medina-Rincón, A., Dagher, A., Postuma, R. B., Huber, R., Doyon, J., Rosa-Neto, P., Carrier, J., Amara, A. W., & Roig, M. (2021). The effects of exercise on sleep quality in persons with Parkinson's disease: A systematic review with meta-analysis. *Sleep Medicine Reviews, 55*, 101384.

Dixon-Ibarra, A., Krahn, G., Fredine, H., Cahill, A., & Jenkins, S. (2016). Adults aging 'with' and 'into' paralysis: Epidemiological analyses of demography and health. *Disability and Health Journal, 9*(4), 575-583.

Drum, C. E. (2009). Models and approaches to disability. In C. E. Drum, G. L. Krahn, & H. Bersani (Eds.), *Disability and public health* (pp. 27-44). American Public Health Association.

Ekelund, U., Tarp, J., Fagerland, M. W., Johannessen, J. S., Hansen, B. H., Jefferis, B. J., Whincup, P. H., Diaz, K. M., Hooker, S., Howard, V. J., Chernofsky, A., Larson, M. G., Spartano, N., Vasan, R. V., Dohrn, I., Hagströmer, M., Edwardson, C., Yates, T., Shiroma, E. J., Dempsey, P., Wijndaele, K., & Anderssen, S. A. (2020). Joint associations of accelerometer-measured physical activity and sedentary time with all-cause mortality: A harmonised meta-analysis in more than 44000 middle-aged and older individuals. *British Journal of Sports Medicine, 54*, 1499-1506. https://doi: 10.1136/bjsports-2020-103270

Flynn, A., Allen, N. E., Dennis, S., Canning, C. G., & Preston, E. (2019). Home-based prescribed exercise improves balance-related activities in people with Parkinson's disease and has benefits similar to centre-based exercise: A systematic review. *Journal of Physiotherapy, 65*(4), 189-199.

Hall, B. (2005). *Why BMI is not fair to athletes.* www.stack.com/a/athlete-bmi

Haskell, W. L., Lee, I. M., Pate, R. R., Powell, K. E., Blair, S. N., & Franklin, B. A. (2007). Physical activity and public health: Updated recommendation for adults from the American College of Sports Medicine and the American Heart Association. *Medicine and Science in Sports and Exercise, 39*, 1423-1434.

Healthline.com. (2023). *What exactly are METs, and what should you know about them?* www.healthline.com/health/what-are-mets

Healthy People 2030. (2021). *Home page.* https://health.gov/healthypeople

Heller, T., Ying, G., Rimmer, J., & Marks, B. (2002). Determinants of exercise in adults with cerebral palsy. *Public Health Nursing, 19*(3), 223-231.

Hoehn, M., & Yahr, M. (1967). Parkinsonism: Onset, progression and mortality. *Neurology, 17*(5), 427-442. https://doi.org/10.1212/wnl.17.5.427 PMID 6067254

Kennedy, W., Fruin, R., Lue, A., & Logan, S. W. (2021). Using ecological models of health behavior to promote health care access and physical activity engagement for persons with disabilities. *Journal of Patient Experience, 8.* https://doi.org/10.1177/23743735211034031

Koop, M. M., Rosenfeldt, A. B., & Alberts, J. L. (2019). Mobility improves after high intensity aerobic exercise in individuals with Parkinson's disease. *Journal of the Neurological Sciences, 399*, 187-193.

Krahn, G. L., Robinson, A., Murray, A. J., Havercamp, S. M., & The Nisonger RRTC on Health and Function. (2021). It's time to reconsider how we define health: Perspective from disability and chronic condition. *Disability and Health Journal, 14*(4), 1-5. https://doi.org/10.1016/j.dhjo.2021.101129

Krahn, G. L., Walker, D. K., & Correa-De-Araujo, R. (2015). Persons with disabilities as an unrecognized health disparity population. *American Journal of Public Health, 105*(S2), S198-S206.

Kraus, L. E., & Jans, L. (2014). *Implementation manual for guidelines for disability inclusion in physical activity, nutrition, and obesity programs and policies. Center on Disability at the Public Health Institute.* http://committoinclusion.org/wp-content/uploads/2014/10/Guidelines-Implementations-Manual_final_8MB.pdf

Levinger, P., Panisset, M., Parker, H., Batchelor, F., Tye, M., & Hill, K. D. (2021). Guidance about age-friendly outdoor exercise equipment and associated strategies to maximise usability for older people. *Health Promotion Journal of Australia, 32*(3), 475-482.

Mayo Clinic. (2022a). *Arthritis.* www.mayoclinic.org/diseases-conditions/arthritis/symptoms-causes/syc-20350772

Mayo Clinic. (2022b). *Parkinson's disease.* www.mayoclinic.org/diseases-conditions/parkinsons-disease/symptoms-causes/syc-20376055

Metsios, G. S., Moe, R. H., van der Esch, M., van Zanten, J. J. C. S., Fenton, S. A. M., Koutedakis, Y., Vitalis, P., Kennedy, N., Brodin, N., Bostrom, C., Swinnen, T. W., Tzika, K., Niedermann, K., Nikiphorou, E., Fragoulis, G. E., Vlieland, T. P. V. M., Van den Ende, C. H. M., Kitas, G. D., & IMPACT-RMD Consortium. (2020). The effects of exercise on cardiovascular disease risk factors and cardiovascular physiology in rheumatoid arthritis. *Rheumatology International, 40*(3), 347-357.

Minnis, G. (2020). *What is delayed onset muscle soreness (DOMS) and what can you do about it?* Healthline.com/health/doms

Molton, I. R., & Jensen, M. P. (2010). Aging and disability: Biopsychosocial perspectives. *Physical Medicine and Rehabilitation Clinics of North America, 21*, 253-265.

Molton, I. R., & Yorkston, K. M. (2017). Growing older with a physical disability: A special application of the successful aging paradigm. *Journals of Gerontology: Social Sciences, 72*(2), 290-299. https://doi.org/10.1093/geronb/gbw122

Moore, G. M., Durstine, J. L., & Painter, P. L. (Eds.). (2016). *ACSM's exercise management for persons with chronic diseases and disabilities* (4th ed.). Human Kinetics.

National Center on Health, Physical Activity and Disability (NCHPAD). (2023). *Exercise guidelines for people with disabilities.* https://www.nchpad.org/14/75/Exercise~Guidelines~for~People~with~Disabilities

Norton, K., Norton, L., & Sadgrove, D. (2010). Position statement on physical activity and exercise intensity terminology. *Journal of Science and Medicine in Sport, 13*(5), 496-502.

Oppewal, A., Maes-Festen, D., & Hilgenkamp, T. I. M. (2020). Small steps in fitness, major leaps in health for adults with intellectual disabilities. *Exercise and Sport Sciences Reviews, 48*(2), 92-97.

Palisano, R., Rosenbaum, P., Walter, S., Russell, D., Wood, E., & Galuppi, B. (1997). Gross Motor Function Classification System for cerebral palsy. *Developmental Medicine & Child Neurology, 39*(4), 214-223.

Piercy, K. L., Troiano, R. P., Ballard, R. M., Carlson, S. A., Fulton, J., Galuska, D. A., George, S. M., & Olson, R. D. (2018). The physical activity guidelines for Americans. *JAMA.* https://doi.org/10.1001/jama.2018.14854

Resnick, B., Galik, E., Dorsey, S., Scheve, A., & Gutkin, S. (2011). Reliability and validity testing of the physical resilience measure. *The Gerontologist, 51*(5), 643-652.

Rethorn, Z. D., Covington, J. K., Cook, C., & Bezner, J. R. (2021). Physical activity promotion attitudes and practices among outpatient physical therapists: Results of a national survey. *Journal of Geriatric Physical Therapy, 44*(1), 25-34.

Rimmer, J. H. (1994). *Fitness and rehabilitation programs for special populations.* Brown and Benchmark.

Saint-Maurice, P. F., Graubard, B. I., Troiano, R. P., Berrigan, D., Galuska, D. A., Fulton, J. E., & Matthews, C. E. (2022). Estimated number of deaths prevented through increased physical activity among US adults. *JAMA Internal Medicine.* https://doi.org/10.1001/jamainternmed.2021.7755

Schlicht, J. A., Inskip, M., & Fiatarone Singh, M. (2021). Just what the doctor ordered: A guide to robust assessment and exercise prescription in older adults. *ACSM's Health & Fitness Journal, 25*(6), 18-27. https://doi.org/10.1249/FIT.0000000000000718

Schootemeijer, S., van der Kolk, N. M., Bloem, B. R., & de Vries, N. M. (2020). Current perspectives on aerobic exercise in people with Parkinson's disease. *Neurotherapeutics, 17*(4), 1418-1433.

Sørensen, L., Larsen, K. S. R., & Petersen, A. K. (2020). Validity of the talk test as a method to estimate ventilatory threshold and guide exercise intensity in cardiac patients. *Journal of Cardiopulmonary Rehabilitation and Prevention, 40*(5), 330-334. https://doi.org/10.1097/HCR.0000000000000506

Thompson, P. D., & Eijsvogels, T. M. (2018). New physical activity guidelines: A call to activity for clinicians and patients. *JAMA, 320*(19), 1983-1984.

U.S. Department of Health and Human Services (USDHHS). (2018). *Physical activity guidelines for Americans* (2nd ed.). U.S. Department of Health and Human Services.

Winnick, J. P., & Porretta D. L. (Eds). (2022). *Adapted physical education and sport* (7th ed). Human Kinetics.

World Health Organization. (1948). *WHO constitution.* www.who.int/about/who-we-are/constitution

CHAPTER 15

American Psychiatric Association (APA) (Ed.). (2022). *Diagnostic and statistical manual of mental disorders* (5th ed., Text Revision). American Psychiatric Publishing.

American Volkssport Association. (2022). *America's walking club.* https://ava.org

Amireault, S., Baier, J. M., & Spencer, J. R. (2019). Physical activity preferences among older adults: A systematic review. *Journal of Aging and Physical Activity, 27*(1), 128-139.

Aquatic Exercise Association (AEA). (2022). *Aquatic fitness programming: Standards and guidelines.* https://aeawave.org/Portals/0/AEA_Cert_Docs/AEA_Standards_Guidlines_2020.pdf?ver=2019-12-18-131623-417%C3%97tamp=1576696862726

Bowling ramp. (2022). *Silver Spring EZ-Bowler bowling ramp.* www.discountramps.com/bowling-ramp/p/BWL-RAMP/

Centers for Disease Control and Prevention (CDC). (n.d.). *Step it up!* https://www.cdc.gov/physicalactivity/walking/call-to-action/index.htm

Giandonato, J. A., Tringali, V. M., & Thoms, R. C. (2021). Improving mental health through physical activity: A narrative literature review. *Physical Activity and Health, 5*(1), 146-153. DOI: https://doi.org/10.5334/paah.108

Hampl, P. (2019). *The art of a wasted day.* Penguin Books.

Harvard. (2022). *Fitness trend: Nordic walking.* www.health.harvard.edu/staying-healthy/fitness-trend-nordic-walking

Hurd, A., & Anderson, D. (2011). *Park and recreation professional's handbook.* Human Kinetics.

Jin, J., Yun, J., & Agiovlasitis, S. (2018). Impact of enjoyment on physical activity and health among children with disabilities in schools. *Disability and Health Journal, 11*, 14-19.

Johns Hopkins. (2023). *5 health problems you're actually not too young for.* www.hopkinsmedicine.org/health/wellness-and-prevention/5-health-problems-youre-actually-not-too-young-for

Kennedy, W., Fruin, R., Lue, A., & Logan, S. W. (2021). Using ecological models of health behavior to promote health care access and physical activity engagement for persons with disabilities. *Journal of Patient Experience, 8*, 1-3. https://doi.org/10.1177/23743735211034031

Kunysz-Rozborska, M., & Rejman, A. (2019). Nordic walking as a form of recreation. *Central European Journal of Sport Sciences and Medicine, 26*(2), 77-82. https://doi.org/10.18276/cej.2019.2-08

Lee, I. M., & Buchner, D. M. (2008). The importance of walking to public health. *Medicine & Science in Sports & Exercise, 40*(7), S512-S518.

Li, F., Harmer, P., Fisher, K. J., & McAuley, E. (2004). Tai chi: Improving functional balance and predicting subsequent falls in older persons. *Medicine & Science in Sports & Exercise, 36*(12), 2046-2052.

Madhivanan, P., Krupp, K., Waechter, R., & Shidhaye, R. (2021). Yoga for healthy aging: Science or hype? *Advances in Geriatric Medicine and Research, 3*(3), e210016. https://doi.org/10.20900/agmr20210016

Martin-Diener, E., Meyer, J., Braun, J., Tarnutzer, S., Faeh, D., Rohrmann, S., & Martin, B. W. (2014). The combined effect on survival of four main behavioural risk factors for non-communicable diseases. *Preventive Medicine, 65*, 148-152.

Mayo Clinic. (2022). *Exercise helps ease arthritis pain and stiffness.* https://www.mayoclinic.org/diseases-conditions/arthritis/in-depth/arthritis/art-20047971

Mayo Clinic Staff. (2022). *Tai chi: A gentle way to fight stress.* www.mayoclinic.org/healthy-lifestyle/stress-management/in-depth/tai-chi/art-20045184#:~:text=Tai%20chi%20is%20a%20series,connecting%20the%20mind%20and%20body

Merrick, D., Hillman, K., Wilson, A., Labbé, D., Thompson, A., & Mortenson, W. B. (2021). All aboard: Users' experiences of adapted paddling programs. *Disability and Rehabilitation, 43*(20), 2945-2951. https://doi.org/10.1080/09638288.2020.1725153

Moore, G. M., Durstine, J. L., & Painter, P. L. (Eds.). (2016). *ACSM's exercise management for persons with chronic diseases and disabilities* (4th ed.). Human Kinetics.

Morris, A. (2022, February 3). "I wanted that self-reliance back": Disabled hikers forge a new path. *New York Times.* https://www.nytimes.com/2022/02/03/travel/disabled-hikers-outdoor-access.html

National Center on Health, Physical Activity and Disability (NCHPAD). (2022). *Inclusive recreation on campus.* www.nchpad.org/1834/7019/Creating~an~Inclusive~College~Recreation~Program

National Council on Aging (NCOA). (2021). *10 common chronic conditions for adults 25+.* www.ncoa.org/article/the-top-10-most-common-chronic-conditions-in-older-adults

Palat, P., Hickey, F., Patel, L., & Sannar, E. (2018). Levodopa-responsive early-onset Parkinsonism in Down syndrome. *Case Reports in Neurological Medicine,* article ID 2314791. https://doi.org/10.1155/2018/2314791

Park, J., McCaffrey, R., Newman, D., Liehr, P., & Ouslander J. G. (2017). A pilot randomized controlled trial of the effects of chair yoga on pain and physical function among community-dwelling older adults with lower extremity osteoarthritis. *Journal of the American Geriatric Society, 65*(3), 592-597. https://doi.org/10.1111/jgs.14717

Rutlin, T. (2022). *Exerstriders poles.* www.exerstrider.com

Stebbins, R. A. (2020). *The serious leisure perspective: A synthesis.* Springer Nature.

Thompson, P. D., & Eijsvogels, T. M. H. (2018). New physical activity guidelines: A call to activity for clinicians and patients. *JAMA, 320*(19), 1983-1984.

U.S. Department of Health and Human Services (USDHHS). (2018). *Physical activity guidelines for Americans* (2nd ed.). U.S. Department of Health and Human Services.

Wilderness Inquiry. (2022). *Home page.* www.wildernessinquiry.org

World Bocce League. (n.d.). *How to play bocce ball.* https://worldbocce.org/free-bocce-instructions-book.pdf

CHAPTER 16

Busse, S. (2014). Eligibility and classification in Paralympic sports. *Palaestra, 28*(2), 20-24.

Cash, S. (2021). *Steve Cash: United States of America.* www.paralympic.org/steve-cash

Davis, R. W. (2017), Adapted sport. In J. P. Winnick & D. L. Porretta (Eds.), *Adapted physical education and sport* (6th ed., pp. 41-57). Human Kinetics.

Deaflympics. (2022). *Sports.* www.deaflympics.com/sports

International Table Tennis Federation (ITTF). (n.d.). *Home.* https://www.ittf.com/

Kennedy, W., Fruin, R., Lue, A., & Logan, S. W. (2021). Using ecological models of health behavior to promote health care access and physical activity engagement for persons with disabilities. *Journal of Patient Experience, 8*, 23743735211034031.

Long, J. (2021). *Multiple medal winner Jessica Long reveals "extra vertebra" so swims in pain.* www.paralympic.org/feature/multiple-medal-winner-jessica-long-reveals-extra-vertebra-so-swims-pain

Molton, I. R., & Jensen, M. P. (2010). Aging and disability: Biopsychosocial perspectives. *Physical Medicine and Rehabilitation Clinics of North America, 21*, 253-265.

Molton, I. R., & Yorkston, K. M. (2017). Growing older with a physical disability: A special application of the successful aging paradigm. *Journals of Gerontology: Social Sciences, 72*(2), 290-299. https://doi.org/10.1093/geronb/gbw122

Össur. (2022). *Sport solutions.* www.ossur.com/en-us/prosthetics/sport-solutions

Paralympics. (2018). *Classifications.* www.paralympic.org/athletics/classification

Paralympics. (2021a). *Paralympics home page.* www.paralympic.org

Paralympics. (2021b). *Rules and regulations.* www.paralympic.org/athletics/classification/rules-and-regulations

Rubenstein, E., DuBois, L., Sadowsky, M., Washburn, K., Forquer, M., Stanish, H., & Shriver, T. (2020). Evaluating the potential of Special Olympics fitness models as a health intervention for adults with intellectual disabilities.

Disability and Health Journal, 13(2), 100850. https://doi.org/10.1016/j.dhjo.2019.100850

Special Olympics. (2021). *Special Olympics.* http://special olympics.org

Team USA. (2022). *Home page.* http://teamusa.org

Thomas, J. D., Kennedy, W., & Cardinal, B. J. (2020). Do written resources help or hinder equitable and inclusive physical activity promotion? *International Journal of Kinesiology in Higher Education, 6*(1), 39-55.

Winnick, J. (2017). Program organization and management. In J. Winnick, & D. L. Porretta (Eds.), *Adapted physical education and sport* (6th ed., pp. 23-57). Human Kinetics.

Winnick, J., & Porretta, D. L. (2022). *Adapted physical education and sport* (7th ed.). Human Kinetics.

Note: The italicized *f* and *t* following page numbers refer to figures and tables, respectively.

Carol Leitschuh, PhD, is a consultant. She is a former faculty member of the University of Minnesota (UMN) School of Kinesiology, where she taught in the doctoral, master's, and bachelor's degree programs. She was also coordinator of the UMN master's program in developmental and adapted physical education, affiliated with the Center for Early Education and Development (CEED) and Center for Neurobehavioral Development (CNBD). Dr. Leitschuh received an Initial Career Award from the Office of Special Education Programs. She developed a tool that monitored the early movement skills of infants and toddlers. Twice she was a visiting scholar of the Erasmus Mundus Program in Adapted Physical Activity. As a Fulbright Scholar in child development, she was a lecturer in the Czech Republic. She received her PhD in human performance, focusing on movement studies in disability. She was awarded a postdoctoral research fellowship at Juniper Gardens Children's Program at the University of Kansas.

Marquell Johnson, PhD, is a professor at the University of Wisconsin–Eau Claire (UWEC) and is the director of the rehabilitation science program and the director of the physical activity and recreation for individuals with disabilities in the university's P.R.I.D.E. and P.R.I.D.E.4Adults outreach programs. He received his PhD in nutrition and exercise science, focusing on movement studies in disability. He has received the Dr. Ron Satz Teacher/Scholar Award (2017); an Excellence in Mentoring in Research, Scholarship, and Creative Activity Award (2016); the UWEC Excellence in Service-Learning as a Faculty Mentor Award (2014); and numerous other awards. His teaching focuses on adapted physical activity and motor development, rehabilitation science, research methods, research and creative activities, physical activity and health behaviors of individuals with disabilities, and related areas.